Capital Investment Decision Analysis for management and engineering

John R. Canada

North Carolina State University
Raleigh, NC

John A. White

Georgia Institute of Technology
Atlanta, GA

Prentice-Hall Inc., Englewood Cliffs, NJ 07632

Library of Congress Cataloging in Publication Data

Canada, John R
    Capital investment decision analysis for management
and engineering.

    Edition of 1971 published under title: Intermediate
economic analysis for management and engineering.
    Bibliography: p.
    Includes index.
    1. Capital investments--Evaluation. I. White,
John A., 1939-   joint author. II. Title.
HG4028.C4C3 1980   658.1'527   79-21228
ISBN 0-13-113555-4

Editorial/production supervision and interior design by STEVEN BOBKER
Manufacturing buyer: GORDON OSBOURNE

©1980 by Prentice-Hall, Inc., Englewood Cliffs, N.J. 07632

Printed in the United States of America

10 9 8 7 6 5 4 3 2 1

Prentice-Hall International, Inc., *London*
Prentice-Hall of Australia Pty. Limited, *Sydney*
Prentice-Hall of Canada, Ltd., *Toronto*
Prentice-Hall of India Private Limited, *New Delhi*
Prentice-Hall of Japan, Inc., *Tokyo*
Prentice-Hall of Southeast Asia Pte. Ltd., *Singapore*
Whitehall Books Limited, *Wellington, New Zealand*

To our wives, Wanda and Mary Lib

contents

PART 2 CAPITAL PROJECT EVALUATION UNDER RISK AND UNCERTAINTY CONDITIONS, 249

preface

This book is an extensive revision of *Intermediate Economic Analysis for Management and Engineering*, published by Prentice-Hall in 1971. It continues as a text and reference on capital project economic evaluation that is more concise and yet more advanced than the traditional applied works and that contains abundant example problems and solutions.

In addition to concisely covering the basic principles of interest computations and basic analysis methods, this book extensively treats techniques for the quantitative analysis of investment problems involving risk and uncertainty. Almost all of these techniques are candidates for straightforward and widespread application in practice, while some are presented in the belief that they will prove valuable as progressive analysts and management personnel work to develop their usefulness. This book is significantly more complete than its predecessor because of the inclusion of additional quantitative techniques, particularly mathematical programming for handling capital budgeting problems, and sensitivity and risk analysis techniques.

The book is intended primarily for advanced undergraduate or graduate study and for students of all disciplines, particularly business and engineering. The concise explanatory features also make the book suitable as a reference in industry. It contains a rather succinct summary of basic capital project evaluation techniques (Part I), and it emphasizes more advanced techniques, concepts, and analysis procedures (Parts II and III).

For the use of Part I, only a knowledge of first year algebra is required, while for much of Parts II and III it is assumed that the student understands the basic analysis procedures of Part I and has a fair knowledge of elementary probability. Some fundamental probability concepts are explained in the text, but those who need further background will find that the first half of most probability and statistics texts will provide adequate review material. Complete understanding of the application of some specialized quantitative techniques to investment economic analyses will be facilitated by prior exposure to the theory underlying those techniques. For an abbreviated first course on the fundamentals of engineering or project economy, Part I can serve as an applications-oriented text which contains essentially the same breadth of coverage as traditional undergraduate texts. The integration of project economic analysis into the larger picture of capital budgeting within the firm is accomplished in Chapter 10, which contains an appendix on procedures and forms used in practice.

For a course in economic evaluation of alternative projects at the advanced undergraduate or initial graduate level, Part I can be used for review purposes as needed, with Parts II and III providing the primary study material. Since the chapters in Parts II and III are largely independent of one another, one can include or delete chapters according to the needs of individuals or classes.

Chapter 11 introduces risk and uncertainty concepts with some emphasis on estimating. Chapter 12 illustrates a wide range of tabular and graphical menas for exploring sensitivity. Chapters 13 and 14 include techniques for considering variability of outcomes, particularly when probabilities can be estimated. Chapter 15 provides a rather detailed explanation of decision techniques utilizing Bayesian statistics; Chapter 16 focuses on the use of decision tree concepts as a means of taking into account future outcomes, alternatives, and decisions in determining the best initial choice. Chapter 17 presents optimization models for replacing assets that either deteriorate gradually or fail suddenly. Chapter 18 provides useful concepts and solution techniques for applying mathematical programming to capital budgeting analyses involving interrelated sets of alternatives. Chapter 19 illustrates simple quantitative means for weighting objectives and nonmonetary factors.

Innumerable persons—friends, colleagues, and helpers—have contributed to the development of this work, so complete acknowledgment is not possible. Once again, the preparation of this work was made much more tolerable than would have otherwise been possible by the extremely competent secretarial services of Mrs. Martha Jackson and Mrs. Vicki DeLoach. Our wives, Wanda and Mary Lib, helped by providing encouragement and (usually) good working conditions. Dr. Jack Turvaville of Tennessee Technological University and Mr. Nathan Wolf of the International Business Machines Corporation supplied valuable additions to the book. To all these, as well as to the authors and publishers providing reprint permissions, and to many others unnamed, we wish to express our gratitude.

John R. Canada
John A. White

*Basic
Capital Project
Evaluation
Techniques*

Chapter
1

introduction and cost concepts

Project economic analysis involves techniques for comparing and deciding between alternatives on the basis of monetary or economic desirability. With the increasing complexity of our industrial technology, economic decision-making is becoming more difficult and at the same time more critical. Economic analyses serve to quantify differences between alternatives and reduce them to bases which provide for ease of project comparison. The importance of use of these methods varies with alternatives under consideration. In general, the use of these techniques is vitally important, for there is much to be saved or lost by virtue of the particular alternative chosen in usual project investment decisions. Indeed, project investment decisions are critically important factors in determining the success or failure of a firm.

Recognition of a Problem Opportunity

The starting point in any conscious attempt at rational decision-making must be recognition that a problem or opportunity exists. In typical situations, problem recognition is obvious and immediate. A broken machine or completely inadequate production capability, for example, causes awareness rather readily. But there usually exist numerous significant opportunities for improvement or alleviation of what would become future problems which are not obvious without search and thought. Once one is aware of the problem or opportunity, action can be taken to solve or take advantage of it.

It has been long acknowledged that economic analysis of complex alternatives should be most valuable when performed as an integral part of the "big picture" of relevant considerations facing the decision-maker. This is often called the "systems analysis" approach.

Systems Analysis

Systems analysis is a coordinated set of procedures that addresses the fundamental issues of design and management: that of specifying how people, money, and materials should be combined to achieve a larger purpose. It includes investigation of proper objectives; comparing quantitatively, where possible, the cost, effectiveness, and risks associated with the alternative policies or strategies for achieving them; and formulating additional alternatives if those examined are found wanting.

Systems analysis seeks to deal with problems by methodologically exploring the objectives, alternatives, assumptions, criteria, and risks as an integral whole. It recognizes the interrelationships that tie a system together. A system can be as broad as one chooses to define it—from a department within an organization, to the organization as a whole, to the national economy, to the world as a whole. Systems analysis requires that the boundaries of the system be extended outward as far as is required to determine which interrelationships are significant to the solution of the problem. This allows one the opportunity to obtain greater optimization to replace sub-optimization for components or subsystems of the system.

Systems analysis at its core consists of the application of classical micro-economic concepts to the problems of resource allocation. It generally involves the use of a number of analytic tools, such as marginal analysis concepts and optimization techniques to determine preferable alternatives; utility and decision theory to define optimally desirable configurations; and sensitivity analysis to investigate the reliability of the conclusions. A good system analysis—whether or not it includes the use of sophisticated techniques and at whatever level it is done—is one that carefully identifies the important issues and alternatives and relates the several costs and benefits

4

of each project in a way that is meaningful to the people responsible for making final selections.

The five basic elements of a systematic analysis are:

1. definition of objectives;
2. formulation of measures of effectiveness;
3. generation of alternatives;
4. evaluation of alternatives;
5. selection.

The interrelationships of these five basic elements, together with the dynamic elements of feedback, are illustrated in Fig. 1-1. The figure shows that dynamic systems analysis can, in a sense, be considered as ordered information flow.

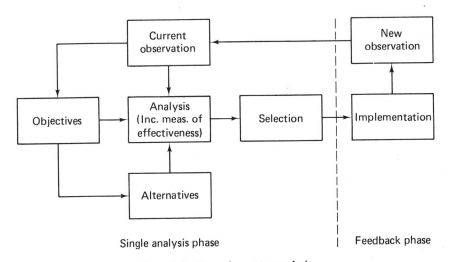

Figure 1-1. Dynamic system analysis.

There are pitfalls in the systems analysis approach. As the degree of comprehensiveness or breadth of the system increases, the number of variable factors or parameters becomes larger. Hence, it is important to define carefully the system boundaries. Analysis of broad systems needs highly developed, tacit knowledge and intuition to arrive at the estimates and judgments for the many situations in which uncertainty cannot be readily reduced or contained.

Generation of Alternatives

The need for imagination and creativity in the generation of alternatives cannot be overstated, for its lack is a common defect of many analyses. To emphasize the point, no matter how good an analysis and selection among two or more alternatives is made, if there exists some yet unidentified alternative that is superior to any of the alternatives considered, then the solution will be suboptimal—indeed, it may be drastically less than optimal.

The search for alternatives may be thought of as involving two kinds of tasks—the identification of *classes* or functionally different alternatives and the identification of the most attractive variations or operationally different alternatives for each particular class. For example, a crowded plant space problem might be alleviated by classes of alternatives such as building more space, leasing more space, relayout of existing space, subcontracting work, reducing product lines, increasing shift work, etc. Within each of these classes of alternatives there may be any number of variations to be considered. The analyst can create great benefits to the organization by ensuring that the problem and objectives are clearly stated. Such statements facilitate the identification of applicable classes of alternatives. Also, variations for each class must be judiciously selected for analysis so that no significantly superior alternative is overlooked or eliminated from consideration.

Importance of Estimates in Economic Analyses

Since economic analyses are concerned with which alternative or alternatives are best for future use, they are, by nature, based on estimates of what is to happen in the future. The most difficult part of an economic analysis is estimating relevant quantities for the future, for the analysis is no better than the estimates comprising it. Most estimates are based on past results, and the usual best source of information on past results is the accounting records of the enterprise. Accounting data must frequently be supplemented by statistical, economic, and engineering data as well as good judgment and mature analysis to arrive at valid cost estimates. Chapter 9 focuses on the vital subject of estimation, including consideration of inflation in some detail. Cost concepts important to economic analyses in general are described below.

Cost Concepts

The word *cost* has many meanings in many different settings. The kinds of cost concepts that should be used depend on the decision problem at hand.

6

There are two facets to estimating for economic analyses: (1) determining the appropriate quantity to estimate, and (2) making the estimate itself. Most estimates to be made are costs and revenues (negative costs).

For economic analyses, the analyst should be concerned with the *marginal* costs of using resources for the alternative. What actually constitutes the appropriate marginal cost depends on both the scale and timing of the alternative. To determine this quantity, the term "cost" should be defined as follows:

> The cost of a resource is the decrease in wealth which results from committing this resource to a particular alternative; that is, before any of the benefits of the alternative are calculated.

This definition avoids unquestioning use of normal accounting information such as book values and one-time costs and focuses on what is the change in value of assets affected by a particular action or decision. The following section discusses major cost concepts and issues useful for determining the marginal costs applicable in economic analyses.

Past Versus Future Costs

Costs and other financial events which previously have occurred or have been presumed are tabulated and summarized within the accounting function of an organization. Past costs can be no more than a guide or source of information for the prediction of future costs. Specifically, the analyst should resist the temptation to rely unquestioningly on what may be described as the "actual cost" data from the accounting function. Even if it is accurate, it will be at best recorded historical costs for similar circumstances.

Future costs are often significantly different from the costs of similar activities in the past. The analyst should be prepared to adjust past costs to reflect probable changes by the time a proposed alternative is to be implemented, taking into account changes in both the prices of the resources and in the amount of each to be required. Prices of resources can be affected by innumerable factors such as climate, geography, and labor regulations.

In economic analyses one is concerned with projecting what is expected to happen in the future as a result of alternative courses of action. Past costs often serve as a useful guide for such projections. It should be remembered that the viewpoints of the accountant and of the economic analyst are generally very opposite—one is a historian and the other is a fortuneteller.

Joint Costs

One of the difficulties in using accounting records is that some of the costs may be recorded in a single category even though they are in fact joint (or common) costs for many different activities. This may be true for labor and material as well as overhead cost items. These joint costs are often allocated to different products, services, or projects using more or less arbitrary formulas.

Any such formula should be scrutinized most carefully by the analyst interested in determining true marginal costs, that is, in the prediction of how total costs are affected by the alternatives under consideration. To determine applicable costs for any alternative, the analyst must both trace out each of the costs unique to the alternative and determine the portion of joint costs that is due to the alternative being examined. It is likely that the results will be very different from cost data readily available from the accounting function.

Usual Accounting Classification of Production Costs

The accounting function of an enterprise keeps records of happenings affecting the finances of the enterprise. Accounting records of production costs normally are separated into three main categories:

1. Direct labor
2. Direct material
3. Overhead

Direct labor costs or *direct materials costs* are those labor or materials costs which can be conveniently and economically charged to products or jobs on which the costs are incurred. Examples are, respectively, the cost of a turret lathe operator and the cost of the bar stock required to produce a large number of a given part.

By contrast, indirect labor cost and indirect materials cost are those costs which cannot be conveniently and economically charged to particular products or jobs on which the costs are incurred. Examples are, respectively, the cost of a janitor serving several departments or products and the cost of tool bits used on different products. Indirect labor and indirect material costs are part of the third category, *overhead costs*, which includes all production costs other than the costs of direct labor and direct material. Examples of other types of overhead costs are power, maintenance, depreciation, insurance, etc. Overhead costs are often referred to as "indirect costs" or "burden." An example of ways in which overhead costs are allocated and should be taken into account in economic analyses is given in Chapter 9.

Appendix 1-A contains a very brief exposition of accounting fundamentals for those who have had no previous exposure to the subject. While understanding of accounting fundamentals is not essential to progress in understanding the content of this book, this appendix should be useful to students with no previous exposure, at least to help provide the framework of the economic setting within which business decisions are made.

Fixed and Variable Costs

The difficult problem in calculating marginal costs is determining which costs are fixed and which vary as a result of decisions under consideration. Fixed costs are, at any time, the inevitable costs that must be paid regardless of the level of output and/or the resources used as the result of a particular alternative. A fixed cost represent an outlay of money, but not necessarily a change in wealth as a result of a particular choice. A variable (also called marginal or incremental) cost is a cost which is affected by the level of output and/or the resources used as a result of a particular alternative.

It is difficult to estimate costs because no cost is fixed for all time. What may be considered fixed over one period may be a variable cost for another period. The distinction between fixed and variable costs depends on the decision at hand and the time horizon relevant to them and should be re-examined for every particular decision.

To illustrate the problem, suppose a contractor has a backhoe for which the total costs for year are the sum of depreciation, fuel, insurance, and operator wages. If the machine is idle for a slack period of the year, then the fuel and wages are the only variable (marginal) costs, since the depreciation and insurance are fixed for that period of time regardless of how much the backhoe is used. Neglecting the effect of pricing during slack periods on prices and business which can be obtained during other periods, the decision-maker should be willing to sell the services of the backhoe for any price greater than the cost of fuel and wages. If, however, the contractor were offered a yearly rental on the machine at a price which essentially covers only the cost of fuel and wages, he should not accept. The relevant marginal costs over a year should also include the insurance costs which could be eliminated if the backhoe were not to be used for that time. Over an even longer term, even the depreciation expenses should be considered variable since the contractor may choose not to buy a new backhoe. This example illustrates the general principle that the proportion of total costs that may be considered variable increases as the period of time for the decision under consideration increases.

If one is making an economic analysis of a proposed change, only the variable (marginal) costs need be considered, since only prospective differences between alternatives need be taken into account.

Long- and Short-Run Costs

If an alternative system entails use of otherwise idle capacity, then the immediate opportunity costs and marginal costs will be low compared to the average costs. If, however, the system is already operating near capacity, the opportunity costs of additional output are likely to be high compared to the average costs. In either case, the long-run marginal costs will tend

to be less extreme than the short-run marginal costs and will tend to somewhat approach, but not necessarily equal, the average costs.

Long-run marginal costs also depend on the changes in technology
associated with shifts in level of production. In many industries marginal
costs decrease with increasing production over time as more efficient facilities are placed into operation. In many other industries both the long-run
and short-run marginal costs may increase with increasing output as added
resources become more scarce.

Determination of long-run marginal costs rests upon an adequate identification of the opportunties that will appear and disappear in the future.
Although some industries may have been characterized by particular cost
trends in the past, these may well not apply in any particular situation
projected into the future. Indeed, past trends may well be reversed by future
events.

Opportunity Costs

An opportunity (or alternative) cost is the value of that which is foregone
(prior to the calculation of any benefits) because limited resources are used
in a particular alternative, thereby causing one to give up the opportunity or
chance to use the resources for other possible income-producing or expense-
reducing alternatives. It is the same as the *shadow price* of a resource in
classical economics. The opportunity cost is the usual appropriate measure
of the marginal cost of a resource for economic analyses of alternatives.
While it can be equal to the price paid for a resource, it is often very different
from that actual outlay. Indeed, the use of a resource normally entails an
opportunity cost even if the resource were obtained without cost.

As an example, suppose a particular project involves the use of firm-
owned warehouse space which is presently vacant. The cost for that space
which should be charged to the project in question should be the income
or savings which the best perceived alternative use of the space would bring
to the firm. This may be much more or much less than the average cost of
that space which might be obtained from accounting records.

The opportunity cost of a resource is often fairly nebulous and hard to
estimate. It may be the sacrifice of future earnings rather than present cash.
In the most general sense, the cost of using a resource on one project is the
cost of not having it avaliable for the best alternative, whether that alternative is to sell the resource or to invest it productively in some other alternative which will bring benefits in the future. Extending the warehouse
example from above, for instance, the opportunity cost of the space could
be either related to the cash value that could be obtained from the outright
sale of the space or the value associated with some other productive use
of the space over time.

In estimating opportunity costs, it is useful to distinguish between resources which can be identically replaced, such as loads of sand or pieces of steel, and those that are somehow unique, such as a specific piece of real estate. For identically replaceable resources, for which there is a ready market, the opportunity cost for the resource is merely the market cost of the replacement or, equivalently, the salvage price of the resource if it is already possessed and will not be replaced.

For a resource which is somehow irreplaceable, the opportunity cost for the resource can be estimated as the cost of replacing the unique resource with the least undesirable substitute available. For example, suppose that the unique resource is an engineer who is especially talented at designing improved methods to reduce costs. The opportunity cost of using him on any project X is his particular value on some alternative project(s) Y where he could make the best improvements with the time available. If, however, the assignment of the especially talented engineer to this project X will cause one or more engineers to be hired to substitute for him on the project(s) he would have done otherwise, then the total cost of assigning him to project X is the net savings foregone plus the salaries of the substitute engineer(s).

As another example, consider a student who could earn $5,000 for working during a year and who chooses instead to go to school and spend $2,000 to do so. The total cost of going to school for that year is $7,000: $2,000 cash outlay and $5,000 for income foregone. (*Note*: This neglects the influence of taxes, and assumes that the student has no earning capability while in school.)

Opportunity cost in determination of interest rates for economic analyses. A very important use of the opportunity cost principle is in the determination of the interest cost chargeable to a proposed capital investment project. The proper interest cost is not just the amount which would be paid for the use of borrowed money, but is rather the opportunity cost, i.e., the return foregone or expense incurred because the money is invested in this project rather than in other possible alternative projects. Even when internally owned funds rather than borrowed funds are used for investing, the interest cost chargeable is determined by the same opportunity cost principle. In classical economics terminology, the opportunity cost is a measure of the maximum benefit that, for any given situation, can be obtained from an extra unit of capital.

As an example, suppose a firm always has available certain investment opportunities such as expansion or bonds purchases which will earn a minimum of, say, $X\%$. This being the case, the firm would be unwise to invest in other alternative projects earning less than $X\%$. Thus, in computing the cost of various alternatives, the analyst may simply add in $X\%$ of the amount invested for each. Such a cost may be thought of as the opportunity cost of not investing in the readily available alternatives.

In economy studies, it is necessary to recognize the time value of money irrespective of how the money is obtained, whether it be through debt financing, through owners' capital supplied, or through reinvestment of earnings generated by the firm. Interest on project investments is a cost in the sense of an opportunity foregone, an economic sacrifice of a possible income that might have been obtained by investment of that same money elsewhere.

Opportunity cost in replacement analyses. As another illustration of the opportunity cost principle, suppose a firm is considering replacing an existing piece of equipment which originally cost $50,000, presently has an accounting book value of $20,000, and can be salvaged now for $5,000. For purposes of an economic analysis of whether or not to replace the existing piece of equipment, the investment in that equipment should be considered as $5,000; for by keeping the equipment, the firm is giving up the *opportunity* to obtain $5,000 from its disposal. This principle is elaborated upon in Chapter 7.

Sunk Costs

Sunk costs are costs resulting from past decisions and which are therefore irrelevent to the consideration of alternative courses of action. Thus, sunk costs should *not* be considered directly in economic analyses.

As an example, suppose Joe Student finds a car he likes on a Saturday and pays $50 as a "down payment" which will be applied toward the $1,000 purchase price but which will be forfeited if he decides not to take the car. Over the weekend, Joe finds another car which he considers equally desirable for a purchase price of $910. For purposes of deciding which car to purchase, the $50 is a sunk cost and thus such should not enter into the decision. The decision then boils down to paying $1,000 minus $50, or $950, for the first car versus $910 for the second car.

A classical example of a sunk cost occurs in the replacement of assets. Suppose that the piece of equipment in the last section, which originally cost $50,000, presently has an accounting book value of $20,000 and can be salvaged now for $5,000. For purposes of an economic analysis, the $50,000 is actually a sunk cost. However, the viewpoint is often taken that the sunk cost should be considered to be the difference between the accounting book value and the present realizable salvage value, which is called "book loss" or "capital loss." According to this viewpoint, the sunk cost is $20,000 minus $5,000, or $15,000. Neither the $50,000 nor the $15,000 should be considered in an economic analysis, except for the manner in which the $15,000 affects income taxes, as discussed in Chapter 7.

Postponable Costs

A *postponable cost* is a cost which can be avoided or delayed for some period of time. As an example, the costs of certain types of maintenance or of personnel for certain planning functions may be postponable, while the cost of direct labor is unavoidable or not postponable if production is to continue.

Escapable Costs

When a reduction or elimination of business activity will result in certain costs being eliminated (with perhaps others increased), the net reduction in costs is considered the *escapable* cost. Escapable costs are related to declines in activity in a manner similar to the way variable costs are related to increases in business activity. The escapable cost when a business activity is decreased from X_2 to X_1 is frequently smaller than the variable cost which originally resulted when business level was expanded from X_1 to X_2. For example, it is usually a more difficult management task to reduce labor and other costs and commitments during a contraction than to increase them during an expansion. It is important in estimating net escapable costs that the amount of eliminated costs be reduced by the amount of any additional costs which would be incurred in related activities as a result of the change.

Replacement Costs

Replacement cost is, as the name implies, the cost of replacing an item. It is important to economic analyses because replacement cost rather than historical original cost is the relevant cost factor for most economic decisions. For example, if a storekeeper has been stocking an item costing $8, and selling that item for $12, and the price to the storekeeper for replacing the item is suddenly increased to $14, then the selling price should be raised to at least $14 before any additional units of that item are purchased.

Cash Costs Versus Book Costs

Costs which involve payments of cash or increases in liability are called *cash costs* to distinguish them from noncash (*book*) costs. Other common terms for cash costs are "out-of-pocket costs" or costs which are "cash flows." Book costs are costs which do not involve cash payments, but rather represent the amortization of past expenditures for items of lengthy durability. The most common examples of book costs are depreciation and depletion charges for the use of assets such as plant and equipment. In economic analyses, only those costs need be considered which are cash flows or poten-

13

tial cash flows. Depreciation, for example, is not a cash flow and is important only in the way it affects income taxes, which are cash flows.

Cost Factors

In an economic analysis, a listing of main factors which may be relevant for projects under consideration is as follows:

First cost, installed and ready to run (or net realizable value).

Insurance and property tax.

The life period of the machine until displaced from the proposed job.

The salvage value at the date of displacement.

The degree and the pattern of utilization; that is, the percent of capacity at which the machine will operate on the intended job with allowances for possible future changes in utilization.

Routine maintenance and repair costs.

Major repair items or periodic overhauls.

Direct operating costs, including operating labor, fuel or power, scrap material and rework.

Indirect costs: indirect labor, tooling, supplies, floor space, inventory.

Fringe benefits.

Hazards and losses relative to equipment, material, and labor time.

Changes in sales volume or price resulting from the choice.

Changes in unit cost of labor, power, supplies, etc., resulting in changes in operating costs.

Objectives of Firm and Nonmonetary Factors

While the primary concern of this book is techniques for considering economic or monetary desirability, it should be recognized that the usual decision between alternatives involves many factors other than those which can be reasonably reduced to monetary terms. For example, a limited listing of objectives other than profit maximization or cost minimization which may be important to a firm are

Minimization of risk of loss

Maximization of safety

Maximization of sales

Maximization of service quality

Minimization of cyclic fluctuation of firm

Minimization of cyclic fluctuation of economy

Maximization of well-being of employees

Creation or maintenance of a desired public image

Economic analyses provide only for the consideration of those objectives or factors which can be reduced to monetary terms. The results of these analyses should be weighed together with other nonmonetary (irreducible) objectives or factors before a final decision can be made. Techniques for weighting objectives and nonmonetary as well as monetary factors are given in Chapter 19.

The Role of the Engineer and Manager in Economic Decision-Making

Economic analyses and decisions between alternatives can be made by the engineer considering alternatives in the design of equipment, facilities, or man-machine systems. However, the decisions are more commonly made by a manager acting upon a number of investment opportunities and alternatives within each opportunity. Whenever the alternatives involve technical considerations, the engineer serves to provide estimates and judgment for the analyses upon which the final managerial decision can be made.

Scope and Importance

All analysis procedures covered in Chapters 2 through 8 are based on single estimates or amounts for each of the variable quantities considered. That is, if an analysis involves estimates of project investment, life, salvage value, operating expenses, etc., only single estimates for each are made even though it is recognized that each of the estimates may be subject to considerable variation or error. Analyses under these conditions are often called "assumed certainty" analyses. Parts II and III, beginning with Chapter 11, will show methods which explicitly consider the variation in estimated quantities and incorporate many refinements for rational economic analyses.

Regardless of who performs economic analyses or who makes the final investment decisions, the proper performance of these functions is critical to the economic progress of our country and of the world, as well as to the economic health or even survival of the individual firm. Business decisions frequently involve investments which must be planned and executed many years before the expected returns will be realized. Moreover, the scale of the investments in research and capital assets required for our expanding economy grows as new technologies develop. Hence, knowledge of the principles and techniques underlying economic analyses is extremely important.

PROBLEMS

1-1. A supplier purchased an Ajax charger five years ago for $5,000, intending to sell it at its usual markup for $5,800.

    Before they were able to obtain delivery, a competitor brought out a radically new charger for the same type of service, better in every way, but selling at a retail price of only $3,000. As a result, the Ajax charger has been a white elephant in the supplier's hands—it is a large piece of obsolete equipment that has been occupying valuable floor space which is now vitally needed.

    In discussing what to do, two members of the firm find themselves in disagreement. The president feels that the charger should be kept unless the $5,000 purchase price is realized on the sale. The accountant feels that the equipment should not be sold unless both the $5,000 cost and $500 cost of storage to date can be realized.

    Which course of action would you recommend? Why?

1-2. Smith purchased his house several years ago for $20,000, and was just offered $25,000 cash for it. Smith and his family had not been planning to sell and move, even though they are willing to do so. A neighborhood economist has correctly computed that the pretax annual rate of profit on the cash Smith has invested in the house would be 45%, and on this basis he recommends that Smith sell the house. What additional information does Smith need to make a decision? What irrelevant information was given?

1-3. A merchant has been attempting to maintain his stock of goods at a constant physical volume even though prices have been rising. His stock of one item was originally purchased for $10 per unit. He sold these goods at $16 per unit (applying his usual markup) and immediately replaced them by identical ones purchased at the new wholesale price of $18 per unit. What do you think of the profitableness of this transaction?

1-4. Certain factory space cost $10.00 per square foot to build and is estimated to have an economic life of 25 years and 0 salvage value. The minimum attractive rate of return on invested capital is 10%. The annual out-of-pocket cost of property taxes, heat, lights, and maintenance is $0.50 per square foot whether or not the space is being used. What should be the cost per square foot considered in an economic analysis of a certain new project A which entails proposed use of that space under each of the following conditions?

    a. The space is now being used for another project B which will have to be moved to new quarters costing $2.00 per square foot per year.

   b. The space is idle and there is no alternative use of it expected for the entire period in which the project under consideration would exist.
   c. The space is part of a large area which is used normally; hence, it is thought reasonable to charge only long-run average costs.

1-5. A firm has a manufacturing division with a normal manufacturing capacity of 1,000,000 units which sell for $120 each. The price consists of variable labor and material costs, $60; fixed costs, $40; and profit, $20. During a severe recession only 200,000 units can be sold annually, and then only if the price is reduced to $100 each. The total fixed cost can be reduced 15% below normal if the plant remains open and 30% below normal if it closes. The variable cost is directly proportional to output.

   Disregard irreducible considerations. Should the plant remain open for the next year or two to produce 200,000 units a year or should it shut down and reopen when business improves?

   At the 200,000 unit production rate, to what level may the price be reduced during the recession before shutting down the plant becomes more economical than operating it?

1-6. Process A, designed to produce 10,000 units a year, has a fixed cost of $100,000 a year. Process B, with the same design capacity has a fixed cost of $80,000 a year. Process A produces the initial 4,000 units at a variable cost of $10 and the next 6,000 units at a variable cost of $17. Process B produces the first 5,000 units at a variable cost of $9 each and produces the next 5,000 at $8 each. Show what load should be assigned to each plant if the demand for the product is varied from zero to 20,000 units. Assume that at no load the fixed costs will not be reduced.

1-7. A firm is considering whether to contract with vendors or use in-house crews for a type of maintenance work. The cost accounting system yields estimates per job as follows:

Direct labor	$500
Materials	220
Overhead	400
Total	$1,120

   A vendor has offered to do the work for $1,000 per job. Discuss whether the firm should contract with the vendor under each of the following conditions:
   a. The "in-house" crews would still be on the payroll and would be otherwise unoccupied if they were not doing this work.
   b. The "in-house" crews on the payroll will always be productivity occupied whether or not this maintenance work is done by them. That is, their labor time is worth $500 elsewhere if they do not work on this job. Of the standard overhead charge given, one-half is fixed and one-half is avoidable if the "in-house" crews do not do the job.

1-8. For the coming period overhead costs for a firm are estimated to be $600,000 for production which is expected to sell for $2,800,000 and to require 200,000 direct labor hours costing $800,000 and direct materials costing $200,000. The firm allocates its overhead to various jobs on the basis of the following relation.

Overhead cost = $100,000 + 0.5 (Direct labor + Direct materials)

The firm is considering changing its method of manufacturing a particular job with estimates as follows:

	Old Method	New Method
Direct labor	$100,000	$90,000
Direct material	8,000	16,000

Which method is most economical if actual overhead costs for the two methods are thought to:
a. Vary according to the allocation formula
b. Be the same for each method
c. Be $5,000 more for the new method than for the old method

1-9. Explain by example the difference between book costs and sunk costs.

1-10. What is the difference between postponable costs and escapable costs?

1-11. Formulate a one-sentence rule for an engineering group indicating when they may eliminate consideration of overhead costs in the analysis of investment decisions.

1-12. List the costs associated with owning an automobile that you would classify as fixed costs and those that you would classify as variable costs according to miles driven during the next year. Assume that you plan to keep the car for many years.

accounting fundamentals

This section contains an extremely brief and simplified exposition of the elements of accounting in recording and summarizing transactions affecting the finances of the enterprise. These fundamentals apply to any entity (such as an individual, corporation, governmental unit, etc), called here just a "firm."

All accounting is based on the so-called *fundamental accounting equation*,

$$\text{Assets} = \text{Liabilities} + \text{Ownership} \qquad (1\text{-}A\text{-}1)$$

where "Assets" are those things of monetary value which the firm *possesses*, "Liabilities" are those things of monetary value which the firm *owes*, and "Ownership" is the worth of what the firm *owns* (also referred to as "equity," "net worth," etc.).

The fundamental accounting equation defines the format of the *balance sheet*, one of the two most common accounting statements. It shows the financial position of the firm *at any given point in time*.

Another important, and rather obvious, accounting relationship is

$$\text{Revenue} - \text{Expenses} = \text{Profit(or Loss)}. \qquad (1\text{-}A\text{-}2)$$

This relationship defines the format of the *income statement* (also commonly known as "profit-and-loss statement"), which summarizes the revenue and expense results of operations *over a period of time*.

It is useful to note that a revenue serves to increase the ownership amount for a firm, while an expense serves to decrease the ownership amount for a firm.

To illustrate the workings of accounts in reflecting the decisions and actions of a firm, suppose you decide to undertake an investment opportunity and that the following sequence of events occurs over a period of a year.

1. Organize a firm and invest $3,000 cash as capital.
2. Purchase equipment for a total cost of $2,000 by paying cash.
3. Borrow $1,500 through note to bank.
4. Manufacture year's supply of inventory through the following:
   a. Pay $1,200 cash for labor.

    b. Incur $400 account payable for material.

    c. Recognize the partial loss in value (depreciation) of the equipment amounting to $500.

5. Sell on credit all goods produced for year, 1,000 units at $3.00 each. Recognize that the accounting value of these goods is $2,100, resulting in an increase in equity (through profits) of $900.

6. Collect $2,200 of account receivable.

7. Pay $400 account payable and $1,000 of bank note.

A simplified version of the accounting entries recording the same information in a format that reflects the effects on the fundamental accounting equation (with a "+" denoting an increase and a "−" denoting a decrease) is shown in Table 1-A-1.

A balance sheet at the end of the year of enterprise operation would appear as follows:

Your Firm

Balance sheet as of end of year 19xx

Assets		Liabilities and Ownership	
Cash:	$2,100	Bank note:	$ 500
Accounts receivable:	800		
Equipment:	1,500	Equity:	3,900
Total:	$4,400	Total:	$4,400

An income statement is not so directly determinable from the above simplified format as was the balance sheet. In this case, the statement for the year would appear as follows:

Your Firm

Income statement for year ending 19xx

Operating revenues (Sales):		$3,000
Operating costs (Inventory depleted):		
Labor:	$1,200	
Material:	400	
Depreciation:	500	
		$2,100
Net income (Profits):		$ 900

It should be noted that the profit for a period serves to increase the value of the ownership in the firm by that amount. Also, it is worth noting that the net cash flow of $1,400 (= $3,000 − $1,200 − $400) is not all profit. This was recognized in transaction 4c, in which a capital consumption for equipment of $500 was declared. Thus, the profit was $900, or $500 less than the net cash flow.

Table 1-A-1

ACCOUNTING EFFECTS OF TRANSACTIONS

	Account	1	2	3	4	5	6	7	Balances at end of year
ASSETS	Cash	+$3,000	−$2,000	+$1,500	−$1,200		+$2,200	−$1,400	+$2,100
	Account receivable					+$3,000	−$2,200		+$ 800
	Inventory		+$2,000		+$2,100	−$2,100			0
	Equipment				−$ 500				+$1,500
equals									
LIABILITIES	Account payable				+$ 400			−$ 400	
plus	Bank note			+$1,500				−$1,000	+$ 500
OWNERSHIP	Equity	+$3,000				+$ 900			+$3,900

Transaction

21

Figure 1-A-1 shows the interrelationships of many asset and cost categories commonly used by accounting functions. Note that these are shown to result in "return on investment," which is merely profit expressed as a percent of capital investment or rate of return for a period and which is a common measure of financial performance.

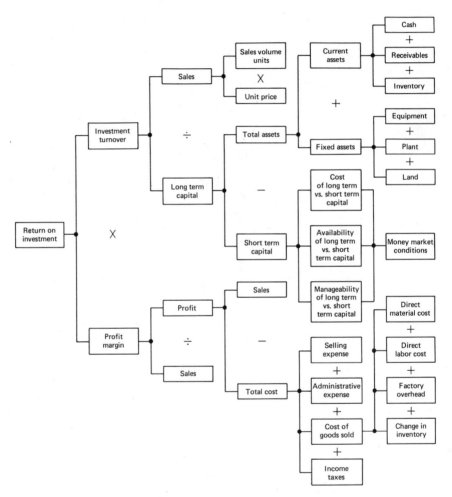

Figure 1-A-1. Interrelationships among many financial categories and terms commonly used in accounting and management practice.

computations involving interest

Just as the spacing of forces is a primary consideration in mechanics, the spacing of cash flows (receipts and disbursements) is important in economic analyses. The timing of cash flows influences what is termed "the time value of money." Because of the opportunities for investing money and increasing its value, a sum of money today is worth more than the same amount at some time in the future. Failure to consider the effect of timing of money involved in investment alternatives may yield poor investment decisions.

Equivalence

An item of money (single sum or uniform series) has an infinite range of equivalent and potential values over time, although it can have actual existence at only one point in time. Thus, to have precise meaning, an item of money must be identified in terms of timing as well as of amount. For purposes of definition, two amounts of money or series of monies at different points in time are said to be equivalent if they are equal to each other at some point in time at a given interest rate. This chapter deals with the use of interest formulas for equivalence conversions.

Interest Calculations

Interest calculations may be based on interest rates which are either *simple* or *compound.*

Simple Interest

Whenever the interest charge for any period is based on the principal amount only and not also on any accumulated interest charges, the interest is said to be *simple.* Calculations involving simple interest may be performed utilizing the following formula:

$$I = P \times s \times N$$

where P = Amount borrowed (invested)
s = Simple interest rate
N = Number of periods before repayment (withdrawal)

Example:
> An individual borrows $1,000 at a simple interest rate of 8% per year and wishes to repay the principal and interest at the end of 4 years. How much must be repaid?

Solution:

$$I = P \times s \times N$$

$$I = (\$1,000)(0.08)(4)$$

$$I = \$320$$

Therefore, $1,000 + $320 = $1,320 is repaid in 4 years.

Compound Interest

Whenever the interest charge for any interest period is based on the remaining principal amount plus any accumulated interest charges up to the beginning of that period, the interest is said to be *compound.* To illustrate the effect of compounding, the following example is given.

Example:
> An individual borrows $1,000 at a compound interest rate of 8% per yr and wishes to repay the principal and interest in 4 years. How much must be repaid?

Solution:

Year	Amount owed at beginning of year	Interest charge for year	Amount owed at end of year
1	$1,000.00	$1,000.00 × 0.08 = $ 80.00	$1,080.00
2	$1,080.00	$1,080.00 × 0.08 = $ 86.40	$1,166.40
3	$1,166.40	$1,166.40 × 0.08 = $ 93.31	$1,259.71
4	$1,259.71	$1,259.71 × 0.08 = $100.78	$1,360.49

Thus, $1,360.49 is repaid. The difference between this and the $1,320.00 answer in the previous example utilizing simple interest is due to the effect of compounding of interest over the 4 years.

Compound Interest Formulas

Compound interest is much more often encountered in practice than is simple interest. Hence, compound interest will be used throughout this book unless otherwise stated. Basic compound interest formulas and tables assuming discrete (lump sum) payments and discrete interest periods are discussed below.

Notation and Cash Flow Diagram

The following notation is used throughout this book for compound interest calculations:

i = Effective interest rate per interest period

N = Number of compounding periods

P = Present sum of money
(the equivalent worth of one or more cash flows at a relative point in time called the present)

F = Future sum of money
(the equivalent worth of one or more cash flows at a relative point in time called the future)

A = End-of-period cash flows (or equivalent end-of-period values) in a uniform series continuing for a specified number of periods

and

G = Uniform period-by-period increase or decrease in cash flows or amounts (the arithmetic gradient)

The use of time or cash flow diagrams is strongly recommended for most problems, at least whenever the analyst desires to visualize the cash flow situation. Whenever some distinction between types of cash flows seems desirable, it is recommended to use an upward arrow for a cash inflow and a downward arrow for a cash outflow.

Interest Formulas Relating Present and Future Sums

Figure 2-1 shows a time diagram involving a present single sum P and a future single sum F separated by N periods with interest at $i\%$ per period. Two formulas relative to those sums are presented below.

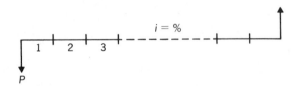

Figure 2-1. Time diagram for single sums.

Find F When Given P

If P dollars are deposited now in an account earning $i\%$ per period, the account will grow to $P(1 + i)$ by the end of one period; by the end of two periods, the account will be $P(1 + i)(1 + i) = P(1 + i)^2$; and by the end of N periods, the account will have grown to a future sum F, as given by

$$F = P(1 + i)^N \qquad\qquad 2\text{-}1$$

where the quantity $(1 + i)^N$, designated (F/P), is tabled in Appendix A-A for numerous values of i and N. Symbolically, we shall use the notation

$$F = P(F/P, i\%, N) \qquad\qquad 2\text{-}2$$

where the symbol in parentheses denotes the unknown and known, the interest rate, and the number of periods, respectively.

Find P When Given F

The reciprocal of the relationship between P and F, from above, is given mathematically as

$$P = F\left(\frac{1}{1 + i}\right)^N \qquad\qquad 2\text{-}3$$

where the quantity $1/(1 + i)^N$ is tabled in Appendix A-A. Symbolically,

$$P = F(P/F, i\%, N) \qquad 2\text{-}4$$

Applying Interest Formulas to Cash Flow Series

Figure 2-2 depicts a time diagram involving a present single sum P and single sums $A_1, A_2, \ldots, A_N$ occurring at the end of periods $1, 2, \ldots, N$, respectively. With interest at $i\%$ per period, the *present worth equivalent* of

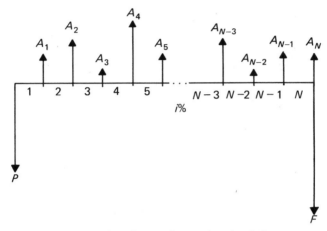

Figure 2-2. Time diagram for a series of cash flows.

the cash flow series $\{A_1, A_2, \ldots, A_N\}$ can be obtained by summing the present worth equivalents of each individual cash flow in the cash flow series. Hence,

$$P = A_1(P/F, i\%, 1) + A_2(P/F, i\%, 2) + \cdots + A_N(P/F, i\%, N) \qquad 2\text{-}5$$

Similarly, the *future worth equivalent* of the cash flow series is given by the sum of the future worth equivalents of the individual cash flows,

$$F = A_N + A_{N-1}(F/P, i\%, 1) + \cdots + A_1(F/P, i\%, N - 1) \qquad 2\text{-}6$$

In a number of instances the present worth and future worth equivalents of cash flow series can be obtained in a closed mathematical form by using summation of series relations. In particular, if each cash flow in the series has the same value, A, then the series is referred to as a *uniform series*. If the value of a given cash flow differs from the value of the previous cash flow by a constant amount, G, then the series is referred to as a *gradient series*. When the value of a given cash flow differs from the value of the previous cash flow by a constant percentage, $j\%$, then the series is referred to as a *geometric series*. Closed form expressions are available for P and F for uniform, gradient, and geometric series and will be presented in subsequent sections. Additional series for which closed form series can be developed are explored in the exercises at the end of the chapter.

Interest Formulas Relating Uniform Series of Payments to Their Present Worth and Future Worth

Figure 2-3 shows a time diagram involving a series of uniform cash flows of amount A occurring at the end of each period for N periods with interest at $i\%$ per period. As depicted in Fig. 2-3, the formulas and tables below are derived such that

1. P occurs one interest period before the first A; and
2. F occurs at the same point in time as the last A, and N periods after P.

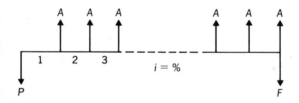

Figure 2-3. Standard time diagram for uniform series.

Four formulas relating A to F and P are given below.

Find F When Given A

If A dollars are deposited at the end of each period for N periods in an account earning $i\%$ per period, the future sum F accrued at the end of the Nth period is

$$F = A[1 + (1 + i) + (1 + i)^2 + \cdots + (1 + i)^{N-1}]$$

It can be shown that this reduces to

$$F = A\left[\frac{(1 + i)^N - 1}{i}\right] \qquad 2\text{-}7$$

where the quantity $\{[(1 + i)^N - 1]/i\}$ is tabled in Appendix A-A. Symbolically,

$$F = A(F/A,i\%,N) \qquad 2\text{-}8$$

Find A When Given F

The reciprocal of the relationship between A and F, from above, is given mathematically as

$$A = F\left[\frac{i}{(1+i)^N - 1}\right] \qquad 2\text{-}9$$

where the quantity $\{i/[(1+i)^N - 1]\}$ is tabled in Appendix A-A. Symbolically,

$$A = F(A/F,i\%,N) \qquad 2\text{-}10$$

Find P When Given A

If we take the relation

$$F = A\left[\frac{(1+i)^N - 1}{i}\right]$$

and substitute

$$F = P(1+i)^N$$

then we find that

$$P = A\left[\frac{(1+i)^N - 1}{i}\right]\left[\frac{1}{1+i}\right]^N$$

which simplifies to

$$P = A\left[\frac{(1+i)^N - 1}{i(1+i)^N}\right] \qquad 2\text{-}11$$

The factor in the brackets is tabled in Appendix A-A. Symbolically,

$$P = A(P/A,i\%,N) \qquad 2\text{-}12$$

Find A When Given P

The reciprocal of the relationship between A and P, from above, is given mathematically as

$$A = P\left[\frac{i(1+i)^N}{(1+i)^N - 1}\right] \qquad 2\text{-}13$$

Again, the factor in brackets is tabled in Appendix A-A. Symbolically,

$$A = P(A/P,i\%,N) \qquad 2\text{-}14$$

A summary of the formulas and their symbols, together with example problems, is given in Table 2-1. It should be noted that for all problems in this book involving uniform series, end-of-year payments are assumed unless stated otherwise.

Table 2-1

SUMMARIZATION OF DISCRETE COMPOUND INTEREST FACTORS AND SYMBOLS

To find	Given	Multiply "Given" by factor below	Factor name	Factor functional symbol	Example (answer for i = 5%) (Note: All uniform series problems assume end of period payments.)
F	P	$(1+i)^N$	Single sum compound amount	$(F/P,i\%,N)$	A firm borrows $1,000 for 5 years. How much must it repay in a lump sum at the end of the fifth year? Ans.: $1,276
P	F	$\dfrac{1}{(1+i)^N}$	Single sum present worth	$(P/F,i\%,N)$	A company desires to have $1,000 8 years from now. What amount is needed now to provide for it? Ans.: $676.84
P	A	$\dfrac{(1+i)^N - 1}{i(1+i)^N}$	Uniform series present worth	$(P/A,i\%,N)$	How much should be deposited in a fund to provide for 5 annual withdrawals of $100 each? Ans.: $432.95
A	P	$\dfrac{i(1+i)^N}{(1+i)^N - 1}$	Capital recovery	$(A/P,i\%,N)$	What is the size of 10 equal annual payments to repay a loan of $1,000? First payment 1 year after receiving loan. Ans.: $129.50
F	A	$\dfrac{(1+i)^N - 1}{i}$	Uniform series compound amount	$(F/A,i\%,N)$	If 4 annual deposits of $2,000 each are placed in an account, how much money has accumulated immediately after the last deposit? Ans.: $8,620
A	F	$\dfrac{i}{(1+i)^N - 1}$	Sinking fund	$(A/F,i\%,N)$	How much should be deposited each year in an account in order to accumulate $10,000 at the time of the fifth annual deposit? Ans.: $1,809.70

Key: i = Interest rate per interest period A = Uniform series amount P = Present worth
  N = Number of interest periods F = Future worth

Interest Factor Relationships

The following relationships exist among the six basic interest factors:

$$(P/F,i\%,N) = \frac{1}{(F/P,i\%,N)} \qquad\qquad 2\text{-}15$$

$$(A/P,i\%,N) = \frac{1}{(P/A,i\%,N)} \qquad\qquad 2\text{-}16$$

$$(A/F,i\%,N) = \frac{1}{(F/A,i\%,N)} \qquad\qquad 2\text{-}17$$

$$(A/P,i\%,N) = i\% + (A/F,i\%,N) \qquad\qquad 2\text{-}18$$

$$(F/A,i\%,N) = (P/A,i\%,N)(F/P,i\%,N) \qquad\qquad 2\text{-}19$$

$$(P/A,i\%,N) = \sum_{j=1}^{N} (P/F,i\%,j) \qquad\qquad 2\text{-}20$$

$$(F/A,i\%,N) = \sum_{j=0}^{N-1} (F/P,i\%,j) \qquad\qquad 2\text{-}21$$

Interest Formulas for Uniform Gradient Series

Some economic analysis problems involve receipts or disbursements that are projected to increase by a constant amount each period. For example, maintenance and repair expenses on specific equipment may increase by a relatively constant amount of change, G, each period.

Figure 2-4 is a cash flow diagram of a series of end-of-period disbursements increasing at the constant amount of change, G dollars per period. For convenience in derivation of the formulas it is assumed that a series of uniform payments of amount G is started at the end of the second period, another series of amount G is started at the end of the third period, and so on. Each of these series terminates at the same time, the end of the Nth period. The future sum (at the end of the Nth period) equivalent to the gradient series shown in Fig. 2-4 is

$$F = G[(F/A,i\%,N-1) + (F/A,i\%,N-2) + \cdots + (F/A,i\%,2) + (F/A,i\%,1)]$$

$$= \frac{G}{i}[(1+i)^{N-1} + (1+i)^{N-2} + \cdots + (1+i)^2 + (1+i) - (N-1)]$$

$$= \frac{G}{i}[(1+i)^{N-1} + (1+i)^{N-2} + \cdots + (1+i)^2 + (1+i) + 1] - \frac{NG}{i}$$

The expression in the brackets reduces to

$$\frac{(1+i)^N - 1}{i} = (F/A,i\%,N)$$

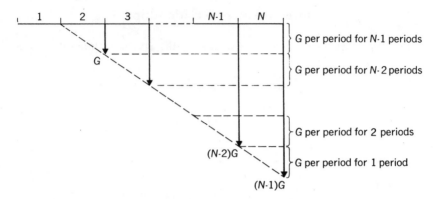

Figure 2-4. Cash flow diagram for uniform gradient of G dollars per period.

Hence,

$$F = \frac{G}{i}\left[\frac{(1 + i)^N - 1}{i} - N\right]$$

                                                                        2-22

The equivalent uniform annual worth of the gradient series may be found by multiplying the above sum of compound amounts by $(A/F,i\%,N)$. Hence,

$$
\begin{aligned}
A &= F(A/F,i\%,N) \\
&= \frac{G}{i}\left[\frac{(1 + i)^N - 1}{i} - N\right]\left[\frac{i}{(1 + i)^N - 1}\right] \\
&= \frac{G}{i} - \frac{NG}{i}\left[\frac{i}{(1 + i)^N - 1}\right] \\
&= G\left\{\frac{1}{i} - \left[\frac{N}{(1 + i)^N - 1}\right]\right\}
\end{aligned}
$$

                                                                        2-23

The factor in the braces is given in Table A-A-17 for a wide range of i and N. Symbolically, the relationship to find the uniform series equivalent to the gradient series is

$$A = G(A/G,i\%,N)$$

                                                                        2-24

Interest Formulas for Geometric Series

Some economic analysis problems involve cash flows that are anticipated to increase over time by a constant percentage. Labor, energy, and material costs are examples of items that may increase by a constant $j\%$ each period.

Figure 2-5 gives a cash flow diagram of a series of end-of-period disbursements increasing at a constant rate of $j\%$ per period. If A_1 represents

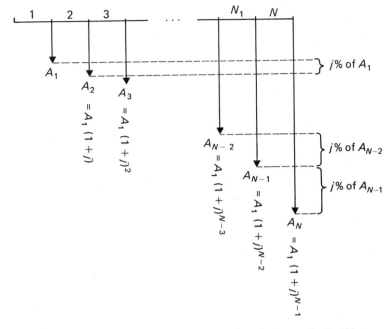

Figure 2-5. Cash flow diagram for geometric series increasing by $j\%$ per period.

the size of the disbursement at the end of period 1, it can be seen that the size of the disbursement at the end of period k, A_k, is equal to $A_1(1+j)^{k-1}$. The present sum equivalent to the geometric series shown in Fig. 2-5 is

$$
\begin{aligned}
P &= A_1(P/F,i\%,1) + A_2(P/F,i\%,2) + A_3(P/F,i\%,3) \\
&\quad + \cdots + A_N(P/F,i\%,N) \\
&= A_1(1+i)^{-1} + A_2(1+i)^{-2} + A_3(1+i)^{-3} \\
&\quad + \cdots + A_N(1+i)^{-N} \\
&= A_1(1+i)^{-1} + A_1(1+j)(1+i)^{-2} + A_1(1+j)^2(1+i)^{-3} \\
&\quad + \cdots + A_1(1+j)^{N-1}(1+i)^{-N} \\
&= A_1(1+i)^{-1}[\,1 + x + x^2 + \cdots + x^{N-1}\,]
\end{aligned}
$$

$$2\text{-}25$$

where $x = (1+j)/(1+i)$. The expression in brackets in Eq. 2-25 reduces to $(1-x^N)/(1-x)$ when $x \neq 1$ or $j \neq i$. If $j = i$, then $x = 1$ and the expression in brackets reduces to N, the number of terms in the summation. Hence,

$$
P = \begin{cases} A_1(1+i)^{-1}(1-x^N)/(1-x) & j \neq i \\ A_1 N(1+i)^{-1} & j = i \end{cases}
$$

$$2\text{-}26$$

which reduces to

$$P = \begin{cases} \dfrac{A_1[1 - (1 + i)^{-N}(1 + j)^N]}{i - j} & j \neq i \\ A_1 N(1 + i)^{-1} & j = i \end{cases} \qquad 2\text{-}27$$

or

$$P = \begin{cases} \dfrac{A_1[1 - (P/F,i\%,N)(F/P,j\%,N)]}{i - j} & j \neq i \\ A_1 N(P/F,i\%,1) & j = i \end{cases} \qquad 2\text{-}28$$

By employing the appropriate interest formula from Table 2-1 the present sum equivalent for the geometric series can be converted to a future sum equivalent or a uniform series equivalent. In terms of the basic interest factors, the future sum equivalent is

$$F = \begin{cases} \dfrac{A_1[(F/P,i\%,N) - (F/P,j\%,N)]}{i - j} & j \neq i \\ A_1 N(F/P,i\%,N - 1) & j = i \end{cases} \qquad 2\text{-}29$$

With the advent of computer terminals, minicomputers, and pocket calculators, the present worth equivalent of a cash flow series normally can be determined quickly by summing the present worths of the individual cash flows, regardless of the form of the cash flow series. For this reason, some may not have a need for the interest formulas for uniform series, gradient series, and geometric series. Various methods for comparing investment alternatives will be presented later, as will be discussions of economic analyses in an inflationary economy and considering income taxes. In those discussions, we will find it convenient to use the interest formulas for the three types of cash flow series presented above.

SOLVED PROBLEMS

1. Ms. Smith loans Mr. Brown $10,000 with interest compounded at a rate of 8% per year. How much will Mr. Brown owe Ms. Smith if he repays the loan at the end of 5 years?

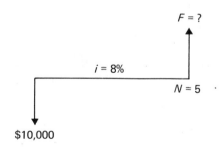

Since the problem is of the form "Find F when given P," the formula to use is

$$F = P(F/P,8\%,5)$$
$$= \$10,000(1.4693)$$
$$= \$14,693$$

2. Mr. Thomas wishes to accumulate $10,000 in a savings account in 10 years. If the bank pays 5% compounded annually on deposits of this size, how much should Mr. Thomas deposit in the account?

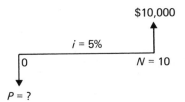

This problem is of the form "Find P when given F," and the formula to use is

$$P = F(P/F,5\%,10)$$
$$= \$10,000(0.6139) = \$6,139$$

3. An individual has been making annual payments of $2,000 to repay a loan. The individual wishes to pay off the loan immediately after having made an annual payment. Four payments remain to be paid. With an interest rate of 8%, how much should be paid in the final payment?

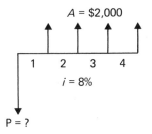

$$P = A(P/A,8\%,4)$$
$$= \$2,000(3.3121) = \$6,624$$

4. A person borrows $10,000 at 6% compounded annually. If the loan is repaid in ten annual payments, what will be the size of the payments if the first payment is made 1 year after borrowing the money?

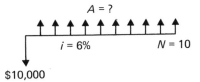

$$A = P(A/P, 6\%, 10)$$
$$= \$10,000(0.1359) = \$1,359$$

5. If \$800 is deposited annually for 10 years in an account which pays 6% compounded annually, how much money will be in the fund immediately after the tenth deposit?

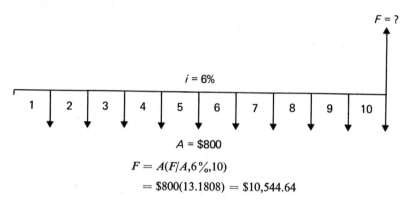

$$F = A(F/A, 6\%, 10)$$
$$= \$800(13.1808) = \$10,544.64$$

6. An individual wishes to accumulate \$100,000 in 30 years. If 30 end-of-year deposits are made into an account which pays interest at a rate of 10% compounded annually, what size deposit is required to meet the stated objective?

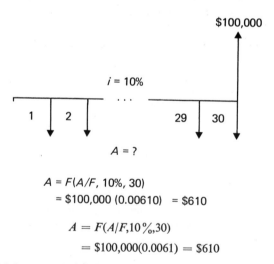

$$A = F(A/F, 10\%, 30)$$
$$= \$100,000 (0.00610) = \$610$$

$$A = F(A/F, 10\%, 30)$$
$$= \$100,000(0.0061) = \$610$$

7. It is expected that a machine will incur operating costs of \$4,000 the first year and that these costs will increase \$500 each year thereafter for the 10-year life of the machine. If money is worth 15% per year to the firm, what is the equivalent annual worth of the operating costs?

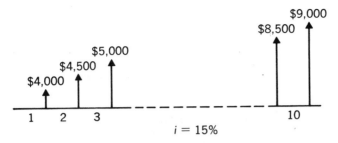

$$i = 15\%$$

The problem reduces to a constant $4,000 per year plus the $500 gradient:

$$A = \$4,000 + G(A/G,i\%,N)$$
$$= 4,000 + \$500(A/G,15\%,10)$$
$$= 4,000 + \$500(3.3832) = \$5,692$$

8. Work problem 7 (above) if the timing of the costs is reversed as shown in the following diagram:

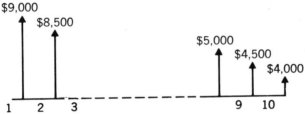

The problem reduces to a constant $9,000 per year minus a $500 gradient of payments (which do not occur)

$$A = \$9,000 - \$500(A/G,15\%,10)$$
$$= 9,000 - \$500(3.3832) = \$7,308$$

9. In Problem 7 suppose the operating cost the first year is $4,000 and each year thereafter for the 10-year life of the machine operating costs increase by 6% per year. If money is worth 15% per year to the firm, what is the equivalent annual worth of the operating costs?

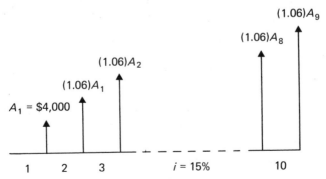

Since $j = 6\%$ and $i = 15\%$,

$$F = \frac{A_1[(F/P,15\%,10) - (F/P,6\%,10)]}{0.15 - 0.06}$$

$$= \frac{\$4,000[4.0456 - 1.7908]}{0.09} = \$100,213$$

and

$$A = F(A/F,15\%,10)$$

$$= \$100,213(0.0493) = \$4,941$$

Deferred Uniform Payments

Frequently, uniform payments occur at points in time such that more than one interest formula must be applied in order to obtain the desired answer. For example, suppose a person borrows \$50,000 to purchase a small business and does not wish to begin repaying the loan until the end of the third year after purchasing the business. With an interest rate of 5% compounded annually, it is desired to determine the amount of the annual payment if 15 payments are made.

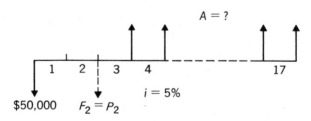

From the cash flow diagram it is apparent that direct use of the formula "Find A when given P" is not possible, since P does not occur one period prior to the first A. However, the problem can be logically solved in two steps. First, the amount of the loan, plus interest, after 2 years is

$$F_2 = P(F/P,5\%,2)$$

$$= \$50,000(1.1025) = \$55,125$$

Note the use of the subscript to denote the point in time. The direct use of $A = P(A/P,i\%,N)$ is now possible, since the amount to be repaid (\$55,125) occurs one period prior to the first loan payment. Therefore, the loan payment size will be

$$A = P_2(A/P,5\%,15)$$

$$= \$55,125(0.0963) = \$5,309$$

Compounding Frequency; Nominal and Effective Rates

In most economy studies, interest is accounted for as if compounding occurs once a year. In practice, the interest accumulation may take place more frequently, so it is important to note the effects of compounding frequency and to treat properly those problems where the assumption of annual compounding is not appropriate.

As an example, an interest rate may be stated as 12% compounded quarterly. In this case, the 12% is understood to be an annual rate, and is called the *nominal interest rate*. The number of compounding periods in a year is four. Hence, the interest rate per interest period is $12\% \div 4 = 3\%$ per quarter. The *effective interest rate* is the exact annual rate that takes into account the compounding which occurs within the year. The following formula may be used to calculate the effective interest rate:

$$\text{Effective rate} = (1 + r/M)^M - 1 \qquad\qquad 2\text{-}30$$

where M = Number of interest periods per year

r = Nominal interest rate

Recalling that $(1 + r/M)^M$ is the single sum compound amount factor, the effective interest rate may be determined directly from the interest tables using the relation

$$\text{Effective rate} = (F/P, r/M\%, M) - 1 \qquad\qquad 2\text{-}31$$

Hence, for our example, the effective rate is $(F/P, 3\%, 4) - 1 = 12.55\%$.

The effective interest rate can be determined for the case of an infinite number of compounding periods from Eq. (2-30) by letting M, the number of interest periods per year, become infinitely large. Such a condition is termed *continuous compounding*. Thus, the effective rate of interest with continuous compounding is $e^r - 1$, where e is the base of the Naperian or natural logarithms and equals 2.7183. As an example, the effective rate of 12% compounded continuously is $e^{0.12} - 1 = 12.75\%$.

The effect of compounding frequency on the effective interest rate for a nominal rate of 12% is given Table 2-2.

Continuous Compounding Interest Formulas

In some instances, particularly when payments are flowing rather frequently within periods rather than at the beginning or end of periods, the additional theoretical accuracy of continuous compounding may be significant. Continuous compounding means that the interest or profit growth

Table 2-2

IMPACT OF COMPOUNDING FREQUENCY UPON EFFECTIVE INTEREST RATE

		For a nominal rate of 12%	
Frequency of compounding	*No. of compounding periods per year*	*Interest rate per period*	*Effective rate*
Annual	1	12%	12.00%
Semiannual	2	6	12.36%
Quarterly	4	3	12.55%
Monthly	12	1	12.68%
Continuously	$\rightarrow \infty$	$\rightarrow 0$	12.75%

is proportional to the amount of total principal and interest at each instant.

To find the future worth of a present single sum under continuous compounding, we let N denote the number of years involved and substitute for i the effective interest rate for continuous compounding. Thus,

$$F = P(1 + i_{eff})^N$$
$$= P[1 + (e^r - 1)]^N \qquad \qquad 2\text{-}32$$
$$= Pe^{rN}$$

To find the present worth of a single sum under continuous compounding, the above equation can be transposed to

$$P = Fe^{-rN} \qquad \qquad 2\text{-}33$$

As an example, the future worth of a present amount of $10,000 at 20% nominal interest compounded continuously for 5 years is $10,000e^{0.20(5)} =$ $27,183.

The effective rate of interest in this case can be calculated as $e^r - 1 = e^{0.20} - 1 = 22.14\%$.

We can find that the future worth of the same $10,000 at effective interest of 22.14% compounded at the end of each year for 5 years is

$$F = P(F/P,22.14\%,5) = \$10,000(1 + 0.2214)^5 = \$27,183$$

This illustrates the general principle that continuous compounding at a given nominal interest rate is equivalent to discrete annual compounding at the corresponding effective rate for continuous compounding. Hence, by letting i equal $e^r - 1$ and N be expressed in years, the discrete interest factors can be used to deal directly with continuous compounding. The continuous compounding interest factors for discrete payments are given by the first six entries in Table 2-3. To distinguish between discrete and continuous compounding, the interest rate is underlined in the appropriate symbolic representation of the interest factor. Notice that the interest rate used in Table 2-3 is the nominal interest rate, r.

Table 2-3

SUMMARY OF CONTINUOUS COMPOUNDING INTEREST FACTORS AND SYMBOLS

To find	Given	Multiply "given" by factor below	Factor name	Factor functional symbol
Discrete payments				
F	P	e^{rN}	Continuous compounding compound amount factor (Discrete, single sum)	$(F/P,r\%,N)$
P	F	e^{-rN}	Continuous compounding present worth factor (Discrete, single sum)	$(P/F,r\%,N)$
P	A	$\dfrac{e^{rN} - 1}{e^{rN}(e^r - 1)}$	Continuous compounding present worth factor (Discrete, uniform series)	$(P/A,r\%,N)$
A	P	$\dfrac{e^{rN}(e^r - 1)}{e^{rN} - 1}$	Continuous compounding capital recovery factor (Discrete, uniform series)	$(A/P,r\%,N)$
F	A	$\dfrac{e^{rN} - 1}{e^r - 1}$	Continuous compounding compound amount factor (Discrete, uniform series)	$(F/A,r\%,N)$
A	F	$\dfrac{e^r - 1}{e^{rN} - 1}$	Continuous compounding sinking fund factor (Discrete, uniform series)	$(A/F,r\%,N)$
Continuous payments				
P	$\bar{A}$	$\dfrac{e^{rN} - 1}{re^{rN}}$	Continuous compounding present worth factor (Continuous, uniform flow)	$(P/\bar{A},r\%,N)$
$\bar{A}$	P	$\dfrac{re^{rN}}{e^{rN} - 1}$	Continuous compounding capital recovery factor (Continuous, uniform flow)	$(\bar{A}/P,r\%,N)$
F	$\bar{A}$	$\dfrac{e^{rN} - 1}{r}$	Continuous compounding compound amount factor (Continuous, uniform flow)	$(F/\bar{A},r\%,N)$
$\bar{A}$	F	$\dfrac{r}{e^{rN} - 1}$	Continuous compounding sinking fund factor (Continuous, uniform flow)	$(\bar{A}/F,r\%,N)$

Continuous Payments Throughout the Year

In some cases, money is disbursed uniformly throughout the year. Consequently, rather than depicting a cash flow of, say, $1,000 occurring at the end of the year, it is assumed that the $1,000 is spread uniformly over the year, as depicted in Fig. 2-6. To distinguish the discrete cash flow

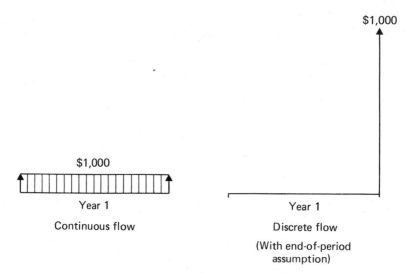

Figure 2-6. Comparison of continuous and discrete flows.

from the continuous cash flow, a bar above the symbol is used. Thus, $\bar{A}_k$ will denote the continuous cash flow spread uniformly over period k.

Suppose a total of $\bar{A}_1$ dollars flows uniformly and continuously throughout period 1. Divide $\bar{A}_1$ into M equal amounts to be deposited at equally spaced points in time during a year. The interest rate per period is r/M, and the future worth of the series of M equal amounts is

$$F = \frac{\bar{A}_1}{M}(F/A,r/M\%,M)$$

which reduces to

$$F = \frac{\bar{A}_1}{r}\left[\left(1 + \frac{r}{M}\right)^M - 1\right]$$

Letting M approach infinity yields

$$F = \bar{A}_1\frac{(e^r - 1)}{r} \qquad\qquad 2\text{-}34$$

Hence, a continuous and uniform flow of $\bar{A}_k$ over year k is equivalent to a single discrete sum of $\bar{A}_k(e^r - 1)/r$ at the end of year k. Employing the previous convention of denoting by A_k the value of a single sum of money occurring at the end of year k, it is evident that a set of continuous cash flows $\{\bar{A}_1, \bar{A}_2, \ldots, \bar{A}_N\}$ spread uniformly over years 1 through N, respectively, is equivalent to a set of discrete cash flows $\{A_1, A_2, \ldots, A_N\}$ occurring at the end of years 1 through N, respectively, with $A_k = \bar{A}_k(e^r - 1)/r$.

In order to obtain the appropriate continuous compounding interest formulas for continuous flows of money, substitute $\bar{A}_k(e^r - 1)/r$ for A_k in the equation for continuous compounding of discretely spaced cash flows. The resulting interest formulas are summarized in Table 2-3. Tables at the end of Appendix A-A provide factors for continuous compounding.

SOLVED PROBLEMS

1. A person makes six end-of-year deposits of $1,000 in an account paying 5% compounded annually. If the accumulated fund is withdrawn 4 years after the last deposit, how much money will be withdrawn?

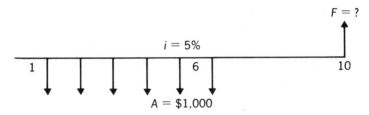

Since F does not occur at the time of the last A, it is necessary that the solution proceed in two steps. The amount of money in the account at the time of the last deposit may be computed as

$$F_6 = A(F/A,5\%,6)$$
$$= \$1,000(6.8019) = \$6,802$$

The problem now is to find F_{10}, given $F_6 = P_6 = \$6,802$

$$F_{10} = P_6(F/P,5\%,4)$$
$$= \$6,802(1.2155) = \$8,268$$

2. What is the effective interest rate for 4.75% compounded annually and 4.60% compounded quarterly?

$$\text{Effective rate} = (1 + r/M)^M - 1$$
$$= (1 + 0.0475)^1 - 1$$
$$= 4.75\%$$
$$\text{Effective rate} = (1 + r/M)^M - 1$$
$$= \left[1 + \frac{0.046}{4}\right]^4 - 1$$
$$= 4.68\%$$

3. A loan company advertises that it will loan $1,000 to be repaid in 30 monthly installments of $44.60. What is the effective interest rate?

$$A = P(A/P,i\%,30)$$
$$\frac{\$44.60}{\$1,000.00} = (A/P,i\%,30) = 0.0446$$

By inspection (with interpolation in tables), $i = 2\%$, and

Effective rate $= (F/P,2\%,12) - 1 = 0.2682 = 26.82\%$

4. Annual deposits of $1,000 are made in an account which pays 4% compounded quarterly. How much money should be in the account immediately after the fifth deposit?

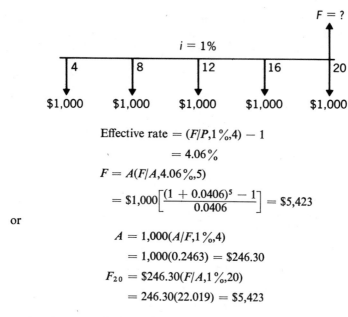

Effective rate $= (F/P,1\%,4) - 1$

$$= 4.06\%$$

$$F = A(F/A,4.06\%,5)$$

$$= \$1,000\left[\frac{(1 + 0.0406)^5 - 1}{0.0406}\right] = \$5,423$$

or

$$A = 1,000(A/F,1\%,4)$$

$$= 1,000(0.2463) = \$246.30$$

$$F_{20} = \$246.30(F/A,1\%,20)$$

$$= 246.30(22.019) = \$5,423$$

An alternate solution method is to treat the five annual deposits as single sums of money. Therefore,

$$F = \$1,000[(F/P,1\%,16) + (F/P,1\%,12) + (F/P,1\%,8) + (F/P,1\%,4) + 1]$$

$$= \$1,000[1.1726 + 1.1268 + 1.0829 + 1.0406 + 1.000] = \$5,423$$

5. Given the payments shown in the cash flow diagram, what is the equivalent worth at 1979 with interest at 6%?

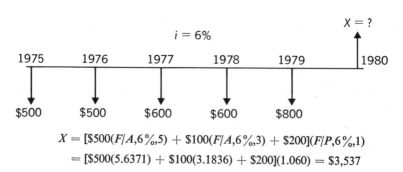

$$X = [\$500(F/A,6\%,5) + \$100(F/A,6\%,3) + \$200](F/P,6\%,1)$$

$$= [\$500(5.6371) + \$100(3.1836) + \$200](1.060) = \$3,537$$

6. With interest at 8% compounded annually, how long does it take for a certain amount to double in magnitude?

$$2 = 1(F/P,8\%,N)$$
$$(F/P,8\%,N) = 2.00$$

By inspection of 8% interest tables, $N = 9$ years.

7. An individual approaches the Loan Shark Agency for $1,000 to be repaid in 24 monthly installments. The agency advertises interest at $1\frac{1}{2}\%$ per month. They proceed to calculate the size of his payment in the following manner:

Amount requested:	$1,000	
Credit investigation:	25	
Credit risk insurance:	· 5	
Total:	$1,030	

Interest:	$(1030)(24)(0.015) = \$371$
Total owed:	$\$1,030 + \$371 = \$1,401$
Payment:	$\dfrac{\$1,401}{24} = \$58.50$

What effective interest rate is the individual paying?

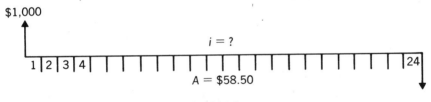

$$A = P(A/P,i\%,24)$$
$$\$58.50 = \$1,000(A/P,i\%,24)$$

By interpolation in tables, $i = 2.9\%$ per month, and

$$\text{Effective rate} = (F/P,2.9\%,12) - 1 = 1.41 - 1 = 41\%$$

8. Money is to be invested for a child's college expenses. Annual deposits of $1,000 are made in a fund that pays 5% compounded annually. If the first deposit is made on the child's 5th birthday and the last on the child's 15th birthday, what is the size of 4 equal withdrawals on the child's 18th, 19th, 20th, and 21st birthdays that will just deplete the account?

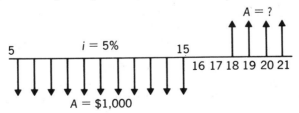

Amount in fund at $t = 15$:

$$F_{15} = A(F/A,5\%,11)$$
$$= \$1,000(14.2068) = \$14,207$$

Amount in fund at $t = 17$:

$$F_{17} = P_{15}(F/P,5\%,2)$$
$$= \$14,207(1.1025) = \$15,663$$

Amount of withdrawals:

$$A = P_{17}(A/P,5\%,4)$$
$$= \$15,663(0.2820) = \$4,417$$

9. A college student borrows money in her senior year to buy a car. She defers payments for 6 months and makes 36 beginning-of-month payments thereafter. If the original note is for \$3,000 and interest is $\frac{1}{2}\%$ per month on the unpaid balance, how much will her payments be?

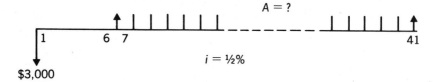

$$i = \tfrac{1}{2}\%$$

\$3,000

Amount owed at $t = 5$:

$$F_5 = P_0(F/P,\tfrac{1}{2}\%,5)$$
$$= \$3,000(1.0253) = \$3,076$$

Amount of monthly payments:

$$A = P_5(A/P,\tfrac{1}{2}\%,36)$$
$$= \$3,075\left[\frac{i(1 + i)^N}{(1 + i)^N - 1}\right]$$
$$= \$3,075\left[\frac{(0.005)(1.005)^{36}}{(1.005)^{36} - 1}\right] = \$93.50$$

10. What is the present worth of \$100,000 ten years hence if interest is (a) 15% compounded annually? (b) 15% compounded continuously?
    a. $P = F(P/F,15\%,10) = \$100,000(0.2472) = \$24,720$
    b. $P = F(P/F,15\%,10) = \$100,000(0.2231) = \$22,310$

11. A firm spends \$10,000 per year on materials, with the cost spread uniformly over each year. Annual rental payments for building and equipment total \$30,000 per year, with the payments being made at the beginning of each year.

Using an interest rate of 10% compounded continuously, what is the present worth equivalent for 10 year's of activity?

$$P = \bar{A}(P/\bar{A},10\%,10) + A(P/A,\underline{10\%},9) + A$$
$$= \$10,000(6.3212) + \$30,000(5.6425) + \$30,000 = \$262,487$$

or

$$P = \frac{\$10,000(e^{0.10} - 1)}{0.10}(P/A,\underline{10\%},10) + \$30,000(5.6425) + \$30,000$$

$$= \$10,517.09(6.0104) + \$30,000(5.6425) + \$30,000 = \$262,487$$

PROBLEMS*

2-1. How much money today is equivalent to $10,000 in 8 years, with interest of 6% compounded annually?

2-2. How much money must be deposited today in a fund paying 8% compounded annually in order to accumulate $50,000 in 20 years?

· 2-3. How much money should be placed in a fund today and every year thereafter to accumulate $3,500 in 5 years? (Assume an interest rate of 5% compounded annually and the $3,500 includes the deposit made at the end of the fifth year.)

2-4. How many monthly payments are necessary to repay a loan of $5,000 with an interest rate of 1% per month and payments of $235.35? (The first payment is made 1 month after receipt of the $5,000.)

2-5. An individual borrows $5,000 and repays the loan with annual payments of $1,319 for 5 years. What was the annual interest rate for the loan transaction?

2-6. An individual purchased a refrigerator for $750 from a department store. The refrigerator was paid for using the department store's revolving charge account. The store charges 1% on the unpaid monthly balance. If the refrigerator is paid for in 30 months, what will be the size of the monthly payment? What is the effective interest rate for the charge account?

2-7. What interest rate makes an investment of $1,000 today equivalent to five annual withdrawals of $400 each with the first $400 occurring 6 years from now?

2-8. How much money today is equivalent to $20,000 in 20 years, with interest of 8% compounded semiannually?

2-9. What is the effective interest rate for 8% compounded (a) annually? (b) semiannually? (c) quarterly? (d) continuously?

2-10. An individual borrows $10,000 at 8% compounded annually. Equal annual payments are to be made for 6 years. However, at the time of the fourth payment, the individual elects to pay off the loan. How much should be paid?

*Unless stated otherwise, assume discrete compounding and end-of-period payments.

2-11. Over a 5-year period, a firm spends $16,000 per year for supplies with the cost occurring continuously and uniformly over each year. Using an interest rate of 8% compounded continuously, determine the present sum of money that is equivalent to the expenditures?

2-12. An individual receives an annual bonus and deposits it in a savings account paying interest at a rate of 6% compounded annually. The size of the annual bonus increases at a rate of 4% per year. How much money will be in the account immediately after the tenth deposit if the first deposit equals $400?

2-13. An individual borrows $10,000 and wishes to repay it with 10 annual payments. Each payment is to be $100 greater than the previous payment. With an interest rate of 8% compounded annually, what will be the size of the last payment?

2-14. A person deposits $1,000 in an account each year for 5 years; at the end of 5 years, one-half of the account balance is withdrawn; $2,000 is deposited annually for 5 more years, with the total balance withdrawn at the end of the fifteenth year. If the account earns interest at a rate of 5%, how much is withdrawn (a) at the end of 5 years? (b) at the end of 15 years?

2-15. Given the cash flow diagram shown below and an interest rate of 8% per period, solve for the value of an equivalent amount at (a) $t = 5$, (b) $t = 12$, (c) $t = 15$. (*Note:* Upward arrows represent cash inflows and downward arrows represent cash outflows.)

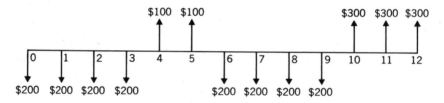

2-16. Revenues from a certain project are expected to be $20,000 at the end of the first year and to decrease at the rate of $1,000 per year through the 15-year life of the project. If interest is 20%, (a) what is the equivalent annual worth of those revenues? (b) what is the equivalent present worth?

2-17. What is the equivalent worth at the end of 6 years of a present expenditure of $5,000 if interest is 25% nominal compounded continuously?

2-18. What is the present worth of operating expenditures of $100,000 per yr which are assumed to be incurred continuously throughout an 8-year period if the effective annual rate of interest is 12%?

2-19. What is the equivalent present worth of $1,000 obligations at the beginning of each year for 5 years if interest is 9.53% nominal, compounded continuously; i.e., the effective rate is 10%?

2-20. A person deposits $1,000 per year into an account which pays interest at a continuous compound rate of 5% the first year after the initial deposit. The annual nominal rate increases by 0.25% each year. If 10 annual deposits are made, what will be the worth of the fund immediately after the last deposit?

2-21. An individual borrows $4,000 and repays the loan with three equal annual payments. The interest rate for the first year of the loan is 5% compounded annually, for the second year of the loan is 6% compounded annually, and for the third year of the loan is 8% compounded annually. Determine the size of the equal annual payment.

2-22. An individual deposits $2,000 in a savings account each year for 5 years. The first year after the initial deposit the account pays interest at a rate of 5% compounded annually; the second year after the initial deposit the interest rate is 5% compounded continuously; the third year the interest rate is 6% compounded annually; an interest rate of 6% compounded semiannually exists the fourth year; and 6% compounded continuously is the interest rate the fifth year. How much money is accumulated in the account one year after the fifth deposit?

2-23. An individual makes semiannual deposits of $800 into an account which pays interest equivalent to 8% compounded quarterly. Determine the account balance immediately after the eighth deposit.

2-24. A firm purchases a unit of equipment for P, keeps it for N years, and sells it for F. With an interest rate of i%, show that the equivalent uniform annual cost for the transaction is given by either

$$P(A/P,i\%,N) - F(A/F,i\%,N)$$

or

$$(P - F)(A/P,i\%,N) + Fi$$

or

$$(P - F)(A/F,i\%,N) + Pi$$

2-25. Consider a cash flow series $\{A_1, \ldots, A_N\}$ consisting of N discrete cash flows. Suppose $A_k = pA_{k-1}$ when $0 < p < 1$. Develop a closed form expression for the present sum equivalent based on an interest rate of i% per period.

2-26. Consider a cash flow series $\{A_1, \ldots, A_N\}$ consisting of N discrete cash flows. Suppose $A_k = kC$ where C is a positive constant. Develop a closed form expression for the present sum equivalent based on an interest rate of i% per period.

2-27. Consider a cash flow series $\{A_1, \ldots, A_N\}$ consisting of n discrete cash flows. Suppose $A_k = A_1 e^{(k-1)C}$ where $0 < C < 1$. Develop a closed form expression for the future sum equivalent based on an interest rate of r% compounded continuously.

2-28. In Problem 2-27 suppose $A_k = k(1 + j)^{k-1}A_1$. Develop a closed form expression for the future sum equivalent based on an interest rate of i% per period.

2-29. Consider a cash flow series $\{A_1, A_2, \ldots\}$ consisting of an infinite number of discrete cash flows. Suppose $A_k = A_1(1 + j)^{k-1}/k!$ where ! denotes the factorial operation. Develop a closed form expression for the present sum equivalent based on an interest rate of $i\%$ per period.

2-30. If $\$P$ is borrowed and repaid with N equal annual payments of $\$A$, based on an interest rate of $i\%$, then show that the amount of payment k that is an interest payment is given by

$$I_k = A[1 - (P/F,i\%,N - k + 1)]$$

and the amount of payment k that is a payment against the principal amount borrowed is given by

$$E_k = A(P/F,i\%,N - k + 1)$$

Chapter

3

equivalent worth methods for comparing alternatives

In comparing investment alternatives a number of different measures of economic effectiveness are often used. This and the following two chapters consider various methods for studying the economic desirability of an individual project and for comparing the relative economic desirabilities of two or more projects. The methods are as follows:

1. present worth;
2. annual worth;
3. future worth;
4. rate of return;
5. benefit-cost ratio.

The first three methods are treated in this chapter, rate of return methods are presented in Chapter 4, and benefit-cost methods are the subject of

Chapter 5. All of the methods are based on the concept of the time value of money. Hence, the mathematical operations described in Chapter 2 will be continued in the following chapters.

Measures of Economic Effectiveness

The various measures of economic effectiveness that will be used in this text are defined as follows:

Present worth: A determination of the present worth (P.W.) involves the conversion of each individual cash flow to its present worth equivalent and the summation of the individual present worths to obtain the net present worth.

Annual worth: The annual worth (A.W.) is determined by converting all cash flows to an equivalent uniform annual series of cash flows.

Future worth: The future worth (F.W.) is obtained by converting each individual cash flow to its future worth equivalent and determining the net future worth for the project.

Rate of return: Among the many definitions of rate of return, the most popular definition is that interest rate which yields a net present worth of zero; such a rate of return is referred to as the *internal rate of return* (I.R.R.).

Benefit-cost ratio: There are several definitions of the benefit-cost ratio (B/C), but, in general, it can be defined as the ratio of the equivalent worth of benefits to the equivalent worth of costs.

Defining Investment Alternatives

In defining investment *alternatives* it is important to ensure that the set of alternatives is mutually exclusive; the term mutually exclusive signifies that an "either-or, but not both" situation exists. That is, the choice of one excludes the choice of any other. Investment *opportunities* will denote projects, proposals, and other options available for investment. Distinct combinations of investment opportunities will be used to define the investment alternatives.

As an illustration, suppose two investment opportunities, A and B, are available. In this case, four mutually exclusive alternatives can be formed: neither A nor B, A only, B only, and both A and B. In general, if there are m investment opportunities then 2^m investment alternatives can be formed. Of course, not all of the 2^m alternatives are necessarily feasible because there are budget limitations, dependencies among investment opportunities, and other restrictions.

Example:

Two industrial trucks, A and B, are being considered by the warehouse manager. In addition, two industrial truck attachments, C and D, are being considered. Opportunities A and B are mutually exclusive; opportunities C and D are mutually exclusive; and the purchase of an attachment is *contingent* upon the purchase of one of the trucks. The 16 possible alternatives are:

Do nothing	D only*	B and C	A, B, and D*
A only	A and B*	B and D	A, C, and D*
B only	A and C	C and D*	B, C, and D*
C only*	A and D	A, B, and C*	A, B, C, and D*

*Denotes an infeasible alternative.

Nine alternatives are infeasible because of the mutually exclusive and contingent dependencies among the investment opportunities. Thus, only seven alternatives must be considered.

A Systematic Procedure for Comparing Investment Alternatives

A systematic procedure for comparing investment alternatives can be stated as follows:

1. define the alternatives;
2. determine the study period;
3. provide estimates of the cash flows for each alternative;
4. specify the time value of money or interest rate;
5. select the measure(s) of effectiveness;
6. compare the alternatives;
7. perform sensitivity analyses;
8. select the preferred alternative.

As noted in the previous sections, one may wish to aggregate investment opportunities in various combinations to arrive at the alternatives to be compared. As an illustration, suppose exactly one tractor-trailer combination is to be purchased. There might exist two tractor alternatives (A and B) and two trailer alternatives (C and D). Hence, there can be formed four tractor-trailer alternatives (AC, AD, BC, BD). Additionally. the do-nothing alternative (maintain the status quo) should not be overlooked.

The study period defines the period of time over which the analysis is to be performed. Cash flows that occur prior to and after the study period are not considered, except as they might influence cash flows during the study period. The study period may or may not be the same as the useful lives for equipment involved. If the study period is less than the useful life of an asset, then an estimate should be provided of its salvage value at the end of the study period; if the study period is longer than the useful life of an asset, then estimates of cash flows should be provided for subsequent replacements for the asset.

Estimates of the cash flows should be provided for each alternative by using the approaches described in Chapter 9. Even though an asset may continue to be used for a period of time beyond the study period, an estimate of its salvage value should be provided assuming it will be disposed of at the end of the study period.

The interest rate or discount rate to be used is the minimum attractive rate for the firm. The *minimum attractive rate of return* (M.A.R.R.), treated in detail in Chapter 10, is defined to be the return that could be earned by investing elsewhere (opportunity cost concept).

As mentioned previously, a number of different measures of economic effectiveness can be selected. All of the methods we consider will yield the same choices. The recommended basis for selecting a particular measure of economic effectiveness is communication. Namely, the method which is best understood by management should be used so long as it yields recommendations consistent with those based on correct time value of money analyses. We will have more to say about this matter at the end of Chapter 4.

When the measure of economic effectiveness is used, the alternatives should be compared and the most economic alternative identified. In the case of present worth, annual worth, and future worth comparisons, one can rank the alternatives on the basis of their worths. When rate of return and benefit-cost ratio comparisons are used, an incremental approach is used.

Since the comparison of investment alternatives involves the use of estimates of future economic conditions, errors can occur. Consequently, it is worthwhile to consider the consequences of such errors on the decision to be made. Sensitivity analyses can be performed to determine the effect of estimation errors on the economic performance of each alternative. Methods for performing sensitivity analyses are presented in Chapters 12 and 13.

The final selection of the preferred alternative is complicated by the presence of nonmonetary factors, multiple objectives, and risk and uncertainties concerning future outcomes. Methods for treating such conditions are presented in Chapters 9, 14, and 15.

Judging the Economic Worth of Investment Opportunities

The measures of economic effectiveness can be used to judge the economic worth of individual investment opportunities. In this section, it will be assumed that each investment opportunity is independent of other opportunities that may be under consideration. Furthermore, it is assumed that there are no restrictions on the number of such investment opportunities to be undertaken. The decision is not which of several opportunities is best, but rather, is an individual opportunity a worthwhile investment. We define an opportunity as being worthwhile if it either has a non-negative present worth, annual worth, or future worth, a rate of return at least equal to the minimum attractive rate of return, or a benefit-cost ratio at least equal to one.

Example:

Given the following investment opportunities, and using each of the five methods, determine which are worthwhile investment opportunities. A minimum attractive rate of return of 10% is to be used in the analysis.

Opportunity	Investment (P)	Study period (N)	Salvage value (F)	Net annual Cash flow (A)
A	$10,000	5 yr	$10,000	+$2,000
B	12,000	5 yr	-0-	+ 3,000
C	15,000	5 yr	-0-	+ 4,167

Solution:

By using methods to be described subsequently, the following values are obtained:

Opportunity	Present worth	Annual worth	Future worth	Rate of return	Benefit-cost ratio
A	+3,790	+1,000	+6,106	20%	2.0000
B	− 630	− 170	−1,015	8%	0.9475
C	+ 850	+ 217	+1,369	12%	1.0567

Thus, investments A and C (in that order) are deemed worthwhile.

Present Worth (P.W.) Method

The term *present worth* (P.W.) means an amount at some beginning or base time that is equivalent to a particular schedule of receipts and/or disbursements under consideration. If disbursements only are considered, the term can be best expressed as *present worth-cost*.

Study Period in Comparisons of Alternative Projects

In comparing alternatives by the present worth method, it is essential that all alternatives be considered over the same length of time. If the alternatives each have the same expected life, there is no problem, for that life can be used. When the alternatives have different expected lives, it is common to use a study period equal to the lowest common multiple of the lives, or the length of time during which the services of the chosen alternative will be needed, whichever is less. For example, if two alternatives have expected lives of 3 and 4 years respectively, then the lowest common multiple of the lives to use as a study period is 12 years. However, if the service for which the alternatives are being compared is expected to be needed for only 9 years, then 9 years should be the study period used.

Comparing Alternatives Using Present Worth Analysis When Receipts and Disbursements Are Known

When receipts (cash inflow) as well as disbursements (cash outflow) figures for more than one mutually exclusive project are known, that project should be chosen which has the highest net present worth, as long as that present worth is greater than zero. As an example, consider two alternative lathes A and B, only one of which should be selected, if any.

Example:

	Lathe	
	A	B
First cost:	$10,000	$15,000
Life:	5 yr	10 yr
Salvage value:	$2,000	0
Annual receipts:	$5,000	$7,000
Annual disbursements:	$2,200	$4,300
Minimum attractive rate of return = 8%		
Study period = 10 yr		

Solution:

The lowest common multiple of the lives is 10 years. Assuming that the service will be needed for at least that long and that what is estimated to happen in the first 5 years for project A will be repeated in the second 5 years, the solution is

56

	Lathe	
	A	B
Annual receipts = $5,000(P/A,8%,10)$:	$33,550	
7,000$(P/A,8%,10)$:		$46,970
Salvage value at year 10 = $2,000$(P/F,8%,10)$:	926	
Total P.W. of cash inflow:	$34,476	$46,970
Annual disbursements = $2,200$(P/A,8%,10)$:	−$14,762	
4,300$(P/A,8%,10)$:		−$28,853
First cost:	− 10,000	− 15,000
Replacement = ($10,000 − $2,000)$(P/F,8%,5)$:	− 5,445	
Total P.W. of cash outflow:	−$30,207	−$43,853
Net P.W.:	$4,269	$3,117

Thus, project A, having the highest net present worth which is greater than zero, is the better economic choice.

Comparing Alternatives Using Present Worth Analysis When Receipts Are Constant or Not Known

When alternatives which perform essentially identical services involve only known cash outflows, it is possible to compare the alternatives on the basis of present worth-cost (P.W.–cost). The method of study is the same as illustrated for the example above except, of course, the alternative with the lowest present worth-cost is best. As an example, consider the following situation involving two compressors, each of which will do the desired job but differ as shown.

Example:

	Compressor	
	I	II
First cost:	$3,000	$4,000
Life:	6 yr	9 yr
Salvage value:	$500	0
Annual operating disbursements:	$2,000	$1,600
Minimum return on investment = 15%		
Study period = 18 yr		

Solution:

Again, assuming a study period equal to the lowest common multiple of lives, i.e., 18 years:

	I	*II*
First cost:	$ 3,000	$ 4,000
First replacement = ($3,000 — $500)($P/F$,15%,6):	1,080	
$4,000($P/F$,15%,9):		1,138
Second replacement = ($3,000 — $500)($P/F$,15%,12):	468	
Operating disbursements = $2,000($P/A$,15%,18):	12,225	
$1,600($P/A$,15%,18):		9,800
Less Salvage value @ 18 = $500($P/F$,15%18):	— 41	
Net P.W.–cost:	$ 16.732	$ 14,938

Since compressor II has the lowest net present worth–cost, it is the better economic choice.

Annual Worth (A. W.) Method

The term *annual worth* (A.W.) means a uniform annual series of money for a certain period of time which is equivalent in amount to a particular schedule of receipts and/or disbursements under consideration. If disbursements only are considered, the term is usually expressed as annual cost (A.C.) or equivalent uniform annual cost (E.U.A.C.).

Calculation of Capital Recovery Cost

The *capital recovery cost* (C.R.) for a project is the equivalent uniform annual cost of the capital invested. It is an annual amount which covers the following two items:

1. depreciation (loss in value of the asset);
2. interest (minimum attractive rate of return) on invested capital.

As an example, consider a machine or other asset which will cost $10,000, last 5 years, and then have a salvage value of $2,000. Further, the interest on invested capital, i, is 8%.

It can be shown that no matter which method of calculating depreciation is used, the equivalent annual cost of the capital recovery is the same. For example, if straight line depreciation is used, the equivalent annual cost of interest is calculated to be $564 as shown in Table 3-1. The annual depreciation cost by the straight line method is ($10,000 − $2,000)/5 = $1,600. The $564 added to $1,600 results in a calculated capital recovery cost of $2,164.

Table 3-1

CALCULATION OF EQUIVALENT ANNUAL COST OF INTEREST
ASSUMING STRAIGHT LINE DEPRECIATION

Year	Investment at beginning of year	Interest on beginning-of-year investment @8%	Present worth of interest @8%	
1	$10,000	$800	$800(P/F,8%,1) =	$741
2	8,400	672	672(P/F,8%,2) =	576
3	6,800	544	544(P/F,8%,3) =	434
4	5,200	416	416(P/F,8%,4) =	306
5	3,600	288	288(P/F,8%,5) =	196
			Total:	$2,253

Annual equivalent of interest = $2,253(A/P,8%,5) = $564

There are several convenient formulas by which capital recovery cost may be calculated in order to obtain the same answer as above. The most apparent formula is (using the same figures as for the machine above)

$$\text{C.R.} = P(A/P,i\%,N) - F(A/F,i\%,N)$$
$$= \$10,000(A/P,8\%,5) - \$2,000(A/F,8\%,5)$$
$$= \$10,000(0.2505) - \$2,000(0.1705) = \$2,164$$

Two other convenient formulas for calculating the capital recovery cost are

$$\text{C.R.} = P(i\%) + (P - F)(A/F,i\%,N)$$
$$= P(0.08) + (P - F)(A/F,8\%,5)$$
$$= \$10,000(0.08) + \$8,000(0.1705) = \$2,164$$

and

$$\text{C.R.} = (P - F)(A/P,i\%,N) + F(i\%)$$
$$= (P - F)(A/P,8\%,5) + F(8\%)$$
$$= \$8,000(0.2505) + \$2,000(0.08) = \$2,164$$

The last of the above formulas will be used primarily for the calculation of capital recovery cost throughout the rest of this book.

Comparing Alternatives Using Annual Worth Analysis When Receipts and Disbursements Are Known

When receipts as well as disbursements figures are known for more than one mutually exclusive project, that project should be chosen which has the highest net annual worth, as long as that net annual worth is greater than zero.

As an example, consider the following two alternative lathes treated previously.

Example:

	Lathe	
	A	B
First cost:	$10,000	$15,000
Life:	5 yr	10 yr
Salvage value:	$2,000	0
Annual receipts:	$5,000	$7,000
Annual disbursements:	$2,200	$4,300
Minimum attractive rate of return = 8%		
Study period = 10 yr		

Solution:

	Lathe			
	A			B
Annual receipts:	$5,000			$7,000
Annual disbursements:	−$2,200			−$4,300
C.R. Cost = $8,000(A/P,8%,5)				
+ $2,000(8%):	−$2,164	$15,000(A/P,8%,10):		−$2,235
Net A.W.:	$ 636			$ 465

Thus project A, having the higher net annual worth, is the better economic choice.

Comparing Alternatives Using Annual Worth Analysis When Receipts Are Constant or Not Known

Very often alternative projects are expected to perform almost identical functions so that each results in the same receipts, savings, or benefits. Sometimes the savings or benefits are intangible or cannot be estimated;

hence, the alternatives are judged on the basis of negative net annual worth, or annual cost. As an example, consider the same alternative compressors as were compared earlier using the P.W. method:

Example:

	Compressor	
	I	*II*
First cost:	$3,000	$4,000
Life:	6 yr	9 yr
Salvage value:	$500	0
Annual operating disbursements:	$2,000	$1,600
Minimum return on investment = 15%		
Study period = 18 yr		

Solution:

	Compressor	
	I	*II*
C.R. Cost = ($3,000 − $500)($A/P$,15%,6) + $500(15%):	−$ 735	
C.R. Cost = $4,000($A/P$,15%,9):		−$ 838
Annual operating disbursements:	−$2,000	−$1,600
Net A.W.:	−$2,735	−$2,438

Thus, compressor II, having the lower annual cost (least negative annual worth), is apparently the more economic choice. It should be noted that this analysis of competing alternatives with different lives makes certain assumptions to be discussed subsequently.

Future Worth (F. W.) Method

The term *future worth* (F.W.) means an amount at some ending or termination time which is equivalent to a particular schedule of receipts and/or disbursements under consideration. If disbursements only are considered, the term can best be expressed as *future worth–cost* (F.W.–cost) or *future cost*. The future worth is also referred to as the *terminal worth*.

Comparing Alternatives Using Future Worth Analysis When Receipts and Disbursements Are Known

When receipt as well as disbursement figures are known for more than one mutually exclusive project, that project should be chosen which has the highest net future worth, as long as that net future worth is greater than zero.

As an example, consider the same two alternative lathes treated previously:

Example:

	Lathe A	Lathe B
First cost:	$10,000	$15,000
Life:	5 yr	10 yr
Salvage value:	$2,000	0
Annual receipts:	$5,000	$7,000
Annual disbursements:	$2,200	$4,300
Minimum attractive rate of return = 8%		
Study period = 10 yr		

Solution:

	Lathe A	Lathe B
Annual receipts = $5,000(F/A,8%,10):	$72,433	
$7,000(F/A,8%,10):		$101,406
Salvage value at year 10:	$2,000	
Total F.W. of cash inflow:	$74,433	$101,406
Annual disbursements = $2,200(F/A,8%,10):	−$31,871	
= 4,300(F/A,8%,10):		−$62,292
First cost = 10,000(F/P,8%,10):	−$21,589	
= 15,000(F/P,8%,10):		−$32,384
Replacement = ($10,000 − $2,000)(F/P,8%,5):	−$11,754	
Total F.W. of cash inflow:	−$65,214	−$94,676
Net F.W.:	$ 9,219	$ 6,730

Thus, project A, having the highest net future worth, is the better economic choice.

Comparing Alternatives Using Future Worth Analysis When Receipts Are Constant or Not Known

As noted for present worth and annual worth analyses, alternative projects can be expected to perform identical functions such that only known cost outflows are given. It is possible to compare the alternatives on the basis of future worth–cost. The method of study is the same as illustrated for the above example; however, the alternative with the lowest future worth–cost is best. As an example, consider the same two compressors treated earlier.

Example:

	Compressor	
	I	II
First cost:	$3,000	$4,000
Life:	6 yr	9 yr
Salvage value:	$500	0
Annual operating disbursements:	$2,000	$1,600
Minimum attractive rate of return = 15%		
Study period = 18 yr		

Solution:

It is assumed that replacements have identical cash flows.

	Future worth–cost compressor	
	I	II
First cost = $3,000(F/P,15%,18):	$ 37,127	
$4,000(F/P,15%,18):		$ 49,502
First replacement = ($3,000 − $500) (F/P,15%,12):	$ 13,375	
$4,000(F/P,15%,9):		$ 14,072
Second replacement = ($3,000 − $500) (F/P,15%,6):	$ 5,783	
Operating disbursements = $2,000(F/A,15%,18):	$151,673	
$1,600(F/A,15%,18):		$121,338
Less salvage value @yr 18:	− $ 500	
Net F.W. − cost:	$207,458	$184,912

Since compressor II has the lowest net future worth–cost, it is the better economic choice.

Assumptions in Comparisons of Alternatives
with Different Lives

In the comparison of projects A and B and also the comparison of compressors I and II, the alternatives compared had different expected lives. The solutions as shown are fully valid only if the following assumptions are reasonable:

1. The period of needed service for which the alternatives are being compared (study period) is either indefinitely long or a length of time equal to a common multiple of the lives of the alternatives.
   Note: The student should recognize that any point in time equal to a common multiple of lives would be a point at which each alternative would have just exhausted a life cycle.
2. What is estimated to happen in the first life cycle will happen in all succeeding life cycles, if any, for each alternative.

These assumptions are commonly made in economic analyses by default; i.e., they are made because there is no good basis for estimates to the contrary. The assumptions are sometimes referred to as the *repeatability* assumptions. They are implicitly contained in all examples and problems illustrating all methods of economic evaluations herein unless there is a statement to the contrary.

Applied to the earlier examples in which the compressors were compared, the assumptions mean the following:

1. The services of a compressor will be needed either 18 years, 36 years, 54 years, etc., or indefinitely.
2. When either compressor I or II is replaced at the end of a life cycle, it will be replaced with a compressor having characteristics affecting cost (i.e., first cost, life, salvage value, and annual operating disbursements) identical to the estimates used for the first life cycle.

Whenever alternatives to be compared have different lives and one or both of the conditions are not appropriate, then it is necessary to enumerate what receipts and what disbursements are expected to occur at what points in time for each alternative for as long as service will be needed or the irregularity is expected to exist (i.e., the study period.) This is sometimes referred to as the *coterminated* assumption. The enumerated information can then be converted into an equivalent P.W.,A.W.,F.W., or other measure of merit by ordinary time value of money computations.

Example:

Suppose that for the compressor illustration above it is expected that the standard assumptions are not met as follows: (a) a compressor is needed for only 12 years; (b) the replacement for compressor II is expected to cost $7,000 rather than $4,000, and its salvage value after 3 years' service (end of the twelfth year of study) is expected to be $200. Compare the two compressors by the annual cost method.

Solution:

The annual cost (A.C.) for compressor I remains the same at $2,735. For compressor II, the cash flow diagram and solution are

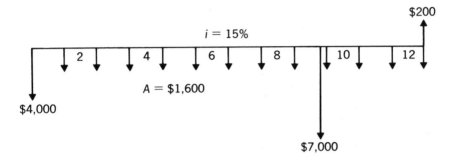

$$A.C. = [\$4,000 + \$7,000(P/F,15\%,9) - \$200(P/F,15\%,12)](A/P,15\%,12)$$
$$+ \$1,600$$
$$= [\$4,000 + \$7,000(0.2843) - \$200(0.1869)](0.1845) + \$1,600$$
$$= \$2,698$$

Thus, under the changed conditions, compressor II is still the least costly, but by less margin.

The easiest way to calculate the present worths (at time 0) and the future worths (at time 12) for comparison of the alternatives, given the above annual costs, is as follows:

Alternative	P.W.–cost = A.C. $(P/A,15\%,12)$
I	$2,735 (5.4206) = $14,825
II	$2,698 (5.4206) = $14,625

Alternative	F.W.–cost = A.C. $(F/A,15\%,12)$
I	$2,735 (29.0017) = $79,320
II	$2,698 (29.0017) = $78,247

Relationship of Various Analysis Methods

All methods of economic evaluation considered to this point have the reassuring property of providing consistent results regarding the economic desirability or relative ranking of projects compared. In fact, it can be shown that the annual worths, present worths, and future worths for any projects under comparison are linearly proportional to each other.

Example:

Show the consistency of economic comparison results for compressors I and II by the various methods given in this chapter.

Solution:

$$\frac{P.W._I}{P.W._{II}} = \frac{A.W._I}{A.W._{II}} = \frac{F.W._I}{F.W._{II}}; \frac{\$16,732}{\$14,938} = \frac{\$2,735}{\$2,438} = \frac{\$207,458}{\$184,912} = 1.12$$

PROBLEMS

3-1. What is the maximum you would be willing to pay now for each of the alternatives A, B, and C if your minimum expected return is 8% and the alternatives yield receipts as below?

	Alternative		
	A	*B*	*C*
Receipts 1 yr hence	$ 100	$ 500	$ 300
Receipts 2 yr hence	200	400	300
Receipts 3 yr hence	300	300	300
Receipts 4 yr hence	400	200	300
Receipts 5 yr hence	500	100	300
Totals:	$1500	$1500	$1500

3-2. A machine can be repaired today for $2,500. If repairs are not made, operating expenses are expected to increase by $400 each year for the next 5 years. The minimum acceptable rate of return is 12%. Compare the present worths of the costs of repairing versus not repairing, assuming that the machine will have no value at the end of the 5-year period.

3-3. The following alternatives are available to fill a given need which is expected to exist for 12 years. Each is expected to have 0 salvage value at the end of each life cycle.

	Plan A	*Plan B*	*Plan C*
First cost:	$2,000	$6,000	$12,000
Life cycle:	6 yr	3 yr	4 yr
Annual disbursements:	$3,500	$1,000	$400

If the minimum attractive rate of return is 10%, compare the alternatives using the following methods:

a. Present worth method
b. Annual worth method
c. Future worth method

3-4. A processing firm entered into a contract for raw materials by agreeing to pay $50,000 immediately and $10,000 per year for 5 years beginning at the end of 7 years from the date of the contract. At the end of the fourth year, the firm requested that it be allowed to make a lump sum payment in advance for the rest of the contract. What was the amount of the lump sum if interest at the settlement was agreed to be 8%?

3-5. Two manufacturing methods have been proposed for a new production requirement. One method involves two general-purpose machines that cost $15,000 each, installed. Each will produce 10 pieces per hr and will require an operator costing $3.00 per hr during operation. The other method requires a special-purpose machine costing $45,000 which will produce 20 pieces per hr and will require an operator costing $2.50 per hr during operation. Both types of machines are expected to last 10 years and have 0 salvage values. Other relevant data are as follows:

	General-purpose machine (each)	Special-purpose machine
Power cost per hr:	$0.25	$0.40
Fixed maintenance per yr:	$350.00	$500.00
Variable maintenance per hr:	$0.15	$0.10
Insurance and floor space per yr:	$1,800.00	$2,200.00

a. If the expected output is 20,000 pieces per yr and the minimum before-tax rate of return is 20%, which method has the lower total annual cost?
b. At what annual output rate would one be indifferent between the two methods?

3-6. It is desired to determine the most economic thickness of insulation for a large cold-storage room. Insulation is expected to cost $150 per 1,000 sq ft of wall area per in. of thickness installed and to require annual property taxes and insurance of 5% of first cost. It is expected to have 0 net salvage value after a 20-year life. The following are estimates of the heat loss per 1,000 sq ft of wall area for several thicknesses:

Insulation, in.	Heat loss, Btu per hr
3	4,400
4	3,400
5	2,800
6	2,400
7	2,000
8	1,800

The cost of heat removal is estimated at $0.01 per 1,000 Btu per hr. The minimum required yield on investment is 20%. Assuming continuous operation throughout the year, which thickness is the most economic?

3-7. Alternative methods I and II are proposed for a plant operation. The following is comparative information:

	Method I	Method II
Initial investment:	$10,000	$40,000
Life:	5 yr	10 yr
Salvage value:	$1,000	$5,000
Annual disbursements		
Labor:	$12,000	$4,000
Power:	$250	$300
Rent:	$1,000	$500
Maintenance:	$500	$200
Property taxes and insurance:	$400	$2,000

All other expenses are equal for the two methods and the income from the operation is not affected by the choice. If the minimum attractive rate of return is 20% and the study period is 10 yr, which is the better choice using the annual worth method?

3-8. Compare the net future worths of two temporary structures that will be retired at the end of 10 years. One has a negative net salvage value. Assume the minimum attractive rate of return = 8%, and that estimates are as follows:

	Structure A	Structure B
First cost:	$14,000	$20,000
Net salvage value:	3,000	−1,000
Annual maintenance and property taxes:	1,500	700

3-9. A proposed material for covering the roof of a building will have an estimated life of 10 years and will cost $5,000. A heavier grade of this roofing material will cost $800 more but will have estimated life of 15 years. Installation costs for either material will be $1,300. Compare the annual costs using a minimum attractive return of 10% and a study period of 30 years.

3-10. A small tractor is required for snow removal. It can be purchased for $3,000 and is expected to have a $500 salvage value at the end of its economic life of 5 years. Its annual operating cost is $1,000 and maintenance will be $300 the first year and increase by $100 per yr. If the minimum attractive rate of return is 10%, and if a contractor will provide this service for $2,000 per yr, which alternative has lower total present worth cost?

3-11. Compare the annual costs of pumps A and B for a 15-year service life using an interest rate of 10%.

	Pump A	*Pump B*
First cost:	$3,500	$5,000
Estimated salvage value:	0	2,000
Annual pumping cost:	450	300
Annual repair cost:	150	80

3-12. It is desired to determine the optimal height for a proposed building which is expected to last 40 years and then be demolished at zero salvage. The following are pertinent data:

	Number of floors			
	2	*3*	*4*	*5*
Building first cost:	$200,000	$250,000	$320,000	$400,000
Annual revenue:	40,000	60,000	85,000	100,000
Annual cash disbursements:	15,000	25,000	25,000	45,000

In addition to the building first cost, the land requires an investment of $50,000 and is expected to retain that value throughout the life period. If the minimum required rate of return is 15%, show which height, if any, should be built based on future worth comparisons.

3-13. A manufacturing process can be designed for varying degrees of automation. The minimum required rate of return is 20%. Which degree should be selected if the economic life is 5 years and the salvage value is 0? Use a present worth analysis.

	Machine A	*Machine B*
First cost:	$20,000	$25,000
Life:	10 yr	8 yr
Salvage value:	$2,000	0
Annual receipts:	$150,000	$180,000
Annual disbursements:	$138,000	$170,000

3-14. An individual is faced with two mutually exclusive investment alternatives. By investing $10,000 a single sum of $15,000 will be received 4 years after the investment; alternatively, by investing $15,000 a single sum of $18,500 will be received 2 years after the investment. Using a M.A.R.R. of 10% and P.W., A.W., and F.W. methods determine the preferred alternative.

3-15. Use P.W., A.W., and F.W. methods to determine which of the following independent investment opportunities should be undertaken. Use a M.A.R.R. of 10%.

	Investment opportunity				
	A	*B*	*C*	*D*	*E*
Initial investment:	$8,000	$10,000	$12,000	$15,000	$16,000
Annual net receipts:	2,000	3,000	3,200	3,500	4,000
Salvage value:	−1,000	2,000	1,000	2,000	0
Study period = 5 yr					

3-16. Use P.W., A.W., and F.W. methods to determine which of the following independent (nonrepeating) investment opportunities are economically worthwhile. Use a M.A.R.R. of 15% and a study period of 10 years.

End of	*Cash Flows for Investment Opportunity*					
year	*A*	*B*	*C*	*D*	*E*	*F*
0	−$10,000	−$5,000	−$8,000	−$12,000	−$6,000	−$15,000
1	1,000	500	1,000	1,500	2,000	400
2	1,000	1,000	1,000	1,500	2,000	800
3	2,000	1,500	1,000	1,500	2,000	1,200
4	2,000	2,000	1,000	1,500	2,000	1,600
5	3,000	2,500	1,000	1,500	—	2,000
6	3,000	3,000	1,000	1,500	—	2,400
7	—	—	1,000	1,500	—	2,800
8	—	—	1,000	1,500	—	3,200
9	—	—	1,000	1,500	—	3,600
10	—	—	3,000	3,000	—	4,000

Chapter

4

rate of return methods
for comparing alternatives

In the previous chapter, present worth, annual worth, and future worth analyses were considered in the comparison of investment alternatives. In this chapter rate of return methods are presented. The use of rate of return methods in measuring the acceptability of individual investment *opportunities* was mentioned at the beginning of Chapter 3. It was noted that an individual investment opportunity was *worthwhile* if its rate of return was not less than the minimum attractive rate of return (M.A.R.R.).

Any *rate of return* (R.R.) method of economic comparison involves the calculation of a rate or rates of return and comparison against a minimum standard of desirability (i.e., the M.A.R.R.).

There are three common techniques for calculating rates of return which can be said to be theoretically sound because they directly take into account the effects of any particular timing of cash flows throughout the study period considered. These methods, which can lead to slightly different calculated results, will be referred to as follows:

1. internal rate of return (I.R.R.) method
2. explicit reinvestment rate of return (E.R.R.R.) method;
3. external rate of return (E.R.R.) method.

The most common method of calculation of the internal rate of return for a single project involves merely finding the interest rate at which the present worth of the cash inflow (receipts or cash savings) equals the present worth of the cash outflow (disbursements or cash savings foregone). That is, one finds the interest rate at which P.W. of cash inflow equals P.W. of cash outflow; or, at which P.W. of cash inflow minus P.W. of cash outflow equals 0; or, at which P.W. of net cash flow equals 0. The I.R.R. could also be calculated by using the same procedures applied to either A.W.'s or F.W.'s.

The method of solving for the I.R.R. normally involves trial and error until the rate is found or can be interpolated. The procedure will be described below for several situations. (When both cash inflows and outflows are involved, the convention of using a "$+$" sign for inflows and a "$-$" sign for outflows in the solution will be followed.)

Computation of Internal Rate of Return (I.R.R.) for a Single Investment Opportunity

Example:

First cost:	$10,000
Project life:	5 yr
Salvage value:	$2,000
Annual receipts:	$5,000
Annual disbursements:	$2,200

Solution:

Expressing P.W. of net cash flow:

$-\$10,000 + (\$5,000 - \$2,200)(P/A,i\%,5) + \$2,000(P/F,i\%,5) = 0$

$@i = 15\%: -\$10,000 + \$2,800(P/A,15\%,5) + \$2,000(P/F,15\%,5) \overset{?}{=} 0$

$\$365 \neq 0$

$@i = 20\% : -\$10,000 + \$2,800(P/A,20\%,5) + \$2,000(P/F,20\%,5) \overset{?}{=} 0$

$-\$598 \neq 0$

Since we have both a positive and a negative P.W. of net cash flow, the answer is bracketed. Linear interpolation for the answer can be set up as follows:

i	P.W. of net cash flow
15%	$365
x%	0
20%	−$598

The answer x% can be found by solving either

$$\frac{15\% - x\%}{15\% - 20\%} = \frac{\$365 - 0}{\$365 - (-\$598)}$$

or

$$x\% = 15\% + \frac{\$365}{\$365 + \$598}(20\% - 15\%)$$

Solving, $x\% = 16.9\%$.

Principles in Comparing Alternatives by a Rate of Return Method

When comparing alternatives by a R.R. method when at most one alternative will be chosen, there are two main principles to keep in mind:

1. Each increment of investment capital must justify itself (by sufficient R.R. on that increment).
2. Compare a higher investment alternative against a lower investment alternative only if that lower investment alternative is justified.

The usual criterion for choice when using a R.R. method is: "Choose the alternative requiring the highest investment for which each increment of investment capital is justified."

This choice criterion assumes that the firm wants to invest any capital needed as long as the capital is justified by earning a sufficient R.R. on each increment of capital. In general, a sufficient R.R. is any R.R. greater than the M.A.R.R.

Alternative Ways to Find the Internal Rate of Return on Incremental Investment

The internal rate of return on the incremental investment for any two alternatives can also be found by

1. Finding the rate at which the P.W. (or A.W. or F.W.) of the net cash flow for the difference between the two alternatives is equal to zero, or

2. Finding the rate at which the P.W.'s (or A.W.'s or F.W.'s) of the two alternatives are equal.

Comparing Alternatives When Receipts
and Disbursements Are Known

Consider the same two alternative lathes A and B compared in the last
chapter, and determine which is better by the internal rate of return method,
using the first way outlined above.

Example:

	Lathe	
	A	*B*
First cost:	$10,000	$15,000
Life:	5 yr	10 yr
Salvage value:	$2,000	0
Annual receipts:	$5,000	$7,000
Annual disbursements:	$2,200	$4,300
Minimum attractive rate of return $= 8\%$		
Study period $= 10$ yr		

Solution:

The first increment of investment to be studied is the $10,000 for lathe A. This
project is the same as illustrated in the "single project" solution shown earlier
in this chapter. The I.R.R. for the lathe, and hence the first increment of
investment, was shown to be approximately 16.9%. Since 16.9% is greater
than the minimum required rate of return of 8%, the increment of investment
in lathe A is justified.

The next step is to determine if the second increment of investment (i.e.,
increasing the investment from $10,000 in lathe A to $15,000 in lathe B) is
justified. An easy way to obtain the solution is to calculate the year-by-
year difference in net cash flow for the two projects and then to find the I.R.R.
on the difference. In order for this year-by-year difference in net cash flow
to be computed, the cash flows for each project must be shown for the same
number of years (length of study period). The study period should be a common multiple of the lives of the projects under consideration, or the length of
time during which the services of the chosen alternatives will be needed, whichever is less. For the example lathes, a study period of 10 years will be used.

Year	Lathe A	Lathe B	Difference Lathe B — Lathe A
0	− $10,000	− $15,000	− $5,000
1	+ 2,800	+ 2,700	− 100
2	+ 2,800	+ 2,700	− 100
3			
4			
5	− $8,000		+ $8,000
6			
7			
8			
9			
10	+ 2,800 + $2,000	+ 2,700	− 100 − $2,000

The equation expressing the present worth of the net cash flow for the difference between the two lathes is

$$-\$5,000 - \$100(P/A,i\%,10) + \$8,000(P/F,i\%,5) - \$2,000(P/F,i\%,10) = 0$$

$$@0\%: \ -\$5,000 - \$100(10.0) + \$8,000(1.0) - \$2,000(1.0) = 0$$

Thus, the I.R.R. on the incremental investment is 0%. Since the minimum rate of return is 8%, the extra investment in lathe B is not justified, and lathe A would be chosen.

In this particular problem, one could have calculated the I.R.R. for lathe B alone. This can be found by solving the following equation:

$$-\$15,000 + \$2,700(P/A,i\%,10) = 0$$

Since there is only one unknown factor in the equation, we can solve directly to find $(P/A,i\%,10) = \$15,000/\$2,700 = 5.55$. We can then observe in the tables that $(P/A,12\%,10) = 5.6502$, and $(P/A,15\%,10) = 5.0188$ and interpolate to find that the $(P/A,i\%,10) = 5.55$ at $i\% \approx 12.7\%$. Thus, the I.R.R. for lathe B alone is greater than 8%. However, this is irrelevant to this decision and certainly not grounds to choose lathe B rather than lathe A, as it was previously shown that the incremental investment required for lathe B was not justified. It should be noted that the indicated decision is the same using the I.R.R. method as when using either the annual worth method or present worth method.

The I.R.R. on the incremental investment can also be calculated by the second alternative way outlined in the last section, i.e., finding the rate at which the present worths of the two alternatives are equal. The equation for the two lathes is

$$-\$10,000 + \$2,800(P/A,i\%,10) - \$8,000(P/F,i\%,5) + \$2,000(P/F,i\%,10)$$

$$= -\$15,000 - \$2,700(P/A,i\%,10)$$

This can be solved to find that $i = 0\%$.

To find the I.R.R. on the incremental investment using A.W. calculations, one needs only to find the interest rate at which annual worths of the two alternatives are equal. The equation for the two lathes is

$$(-\$10,000 + \$2,000)(A/P,i\%,5) - \$2,000(i\%) + \$2,800$$
$$= -\$15,000(A/P,i\%,10) + \$2,700.$$

This too can be solved to find that $i = 0\%$, again indicating that the incremental investment is not justified.

Comparing Numerous Alternatives

The following example is given to further illustrate the principle that the return on each increment of investment capital should be justified. To make the computations easier, each alternative in this example has a salvage value equal to the investment. In such cases, the I.R.R. can be calculated directly by dividing the annual net cash inflow or savings by the investment amount. In the tabulated solution shown, the symbol Δ is used to mean "incremental" or "change in." The letters on each end of the arrows designate the projects for which the increment is considered.

Example:

	Alternative project					
	A	*B*	*C*	*D*	*E*	*F*
Investment:	$1,000	$1,500	$2,500	$4,000	$5,000	$7,000
Annual savings in cash disbursements:	150	375	500	925	1,125	1,425
Salvage value:	1,000	1,500	2,500	4,000	5,000	7,000

If the company is willing to invest any capital which will earn at least 18%, find which alternative, if any, should be chosen using the I.R.R. method.

Solution:

It should be noted that the alternatives are arranged in order of increasing investment amount and that calculations regarding an increment must be completed before one knows which increment to consider next. The symbol ΔI.R.R. means internal rate of return (I.R.R.) on incremental investment.

Increment considered	*A*	*B*	*B → C*	*B → D*	*D → E*	*E → F*
ΔInvestment:	$1,000	$1,500	$1,000	$2,500	$1,000	$2,000
ΔAnnual savings:	$150	$375	$125	$550	$200	$300
ΔI.R.R.:	15%	25%	12.5%	22%	20%	15%
Is increment justified?	No	Yes	No	Yes	Yes	No

By the above analysis, alternative E would be chosen because it is the alternative requiring the highest investment for which each increment of investment capital is justified. Note that the analysis was performed without even considering the I.R.R. on the total investment for each of the alternatives.

In choosing alternative E, several increments of investment were justified as shown below:

Increment	Investment	Internal rate of return on increment (ΔI.R.R.)
B	$1,500	25%
B → D	2,500	22
D → E	1,000	20
Total:	$5,000	

As a side note, the I.R.R. on the total investment for each alternative is as follows

	Alternative					
	A	*B*	*C*	*D*	*E*	*F*
I.R.R.:	15%	25%	20%	23%	22.5%	20.4%

Note that alternative B has the highest overall I.R.R. and that alternative F has an overall I.R.R. which is greater than the minimum of 18%. Nevertheless, alternative E would be chosen on the rationale that the company wants to invest any increment of capital when and only when that increment will earn at least the minimum return.

Comparing Alternatives When Disbursements Only Are Known

When disbursements only are known, I.R.R.'s can be calculated for incremental investments only and not for the investment in any one alternative. Thus, the lowest investment has to be assumed to be justified (or necessary) without being able to calculate the I.R.R. on that alternative. As an example, consider the same alternative compressors compared in the last chapter, and determine which is the better alternative.

Example:

| | Compressor ||
	I	II
First cost:	$3,000	$4,000
Life:	6 yr	9 yr
Salvage value:	$500	0
Annual operating disbursements:	$2,000	$1,600
Minimum rate of return = 15%		
Study period = 18 yr		

Solution:

Listing the cash flows for the lowest common multiple of the lives:

Year	Compressor I	Compressor II	Difference (Compr. II − Compr. I)
0	− $3,000	− $4,000	− $1,000
1	− 2,000	− 1,600	+ 400
2			
3			
4			
5			
6	− $2,500		+ $2,500
7			
8			
9		− $4,000	− $4,000
10			
11			
12	− $2,500		+ $2,500
13			
14			
15			
16			
17			
18	− 2,000 + $500	− 1,600	+ 400 − $500

The I.R.R. for the difference between the compressors (i.e., on the incremental investment) can be obtained by solving the following equation for the difference in the net cash flows:

$$-\$1,000 - \$4,000(P/F,i\%,9) - \$500(P/F,i\%,18) + \$400(P/A,i\%,18)$$
$$+ \$2,500(P/F,i\%,6) + \$2,500(P/F,i\%,12) = 0$$

The I.R.R. can be found to be approximately 47%. Since this return on the increment is greater than the minimum required, 15%, compressor II is justified.

The use of A.W. calculations in determining the I.R.R. on incremental investment provides a convenient shortcut for problems where the two main assumptions stated in Chapter 3 (regarding the period of needed service and the repeatability of cost factors) hold true. For the compressor problem above, the I.R.R. may be found by solving the following:

$$(\$3,000 - \$500)(A/P,i\%,6) + \$500(i\%) + 2,000$$
$$= \$4,000(A/P,i\%,9) + \$1,600.$$

The equation is satisfied for an interest rate of approximately 47%, which is the same answer as obtained by the solution based on the differences in cash flows.

Differences in Ranking of Investment Opportunities

It was pointed out previously that the I.R.R. method will always give results which are consistent (regarding project acceptance or rejection) with results using the P.W., A.W., or F.W. method. However, the I.R.R. method can give a different *ranking* of the order of desirability of individual investment opportunities than the P.W., A.W. or F.W. method. As an example, consider Fig. 4-1 depicting the relation of I.R.R. to net present worth for two investment opportunities, project X and Y.

The I.R.R. for each project is the rate at which the net present worth for that project is zero. The net present worth for each project is shown for a

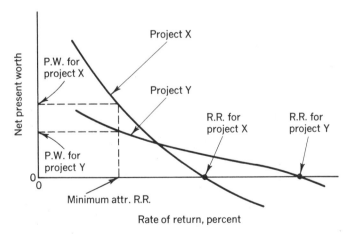

Figure 4-1. Relation of I.R.R. to P.W. for projects X and Y.

typical interest rate. For the hypothetical but quite feasible relationship shown in Fig. 4-1, project Y has the higher I.R.R. while project X has the higher net present worth for all I.R.R.'s less than the rate at which the net present worths are equal. This illustrates a case in which the I.R.R. method does result in a different *ranking* of alternatives as compared to the P.W. (A.W. or F.W.) method. However, since both projects had a net present worth greater than zero, and the I.R.R. for both projects is greater than the minimum attractive rate of return, the determination of acceptance of both projects is consistently shown by either method.

Problems in Which Either No Solution or Several Solutions for Rate of Return Exist

It is possible, but not commonly experienced in practice, to have situations in which there is no single I.R.R. solution by the discounted cash flow method. Descartes' rule of signs indicates that multiple solutions can occur whenever the cash flow series reverses sign (from net outflow to net inflow or the opposite) more than once over the period of study. As an example, consider the following project for which the I.R.R. is desired.

Example:

Year	Net cash flow
−1	+$ 500
0	− 1,000
1	0
2	+ 250
3	+ 250
4	+ 250

Solution:

Year	Net cash flow	P.W. @35%		P.W. @63%	
		Factor	Amount	Factor	Amount
−1	+$ 500	1.35	+$ 676	1.63	+$ 813
0	− 1,000	1.00	− 1,000	1.00	− 1,000
1	0				
2	+ 250	0.55	+ 137	0.38	95
3	+ 250	0.41	+ 102	0.23	57
4	+ 250	0.30	+ 75	0.14	35
		Net P.W.:	Σ = 0		Σ = 0

Thus, the present worth of the net cash flows equals 0 for interest rates of 35% and 63%. Whenever multiple answers such as these exist, it is likely that neither is correct.

An effective way to overcome this difficulty and obtain a "correct" answer is to manipulate cash flows as little as necessary so that there is only one reversal of the cumulative net cash flow. This can be done by using the minimum attractive rate of return to manipulate the funds, and then solving by the discounted cash flow method. For the above example, if the minimum attractive rate of return is 10%, the +$500 at year −1 can be compounded to year 0 to be $500 $(F/P,10\%,1) = +\$550$. This, added to the −$1,000 at year 0, equals −$450. The −$450, together with the remaining cash flows, which are all positive, now fits the condition of only one reversal in the cumulative net cash flow. The interest rate at which the present worth of the net cash flows equals 0 can now be shown to be 19% per the following table:

Timing	Net cash flow	P.W. @19% Factor	P.W. @19% Amount
0	− $450	1.00	− $450
2	+ 250	0.70	+ 177
3	+ 250	0.59	+ 150
4	+ 250	0.48	+ 123
	Net P.W.:		$\Sigma = 0$

It should be noted that whenever a manipulation of net cash flows is performed, the calculated I.R.R. will vary depending on what cash flows are manipulated and at what interest rate. The less manipulation and the closer the minimum rate of return to the calculated rate of return, the less the variation in the final calculated rate of return.

Appendix 4-A gives another example of the above type problem and shows how the E.R.R. method can be used to obtain a solution.

Explicit Reinvestment Rate of Return Method

The explicit reinvestment rate of return (E.R.R.R.) method involves dividing a "net profit" amount by the initial investment, where the net profit is calculated using a depreciation charge based on the sinking fund method of depreciation. As will be explained in Chapter 6, the sinking fund depreciation charge is obtained by multiplying the depreciable investment by the sinking fund factor, A/F. The interest rate used is the explicit rate at which recovered depreciation monies are assumed to be reinvested. To illustrate, consider the same single project for which the internal rate of return was calculated at the beginning of the chapter.

Example:

First cost:	$10,000
Project life:	5 yr
Salvage value:	$ 2,000
Annual receipts:	$ 5,000
Annual disbursements:	$ 2,200

Solution:

The following solution by the explicit reinvestment rate of return method uses a reinvestment rate of 10%.

Annual receipts:		$5,000
Annual expenses:		
Disbursements:	$2,200	
Depreciation $= (\$10,000 - \$2,000)(A/F,10\%,5)$:	1,310	
		3,510
Net annual profit:		$1,490

$$\text{Explicit reinvestment rate of return} = \frac{\$1,490}{\$10,000} = 14.9\%$$

If a reinvestment rate of, say, 20% were used for the sinking fund in the above example, the explicit reinvestment rate of return could be calculated to be 17.3%. If a reinvestment rate of 16.9% had been used, then the explicit reinvestment rate of return would have been 16.9%, which is the same as the I.R.R. From this, it can be inferred that the I.R.R. method involves the assumption that monies recovered for depreciation purposes can be reinvested at the same rate as the calculated rate of return.

In general, it can be said that calculated rate of return results using the explicit reinvestment method do not differ significantly from the I.R.R. method. Even though the explicit reinvestment method is not used commonly, it does have the advantage of computational ease when there is a single beginning investment and there are constant receipts and disbursements each year.

Comparing Alternatives Using the Explicit Reinvestment Rate of Return Method

When comparing investment alternatives using the explicit reinvestment rate of return method, an incremental approach is required (just as for the I.R.R. method). Specifically, the explicit reinvestment rate of return on the incremental investment is obtained by dividing the incremental net annual profit by the incremental investment. To illustrate, consider the lathe example presented previously.

Example:

	Lathe	
	A	B
First cost:	$10,000	$15,000
Life:	5 yr	10 yr
Salvage value:	$2,000	0
Annual receipts:	$5,000	$7,000
Annual disbursements:	$2,200	$4,300
Minimum attractive rate of return $= 8\%$		
Study period $= 10$ yr		

Solution:

It was shown previously that the explicit reinvestment rate of return for lathe A is 14.9%, which is greater than the minimum attractive rate of return. Hence, it is only necessary to compute the incremental explicit reinvestment rate of return.

	A		B	
Annual receipts:		$5,000		$7,000
Annual expenses:				
Disbursements:	$2,200		$4,300	
Depreciation:	1,310		941	
		3,510		5,241
Net annual profit:		$1,490		$1,759

Incremental net annual profit $= \$1,759 - \$1,490 = \$269$

Incremental investment $= \$15,000 - \$10,000 = \$5,000$

$$\text{Incremental explicit reinvestment rate of return} = \frac{\$269}{\$5,000} = 5.38\%$$

Since the incremental explicit reinvestment rate of return is less than the minimum attractive rate of return, the incremental investment cannot be justified economically. Hence, lathe A is the best choice.

Comparing Alternatives When Disbursements Only Are Known

When disbursements only are known, rates of return can be calculated only for incremental investments. Thus, the lowest investment must be assumed to be justified (or necessary). As an example, consider the situation involving the two compressors presented previously.

Example:

	Compressor	
	I	II
First cost:	$3,000	$4,000
Life:	6 yr	9 yr
Salvage value:	$500	0
Annual operating disbursements:	$2,000	$1,600
Minimum attractive rate of return $= 15\%$		
Study period $= 18$ yr		

Solution:

Annual operating disbursements:	$2,000	$1,600
Annual depreciation $=$		
($3,000 $-$ $500)($A/F$,15%,6):	286	
$4,000($A/F$,15%,9):		238
Net annual profit:	$-$2,286	$-$1,838

Incremental explicit reinvestment rate of return

$$= \frac{-\$1,838 - (-\$2,286)}{\$4,000 - \$3,000} = 44.8\%$$

Since the incremental explicit reinvestment rate of return is greater than the minimum attractive rate of return, the increment of investment is justified and compressor II is the recommended alternative.

External Rate of Return (E.R.R.) Method

Implicit in the internal rate of return method is the assumption that recovered funds are reinvested at a rate equal to the internal rate of return. Since it is often the case that opportunities do not exist for investing recovered funds and earning such a rate, the notion of explicit reinvestment rate of return methods has appeal. Additionally, the possibility of multiple solutions using the internal rate of return method can result in misinterpretations and misunderstandings of the rate of return figure obtained.

Because of the desire to incorporate explicitly the reinvestment rate in rate of return calculations and the desire to use a method that will yield a unique solution, an external rate of return method was developed. If complicated manipulations are to be avoided, the explicit reinvestment rate of return method is limited to a single investment (negative cash flow) and a uniform series of returns (positive cash flows). A more general approach is to define the external rate of return as the interest rate which equates the future worth of investments to the accumulation of reinvested returns. Recovered funds are assumed to be reinvested at the minimum attractive rate of return, based on the opportunity cost concept. To illustrate, consider the same single project for which rates of return were calculated at the beginning of the chapter.

Example:

First cost:	$10,000
Project life:	5 yr
Salvage value:	$2,000
Annual receipts:	$5,000
Annual disbursements:	$2,200

Solution:

The following solution by the external rate of return (E.R.R.) method uses a reinvestment rate or minimum attractive rate of return (M.A.R.R.) of 10%:

Yr	Net annual cash flow
0	−$10,000
1–5	$2,800
5	$2,000

Future accumulation of recovered monies $= \$2,800 \ (F/A,10\%,5) + \$2,000$ $= \$19,094$. Future worth of investments $= \$10,000 \ (F/P,i\%,5)$. Thus,

$$\$10,000(F/P,i\%,5) = \$19,094$$

or

$$(F/P,i\%,5) = 1.9094$$

From the interest tables it is seen that

$i\%$	$(F/P,i\%,5)$
12%	1.7623
15%	2.0114

By using linear interpolation, a value of 1.9094 is obtained for the $(F/P,i\%,5)$ factor when $i\%$ equals, approximately, 13.77%. The exact value of $i\%$ can be obtained by using logarithms and recalling the mathematical relation repre-sented by the $(F/P,i\%,N)$ factor. Namely,

$$(1 + i)^N = (F/P,i\%,N)$$

Hence, for the example

$$(1 + i)^5 = 1.9094$$
$$5 \ln(1 + i) = \ln 1.9094$$
$$\ln(1 + i) = 0.1293$$
$$\ln^{-1}(1 + i) = 1.138$$
$$i = 0.138$$

Hence, an external rate of return of 13.8% will result from the project. Since 13.8% is greater than the minimum attractive rate of return of 10%, the pro-ject is justified economically.

In general, a project justified economically using the internal rate of return method will also be justified when using the external rate of return method. A unique solution always occurs using the E.R.R. method.

Comparing Alternatives Using the External Rate of Return Method

An incremental approach is required when comparing investment alter-natives using the E.R.R. method. Specifically, the external rate of return on incremental investment is defined to be the interest rate that equates the future worth of the incremental investment and the future accumulation of incremental positive valued cash flows. To illustrate, consider the lathe example presented previously.

Example:

| | Lathe | |
	A	B
First cost:	$10,000	$15,000
Life:	5 yr	10 yr
Salvage value:	$2,000	0
Annual receipts:	$5,000	$7,000
Annual disbursements:	$2,200	$4,300
Minimum attractive rate of return = 8%		
Study period = 10 yr		

Solution:

It was shown previously that lathe A has an E.R.R. of 13.8% and is economically justified. It remains to determine if the incremental investment required to purchase lathe B is justified. Over the 10-year study period the incremental cash flows have the following profile:

End of Year	B − A
0	−$5,000
1–5	−100
5	+$8,000
6–10	−100
10	−$2,000

Future accumulation of positive valued cash flows = $8,000(F/P,8%,5) = $11,752. Future worth of negative valued cash flows = $5,000(F/P,i%,10) + $100(F/A,i%,10) + $2,000.

Hence, $5\,000(F/P,i\%,10) + \$100(F/A,i\%,10) + \$2,000 = \$11,752$

$$@i = 8\% \quad \$12,244 > \$11,752$$
$$@i = 7\% \quad \$11,218 < \$11,752$$

Interpolation gives $i = 7.52\%$ which is less than the M.A.R.R.; hence, the incremental investment required for B is not justified.

Comparing Alternatives When Disbursements Only Are Known

When disbursements only are known, the external rate of return method is applied to incremental cash flows in the same manner as other rate of return methods. Thus, the alternative having the lowest investment is assumed to be justified (or necessary). As an illustration, consider again the compressor example.

Example:

	Compressor	
	I	II
First cost	$3,000	$4,000
Life:	6 yr	9 yr
Salvage value:	$500	0
Annual operating disbursements:	$2,000	$1,600
Minimum attractive rate of return = 15%		
Study period = 18 yr		

Solution:

End of Year	II − I
0	−$1,000
1	$400
2	$400
3·	$400
4	$400
5	$400
6	$400 + $2,500
7	$400
8	$400
9	$400 − $4,000
10	$400
11	$400
12	$400 + $2,500
13	$400
14	$400
15	$400
16	$400
17	$400
18	$400 − $500

Future accumulation of positive valued cash flows $= \$400(F/A,15\%,18)$ $+ \$2,500(F/P,15\%,12) + \$2,500(F/P,15\%,6) = \$49,493$.
Future worth of negative valued cash flows $= \$1,000(F/P,i\%,18)$ $+ \$4,000(F/P,i\%,9) + \$500$.

$$@i = 20\% \qquad \$47,763 < \$49,493$$
$$@i = 25\% \qquad \$85,814 > \$49,493$$

Interpolation gives E.R.R. $= 20.22\%$ which is greater than the M.A.R.R. of 15%; hence, compressor II is recommended.

PROBLEMS

4-1. A construction firm is considering leasing a crane needed on a project for 4 years for $200,000 payable now. The alternative is to buy a crane for $250,000 and sell it at the end of 4 years for $100,000. Annual maintenance costs for ownership only are expected to be $10,000 per yr for the first 2 years and $15,000 per yr for the last two years. At what interest rate are the two alternatives equivalent?

4-2. An industrial machine costing $1,000 will produce net savings of $400 per year. The machine has a 5-year economic life but must be returned to the factory for major repairs after 3 years of operation. These repairs cost $500. The company's M.A.R.R. is approximately 10%. What I.R.R. will be earned on purchase of this machine? Would you recommend it?

4-3. An improved facility costing $50,000 has been proposed. Construction time will be 2 years with expenditures of $20,000 the first year and $30,000 the second year. Savings beginning the first year after construction completion are as follows:

Year	Savings
1	$10,000
2	14,000
3	18,000
4	22,000
5	26,000

The facility will not be required after 5 years and will have a salvage value of $5,000. Determine the (a) I.R.R. and (b) E.R.R. using a reinvestment rate of 10%.

4-4. A distillery is considering the erection of a bottle-making plant. The number of bottles needed annually is estimated at 600,000. The initial cost of the facility would be $50,000 with estimated life of 20 years. Annual operation and maintenance costs are expected to be $7,500, and annual taxes and insurance $2,500. Should the distillery erect the bottle-producing facility or buy the bottles from another company at $0.03 each? Use the three rate of return methods with a minimum attractive rate of 12%.

4-5. What is the internal rate of return on an investment of $1,000 which will yield $325 per year for 5 years?

4-6. There are five alternative machines to do a given job. Each is expected to have a salvage value of 100% of the investment amount at the end of its life of 4 years. If the firm's minimum attractive rate of return is 12%, which machine is the best choice based on the following data? Use an internal rate of return comparison, as well as an external rate of return comparison.

	Machine				
	A	B	C	D	E
Investment:	$1,000	$1,400	$2,100	$2,700	$3,400
Net cash flow per yr:	110	180	280	340	445

4-7. Consider two investment alternatives having cash flow profiles as given below. Use both an internal and an external rate of return comparison to determine the recommended alternative. Base your analysis on a study period of 5 years and a minimum attractive rate of return of (a) 8%, (b) 15%, and (c) 25%.

End of Year	A	B
0	0	−10,000
1	−20,000	5,000
2	30,000	3,500
3	250	40,000
4	20,000	2,576
5	3,864	30,000

4-8. Two alternative machines will produce the same product, but one machine will produce higher-quality items, which can be expected to return greater revenue. Given the following data, determine which machine is better using the three rate of return methods, a minimum attractive rate of return of 15%, and a study period of 10 years.

	Machine A	Machine B
First cost:	$20,000	$30,000
Salvage value:	$2,000	0
Annual receipts	$150,000	$180,000
Annual disbursements:	$138,000	$163,000

4-9. An individual is faced with two mutually exclusive investment alternatives. By investing $15,000 a single sum of $18,500 will be received 2 years after the investment; alternately, by investing $10,000 a single sum of $15,000 will be received 4 years after the investment. Using I.R.R. and E.R.R. methods, determine the preferred alternative based on a M.A.R.R. of (a) 5%, (b) 10%, and (c) 20%.

4-10. Use E.R.R.R., E.R.R. and I.R.R. methods to determine which of the following independent investment opportunities should be undertaken. Use a M.A.R.R. of 10%.

	Investment opportunity				
	A	B	C	D	E
Initial investment:	$8,000	$10,000	$12,000	$15,000	$16,000
Annual net receipt:	2,000	3,000	3,200	3,500	4,000
Salvage value:	−1,000	2,000	1,000	2,000	0
Study period = 5 yrs					

4-11. Use E.R.R. and I.R.R. methods to determine which of the following independent (nonrepetitive) investment opportunities are economically worthwhile. Use a M.A.R.R. of 15% and a study period of 5 years.

End of year	Cash flows for investment opportunity					
	A	*B*	*C*	*D*	*E*	*F*
0	−$10,000	−$5,000	−$8,000	−$12,000	−$6,000	−$15,000
1	2,000	1,000	3,000	5,000	1,000	4,500
2	2,000	1,500	3,000	5,000	1,500	4,500
3	2,000	2,000	5,000	6,000	2,000	4,500
4	3,000	2,500	0	0	2,500	4,500
5	3,000	0	0	0	3,000	0

4-12. Use E.R.R.R., E.R.R., and I.R.R. methods to determine the preferred incinerator alternative.

	Incinerator			
	A	*B*	*C*	*D*
First cost:	$3,000	$3,800	$4,500	$5,000
Life:	10 yr	10 yr	10 yr	10 yr
Salvage value:	0	0	0	0
Annual operating disbursements:	$1,800	$1,770	$1,470	$1,320
M.A.R.R.=10%				

4-13. For the case of a zero salvage value, single negative cash flow at $t = 0$, and a uniform series of cash flows for $t = 1, \ldots, N$, show that If I.R.R. > M.A.R.R., then I.R.R. > E.R.R. > M.A.R.R. and if I.R.R. < M.A.R.R. (where I.R.R. $\geq$ 0), then I.R.R. < E.R.R. < M.A.R.R.

4-14. Let $\{C_t\}$ denote the set of investments and $\{R_t\}$ denote the set of returns for an investment alternative. Given below are various plots of future worth versus the discount rate. What would be the recommendation in each case using the I.R.R. and the E.R.R. methods?

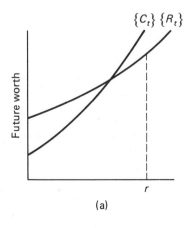

(a)

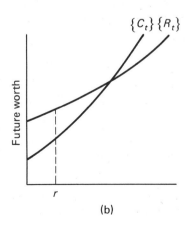

(b)

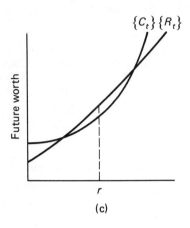

(c)

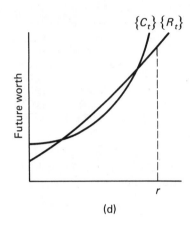

(d)

APPENDIX 4-A

use of E.R.R. method to overcome multiple solutions difficulty with the I.R.R. method

In order to illustrate the differences in approach using the I.R.R. and E.R.R. methods, consider Solomon's classic pump problem.*

Example:

   A firm is considering installing a new pump that will move oil faster than the present pump. The new pump will finish the job in one year; the present pump will require two years. The total value of the oil to be pumped is $20,000. The new pump costs $1,600, and neither pump will have any salvage value.

   The cash flow profiles for each pump and the incremental cash flow of the new pump over the old are presented in Table 4-A-1. If the firm's M.A.R.R. is 25%, determine which pump is most economical using the I.R.R. and E.R.R. methods.

*Solomon, Ezra, "The Arithmetic of Capital Budgeting Decisions" *The Journal of Business*, Vol. 29, No. 2, 1956, pp. 124–129.

Table 4-A-1

CASH FLOW PROFILES

End of year	Old pump	New pump	Increment New pump — Old pump
0	0	−1,600	−1,600
1	10,000	20,000	10,000
2	10,000	0	−10,000

Solution:

Using F.W. calculations to solve for the internal rate of return on the incremental net cash flows gives

$$-1,600(1 + i)^2 + 10,000(1 + i) - 10,000 = 0$$

This equation has two roots yielding internal rates of return of $i = 0.25$, (25%) and $i = 4.0$, (400%). With two (or more) roots, there may be some confusion as to which should be compared to the M.A.R.R. in order to select the correct alternative. Actually, neither may be correct.

Using the same incremental net cash flows to compute the external rate of return results in

$$1,600(1 + i)^2 + 10,000 = 10,000(1 + r)$$

Solving for i as a function of the reinvestment rate r,

$$i = 2.5\sqrt{r} - 1$$

Table 4-A-2 gives different values of r, the corresponding external rate of return i, and the recommended alternative to select.

Table 4-A-2

VALUES OF r, i, AND RECOMMENDED ALTERNATIVE

r Reinvestment rate	$i = $ E.R.R. External rate of return	Recommended alternative
0.10	−0.209	Old pump
0.15	−0.032	Old pump
0.20	0.118	Old pump
0.25	0.250	Either pump
0.30	0.369	New pump
0.50	0.768	New pump
1.00	1.500	New pump
2.00	2.536	New pump
3.00	3.330	New pump
4.00	4.000	Either pump
5.00	4.590	Old pump

Note that for those E.R.R. values in excess of the reinvestment rate, the decision is to purchase the new pump. Also, note the correspondence between the internal rates of return (25 % and 40 %) and the values of the external rate of return at which one is indifferent about the alternatives. Naturally, for E.R.R. values less than r, it is preferable to invest elsewhere and earn the M.A.R.R., r, rather than invest in the new pump.

Chapter

5

benefit–cost ratio methods of comparing alternatives

A method of comparing investment alternatives that has experienced considerable usage in the public sector is the benefit–cost ratio method. Many federal government agencies and departments, as well as the United States Postal Service and a number of public utilities, use benefit–cost ratio methods in performing economic analyses. In Chapter 8 we examine in detail the process of conducting economic analyses for governmental agencies and public utilities; in that discussion, benefit–cost ratios are employed.

The *benefit–cost ratio* (B/C) can be defined as the ratio of the equivalent worth of benefits to the equivalent worth of costs. The equivalent worths can be P.W.'s, A.W.'s, or F.W.'s, The B/C method is often used by a government agency to measure the economic effectiveness of an investment that will benefit some segment of the general public; hence, the B/C is sometimes defined as the ratio of the present or annual worth of benefits for the user public to the present or annual worth of the total costs of supplying the benefits. The B/C is also referred to as the *savings-investment ratio* (S.I.R.) by some government agencies and departments.*

Two commonly used formulations of the B/C ratio are as follows:

1. Conventional B/C:

$$B/C = \frac{\text{P.W.(benefits to user)}}{\text{P.W.(total costs to supplier)}} = \frac{\text{P.W.}(B)}{\text{P.W.(C.R.} + O + M)} \qquad 5\text{-}1$$

or

$$B/C = \frac{\text{A.W.(benefits to user)}}{\text{A.W.(total costs to supplier)}} = \frac{B}{\text{C.R.} + (O + M)} \qquad 5\text{-}2$$

where B = annual worth of benefits to user
C.R. = capital recovery cost or the equivalent annual cost of the initial investment, considering any salvage value
O = uniform annual operating cost
M = uniform annual maintenance cost

2. Modified B/C:

$$B/C = \frac{\text{P.W.}[B - (O + M)]}{\text{P.W.(C.R.)}} \qquad 5\text{-}3$$

or

$$B/C = \frac{B - (O + M)}{\text{C.R.}} \qquad 5\text{-}4$$

The numerator of the modified B/C expresses the present or annual worth of the net of benefits and operating and maintenance costs; the denominator includes only the investment costs, expressed on a present or an annual basis.

The conventional B/C method appears to have been supplanted by the modified B/C method among a number of user groups. Although both B/C methods yield the same recommendation when comparing investment alternatives, they can yield different rankings for independent investment opportunities. The modified B/C method will always yield the same ranking as obtained by using either the P.W., A.W., or F.W. methods.

An individual investment *opportunity* is deemed a worthwhile investment if its B/C $\geq$ 1.0. When comparing investment *alternatives*, however, an incremental approach is required. As with rate of return methods, each increment of investment must be justified economically by having a B/C $\geq$ 1.0.

Economic Analysis Handbook, Publication P-442 (Washington, D.C.: Department of the Navy, Naval Facilities Engineering Command, 1971).

Computation of B/C for a Single Investment Opportunity

Example:

First cost:	$10,000
Project life:	5 yr
Salvage value:	$2,000
Annual receipts:	$5,000
O and M disbursements:	$2,200
M.A.R.R.	8%

Solution:

By interpreting annual receipts as annual benefits, the conventional B/C and modified B/C are computed as follows:

$$C.R. = (\$10,000 - \$2,000)(A/P, 8\%, 5) + \$2,000(0.08) = \$2,163$$

$$\text{Conventional B/C} = \frac{B}{C.R. + (O + M)} = \frac{\$5,000}{\$2,163 + \$2,200} = 1.146 > 1.0$$

$$\text{Modified B/C} = \frac{B - (O + M)}{C.R.} = \frac{\$5,000 - \$2,200}{\$2,163} = 1.294 > 1.0$$

Since B/C > 1.0, the individual investment opportunity is a worthwhile investment. Hereafter, only the modified B/C will be used unless otherwise stated and it will be denoted, simply, B/C.

Comparing Alternatives Using Benefit—Cost Analysis When Receipts and Disbursements Are Known

In order to illustrate the use of the B/C method in comparing alternatives when both receipts and disbursements are known, the example involving two alternative lathes presented in Chapters 3 and 4 will be considered. Annual receipts are treated as annual benefits in the analysis; annual disbursements are treated as annual operating and maintenance costs.

Example:

	Lathe	
	A	*B*
First cost:	$10,000	$15,000
Life:	5 yr	10 yr
Salvage value:	$2,000	0
Annual receipts:	$5,000	$7,000
Annual disbursements:	$2,200	$4,300
Minimum attractive rate of return = 8%		
Study period = 10 yr		

Solution:

As previously, it is assumed that after 5 years lathe A will be replaced with another lathe having an identical cash flow profile. Hence, annual worths for individual life cycles can be used in computing the benefit–cost ratio.

The first increment of investment (the $10,000 for lathe A) was shown, in the previous example, to have a B/C of 1.294 > 1.0. Hence, the increment of investment in lathe A is justified. The next step is to determine if the second increment of investment is justified. The simplest approach is to divide the difference in the annual worths of net annual benefits by the differences in the capital recovery costs.

For lathe B,

$$\text{C.R.} = \$15,000(A/P,8\%,10) = \$2,220$$

For the second increment of investment,

$$\Delta\text{B/C} = \frac{(\$7,000 - \$4,300) - (\$5,000 - \$2,200)}{\$2,200 - \$2,163}$$

$$= \frac{\$2,700 - \$2,800}{\$2,220 - \$2,163}$$

$$= \frac{-\$100}{\$57} = -1.75 < 1.0$$

Since the B/C for the increment of investment from lathe A to lathe B has a value less than one, the increment cannot be justified and thus lathe A is recommended.

Comparing Numerous Alternatives

The following example is given to further illustrate the principle that each increment of investment capital must be justified when using the B/C ratio method. To simplify the computations involved, the alternatives each have a salvage value equal to the investment. Hence, there is no depreciation cost, and the incremental capital recovery cost equals the product of the M.A.R.R. and the incremental investment.

Example:

	Alternatives					
	A	*B*	*C*	*D*	*E*	*F*
Investment:	$1,000	$1,500	$2,500	$4,000	$5,000	$7,000
Annual savings in cash disbursements:	150	375	500	925	1,125	1,425
Salvage value:	1,000	1,500	2,500	4,000	5,000	7,000
M.A.R.R. = 18%						

Solution:

The alternatives are listed in increasing order of investment. The two primary principles employed are the same as for rate of return methods, i.e., each increment of capital investment must justify itself and an alternative should be compared with an alternative requiring a lower investment only if the latter investment is justified. The symbol ΔB/C means the benefit–cost ratio on the incremental cost.

Increment considered	A	B	B → C	B → D	D → E	E → F
ΔInvestment	$1,000	$1,500	$1,000	$2,500	$1,000	$2,000
ΔC.R.	180	270	180	450	180	360
ΔAnnual savings (ΔB)	150	375	125	550	200	300
ΔB/C	0.833	1.389	0.694	1.222	1.111	0.833
Is increment justified?	No	Yes	No	Yes	Yes	No

Since the last increment of cost which is justified is that required to obtain alternative E, it is recommended. It is interesting to note that alternative E does not have the greatest individual B/C, just as it did not have the greatest individual rate of return.

			Alternatives			
	A	B	C	D	E	F
B/C ratio	0.833	1.389	1.111	1.285	1.250	1.131

Note that alternative B has the highest B/C and that alternative F has a B/C > 1.0. Nevertheless, alternative E would be recommended on the basis that the firm wishes to expend incremental cost if and only if it has a ΔB/C ≥ 1.0.

Comparing Alternatives When Disbursements Only Are Known

When disbursements only are known, benefit–cost ratios are to be calculated for incremental investments only and not for the investment in any one alternative. The alternative requiring the smallest initial investment is assumed to be justified (or necessary). As an illustration, consider the compressor example presented in the two previous chapters.

Example:

	Compressor	
	I	*II*
First cost:	$3,000	$4,000
Life:	6 yr	9 yr
Salvage value:	$500	0
Annual operating disbursements:	$2,000	$1,600
M.A.R.R. = 15%		
Study period = 18 yr		

Solution:

$$\text{C.R. (I)} = (\$3{,}000 - \$500)(A/P,15\%,6) + \$500(0.15) = \$735$$
$$\text{C.R. (II)} = \$4{,}000(A/P,15\%,9) = \$840$$
$$\Delta B/C = \frac{(0 - \$1{,}600) - (0 - \$2{,}000)}{\$840 - \$735}$$
$$= \frac{-\$1{,}600 + \$2{,}000}{\$840 - \$735}$$
$$= \frac{\$400}{\$105} = 3.81 > 1.0$$

Since $\Delta B/C > 1.0$, then the incremental cost is justified and compressor II is recommended. Notice, the repeatability assumption was again used. Furthermore, negative net annual benefits exist for each individual alternative; however, the incremental annual benefit ($-\$1{,}600 + \$2{,}000$) is positive.

Which Method of Comparing Alternatives Should Be Used?

Since all of the methods of comparing alternatives that have been considered will yield the same recommendation, an obvious question is which method should be used? The factors that contribute to an answer to the question include the following:

1. Does management in the organization have a preference?
2. Are individuals involved in the decision accustomed to using one of the methods?
3. Does the study period coincide with the useful lives of the alternatives? Are the useful lives of the alternatives equal?
4. How are the computations to be performed?

The methods of comparing investment alternatives considered thus far included the following *discounted cash flow methods:*

1. present worth;
2. annual worth;
3. future worth;
4. rate of return;
   a. internal rate of return;
   b. explicit reinvestment rate of return;
   c. external rate of return;
5. benefit–cost ratio:
   a. conventional benefit–cost ratio;
   b. modified benefit–cost ratio.

The primary reason for selecting a particular method of comparing alternatives appears to be management preference. Some prefer to express the net economic worth of an alternative as a single sum; hence, either the present worth method or the future worth method is used. Others prefer the annual worth method, since the cash flows are spread out uniformly over the study period; the annual worth is felt, by some, to provide greater insight into the impact of the alternative on annual budgets during the study period. Yet another group prefers to express the profitability of an investment in such finacial terms as "yield on investment," "return on investment," and "percentage return"; a rate of return method would be preferred by such a group. As an alternative to the rate of return method, the benefit–cost ratio method expresses the net economic worth as a percentage of the investment required; as an example, a B/C of 1.10 means that the net present worth of the investment is 10% greater than the investment.

Organizations sometimes adopt a particular method of comparing investment alternatives. So long as the method provides a rational basis for comparing investment alternatives, it is recommended that it be used; in this case, *rational* means that the method yields the same recommendation as would be obtained using one of the discounted cash flow methods listed above. If the method adopted by the organization does not yield the same recommendation as would be obtained by using one of the discounted cash flow methods, then further investigation should be performed to determine why management prefers such a system.

Some of the alternatives to discounted cash flow methods reflect a highly conservative fiscal policy; as examples, a minimum attractive rate of return of zero and a study period of 2 to 3 years are implicitly assumed by some methods.

The *payback period method* is a popular method for comparing investment alternatives, but it does not necessarily result in the same recommendation as obtained using a discounted cash flow method. The payback period is defined to be the number of years required to recover the initial investment. A zero interest rate is assumed. The alternative having the smallest payback period is recommended. Both the timing of cash flows and the duration of time the flows are expected are ignored.

Example:

		Alternatives	
End of Year	*A*	*B*	*C*
0	−$1,000	−$1,000	−$1,000
1	$250	$500	$900
2	$250	$500	0
3	$500	0	$100
4	$1,000	0	0
5	$2,000	$100	$100

Solution:

	A	*B*	*C*
Payback period:	3 yr	2 yr	3 yr

Using the payback period method, alternative B is recommended. Furthermore, alternatives A and C are interpreted to be equivalent, since they both have a payback period of 3 years. In contrast, the I.R.R. for alternative A is by far the highest of the group, while the I.R.R. for alternative B is the lowest.

Despite its obvious deficiencies, the payback period method continues to be one of the most popular methods of comparing investment alternatives. It serves as an indicator of risk when used in conjunction with a discounted cash flow method; the shorter the payout period, the less the apparent risk. Some other reasons for its popularity include:

1. ease of computation and understanding;
2. absence of interest rate calculations;
3. investment capital is limited and must be recovered quickly;
4. hedge against errors in estimating future cash flows; and
5. the difficulty of determining the minimum attractive rate of return.

Although the authors prefer the use of discounted cash flow methods, it is realized that one does not always have the freedom to choose the method to be used. If such freedom does exist, then the present worth method is suggested. It is felt that the present worth method encourages a careful consideration of the cash flows that are likely to occur during the study period. When the study period exceeds the useful life of an individual alternative, then the cash flows must be made explicit for any replacements during the study period. Similarly, if the study period ends prior to the end of the useful life of an individual alternative, then an estimate of the unused value must be made explicit in the form of a salvage value.

One of the primary reasons for using the annual worth method is its ease of computation when unequal useful lives exist for the alternatives and the repeatability assumption is used. This particular strength of the annual worth method is also its primary weakness because it can be applied without thought being given to the length of the study period and any differences in the length of the study period and the useful lives of each alternative. However, the development and widespread use of minicomputers, computer terminals, and calculators has served to diminish the concern for computational aspects of the various methods.

PROBLEMS

5-1. Consider the two alternatives given below. Using the modified benefit–cost ratio, which (if any) should be selected?

	Alternatives	
	I	II
First cost	$20,000	$20,500
Life:	10 yr	10 yr
Salvage value:	$1,000	$1,500
Annual receipts:	$4,740	$4,800
M.A.R.R. = 10%		
Study period = 10 yr		

What are the B/C values for the individual alternatives?

5-2. A construction firm is considering leasing a crane for 4 years for $200,000 payable now. As an alternative, the crane can be purchased for $250,000 and sold for $100,000 at the end of 4 years. Annual maintenance costs for ownership are expected to be $10,000 per year for the first 2 years and $15,000 per year for the last 2 years. Using a study period of 4 years and a M.A.R.R. of 10%, perform a B/C analysis to determine the preferred alternative.

5-3. Perform a conventional B/C analysis for the example involving the following alternatives (A-F). Also, compute the conventional B/C values for the individual alternatives; compare the values obtained with the modified B/C values. M.A.R.R. = 10%.

			Alternative project			
	A	B	C	D	E	F
Investment:	$1,000	$1,500	$2,500	$4,000	$5,000	$7,000
Annual savings in						
cash disbursements:	150	375	500	925	1,125	1,425
Salvage value:	1,000	1,500	2,500	4,000	5,000	7,000

5-4. A machine can be repaired today for $2,500. If repairs are not made, operating expenses are expected to increase by $400 each year for the next 5 years Using a M.A.R.R. of 12% and a B/C analysis, should the machine be repaired?

5-5. The following alternatives are available. Each alternative is expected to have a zero salvage value at the end of each life cycle.

	A	B	C
First cost:	$2,000	$6,000	$12,000
Life cycle:	6 yr	3 yr	4 yr
Annual disbursements:	$3,500	$1,000	$400
M.A.R.R. = 10%			
Study period = 12 yr			

Assume replacements are identical in cash flow profile to the asset replaced. Use a B/C analysis to determine the preferred alternative.

5-6. Alternative methods I and II are proposed for a plant operation. The following is comparative information:

	Method I	Method II
Initial investment	$10,000	$40,000
Life:	5 yr	10 yr
Salvage value:	$1,000	$5,000
Annual disbursements:	$14,150	$7,000
M.A.R.R. = 20%		
Study period = 10 yr		

Using a B/C analysis to determine the preferred alternative, compare the alternatives.

5-7. Two alternative machines will produce the same product, but one will produce higher-quality items which can be expected to return greater revenue. Given the following data, determine which machine is better. Use the B/C method, a study period of 10 years, and a M.A.R.R. of 15%.

	Machine A	Machine B
First cost:	$ 20,000	$ 30,000
Salvage value:	2,000	0
Annual receipts:	150,000	180,000
Annual disbursements:	138,000	170,000

Determine the B/C values for each machine by using both the conventional and the modified formulations.

5-8. Five alternative machines are being considered for a particular job. Each is expected to have a salvage value of 100% of the investment amount at the end of the 4-year study period. Using a B/C analysis, with a M.A.R.R. of 12%, which machine should be selected on the basis of the following data?

	Alternatives				
	A	B	C	D	E
Investment:	$2,100	$3,400	$1,000	$2,700	$1,400
Net cash flow per yr:	280	445	110	340	180

5-9. A distillery is considering constructing a bottle-making plant. The number of bottles needed annually is estimated at 600,000. The initial cost of the facility will be $50,000, with an estimated life of 20 years. Annual operating and main-tenance costs are expected to be $7,500, and annual taxes and insurance are expected to total $2,500. Using a B/C analysis with a M.A.R.R. of 12% and a study period of 20 years, should the distillery erect the bottle-producing facility or buy the bottles at a cost of $0.03 each?

5-10. Given the following alternatives, show which is best considering a savings in operating disbursements as ΔB and using M.A.R.R. $= 10\%$.

	Incinerator			
	A	B	C	D
First cost:	$3,000	$3,800	$4,500	$5,000
Life:	10 yr	10 yr	10 yr	10 yr
Salvage value:	0	0	0	0
Annual operating disbursements:	$1,800	$1,770	$1,470	$1,380

consideration of income taxes and depreciation

This chapter provides a brief overview of main tax and depreciation considerations and a general technique for including the effect of income taxes in economy studies.

Only cash flows need be considered in determining the economic desirability of an alternative in an economic analysis. Income taxes are relevant cash flows and should be considered whenever their omission may cause the selection of an uneconomical alternative. Although depreciation write-offs are not, in themselves, cash flows, they do affect income taxes, and hence affect cash flows.

Introduction to Depreciation

The primary purpose of depreciation accounting is to provide for the recovery of capital invested in property which is expected to decline in value as a result of time and/or use. This is done through the mechanism of *depreciation charges*, which are allocations or noncash charges made periodically. Depreciation accounting also provides a systematic means for placing a declared or unamortized value, commonly called *book value*, on property.

The purpose of the following sections is primarily to acquaint the student with the computational mechanics of four common depreciation plans or methods so that they can be applied appropriately in the computation of after-tax cash flows .The four depreciation methods are:

1. straight line;
2. declining balance;
3. sum-of-years-digits;
4. sinking fund.

Straight Line Depreciation

The *straight line depreciation plan* provides for uniform periodic depreciation charges over the write-off period.

Letting P = Cost of asset,

F = Salvage value, and

W = Write-off period (in years),

the depreciation charge, denoted by D, may be given as $D = (P - F)/W$, where $(P - F)$ is known as the *depreciable investment*.

The value of the asset on the books of account at the end of year x is termed the *book value*, denoted B.V.$_x$, and is given as

$$\text{B.V.}_x = P - \left[\frac{P - F}{W}\right] \times x \qquad\qquad 6\text{-}1$$

Example:

A machine costs \$15,000 installed. The allowable write-off period is 12 years, at which time the salvage value is assumed to be \$1,500. What will be the annual depreciation charge and what will be the book value at the end of the third year?

Solution:

$$D = \frac{P - F}{W} = \frac{\$15,000 - \$1,500}{12} = \$1,125$$

$$\text{B.V.}_3 = P - \left[\frac{P - F}{W}\right] \times 3 = \$15,000 - \left[\frac{\$15,000 - \$1,500}{12}\right] \times 3$$

$$= \$11,625$$

Declining Balance Depreciation

The *declining balance method* of depreciation provides for an accelerated write-off (depreciation) during the early years of the life of an asset, with progressively smaller depreciation charges with increasing years. For this method, the depreciation charge for the xth year, D_x, is equal to a fixed percentage d_r of the book value at the beginning of the xth year [end of $(x - 1)$th year]. Thus,

$$D_x = \text{B.V.}_{x-1}(d_r) \qquad\qquad 6\text{-}2$$

It can be shown that the book value at the end of the $(x - 1)$th year is given by

$$\text{B.V.}_{x-1} = P(1 - d_r)^{x-1} \qquad\qquad 6\text{-}3$$

Thus,

$$D_x = P(1 - d_r)^{(x-1)}(d_r) \qquad\qquad 6\text{-}4$$

In order for the book value to equal the estimated salvage value at the end of the write-off period, W years, d_r should be calculated as

$$d_r = 1 - \sqrt[W]{\frac{F}{P}} \qquad\qquad 6\text{-}5$$

Example:
>   For the previous example using straight line depreciation, determine the book value at the end of the third year and the depreciation charge for the fourth year using the declining balance method of depreciation.

Solution:

$$d_r = 1 - \sqrt[W]{\frac{F}{P}} = 1 - \sqrt[12]{\frac{1,500}{15,000}} = 1 - 0.826 = 0.174$$

$$\text{B.V.}_3 = \$15,000(1 - 0.174)^3 = \$8,460$$

$$D_4 = \$8,460(0.174) = \$1,470$$

A special version of the declining balance depreciation method is called the *double declining balance method.* For this method, Internal Revenue Service (IRS) regulations allow the rate, d_r, to be computed as 200% of the straight line rate for new property used in a trade or business. For used property, the rate allowable is 150% of the straight line rate. The straight line rate is $1/W$.

All other computations are comparable. Using this version of the method, the book value at the end of the write-off period, W years, will not normally equal the salvage value. Because of this, the taxpayer is generally permitted to switch later to straight line depreciation for the remaining years.

Example:
>   Work the same problem as above except using the double declining balance method. Also, assume that it is desired to switch to the straight line method after the fourth year. What is the depreciation charge for all remaining years?

Solution:

$$d_r = \frac{200\%}{12} = 0.167$$

$$\text{B.V.}_3 = \$15,000(1 - 0.167)^3 = \$8,670$$

$$D_4 = 8,670(0.167) = \$1,448$$

$$\text{B.V.}_4 = \$8,670 - \$1,448 = \$7,222$$

$$D = \frac{\$7,222 - \$1,500}{12 - 4} = \$715 \text{ per yr after the fourth year}$$

Sum-of-Years-Digits Depreciation

The *sum-of-years-digits method* is an alternative depreciation method for achieving accelerated write-off during the early years of life of an asset.

To use this method, the digits corresponding to the number of years of estimated life are added together. This sum can also be conveniently obtained by use of the formula $\text{S.Y.D.} = (W)(W + 1)/2$. The depreciation charge for the first year is $(W/\text{S.Y.D.})(P - F)$; for the second year is $[(W - 1)/\text{S.Y.D.}]$ $\cdot (P - F)$; for the third year $[(W - 2)/\text{S.Y.D.}]/(P - F)$; and so forth until the Wth year it is $(1/\text{S.Y.D.})(P - F)$.

Example:
  Work the same problem as above except using the S.Y.D. method.

Solution:

$$\text{S.Y.D.} = 1 + 2 + \cdots + 12 = \frac{12(13)}{2} = 78$$

$$\text{B.V.}_3 = \$15,000 - \left[\frac{12}{78}(\$13,500) + \frac{11}{78}(\$13,500) + \frac{10}{78}(\$13,500) \right]$$

$$= \$15,000 - \$5,700 = \$9,300$$

$$D_4 = \frac{9}{78}(\$13,500) = \$1,580$$

Sinking Fund Depreciation

The sinking fund depreciation method is of more interest in some special types of economy studies than for its use for normal accounting and income tax purposes. Its historical origin stems from times when it was fairly common for public utilities and other regulated firms to set aside depreciation charges in an interest-bearing account so that the accumulated charges and interest would just equal the estimated depreciable part of the asset investment as of the end of the investment life.

The annual sinking fund deposit, d, which is assumed to earn interest at $i\%$ per year can be calculated as:

$$d = (P - F)(A/F, i\%, W) \qquad\qquad 6\text{-}6$$

The total depreciation charge for any year is the sinking fund deposit plus accumulated interest for that year. It is also the difference in book value for that year and the previous year. Thus,

$$D_x = \text{B.V.}_x - \text{B.V.}_{x-1}$$

The book value for any year is the first cost minus the accumulated sinking fund deposits and interest. Thus,

$$\text{B.V.}_x = P - d(F/A, i\%, x) \qquad\qquad 6\text{-}7$$

Example:

Work the same problem as above except use the sinking fund depreciation method with an interest (fund or reinvestment) rate of 6%.

Solution:

$$d = (\$15,000 - \$1,500)(A/F,6\%,12) = \$800$$

$$\text{B.V.}_3 = P - d(F/A,6\%,3)$$

$$= \$15,000 - \$800(F/A,6\%,3) = \$12,453$$

Similarly, $\text{B.V.}_2 = \$13,352$; so $D_3 = \$13,352 - \$12,453 = \$899$.

Additional First-Year Depreciation

In addition to the ordinary first-year depreciation deduction, taxpayers can elect to take an intial extra deduction equal to 20% of the cost of new or used "qualifying" tangible personal property to be used in a business and having a useful life of at least 6 years. The 20% is computed on the first cost without reducing the cost of the asset by the anticipated salvage value at the end of its anticipated life. Regular depreciation is then computed on a cost basis reduced by the extra deduction.

The full cost or a fractional part of the cost of an item may be selected for the extra write-off but only up to an aggregate amount for all items of $10,000 per year for each individual or corporation. Thus, the extra write-off or deduction is limited to $10,000(20%) = \$2,000$. Because of this limitation, economy studies involving depreciation in the remainder of this book will normally assume that the extra first-year depreciation does not apply unless it is stated otherwise.

Example:

Work the same problem as above using the straight line method of depreciation and assuming that advantage of the extra first-year depreciation is taken. by an individual taxpayer or corporation.

Solution:

$$\text{Extra first-year depreciation} = \$15,000(20\%) = \$3,000$$
$$= \$2,000 \text{ possible maximum}$$

$$D = \frac{P - \$2,000 - F}{W} = \frac{\$15,000 - \$2,000 - \$1,500}{12} = \$958$$

$$\text{B.V.}_3 = P - \$2,000 - (\$958)(3) = \$10,125$$

Comparison of Depreciation Methods

To provide a common basis for comparing the four methods of depreciation, Table 6-1 shows year-by-year depreciation charges for a typical asset which costs $16,000, is expected to last 5 years, and then be sold for a net of $1,000.

Figure 6-1 provides a graphical comparison of the year-by-year book

Table 6-1

COMPARISON OF DEPRECIATION CHARGES USING FOUR METHODS FOR EXAMPLE
MACHINE HAVING $16,000 INVESTMENT, FIVE-YEAR LIFE, AND $1,000
SALVAGE VALUE

End of year	Straight line	Double declining balance	Sum-of-years digits	Sinking fund @ 10%
1	$ 3,000	$ 6,000	$ 5,000	$ 2,457
2	3,000	3,750	4,000	2,703
3	3,000	2,344	3,000	2,973
4	3,000	1,465	2,000	3,270
5	3,000	1,441*	1,000	3,597
Totals	$15,000	$15,000	$15,000	$15,000

*Based on exercising option of switching to straight line depreciation to adjust to final
salvage value. In this example, the change in method occurs in the fifth year.

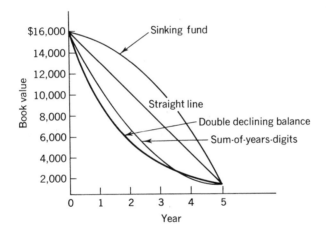

Figure 6-1. Comparison of book values using four depreciation methods
for example machine in Table 6-1.

values for the above example machine using each of the four depreciation
methods. It assumes depreciation is occurring throughout each year, even
though it is normally accounted for on a year-by-year basis.

Units-of-Production Depreciation

All the depreciation methods discussed to this point are based on elapsed
time on the theory that the decrease in value of property is mainly a function
of time. When the decrease in value is mostly a function of use, depreciation
may be based on the *units-of-production method.*

This method results in the total depreciable investment being allocated equally over the units produced and requires an estimate of the total lifetime of productive use. The depreciation rate is calculated as

$$\text{Depreciation per unit of production} = \frac{P - F}{\text{Estimated lifetime production}} \qquad \text{6-8}$$

Example:

An auto has a first cost of $5,000 and is expected to have $1,000 salvage value when traded after 100,000 miles of use. It is desired to find its depreciation rate based on functional use and to find its book value after 20,000 miles of use.

Solution:

$$\text{Depreciation per unit of production} = \frac{\$5,000 - \$1,000}{100,000 \text{ miles}} = \$0.04 \text{ per mile}$$

$$\text{B.V.} = \$5,000 - \$0.04(20,000 \text{ miles}) = \$4,200$$

Choosing a Depreciation Method

There are many factors to be considered in the choice of a method of depreciation. Generally, the most important factor is the effect of the method on the timing of income taxes paid.

If income tax rates are constant and the firm has taxable income over the depreciable life, then the total income taxes paid is identical regardless of the depreciation method employed. However, given the choice of paying a dollar of income tax now versus a dollar of income tax later, the time-value-of-money effect encourages one to choose the postponement. Indeed, this postponement is achieved by depreciation methods which result in higher depreciation charges (and thus lower taxable incomes and taxes) in the early years of an asset, as in the sum-of-years-digits and declining balance methods.

The choice between depreciation methods for income tax purposes can be quite important to the firm. Among the factors which should be considered in this decision are (a) the expected trend of income tax rates as the result of legislation and variability of the firm's earnings, (b) whether or not the firm has losses to be carried forward to future years, and (c) the effects on future after-tax earnings reported to the stockholders or owners.

Decisions on depreciation method are not irrevocable for federal income tax purposes. In general, if at any time after the first year one wants to switch from an "accelerated" method (like the declining balance) to a slower method (like straight line), this can be done without obtaining permission of the IRS. However, if the reverse is desired, IRS permission must be obtained.

Items Not Depreciable for Tax Purposes

It should be recognized that all items constituting a one-time-only first cost or capital expenditure are not necessarily depreciable for income tax purposes. These include the following:

1. items which supposedly do not diminish in value over time, such as working capital and land;
2. items which are charged as expenses in year of incurrence, such as advertising, training, and research;
3. items which are only an implied or opportunity cost;
4. moves and rearrangements of facilities.

Useful Life and Salvage Value for Tax Purposes

The depreciable life which is used for tax reporting purposes is of great concern to taxpayers and taxing agencies alike. Federal tax law provides a choice between the following two methods of estimating useful lives for all depreciable property bought in a taxable year.

1. *Class life system (ADR).* This involves using lives fixed by the IRS for various classes of assets, except that the lives can be shortened or lengthened to deviate from the IRS guidelines by up to 20%.
2. *Your estimate of useful life.* This involves using taxpayers' estimates and is subject to challenge by the IRS if it is thought to be too short based on the experience of other taxpayers. The life to be estimated is the period over which the asset is thought to be useful to the taxpayer, not its expected physical life.

The salvage value is the estimated remaining net value of the asset at the end of its useful life. Net salvage value is the resale (or scrap or junk) value minus any cost of removing and selling the asset.

Because the selection of useful lives and salvage values affects year-by-year depreciation charges and tax payments so much, the IRS is continually interested in proving that the accrued depreciation for assets in a guideline class bears a reasonable relationship to the basis (first cost minus present salvage value) of those assets. When the test is not met, the question of whether or not the taxpayer's retirement and replacement values are consistent with the class life or estimated life being used must be determined on the basis of the facts and circumstances.

Main Types of Taxes

Below are described the main types of taxes important to economic analyses.

1. *Property taxes* are based on the valuation of property owned, such as land, equipment, buildings, inventory, etc., and the established tax rates. They do not vary with income and are usually much lower in amount than income taxes.

2. *Sales taxes* are taxes imposed on product sales, usually at the retail level. They are not normally relevant in economy studies.

3. *Excise taxes* are taxes imposed upon the manufacture of certain products, such as alcohol and tobacco. They are not normally significant in economy studies.

4. *Income taxes* are taxes on profits or income in the course of regular business as well as on gains on the disposal of capital property. They are the most significant type of tax to consider in usual economic analyses and are the subject of the remainder of this chapter.

When Income Taxes Should Be Considered

In the preceding chapters we have treated income taxes either as if they are not applicable or only implicitly, i.e., by using a before-tax rate of return which is larger than the after-tax rate of return, with the intention that the resulting cash flows will be sufficient to provide for both the after-tax rate of return and the income tax.

An approximation of the before-tax rate of return requirement to include the effect of income taxes in studies using before-tax cash flows can be determined from the following relationship:

[Before-tax R.R.][1 − {Effective income tax rate}] = [After-tax R.R.]

Thus,

$$[\text{Before-tax R.R.}] = \frac{[\text{After-tax R.R}]}{[1 - \{\text{Effective income tax rate}\}]} \qquad 6\text{-}9$$

If the property is nondepreciable and there is no capital gain or loss or investment tax credit, then the above relationship is exact, not an approximation. If salvage value is less than 100% of first cost and if life of the property is finite, then the depreciation method selected for income tax purposes affects the timing of income tax payments and, therefore, error can be introduced by use of the relationship in Eq. 6-9. In practice, it is usually desirable to make after-tax analyses for any income-tax-paying enterprise unless one knows that income taxes would have no effect on the relative desirability of alternatives being considered.

After-tax analyses can be performed by exactly the same methods as before-tax analyses. The only difference is that after-tax cash flows should be used in place of before-tax cash flows by mere adjustment for either disbursements or savings in taxes; the calculation should be made using an after-tax minimum attractive rate of return.

Understanding Income Taxes

One way to help understand the effect of federal and state income taxes is to consider the taxing governments as partners in most every individual or business income or profit-seeking activity. As partners, the government organizations share in the profits from financially successful ventures, and they also normally share in the losses of unprofitable ventures (via reduced taxes, subject to some restrictions). The mystery behind the sometimes-complex computations of income taxes is lessened when one recognizes that income taxes paid are just another type of disbursement, while income taxes saved (due to business deductions or losses) are the same as any other kind of disbursement savings.

The federal (and most state) income tax regulations can be very complex, but the provisions that apply to most economic analyses of capital investments generally can be understood and applied without great difficulty. However, sometimes the help of a tax specialist is needed. This chapter is not intended to be a comprehensive treatment of federal tax law. Rather, herein are described only some main provisions of the tax law as of 1976,* followed by illustrations of general procedures for computing after-tax cash flows and making after-tax economic analyses.

Because income tax rates and many of the applicable regulations are changed rather frequently, it is not possible to have the rates or regulations always up-to-date in a textbook. In making actual economy studies, the analyst should use the existing or anticipated applicable rates and regulations.

Some Basic Principles Relating to Income Taxes

Income taxes are levied on both personal and corporate incomes. Although the regulations of most of the states that have income taxes have the same basic features as in the federal regulations, there is a great variation in the tax rates. State income taxes are in most cases much less than the federal taxes, and very often they can be closely estimated as a constant percent of federal taxes. Therefore, no attempt will be made to discuss state income taxes. An understanding of the applicable federal income tax regulations

*Some specific changes since 1976 are discussed.

usually will enable the analyst to apply the proper procedures if state taxes must be considered.

As an example of an effective (combined federal and state) incremental tax rate for a corporation, suppose the federal income tax rate is 48% and the state income tax rate is 10%. Futher assume the common case in which income is computed the same way for both taxes except that state tax paid is deductible from taxable income for federal tax purposes, but the federal tax paid is not deductible from taxable income for state tax purposes. Thus, the net effective tax rate is

$$48\% + 10\% - 0.48(10\%) = 53.2\%$$

Income taxes are disbursements, as are any other costs, and thus reduce the profits available to owners and stockholders. However, there is an important difference in that income taxes are computed as a percentage of *taxable income*, which is defined below.

Taxable Income of Individuals

An individual's total earned income is essentially what is called *adjusted gross income* for federal tax purposes. From this amount individuals may subtract for personal exemptions and allowable deductions to determine the *taxable income*. Personal exemptions are provided at the rate of $750 for the taxpayer and each dependent, with extra exemptions permissible for blind persons and persons 65 years of age or over. Allowable deductions are provided for such items as excessive medical costs, state and local taxes, interest on borrowed money, charitable contributions, casualty losses, etc., within some limits. Thus, for individual taxpayers,

Taxable income = Adjusted gross income − Personal exemption
deductions − Other allowable deductions

Taxable Income of Business Firms

The revenue of a firm is essentially what is called its *gross income*. From this amount firms may subtract all ordinary expenses to conduct the business (including very restricted contributions) except for capital expenditures. Business capital expenditures can be declared as an expense for each period (year) only to the extent of allowable depreciation or depletion charges on those capital expenditures. Thus, for business firms,

Taxable income = Gross income − All expenditures except capital
expenditures − Depreciation and depletion charges

The taxable income of a firm is often the same as the so-called *before-tax net profit*. After income taxes are subtracted (from the before-tax net profit), the remainder is often called the *after-tax net profit*.

Income Tax Effects and Rates

There are two types of income for tax computation purposes: *ordinary income* (*and losses*) and *capital gains* (*and losses*). Each of these will be explained below.

Ordinary Income (and Losses)

Ordinary income is the net profit that results from the regular business operations (such as the sale of products or services) performed by a corporation or individual. For federal tax purposes, virtually all ordinary income is taxable income and is subject to a graduated rate scale with provision for higher rates with higher income. For corporations in 1976, the federal rates for taxable income were:

20% for taxable income up to $25,000

22% for taxable income between $25,000 and $50,000

48% for taxable income in excess of $50,000

For individuals, the federal rates increase progressively from 14% to 70% of taxable income, as shown in Table 6-2, which happens to be for single taxpayers. The effect of these rates on income taxes for both single individuals and corporations is graphically illustrated in Fig. 6-2. In general, married taxpayers qualifying who file a joint tax return are allowed to have approximately twice as much of their combined (joint) taxable income taxed at a given rate as compared to single taxpayers.

Capital Gains (and Losses)

When an asset other than assets sold as part of normal business operation is disposed of for more (or less) than its book value, the resulting so-called capital gain (or capital loss) often affects taxes at a rate which is different from that for ordinary income. The amount of tax effect depends upon the amount of capital gain or loss, type of property, whether it is long-term or short-term, whether other capital gains or losses are involved, and the applicable rate or rates.

Table 6-2

1976 FEDERAL INCOME TAX RATES FOR PERSONS CATEGORIZED AS SINGLE TAXPAYERS

If the taxable income is:		The tax is:		Of the amount over
Over	But not over			
$ 0	$ 500	$ 0	+14%	$ 0
500	1,000	70	+15%	500
1,000	1,500	145	+16%	1,000
1,500	2,000	225	+17%	1,500
2,000	4,000	310	+19%	2,000
4,000	6,000	690	+21%	4,000
6,000	8,000	1,110	+24%	6,000
8,000	10,000	1,590	+25%	8,000
10,000	12,000	2,090	+27%	10,000
12,000	14,000	2,630	+29%	12,000
14,000	16,000	3,210	+31%	14,000
16,000	18,000	3,830	+34%	16,000
18,000	20,000	4,510	+36%	18,000
20,000	22,000	5,230	+38%	20,000
22,000	26,000	5,990	+40%	22,000
26,000	32,000	7,590	+45%	26,000
32,000	38,000	10,290	+50%	32,000
38,000	44,000	13,290	+55%	38,000
44,000	50,000	16,590	+60%	44,000
50,000	60,000	20,190	+62%	50,000
60,000	70,000	26,390	+64%	60,000
70,000	80,000	32,790	+66%	70,000
80,000	90,000	39,390	+68%	80,000
90,000	100,000	46,190	+69%	90,000
100,000		53,090	+70%	100,000

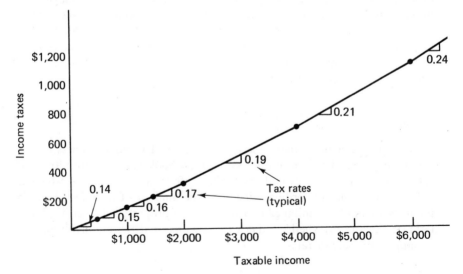

Figure 6-2. (a) 1976 Federal income taxes for individuals.

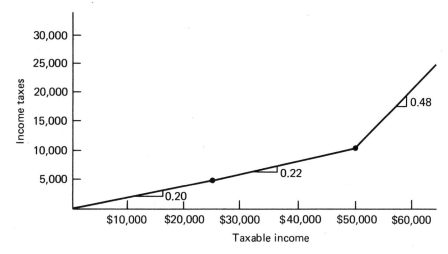

Figure 6-2. (b) 1976 Federal income taxes for corporations.

In formula form,

Capital gain (loss) = Net selling or disposal price − Book value
= Net selling or disposal price − Original first cost
+ Accumulated depreciation charges

Table 6-3 summarizes the tax treatment by type of asset (property being sold or disposed of). Table 6-4 summarizes the tax treatment applied to capital gains and losses for individuals and for corporations. The following are brief descriptions and examples of how short-term and long-term gains and

Table 6-3

TAX TREATMENT FOR GAINS AND LOSSES ON SALE OR EXCHANGE
OF ASSETS FOR FEDERAL TAX PURPOSES

If property sold was held for:	*Such as:*	*Any gain is taxed as:*	*Any loss is taxed as:*
Sale to customers	Merchandise inventory	Ordinary income	Ordinary income
Investment	Stock, bonds, land	Capital gain	Capital loss
Personal use	Home, car, jewelery	Capital gain	Nondeductible
Use in business	Buildings, land, equipment	Capital gain or ordinary income*	Capital loss or ordinary income loss

*Depends on whether recovery of previously charged depreciation and other capital gains or losses are involved. See subsequent section.

Table 6-4
TAX TREATMENT OF CAPITAL GAINS AND LOSSES

	Short-term	*Long-term*
FOR INDIVIDUALS:		
Capital gain	Taxed as ordinary income	50% of the capital gain taxed as ordinary income. Alternatively, up to $50,000* of the capital gain can be taxed at 25%, and the balance of the gain taxed at a higher rate if that is to the tax-payers advantage.
Capital loss	Subtract capital losses from any capital gains; balance may be deducted from ordinary income, but not more than $3000* per year. Any balance may be carried over to succeeding year(s).	Subtract capital losses from any capital gains; half the balance may be deducted from ordinary income, but not more than $3000* per year. Any balance may be carried over to succeeding years.
FOR CORPORATIONS:		
Capital gain	Taxed as ordinary income	Taxed at ordinary income tax rate (20%, 22%, or 48%) or 30%, whichever is smaller.
Capital loss	Corporations may deduct capital losses only to the extent of capital gains. Any capital loss in the current year that exceeds capital gains is carried back for up to 3 years and, if not completely absorbed, is then carried forward for up to 7 years.	

*Limitations given are for married taxpayers filing a joint return. Married persons filing separate returns and single taxpayers are entitled to only one-half of the limitations shown. The $3,000 limitation on capital losses was instituted in 1978 and was formerly $2,000 for property sold in 1977 and $1,000 for property sold in 1976 or before.

losses are taxed. The holding period required for a gain or loss to qualify for "long-term" tax treatment is:

For property sold	*Minimum holding period*
1976 or before	6 months
In 1977	9 months
1978 and after	12 months

Gains or losses on capital assets sold after holding for a period less than the applicable minimum (above) are subject to "short-term" tax treatment.

For tax computation purposes, short-term gains and losses are added separately, and the total of one is subtracted from the total of the other to determine whether a net short-term gain or loss results. The long-term gains and losses are treated in the same manner to determine the net long-term gain or loss. The *total net gain or loss* is then determined by merging the net short-term capital gain or loss with the net long-term capital gain or loss. A numerical example for one specific case is given below.

During the year an individual had the following transactions:

Long-term capital gain:	$5,400	
Long-term capital loss:	(1,750)	
Net long-term capital gain:		$3,650
Short-term capital gain:	$2,600	
Short-term capital loss:	(3,790)	
Net short-term capital loss:		($1,190)
Excess of net long-term capital gain over net short-term capital loss:		$2,460

The $2,460 would be taxed as a long-term capital gain. Tax rates are explained in the next section.

Taxes on Capital Gains and Losses for Individuals

The effects of capital gains and losses are somewhat different for individuals and corporations. For individual taxpayers, a net short-term capital gain is treated the same as ordinary income, and a net short-term capital loss is directly deductible from other ordinary taxable income subject to limitations described at the end of this section. If there is a total net long-term gain (net long-term gain exceeds net short-term loss), 50% of the excess is added to the ordinary income to comprise the taxable income. However, there is an alternative tax computation which may result in a lower tax as follows:

If the net long-term capital gain does not exceed $50,000 ($25,000 for individual taxpayers):

Pay at the regular income tax rate on the ordinary income and at a flat rate of 50% on one-half of the net long-term capital gain. The effect of this computation is to tax the net long-term capital gain at a maximum rate of 25% (i.e., 50% × ½).

If the net long-term capital gain exceeds $50,000 ($25,000 for individual taxpayers):

Pay at the regular income tax rate on the ordinary income, plus $12,500 (25% of the first $50,000 net long-term capital gain), and the difference between the regular tax on all taxable income (or one-half the capital gain if that amount is greater than the amount of taxable income) and the regular tax on the sum of ordinary income and $25,000.

The effect of this computation is to tax the first $50,000 of net long-term capital gain at 25% and the balance of the gain at a higher rate.

Example:

An individual taxpayer has a taxable income of $100,000. This includes $20,000 of ordinary income and one-half of $160,000 long-term capital gain added to taxable income (one-half of $160,000 long-term capital gain). Determine the income tax.

Solution:

Regular Tax Computation:

Tax on $100,000 ordinary income (from Table 6-2) = $53,090

Alternative Tax Computation:

1. Tax on $20,000 ordinary income:		$5,230
2. 25% of $50,000 long-term capital gain:		12,500
3. Regular tax on $100,000 taxable income	$53,090	
Less: Regular tax on $20,000 ordinary income and $25,000 (1/2 of first $50,000 of capital gain):	17,190	
		35,900
4. Alternative tax:		$53,630

Thus, the alternative tax of $53,630 is slightly greater than the regular tax of $53,090 as shown above. Hence, the alternative tax would not be chosen by the taxpayer.

There is a limitation on the deduction that an individual may make for net capital losses. Capital losses first must be offset against any capital gains. In any year, any excess of short-term capital losses or of one-half long-term capital losses then is deductible from ordinary income to the extent of the taxable income for that year or $3,000,* whichever is less. However, any excess capital loss above this limitation may be carried forward to future years as an offsetting loss until it is absorbed, but it is subject to the same limitation each year. Any amount that is carried over retains its long-term or short-term character.

Taxes on Capital Gains and Losses for Corporations

For tax purposes, corporations, as well as individuals, treat a net short-term capital gain the same as ordinary income. Corporations are not permitted to add only 50% of their total net long-term capital gain to taxable income as can be done by individuals. Instead, all of the long-term capital gain should be taxed at the full rate. However, there is also an alternative capital gains tax rate for corporations which is a flat 30% of the excess of net long-term capital gains over net short-term capital losses. Consequently, in no case does the tax on capital gains for corporations exceed 30%.

---

*The $3,000 limitation was instituted in 1978 and was formerly $2,000 for property sold in 1977 and $1,000 for property sold in 1976 or before.

In the year in which they occur, a corporation may deduct capital losses only to the extent of its capital gains of that year. However, any capital loss in the current year that exceeds its capital gains for that year may be carried back to the 3 years preceding the year of loss and, if not completely absorbed, it may be carried over for up to 5 succeeding years; and it then is treated as a short-term loss, regardless of whether it was a short-term or long-term loss in the year in which it occurred. This results in the interesting situation that if a corporation does not have any capital gains against which the capital losses of a current year can be charged (so as to save capital gain taxes at, say, 30%), it can recover the loss through income tax offset in a prior or succeeding year. The loss is considered to be short-term and thus is deductible from other income (thus, saving taxes at, say, 48%).

Example:

A corporation had a taxable income of $120,000, which included the following:

Long-term capital gain:		$65,000
Long-term capital loss:		(18,000)
Net long-term capital gain:		$47,000
Short-term capital gain:	$10,000	
Short-term capital loss:	(27,000)	
Net short-term capital loss:		(17,000)
Excess of net long-term capital gain over net short-term capital loss:		$30,000

What is the income tax to be paid?

Solution:

Regular Tax Computation:

First $25,000 @ 20%:	$ 5,000
Next $25,000 @ 22%:	5,500
Remaining ($120,000 − $50,000) @ 48%:	33,600
	$44,100

Alternative Tax Computation:

Taxable income:	$120,000
Less: Excess of net long-term capital gain over net short-term capital loss (see above):	30,000
Ordinary income:	$ 90,000
Tax on ordinary income:	
First $25,000 @ 20%:	5,000
Next $25,000 @ 22%:	5,500
Remaining ($90,000 − $50,000) @ 48%:	19,200
Total:	$29,700
Tax on capital gain:	
30% of $30,000:	9,000
Total:	$38,700

Since the alternative tax of $38,700 is less than the regular tax of $44,100, the corporation would doubtless choose to pay the alternative tax.

Gains and Losses from Disposal of Depreciable Property

For depreciable property such as buildings and equipment used in a business, the determination of how a gain or loss affects taxes can be complicated and can be explained best by reference to Fig. 6-3 and by assuming that straight line depreciation has been used for accounting and tax purposes.* If we sell the asset for a price less than the original cost but greater than the book value (S.P.$_1$ in Fig 6-3), the excess of selling price over book value represents a recovery of previously charged, and deducted, depreciation cost. Consequently, this excess is considered to be ordinary income and is taxed as such, since this amount had been deducted from ordinary income in prior years. If the selling price is greater than the original cost (S.P.$_2$ in Fig. 6-3), the difference between the original cost and the book value again

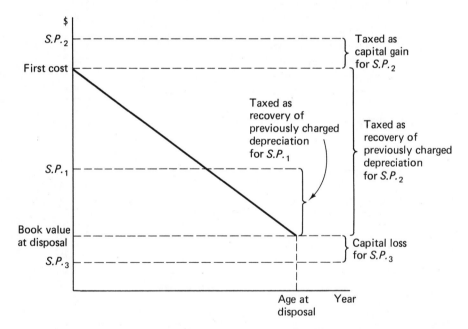

Figure 6-3. Illustration of various possible gains and losses on disposal of depreciable property used in a business.

*Some complications exist for assets purchased prior to 1964 and for cases in which accelerated depreciation methods are used. When such conditions are encountered, the specific IRS rules should be consulted.

is recovery of previously charged depreciation, and it is taxed as ordinary income, but the excess of the selling price above the original cost is taxed in a manner similar to a capital gain On the other hand, if we sell the asset for a price that is less than the book value (S.P.$_3$ in Fig. 6-3), a loss results which is treated as a capital loss.

Example:

A corporation has equipment which cost $100,000 five years ago. At that time a straight line depreciation schedule was set up based on an estimated 15-year life and $10,000 salvage value. The incremental tax rate on ordinary income is 48% and on capital gains or losses is 30%. Determine the taxes to be paid (or saved) on the gain (or loss) if the property is sold now for (a) $80,000, (b) $120,000, and (c) $45,000.

Solution:

Total depreciation charged to now $= (5/15)($100,000 - $10,000) = $30,000$
Book value now $= $100,000 - $30,000 = $70,000$

a. $80,000 - $70,000 = $10,000 gain due to recovery of previously charged depreciation.
   $10,000 @ 48% = $4,800 taxes to be paid.
b. $120,000 - $70,000 = $50,000 gain.
   $100,000 - $70,000 = $30,000 is recovery of previously charged depreciation.
   $120,000 - $100,000 = $20,000 is gain subject to capital gain rate.
   $ 30,000 \times 0.48 + $20,000 \times 0.30 = $20,400 taxes to be paid.
c. $ 70,000 - $45,000 = $25,000 capital loss.
   $ 25,000 \times 0.30 = $7,500 taxes saved.

The above example was for the sale or disposal of an individual asset. The tax rate that would apply to the gain or loss on any particular asset depends on the net gain or loss realized for all sales of such property made during the tax year. The net result of such sales determines the tax treatment on a given individual sale. This is illustrated for various situations by the two examples at the end of this chapter.

Investment Tax Credit

A special provision of the federal tax law which, when in force,* may have direct bearing on economic analyses is the investment tax credit. This allows businesses to subtract from their tax liability as much as 10%* of what they invest in "qualifying" property. By "qualifying" is meant depreci-

---

*During the 1960's and early 1970's the investment tax credit (with a maximum rate of 7% (instead of 10% as shown above) was made law and then later repealed at least two times. The maximum rate was increased from 7% to 10% in the mid-1970's, and at that time the law provided that the maximum rate would revert to 7% (4% for public utilities) for property acquired after December 31, 1980.

able equipment or tangible personal property (not including buildings) used in a business. This is subject to limitations according to the expected life of the qualifying assets, the amount of used property, and the total tax credit claimed. The limitation according to expected life per 1978 federal tax law is summarized below:

If the expected life is:		*The maximum possible investment credit (as a percentage of investment) is:*
At least, but less than		
7 yr		10%
5 yr	7 yr	$\frac{2}{3}$ of 10%
3 yr	5 yr	$\frac{1}{3}$ of 10%
0 yr	3 yr	0%

Example:

A firm invested $500,000 in property expected to last for 10 years, $300,000 in property expected to last 5 years, and $900,000 in property expected to last 4 years. What is the maximum possible tax credit?

Solution:

$$
\begin{array}{ll}
\$500,000 \times 10\% & = \$\ 50,000 \\
\$300,000 \times \frac{2}{3} \times 10\% & = \$\ 20,000 \\
\$900,000 \times \frac{1}{3} \times 10\% & = \$\ 30,000 \\
\hline
\text{Total:} & \$100,000
\end{array}
$$

A further limitation is that at most $100,000 of the cost of used property may be counted in any one year for purposes of the investment credit.

The allowable investment tax credit in any year cannot exceed the tax liability. If the tax liability is more than $25,000, the tax credit cannot exceed $25,000 plus 50% of the tax liability above $25,000. However, the investment tax credit can be carried back as many as 3 years and forward as many as 7 years.

Example:

Suppose that a firm in a given year has a tax liability of $105,000 before consideration of credits and a maximum possible investment credit of $100,000 (such as calculated in the last example). What is the firm's tax liability for that year?

Solution:

Maximum allowable investment credit:

$$\$25,000 + 50\%(\$105,000 - \$25,000) = \$65,000$$

Tax liability for year:

$$\$105,000 - \$65,000 = \$40,000$$

It should be noted that for the above two examples the difference between the maximum possible tax credit and the allowable investment credit for the year is $35,000 (= $100,000 − $65,000) and can be carried backward or forward to reduce taxes paid or payable in other years.

As an additional side note, even though the investment tax credit results in a cash savings and, therefore, in a reduction in the net investment, 1976 federal tax law provides that the credit does not reduce the investment to be depreciated.

Example:

Given a $10,000 investment which is expected to have a life of 10 years and a $300 salvage value, what is the net investment assuming that the full investment tax credit can be used? What is the depreciable investment and the annual straight line depreciation charge?

Solution:

Investment tax credit:

$$\$10,000 \times 10\% = \$1,000$$

Net (effective) investment:

$$\$10,000 - \$1,000 = \$9,000$$

Depreciable investment:

$$\$10,000 - \$300 = \$9,700$$

Depreciation charge/year:

$$\$9,700/10 = \$970$$

The above discussion of income taxes is a minimal description of some main provisions of the federal income tax law which are important to economic analyses. It is by no means complete, but it is intended to provide a basis for illustrating after-tax (i.e., after income tax) economic analyses. In general, the analyst should either know how to determine the specific provisions of the state and federal income tax law that affect the projects being studied or seek the information from persons qualified in tax laws.

The remainder of the chapter illustrates various after-tax economy studies using a suggested tabular form for computing after-tax cash flows.

Tabular Procedure for Computing After-Tax Cash Flow

Below is a suggested table to facilitate the computation of after-tax cash flows.

(1)	(2)	(3)	(4) = (2) + (3)	(5) = −(4) × Rate	(6) = (2) + (5)
Year	Before-tax cash flow	Depreciation for tax purposes	Taxable income	Cash flow for income taxes	After-tax cash flow

Column (2) contains the same information used in "before-tax" analyses. Column (3) is for the write-off of asset value which can be declared as an expense for tax purposes. Column (4) is the income or amount subject to taxes. Column (5) is the taxes paid or saved. Column (6) contains the "after-tax" cash flows to be used directly in after-tax economic analyses just the same as the cash flows in column (2) are used in before-tax economic analyses. The column headings indicate the arithmetic operations for computing columns (4), (5), and (6). It is intended that the table be used with the conventions of "+" for cash inflow or savings and "−" for cash outflow or opportunity foregone. A slight deviation from this is the convention of assigning a "−" to a depreciation charge even though it is not a cash expense item.

Illustration of Computations of After-Tax Cash Flows for Various Common Situations

The following series of example problems illustrates the computation of after-tax cash flows as well as various common situations affected by taxes. All problems herein include the common assumption that any tax disbursement or savings occurs at the same time (year) as the income or expense which affects the taxes. For purposes of comparison of the effect of various situations, the after-tax rate of return will be shown for each example. One can observe from the results of Examples 1 through 5 below that the faster (sooner) the depreciation write-off, the higher the after-tax rate of return.

Example 1:

Certain new machinery is estimated to cost $120,000 installed. It is expected to reduce net annual operating disbursements by $24,000 per yr for 10 years and to have $20,000 salvage value at the end of the tenth year. (a) What is the before-tax rate of return? (b) Show the cash flow tabulation and the after-tax rate of return if straight line depreciation is used and the ordinary income tax rate is 48%. Assume an investment tax credit is not applicable except in Example 3.

Solution:

a. Before-tax rate of return:

$-\$120,000 + \$24,000(P/A,i\%,10) + \$20,000(P/F,i\%,10) = 0$

@15%: $-\$120,000 + \$24,000(5.019) + \$20,000(0.2472) = +\$5,050$

@20%: $-\$120,000 + \$24,000(4.192) + \$20,000(0.1615) = -\$16,300$

$i = 15\% + \left(\dfrac{5,050}{5,050 + 16,300}\right)(20\% - 15\%) = 16.2\%$

b.

(1)	(2)	(3)	(4) = (2) + (3)	(5) = −(4) × Rate	(6) = (2) + (5)
Year	*Before-tax cash flow*	*Depreciation for tax purposes*	*Taxable income*	*Cash flow for income taxes*	*After-tax cash flow*
0	− $120,000				− $120,000
1–10	+ 24,000	− $10,000	+ $14,000	− $6,720	+ 17,280
10	+ 20,000				+ 20,000

$$-\$120,000 + \$17,280(P/A,i\%,10) + \$20,000(P/F,i\%,10) = 0$$
By trial and error, $i = 8.9\%$.

Example 2:

Same problem as Example 1(b) above except that sum-of-years-digits depreciation is used.

Solution:

$$\text{S.Y.D.} = \frac{N(N+1)}{2} = \frac{10(11)}{2} = 55$$

First-year depreciation: $\frac{10}{55}(\$120,000 - \$20,000) = \$18,200$

Decrease in depreciation each year thereafter:

$$\frac{1}{55}(\$120,000 - \$20,000) = \$1,820$$

(1)	(2)	(3)	(4) = (2) + (3)	(5) = −(4) × Rate	(6) = (2) + (5)
Year	*Before-tax cash flow*	*Depreciation for tax purposes*	*Taxable income*	*Cash flow for income taxes*	*After-tax cash flow*
0	− $120,000				− $120,000
1	+ 24,000	− $18,200	+ $5,800	− $2,780	+ 21,220
Each Year 2–10	+ 24,000	Decreases $1,820	Increases $1,820	$875 more negative	Decreases $875
10	+ 20,000				+ 20,000

$$-\$120,000 + \$21,220(P/A,i\%,10) - \$875(A/G,i\%,10)(P/A,i\%,10)$$
$$+ \$20,000(P/F,i\%,10) = 0$$
By trial and error, $i = 12.9\%$.

Example 3:

Same problem as Example 1(b) above except assume that the full investment tax credit can be taken at the same time the investment is made.

Solution:

(1)	(2)	(3)	(4) = (2) + (3)	(5) = −(4) × Rate	(6) = (2) + (5)
		Depreciation			
	Before-tax	*for tax*	*Taxable*	*Cash flow for*	*After-tax*
Year	*cash flow*	*purposes*	*income*	*income taxes*	*cash flow*
0	−$120,000			+12,000*	−$108,000
1–10	+ 24,000	−$10,000	+$14,000	− 6,720	+ 17,280
10	+ 20,000				+ 20,000

*$120,000 × 10% = $12,000

$$-\$108,000 + \$17,280(P/A,i\%,10) + \$20,000(P/F,i\%,10) = 0$$

By trial and error, $i = 11.3\%$

Example 4:

Same problem as Example 1(b) above regarding the cash flows expected to happen. However, tax regulations will permit the equipment to be depreciated over a 4-year period using straight line depreciation and zero salvage value. Assume that any annual loss reduces taxable ordinary income and that any capital gain is taxable at 25%.

Solution:

$$\text{Annual depreciation:} \frac{\$120,000 - \$0}{4} = \$30,000$$

(1)	(2)	(3)	(4) = (2) + (3)	(5) = −(4) × Rate	(6) = (2) + (5)
		Depreciation			
	Before-tax	*for tax*	*Taxable*	*Cash flow for*	*After-tax*
Year	*cash flow*	*purposes*	*income*	*income taxes*	*cash flow*
0	−$120,000				−$120,000
1–4	+ 24,000	−$30,000	−$ 6,000	+$ 2,880	+ 26,880
5–10	+ 24,000	0	+ 24,000	− 11,500	+ 12,500
10	+ 20,000		+ 20,000*	− 5,000†	+ 15,000

*Capital gain = $20,000 − $0 = $20,000.
†Tax on capital gain: $20,000 × 25% = $5,000.

$$-\$120,000 + \$26,880(P/A,i\%,4) + \$12,500(P/A,i\%,6)(P/F,i\%,4)$$
$$+ \$15,000(P/F,i\%,10) = 0$$

By trial and error, $i = 12.5\%$.

Example 5:

Same problem as Example 1(b) above regarding expected cash flows except that the equipment is expected to have no salvage value after 10 years. Even though the equipment is serviceable for only 10 years, assume that tax regulations now require that the equipment be amortized over a 15-year period using straight line depreciation. As in Example 4, assume that any annual loss reduces taxable ordinary income and that any capital gain is taxable at 25%.

Solution:

$$\text{Annual depreciation: } \frac{\$120,000}{15} = \$8,000$$

(1)	*(2)*	*(3)*	*(4) = (2) + (3)*	*(5) = −(4) × Rate*	*(6) = (2) + (5)*
		Depreciation			
	Before-tax	*for tax*	*Taxable*	*Cash flow for*	*After-tax*
Year	*cash flow*	*purposes*	*income*	*income taxes*	*cash flow*
0	−$120,000				−$120,000
1–10	+ 24,000	−$8,000	+$16,000	−$7,680	+ 16,320
11–15		− 8,000	− 8,000	+ 3,840	+ 3,840

$$-\$120,000 + \$16,320(P/A,i\%,10) + \$3,840(P/A,i\%,5)(P/F,i\%,10) = 0$$

By trial and error, $i = 7.5\%$.

The after-tax rate of return results from Examples 1(b) through 5 above are summarized in Table 6-6. Note the marked increase in this return with increased rates of depreciation.

Table 6-6

SUMMARIZATION OF AFTER-TAX RATES OF RETURN
FOR EXAMPLES 1(b) THROUGH 5

Example	*Method of depreciation (with special treatment)*	*After-tax rate of return*
1(b)	Straight line	8.9%
2	Sum-of-years-digits	12.9
3	Straight line (investment tax credit taken)	11.3
4	Straight line (over 4 yr)	12.5
5	Straight line (over 15 yr)	7.5

Illustration of After-Tax Analyses Using Different Economic Analysis Methods

Example:

It is desired to compare the economics of wooden vs. brick construction for a certain building. Below are given the pertinent data.

	Wood	*Brick*
First cost:	$40,000	$100,000
Life:	20 yr	40 yr
Salvage value:	$10,000	$20,000
Annual before-tax		
cash disbursement:	$9,000	$3,000

Use a table to compute the after-tax cash flows based on straight line depreciation and a 30% tax rate to cover both state and federal income taxes. Assuming a 6% minimum attractive after-tax rate of return, show which alternative is best by the (a) annual worth method, (b) present worth method, and (c) rate of return method.

Solution:

Annual depreciation for wood: $\dfrac{\$40,000 - \$10,000}{20} = \$1,500$

Annual depreciation for brick: $\dfrac{\$100,000 - \$20,000}{40} = \$2,000$

	(1) Year	(2) Before-tax cash flow	(3) Depreciation for tax purposes	(4) = (2) + (3) Taxable income	(5) = −(4) × Rate Cash flow for income taxes @30%	(6) = (2) + (5) After-tax cash flow
Wood	0	−$ 40,000				− $40,000
	1–20	− 9,000	−$1,500	−$10,500	+$3,150	− 5,850
	20	+ 10,000				+ 10,000
Brick	0	− 100,000				− 100,000
	1–40	− 3,000	− 2,000	− 5,000	+ 1,500	− 1,500
	40	+ 20,000				+ 20,000

a. *Annual worth comparison:*
   Wood:
$$-\$40,000(A/P,6\ \%,20) + \$10,000(A/F,6\ \%,20) - \$5,850$$
$$= -\$40,000(0.087) \quad\quad + \$10,000(0.027) \quad\quad - \$5,850 = -\$9,060$$
   Brick:
$$-\$100,000(A/P,6\ \%,40) + \$20,000(A/F,6\ \%,40) - \$1,500$$
$$= -\$100,000(0.0664) \quad\quad + \$20,000(0.0064) \quad\quad - \$1,500 = -\$8,012$$
   Thus, the brick is more economical.

b. *Present worth comparison:*

		Wood	*Brick*
First cost:		−$ 40,000	−$100,000
Annual disbursement:	−$ 5,850(P/A,6%,40) =	− 88,000 − $1,500(P/A,6%,40) =	− 22,600
Replacement:	−$30,000(P/F,6%,20) =	− 9,350	
Salvage value:	+$10,000(P/F,6%,40) =	+ 970 + $20,000(P/F,6%,40) =	+ 1,930
	Net P.W.: =	−$136,380	−$120,670

Thus, the brick again is shown to be more economical.

c. *Rate of return (I.R.R.) comparison:*
Equating the annual costs to obtain the return on the extra investment:

$$-\$40,000(A/P,i\%,20) + \$10,000(A/F,i\%,20) - \$5,850$$
$$= -\$100,000(A/P,i\%,40) + \$20,000(A/F,i\%,40) - \$1,500$$

By trial and error, $i \approx 8\%$, which means that the extra investment for the brick, having an after-tax return of more than 6%, is justified and thus, the brick is again shown to be the better alternative.

Note: The signs (positive and negative) could have been reversed in the computations for each of the above three methods. This is commonly done when it is understood that one is dealing with costs rather than savings or incomes.

Illustration of After-Tax Analyses with Receipts Known, Different Lives, Capital Gains and Capital Losses, and Applicable Investment Tax Credits

Example:
Consider the same alternative lathes A and B for which before-tax economic comparisons were made in Chapters 3 and 4. The following before-tax data were given:

	Lathe	
	A	B
First cost:	$10,000	$15,000
Life:	5 yrs.	10 yr
Salvage value:	2,000	0
Annual receipts:	5,000	7,000
Annual disbursements:	2,200	4,300
Minimum attractive rate of return = 8% (before-tax)		

It is desired to compare the economics of both alternatives on an after-tax basis if both alternatives are to be depreciated using the straight line method and $1,500 salvage value and the above-estimated lives. (*Note:* The $2,000 and $0 are estimated actual salvage values (cash flows) whereas the $1,500 is the assumed salvage value for each for purposes of determining depreciation charges.) The effective tax rate on ordinary income is 55% and the effective rate on capital gains and losses is 35%. A 10% investment tax credit is used and the after-tax minimum attractive rate of return = 5%. Make the "repeatability" assumption. Use the (a) A.W. method, (b) P.W. method, and (c) E.R.R. method.

Solution:

(1)	(2) Before-tax cash flow	(3) Depreciation for tax purposes	(4) = (2) + (3) Taxable income	(5) = −(4) + Rate Cash flows for income taxes	(6) = (2) + (5) After-tax cash flow
Year					
Lathe A 0	−$10,000			+$ 333[1]	−$ 9,667
1–5	+ 2,800	−$1,700[2]	$1,100	− 605	+ 2,195
5	+ 2,000		+ 500[3]	− 275[4]	+ 1,725
Lathe B 0	−$15,000			+ 1,500[5]	− 13,500
1–10	+ 2,700	− 1,350[6]	− 1,350	− 743	+ 1,957
10	0		− 1,500[7]	+ 525[8]	+ 525

(1) Investment tax credit = $10,000 × 10% × 1/3 = $333.
(2) Depreciation = ($10,000 − $1,500)/5 = $1,700.
(3) Capital gain = $2,000 − $1,500 = $500.
(4) Tax on capital gain (recovery of previously charged depreciation) = −$500 × 0.55 = $275.
(5) Investment tax credit = $15,000 × 10% = $1,500.
(6) Depreciation = ($15,000 − $1,500)/10 = $1,350.
(7) Capital loss = $1,500 − $0 = $1,500.
(8) Tax on capital loss = $1,500 × 0.35 = $525.

a. *Annual Worth Comparison:*
   Lathe A:

$$-\$9,667(A/P,5\%,5) + \$1,725(A/F,5\%,5) + \$2,195 = \$274$$

   Lathe B:

$$-\$13,500(A/P,5\%,10) + \$525(A/F,5\%,10) + \$1,957 = \$51$$

   Thus, lathe A, having the highest net A.W., is best.

b. *Present Worth Comparison:*
   The easiest way is to use the following relation for a study period equal to the lowest common multiple of the lives:

   P.W. = A.W.$(P/A,5\%$, study period)

   For Lathe A: P.W. = $274(P/A,5\%,10) = $2,116.
   For Lathe B: P.W. = $51(P/A,5\%,10) = $394.
   Thus, lathe A is again shown to be best.

c. *Rate of Return (E.R.R.) Comparison:*
   The E.R.R. for the lowest investment (in lathe A) can be found by solving:

$$\$9,667(F/P,i\%,5) = \$1,725 + \$2,195(F/A,5\%,5)$$
$$\$9,667(F/P,i\%,5) = \$1,725 + \$12,130$$
$$(F/P,i\%,5) = 1.433$$

From tables,

@ $i\%$	$(F/P,i\%,5)$
5%	1.276
$X\%$	1.433
8%	1.469

By linear interpolation, X is slightly less than 8%. Since 8% > 5% M.A.R.R., the investment in lathe A is justified.

The return on the extra investment required for B instead of A can be found by analyzing the difference in cash flows as follows:

Year	A	B	Diff. $(B - A)$
0	−$9,667	−$13,500	−$3,833
1	+ 2,195	+ 1,957	− 238
2			
3			
4			
5	+$1,725 − $9,667		+$7,942
6			
7			
8			
9			
10	+$2,195 + $1,725	+$1,957 + $525	−$ 238 − $1,200

The E.R.R. for diff. (B − A) can be found by solving:

$$\text{F.W. of outflows} = \text{F.W. of inflows}$$

$$\$3,833(F/P,i\%,10) + \$238(F/A,i\%,10) + \$1,200 = \$7,942(F/P,5\%,5)$$

By trial and error, i can be found to be between 4% and 5%. Since this is less than the 5% M.A.R.R., the extra investment in B rather than A is not justified; therefore, A would be the indicated choice.

Tax Rates on Gains or Losses on Disposal of Old Assets

Figures 6-2 and 6-3 and Table 6-4 summarize in gross form the tax rates involved in both capital and ordinary income gains and losses for individuals and for corporations, respectively. These will be illustrated for various situations using the table for computation of after-tax cash flows by the next two example problems.

Example:

An individual taxpayer for whom applicable incremental ordinary income is taxed at 40% has an asset with a book value of $4,500 that is disposed of for $1,500. Show the net after-tax cash flow of this transaction if the loss is treated as:

a. ordinary income loss;

b. capital loss—and the individual has $4,000 in net long-term capital gains from disposal of other assets; and

c. capital loss—and the individual has no capital gains from other sources.

Solution:

Using Table 6-4 for the applicable tax rates:

	(2) Before-tax cash flow	(3) Depreciation for tax purposes	(4) = (2) + (3) Taxable income	(5) = −(4) × Rate Cash flow for income taxes	(6) = (2) + (5) After-tax cash flow
(a)	+$1,500		− $3,000	+$1,200*	+$2,700
(b)	+ 1,500		− 3,000	+ 600†	+ 2,100
(c)	+ 1,500		− 3,000	+ 1,000‡	+ 2,500

*$3,000 book loss × 40% = $1,200 tax reduction.

†$3,000 reduction in capital gains × 40%/2 = $600 tax reduction.

‡$3,000 book loss × 40% = $1,200 possible tax reduction; however, this is limited to a maximum of $1,000 in the year. The remaining $200 can be carried back as many as 3 years or forward up to 5 years.

Example:

A corporation paying taxes in the 48% bracket owns an old asset with a book value of $500 which is disposed for $1,500. Show the net after-tax cash flow for this transaction if the gain is treated as

a. ordinary income;

b. long-term capital with a rate of 30%; and

c. short-term capital.

Solution:

	(2) Before-tax cash flow	(3) Depreciation for tax purposes	(4) = (2) + (3) Taxable income	(5) = −(4) × Rate Cash flow for income taxes	(6) = (2) + (5) After-tax cash flow
(a)	+$1,500		+$1,000	−$480*	+$1,020
(b)	+ 1,500		+ 1,000	− 300†	+ 1,200
(c)	+ 1,500		+ 1,000	− 480‡	+ 1,020

*−$1,000(0.48) = −$480.

†−$1,000(0.30) = −$300.

‡−$1,000(0.48) = −$480.

PROBLEMS

(*Note*: In each of the problems involving after-tax studies, assume that any salvage values are both the cash flows expected at the end of the project lives and the amounts used for computation of depreciation charges, unless the problem states to the contrary. Also, assume that any investment tax credit and any extra first-year depreciation are not applicable unless stated otherwise.)

6-1. A machine tool costs $40,000. Its life for depreciation purposes is estimated at 10 years, and its salvage value is assumed to be $4,000. Determine (1) the depreciation charge for the fifth year and (2) the book value at the end of the fifth year using each of the following methods:
   a. Straight line
   b. Sum-of-years-digits
   c. Double declining balance

6-2. Work Prob. 6-1 assuming that the 20% additional first-year depreciation is taken.

6-3. A new machine has just been purchased by a manufacturer for $25,000. Freight and trucking charges were $500, and the installation cost was $300. The machine has an estimated useful life of 8 years, at which time it is expected that $1,000 dismantling costs will have to be paid in order to sell it for $5,000. Compute (1) the depreciation charge for the first year and (2) the book value at the end of the first year using each of the following methods:
   a. Straight line
   b. Sum-of-years-digits
   c. Declining balance
   d. Sinking fund with reinvestment rate of 12%

6-4. An asset costs $10,000 and is expected to have $1,000 salvage value at the end of 5 years. Graph its book value as a function of year using each of the following methods:
   a. Straight line
   b. Sum-of-years-digits
   c. Double declining balance

6-5. Compute the depreciation on an automobile—your own car or one in which you are interested. Obtain from a dealer the cost of the new car and the "Blue Book" values of this car, or its equivalent, at the ages of 1, 2, 3, 4, and 5 years. Note that these are average market values based on average mileage and maintenance. From the values obtained, compute the year-by-year depreciation costs. Compare the results with depreciation costs computed by the depreciation method in this chapter that most nearly approximates the above values.

6-6. A special-purpose machine is to be depreciated as a linear function of use. It costs $25,000 and is expected to produce 100,000 units and then be salvaged for $5,000. Up to the end of the third year it had produced 60,000 units and during the fourth year it produced 10,000 units. What is the depreciation charge for the fourth year and the book value at the end of the fourth year?

6-7. Determine the more economical means of acquiring a business machine if you may either (1) purchase the machine for $5,000 with a probable resale value of $2,000 at the end of 5 years or (2) rent the machine at an annual rate of $900 per yr for 5 years with an initial deposit of $500 refundable upon returning the machine in good condition. If you own the machine, you will depreciate it for tax purposes at the annual rate of $600. Of course, all leasing rental charges are deductible from taxable income. As either owner or lessee you will assume liability for all expenses associated with the operation of the machine. Compare the alternatives using the annual cost method. The after-tax minimum attractive rate of return is 10% and the income tax rate is 40%.

6-8. A corporation in year 19X1 expects a gross income of $500,000 and total operating (cash) expenditures of $400,000 and capital expenditures of $20,000. In addition, the corporation is able to declare $60,000 depreciation charges for the year. What is the expected taxable income and total federal income taxes owed for the year?

6-9. BIG Corporation is considering making an investment of $100,000 which will increase its annual taxable income from $40,000 to $70,000. What annual federal income taxes will be owed as a result of this investment? What is the average rate to be paid on the taxable income?

6-10. Suppose the investment by BIG Corporation (above) has expected results as follows:

Annual receipts:	$75,000
Annual disbursements:	$45,000
Life:	8 yr
Salvage value	$20,000

If straight line depreciation is used and if the after-tax minimum attractive rate of return is 15%, determine if the investment is attractive using the net P.W. method.

6-11. An unmarried taxpayer currently has an adjusted gross income of $25,000 and a taxable income of $19,000. He is considering making an investment which will be either a loser or a winner. Determine the annual amount and rate as percent of taxable income for taxes to be paid or saved if the investment
a. Increases taxable income by $3,000
b. Decreases taxable income by $3,000

6-12. Work Examples 1 and 2 in the text of this chapter except assume that the firm can take full advantage of the 10% investment tax credit and the additional first-year depreciation. Assume that the credit occurs at the same time as the investment and the additional depreciation occurs at the end of the first year.

6-13. A firm is expecting to make the following investments during the coming tax year:

Investment	Expected life
$500,000	10 yr
50,000	6 yr
80,000	4 yr
200,000	2 yr

a. What is the investment tax credit?

b. If the firm's total tax liability for the coming year is $70,000, how much of the investment tax credit can be claimed in that year?

6-14. Five years ago a corporation bought an asset for $200,000 which it then estimated would last a total of 10 years and then have a $40,000 salvage value. The company now sells the asset for $95,000. Determine the taxes to be paid or saved as a result of the disposal if:

a. Sum-of-years-digits depreciation had been used and any gain is taxed at 48 % for recovery of previously charged depreciation.

b. Straight line depreciation had been used and any loss is directly deductible from ordinary income for a prior year, thus saving taxes at 48 % rate.

c. Straight line depreciation had been used and any loss reduces the capital gains from other assets being sold in the same year. Those capital gains would have been taxed at 30 %.

6-15. Two alternative machines will produce the same product, but one is capable of higher quality work, which can be expected to return greater revenue. The following are relevant data:

	Machine A	Machine B
First cost:	$20,000	$30,000
Life:	12 yr	8 yr
Salvage value:	$4,000	0
Annual receipts:	$150,000	$188,000
Annual disbursements:	$138,000	$170,000

Determine which is the better alternative based on using straight line depreciation, an income tax rate of 33 %, and a minimum attractive after-tax rate of return of 10 % using the following methods:

a. annual worth,

b. present worth,

c. rate of return (E.R.R.)

6-16. Alternative methods I and II are proposed for a plant operation. The following is comparative information:

	Method I	Method II
Initial investment:	$10,000	$40,000
Life:	5 yr	10 yr
Salvage value:	$1,000	$5,000
Annual disbursements:		
Labor:	$12,000	$4,000
Power:	$250	$300
Rent:	$1,000	$500
Maintenance:	$500	$200
Property taxes and insurance:	$400	$2,000
Total annual disbursements:	$14,150	$17,000

Determine which is the better alternative based on an after-tax annual cost analysis with a tax rate of 50% and a minimum attractive after-tax rate of return of 12% assuming the investment tax credit is used and the following methods of depreciation:
a. Straight line
b. Sum-of-the-years-digits

6-17. A manufacturing process can be designed for varying degrees of automation. The following is relevant cost information:

Degree	First cost	Annual labor cost	Annual power and maintenance cost
A	$10,000	$9,000	$ 500
B	14,000	7,500	800
C	20,000	5,000	1,000
D	30,000	3,000	1,500

Determine which is best by after-tax analyses using a tax rate of 50% and a minimum attractive after-tax rate of return of 15% and straight line depreciation. Assume each has a life of 5 years and 0 salvage value. Use each of the following methods:
a. Annual worth
b. Present worth
c. Rate of return (I.R.R.)

6-18. A certain machine can be installed at a cost of $15,000 and yield annual savings of $4,000 and zero salvage at the end of a 5-year economic life. The

firm's income tax rate is 50%. Determine the after-tax rate of return for this investment using the following methods of depreciation:
a. Straight line
b. Sum-of-years-digits
c. Double declining balance

6-19. Work Prob. 6-18a with the following changes:
a. The whole investment amount can be declared as an expense at the end of the first year of project life without resorting to straight line depreciation.
b. Straight line depreciation is used and the investment tax credit is allowed per the limitations according to expected life.

6-20. A $50,000 investment is expected to cause a reduction in net annual out-of-pocket costs of $11,000 a year for 10 years and then have zero salvage value. The investment will be depreciated for income tax purposes using the sum-of-years-digits method with a life of 10 years and zero salvage value. If the tax rate is 50%, find the after-tax rate of return. Use the gradient formula in the solution.

6-21. Jim Crooner has such a high income that he is in the 70% tax bracket on ordinary income. He buys a farm as a side business for $50,000. He figures that, because of his tax bracket, it would be a good idea to fix up the farm and sell it for a capital gain which is taxed at 25%. He keeps the farm for 5 years, and the annual out-of-pocket costs are $10,000 more than the annual cash revenues. Each year he is able to deduct that loss and also $4,000 depreciable expense from his taxable income. At the end of the fifth year he sells the farm for $100,000. Find the following:
a. The before-tax rate of return
b. The after-tax rate of return

Chapter

7

replacement analyses

Replacement studies are of two general types. The first type involves studies on whether to keep an old asset (sometimes called *defender*) or to replace the old with a new asset (sometimes called *challenger*) at a given point in time. The second general type involves determining, in advance, the economic service life of an asset. The latter type of replacement study is treated briefly in this chapter and in depth in Chapter 17.

The economics of replacement can generally be studied by any of the methods used for economic analyses of alternatives; e.g., rate of return, annual worth, present worth, future worth, or benefit–cost ratio.

Importance of Replacement Studies

The formulation of a replacement policy plays a major part in the determination of the basic technological and economic progress of a firm. Undue or hasty replacement can leave a firm pressed for capital that may be needed for other beneficial uses. Furthermore, if replacement is postponed beyond a reasonable time, the firm may find that its production costs are rising; whereas, the costs of its competitors who are using more modern equipment are declining. This can result in the firm's loss of ability to meet price competition and a consequent technological and economic trap of drastic consequences.

Causes of Retirement

Property retirement for economic study purposes is said to occur whenever the asset is physically removed, abandoned, or reassigned to a secondary service function. The following are common causes of retirement:

1. unsatisfactory functional characteristics, such as deterioration or inadequacy to meet requirements for safety, capacity, style or quality;

2. end of need for output capability of asset; and

3. existence of improved assets which have reduced operating costs to the extent that the old asset is uneconomical.

Replacement Considerations and Assumptions

Below are discussed several important classes of considerations and assumptions inherent in replacement analyses (as well as in most analyses of nonreplacement alternatives) together with some of the alternatives within these classes.

1. The *planning horizon* is the furthest time in the future considered in the analysis. Often, an infinite planning horizon is used if it is difficult or impossible to predict when the activity under consideration will be terminated. Whenever it is clear that the project will have a definite and predictable duration, it is more realistic to base the study on a finite planning horizon.

2. The *technology* is important with respect to the characteristics of machines which are candidates to replace those under analysis. If it is assumed that all future assets will be the same as those presently in service, this implies that there will be no technological progress for that type of asset. It is probably more realistic to expect some obsolescence of old assets with respect to available new assets.

3. *Cost and return patterns over asset life* can take an infinite variety of forms. It is fairly common to assume they are uniform (constant) for lack of ability or willingness to try to estimate more closely. Common alternatives are to assume an increasing or decreasing pattern according to some function of time.

4. The *availability of capital* can be quite important to any replacement analysis, for the alternatives usually involve keeping the old asset so that little or no additional capital is needed as opposed to investing in some replacement asset with a marked capital outlay. Many studies are made assuming infinite capital available at some specified minimum rate of return. On the other hand, it may be desirable to consider some limitation on capital available, at least in the choice between alternative projects in a given time period.

Salvage Value of Old Asset in Trade-in

When equipment is replaced, the old equipment is often accepted as partial payment for its replacement. If the vendor offers an allowance of, say, $3,000 on an older truck when traded for a newer model listed at, say, $5,000, the exchange price ($2,000) is then known, but the true salvage value of the older truck is not necessarily known. It is only by knowing the cash price of the newer model, say $4,200, that we can have a true estimate of the actual salvage value of the old truck ($4,200 − $2,000 = $2,200). Thus, the difference between the "apparent" salvage value based on trade-in quotation and the true salvage value is $3,000 − $2,200 = $800. The erroneous overstatement of challenger and defender costs by this $800 does not result in compensating errors whenever the expected life of the challenger differs from that for the defender and the conventional approach (to be explained later) is used. The added stated investment for the challenger then is spread over a different number of years than for the defender.

Specifying the Planning Horizon for a Replacement Study

As pointed out in Chapter 3, the determination of the study period or planning horizon is an important step in comparing investment alternatives. In this section, aspects of that determination peculiar to replacement studies are examined.

In a replacement study it is very common for the anticipated remaining life of the defender to be different from the anticipated lives of the challengers. In fact, it is usually the case that the remaining life for the defender is less than the useful life of the challenger. For this reason, it is very common to specify a planning horizon equal to the anticipated remaining life of the defender.

If a particular situation dictates that the planning horizon should be greater than the anticipated remaining life of the defender, then forecasts are required for potential future replacements of the defender. Although this is normally the case in comparing any investment alternative, it is commonly assumed that replacements will have identical cash flow profiles. (Recall that the *repeatability* assumptions were used in several of the examples in previous chapters). Such assumptions are questionable because the defender normally would not last more than one life cycle. For this reason, it is often assumed that the defender will be replaced at the end of its useful life with an asset having a cash flow profile equal to or better than the best challenger available currently.

Example:

A lathe has been in use for some time and can be continued in service for at most 4 more years. A new lathe can be purchased for $18,000 and at the end of the 10-year planning horizon it will have a salvage value of $1,500. The defender has a market value of $1,800 currently; at the end of 4 years it will have a negligible salvage value. The annual disbursements for the defender equal $3,500 and for the challenger equal $2,100.

If the defender is continued in service for 4 years and replaced at that time, the replacement is anticipated to cost $18,000 initially, have annual disbursements of $2,100, and have a salvage value of $X after 6 years of service. A before-tax study and a M.A.R.R. of 15% are deemed appropriate.

Solution:

Two approaches come to mind in estimating the value of X. One approach is to specify a value of X such that the capital recovery cost for the replacement is equal to the capital recovery cost of the challenger. While such an approach may, on the surface, appear reasonable, it assumes implicitly that X equals the book value after 6 years using the sinking fund depreciation method. The sinking fund depreciation method does not adequately describe the way in which most equipment truly depreciates in value. Hence, it does not seem proper to select X in this manner. Instead, it is felt that the proper approach is to forecast the value of X directly. For the purpose of this example, the sum-of-years-depreciation book value will be used; hence, $X = \$4,500$. In this case, the capital recovery cost of the replacement for the defender will be greater than that of the challenger.

Year	Defender	Challenger
0	$0	$-$18,000 + $1,800
1–4	$- $3,500	$-$2,100
4	$-$18,000	$0
5–10	$- $2,100	$-$2,100
10	$4,500	$1,500

$$\begin{aligned}
\text{P.W. (Defender)} \; = \; &-\$3,500(P/A,15\%,4) - \$18,000(P/F,15\%,4) \\
&-\$2,100(P/A,15\%,6)(P/F,15\%,4) \\
&+ \$4,500(P/F,15\%,10) \\
= \; &-\$23,716 \\
\text{P.W. (Challenger)} \; = \; &-\$16,200 - \$2,100(P/A,15\%,10) \\
&+ \$1,500(P/F,15\%,10) \\
= \; &-\$26,369
\end{aligned}$$

The defender has the lowest discounted cost, even though a somewhat conservative approach was used to account for the replacement of the defender at the end of its useful life. Technological improvements may well produce replacement candidates in the future that are superior to those available currently.

Cash Flow Approach and Conventional Approach

In performing replacement studies a cash flow approach can usually be employed directly. If such an approach is used, the trade-in or current market value of the defender would be shown as a positive cash flow for the challenger, since the positive cash flow will be realized if the defender is replaced. The cash flow approach allows a direct treatment of a situation in which the current market value for the defender can be different for different challengers. Finally, tax aspects involving capital gains and losses are easily handled when a cash flow approach is used.

Example:
An industrial lift truck has been in service for several years and management is contemplating replacing it. Two replacement candidates (A and B) are under consideration. If new truck A is purchased, the old lift truck will have an actual salvage value of $2,000; if new truck B is purchased, the defender will have an actual salvage value of $1,500.

A planning horizon of 5 years is to be used. If the defender is retained, it is anticipated to have annual operating and maintenance costs of $7,200; it will have a zero salvage value at the end of 5 additional years of service.

Challenger A will cost $12,000 and will have operating and maintenance costs of $4,400; at the end of the planning horizon, it will have a salvage value of $3,000. Challenger B will cost $10,000 and will have operating and maintenance costs of $5,100; at the end of the planning horizon it will have a salvage value of $2,500.

A before-tax analysis is to be used to determine the preferred alternative. A present worth comparison and a minimum attractive rate of return of 20% are to be used.

Solution:

The following cash flow profiles exist for the three alternatives:

End of year	Defender	Challenger	
		A	B
0	$0	−$12,000 + $2,000	−$10,000 + $1,500
1–5	−$7,200	−$4,400	−$5,100
5	0	$3,000	$2,500

P.W. (Defender) $= -\$7,200(P/A,20\%,5) = -\$21,535$

$\quad$ P.W.(A) $= -\$10,000 - \$4,400(P/A,20\%,5) + 3,000(P/F,20\%,5)$

$\quad\quad = -\$21,955$

$\quad$ P.W.(B) $= -\$8,500 - \$5,100(P/A,20\%,5) + 2,500(P/F,20\%,5)$

$\quad\quad = -\$22,749$

Since the defender has the lowest equivalent present cost ($21,535), it would be recommended that the lift truck currently in use be retained.

Example:

Suppose that in the previous example an after-tax analysis is to be performed. Assume the defender has a current book value of $750 and is being depreciated using sum-of-years-digits depreciation with depreciation charges of $500 and $250 remaining. Capital gains are taxed at 25% and ordinary income is taxed at 50%.

The challenger lift trucks will be depreciated using sum-of-years-digits depreciation over an 8-year period to a terminal salvage value equal to 10% of the initial investment. Both challengers qualify for a 10% investment tax credit. An after-tax minimum attractive rate of return of 12% is to be used in the analysis.

Solution:

Defender:

Year	Before-tax cash flow	Depreciation for tax purposes	Taxable income	Cash flow for income taxes	After-tax cash flow
0	0				0
1	−$7,200	−$500	−$7,700	+$3,850	−$3,350
2	− 7,200	− 250	− 7,450	+ 3,725	− 3,475
3	− 7,200		− 7,200	+ 3,600	− 3,600
4	− 7,200		− 7,200	+ 3,600	− 3,600
5	− 7,200		− 7,200	+ 3,600	− 3,600

$$\text{P.W.} = -\$3,600(P/A,12\%,5) + \$250(P/F,12\%,1) + \$125(P/F,12\%,2)$$
$$= -\$12,655$$

Challenger A:

Year	Before-tax cash flow	Depreciation for tax purposes	Taxable income	Cash flow for income taxes	After-tax cash flow
0	−$12,000			+$1,200*	−$10,800.00
	+ 2,000			− 312.50†	+ 1,687.50
1	− 4,400	−$2,400	−$6,800	+ 3,400	− 1,000
2	− 4,400	− 2,100	− 6,500	+ 3,250	− 1,150
3	− 4,400	− 1,800	− 6,200	+ 3,100	− 1,300
4	− 4,400	− 1,500	− 5,900	+ 2,950	− 1,450
5	− 4,400	− 1,200	− 5,600	+ 2,800	− 1,600
	+ 3,000‡				+ 3,000

*10% investment tax credit: 0.10($12,000) = $1,200.

†25% capital gains tax: 0.25($2,000 − $750) = $312.50.

‡Salvage value equals book value; thus, no capital gain or loss.

$$\text{P.W.} = -\$9,112.50 - [\$1,000 + \$150(A/G,12\%,5)](P/A,12\%,5)$$
$$+ \$3,000(P/F,12\%,5) = -\$11,975$$

Challenger B:

Year	Before-tax cash flow	Depreciation for tax purposes	Taxable income	Cash flow for income taxes	After-tax cash flow
0	−$10,000			+$1,000*	−$9,000
	+ 1,500			− 187.50†	+ 1,312.50
1	− 5,100	−$2,000	−$7,100	+ 3,550	− 1,550
2	− 5,100	− 1,750	− 6,850	+ 3,425	− 1,675
3	− 5,100	− 1,500	− 6,600	+ 3,300	− 1,800
4	− 5,100	− 1,250	− 6,350	+ 3,175	− 1,925
5	− 5,100	− 1,000	− 6,100	+ 3,050	− 2,050
	+ 2,500‡				+ 2,500

*10% investment tax credit: 0.10($10,000) = $1,000.

†25% capital gains tax: 0.25($1,500 − $750) = $187.50.

‡Salvage value equals book value; thus, no capital gain or loss

$$\text{P.W.} = -\$7,687.50 - [\$1,550 + \$125(A/G,12\%,5)](P/A,12\%,5)$$
$$+ \$2,500(P/F,12\%,5) = -\$12,656$$

On the basis of an after-tax analysis the recommendation is made to replace the lift truck with challenger A. The example emphasizes the importance of performing after-tax studies.

It should be noted that a cash flow approach is not commonly suggested in the engineering economy literature. The conventional approach is to incorporate the current market value in the determination of the investment in the defender. However, *when they are applied correctly, both the conventional approach and the cash flow approach yield the same recommendations.*

Example:

In the previous example what would be the P.W.'s for the alternatives using the conventional approach of treating the current market value of the defender as a cost of continuing it in service?

Solution:

Since the old lift truck will have a salvage value of $2,000 if traded in for new truck A and a salvage value of $1,500 if traded in for new truck B, a current market value of $2,000 will be used as the opportunity cost of continuing the old truck in service. Consequently, the before-tax cash flow for the defender will be $-$2,000 in year 0; for challenger A a value of $-$12,000 will apply in year 0; and for challenger B values of $-$10,000 and $-$500 are entered for year 0. The latter entry would represent the difference in trade-in values (i.e., opportunity foregone for not having taken the higher trade-in value).

The investment tax credits will remain the same. However, the treatment of capital gains taxes can be handled differently. Namely, a tax savings can be applied to the defender; in such a case, for each alternative one would add the amount $0.25(\$2,000 - \$750) = \$312.50$ in year 0 to the entry denoting the cash flow for income taxes.

Regardless of the market value used to assess the opportunity cost of retaining the defender and the method of assessing the capital gains tax, the differences in the present worths for the alternatives remain unchanged. Using a $2,000 market value and assessing capital gains tax savings as indicated above the reader may wish to show that the following after-tax present worth–costs result:

$$\text{P.W. (Defender)} \quad\; = \$14,343$$
$$\text{P.W. (Challenger A)} = \$13,663$$
$$\text{P.W. (Challenger B)} = \$14,344$$

Indefinite Planning Horizon

Having treated the subjects of specifying the planning horizon for a replacement study and the cash flow approach, it remains to consider the situation in which an indefinite planning horizon is used. When a very long planning horizon is used, it is often assumed that the defender will be replaced at the end of its life with an indefinite sequence of challengers. Hence, the annual worths of a life cycle of the challenger are compared with the annual worth for the remaining life of the defender.

Example:

Consider the example on page 145 involving the replacement of a lathe in a before-tax analysis and assume an indefinite planning horizon is to be used. Show that the cash flow approach and conventional approach yield identical recommendations.

Solution:

The conventional approach would compare the annual worths of a life cycle of the challenger and the remaining life of the defender.

$$\text{A.W. (Defender)} = -\$1,800(A/P,15\%,4) - \$3,500$$
$$= -\$4,130$$
$$\text{A.W. (Challenger)} = -\$18,000(A/P,15\%,10) + \$1,500(A/F,15\%,10)$$
$$- \$2,100 = -\$5,613$$

Thus, the defender should not be replaced at this time.

The cash flow approach would compare the capitalized worth* and/or annual worth for an infinite planning horizon.

$$\text{C.W. (Defender)} = -\$3,500(P/A,15\%,4) - \frac{\$5,613}{0.15}(P/F,15\%,4)$$
$$= -\$31,391$$
$$\text{A.W. (Defender)} = -\$31,391(0.15) = -\$4,709$$
$$\text{C.W. (Challenger)} = \frac{-\$5,613}{0.15} + \$1,800 = -\$35,620$$
$$\text{A.W. (Challenger)} = -\$35,620(0.15) = -\$5,343$$

The capitalized worth of the defender was obtained by considering the $3,500 annual disbursements for the defender for 4 years followed by an indefinite, repeating sequence of challengers. The capitalized worth of the challenger was obtained by considering an indefinite sequence of challengers and the salvage value for the defender. The $270 difference in A.W.'s between the conventional and cash flow approaches for the challenger is the interest cost on the salvage value for the defender ($1,800 \times 0.15$).

The recommendations are identical; do not replace the defender at this time. However, the conventional approach is computationally simpler.

Asset Life Types

Economic studies, since they deal with the future, involve estimated rather than observed lives of properties. The term *life* can have a number of meanings; hence, the following defining distinctions are given:

*Capitalized worth (C.W.) is present worth for infinite planning horizon. The C.W. for any uniform series of amount A assumed to continue forever is A/i.

1. *Economic life* (*service life*) is the period of time from the date of installation to date of retirement from the primary intended service of the asset. An estimate of the economic life of an asset may be based on the period which maximizes the annual worth of the proposed asset, assuming that the asset's service will be needed for that long and that no superior alternatives become available during that period. Retirement, however, is signaled by a future economy study when the annual worth of a prospective new asset becomes greater than the annual worth of retaining the present asset for 1 or more years. Retirement may constitute either disposal or demotion of the asset to a lower, less useful, grade of service than was originally intended (such as for standby service).

2. *Ownership life* is the period of time from the date of installation to the date of actual disposal by a specific owner. The ownership life of an asset may well consist of one or more periods of secondary (downgraded) service in addition to the period of primary service, which constitutes its economic life.

3. *Physical life* is the period of time from the date of installation by the original owner until the asset is ultimately disposed of by its final owner.

There are several reasons underlying the difference between physical life and economic life. The first reason is the technological improvements in reliability or uniformity, the increased output capacities, and the reduced operating costs of successive new models. Secondly, the old equipment may show a pattern of increasing maintenance and operating costs as well as a deterioration in the quality of the goods or services produced. While the above reasons underlie the need for replacement in general, they also should dictate the pattern, if any, of physical life in addition to economic life. It should be kept in mind that we are generally concerned with economic lives in replacement studies.

Calculation of Economic Life—New Asset by Itself

The second general type of replacement study mentioned at the beginning of this chapter is the determination, in advance, of how many years an asset should be kept for most economical service. In determining the economic life of a prospective new asset, there are three main types of costs to be taken into account: (1) costs of capital recovery, (2) costs inherent to the asset, and (3) costs relative to available improved models. Generally, the longer an asset is kept, the lower will be its annual cost of capital recovery and the higher will be its inherent and relative operating costs. An explanation of the meaning and calculation of each of these three types of costs is given in the following sections.

Costs of Capital Recovery

A realistic year-by-year cost of capital recovery can be determined only by estimating the net salvage (resale) value at the end of each year. The capital recovery cost for any year can be calculated as the decline in salvage value plus the interest on the asset value for that year. For example, the expected year-by-year salvage values of an asset X costing $23,000 and the calculation of yearly capital recovery costs, assuming interest at 10%, are shown in Table 7-1.

Table 7-1

YEARLY CAPITAL RECOVERY COST DATA FOR ASSET X

Year	Salvage value at end of year	Decrease in salvage value during year	Interest on investment at beginning of year (@10%)	Capital recovery cost for year
1	$15,000	$8,000	$2,300	$10,300
2	8,500	6,500	1,500	8,000
3	3,000	5,500	850	6,350
4	1,000	2,000	300	2,300
5	1,000	0	100	100

Costs Inherent to the Asset

Asset inherent costs include the cost of operation and maintenance, the cost of capacity decreasing compared to when the asset was new, and the cost of quality declining compared to when the asset was new. Decreasing capacity cost is the loss in output due to downtime and reduced operating rate. Declining quality cost is the cost of lost sales, and reduced sales price or scrap rework due to the reduced quality capability of the asset. It should be kept in mind that the costs of decreasing capacity and declining quality are costs compared to the asset when it was new and not compared to possible improved models of the asset. Consideration of the effect of improved models is included in the next section.

For example, the inherent costs of the asset X for which capital recovery data were given in the preceding section is shown in Table 7-2.

Costs Relative to Improved Models

It is common that improved models of an asset will produce at lower operating costs and/or will produce a higher-quality product than the original models of that asset. There is thus an increase in operating costs and an increase in the cost of declining quality in the old asset relative to the new

Table 7-2

YEARLY INHERENT COST DATA FOR ASSET X

Year	Cost of operation and maintenance	Cost of decreasing capacity	Cost of declining quality	Total inherent costs for year
1	$ 6,000	$ 0	$ 0	$ 6,000
2	6,000	0	0	6,000
3	6,000	500	500	7,000
4	8,000	1,000	4,000	13,000
5	10,000	2,000	5,000	17,000

improved model of the asset. These increases in costs are alternative or opportunity costs. Another relative cost is the decreasing net income caused by obsolescence affecting the demand for the asset's products or services.

For example, the relative costs for the same asset X as in the preceding two sections are shown in Table 7-3.

Table 7-3

YEARLY RELATIVE COST DATA FOR ASSET X

Year	Operating cost inferiority	Quality inferiority	Obsolescence	Total relative costs for year
1	$ 0	$ 0	$ 0	$ 0
2	500	0	0	500
3	800	850	0	1,650
4	2,000	3,000	0	5,000
5	2,500	3,500	1,000	7,000

Table 7-4 summarizes the data of Tables 7-1, 7-2, and 7-3 to provide for the calculation of total costs for each year and total equivalent annual costs for purposes of determining the most economical life for the asset X.

Thus, from Table 7-4, it can be seen that the equivalent annual cost is at a minimum if asset X is retired at the end of 3 years. It can also be observed that the total marginal cost (shown in the fifth column as "Total cost for year") exceeds the equivalent annual cost after the third year. This illustrates the general principle for the determination of economic life, which may be stated as follows for the general case in which year-by-year costs are increasing:

Replace at the end of any period for which the total cost in the next period exceeds the average cost up to that period. Do not replace as long as the total cost in a period does not exceed the average cost to the end of that period.

Table 7-4

ECONOMIC LIFE CALCULATION FOR ASSET X

Year	Capital recovery cost for year	Total inherent cost for year	Total relative cost for year	Total cost for year	$(P/F,10\%,N)$	P.W. of cost for year [Total cost × $(P/F,10\%,N)$]	Cumulative P.W. of cost since placed in service $(\Sigma\ P.W.)$	$(A/P,10\%,N)$	Equivalent (average) annual cost if retired at end of year [$\Sigma\ P.W. \times (A/P,10\%,N)$]
1	$10,300	$ 6,000	$ 0	$16,300	0.909	$14,790	$14,790	1.100	$16,300
2	8,000	6,000	500	14,500	0.826	12,700	27,400	0.576	15,800
3	6,350	7,000	1,650	15,000	0.751	11,300	38,700	0.402	15,570 (minimum)
4	2,300	13,000	5,000	20,300	0.683	13,900	52,600	0.315	17,800
5	100	17,000	7,000	24,100	0.621	15,000	67,600	0.264	17,850

Example:

As an additional example of calculation of economic life without consideration of income taxes, suppose a certain machine has an installed price of $10,000 and the projected year-by-year operating costs and salvage values shown in the tables below.

Year	Total annual inherent and relative operating cost	Salvage value
1	$3,000	$6,000
2	3,500	3,000
3	8,000	1,000

Neglecting income taxes and assuming an interest rate of 0%, below are shown calculations for determining the most economic replacement interval.

A.C. (for 1-yr interval):

$$(\$10,000 - \$6,000)(A/P,0\%,1) + \$6,000(0\%) + \$3,000 = \$7,000$$

A.C. (for 2-yr interval):

$$(\$10,000 - \$3,000)(A/P,0\%,2) + \$3,000(0\%)$$
$$+ [\$3,000 + \$3,500(P/F,0\%,2)](A/P,0\%,2) = \$6,750$$

A.C. (for 3-yr interval):

$$(\$10,000 - \$1,000)(A/P,0\%,3) + (\$1,000)(0\%) + [\$3,000(P/F,0\%,1)$$
$$+ \$3,500(P/F,0\%,2) + \$8,000(P/F,0\%,3)](A/P,0\%,3) = \$7,830$$

Thus, replacement at 2-yr intervals is apparently slightly more economical than 1-yr or 3-yr intervals.

Calculation of Remaining Economic Life—Existing Asset

Example:

As an example of replacement analysis involving determination of the optimal remaining life of an old asset considering how it compares with a prospective challenger and including effect of income taxes, suppose the replacement of a spray system is being considered by the Hokie Metal Stamping Company. The new improved system will cost $60,000 installed and will have an estimated economic life of 12 years and $6,000 salvage value. Further, it is estimated that annual operating and maintenance costs will average $32,000 per yr for the new system and that straight line depreciation will be used. The present system has a book value of $12,000 and a present realizable salvage value of $8,000. Its estimated costs and book values for the next 3 years are as follows:

Year	Salvage value at end of year	Book value at end of year	Inherent and relative operating costs during year
1	$6,000	$9,000	$40,000
2	5,000	6,000	50,000
3	4,000	3,000	60,000

Table 7-5 shows calculations to determine relevant after-tax cash flows for this problem. It is assumed that the ordinary income tax rate is 50% and that any gain or loss on disposal of the old asset affects taxes at the full ordinary rate.

After-tax annual cost calculations for each alternative utilizing the results in column (6) of Table 7-5 (with the signs reversed) and a 15% minimum after-tax rate of return are:

New system,

$$(\$60,000 - \$6,000)(A/P,15\%,12) + \$6,000(15\%)$$
$$+ \$13,750 = \$24,600$$

Old system,
keep 1 yr:

$$(\$10,000 - \$7,500)(A/P,15\%,1) + \$7,500(15\%)$$
$$+ \$18,500 = \$22,500$$

Old system,
keep 2 yr:

$$(\$10,000 - \$5,500)(A/P,15\%,2) + \$5,500(15\%)$$
$$+ [\$18,500(P/F,15\%,1)$$
$$+ \$23,500(P/F,15\%,2)](A/P,15\%,2) = \$24,400$$

Old system,
keep 3 yr:

$$(\$10,000 - \$3,500)(A/P,15\%,3) + \$3,500(15\%)$$
$$+ [\$18,500(P/F,15\%,1) + \$23,500(P/F,15\%,2)$$
$$+ \$28,500(P/F,15\%,3)](A/P,15\%,3) = \$26,475$$

On the basis of the above analysis, one would tend to say that the old system should be replaced at the end of the first year. But the above analysis procedure is deceiving, for it is not generally correct. Instead, one should examine marginal costs. The valid economic criterion is to keep the old system as long as the marginal cost of an additional year of service is less than the equivalent annual cost of the new system. The marginal cost of keeping the old system for the first year is the $22,500 previously computed. This $22,500 is less than the $24,550 average annual cost of the new system, thus justifying keeping the old system for the first year.

Table 7-5

CALCULATION OF AFTER-TAX CASH FLOWS FOR EXAMPLE REPLACEMENT ANALYSIS

(1) Year	(2) Before-tax cash flow	(3) Depreciation for tax purposes	(4) = (2) + (3) Taxable income	(5) = -(4) × Rate Cash flow for income taxes -(4) × 50%	(6) = (2) + (5) After-tax cash flow
New system					
0	− $60,000				− $60,000
1–12	− 32,000	−$4,500	− $36,500	+ $18,250	− 13,750
12	+ 6,000				+ 6,000
Old system, keep 1 yr					
0	(−)$ 8,000		(−)($ 8,000 − 12,000)	(−)$ 2,000	(−)$10,000
1	− 40,000	−$3,000	− 43,000	+ 21,500	− 18,500
1	+ 6,000		+ 6,000 − 9,000	+ 1,500	+ 7,500
Old system, keep 2 yr					
0	(−)$ 8,000		(−)($ 8,000 − 12,000)	(−)$ 2,000	(−)$10,000
1	− 40,000	−$3,000	− 43,000	+ 21,500	− 18,500
2	− 50,000	− 3,000	− 53,000	+ 26,500	− 23,500
2	+ 5,000		+ 5,000 − 6,000	+ 500	+ 5,500
Old system, keep 3 yr					
0	(−)$ 8,000		(−)($ 8,000 − 12,000)	(−)$ 2,000	(−)$10,000
1	− 40,000	−$3,000	− 43,000	+ 21,500	− 18,500
2	− 50,000	− 3,000	− 53,000	+ 26,500	− 23,500
3	− 60,000	− 3,000	− 63,000	+ 31,500	− 28,500
3	+ 4,000		+ 4,000 − 3,000	− 500	+ 3,500

Note: Negative signs in parentheses represent the result of "opportunity foregone"—i.e., if the old system were sold, a certain cash flow would result, but by keeping it the opportunity for the cash flow is foregone; hence, the reversal of cash flow sign.

157

The marginal cost of keeping the old system for the second year is ($7,500 − $5,500) + 7,500(15%) + $23,500 = $26,625. This is greater than the $24,600 average annual cost of the new system, thus indicating that the old system should not be kept the second year, but rather that it be replaced at the end of the first year. (Incidentally, the student may want to see that the marginal cost of keeping the old system for the third year is ($5,500 − $3,500) + $5,500(15%) + $28,500 = $31,325.

The above example assumes that there is only one new asset (challenger) alternative available. It shows the general relationship that if the old asset (defender) is retained beyond the break-even point, its costs continue to grow and replacement becomes more urgent as illustrated in Fig. 7-1.

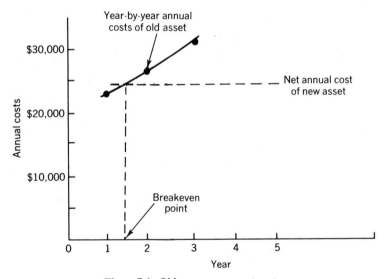

Figure 7-1. Old versus new asset costs.

Figure 7-2 illustrates the effect of improved new challengers in the future. If an improved challenger X becomes available before replacement with the new asset of Fig. 7-1, then a new replacement study probably should take place to consider that improved challenger. If there is a possibility of a further improved challenger Y as of, say, 4 years later, it may be still better to postpone replacement until that challenger becomes available. Thus, retention of the old asset beyond the break-even point has a cost which may well grow with time, but this cost of waiting can, in some instances, be worthwhile if it permits purchase of an improved asset having economies that offset the cost of waiting. Of course, a decision to postpone a replacement may also "buy time and information." Because technological change tends to be sudden and dramatic rather than uniform and gradual, new challengers

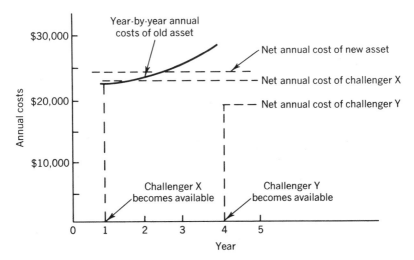

Figure 7-2. Old versus new asset costs with improved challengers becoming available in future.

with significantly improved features can arise sporadically and can change replacement plans substantially.

Relationship of Economic Life to the Planning Horizon (Study Period)

The preceding discussion of economic life of a new asset by itself was based on the assumption that the planning horizon either equals the economic life or it is an integer multiple of the economic life. In the latter case, it is further assumed that subsequent replacements are identical in cash flow profiles (i.e., the *repeatability* assumptions). Such may not always be the case and deserves consideration.

Example:
Consider a compressor that costs $5,000. Annual costs, excluding capital recovery costs, increase by 10% per year, with the first such cost being $1,400. Salvage values for the compressor are reasonably approximated by the corresponding sum-of-years-digits depreciation book value based on a maximum useful life of 9 years and a terminal salvage value of $500. A before-tax analysis is to be performed using a M.A.R.R. of 10%.

Solution:
By performing a considerable number of computations, the following equivalent uniform annual costs (E.U.A.C.'s) are obtained for each possible life:

N	Book (salvage) value	(1) Capital recovery	(2) Annual disbursements	(3) = (1) + (2) E.U.A.C.
1	$4,100	$1,400	$1,400	$2,800
2	3,300	1,310	1,466	2,776
3	2,600	1,225	1,536	2,761
4	2,000	1,147	1,606	2,753
5	1,500	1,073	1,678	2,751
6	1,100	1,005	1,754	2,759
7	800	943	1,830	2,773
8	600	885	1,908	2,793
9	500	831	1,988	2,819

The minimum annual cost is $2,751 and corresponds to an economic life of 5 years. The E.U.A.C. computation for $N = 5$ was performed as follows:

First cost:	$5,000
Life:	5 yr
Salvage value:	$1,500
First yr. disb. (A_1):	$1,400
Growth rate ($j\%$):	10%
M.A.R.R.	10%

From Eq. 2-28, since $j = i$, then $P = A_1 N(P/F,i\%,1)$ or $P = 1,400(0.9091)N$ and $A = 1,400(0.9091)N(A/P,10\%,N)$. Hence, the annual worth equivalent for the annual disbursements is

$$A = \$1,400(0.9091)(5)(A/P,10\%,5)$$
$$= \$1,678$$

The capital recovery cost is

$$\text{C.R.} = (\$5,000 - \$1,500)(A/P,10\%,5) + \$1,500(0.10)$$
$$= \$1,073$$

Combining the two annual amounts gives the E.U.A.C. of $2,751.

Example:

In the previous example, suppose a 7-year planning horizon is to be used. Assume replacements are identical in cash flow profile.

Solution:

The alternatives to be considered include the following economic life combinations: (7,0), (6,1), (5,2), and (4,3). By using a present worth analysis the following results are obtained:

$$\text{P.W.}(7,0) = \$2,773(P/A,10\%,7) = \$13,499$$
$$\text{P.W.}(6,1) = \$2,759(P/A,10\%,6) + \$2,800(P/F,10\%,7) = \$13,452$$
$$\text{P.W.}(5,2) = \$2,751(P/A,10\%,5) + \$2,776(P/A,10\%,2)(P/F,10\%,5)$$
$$= \$13,421$$

P.W.(4,3) = $2,753(P/A,10\%,4)$ + $2,761(P/A,10\%,3)(P/F,10\%,4)$

= \$13,417

The optimum combination of service lives is (4,3) with a present cost of \$13,417. [The reader should recognize that time-value-of-money effects make it unnecessary to consider such combinations as (3,4), (2,5), and (1,6)].

Intangibles in Replacement Problems

As in other management decisions, replacement problems have intangible aspects that may have sufficient weight to control the decision. Intangibles in replacement analysis may include competing needs for capital, future uncertainties in market and costs, possibilities of product change, financial condition of the business, attitudes and limitations of personnel, labor shortage or surplus, ethical and social problems, etc. Intangibles are notably reflected in two of the quantitative factors or elements used in the illustrations above, namely the study period and the minimum required rate of return on investment.

Models for Replacement Analysis

There is an infinite variety of possible mathematical models for analysis of replacement situations. These models vary even in calculated results because of varying assumptions and degrees of complexity. Models for determining optimum replacement policy (e.g., economic life or when to replace in advance) are presented in Chapter 17. However, one popular replacement model, MAPI, is considered in Appendix 7-A.

Economic Replacement Point and MAPI Method

Because the decision to retire and replace an asset is made at a time subsequent to installation, the accumulation of better information upon which to estimate the most economic life is possible. Then, as an old asset (defender) is compared to a proposed new asset (challenger), the problem may be one of comparing the cost of keeping the defender one more year vs. the annual equivalent cost of the challenger. This is essentially what is done using the MAPI method developed by the Machinery and Allied Products Institute.

PROBLEMS

7-1. A firm is contemplating replacing a computer it purchased 3 years ago for \$450,000. Operating and maintenance costs have been \$85,000 per year. Currently the computer has a trade-in value of \$300,000 toward a new computer which costs $650,000 and has a life of 5 years, with a value of $200,000 at that time. The new computer will have annual operating and maintenance costs of $80,000.

If the current computer is retained, another small computer will have to be purchased in order to provide the required computing capacity. The smaller computer will cost $300,000, have a value of $50,000 in 5 years, and have annual operating and maintenance costs of $55,000.

Using a before-tax analysis, with a minimum attractive rate of return of 30%, determine the preferred course of action.

7-2. A firm owns a pressure vessel which it is contemplating replacing. The old pressure vessel has annual operating and maintenance costs of $6,000 per year, it can be kept for 5 more years, and it will have a zero salvage value at that time.

The old pressure vessel can be traded in on a new one; the trade-in value is $3,000; the purchase price for the new pressure vessel is $12,000. The new pressure vessel will have a value of $5,000 in 5 years and will have annual operating and maintenance costs of $3,000 per year. Using a minimum attractive rate of return of 20% and a before-tax analysis, determine whether or not the pressure vessel should be replaced.

7-3. A building supplies distributor purchased a gasoline-powered fork-lift truck 5 years ago for $10,000. At that time, the estimated useful life was 10 years with a salvage value of $1,000. The truck can now be sold for $2,500. For the old truck, annual average operating expenses for year j have been in accordance with

$$C_j = \$2,000(1.10)^{j-1}$$

The distributor is considering replacing the lift truck with a smaller battery-powered truck costing $8,000. The estimated life is 10 years with the salvage value decreasing by $600 each year. Annual average operating expenses are expected to be $2,000. If a M.A.R.R. of 10% is assumed and a 5-year planning horizon is adopted, should the replacement be made?

7-4. The Ajax Corp. has an overhead crane which has an estimated remaining life of 10 years. The crane can be sold for $8,000. If the crane is kept in service, it must be overhauled immediately at a cost of $4,000. Operating and maintenance costs will be $3,000 per year after the crane is overhauled. After the crane is overhauled, it will have a zero salvage value at the end of the 10-year period. A new crane will cost $18,000, will last for 10 years, and will have a $4,000 salvage value at that time. Operating and maintenance costs are $1,000 for the new crane. The company uses an interest rate of 10% in evaluating investment alternatives. Should the company replace the old crane?

7-5. A firm is considering replacing a compressor which was purchased 4 years ago for $50,000. Currently, the compressor has a book value of $30,000 based on straight line depreciation. If the compressor is retained, it will probably be used for 4 more years, at which time it is estimated to have a salvage value of $10,000. If the old compressor is retained for 8 more years, it is estimated that its salvage value will be negligible at that time. Operating and maintenance costs for the compressor have been increasing at a rate of $1,000 per year, with the cost during the past year being $8,000.

A new compressor can be purchased for $60,000. It is estimated to have uniform annual operating and maintenance costs of $8,000 per year. The salvage value for the compressor is estimated to be $30,000 after 4 years and $15,000 after 8 years. If a new compressor is purchased, the old compressor will be traded in for $20,000.

Using an after-tax analysis with straight line depreciation and a minimum attractive rate of return of 10%, determine the preferred alternative using a planning horizon of (a) 4 years and (b) 8 years. Assume a 50% ordinary income tax rate and a 25% capital gain or loss tax rate.

7-6. A new numerically controlled drill press can be used to replace three manual drill presses now in use. The N/C drill press will cost $55,000, will last 10 years and have a negligible salvage value, and will have annual operating and maintenance costs of $10,000 per year.

The manual drill presses were purchased 5 years ago for $11,000 each; they were estimated to have lives of 10 years, with negligible salvage values. Currently, the manual drill presses are worth $1,500 each. Annual operating and maintenance costs are $6,000 per drill press.

A study period of 5 years is to be used in the replacement study. A salvage value of $15,000 is estimated for the N/C drill press at the end of the study period. An after-tax M.A.R.R. of 15%, a tax rate of 50%, an investment tax credit of 10%, and a capital gains tax rate lf 30% are to be used. Any capital losses will be assumed to be deducted from taxable income in the year they occur. Sum-of-the-years digits depreciation is to be used for both alternatives. What action do you recommend?

7-7. Machine X has been used for 10 years and currently has a book value of $2,000. A decision must be made concerning the most economic action to take: keep X, replace X with Y, or replace X with Z. A before-tax analysis is to be performed.

If Machine X is continued in service, it can be used for 6 years and scrapped at zero value. Annual operating and maintenance costs will equal $9,500.

If Machine X is replaced with machine Y, a trade-in allowance of $2,500 will be provided for X. The original purchase price for Y, excluding the trade-in allowance, is $12,000. At the end of the 6-year planning horizon, Y will have a salvage value of $3,000. Annual operating and maintenance costs will total $8,000.

If machine X is replaced with machine Z, no trade-in allowance will be provided for X. The purchase price for Z is $15,000. At the end of the 6-year planning horizon, Z will have a salvage value of $5,000. Annual operating and maintenance costs will total $6,000.

Using a M.A.R.R. of 15% and a before-tax analysis, determine the preferred course of action.

7-8. A recent flood indicates the need for a larger drainage structure. Three possibilities are considered:

A. Leave the existing 2-ft pipe in place (it is undamaged) and install another of equal size alongside.

B. Remove the existing 2-ft pipe and replace it with a single 3-ft pipe.

C. Remove the existing 2-ft pipe and replace it with a concrete box culvert.

If the present 2-ft pipe is removed, it will have a salvage value of $400. Estimates regarding the new installations are as follows:

	A	B	C
Cost installed:	$1,500	$2,700	$2,800
Estimated life:	15 yr	15 yr	30 yr

Comparing annual costs with interest at 10% before taxes, which alternative is recommended? Assume that the existing pipe will have the same life as the one proposed for installation under alternative A and that a drainage system is needed indefinitely.

7-9. A man owns a side business which he purchased 10 years ago for $46,000. Straight line depreciation has been charged assuming a 25-year life and $6,000 salvage value. He now has an offer to sell the business for $50,000. He estimates that if he does not sell now, he will hold the property for another 7 years and sell it at that time for $45,000. If he keeps the business, he estimates he will pay taxes at the rate of 60% on an annual net taxable income of $5,000 due to this side business. (Any capital gain or capital loss will affect taxes at the rate of 25%. The business will have an annual net cash flow of $6,600, from which $1,600 depreciation is deducted.) (a) Compute the before-tax rate of return from continued ownership of the side business. (b) If he can get 8% after taxes from the use of his capital in some other venture of comparable risk, should he sell now, or wait 7 years? Compute the after-tax rate of return on continued ownership.

7-10. An individual owns a rental property in an industrial district of a city. This is rented to a single tenant at an annual rate of $10,000. The present lease is about to expire. The tenant is willing to renew the lease for a long term at the present figure but not at a higher one. A manufacturing company adjoining the building site has made an offer of $120,000 for this property. Because of the particular needs of this manufacturer for an area to expand, the property owner believes that this is a better offer than can be secured from any other buyer. If the offer is not accepted at once, it is considered likely that the manufacturer will make other plans for plant expansion and that the offer will therefore not be renewed at a later date. A decision must therefore be made at once whether or not to accept this offer.

It is believed that if the property is not sold at once, ownership will be continued for a fairly long time. For purposes of the economy study to guide the decision, assume that ownership will continue for 20 years and that the net resale value before income taxes at the end of that period will be $50,000. The original cost of the property 5 years ago was $80,000, divided for accounting and tax purposes into $20,000 for land and $60,000 for the building. Since purchase, the building has been depreciated for accounting and tax purposes at $1,500 per yr on the basis of an estimated remaining life of 40 years from the purchase date and a terminal salvage value of zero.

If ownership is continued, it is estimated that receipts from rental will continue at $10,000 per yr. Annual disbursements are estimated to be $1,500 for upkeep, $2,100 for property taxes, and $400 for insurance.

a. Compute a rate of return before income taxes that provides a basis for comparison between the alternatives of continued ownership and immediate sale.

b. Compute a rate of return after income taxes that provides a basis for comparison between these two alternatives. Consider the income taxes both on any capital gain and on annual taxable income. Assume a 48% tax rate on ordinary income and a 30% tax rate on capital gains.

APPENDIX 7A

the MAPI method for replacement and general investment analyses*

This appendix is intended to provide a brief summarization of the main provisions, strengths, and weaknesses of the current (third) version of the MAPI method and to illustrate its use for a typical project analysis. The MAPI method or system for investment analysis has evolved over the past 30 years through several major works by George Terborgh, Research Director of the Machinery and Allied Products Institute. The first version, which applied only to replacement problems, was described in *Dynamic Equipment Policy* and the *MAPI Replacement Manual* both published in 1950. The second and more general-purpose MAPI system was published in *Business Investment Policy* in 1958. The current (third) version was summarized in 1967 in *Business Investment Management*. All the above works were published by the Machinery and Allied Products Institute, Washington, D.C.

Basically, the MAPI method provides a series of charts and forms to facilitate ease in investment analysis computation. One of its main strengths is the inclusion of provision for consideration of obsolescence and deteriora-

---

*By Dr. Jack Turvaville, Associate Professor of Industrial Engineering, Tennessee Technological University. Based largely on pp. 149–158 of George Terborgh's *Business Investment Management* (Machinery and Allied Products Institute, 1967). Reproduced by permission of the publisher.

tion which affect operating results as a linear function of time. The MAPI charts provide for ease in determining the percentage retention value. These charts are computed for various service lives, salvage values, and tax write-off methods. They are available for straight line, double declining balance, sum-of-years-digits and current expensing depreciation methods for either a 1-year or longer-than-1-year comparison period—a total of eight charts. Figures 7-A-1 and 7-A-2 illustrate two such charts as given for a wide range

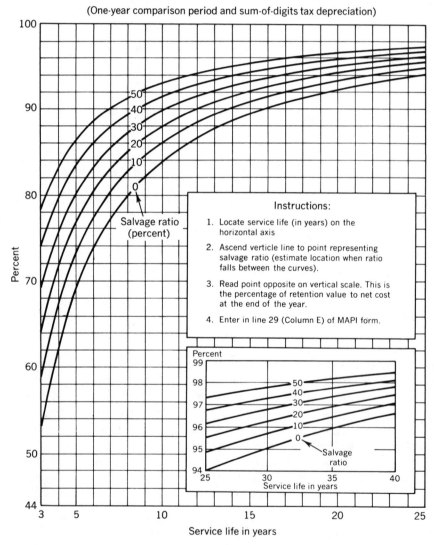

Figure 7-A-1. Example MAPI Chart. Copyright © 1967, Machinery and Allied Products Institute.

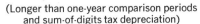

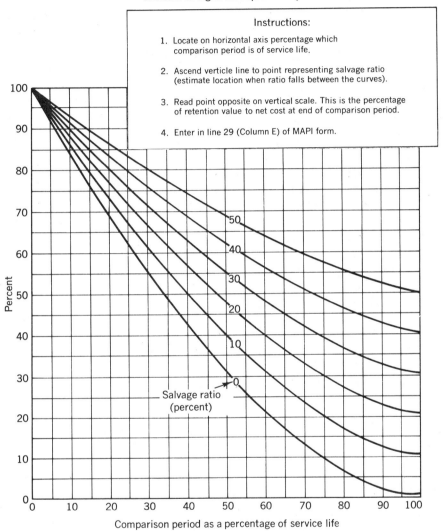

Figure 7-A-2. Example MAPI Chart. Copyright 1967, Machinery and Allied Products Institute.

of service lives and salvage value ratios. Assumptions on which the charts are based include 50% income tax rate, a 25–75% debt-to-equity-capital ratio, an average debt capital interest rate of 3%, and an after-tax equity return of 10%.

It should be recognized that allowance for deterioration and obsolescence is built into the chart retention values. According to Terborgh, the function of computation for the retention values

...is to project a stream of pretax earnings over the estimated service life that conforms in shape to the projection pattern, and in size to the following requirements: (1) it must include the income tax, payable at the specified rate, on the excess of the earnings over the deductions provided by tax depreciation and interest; (2) the remainder of the earnings after tax (with terminal salvage, if any) must suffice to permit a full recovery of the investment over the service life, and to provide a return throughout on the unrecovered balance of equity at the prescribed after-tax return rate and on the unrecovered balance of debt at the prescribed interest rate.

The use of the MAPI method is consummated through a standard form as shown in Figs. 7-A-3 and 7-A-4 with example amounts entered therein. The example amounts are based upon the following example project taken from page 156 of Terborgh's *Business Investment Management* (op. cit.): An analyst desires to investigate whether it would be more economical for the company to make its own corrugated containers. To do this the company will have to purchase a large box machine and a box-stitcher at combined cost of $29,800.

It is estimated that direct labor cost will be increased by $900 per yr, indirect labor (supervision) by $50, and fringe benefits by $190. Maintenance will be higher by $200, tool costs by $80, power consumption by $40, and property taxes and insurance by $320. On the other hand, there will be a saving of $16,800 in the cost of puchased materials, $1,100 in inventory carrying costs (other than floor space), and $1,000 in floor space. The net cost reduction is therefore $17,020.

In addition to this operating advantage, the equipment will permit a reduction of $4,000 in inventory investment. After consulting with operating officials and others, the analyst comes up with the following stipulations:

Comparison period:	1 yr
Project operating rate:	1,200 hr
Service life:	13 yr
Terminal salvage ratio:	10% of net cost
Tax depreciation method:	sum-of-years-digits
Tax rate:	50%
Debt ratio:	30%
Debt interest rate:	5%
Investment credit:	7%

The results shown on line 40 of Fig. 7-A-4 indicate an after-tax return of 34.5% for the above project.

In reviewing the application of the MAPI method to the example project, it should be observed that all of the considerations given to the determina-

PROJECT NO. _____	**MAPI SUMMARY FORM** (AVERAGING SHORTCUT)		SHEET 1

PROJECT	Box Machine and Stitcher		
ALTERNATIVE	Continuing as is		
COMPARISON PERIOD (YEARS)		(P)	1
ASSUMED OPERATING RATE OF PROJECT (HOURS PER YEAR)			1,200

I. OPERATING ADVANTAGE

(NEXT-YEAR FOR A 1-YEAR COMPARISON PERIOD,* ANNUAL AVERAGES FOR LONGER PERIODS)

A. EFFECT OF PROJECT ON REVENUE

	INCREASE	DECREASE	
1. FROM CHANGE IN QUALITY OF PRODUCTS	$	$	1
2. FROM CHANGE IN VOLUME OF OUTPUT			2
3. TOTAL	$ X	$ Y	3

B. EFFECT ON OPERATING COSTS

	INCREASE	DECREASE	
4. DIRECT LABOR	$ 900	$	4
5. INDIRECT LABOR	150		5
6. FRINGE BENEFITS	190		6
7. MAINTENANCE	200		7
8. TOOLING	80		8
9. MATERIALS AND SUPPLIES		16,800	9
10. INSPECTION			10
11. ASSEMBLY			11
12. SCRAP AND REWORK			12
13. DOWN TIME			13
14. POWER	40		14
15. FLOOR SPACE		1,000	15
16. PROPERTY TAXES AND INSURANCE	320		16
17. SUBCONTRACTING			17
18. INVENTORY		1,100	18
19. SAFETY			19
20. FLEXIBILITY			20
21. OTHER	$		21
22. TOTAL	1,880 Y	$ 18,900 X	22

C. COMBINED EFFECT

23. NET INCREASE IN REVENUE (3X—3Y)	$	23
24. DECREASE IN OPERATING COSTS (22X—22Y)	$ 17,020	24
25. ANNUAL OPERATING ADVANTAGE (23 + 24)	$ 17,020	25

*Next year means the first year of project operation. For projects with a significant break-in period, use performance after break-in.

Figure 7-A-3. MAPI Summary Form, Sheet 1 (with entries for example project).

tion of the operating advantage would be necessary regardless of what technique were to be used in developing a measure of comparison. It must be further noted that line 29 of Fig. 7-A-4 states that an estimate of the retention value does not have to come from the MAPI charts. If the analyst has a better estimate, then it can be used.

II. INVESTMENT AND RETURN

A. INITIAL INVESTMENT

26. INSTALLED COST OF PROJECT $ 29,800
       MINUS INITIAL TAX BENEFIT OF $ 2,100   (Net Cost) $ 27,700   26

27. INVESTMENT IN ALTERNATIVE
       CAPITAL ADDITIONS MINUS INITIAL TAX BENEFIT $ _____
       PLUS: DISPOSAL VALUE OF ASSETS RETIRED
           BY PROJECT* $ 4,000 $ 4,000   27

28. INITIAL NET INVESTMENT (26—27) $ 23,700   28

B. TERMINAL INVESTMENT

29. RETENTION VALUE OF PROJECT AT END OF COMPARISON PERIOD
       (ESTIMATE FOR ASSETS, IF ANY, THAT CANNOT BE DEPRECIATED OR EXPENSED. FOR OTHERS, ESTIMATE
                 OR USE MAPI CHARTS.)

Item or Group	Installed Cost, Minus Initial Tax Benefit (Net Cost) A	Service Life (Years) B	Disposal Value, End of Life (Percent of Net Cost) C	MAPI Chart Number D	Chart Percentage E	Retention Value $\frac{A \times E}{100}$ F
Box Machine and Stitcher	$ 27,700	13	10	A1	89.4	$ 24,760

ESTIMATED FROM CHARTS   (TOTAL OF COL. F) $ 24,760
       PLUS: OTHERWISE ESTIMATED $ _____ $ 24,760   29

30. DISPOSAL VALUE OF ALTERNATIVE AT END OF PERIOD* $ 4,000   30

31. TERMINAL NET INVESTMENT (29—30) $ 20,760   31

C. RETURN

32. AVERAGE NET CAPITAL CONSUMPTION $\left(\frac{28-31}{P}\right)$ $ 2,940   32

33. AVERAGE NET INVESTMENT $\left(\frac{28+31}{2}\right)$ $ 22,230   33

34. BEFORE-TAX RETURN $\left(\frac{25-32}{33} \times 100\right)$ % 63.3   34

35. INCREASE IN DEPRECIATION AND INTEREST DEDUCTIONS $ 4,190   35

36. TAXABLE OPERATING ADVANTAGE (25—35) $ 12,830   36

37. INCREASE IN INCOME TAX (36 × TAX RATE) $ 6,415   37

38. AFTER-TAX OPERATING ADVANTAGE (25—37) $ 10,605   38

39. AVAILABLE FOR RETURN ON INVESTMENT (38—32) $ 7,665   39

40. AFTER-TAX RETURN $\left(\frac{39}{33} \times 100\right)$ % 34.5   40

*After terminal tax adjustments.

Figure 7-A-4. MAPI Summary Form, Sheet 2 (with entries for example project).

An after-tax cash flow diagram using the information from the MAPI forms in Fig. 7-A-3 and 7-A-4 would be

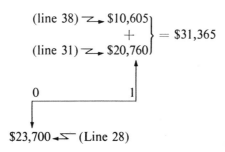

$$\left.\begin{array}{l}\text{(line 38) } \rightarrow \$10,605 \\ \qquad + \\ \text{(line 31) } \rightarrow \$20,760\end{array}\right\} = \$31,365$$

$23,700 ← (Line 28)

Solving, $-\$23,700 + \$31,365(P/F,i\%,1) = 0$, and from interest tables, i can be interpolated to be 32.4%. This is close to the 34.5% return by the MAPI method. Generally, if the MAPI assumptions are not violated substantially, the return calculated by the MAPI method is a good approximation of the internal rate of return.

The MAPI method can be applied to problems involving a comparison period of more than one year in a manner very similar to the above example.

To most people trained in engineering economy principles, the use of a formula approach such as the MAPI method is too rigid. The assumptions built into the method can be significantly inappropriate and cause error in the analysis result. Furthermore, the development of the MAPI charts is complicated to understand. However, the MAPI method does provide for obsolescence and deterioration, offers an excellent checklist, will provide consistent results, and is relatively easy to use.

Chapter

8

analyses for government agencies and public utilities

Public organizations such as government agencies and privately owned public utilities are confronted with selections between alternatives which involve differing patterns of cash flows and intangible considerations much the same as within private competitive enterprises. Some differences in methods and emphases for economy studies applicable to these organizations will be described herein, first for government agencies and then for public utilities.

Investments by Government Agencies

The government (public sector) analyst has a somewhat more difficult problem of measuring benefits than does the private sector analyst because the government sector analyst knows he should include the social benefits (and costs) of the project. The private sector manager may choose to take refuge in profit maximization or cost minimization for the firm and not include the social costs and benefits.

On the other hand, economy studies for government agencies are made easier because such agencies are not subject to income taxes. While funds for many such agencies are obtained through income taxes, none of the agencies pay income taxes to others, and thus the relative economic merits of alternatives considered by the agencies are not affected by income taxes.

The bulk of government expenditures is not allocated on the basis of economic criteria. However, economic analysis is used to a considerable extent for such expenditures as water resource development, highway location and sizing, and weapons systems selection.

When capital expenditures are involved, government analyses notably include:

1. measuring benefits and costs, often under conditions in which no market yardstick is available, and sometimes weighting the incidence of benefits on different individuals and groups;
2. determining criteria for judging acceptability;
3. selecting the appropriate interest rate to convert benefits and costs into equivalent terms.

The latter two are discussed in the following sections.

Criteria for Judging Acceptability of Government Projects

Capital expenditures by various agencies of government are applied to a vast array of purposes, such as for the control and preservation of natural resources, providing economic services, protection, and cultural development.

Analyses of capital expenditures for government purposes can take many forms, such as:

1. maximization of the ratio of benefits to costs on an annual or present equivalent basis;
2. minimization of combined annual cost to the public user and the agency supplier of the facility when benefits are fixed;
3. minimization of the present value sacrificed if the program were cut;
4. optimization of cost-effectiveness function(s).

The very difficult, subjective part of most decisions involving competing classes of projects revolves around divergent views on what is the "general welfare" of the public. What is perceived to be in the best interests of the public may vary sharply over time, depending on changes in such conditions as the state of the economy, foreign relations, public health, environmental degradation, and public service needs. Further, intangibles or irreducibles are generally much more important in public works than they are in private enterprises.

Judging the importance of irreducibles for public projects in many respects presents the same kinds of problems as occur in private economy studies. The best that an individual can do in dealing with personal problems of economy may be to note the satisfactions that will come from particular alternatives and to consider them in the light of their long-run costs and in the light of the individual's capacity to pay.

Analysts who perform economy studies for a government agency sometimes fall into the trap of making the study based on just the disbursements and receipts, if any, for that particular agency or government body it represents. Thus, for example, a state or local government might rationalize that a particular project is justified if the federal government pays most of the cost, even though the project is grossly unjustified based on total costs and benefits. In principle, if the ideal of democratic government to "promote the general welfare" is to be followed, one should consider the effects of governmental alternatives on all of the people, not merely on the economic considerations of a particular unit of the government.

Example:
   A county is considering installing a water treatment system which is expected to cause environmental and direct benefits of $1,000,000 per year for its inhabitants. The system would require an investment of $9,000,000 and have operating and maintenance costs of $300,000 per year for an expected life of 20 years, after which it would have no value. If money for this type of project costs the county 6%, is the project justified on an economic basis? Suppose the state government is willing to pay $4,000,000 of the investment. Now is it justified?

Solution:
   Using the net present worth method based on total benefits and costs, we get:

Net P.W. $= (\$1,000,000 - \$300,000)(P/A,6\%,20) - \$9,000,000 = -\$971,000.$

$\qquad = -\$971,000 < \$0$

Thus, it is not justified in total.
Based only on benefits and costs to the county:

Net P.W. $= (\$1,000,000 - \$300,000)(P/A,6\%,20)$

$\qquad - (\$9,000,000 - \$4,000,000) = \$3,029,000$

$\qquad = \$3,029,000 > \$0$

Thus, it is apparently justified to the county.

   It would be common for county decision makers to consider only the net P.W. $= \$3,029,000$ on the county investment and conclude that the project must be worthwhile, never seriously considering that the net P.W. on the total investment is well below zero. This is the equivalent of considering the state's money as free, which is sometimes rationalized on the basis that "... we ought to get it, because if we don't some other agency or organization will." Nevertheless, in principle, one should consider the total benefits and costs to determine if the investment of state, as well as county, funds is justified.

Interest Rate for Government Projects

The interest rate plays the same formal role in the evaluation of public sector investment projects that it does in the private sector. The rationale for its use is somewhat different. It is used in the private sector, because it leads directly to the private sector goal of profit maximization or cost minimization. Its basic function in the public sector is similar, in that it should lead to an optimization of economic and social net benefits, providing these have been appropriately measured. It will lead to the determination of how available funds may be allocated best among competing projects, particularly considering the scale and capital intensity of those projects.

Three main choices for the interest rate to use in government economy studies are as follows:

1. borrowing rate;
2. the opportunity cost to the governmental agency;
3. the opportunity cost to the taxpayer;

In general, it is appropriate to use the borrowing rate only for cases in which money is borrowed specifically for the project(s) under analysis and use of that money will not cause other worthy projects to be foregone.

Opportunity cost is the interest rate on the best investment opportunity foregone. If projects are chosen so that the return rate on all accepted projects is higher than the return rate on any of the rejected projects, then the interest rate for use in the economic analysis is equal to the opportunity cost.

If this is done for all projects and investment capital available within a government agency, then the result is a *government opportunity cost*. If, on the other hand, one considers the best opportunities available to the taxpayers if the money were not obtained through taxes for use by the government agency, the result is a *taxpayers opportunity cost*.

Theory suggests that in government economic analyses the interest rate should be the largest of the three listed above. Generally, the taxpayers opportunity cost is substantially the highest of the three. As an indicative example, a federal government directive in 1972 specified that an interest rate of 10% should be used in economy studies for a wide range of federal projects. This 10%, it can be argued, was at least a rough approximation of the average return taxpayers could be obtaining from the use of that money. In any case, it was substantially greater than the 6% to 8% the federal government was paying for the use of borrowed money at that time.

Benefit–Cost Ratios

Chapter 5 described the B/C ratio as a method for determining the desirability of a project by itself or for comparing alternatives. It is particularly applicable to public projects in which the benefits are difficult to estimate in monetary terms and/or the benefits accrue to people or groups other than the agency which pays most or all of the cost. In general, if the ratio of equivalent benefits to equivalent costs is ≥ 1.0, the project or incremental cost is deemed to be justified using this method. If the modified B/C ratio (Eqs. 5-3 and 5-4) is used, then the results will always be consistent with results using either the P.W., A.W., or F.W. method.

Example:
> The above example regarding a water treatment system could have been analyzed using the B/C ratio method, with the same conclusions, as follows:

Solution:
> Based on total benefits and costs:

$$\text{B/C ratio} = \frac{(\$1,000,000 - \$300,000)(P/A,6\%,20)}{\$9,000,000} = 0.89$$

Since $0.89 < 1.0$, it is not justified.
Based only on benefits and costs to the county:

$$\text{B/C ratio} = \frac{(\$1,000,000 - \$300,000)(P/A,6\%,20)}{\$9,000,000 - \$4,000,000} = 1.61$$

Since $1.61 > 1.0$, it is apparently justified.

Cost-Effectiveness Analysis

Cost-effectiveness analysis became popular in the 1960's, especially for the evaluation of complex defense and space systems. Much of the philosophy and methodology of the cost-effectiveness approach was derived from benefit–cost analysis. The basic concepts inherent in cost-effectiveness analysis are now being brought to a broad range of public investment-type problems.

The requirements for cost-effectiveness analysis are essentially the same as for any other type of economic analysis. That is, the following three requirements must be satisfied:

1. Alternate means for meeting the goals must exist.
2. The alternatives to be evaluated must have common goals or purposes.
3. Measures of cost as well as effectiveness must be estimable.

The cost-effectiveness approach is distinctive because effectiveness can be expressed in whatever terms or scales are appropriate instead of having to be reduced to dollars. Decision criteria using this approach involve subjective or objective trade-offs between various levels of cost and various levels of effectiveness to judge the optimal combination. Examples of measures of effectiveness are speed, maintainability, reliability, and convenience.

To select between alternatives for cases in which there is only one significant measure of effectiveness, the fixed-cost or fixed-effectiveness approach can be used. In the fixed-cost approach, the basis for selection is the amount of effectiveness obtained at a given cost. The selection criterion in the fixed-effectiveness approach is the cost incurred to obtain a given level of effectiveness.

The following is a description of the selection procedure which could be employed when using the cost-effectiveness approach for evaluating mutually exclusive alternatives and there are several measures of effectiveness. The alternatives can first be ranked in order of their capability to satisfy the most important criterion or measure of effectiveness. For example, in determining the choice of alternative dam systems, the most important measure of effectiveness may be flood protection as measured by the probability of a flood in any given year. Other criteria, such as navigability and recreation, would be ranked in secondary positions. Often this procedure will result in elimination of the least promising candidates. If the cost and effectiveness for the top contender are both superior to the respective values for other remaining candidates, the choice is obvious. However, it is more common for the costs as well as the effectiveness of various candidates to differ significantly in conflicting directions; therefore, selection must be made or based on judgmental trade-offs using the incremental approach. That is, one should start with the lowest-cost alternative as a base and judgmentally determine if the incremental cost is justified by the incremental effectiveness for each successively higher-cost alternative.

Example:

To carry through the example of the last paragraph, suppose there are four alternative dam systems under consideration for a given location. The costs and measures of effectiveness for the most important criterion are as follows:

Dam system	*P.W. of costs*	*Probability of flood/year*
A	$1.0MM	0.30
B	2.5MM	0.10
C	3.7MM	0.06
D	5.5MM	0.01

It may be judged that dam system A would result in unacceptably poor flood control effectiveness, and that thus only dam systems B, C, and D are worthy of more extensive consideration. The secondary measures of effectiveness of the remaining systems may now be thought worthwhile to estimate. All relevant data are summarized as follows:

Dam system	P.W. of costs	Effectiveness measures		
		Probability of flood/year	Navigability (on 0–10 scale)	Recreation (people-days/yr)
B	$2.5MM	0.10	5	100,000
C	3.7MM	0.06	7	150,000
D	5.5MM	0.01	10	275,000

Solution:

Dam system B is the lowest cost alternative and should be compared against doing nothing. Let us assume that some dam system is considered better than no dam system; thus dam system B would be justified.

Next, the incremental cost of selecting C rather than B ($3.7MM − $2.5MM = $1.2MM) should be judged in view of the incremental effectiveness of reducing the probability of flood by 0.04 (= 0.10 − 0.06), increasing navigability from 5 to 7 and increasing recreation use by 50% [= (150,000 − 100,000)/100,000]. Suppose that the incremental cost is judged not to be justified, so that B is still the leading contender. Dam system C should then be dropped from further consideration.

Next, the incremental cost of selecting D rather than B ($5.5MM − $2.5MM = $3.0MM) should be judged in view of the incremental effectiveness of reducing the probability of flood by 0.09 (= 0.10 − 0.01), increasing navigability from 5 to 10 and increasing recreation use by 175%. Let us suppose that this increment of cost is judged to be justified by the incremental effectiveness. Hence, dam system D is the final best choice.

The above example assumed that there were no factors important to the choice between the alternatives other than cost and the three measures of effectiveness. In normal practice, there would be other intangible or irreducible factors that should be considered in addition to these quantifiable measures before the selection decision is made.

Investments by Privately Owned Public Utilities

Privately owned, regulated public utilities are an important part of the United States economy. These include many suppliers of electricity, gas, water, telephone service, and various types of transportation services. Regulation is conducted by various local, state, and federal commissions and includes such matters as rate structures, standards of service, and financing allowable.

Because a utility typically requires large amounts of capital to be invested in fixed plant and equipment, economy of operation for the company and low rates to the public are possible only if there are high use factors for such assets. This is generally achieved through government bodies that limit competition and in many cases grant the utility company a virtual monopoly for providing the service in a given locale. Public regulation of utility companies and the prices they charge is a substitute for regulation by competition. Limiting competition not only results in reducing uneconomical duplication of facilities, but it can also reduce public nuisances such as the duplication of utility service lines and transportation facilities.

Utility firm earnings, after income taxes, usually are not permitted to exceed 10% to 15% on owners' equity capital. It should be noted that, although there is a maximum limit put on utility earnings by regulatory bodies, there is no guarantee of any such profits, and there is no assurance against loss. However, if the utility can show that it is operating efficiently, it usually can obtain permission to earn whatever is necessary to attract needed capital.

Utilities have much greater stability of income than normal competitive enterprises. Because of their relative stability and great capital needs, utilities commonly use a much higher proportion of debt capital to total capital than do normal competitive businesses. Whereas non-utility firms seldom use more than 30% debt capital, it is very common for utilities to borrow over 50% of their total capital.

Differences Between Economy Studies in Regulated Public Utilities and in Competitive Industry

Economy studies for public utilities can be performed by virtually the same methods as for non-utility firms. The following are several main differences in circumstances that can affect the numbers used and the simplicity with which economy studies for utilities can be made.

First, funds for investment in new fixed assets are generally much more available for utilities than they are for competitive firms. Public utilities commonly raise new capital for expansion at frequent intervals and consideration of capital rationing due to limitation of funds does not enter into the determination of the minimum attractive rate of return. The M.A.R.R. for such expansion projects is likely to be at or only slightly higher than the weighted average cost of capital.* On the other hand, if the utility has numerous cost reduction proposals and limited capital, such proposals are

---

*For example, if the firm is using 60% debt capital costing 10% per year and 40% equity capital for which the owners expect a return of 14% per year, the weighted average cost of capital is $0.60 \times 10\% + 0.40 \times 14\% = 11.6\%$.

likely to be subject to capital rationing concepts, with the M.A.R.R.'s for such proposals usually determined by the opportunity costs. These opportunity costs of capital are normally not much higher than the weighted average cost of capital for a public utility, but for a competitive firm they can be very high.

Another distinction is that the utility is supposed to select alternatives that will minimize the revenue requirements from customers paying for the services of the utility, whereas the competitive firm is expected to select alternatives that will be most beneficial to the owners of the firm. The interests of customers and stockholders of a utility firm are generally the same in the long run, but this may not be true in the short run.

Utilities do not normally undertake economy studies to determine whether or not a given service should be provided as competitive firms commonly do. Instead, utility economy studies are normally focused on which alternative for providing the service is preferable, that is, which alternative minimizes the revenue required to pay for the service.

A final difference is that because of the stability of utilities it is common in utility economy studies to express annual income taxes and certain other costs as a percent of the investment as a computational convenience. This will be explained in the next two sections.

Computation of Income Taxes as Percent of Investment for Utility Economy Studies

Figure 8-1 shows the relationship of operating revenues and costs for a public utility, with emphasis on taxable income (i.e., profit before taxes) and income taxes as a cost.

It is common in the United States that utilities are allowed to earn a certain return (i.e., "fair" return) on their so-called rate base, which is generally increased by the amount of any new investment. If the taxable income is a constant proportion of investment and if the income tax rate (i.e., income taxes/taxable income) is constant, then income taxes are a constant proportion of investment. That is, each of the ratios in Eq. 8-1 would be a constant.

$$\frac{\text{Income taxes}}{\text{Investment}} = \frac{\text{Taxable income}}{\text{Investment}} \times \frac{\text{Income taxes}}{\text{Taxable income}} \qquad 8\text{-}1$$

This results in a great computational convenience for making most after-tax utility economy studies. That is, instead of having to go through the tabular method for determining after-tax cash flows for all alternatives as explained in Chapter 6, one can merely add in the annual cost for income taxes as a percentage of the investment for each alternative.

The following is a typical formula for determining the annual cost of

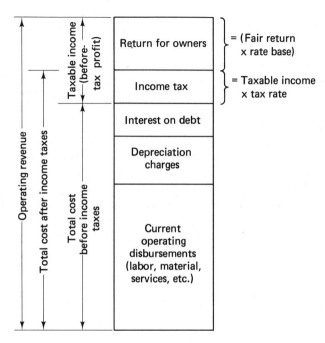

Figure 8-1. Relationship of operating revenues and costs for a public utility.

income taxes as a proportion of investment for a particular set of circumstances:

$$T = \left[\frac{t}{1-t}\right]\left[i + (A/F,i\%,n)(1-c) - \frac{1}{n}(1-c)\right]\left[1 - \frac{Bb}{i}\right] \qquad 8\text{-}2$$

where T = Annual charge rate for income taxes
        (= income taxes/investment)
    t = Effective income tax rate
        (= income taxes/taxable income)
    i = M.A.R.R. on invested capital
        (normally = weighted average cost of capital)
    n = Life of project
    c = Salvage value proportion
        (= salvage value/investment)
    B = Proportion of debt capital
        (= debt capital/total capital)
    b = Average interest rate on debt capital
        (= debt interest/year/debt capital)

Equation 8-2 is applicable to situations in which straight line depreciation is used for determining taxable income and for determining the firm's accounting (or book) profits and a fair return is allowed on a rate base equal to the depreciated book value. The middle term in brackets can be considered a "levelized annual return rate" to cover depreciation and interest over the life of the project; the $[1 - Bb/i]$ term adjusts for the proportion of the return that goes to the owners. Similar equations can be developed for other circumstances* such as when an accelerated depreciation method is used for computing taxable income even though accounting depreciation is based on the straight line method.

The determination of the effective income tax rate, t, when federal and state income taxes are involved is worthy of note. Federal tax laws allow the deduction of state taxes paid in the computation of federal taxes owed, but state tax laws vary considerably regarding how much of federal taxes paid can be deducted in the computation of state taxes owed. For the case in which no federal taxes can be deducted on the computation of state taxes owed, the following is the formula for the effective income tax rate, t:

$$t = t_f + t_s - (t_s)(t_f) \qquad\qquad 8\text{-}3$$

where t_f = federal income tax rate
$\qquad t_s$ = state income tax rate

Calculation of Fixed Charge Rates

Fixed charge rates are a computational convenience used in utility economy studies. These rates normally include two or more annual cost components which can be expressed as a constant percent of the investment. The last section showed a formula for determining a fixed charge rate to cover income taxes. A rate to cover the annual cost of depreciation plus return on investment is merely the capital recovery cost expressed as a percent of the investment. Such annual costs as ad valorem (property) taxes and sometimes maintenance can be legitimately estimated as a constant percent of investment. Further, the effect of any investment tax credit can be converted into an annual percent which *reduces* the annual charge rate because it is a credit against costs.

Example:
The sources and costs of money for the firm are given as follows:

$$
\begin{array}{lll}
55\% \text{ bonded debt @ } 10\% & = 5.5 \\
35\% \text{ common stock @ } 14\% & = 4.9 \\
10\% \text{ preferred stock @ } 10\% & = 1.0 \\
\hline
\text{Weighted average} = \Sigma & = 11.4\% \\
(= i = \text{M.A.R.R.})
\end{array}
$$

---

*See especially P. H. Jeynes, *Profitability and Economic Choice* (Ames: Iowa State University Press), 1968, pp. 181–223, for formal derivations using almost the same notation as in Eq. 8-2.

It is desired to determine a total fixed charge rate for evaluating alternative steam-generating units having an economic life of 28 years and zero salvage value. This fixed charge rate should include the following cost components:
1. depreciation plus minimum return (interest);
2. income taxes;
3. ad valorem taxes;
4. routine maintenance;
5. investment tax credit.

Income tax conditions are such that Eqs. 8-1 and 8-2 are applicable, with $t_f = 48\%$ and $t_s = 6\%$. Annual ad valorem taxes are 1% of investment and annual routine maintenance is 2% of investment. The investment tax credit is assumed to be a one-time 4% of the investment.

Solution:

1. Depreciation plus minimum return $= (A/F,11.4\%,28)(1 - c) + i$
$$= 0.0068 + 0.114$$
$$= 0.121$$

2. Income taxes (from Eq. 8-3):
$$t = 0.48 + 0.06 - 0.06(0.48) = 0.511$$
From Eq. 8-2:
$$T = \left[\frac{0.511}{1 - 0.511}\right]\left[0.114 + (A/F,11.4\%,28)(1 - 0) - \frac{1}{28}(1 - 0)\right]$$
$$\left[1 - \frac{0.55 \times 0.10}{0.114}\right] = 0.046$$

3. Ad valorem taxes (given)   0.01
4. Routine maintenance (given)   0.02
5. Investment tax credit
$$= -0.04(A/P,11,4\%,28) = -0.0048$$ -0.005
                                                                _____
                                                                 0.192

Thus, the fixed charge components total up to an annual rate of 0.192 or 19.2%. This means that for each dollar invested in this type of plant, revenue of 19.2¢ is needed each year over the 28-year life just to cover the costs included in the fixed charge.

Using Fixed Charge Rates in Economy Studies

Fixed charge rates can be used very easily to make after-tax comparisons of alternatives by the A.W., P.W., or C.W. methods if the conditions for which the fixed charge rates are derived are applicable. For cases in which alternatives having different lives are compared using fixed charge rates, the repeatability assumptions discussed in Chapter 3 must be applicable.

Example:

Suppose it is desired to compare the economics of steam versus internal combustion generating units on a per kilowatt basis. We will use a fixed charge rate of 19.2% for the steam unit as calculated in the example above. Similar calculations for internal combustion units having a life of 14 years result in a fixed charge rate of approximately 21.2%. These and other data for the two alternatives are summarized in the table below:

	Steam	Internal combustion
Investment/kW	$350	$150
Life	28 yr	14 yr
Other operating costs/yr not included in fixed charges	$17	$60
Annual fixed charge rate	19.2%	21.2%
Minimum return (interest)	11.4%	11.4%

Solution by A.W. Method:

	Steam	Internal combustion
Fixed charges:		
$350 × 19.2%	$66.50	
$150 × 21.2%		$31.80
Other operating costs:	17.00	60.00
Total annual costs =	$83.50	$91.80
	↑	
	Best	

Solution by P.W. Method:

(*Using a 28-year study period*)

	Steam	Internal combustion
Fixed charges:		
$350 × 19.2% × $(P/A,11.4\%,28)$	$550.60	
$150 × 21.2% × $(P/A,11.4\%,28)$		$263.30
Other operating costs:		
$17(P/A,11.4\%,28)$	140.80	
$60(P/A,11.4\%,28)$		496.80
Total present worth of costs =	$691.40	$760.10
	↑	
	Best	

Solution by C.W. Method:

	Steam	Internal combustion
Fixed charges:		
$350 \times 19.2\% \times (P/A,11.4\%,\infty)$	$583.20	
$150 \times 21.2\% \times (P/A,11.4\%,\infty)$		$278.90
Other operating costs:		
$17(P/A,11.4\%,\infty)$	149.10	
$60(P/A,11.4\%,\infty)$		526.20
Total capitalized worth of costs $=$	$732.30	$805.10
	↑	
	Best	

Problems Involving Investments at Different Points in Time

Public utilities are commonly faced with the need to add service capability at different points in time in order to meet growing demand. Expected service lives of units added at different dates may be approximately the same, or there may be other conditions so that there is no obvious length of study period to use for an economy study to compare different plans. The literature often refers to the two methods commonly used for handling such problems as the *repeated plant* method or assumption and as the *coterminated plant* method or assumption.

The repeated plant method of analysis is rather analogous to using the repeatability assumptions. If a unit added to a system to expand capacity is identical to the first unit, then its equivalent annual cost, once it has been installed, is assumed to be the same as for the first unit. The equivalent annual cost of each added unit starts at a different time and the assumption may be made that this specific annual cost will be repeated indefinitely. Because of the indefinite study period with different costs beginning at different points in time, use of the capitalized cost method of analysis is convenient. However the present worth method can be used as long as the study period chosen is at least as long as the end of the first life cycle for the last type of asset placed in service and it is assumed that all costs continue repeating after the end of the study period.

The coterminated plant method of analysis, on the other hand, assumes that all alternatives will be terminated as of the end of the study period. Both methods will be illustrated below.

Example:

Using Repeated Plant Assumption

Suppose we have the same steam versus internal combustion alternatives given in the above example using fixed charge rates. The only new factor is that the installations may be staggered in time as follows to meet the projected demand growth:

Year	Steam	Internal combustion
0	300 mW	100 mW
5		100 mW
10		100 mW

(Note: mW means "megawatt" and equals 1,000 kW)

Solution by Capitalized Cost Method:

If the total annual costs/kilowatt are the same as in the previous example, the annual costs for each installation "package" would be as follows:

$$\text{Steam:} \quad \$83.50/kW \times 300,000 \text{ kW} = \$25,050,000$$
$$\text{Combustion:} \quad \$91.80/kW \times 100,000 \text{ kW} = \$ 9,180,000$$

Thus the costs would be as shown in Fig. 8-2 to $N = \infty$:

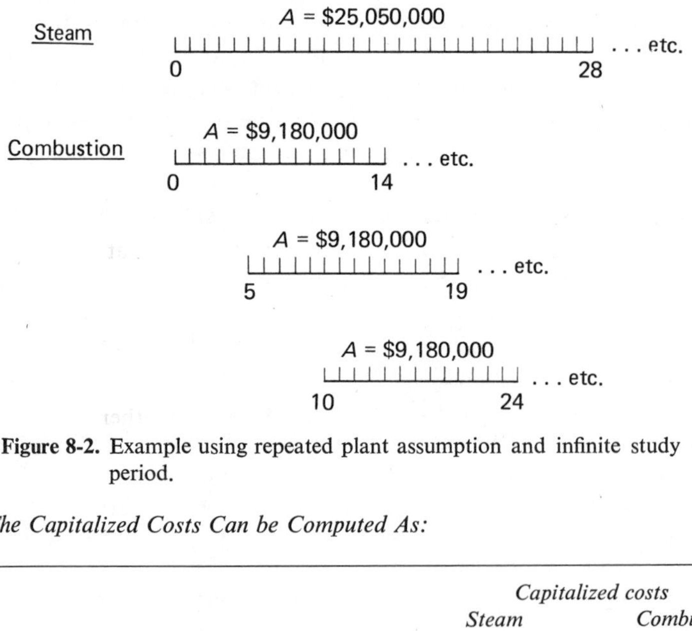

Figure 8-2. Example using repeated plant assumption and infinite study period.

The Capitalized Costs Can be Computed As:

	Capitalized costs	
	Steam	Combustion
$25,050,000 $(P/A,11.4\%,\infty)$	$219,736,000	
$ 9,180,000 $(P/A,11.4\%,\infty)$		$80,526,000
$ 9,180,000 $(P/A,11.4\%,\infty)(P/F,11.4\%,5)$		46,856,000
$ 9,180,000 $(P/A,11.4\%,\infty)(P/F,11.4\%,10)$		27,454,000
Total	$219,736,000	$154,836,000

Solution by Present Worth Method:

The life cycle for the steam alternative is 28 years, and for the combustion alternative the end of the first life cycle for the last (or third) unit is 24 years. The longest of these is 28 years, which is the minimum study period to be used. Thus, the costs would be as shown in Fig. 8-3.

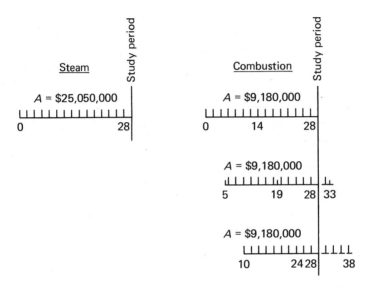

Figure 8-3. Example using repeated plant assumption and 28 year study period.

	Present worths (28-yr study period)	
	Steam	*Combustion*
$25,050,000(P/A,11.4\%,28)$	$209,820,000	
$9,180,000(P/A,11.4\%,28)$		$76,892,000
$9,180,000(P/A,11.4\%,23)(P/F,11.4\%,5)$		42,956,000
$9,180,000(P/A,11.4\%,18)(P/F,11.4\%,10)$		23,311,000
Totals	$209,820,000	$143,159,000

General application of the coterminated plant assumption requires that a salvage value or *residual value* be estimated to reflect the value of the remaining life of any units that actually will or could remain in service at the end of the study period. Such salvage values might be estimated directly or by using some formula such as for remaining book value. In such cases, use of fixed charge rates may still be advantageous, or it may be easier to work with cash flows only.

Example:

Using Coterminated Plant Assumption:

Suppose the above steam versus combustion alternatives are to be compared with one significant change—the period of needed service is limited to, say, 28 years. The salvage values at the end of 28 years are assumed to equal the book values at that time if straight line depreciation were used. It is desired to show the solution using the coterminated assumption and fixed charge rates. The conditions are the same otherwise. Assume that the contribution to the fixed charge rate caused by ad valorem taxes, routine maintenance, and investment tax credit are 0.01, 0.02, and −0.005, respectively, for any replacement combustion units.

Solution:

The fixed charge rates (and annual costs) for all units would remain the same except for:

a. Replacement combustion unit for years 20–28
b. Replacement combustion unit for years 25–28
The following are the calculations of new fixed charge rates.

	Combustion yr 20–28	Combustion yr 25–28
Investment: 100 mW × $150/kW × 10^3 kW/mW $15,000,000		$15,000,000
Book value at year 28		
$15,000,000 − $15,000,000(9/14)	5,357,000	10,714,000
$15,000,000 − $15,000,000(4/14)		
Salvage value as % investment = c		
$5,357,000/$15,000,000	0.357	
$10,714,000/$15,000,000		0.714
Fixed charges:		
Depreciation plus minimum return		
$(A/F,11.4\%,9)(1 - 0.357) + 0.114$	0.159	
$(A/F,11.4\%,4)(1 - 0.714) + 0.114$		0.177
Income taxes (using Eq. 8-2 and $t = 0.511$)		
$T = \left[\frac{0.511}{1 - 0.511}\right]\left[0.114 + (A/F,11.4\%,9)(1 - 0.357)\right.$		
$\left. - \frac{1}{9}(1 - 0.357)\right]\left[1 - \frac{0.55 \times 0.10}{0.114}\right]$	0.047	
$T = \left[\frac{0.511}{1 - 0.511}\right]\left[0.114 + (A/F,11.4\%,4)(1 - 0.714)\right.$		
$\left. - \frac{1}{4}(1 - 0.714)\right]\left[1 - \frac{0.55 \times 0.10}{0.114}\right]$		0.057
Ad valorem taxes (given)	0.01	0.01
Routine maintenance (given)	0.02	0.02
Investment tax credit (given)	−0.005	−0.005
Total fixed charge rate	0.231	0.259

	Combustion yr 20–28	*Combustion yr 25–28*
Annual costs:		
Fixed charges		
$15,000,000 \times 0.231$	$3,465,000	
$15,000,000 \times 0.259$		$3,885,000
Other operating costs		
$100 \text{ mW} \times \$60 \times 10^3$	6,000,000	6,000,000
	$9,465,000	$9,885,000

Thus, the steam versus combustion alternatives can be compared using the equivalent annual costs shown in Fig. 8-4.

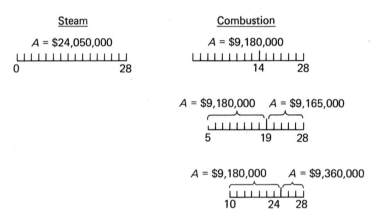

Figure 8-4. Example using coterminated plant assumption. (Service terminated at 28 years.)

A present worth comparison for the above conditions would result in the present worth of costs for the combustion alternative being slightly higher than in the previous example using the repeatability assumption and a 28-year study period. However, the combustion alternative would still be better. In general, the repeated plant assumption is easier computationally, but if it is thought that the period of needed service is limited rather than indefinitely long, then the coterminated plant assumption should be used to be sure of a fair comparison.

PROBLEMS

8-1. What is the benefit-cost ratio for the following project if interest on capital is (a) 5%, (b) 15%?

Initial cost	$100,000
Additional cost at the end of year 5	$ 40,000
Annual benefits at the end of years 2 through 15	$ 15,000

8-2. A city is considering the elimination of a railroad grade crossing by building an overpass. The overpass would cost $1,000,000 and is estimated to have a useful life of 40 years and a $100,000 salvage value. Approximately 2,000 vehicles per day are delayed an average of 2 minutes each due to trains at the grade crossing. Trucks comprise 40% of the vehicles, and the opportunity cost of their delay is assumed to average $20/truck-hour. The other vehicles are cars having an assumed average opportunity cost of $4.00/car-hour. The installation will save the railroad an annual expense of $30,000 for lawsuits and maintenance of crossing guards, but it will not save the railroads anything for time to pass through the intersection. It is estimated that the new overpass will save the city approximately $4,000 per year in expenses directly due to accidents. Should the overpass be built by the city if it is to be the owner and the opportunity cost for its capital is 8%? How much should the railroad reasonably be asked to contribute toward construction of the bridge if its opportunity cost on capital is assumed to be 15%?

8-3. Five alternatives are being considered for providing a sewage treatment facility. The costs and estimated benefits of the alternatives are as follows:

| | Annual equivalents (in Thousands) | |
	Costs	Benefits
Alternative		
A	$1,050	$1,110
B	900	810
C	1,230	1,390
D	1,350	1,500
	990	1,140

Which plan should be adopted, if any, if the Sewage Authority wishes to invest if, and only if, the B-C ratio on any cost is at least 1.0?

8-4. Two alternate locations for a new highway from Ducktown to Apex are to be compared. Location A involves a distance of 12 miles and a total first cost of $4,000,000. Resurfacing will be required every 10 years at an estimated cost of $100,000 per mile and the annual maintenance cost will be $3,000 per mile.

Location B involves a distance of 15 miles and a total first cost of $2,500-000. Costs per mile for resurfacing and annual maintenance are the same as for A.

The average traffic over this highway is estimated to be 1,000 vehicles per day, of which approximately 20% will be trucks, 10% will be commercial passenger cars, and the rest will be noncommercial passenger cars. The incremental cost of vehicle operation is assumed to be $0.50/mile for trucks, $0.15/mile for commercial cars, and $0.05/hour for noncommercial cars. The opportunity value of time saving for occupants of trucks and commercial cars is estimated at $0.20/vehicle-minute, and traffic is estimated to average 45 miles/hour.

a. Assuming that money invested by this government agency has an opportunity cost of 10% and that the highway will be used indefinitely, determine if the extra investment in location A is justified using appropriate B-C ratio(s).

b. Assume that the rate of vehicle use will be 1,000 vehicles in the first year and will increase by 60 vehicles each year thereafter. What is the maximum incremental investment that could be justified in choosing location A rather than location B?

8-5. A steel bridge cost $400,000 when built by the state 15 years ago. Average annual maintenance costs are expected to be $10,000 per year; therefore it has been proposed to replace the steel bridge with a concrete bridge of comparable capacity. A new concrete bridge would cost $700,000, but it would require only $2,000 per year maintenance cost and would last 60 years and cost $40,000 to remove then. The present realizable salvage value for the steel bridge is $50,000 now, which means that the new capital required for the new bridge would be only $650,000. If kept, the old steel bridge would be expected to last 25 more years and have a $15,000 salvage value at that time.

The state has sufficient tax funds on hand to finance the new bridge without borrowing, but some contend that money invested in highway improvements has an opportunity cost to taxpayers of at least 8%. The following is an annual cost economic comparison provided by an engineer:

Keep Present Bridge
Depreciation (based on 15-year life) = $400,000/15 = $26,667
Maintenance   10,000
                Total annual cost $36,000

Replace with Proposed Bridge
Depreciation (based on 60-year life) = $650,000/60 = $10,833
Maintenance   2,000
                Total annual cost $12,833

List any errors you perceive in the engineer's analysis. Make an annual cost comparison that is more valid. Use any assumptions you think are reasonable.

8-6. It is proposed that a new toll bridge be built by a State Highway Department and financed by means of a self-liquidating 30-year bond issue which can be retired as funds are available. The bridge would cost $40,000,000. Conservative estimates indicate that the bridge would be used by an average of 50,000 private cars per day and 4,000 commercial vehicles per day. Estimated annual out-of-pocket costs for maintenance and operation of the bridge would be $2,000,000. If commercial vehicles are to pay five times the charge for private vehicles, what should be the toll fee for both types of vehicles in order for the bridge to be self-liquidating? Interest on bonds is 8%.

8-7. A government highway department is considering the economics of installing a four-lane highway versus a six-lane highway in a certain location now. A four-lane highway would cost $3,000,000 now and would be sufficient to meet requirements for 10 years, at which time it is projected that the highway would have to be expanded by two lanes at a cost of $1,000,000. Alternatively, the full six-lane highway could be built now for $3,400,000 and this would be sufficient for needs into the indefinite future. Average annual maintenance costs would be $100,000 for the four-lane highway and $120,000 for the six-lane highway. If money used by the highway department is assumed to cost 8%, which is the better choice based on an annual cost comparison?

8-8. How much could a city afford to pay now for a new sewage treatment facility that would eliminate contractor charges of $100,000 each year starting this year and would also result in pollution reduction benefits judged to be worth approximately $200,000 beginning at the end of 5 years from now and increasing by $10,000 at the end of each year thereafter until the end of 25 years from now? Assume capital used by the city has an opportunity cost of 10%.

8-9. Four locations are being considered for a new city park. The following are costs and effectiveness measures for each:

Location	First cost	Annual upkeep cost	Effectiveness (on a scale 0 to 100)
A	$ 800,000	$20,000	50
B	500,000	30,000	70
C	600,000	40,000	70
D	1,100,000	10,000	50

If the park is expected to last indefinitely and the opportunity cost for the city's money is 10%, show which alternative must be best even though you don't know the city's cost-effectiveness trade-off faction. Plot present worth of costs versus effectiveness to show graphically the relationships for all alternatives.

8-10. A telephone company has determined that a 800-pair cable is required immediately in a certain area and that a total of 1,400 pairs will be needed by the end of 10 years from now. An underground conduit of sufficient size to handle the cable needs is being installed now at a cost of $20,000. If a 1,400-pair cable is installed now, it will cost $60,000. As an alternative, the telephone company can install a 800-pair cable now at a cost of $40,000 and then install an additional 600-pair cable at the end of 10 years at an estimated cost of $32,000. Because of expected obsolescence, the life of either installation is estimated to end 30 years from the present time, and the salvage value of all cable at that time is estimated to be 10% of the first cost.

Compare the alternatives on the basis of present worth of all relevant costs, including income taxes by the use of fixed charge rates. The company uses 40% borrowed capital for which it pays 8% interest. Its M.A.R.R. is its weighted average cost of capital, which is 10%. Straight line depreciation is used for accounting and tax purposes, and its effective income tax rate is 55%. Annual property taxes for either alternative would be 2% of the installed cost. Annual maintenance would be 4% of the cable investment cost for cable installed now and would be 3% for cable installed 10 years from now.

8-11. A private water utility company has been asked to supply service to a new development. Alternative A would cost $1,000,000 for installation and would involve annual operating costs of $40,000. Alternative B would cost only $450,000 for the initial installation but would require annual operating costs of $160,000. Either alternative would have a life of 25 years and a salvage value of 10% of the first cost. The company has a 48% income tax rate, uses 60% borrowed capital for which it pays 9% interest, and it earns 12% on total capital. It uses straight line depreciation for both accounting and income tax purposes. The company has some doubts as to whether this development will be successful, but it is constrained to install lines. If it is not successful, operating costs will be only 20% of the above projections. Which alternative would you recommend? Compare total annual costs using fixed charge rate(s).

8-12. Two plans for providing a certain telephone service over the next 25 years are under consideration as follows:

Plan I

Year 0	Retire Item A:	No net salvage
	Place Item B:	$100,000 capitalized first cost
		6,000 one-time noncapitalized cost

Plan II

Year 0	Retain Item A:	$ 3,000 per year maintenance and ad valorem tax charges
	Place Item C:	60,000 capitalized first cost
		4,000 one-time noncapitalized cost
Year 10	Retire Item A:	No net salvage
	Place Item D:	Same first cost and noncapitalized expense as Item C

Assume that all items except Item A will be retired at the end of year 25 with no net salvage value. Maintenance for Items B, C, and D is 7%, property taxes are 4%, and income taxes are 3% of the respective first costs. The minimum return on money is 10%.

Calculate the total fixed charge rate(s) for Items B, C, and D. Then compare the economics of the two plans by using the present worth method, i.e., by calculating the present worth of annual charges. (*Note:* Fixed charge rates are applied only to *capitalized* first costs, which become part of the utility's rate base. Noncapitalized first costs, such as for certain labor and supplies, are charged as expenses in the years they occur and thus should be considered in an economy study only as one-time cash outflows.)

8-13. A power company is considering four mutually exclusive alternatives for moving coal. The economic life is 10 years and the salvage value is 0 for each alternative. The minimum required rate of return is 15%. The fixed charge rate to cover all investment-related costs except for labor, power, and maintenance is 25% per year. Given the following data, show which alternative is best by annual cost comparison:

Alternative	Investment	Annual labor cost	Annual power and maintenance cost
A	$100,000	$70,000	$5,000
B	175,000	55,000	6,000
C	210,000	35,000	9,000
D	280,000	20,000	11,000

8-14. A utility company is faced with the following immediate and deferred investment alternatives: Alternative A results in total equivalent annual costs of $10,000 per year starting immediately. Alternative B involves two parts, each part having total equivalent annual costs of $7,000 per year. The first part would be installed immediately and the second part would be installed after 8 years. All investments are expected to have economic lives of 20 years from installation, after which replacements can be made and costs repeated for additional 20-year cycles into the indefinite future.

Compare the alternatives by using the present worth method and a minimum attractive rate of return of 10% for an infinite study period.

estimating for
economic analyses

Probably the most difficult and expensive part of any economic analysis is to determine the estimates needed to complete the analysis. This chapter will attempt to provide a perspective and approaches to estimating, with emphasis on making single-valued estimates for the traditional assumed-certain analyses which have been the topic of Part 1 of this book. Chapter 11 will cover estimating in terms of probabilities and other measures of variability to reflect the risk inherent in predicting future outcomes. First, we will describe how to consider inflation in estimating future monetary inflows and outflows.

Consideration of Inflation

Until now we apparently have assumed that prices are relatively unchanged over substantial periods of time, or that the effect of such changes are the same on any alternatives considered. Unfortunately, these are not generally realistic assumptions. Inflation can, indeed, affect the economic comparison of alternatives. Hence, the nature of inflation and methods of taking inflation into account will be considered below.

Actual Dollars Vs. Real Dollars

Inflation describes the situation in which prices of goods and services are increasing. As prices rise, the value of money, i.e., its purchasing power (in real dollars, as defined below) decreases correspondingly.

Let us define two distinct kinds of dollars (or other monetary units such as pesos or rubles) with which we can work in economic analyses, if done properly:

1. *Actual Dollars:* The actual number of dollars as of the point in time they occur and the usual kind of dollar terms in which people think. Sometimes called *then-current dollars*, they will be denoted as "A$" whenever a distinction needs to be made in this book.

2. *Real Dollars:* Dollars of purchasing power as of some point in time, regardless of the point in time the actual dollars occur. Sometimes called *constant worth dollars*, they will be denoted as "R$" whenever a distinction needs to be made in this book.

Actual dollars as of any time, n, can be converted into real dollars of purchasing power at any time k by the relation:

$$R\$ = A\$\left[\frac{1}{1+f}\right]^{n-k} = A\$(P/F, f\%, n - k) \qquad 9\text{-}1$$

Similarly,

$$A\$ = R\$(1 + f)^{n-k} = R\$(F/P, f\%, n - k) \qquad 9\text{-}2$$

where f is the inflation rate per period over the n periods. It is most common to express real dollars as dollars of purchasing power as of the beginning of the study period under consideration.

As an example, suppose your salary for each of the next 3 years is expected to be as follows:

Year	Salary (in A$)
1	$10,000
2	11,000
3	12,100

Your salary could just as well have been expressed in dollars of purchasing power as of some base point in time. If you assume that the base point in time is year 1, your R$ salary expected for the next 3 years could be expressed as follows:

Year	Salary (*in* R$)
1	$10,000
2	10,000
3	10,000

If the inflation rate is 10% per year, both ways of expressing your expected salary are exactly equivalent! These numbers illustrate a situation which is close to the experience of many people in recent years; i.e., even though salaries or wages (A$) have been increasing, the purchasing power (R$) of those salaries has not increased correspondingly. Indeed, many people have faced declining purchasing power because the rate of salary increases has not been as great as the rate of inflation.

Fixed Vs. Responsive Annuities

Whenever future investment receipts are predetermined by contract, as in the case of a bond or a fixed annuity, these receipts do not respond to inflation. In cases where the future receipts are not predetermined, however, they may respond to inflation. The degree of response varies from case to case. To illustrate the nature of inflation, let us consider two annuities: The first annuity is fixed (unresponsive to inflation) and yields $2,000 per yr for 10 years. The second annuity is of the same duration and yields enough future dollars to be equivalent to $2,000 in the value of dollars of investment (constant worth dollars). Assuming an inflation of 3% per annum, pertinent values for the two annuities over a 10-year period are shown in Table 9-1.

Thus, when the receipts are constant in actual dollars (unresponsive to inflation), their equivalent in value of real dollars of investment declines over the 10-year interval to $1,488 in the final year. When receipts are fixed in value of real dollars of investment (responsive to inflation), their equivalent in actual dollars rises to $2,688 by year 10.

Real Interest Rate, Inflation Rate, and Combined Interest Rate

Let us define several types of rates and show how they are used:

1. *Real Interest Rate:* The increase in real purchasing power expressed as a percent per period. The interest rate at which R$ outflow is equivalent to R$ inflow. Sometimes known as *monetary return* or *real monetary rate*. Denoted as "i."

2. *Inflation Rate:* The increase in price of given goods or services as a percent per period. Denoted as "f."

Table 9-1

ILLUSTRATION OF FIXED AND RESPONSIVE ANNUITY
WITH INFLATION RATE OF 3% PER YR

	Fixed annuity		Responsive annuity	
Year	In actual dollars	In value of dollars of investment (real dollars)*	In actual dollars	In value of dollars of investment (real dollars)*
1	$2,000	$1,942	$2,060	$2,000
2	2,000	1,886	2,122	2,000
3	2,000	1,830	2,186	2,000
4	2,000	1,776	2,252	2,000
5	2,000	1,726	2,318	2,000
6	2,000	1,674	2,388	2,000
7	2,000	1,626	2,460	2,000
8	2,000	1,578	2,534	2,000
9	2,000	1,532	2,610	2,000
10	2,000	1,488	2,688	2,000

*See Eq. 9-1.

3. *Combined Interest Rate:* The increase in amount to cover real interest and inflation expressed as a percent per period. The interest rate at which A$ outflow is
equivalent to A$ inflow. It is often denoted as "i", but it will be denoted as "i_c"
whenever it needs to be distinguished from real interest rate.

Because the real interest rate or monetary return and the inflation rate
have a multiplicative or compounding effect,

$$i_c = (1 + i)(1 + f) - 1 \qquad\qquad 9\text{-}3$$
$$= i + f + (i \times f)$$
$$i_c \cong i + f$$

where i and f are not large relative to the accuracy desired.

What Interest Rate to Use in Economy Studies

In general, the interest rate appropriate for equivalence calculations in
economy studies depends on the type of cash flows as follows:

If cash Flows are in terms of:		Then the interest rate to use is:
(a)	Real $	Real interest rate, i
(b)	Actual $	Combined interest rate, i_c

The above should make intuitive sense as follows: If one is estimating in terms of real (uninflated) dollars, then use a real (uninflated) interest rate. Similarly, if one is estimating in terms of actual (inflated) dollars, then use the combined (inflated) interest rate. Thus, one can make economic analyses using either R$ or A$ with equal validity, provided the appropriate interest rate is used for equivalence calculations.

Example:

To illustrate the relationship of the two approaches to consideration of infla-tion, consider a project requiring an investment of $10,000 which is expected to return, in terms of actual dollars, $3,000 at the end of the first year, $4,000 at the end of the second year, and $6,000 at the end of the third year. The rate of inflation is 5% per yr, and the real monetary interest rate is 10% per yr. (Thus, from Eq. 9-3, the combined discount factor is 15.5%.) Table 9-2 shows how the net present worth of the project would be calculated to be $-$520 using the second (b) method above.

Table 9-2

CALCULATION OF NET PRESENT WORTH
WITH ESTIMATES IN ACTUAL DOLLARS

Year (N)	Outcome in actual dollars	Discount factor for real interest and inflation $(P/F,15.5\%,N)$	Present worth
0	$-$10,000	1.000	$-$10,000
1	3,000	0.867	2,600
2	4,000	0.745	2,990
3	6,000	0.647	3,890
			$\Sigma = -$520

If the first (a) method for considering inflation is used, then the outcomes should be estimated in terms of real dollars.

For the above example, with the inflation rate of 5%, if the estimator is precisely consistent, the outcome estimates in terms of real dollars, as of time of investment, using Eq. 9-1, should be $10,000, $2,860, $3,620, and $5,180 for each year, respectively. Table 9-3 shows how the net present worth of the project would be calculated to be the same $-$520 using the first method, which involves straightforward present worth calculations with the real interest rate of 10%.

It is worthy of note that had the outcomes in actual dollars been dis-counted by only the real interest rate of 10%, then the net present worth would have been calculated to be $540, indicating a favorable project. This

Table 9-3

CALCULATION OF NET PRESENT WORTH
WITH ESTIMATES IN REAL DOLLARS

Year (N)	Outcome in real dollars	Discount factor for real interest only (P/F,10%,N)	Present worth
0	−$10,000	1.000	−$10,000
1	2,860	0.909	2,600
2	3,620	0.826	2,990
3	5,180	0.751	3,890
			$\Sigma = -\$520$

is in contrast with the −$520 net present worth (indicating an unfavorable project) calculated using the correct interest rate.

Equation 2-28 enables one to calculate the present worth of an annuity that is increasing (inflating) at a constant rate. Using f instead of j for the rate of inflation, and i_c instead of i for the combined interest rate, Eq. 2-28 would be changed to:

$$P = \begin{cases} \dfrac{A_1[1 - (P/F,i_c\%,N)(F/P,f\%,N)]}{i_c - f} & \text{for } f \neq i_c \qquad 9\text{-}4 \\[2ex] A_1N(F/P,i_c\%,1) & \text{for } f = i_c \qquad 9\text{-}5 \end{cases}$$

where A_1 is the first year-end payment.

Example:

Calculate the present equivalent and annual equivalent of a series of year-end payments. The first year payment is $10,000; thereafter each payment is 10% greater than the previous one. A total of 12 payments occurs. The combined interest rate is 15%.

Solution:

Using Eq. 9-4, we get:

$$P = \$10,000 \frac{[1 - (P/F,15\%,12)(F/P,10\%,12)]}{15\% - 10\%}$$

$$= \frac{\$10,000[1 - (0.1869)(3.138)]}{0.05} = \$82,702$$

$$A = P(A/P,15\%,12)$$

$$= \$82,702(0.18448) = \$15,256 \text{ (In A\$ because } i_c \text{ was used)}$$

Effect of Inflation on Before-Tax and After-Tax Economy Studies

As illustrated previously, if subsequent benefits from an investment bring constant quantities of A$ over time, then inflation will diminish the real value (R$) of the future benefits and, hence, the real rate of return. If, on the other hand, all before-tax costs and benefits are changing at equal rates, then inflation has no net effect on before-tax economic analyses of alternatives. Unfortunately, however, this is not true for after-tax economic analyses.

In general, given two projects with the same before-tax rate of return, it can be shown that inflation results in a smaller after-tax rate of return than that for a project which does not have benefits which increase with inflation. This is because even though the benefits may increase at the same rate as inflation, the depreciation charges do not increase, which results in larger income tax payments. The net result is that even though the after-tax cash flow in A$ is increased with inflation, that increase is not large enough to offset both the increased income taxes and inflation.

As a side note, inflation might cause equipment to have a salvage value that was not forecast or that is larger than had been projected. This would tend to reduce the unfavorable effect of inflation on the after-tax rate of return.

Deflation

The above section concentrated on inflation because that is the dominant condition experienced in the past and expected in the future. However, we should also recognize deflation. Deflation is the opposite of inflation—a decrease in the monetary price for goods and services, which correspondingly means an *increase* in the real value or purchasing power of money. Deflation can be handled exactly comparably to inflation in economic analyses. That is, estimates can be made either in terms of R$ or A$, and the corresponding interest rate to use should be either the real rate, i, or the composite rate,

$$i_c = (1 + i)(1 - f) - 1 = i - f - i \times f$$

where f is the rate of deflation.

Estimating—Difficulty and Perspective

Chapter 1 described various cost concepts which are important to economic analyses. The key point was that the costs which are important to economic comparisons are the marginal (variable, or incremental) costs for the future, and that these costs may well include opportunities foregone as well as actual cash flows.

The basic difficulty in estimating for economic analyses is that most prospective projects for which estimations are to be made are unique; that is, substantially similar projects have not been undertaken in the past under conditions that are the same as expected for the future. Hence, outcome data that can be used in estimating directly and without modification often do not exist. It may be possible, however, to gather data on certain past outcomes which are related to the outcomes being estimated and to adjust and project that data based on expected future conditions. Techniques for collecting and projecting estimation data and also for making probabilistic estimates are rooted in the field of statistics.

Whenever an economic analysis is for a major new product or process, the estimating for that analysis should be an integral part of comprehensive planning procedure. Such comprehensive planning would require the active participation of at least the marketing, design engineering, manufacturing, finance, and top management functions. It would generally include the following features:

1. a realistic master plan for product development, testing, phase into production, and operation;
2. provision for working capital and facilities requirements;
3. integration with other company plans;
4. evaluation against company objectives for market position, sales volume, profit, and investment; and
5. provision of a sound basis for operating controls if project is adopted.

Obviously, such comprehensive planning is costly in time and effort, but when a new product or process has major implications for the future of a firm, it is generally a sound rule to devote a greater rather than a lesser amount of effort to complete planning, including estimates for the economic analysis that is a partial result of the planning. The application of this rule, of course, is bounded by constraints of limited time and talent; however, following the rule will tend to minimize the chance of poor decisions or lack of preparedness to implement projects once the decision to invest has been made.

Estimation Reliability

Estimates or forecasts, by their nature, are evaluations of incomplete evidence indicating what the future may hold. They may be based on empirical observations of only somewhat similar or analogous situations, adjusted on the basis of the kind of personal hunch that grows out of the accumulation of the experiences. Or they may be inferences drawn from various kinds of available objective data, such as trade statistics, results experienced in analogous situations, or personal observations.

Regardless of the estimate source, the estimate user should have specific recognition that the estimate will be in error to some extent. Even the use of formalized estimation techniques will not, in itself, eliminate error, although it will hopefully reduce error somewhat, or will at least provide specific recognition of the anticipated degree of error.

The level of detail and accuracy of an estimate should depend on the following:

1. the estimability of that which is to be estimated;
2. methods or techniques employed;
3. qualifications of estimator(s);
4. time and effort available and justified by the importance of the study; and
5. sensitivity of study results to the particular estimate.

Types of Estimates

A cost estimate for a project can vary from an instant, top-of-the-head, guess to a detailed estimate prepared from complete drawings and specifications with accuracy depending on how much is known about the project and how much time and effort are spent on the preparation of the estimate.

The American Association of Cost Engineers has proposed five classifications of estimating types:

1. order-of-magnitude (ratio estimate);
2. study (factored estimate);
3. preliminary (budget authorization estimate);
4. definitive (project control estimate); and
5. detailed (firm estimate).

Estimates can also be classified according to probable accuracy such as $\pm 5\%$, $\pm 20\%$, etc.

Figure 9-1 depicts hypothetical curves showing relationships between cost of estimate, probable deviation (actual minus estimated as percent of estimated), and contingencies for various classes of estimates. These seven classes of estimates are arbitrary as given by an ASTME publication.*

Sources of Data

The variety of sources from which information can be obtained is too great for complete enumeration. The following five major sources, which are ordered roughly according to decreasing importance, are described in subsequent sections:

1. accounting records;
2. other sources within the firm;

*ASTME (American Society of Tool and Manufacturing Engineers), *Manufacturing Planning and Estimating Handbook*, New York: McGraw-Hill, 1963, Chapter 3.

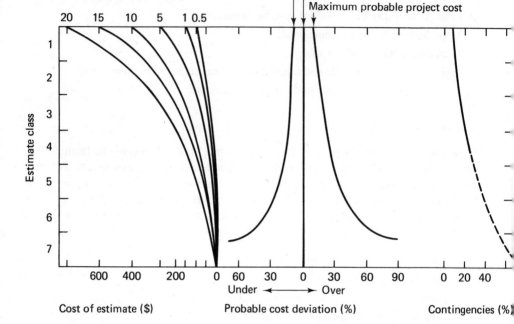

Figure 9-1. Hypothetical curves depicting cost of estimate, probable cost
deviation, and a contingency factor. Reproduced by permis-
sion of ASTME (American Society of Tool and Manufacturing Engineers), *Manufacturing, Planning and Estimating
Handbook*, New York: McGraw-Hill, 1963, Chapter 3.

3. sources outside the firm;
4. research and development.

Accounting Records

It should be emphasized that although data available from the records
of the accounting function are a prime source of information for economic
analyses, these data are very often not suitable for direct, unadjusted use.

A very brief and oversimplified description of the accounting process
was contained in Appendix 1-A. In its most basic sense, accounting consists
of a series of procedures for keeping a detailed record of monetary transactions between established categories of assets, each of which has an accepted
interpretation useful for its own purposes. The data generated by the accounting function are often inherently misleading for economic analyses, not only
because they are based on past results, but also because of the following
limitations.

First, the accounting system is rigidly categorized. These categories for a given firm may be perfectly appropriate for operating decisions and financial summaries, but rarely are they fully appropriate to the needs of economic analyses for longer-term decisions.

Example:

Consider the XYZ Corporation, which experienced certain 19X1 actual overhead costs and has certain 19X2 projected overhead costs as shown in Table 9-4.

Table 9-4

OVERHEAD COSTS FOR XYZ CORPORATION

Type	19X1 actual	19X2 projected
Indirect labor	$40,000	$54,000
Indirect material	30,000	26,000
Supervision	30,000	33,000
Maintenance	20,000	22,000
Depreciation	50,000	50,000
Interest on debt	10,000	15,000
Total:	$180,000	$200,000

To continue the example, the XYZ Corporation allocates its overhead costs to individual projects on the basis of direct labor dollars. For 19X1, the actual direct labor dollars expended was $360,000, which means that the correct "after-the-fact" rate would be $180,000/$360,000, or $0.50 per dollar labor cost. For 19X2, the projected number of direct labor dollars is $500,000. This means that the overhead rate for 19X2 should be $200,000/$500,000, or $0.40 per dollar of direct labor cost. Suppose that a prospective job requires $10,000 of direct labor by the machine generally used, but only $6,000 by a proposed new machine, and it is desired to determine the change in overhead costs due to the proposed change in 19X2.

Solution:

Using the overhead rate directly, the traditionally used machine would show an overhead cost of $10,000 × 0.40, or $4,000, while the new machine would show an overhead cost of $6,000 × 0.40, or $2,400, for the job. Thus, the change in machine will supposedly reduce overhead costs by $1,600. This amount is probably in marked error, for a decrease in direct labor cost due to change in machine will not necessarily result in a corresponding decrease in actual overhead costs for the job. To emphasize this point, it should be recognized that the overhead rate is merely a paper allocation of costs on an average basis for accounting purposes.

The correct approach to estimation of overhead costs in the above situation is to examine how the individual cost types included in the total overhead cost are expected to be affected by the proposed change in machines. Let us assume that the change in machine used is not expected to change the costs of supervision, depreciation, and interest on debt, while it is expected to increase actual expenditure for indirect labor by $600, decrease actual expenditure for indirect material by $200, and increase actual maintenance expenditure by $600. Hence, the change in methods is expected to increase true overhead costs by $1,000 rather than decrease those costs by $1,600, as calculated by straight application of the overhead rate.

Another limitation of accounting data for obtaining estimates is the misstatements imbedded by convention into accounting practice. These underestimates are based philosophically on the idea that management should avoid overstating the value of its assets and should therefore assess them very conservatively. This leads to such practices as not changing the stated value of one's resources as they appreciate due to rising market prices and depreciating assets over a much shorter life than actually expected. As a result of such accounting customs, the analyst should always be careful about treating such resources as cheaply (or, sometimes, as expensively!) as they might be represented.

The final limitations of accounting data are its illusory precision and implied authoritativeness. Although it is usual to present data to the nearest dollar or the nearest cent, the records are not nearly that accurate in general.

In summary, accounting records are a good source of historical data, but they have severe limitations when used in making estimates for economic analyses. Further, accounting records rarely directly contain the marginal costs, especially opportunity costs, appropriate for economic analyses.

Other Sources Within the Firm

The usual firm has a large number of people and records which may be excellent sources of estimates or information from which estimates can be made. Colleagues, supervisors, and workers can provide insights or suggest sources that can be obtained readily.

Examples of records which exist in most firms are sales, production, inventory, quality, purchasing, industrial engineering, and personnel. Table 9-5 provides a list of the types of data which might be needed for cost-estimating purposes together with typical sources (mostly intrafirm) for the data.

Sources Outside the Firm

There are innumerable sources outside the firm that can provide information helpful for estimating. The main problem is to determine which sources are most fruitful potentially for particular needs.

Published information such as technical directories, trade journals, U.S.

Table 9-5

Types and Sources of Cost Estimating Data*

Description of data	Sources
General design specifications	Product engineering and/or sales department
Quantity and rate of production	Request for estimate or sales department
Assembly or layout drawings	Product engineering or sales department or customer's contact man
General tooling plans and list of proposed subassemblies of product	Product engineering or manufacturing engineering
Detail drawings and bill of material	Product engineering or sales department
Test and inspection procedures and equipment	Quality control or product engineering or sales department
Machine tool and equipment requirements	Manufacturing engineering or vendors of materials
Packaging and/or transportation requirements	Sales department or shipping department or product engineering (government specifications)
Manufacturing routings and operation sheets	Manufacturing engineering or methods engineering
Detail tool, gage, machine, and equipment requirements	Manufacturing engineering or material vendors
Operation analysis and workplace studies	Methods engineering
Standard time data	Special charts, tables, time studies, and technical books and magazines
Material release data	Manufacturing engineering and/or purchasing department or materials vendors
Subcontractor cost and delivery data	Manufacturing engineering and/or purchasing department or customer
Area and building requirements	Manufacturing engineering or plant layout or plant engineer
Historical records of previous cost estimates (for comparison purposes, etc.)	Manufacturing engineering or cost department or sales department
Current costs of items presently in production	Cost department or treasurer or comptroller

*Reproduced by permission of ASTME, *Manufacturing Planning and Estimating Handbook*, New York: McGraw-Hill, 1963, pp. 3–20.

government publications, and comprehensive reference books offer a wealth of information to the knowledgeable or persistent searcher.

Personal contacts are excellent potential sources. Vendors, salesmen, professional acquaintances, customers, banks, government agencies, chambers of commerce, and even competitors are often willing to furnish needed information if the request is serious and tactful.

Probably the most valuable estimating sources outside the firm, which are available and updated continuously, are cost indexes. Cost indexes provide a means for converting past costs to present costs through the use of dimensionless numbers, called *indexes*, to reflect relative costs for two or more points in time.

There are many cost indexes and they cover almost every area of interest. Some are based on national averages; others are very specialized. Indicative values for several frequently-used indexes are shown in Table 9-6.

Table 9-6

Some Major Cost Indexes*

	Engineering News-Record		U.S. Dept. of Commerce	U.S. Dept. of Labor	
	Construction	Building	Composite construction cost	Avg. mfg. wage for nonsupervisory workers	
Year	1913 = 100		1967 = 100	$/hr	1967 = 100
1960	824	559	83	$2.26	80
1961	847	568	84	2.32	83
1962	872	580	86	2.39	85
1963	901	594	88	2.46	87
1964	936	612	90	2.53	89
1965	971	627	93	2.61	90
1966	1019	650	96	2.72	96
1967	1070	672	100	2.83	100
1968	1155	721	106	3.01	106
1969	1269	790	114	3.19	113
1970	1386	836	121	3.36	119
1971	1581	948	130	3.57	126
1972	1753	1048	139	3.81	135
1973	1895	1138	152	4.07	144
1974	2020	1204	173	4.40	155

*See *Engineering News-Record*, periodic issues, for descriptions of a number of indexes.

The Bureau of Labor Statistics of the Department of Labor publishes much data on price changes of many types of products and earnings of workers in almost every industry. Some of these data are components of many cost indexes, and others are useful in constructing highly specialized indexes.

Cost indexes are limited in their accuracy and, like all statistical devices, must be used with caution. Most indexes are based on data combined in more or less arbitrary fashion. A cost index, like cost data themselves, normally will reflect only average changes, and an average often has little meaning when applied to a specific case. Under favorable conditions a $\pm 10\%$

accuracy is the most that can be expected in projecting a cost index over a 4-or 5-year period.

Research and Development

If the information is not published and cannot be obtained by consulting someone who knows, the only alternative may be to undertake R&D to generate it. Classic examples are developing a pilot plant and undertaking a test market program. These activities are usually expensive and may not always be successful; thus, this final step is taken only when there are very important decisions to be made and when the sources mentioned above are known to be inadequate.

Ways Estimates Are Accomplished

Estimates can be done by:

1. A *conference* of various people who are thought to or have good information or bases for estimating the quantity in question. A special version of this is the Delphi method which is described subsequently.
2. *Comparison* with similar circumstances or designs which can include formal logic.
3. *Detailed* analysis, using itemized quantitative breakdowns and statistical means as possible. Some of these will be described in later sections.

The Delphi Method of Estimating

The Delphi method is a relatively new technique for the use of a group of persons to make estimates which are of substantial importance, and for which each of the estimators is thought to have some reasonable basis of judgment. It attempts to improve the panel or committee approach in arriving at a forecast or estimate by subjecting the views of individuals to each other's criticism in ways that avoid face-to-face confrontation and provide anonymity of opinions and of arguments in defense of those opinions. Direct debate is generally replaced by the interchange of information and opinion through a carefully designed sequence of questionnaires. The participants are asked to give their opinions and the reasons for their opinions, and at each successive interrogation they are given new and refined information, in the form of opinion feedback, which is derived from a computed consensus. The process continues through successive iterations until further progress toward a consensus appears to be of questionable value in view of the worth of further accuracy of the estimate.

To illustrate this technique, suppose that, say, sales of a new product are critical to the success of a proposed investment project. Further, there are nine persons whose judgments are thought to be approximately equally valid for this critical estimate. Each of these persons is asked to estimate this, and the results on a quantity interval scale are shown as $S_1, S_2, S_3, S_4, S_5, S_6, S_7, S_8, S_9$ in Fig. 9-2. Once these results are known, the median, upper quartile, and lower quartile can be calculated and the results shown as $Q_l, M,$ and Q_u in Fig. 9-2(a).

(a) First round estimates

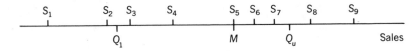

(b) Second round estimates

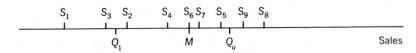

Figure 9-2. Illustration of Delphi method.

The values of $Q_l, M,$ and Q_u should then be communicated to each estimator and each should be asked to reconsider his previous estimate and, if his new estimate lies outside the interquartile range between Q_l and Q_u, to state briefly the reason why, in his opinion, the answer should be lower (or higher) than corresponds to the 75% majority opinion expressed in the first round.

The results of this second round of estimates as depicted in Fig. 9-2(b) (and which will usually be less dispersed than the first round) are again fed back to each estimator in summary form, including the new quartiles and median. In addition, the reasons for raising or lowering the values, elicited in the second round, are given to the estimators in edited form while still preserving the anonymity of the individual estimators. Now the estimators are asked to revise individually their estimates after considering and weighting the reasoning of the others. Moreover, if any revised estimate falls outside the second round's interquartile range, the estimator in question is asked to state briefly why the arguments that might have drawn his estimate toward the median were unconvincing. These revised estimates constitute the third round.

The above process can be continued for as many additional rounds as thought worthwhile. The median (or perhaps computed mean) of the final round can then be taken as the estimated quantity (sales), and the remaining dispersion around this value is generally a conservative indication of the risk involved.

Quantitative Techniques

The quantitative techniques described below do not have unique names, but the names given are suggestive of the approaches.

Unit Technique

The *unit technique* involves using an assumed or estimated per unit factor which can be estimated effectively. Examples are:

Capital cost of plant per kilowatt of capacity

Fuel cost per kilowatt-hour generated

Capital cost per installed phone

Revenue per long-distance call

Operating cost per mile

Maintenance cost per day of use

When multiplied by the appropriate unit, such factors give a total estimate.
There are limitless possibilities for breaking quantities to be estimated into units that can be estimated readily. Examples are:

(a) In different units
   (Example: $/week instead of $/year)

(b) A proportion instead of a number
   (Example: Percent defective, to convert to number of defects)

(c) A number instead of a proportion
   (Example: Number defective and number produced, to convert to percent defective)

(d) A rate instead of a number
   (Example: Miles per gallon, to convert to gallons consumed)

(e) A number instead of a rate
   (Example: Miles and hours traveled, to convert to average speed)

(f) Using an adjustment factor to increase or decrease a known or estimated number
   (Example: Defectives reported, to convert to total defectives)

As a simple example, suppose we need a preliminary estimate of the cost of a particular house. Using a unit factor of, say, $25/sq ft and knowing that the house is approximately 1,500 sq ft, we find that the estimated cost would be $25 \times 1,500 = $37,500.

Although the unit technique is very useful for preliminary estimating purposes, one can be dangerously misled by such average values. In general, more detailed methods can be expected to result in greater accuracy.

Segmenting Technique

The *segmenting technique* involves decomposing an uncertain quantity into parts that can be separately estimated and then added together. As an example, suppose we wish to estimate the sales of product X in the Carolinas. The simplest possible segmenting would be to estimate sales separately in North Carolina and in South Carolina and then to add the two together.

Factor Technique

The *factor technique* is an extension of the unit method and the segmenting method in which one sums the product of several quantities or components and adds these to any components estimated directly. That is,

$$C = \sum C_e + \sum_i f_i \times U_i \qquad 9\text{-}6$$

where C = Value (cost, price, etc.) being estimated
C_e = Cost of selected components estimated directly
f_i = Cost per unit of component i
U_i = Number of units of component i

Example:
Suppose we need a slightly refined estimate of the cost of a house consisting of 1,500 sq ft, two porches, and a garage. Using unit factors of $22/sq ft, $2,000/porch, and $3,000/garage, we can calculate the estimate as

$$\$22 \times 1,500 + \$2,000 \times 2 + \$3,000 = \$40,000$$

Power-Sizing Technique

The *power-sizing technique* is a sophistication of the unit method and is frequently used for costing equipment and plant in which it is recognized that cost varies as some power of the change in capacity or size. That is,

$$(C_A \div C_B) = (S_A \div S_B)^X \qquad 9\text{-}7$$

where C_A = Cost for plant A ⎱ (Both in R$ or A$ at point in time for
C_B = Cost for plant B ⎰ which estimate is desired.)
S_A = Size of plant A ⎱
S_B = Size of plant B ⎰ (Both in same physical units)
X = Cost-capacity factor to reflect economies of scale*

Example:
Suppose it is desired to make a preliminary estimate of the cost of a 350-mW fossil power plant if built now. It is known that a 100-mW plant cost $22 million in 1960 when the appropriate cost index was 800 and that today the

---

*May be calculated/estimated from experience. See p. 137 of Park, W.R., *Cost Engineering Analysis* (New York: Wiley), 1973, for typical factors. For example $X = 0.68$ for nuclear generating plants and 0.79 for fossil steam generating plants.

cost index is 1200. The power-sizing model estimate, with $X = 0.79$, is as follows:

Cost now of 100-mW plant: $22 million $\times$ (1.200 $\div$ 800) = $33 million
   (Call it C_B)
Cost now of 350-mW plant: $C_A \div$ $33 million = (350 $\div$ 100)$^{0.79}$
   (Call it C_A)

$$C_A = \$88.8 \text{ million}$$

Statistical and Mathematical Modeling Techniques

There are numerous statistical and mathematical modeling techniques that can be used for estimating or forecasting the future. Typical of the mathematical modeling techniques that allow one to decompose difficult problems in order to make estimates more knowledgeable and/or reliable; but that will not be described herein; are econometric models, demographic (population characteristic) models, network scheduling models, stochastic process models, mathematical programming models, and Monte Carlo simulation models. Two of the most common techniques, regression and correlation analysis and exponential smoothing, are described below.

Regression and Correlation analysis. Sometimes it is possible to correlate an element, such as revenue for a firm, with one or more economic indices, such as construction contracts awarded, disposable personal income, the Federal Reserve Board Index of Industrial Production, etc. When an index can be found to which an element to be estimated is highly correlated, but with a time lag, formal correlation techniques may be highly useful. In cases where the lag is insufficient for longer-term forecast requirements, correlation of an element to be estimated with the available index still leaves the forecaster with the need to predict or obtain a prediction of future value(s) of the index itself.

As an example, suppose that comparison of Norcar Company sales with many economic indicators shows that sales correlate best with, say, the state's construction volume committed. The nature of the correlation is shown in Table 9-7.

Table 9-7

NORCAR COMPANY SALES AND
CONSTRUCTION VOLUME COMMITTED

Year	Sales ($ million)	Construction volume committed ($ million)
1965	3	40
1966	2	25
1967	5	50
1968	4	45

The volume of sales as a function of the construction volume committed (together with the regression line to be calculated later) is shown in the scatter diagram of Fig. 9-3. Let us assume that a linear regression is thought to express the correlation adequately. A least-squares linear regression line can be fitted to the data to find the equation of the relationship in the general form $Y = a + bX$. Calculations to find a and b can be made by solving the following normal equations:

$$\sum Y = Na + b \sum X \qquad\qquad 9\text{-}8$$

and

$$\sum XY = a \sum X + b \sum X^2 \qquad\qquad 9\text{-}9$$

where N is the number of data points. These equations can be solved to find

$$b = \frac{\sum XY}{\sum X^2} \qquad\qquad 9\text{-}10$$

and

$$a = \frac{\sum Y}{N} - b \frac{\sum X}{N} \qquad\qquad 9\text{-}11$$

The calculations of $\sum Y, \sum X, \sum X^2, \sum Y^2$, and $\sum XY$ are performed in Table 9-8.

Table 9-8

CALCULATIONS FOR LINEAR LEAST-SQUARES REGRESSION—NORCAR COMPANY

Y Sales ($ million)	X Construction volume committed ($ million)	X²	Y²	XY
3	40	1,600	9	120
2	25	625	4	50
5	50	2,500	25	250
4	45	2,025	16	180
$\sum Y = 14$	$\sum X = 160$	$\sum X^2 = 6,750$	$\sum Y^2 = 54$	$\sum XY = 600$

Thus, the solution for the coefficients b and a are:

From Eq. 9, $\qquad b = \dfrac{600}{6,750} = 0.0888$

From Eq. 9, $\qquad a = \dfrac{14}{4} - 0.0888 \left(\dfrac{160}{4}\right) = -0.05$

Thus, the linear relationship is

Sales $= -\$0.05$ million $+ 0.0888$ (Construction volume in $ million)

The line showing this relationship is drawn in Figure 9-4.

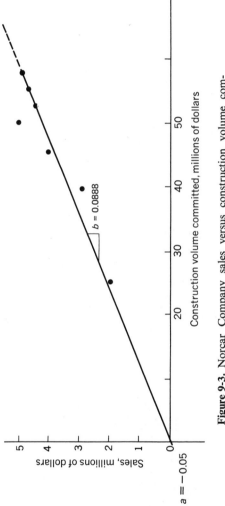

Figure 9-3. Norcar Company sales versus construction volume committed (with least squares regression line shown).

215

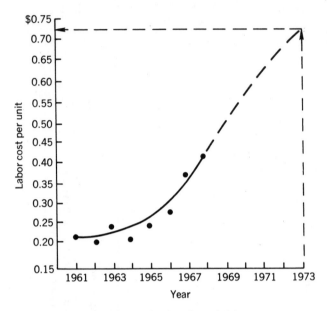

Figure 9-4. Time series data for unit labor cost.

A standard quantitative measure of the "goodness of fit" of a linear regression is called the *coefficient of correlation*. If the absolute value of the coefficient of correlation is 1, this means there is perfect correlation between the dependent and independent variables; while if it is 0, this means no correlation exists; while any absolute value between 1 and 0 gives a measure of relative correlation or lack of it. The coefficient of correlation p for this two-variable case can be most readily calculated from Eq. (9-12).

$$p = \frac{N \sum XY - (\sum X)(\sum Y)}{\sqrt{N \sum X^2 - (\sum X)^2}\sqrt{N \sum Y^2 - (\sum Y)^2}}$$

$$= \frac{4(600) - (160)(14)}{\sqrt{4(6,750) - (160)^2}\sqrt{4(54) - (14)^2}} = 0.981$$

9-12

Thus, a good degree of correlation is indicated.

Correlation analysis should be applied with good judgment, particularly with respect to whether the correlation exhibited in the past can be reasonably expected to continue on the basis of future conditions.

To conclude this section on estimation by correlation analysis, let us consider the topic of extrapolation, which is the process of estimating by projecting outside the range of past data. Extrapolation forecasts can be made by either graphical or mathematical methods. Further, extrapolation can be made for an element correlated to some index or for an element which exhibits a trend over a time series.

As an example of a mathematical linear extrapolation for an element correlated to an index, consider the Norcar Company case above in which the linear regression of Sales, (Y) as a function of construction volume committed, (X) was found to be $Y = -\$0.05$ million $+ 0.0888X$, based on data for the construction volume committed index ranging from \$25 million to \$50 million. Suppose that it is desired to obtain a linear projection of sales for a construction volume committed index of \$70 million. This is easily calculated as

$$Y = -\$0.05 \text{ million} + 0.0888 (\$70 \text{ million}) = \$6.17 \text{ million}$$

As an example of a graphical and nonlinear extrapolation of time series data (i.e., data arranged according to time order), consider the labor cost data in Fig. 9-4. The data show a pronounced increase in unit labor cost over time; indeed, the trend seems to be at a greater rate than a linear increase. Suppose it is desired to obtain an estimate of the unit labor cost in, say, 1983. A possible graphical nonlinear extrapolation which results in an estimate of approximately \$0.72 is shown in Fig. 9-4.

Time series extrapolations are valid only if nonrecurring distortions have been removed from the data. Also, unless the forces which caused the underlying patterns continue into the future unchanged, supplementary analyses of causative factors and sound judgment should be applied to adjust extrapolations for changes which are expected to occur.

Exponential smoothing. It is often the case that more recent data are more relevant to estimates for a given element than are older data, and that the more recent data should receive greater weight. There are many mathematical methods of accomplishing this. One common technique of forecasting with time series data is called exponential smoothing.

The exponential smoothing model gives an estimate of the expected element outcome, $\bar{X}$, as

$$\bar{X} = CX_0 + C(1 - C)X_1 + C(1 - C)^2 X_2 + \cdots + C(1 - C)^n X_n + \cdots$$

$$9\text{-}13$$

where $X_0 =$ Actual outcome for the most recent time period
$X_1 =$ Actual outcome in the first preceding time period
$X_2 =$ Actual outcome in the second preceding time period, etc.
$C =$ Weighting constant, between 0 and 1

The above expression can be reduced for computational simplicity to

$$\bar{X} = CX_0 + (1 - C)\bar{X}_1 \qquad 9\text{-}14$$

where $\bar{X}_1$ is the estimate made at the end of the first preceding period (which applied to the most recent time period).

This means that to obtain a new estimate of the expected outcome, we multiply the estimate for the most recent time period by $(1 - C)$ and add to it the actual outcome during the most recent time period multiplied by C.

As an example, suppose that the cost of an item for last year was estimated to be $600,000 and actually turned out to be $700,000. The estimate for the next year using the exponential smoothing model is $\bar{X} = C(\$700,000) + (1 - C)(\$600,000)$ where C is a subjectively determined weighting constant between 0 and 1.

A great advantage of this technique of forecasting is its flexibility of weighting. If the weighting constant C is 1, the mathematical model reduces to using the most recent period's outcome as the forecast. If C is very close to 0, this is essentially equivalent to using an arithmetic average of actual outcome over a large number of previous periods as the best estimate of the future outcome. Intermediate choices for C between 0 and 1 provide forecasts which have more or less emphasis on long-run average outcomes versus current outcomes.

Triangulation Technique

The *triangulation technique* involves estimating a given quantity by two or more independent methods or techniques, each of which can be subjective or quantitative. This results in two or more estimates that can be compared against each other for reasonableness. A final estimate can then be selected arbitrarily or by some averaging means.

As an example without numbers, real estate appraisers often use two or three of the following methods to aid in estimating the selling price or value of real estate:

1. comparables—what somewhat similar property sold for, adjusted for when it sold;

2. new cost minus depreciation;

3. capitalized value of income potential (such as a multiple of annual net rent).

Having the above three estimates, the appraiser can then take an average and/or make intuitive adjustments to arrive at a final estimate.

PROBLEMS

9-1. Your firm is considering replacing its conventional trucks with turbine-powered vehicles. What information would you like to have in studying the decision? Where would you expect to get the information?

9-2. How would you obtain information needed to study the economics of the following?

a. Leasing vs. purchasing a computer system
b. Maintaining equipment with in-house personnel or purchased services
c. Keeping versus replacing an old machine system
d. Coal-fired steam versus gas turbine generation plant

9-3. Use the conference method or the Delphi method to estimate the following:
   a. The ticket price for a 5,000-mile SST one-way trip.
   b. The cost of a year's college education in a state-supported university in 1985.
   c. The time to dig a trench $2' \times 4' \times 10'$ in soft clay using hand tools.
   d. The average annual growth rate for a particular utility service over the next 10 years.
   e. The price of premium gasoline in 1985.
   f. The average length of time required to change an automobile tire.
   g. The percentage of football (or other) games to be won next year by the team of your choice.

9-4. A certain size plant cost $10,000,000 in 1970. Of this $500,000 was for land, $2,000,000 was for building, and the rest was for equipment. Estimate the cost of a similar plant built in 1990 if land then is expected to cost $1,200,000 and the appropriate cost indexes are as follows:

	1970	1990
Building	110	220
Equipment	90	135

9-5. Estimate the salary you hope to be making 10 years from now expressed in equivalent dollars of purchasing power right now. If the average inflation rate over the 10-year period is expected to be 8% compounded annually, what is the equivalent hoped-for salary expressed in actual dollars 10 years from now?

9-6. The "actual" (then-current) costs for a utility service are expected to be as follows:

End of year	"Actual" costs
1980	$10,000
1981	10,000
1982	12,000

Assume that the average inflation rate is 8%/yr and that the real interest on money is 4%/yr, so the combined interest rate can be approximated as 12%.
   a. Find the equivalent worth of the sum of all costs as of the end of 1980.
   b. Express each of the three costs in "real dollars" of purchasing power as of the end of 1980.

    c. Using the results of (b), find the equivalent worth of the sum of all costs as of the end of 1980. How should this answer compare to the answer to (a)?

9-7. A firm desires to determine the most economic equipment overhauling schedule alternative to provide for service for the next 9 years of operation. The firm's real minimum attractive rate of return is 8% and the inflation rate is estimated at 7%. The following are alternatives with all costs expressed in real (constant worth) dollars.
    a. Completely overhaul for $10,000 now.
    b. A major overhaul for $7,000 now that can be expected to provide 6 years of service and then a minor overhaul costing $5,000 at the end of 6 years.
    c. A minor overhaul costing $5,000 now and at the end of 3 years and 6 years from now.

9-8. A woman bought a 6% tax-free municipal bond. It cost $1,000 and will pay $60 interest each year for 10 years. The bond will mature at the end of 10 years and will return $1,000 to the woman. If there is a 4% annual inflation rate during this period, what real rate of return will the woman receive after considering the effect of inflation?

9-9. Joe Futile wishes to set aside money for his son's college education. His goal is to have a bank savings account containing an amount equivalent to $10,000 of today's purchasing power at the time of his son's eighteenth birthday. The estimated inflation rate is 7% per year. If the bank pays 5% compounded annually, what lump sum of money should Joe deposit in the bank account on his son's fourth birthday?

9-10. Two alternative water supply schemes are being examined. Scheme A costs $250,000 to construct and $8,000 a year to operate. Scheme B costs $150,000 to construct and $15,000 a year to operate. The economic lives of both schemes are 20 years and the salvage values are nil. Finance is by loan money at 8%. Using annual cost comparisons, show which scheme should be adopted if:
    a. All estimates are in terms of "actual" dollars.
    b. All estimates are in terms of "real" dollars and the inflation rate is 5%.
    [*Note:* combined rate $\cong$ inflation rate + real rate.
    Thus, real rate $\cong$ combined rate − inflation rate.]

9-11. Rework Prob. 9-10 if only half of the finance comes from the loan at a fixed 5% rate of interest and the other half comes from equity capital which requires a minimum return of 20% on inflated (actual) currency.

9-12. Operation and maintenance costs for alternatives A and B are estimated on different bases as follows:

Year in which cost incurred	Alternative A in "Actual $"	Alternative B in time 0 "Real $"
1	$110,000	$100,000
2	112,000	100,000
3	114,000	100,000
4	116,000	100,000

If the average inflation rate is 10%/yr and the real interest on money is 5%/yr, show which alternative has the lower equivalent (a) present worth of costs at time 0 and (b) future worth of costs at time 4.

9-13. a. The ENR index for construction costs was 824 for 1960 and 2,020 for 1974. What was the average annual percent increase for the 14 years?

b. Suppose a project which cost $1,000,000 in 1968 is to be built next year, at which time the ENR index is expected to be, say, 3,200. What would be the estimated cost of construction next year?

9-14. A 60-kilowatt diesel electric set, without a precompressor, cost $32,000 in 1974. A similar design, but using 140 kilowatts, is planned for an isolated installation. The cost-capacity factor $X = 0.7$, and the cost index in 1974 was 230. Now the cost index is 350. A precompressor is estimated separately at $1,900 now. Using the power-sizing model, find the estimated total equipment cost now.

9-15. A small plant has been constructed and the costs are known. A new plant is to be estimated using the power-sizing model. Major equipment, costs, and factors are as follows:

Equipment	Reference size	Unit reference cost	Cost-capacity factor	New design size
Two boilers	6 mW	$300,000	0.80	10 mW
Two generators	6 mW	400,000	0.60	9 mW
Tank	80,000 gal	106,000	0.66	91,500 gal

If ancillary equipment for this anticipated line will cost $200,000, find the cost for the proposed plant.

9-16. A firm that manufactures totally enclosed electric motors has known costs on $\frac{1}{4}$, $\frac{1}{3}$, $\frac{3}{4}$, and 1-horsepower sizes of $22.50, $25.00, $29.50, and $35.00, respectively for the 1,725 rpm type. A 3,450 rpm 1-horsepower motor costs $31.50. Estimate the cost for a $1\frac{1}{2}$-horsepower, 1,725-rpm motor using your best judgment.

9-17. Your company is now making a product that has a raw material cost of exactly $0.53 per unit out of a total cost of $1.63 per unit. You are responsible for an analysis of the economics of tripling the present capacity. Should you automatically assume that the raw materials cost for the added capacity will be $0.53 per pound? Why or why not?

9-18. A rule of thumb sometimes used is that when a unit is being operated at 50% capacity the maintenance costs will be approximately 75% of the maintenance costs at 100% capacity.

a. Why would the maintenance costs not be 50% of the maintenance costs at 100% capacity.

b. Is it reasonable that maintenance costs at 120% of capacity could be less than 120% of the maintenance costs at 100% capacity? More than 120%? What might cause the difference?

9-19. The following is an exercise to illustrate the use of various weighting constants for exponential smoothing forecasting. Suppose the actual sales of a firm were 500 units for year 1 and 600 for year 2. You forecasted it would be 550 units for year 2 and now you wish to forecast for year 3 and beyond.

a. What would be your forecast for year 3 if your smoothing constant, C, were, respectively, 0.1, 0.5, and 0.97?

b. Suppose actual sales turn out to be as follows:

Year	Actual sales
3	700
4	800
5	700
6	600
7	600

What would have been the forecast for each year (4, 5, 6, and 7) using each of the three smoothing constants?

c. Distinguish between the actual results and the forecast for each year using each of the three smoothing constants. What are your conclusions on the desirability and nondesirability of using a low value of C?

9-20. Total operating costs and the corresponding production volumes for a particular process has been found to be as follows:

Operating costs (M)	Production volume (hundreds of units)
800	10.0
1,000	11.0
700	9.0
600	8.5

a. Calculate the least-squares linear regression line to relate total operating costs as a function of production volume.

b. From the line in Prob. 10-3(a), estimate the operating costs for a production volume of 950 units.

c. Calculate the coefficient of correlation and comment on whether this indicates a relatively good or poor fit of the regression line to the data.

Chapter

10

capital planning and budgeting

Proper capital planning, budgeting, and management represent the basic top management function of an enterprise and are crucial to its welfare. *Capital budgeting* is commonly understood to be a function which takes place at the highest levels of management, such as office of the controller or corporate executive committee, but it should be recognized that decisions made at the lower levels in the management hierarchy directly affect those proposals which are ultimately considered as contenders in the overall capital budget. For example, before a major project is considered in top management's capital budget, usually many subalternatives of design and specification will have been considered and the related decisions virtually made as part of the recommended project package. Appropriate procedures for evaluation of these subalternatives should be available and uniformly applied to insure that economic consequences are considered at all levels.

Capital budgeting may be defined as the series of decisions by individual economic units as to how much and where resources will be obtained and expended for future use, particularly in the production of future goods and services. The scope of capital budgeting encompasses

1. how the money is acquired and from what sources;
2. how individual capital project opportunities (and combinations of opportunities) are identified and evaluated;
3. how minimum requirements of acceptability are set;
4. how final project selections are made; and
5. how postmortem reviews are conducted.

The above facets of capital budgeting are highly interrelated and will be discussed in turn below.

Sources of Funds

The determination of how much capital and from what sources should be applied toward project investments is a function of the individual project investment amount requirement; prospective profitability, type, and risk; the amount, conditions, and prices of funds to be obtained from internal or external sources; and the firm's financial policies and condition.

Most investment funds are obtained from internal sources: retained earnings and reinvested depreciation reserves. When outside sources are used, it can be to the disadvantage of the present owners to the extent that present ownership control is diluted, as in the case of new equity stock issuance; or to the extent that the company is burdened with new fixed monetary obligations and operating restrictions, as in the case of long-term borrowing. However, outside sources are often used when it is judged to be in the best interests of the existing stockholders.

In general, the more attractive the investment proposals available, the more the company will be willing to go to outside sources to obtain capital in order to take advantage of more investments. However, this has to be balanced against the cost of obtaining outside capital. The more outside capital the company obtains by borrowing, the higher the cost—in terms of both interest and risk—is likely to be.

Identification and Evaluation of Opportunities

Identification

All levels of the organization—operating, staff, supervisory, and engineering, as well as top management—should be encouraged to develop proposals for capital investment projects. For example, the research section may discover new products and processes. The engineering section may create improved designs in product, packaging, or methods. The manufacturing section may propose the installation of more efficient facilities. The marketing section may propose programs of advertising, sales, or inventory expansion for the development of new markets or expansion of existing ones. Finally, top management may, for example, develop plans for major acquisitions leading to integration or diversification.

The importance of identifying all opportunities reasonably worth consideration can hardly be overemphasized. It doesn't matter how thorough and accurate are the evaluations and final selection procedures of a firm; if a project(s) which would have been superior to others accepted is (are) never even considered, then the firm will have suboptimized. That is, the firm will have invested in the project(s) considered which is (are) best, but it will have given up the opportunity to have generated even greater benefits which could have been obtained had the limited capital been invested in that superior opportunity which ". . . might have been."

A dearth of good investment proposals within a firm indicates that the firm lacks a healthy climate for encouraging the search for investment opportunities. This climate should exist in order for the firm to create the best economic opportunities for itself. Indeed, the development of good investment proposals can even become a question of the firm's survival.

Evaluation

Evaluation of opportunities is undertaken to determine which of the opportunities is (are) best and, sometimes, also to determine whether the "best" is (are) good enough. This book has been concerned primarily with methods of evaluation on the basis of monetary criteria, supposedly leading to profit maximization or cost minimization. But it must be recognized again that the objectives of a firm are not necessarily solely, or even dominantly, based on monetary criteria. Some examples of firm objectives other than profit maximization or cost minimization are given in the first part of Chapter 19.

Minimum Requirements of Acceptability

The determination of the *minimum acceptable rate of return* (*M.A.R.R.*), sometimes also called *cost of capital*, for the project proposals of a firm is generally controversial and difficult. From a purely monetary viewpoint this minimum rate of return should be selected to maximize the economic well-being of present owners. The outward manifestation of this viewpoint is that an investment should be undertaken as long as the present value of the existing owners' equity in the firm is enhanced. Even with agreement on this, there are many viewpoints on just how the minimum rate of return should be determined. Several of these viewpoints will be discussed below.

An easy-to-compute method for determining what is alleged to be a "minimum rate of return" is to determine the rate of cost of each source of funds and to weight these by the proportion that each source constitutes of the total. For example, if one-third of a firm's capital is borrowed at 6% and the remainder of its capital is equity earning 12%, then the alleged minimum rate of return is $\frac{1}{3} \times 6\% + \frac{2}{3} \times 12\% = 10\%$.

Another school of thought maintains that if particular projects are to be undertaken using borrowed funds, then the minimum rate of return should be based on the rate of cost of those borrowed funds alone. Yet another school of thought, as exemplified by Solomon,* maintains that the minimum rate of return should be based on the cost of equity funds alone, on the grounds that firms tend to adjust their capitalization structure to the point at which the real costs of new debt and new equity capital are equal.

Great stimulation to thinking on the determination of the minimum rate of return or cost of capital was caused by Modigliani and Miller.† They developed a theory which essentially asserts that the average cost of capital to any firm is completely independent of its capital structure and is strictly the capitalization rate of future equity earnings. Since Modigliani and Miller's article, there have been many articles criticizing their contention on the grounds of oversimplification and unfounded postulation.‡ There has been no clearcut settlement of this issue, and the problem of determining the cost of capital is still one of open controversy in both theory and practice.

Another viewpoint on the determination of the minimum rate of return commonly overlooked and which we feel is most sound is the *opportunity cost* viewpoint; it comes as a direct result of the phenomenon of "capital rationing."

Capital rationing describes what is necessary when there is a limitation of funds relative to prospective proposals to use the funds. This limitation may be either internally or externally imposed. Its parameter is often expressed as a fixed sum of capital; but when the prospective returns from investment proposals together with the fixed sum of capital available to invest are known, then the parameter can be expressed as a minimum acceptable rate of return, or cut-off rate.

---

*Ezra Solomon, *The Management of Corporate Capital* (New York: The Free Press, 1959), p. 136.

†Franco Modigliani and Menton H. Miller, "The Cost of Capital, Corporation Finance, and the Theory of Investment," *American Economic Review* (June 1958), 261–297.

‡See principally D. Durand, "The Cost of Capital in an Imperfect Market: A Reply to Modigliani and Miller," *American Economic Review* (September 1959), 639–655.

Ideally, the cost of capital by the opportunity cost principle can be determined by ranking prospective projects according to a ladder of profitability and then establishing a cut-off point where the capital is used on the better projects. The rate of return earned by the last project before the cut-off point is the cost of capital or minimum rate of return by the opportunity cost principle.

To illustrate the above, Fig. 10-1 ranks projects according to prospective rate of return and the cumulative investment required. For purposes of illustration, the amount of capital shown available is $4 million. By connecting up (to the next whole project within the $4 million) and across, one can read the minimum rate of return under the conditions, which turns out to be 25%.

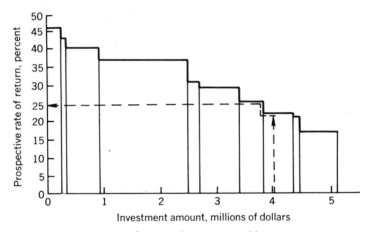

Figure 10-1. Schedule of prospective returns and investment amounts.

It is not uncommon for firms to set two or more M.A.R.R. levels according to risk categories. For example, one major industrial firm defines risk categories for income-producing projects and "normal" M.A.R.R. standards for each as follows:

1. *High Risk* (M.A.R.R. = 40%)
   New products
   New business
   Acquisitions
   Joint ventures
2. *Moderate Risk* (M.A.R.R. = 25%)
   Capacity increase to meet forecasted sales
3. *Low Risk* (M.A.R.R. = 15%)
   Cost improvements

Make versus buy
Capacity increase to meet existing orders

To illustrate how the above set of M.A.R.R. standards could be determined, the firm could rank prospective projects in each risk category according to prospective rates of return and investment amounts. After tentatively deciding how much investment capital should be allocated to each risk category, the firm could then determine the M.A.R.R. for each risk category as illustrated in Fig. 10-1 for a single category. Of course, the firm might reasonably shift its initial allocation of funds according to the opportunities available in each risk category, thereby affecting the M.A.R.R. for each category allocated more or less investment funds.

In principle, it would be desirable for a firm to invest additional capital as long as the return from that capital is greater than the cost of obtaining that capital. In such a case, the opportunity cost would equal the marginal cost (in interest and/or stockholder returns) of the last capital used. In practice, however, the amount of capital actually invested is more limited due to risk and conservative money policies; thus, the opportunity cost is higher than the marginal cost of the capital.

It is often reasonable to argue that since one cannot truly know the opportunity cost for capital in any given period (such as a budget year), it is useful to proceed as if the M.A.R.R. for the upcoming period were the same as in the previous period. In addition to the normal difficulty of projecting the profitability of future projects and the availability of capital, there also may be pressures to manipulate the standards of acceptability to permit the approval of favored, even if economically undesirable, projects or classes of projects.

Project Selection

To the extent that project proposals can be justified through profitability measures, the most common basis of selection is to choose those proposals which offer the highest prospective profitability subject to allowances for intangibles or nonmonetary considerations, risk considerations, and limitations on the availability of capital. If the minimum acceptable rate of return has been determined correctly, one can choose proposals according to the rate of return method, annual worth method, or present worth method.

For certain types of project proposals, monetary justification is not feasible—or at least any monetary return is of minor importance compared to intangible or nonmonetary considerations. These types of projects should require careful judgment and analysis, including how they fit in with long-range policies and plans. Factor weighting methods such as those in Chapter

19 are particularly suited to projects for which monetary justification is not feasible.

The capital budgeting concepts discussed in this chapter are based on the presumption that the projects under consideration are *not* mutually exclusive (i.e., the adoption of one does not preclude the adoption of others, except with regard to the availability of funds). Whenever projects are mutually exclusive, the alternative chosen should be based on justification through the incremental return on any incremental investment(s) as well as proper consideration of nonmonetary factors.

Classifying Investment Proposals

For purposes of study of investment proposals, there should be some system or systems of classification into logical, meaningful categories. Investment proposals have so many facets of objective, form, and competitive design that no one classification plan is adequate for all purposes. Several possible classification plans are given below:

1. according to the kinds and amounts of scarce resources used, such as equity capital, borrowed capital, available plant space, the time required of key personnel, etc.;

2. according to whether the investment is tactical or strategic: a *tactical investment* does not constitute a major departure from what the firm has been doing in the past and generally involves a relatively small amount of funds; *strategic investment* decisions, on the other hand, may result in a major departure from what a firm has done in the past and involve large sums of money;

3. according to the business activity involved, such as marketing, production, product line, warehousing, etc.;

4. according to priority, such as absolutely essential, necessary, economically desirable, or general improvement;

5. according to type of benefits expected to be received, such as increased profitability, reduced risk, community relations, employee benefits, etc.;

6. according to whether the investment involves facility replacement, facility expansion, or product improvement; or

7. according to the way benefits from the proposed project are affected by other proposed projects; this is generally a most important classification consideration, for there quite often exist interrelationships or dependencies between pairs or groups of investment projects.

Of course, all of the above classification systems probably are not needed or desirable. As an example, one major corporation uses the following four major categories for higher management screening:

1. expanded facilities;
2. research and development;
3. improved facilities—for process improvement, cost savings, or quality improvement; and
4. necessity—for service facilities, emergency replacements, or for the removal or avoidance of a hazard or nuisance.

Degrees of Dependency Between Projects

Several main categories of dependency between projects are briefly defined in Table 10-1. Actually, the possible degress of dependency between projects can be expressed as a continuum from "prerequisite" to "mutually exclusive," with the degrees "complement," "independent," and "substitute" between these extremes, as shown in Fig. 10-2.

Table 10-1

DEGREES OF DEPENDENCE BETWEEN PAIRS OF PROJECTS

"If the results of the first project would _____ by acceptance of second project . . .	. . . then the second project is said to be _____ _____ the first project."	Example
be technically possible or would result in benefits only	a prerequisite of	Car radio purchase feasible only with purchase of car
have increased benefits	a complement of	Additional hauling trucks more beneficial if automatic loader purchased
not be affected	independent of	A new engine lathe and a fence around the warehouse
have decreased benefits	a substitute for	A screw machine which would do part of work of a new lathe
be impossible or would result in no benefits	mutually exclusive with	A brick building or a wooden building for a given need

In developing a project proposal to be submitted for review and approval, the sponsor should include whatever complementary projects seem desirable as part of a single package. Also, if a proposed project will be a partial substitute for any projects to which the firm is already committed or which are under consideration, this fact should be noted in the proposal.

In cases where choices involved in planning a proposed project are considered sufficiently important so that the final decision should be made by higher levels of management, the project proposal should be submitted in

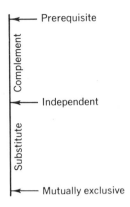

Figure 10-2. Continuum of degrees of dependence between pairs of projects.

the form of a set of mutually exclusive alternatives. For example, if it is to be decided whether to move a plant to a new location and several alternative sites are possible, then separate proposals should be made for each site so as to facilitate the choice of which site, if any, should be chosen.

Whenever capital budgeting decisions involve several groups of mutually exclusive projects and independent projects to be considered within capital availability constraints, mathematical programming models can be useful for selecting the optimal combination of projects. This is illustrated in Chapter 18.

Organization for Capital Planning and Budgeting

In most large organizations project selections are accomplished by sequential review through various levels of the organization. The levels required for approval should depend upon the nature and importance of the individual project, as well as the particular organizational makeup of the firm. In general, a mix of central control and coordination together with authority to make project commitments delegated to operating divisions is considered desirable. Three typical basic plans for delegating investment decisions are listed below.

1. Whenever proposals are clearly "good" in terms of economic desirability according to operating division analysis, the division is given the power to commit as long as appropriate controls can be maintained over the total amount invested by each division and as long as the division analyses are considered reliable.

2. Whenever projects represent the execution of policies already established by headquarters, such as routine replacements, the division is given the power to commit within the limits of appropriate controls.

3. Whenever a project requires a total commitment of more than a certain amount, this request is sent to higher levels within the organization. This is often coupled with a budget limitation regarding the maximum total investment which a division may undertake in a budget period.

To illustrate the concept of larger investments requiring higher administrative approval, the limitations for a particular firm might be as follows:

If the total investment is . . .		*then approval is required through*
more than	*but less than*	
$ 50	$ 1,000	Plant manager
1,000	10,000	Division vice-president
10,000	25,000	President
25,000	——	Board of directors

Communication

The importance of effective communication of capital investment proposals is often overlooked. No matter how great are the merits of a proposed project, if those merits are not communicated to the decision-maker(s) in understandable terms with emphasis on the proper matters, that proposal may well be rejected in favor of less desirable, though better communicated, proposals. Klausner* provides good insight into this problem with emphasis on the differing perspectives of engineers responsible for technical design and proposal preparation and management decision makers responsible for husbanding the firm's capital resources. The proposal preparer should be as aware as possible of the decision-maker's perspective and related informational needs. For example, in addition to basic information such as investment requirements and measures of merit and other expected benefits, the decision-maker may well want clearly presented answers to such questions as:

1. What bases and assumptions were used for estimates?
2. What level of confidence does the proposer have regarding these estimates?
3. How would the investment outcome be affected by variations in these estimated values?

If project proposals are to be transmitted from one organizational unit to another for review and approval, there must be effective means for communication. The means can vary from standard forms to personal appear-

*R. F. Klausner, "Communicating Investment Proposals to Corporate Decision Makers," *The Engineering Economist* (Fall 1971), p. 45.

ances. In communicating proposals to higher levels, it is desirable to use a format which is as standardized as possible to help assure uniformity and completeness of evaluation efforts. In general, the technical and marketing aspects of each proposal should be completely described in a format which is most appropriate to each individual case. However, the financial implications of all proposals should be summarized in a standardized manner so that they may be uniformly evaluated. An example of formats used in practice is given in Appendix 10-A.

Postmortem Review

The provision of a system for periodic postmortem reviews (post-audits) of the performance of consequential projects previously authorized is an important aspect of a capital budgeting system. That is, the earnings or costs actually realized on each such project undertaken should be compared with the corresponding quantities estimated at the time the project investment was committed.

This kind of feedback review serves at least three main purposes as follows:

1. It determines if planned objectives have been obtained.

2. It determines if corrective action is required.

3. It improves estimating and future planning.

Postmortem reviews should tend to reduce biases in favor of what individual divisions or units preparing project proposals see as their own interests. When divisions of a firm have to compete with each other for available capital funds, there is a tendency for them to evaluate their proposals optimistically. Estimating responsibilities can be expected to be taken more seriously when the estimators know that the results of their estimates will be checked. However, this checking function should not be overexercised, for there is a human tendency to become overly conservative in estimating when one fears severe accountability for unfavorable results.

It should be noted that a postmortem audit is inherently incomplete. That is, if only one of several alternative projects is selected, it can never be known exactly what would have happened if one of the other alternatives had been chosen. "What might have been if . . ." is at best conjecture, and all postmortem audits should be made with this reservation in proper perspective.

Figure 10-3 is an example summary form for showing actual versus estimated results for several projects together. Specially designed forms consisting of one or more pages may well be justified to provide greater detail for each major project post-audited.

RECAP OF INVESTMENTS AND SAVINGS
FOR SELECTED 1965 APB ECONOMY ITEMS
(Adjusted to 1967 Volume and Costs)

Project	Better Weighers	Improved Takeaway System	Dust Control	Direct Sugar Feed	Improved Baling	Relocate XYZ Station
Supporting Work Sheets	I	II	III	IV	V	VI
APB Number	65–13	65–3	64–30	65–6	65–9	64–5
P.O. Number	1101	1210	0904	1150	1304	1050
Investment Expenditure: 1st Q. 1965	$150	–	$1,100	–	–	–
2nd Q.	1,230	–	2,700	–	–	2,000
3rd Q.	2,310	$1,980	5,460	$3,480	–	2,700
4th Q.	650	3,720	4,320	2,970	–	5,000
1st Q. 1966	–	520	150	675	$400	67
2nd Q.	–	–	1,275	–	2,300	4
3rd Q.	–	–	–	1150	1,800	–
4th Q.	–	–	–	275	500	–
Total Expended	$4,340	$6,220	15,005	$8,550	$5,000	10,4
Amount Authorized	4,000	6,400	14,500	9,000	5,000	9,50
Under or (Over) Expended	($340)	$180	($505)	$450	–	($950
Annual Savings 1967 Basis	$3,570	$675	$3,000	$8,000	$1,500	$4,
Less Taxes and Insurance	70	100	225	130	75	16
Net Annual Savings	$3,500	$575	$2,785	$7,870	$1,425	$3,83
Original Estimated Savings	$2,400	$1,800	$2,500	$7,000	$1,400	$5,000
Principal Reason for Variance	Better than anti- cipated weights	Mechani- cal trouble with system	–	In- crease in produc- tion re- quire- ments	–	Sub- normal station perfor- mance

Figure 10-3. Example summary form for postmortem review. Reprinted from J. R. Frost, "The Industrial Engineer's Responsibility in the Control and Analyses of Capital Expenditure," *The Journal of Industrial Engineering* May 1968, by permission of the publisher.

Budget Periods

The approved capital budget is limited typically to a 1-or 2-year period or less, but this should be supplemented by a long-range capital plan with provision for continual review and change as new developments occur. The long-range plan (or plans) can be for a duration of from 2 years to 20 years, depending on the nature of the business and the desire of management to force preplanning.

Even when the technological and market factors in the business are so changeable that plans are no more than guesses to be continually revised, it is valuable to plan and budget as far ahead as possible. Planning should encourage the search for investment opportunities, provide a basis for adjusting other aspects of management of the firm as needed, and sharpen management's forecasting abilities. Long-range budget plans also provide a better basis for establishing minimum rate-of-return figures which properly take into account future investment opportunities.

Timing of Capital Investments and Management Perspective

An aspect of capital budgeting which is difficult and often important is deciding how much to invest now as opposed to later. If returns are expected to increase for future projects, it may be profitable to withhold funds from investment for some time. The loss of immediate return, of course, must be balanced against the anticipation of higher future returns.

In a similar vein, it may be advantageous to supplement funds available for present projects whenever returns for future projects are expected to become less than those for present projects. Funds for present investment can be supplemented by the reduction of liquid assets, the sale of other assets, and the use of borrowed funds.

The procedures and practices discussed in this chapter and book are intended to aid management in making sound investment decisions. Management's ability to sense the opportunities for growth and development and to time their investments to achieve optimum advantage is a primary ingredient of success for an organization.

Leasing Decisions

By the term *lease*, we normally are referring to the financial type of lease; that is, a lease in which the firm has a legal obligation to continue making payments for a well-defined period of time for which it has use, but not ownership, of the asset(s) leased. Many financial leases are very similar to debt and should be treated in essentially the same manner as debt. A significant proportion of assets in some firms is acquired by leasing, thus making the firm's capital available for other uses. Buildings, railroad cars, airplanes, production equipment, and business machines are examples of the wide array of facilities that may be leased.

Lease specifications are generally detailed in a formal written contact. The contract may contain such specifications as the amount and timing of rental payments; cancellability and sublease provisions, if any; subsequent purchase provisions; and lease renewability provisions.

Although the financial lease provides an important alternative source of capital, it carries with it certain subtle, but important, disadvantages. Its impact is similar to that of added debt capital. The acquisition of financial leases or debt capital will reduce the firm's ability to attract further debt capital and will increase the variability (leverage) in prospective earnings on equity (owner) capital. Higher leverage results in more fixed charges for debt interest and repayment, and thus will make good conditions even better and poor conditions even worse for the equity owners.

Confused reasoning may be introduced into economy studies in which calculations appropriate for justifying long-run economy of proposed investments in physical assets are combined with calculations related to the financing of those assets. It is recommended that analyses (and decisions) such as these be made separately, not mixed, whenever possible.

Figure 10-4 depicts the types of analyses which should be made for lease-related decisions and also shows what conclusion (final choice) should be made for various combinations of conditions (analysis outcomes). The "buy" versus "status quo" (do nothing) decision is to determine long-run economy or feasibility and is sometimes referred to as an *equipment* decision.

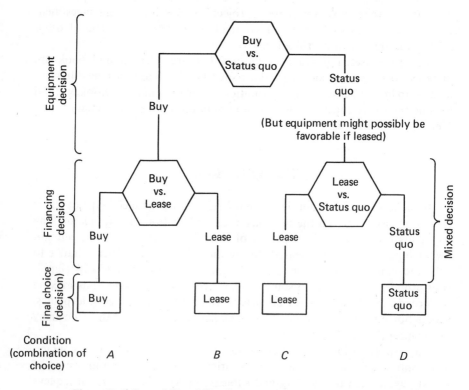

Figure 10-4. Separability of "Buy" vs. "Lease" vs. "Status Quo" decisions, and the choices which should result.

In general practice, only if this is investigated and "buy" is found to be preferable should one be concerned with the "buy" versus "lease" question, which is considered a financing decision. However, we cannot always separate the *equipment* and *financing* decisions. For example, if the *equipment* decision results in "status quo" being preferable and yet it is possible that the equipment might be favorable if leased, then we should compare "status quo" with "lease." This, by definition, is a *mixed* decision involving both *equipment* and *financing* considerations.

The main point one should retain from the above is that one should not merely compare "buy" versus "lease" alternatives; one should also compare, if possible, against the "status quo" alternative to determine if the asset is justified under any financing plan.

A major factor in evaluating the economics of leasing versus buying is the tax deductions (reductions in taxable income) allowable. In the case of leasing, one is allowed to deduct the full cost of normal financial lease payments. In the case of buying (ownership), only depreciation charges and interest payments, if any, are deductible. Of course, other disbursements for operating the property are tax deductible under either financing plan.

Example:

Suppose a firm is considering purchasing equipment for $200,000 which would last for 5 years and have zero salvage value. Alternatively, the same equipment could be leased for $52,000 at the *beginning* of each of those 5 years. The composite income tax rate for the firm is 55% and straight line depreciation is used. The net before-tax cash benefits from the equipment is $56,000 at the end of each year for 5 years. If the after-tax M.A.R.R. for the firm is 10%, using the present worth method show whether the firm should buy or lease or maintain the status quo.

Solution:

Alternative	Yr	Before-tax cash flow	Deprecia-tion	Taxable income	Income taxes @ 55%	After-tax cash flow
Buy	0	−$200,000				−$200,000
	1–5		−$40,000	−$40,000	+$22,000	+$ 22,000
Lease	0	−$ 52,000		−$52,000	+$28,600	−$ 23,400
	1–4	−$ 52,000		−$52,000	+$28,600	−$ 23,400
Status quo	1–5	−$ 56,000		−$56,000	−$30,800	−$ 25,200

Thus, the present worths for the three alternatives are:

Buy: −$200,000 + $22,000(P/A,10%,5) = −$116,600

Lease: −$ 23,400 − $23,400(P/A,10%,4) = −$ 97,600

Status quo: −$ 25,200(P/A,10%,5)   = −$ 95,500

If the sequence of analysis follows that in Fig. 10-4, we would first compare "buy" (P.W. = −$116,600) against "status quo" (P.W. = −$95,500) and find the status quo to be better. Then we would compare "lease" (P.W. = −$97,600) against "status quo" (P.W. = −$95,500) and find the "status quo" to be better. Thus, "status quo" is the better final choice. It should be noted that had we merely compared "buy" versus "lease", "lease" would have been the choice. But the final decision should not have been made without comparision against "status quo."

Another way the problem could have been solved would have been to include the +$56,000 before-tax cash benefits in with both the "buy" and the "lease" alternatives. Then the two alternatives being considered would have been "buy rather than status quo" (P.W. = −$116,600 + $95,500 = −$21,100) and "lease rather than status quo" (P.W. = −$97,600 + $95,500 = −$2,100). Of these alternatives, "lease rather than status quo" is the better, but "lease" is still not justified because of the negative P.W., indicating that the costs of "lease" are greater than the benefits.

Capital Expenditure Practices and Example of Forms for Analysis

There have been a number of extensive surveys of the capital expenditure practices used by mostly large industrial firms. The National Industrial Conference Board published a definitive work in 1963* which included good examples of procedures and forms used by a variety of firms. This was updated somewhat in 1974,† with emphasis on the methods used for evaluating prospective projects as well as the policies and procedures for screening and approval. The 1974 report also reflected a growing trend for firms to incorporate formal techniques for considering risk and uncertainty in project evaluation.

Petty, Scott, and Bird‡ reported on a thorough survey which obtained responses from over 100 of the 500 largest industrial firms in the United States. The following are some highlights:

A. The most important financial objectives were ranked (in decreasing order of importance) as follows:
(1) Target earnings per share growth rate.

*Norman E. Pflomm, *Managing Capital Expenditures*, National Industrial Conference Board Studies in Business Policy, No. 107.

†Patrick J. Davey, *Capital Investments: Appraisals and Limits*, The Conference Board, Report No. 641.

‡Petty, J. W., D. W. Scott, and M. M. Bird, "The Capital Expenditure Decision-Making Process of Large Corporations," *The Engineering Economist* (Spring 1975), p. 159.

(2) Maximize percent return on asset investment.

(3) Maximize aggregate dollar earnings.

(4) Maximize common stock price.

B. The most-used evaluation techniques were ranked as follows:

(1) Internal rate of return.

(2) Accounting return on investment $\left(= \dfrac{\text{accounting profit/yr}}{\text{book value of investment}}\right)$.

(3) Payback period.

(4) Net present value.

C. The most important qualitative (nonmonetary) factors affecting investment decisions were ranked as follows:

(1) Legal.

(2) Image with industry, investor, and customer.

(3) Environmental responsibility.

(4) Employee safety.

D. The most-used definitions of risk were ranked as follows:

(1) Probability of not achieving a target return (in percent or dollars).

(2) Variation in returns.

(3) Payback period uncertain.

E. The most-used methodologies for analyzing the riskiness of a capital investment were ranked as follows:

(1) Payback period.

(2) Risk-adjusted discount rate.

(3) Measuring of expected variation in returns.

(4) Simulation.

F. The minimum return standard (method of determining M.A.R.R.) was ranked as follows:

(1) Management-determined target R.R.

(2) Weighted cost (average) of sources of funds.

(3) Cost of a specific source of funds.

(4) Firm's historical R.R.

Abdelsamad* summarized the results for an early 1970's survey of capital expenditure practices of some 200 of the largest industrial corporations in the United States. The results confirmed other surveys by showing that there is considerable growing sophistication in the use of valid proposal evaluation techniques among the larger industrial firms.

Of particular interest is the following list of six problem areas that were

*M. Abdelsamad, *A Guide to Capital Expenditure Analysis*, AMAACOM, Division of American Management Association, 1973.

considered most important in the evaluation of capital expenditure proposals by the respondent firms:

1. forecasting in general;
2. disclosure of alternatives;
3. inability of accounting department to later confirm or disprove accuracy of original cash flow estimates;
4. qualitative information not subject to quantitative analysis;
5. overestimation of benefits; and
6. lack of standardization in methods and assumptions used by analysts and evaluators.

Appendix 10-A is an illustrative segment of the excellent *Instruction Manual—DCF Plan* by Giddings & Lewis, Inc. Reprinted is primarily an example using their "Shortcut Method" forms. Their "Shortcut Method" differs from their "Long-Form Method" only by assuming an approximately constant "Income From Operations" each year throughout the comparison period. Page 3-S of the forms references certain charts in the *Manual* which contain various discount factors, but which are not shown herein. The full *Manual* also contains comprehensive instructions concerning what to consider and how to complete the forms line-by-line as needed.

Although this example at least partially reflects well-considered analysis and control programs, it should not be interpreted as necessarily the best program available or as a program which should be emulated without modification by any other firm. Indeed, a firm's capital budgeting and control procedures should be built around its own set of business objectives and needs.

PROBLEMS

10-1. Discuss the scope of capital budgeting with particular emphasis on how the various main considerations in capital budgeting are interrelated.

10-2. In your opinion, what is the most valid philosophy on how the minimum acceptable rate of return should be determined?

10-3. Under what circumstances is it reasonable to have more than one minimum acceptable rate of return for a given firm?

10-4. Select the classification systems for investment proposals which you think would be most useful for the typical small (say, fewer than 200 employees) enterprise. Do the same for the typical large (say, more than 2,000 employees) enterprise. Explain the reasonableness of any differences in your selections for the two size groups.

The salesman of the business machine firm has indicated that the expected useful service life of this machine is 5 years, with zero salvage value, but the company is not sure how long the machine will actually be needed. If the machine is rented, the company can cancel the lease at the end of any year. Assuming an income tax rate of 25% and that the firm's after-tax M.A.R.R. is 10%, prepare an appropriate analysis to help the firm decide whether it is more desirable to purchase or rent.

APPENDIX 10-A

Giddings & Lewis DCF Investment Evaluation Plan*

Introduction

The plan has been developed to provide a uniform method of evaluating investment opportunities within the corporation and to provide a standard format for review and grading of projects requiring capital funding.

The Giddings & Lewis DCF Investment Evaluation Plan is a modification of the conventional discounted cash flow technique which is gaining popularity in industry, particularly in multiplant concerns.

The discounted cash flow approach recognizes effective cash flow in business performance and the time value of money as an important factor in financial decisions. A prime feature of the DCF method is that it expresses evaluations in a term of common financial understanding, "compound interest":

> *The discounted cash flow procedure develops a* "True Rate of Return," *sometimes referred to as* "Profitability Rate." *This is equivalent to after-tax compound interest earnings over the analysis period, including full recovery of invested funds (i.e., compound interest earned plus recovery of investment—all after tax).*

*Reprinted from Giddings & Lewis, Inc., *Instruction Manual—DCF Plan* (May 1, 1969) by permission of Giddings & Lewis, Fond Du Lac, Wisconsin. Only certain illustrative segments of the manual are shown herein.

10-5. What is the purpose of a postmortem review? C
unwise commitments made as a result of past

10-6. Explain the various degrees of dependency bet
If there are one or more projects which seem de
tary to a given project, should those complemen
a proposal package or kept separate for review b

10-7. A 4-year-old truck has a present net realizable v
expected to have a salvage value of $1,800 after its
operating disbursements are $720 per year.

An equivalent truck can be leased for $0.40 per
each day the truck is kept. The expected annual utili
30 days. If the before-tax minimum attractive rate
which alternative is better by comparing before-tax e
a. Using only the above information.
b. Using further information that the annual cost
without a truck is $2,000.

10-8. Work Prob. 10-7 by comparing after-tax equivalent
effective tax rate is 60% and the present book value is $
ciation charge is $1,000 per year if the firm continues to
gains or losses on disposal of the old truck affect taxes
and the after-tax M.A.R.R. is 5%.

10-9. A lathe costs $56,000 and is expected to result in net cash
at the beginning of each year for 3 years and then have
$10,000 at the end of the third year. The equipment co
$22,000 a year, with the first payment due immediately. I
does not pay income taxes and its M.A.R.R. is 10%, s
organization should lease or purchase the equipment.

10-10. The Shakey Company can finance the purchase of a new
$2 million with a bond issue, for which it would pay $100,
year, and then repay the $2 million at the end of the life o
Instead of buying in this manner, the company can lease t
paying $190,000 per year, the first payment being due one y
The building would be fully depreciated for tax purposes ov
life of 20 years. The income tax rate is 40% for all expenses and
or losses and the firm's after-tax M.A.R.R. is 5%. Determine
firm should borrow and buy or lease if at the end of 20 years the
the following salvage values for the owner: (a) nothing, (b) $500,
line depreciation will be used, but is allowable only if the compan'
the building.

10-11. The Capitalpoor Company is considering purchasing a business n
$100,000. An alternative is to rent it for $35,000 at the beginnir
year. The rental would include all repairs and service. If the n
purchased, a comparable repair and service contract can be obt
$1,000 per year.

As a separate and additional calculation, the Giddings & Lewis DCF Plan also expresses "Years to Pay Back," or years to recover the investment (after tax), primarily as one measure of risk of investment rather than profitability.

It is not intended that the procedure should replace executive judgment in the company's capital investment program, but it is adopted as an aid to the many investment decisions involved in maintaining and planning growth of the firm's fixed assets.

Policy For Use

Economic evaluations, using the G&L DCF Plan, are to be developed for all proposals involving capital expenditures of $2,000 or more. (Except for projects approved for reasons other than for tangible return on investment.)

Component equipment and all supporting facilities isolatable to a common purpose shall be considered as one project and should be covered by not more than one appropriation request. A single appropriation request may be used for a group of projects serving an overall common purpose and where this approach will simplify analysis.

Approvals

The President and General Manager of Giddings & Lewis Machine Tool Company and of Gisholt Machine Company shall approve all Capital Expenditures of $2,000 and over for their divisions, when not in excess of the approved Capital Budget.

The Chairman of the Board shall approve all Capital Expenditure Projects in excess of $50,000 and also Capital Expenditure Projects of lesser amounts which are not covered by the Capital Budget for a respective Division Company.

Post Audit

The real potential of the DCF Capital Investment Evaluation System will not be realized until a general confidence in the evaluations is achieved.

A Post Audit Procedure will be issued to aid in attaining this confidence.

The plan will be to Post Audit each evaluation, 1 year after the Zero Point, and a report of the findings will be issued to those who have signed the appropriation request.

Example:

Figures 10-A-1 through 10-A-5 provide an example evaluation using the G&L "Short-Cut Method."

Request for Approval of Capital Asset Addition	Location: PLANT #12	
Ⓖ **GIDDINGS & LEWIS** Discounted Cash Flow Capital Investment Evaluation Procedure **SHORT–CUT METHOD** For use only when Annual Income from Operations (exclusive of tax and salvage credits) is assumed to be level, year to year.		Page No. 1-S

1. DESCRIPTION OF PROJECT:		

Replace Model #1. G&L Widget Machine, in North end of plant #12, with New Model #12. Equip with G&L Electronic Inspection device. Propose to have machine available for customer demonstrations an average of 12 hrs/mo. Will involve rearranging 3 machines in Dept 99 as per attached sketch.

2. REASON FOR EXPENDITURE:

☐ NEW PRODUCT ☒ OBSOLESCENCE ☒ PROFIT IMPROVEMENT ☐ SAFETY

☒ REDUCED COSTS ☒ CAPACITY INCREASED ☒ REPLACEMENT ☐ OTHER

Cost reduction detailed on Page 4-5 & covered by attachments shows reduction in direct & Indirect labor, use of less costly alloy, reduced overtime premium. less spoilage, less maunal inspection & reduced maintenance

Note:
(Model #1 is a prototype)

3. ☐ This is part of an approved project See Appropriation No. ___

4. Request Submitted By **S. D. Jones** 4/25	5. Analysis Checked & Approved By **J. E. Smith** 4/10

6. APPROVALS

APPROPRIATION NO.	
CAPITAL PLAN NO.	70-12-1
YEAR TO FUND	1970
Date Submitted	4-25-69
Date Approved	

7. COSTS

CAPITALIZED Items	line 1d page 2S	77,500
EXPENSED Items	line 2d page 2S	1,700
TOTAL TO BE AUTHORIZED		79,200
WORKING FUNDS	line 4c page 4S	1,200

8. CREDITS

INVESTMENT Credit	line 6a page 2S	5,425
EXPENSE Tax Credit	line 6b page 2S	935
SALVAGE Credit --"OLD" ASSETS	line 6c page 2S	4,478
OTHER Credits	line 6d page 2S	

9. NET FUNDS REQUIRED 69,562

10. PROFIT IMPROVEMENT

TRUE (DOF) RATE OF RETURN	line 16 page 16	18.0 %
Equivalent PRE-TAX RATE OF RETURN		40.0 %
YEARS TO PAY BACK		4.5 (After tax)

11. ASSETS REPLACED

Description & Proposed Disposition:

Propose to sell old Model #1 thru Goldberg-Emniernion

Date Acquired	1965
Present Book Value	$ 7200
Potential Salvage Value	$ 9950

Figure 10-A-1. Example form and evaluation (p6.1).

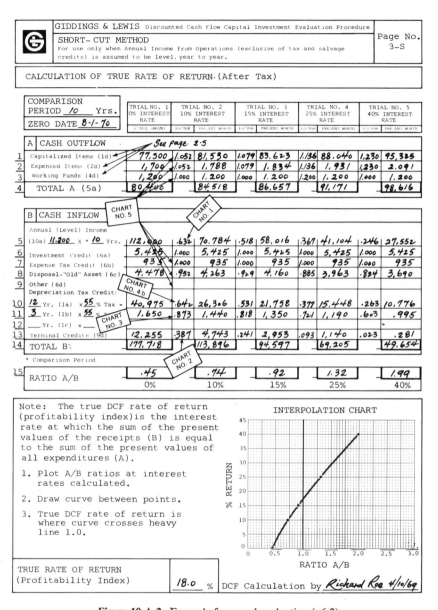

Figure 10-A-2. Example form and evaluation (p6.2).

Page 2-S	SUMMARY OF ACTUAL CASH FLOW (Short Cut Form Procedure)

SUMMARY OF INVESTMENTS

CAPITALIZED ITEMS: (Totals By Depreciation Schedule)

1a	Sched. *12* Yr. *G & L Widget Machine Model #2*	*74,500*	1a
1b	Sched. *3* Yr. *G & L Electronic Inspection Device*	*3,000*	1b
1c	Sched. ___ Yr. ___		1c
1d	TOTAL Capitalized Items	*77,500*	1d

EXPENSED ITEMS: (Site Prep., Relocation, Inventory Loss, etc.)

2a	*Re-arrange 3 machines in Dept 99*	*1,700*	
2b			
2c			
2d	TOTAL Expensed Items	*1,700*	2d
3a	TOTAL TO BE AUTHORIZED	*79,200*	3a

Increase in Working Funds: (Acct.'s Rec., parts supply, Inventory, etc.)

4a	*Spare parts Supply*	*1,200*	
4b			
4c	TOTAL WORKING FUNDS	*1,200*	4c
5a	GROSS FUNDS REQUIRED FOR PROJECT	*80,400*	5a

SUMMARY OF CREDITS IN THE INVESTMENT CASH FLOW (At Start of Operation)

6a	INVESTMENT CREDIT:	(1d) $ *77,500* x *7* %	*5,425*	6a
6b	Tax Credit from Expense:	(2d) $ *1,700* x (Tax Rate) *55* %	*935*	6b
6c	Disposal Value of Assets Replaced: $ *9,750* x (1.0-Tax Rate) *45* %		*4,478*	6c
6d	Other ___			6d
6e	TOTAL CREDITS (Before Depr. Tax Credits)		*10,838*	6e
7a	NET FUNDS REQUIRED FOR PROJECT		*69,562*	7a

EXPECTED TIMING OF EXPENDITURES

Qtr	Yr.	Description	*12* Yr.	*3* Yr.	___ Yr.	Expense Item	Working Funds	TOTAL
1	*70*	*Widget Machine*	*74,500*					*74,500*
1	*70*	*Inspection Device*		*3,000*				*3,000*
1	*70*	*Rearrange Dept*				*1,700*		*1,7000*
3	*70*	*Spare Parts Supply*					*1,200*	*1,200*
		Note - Dispose of old asset by Jan 1971						
		Note - Move facility in operation by - 8-1-70						
		TOTALS	*74,500*	*3,000*		*1,700*	*1,200*	*80,400*

TERMINAL CREDITS:

9a	Salvage Value of New Asset *(10Yr)*	$ *27,055* x (1.0-Tax Rate) *45* %	*12,175*
9b	Return of Working Funds (4c)	$	*1,200*
9c	*(1/4 of 9,950)*	$ *2,488* x (1.0-Tax Rate) *45* %	*(1,120)*
9d	TOTAL TERMINAL CREDITS		*12,255*	9d

10a	ANNUAL (Level) INCOME FROM OPERATIONS--Page 4 (31) $ *24,890* x (1.0-Tax Rate) *45* %		*11,200*	10a

Figure 10-A-3. Example form and evaluation (p6.3). [Charts references are for (P/F) and (F/P) factors].

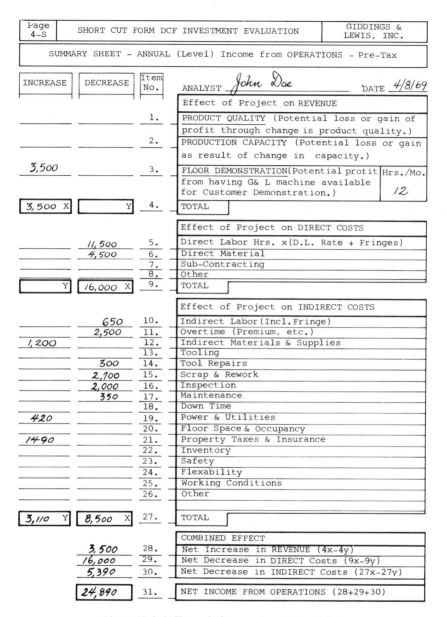

INCREASE	DECREASE	Item No.		
			SHORT CUT FORM DCF INVESTMENT EVALUATION — Page 4-S — GIDDINGS & LEWIS, INC.	
			SUMMARY SHEET – ANNUAL (Level) Income from OPERATIONS – Pre-Tax	
			ANALYST *John Doe* DATE 4/8/69	
			Effect of Project on REVENUE	
		1.	PRODUCT QUALITY (Potential loss or gain of profit through change is product quality.)	
		2.	PRODUCTION CAPACITY (Potential loss or gain as result of change in capacity.)	
3,500		3.	FLOOR DEMONSTRATION(Potential profit from having G& L machine available for Customer Demonstration.)	Hrs./Mo. 12
3,500 X	Y	4.	TOTAL	
			Effect of Project on DIRECT COSTS	
	11,500	5.	Direct Labor Hrs. x(D.L. Rate + Fringes)	
	4,500	6.	Direct Material	
		7.	Sub-Contracting	
		8.	Other	
Y	16,000 X	9.	TOTAL	
			Effect of Project on INDIRECT COSTS	
	650	10.	Indirect Labor(Incl.Fringe)	
	2,500	11.	Overtime (Premium, etc.)	
1,200		12.	Indirect Materials & Supplies	
		13.	Tooling	
	300	14.	Tool Repairs	
	2,700	15.	Scrap & Rework	
	2,000	16.	Inspection	
	350	17.	Maintenance	
		18.	Down Time	
420		19.	Power & Utilities	
		20.	Floor Space & Occupancy	
1490		21.	Property Taxes & Insurance	
		22.	Inventory	
		23.	Safety	
		24.	Flexability	
		25.	Working Conditions	
		26.	Other	
3,110 Y	8,500 X	27.	TOTAL	
			COMBINED EFFECT	
	3,500	28.	Net Increase in REVENUE (4x-4y)	
	16,000	29.	Net Decrease in DIRECT Costs (9x-9y)	
	5,390	30.	Net Decrease in INDIRECT Costs (27x-27y)	
	24,890	31.	NET INCOME FROM OPERATIONS (28+29+30)	

Figure 10-A-4. Example form and evaluation (p6.4).

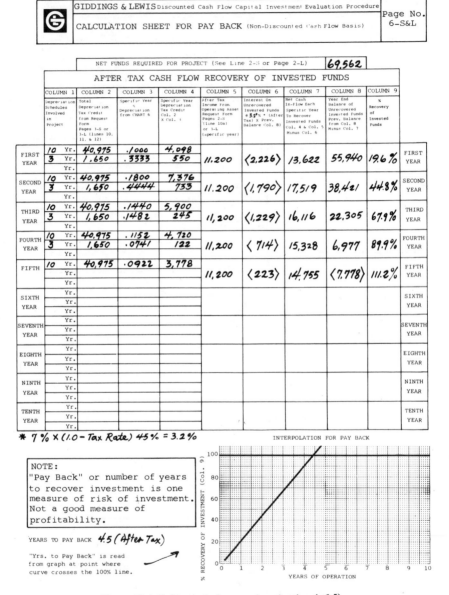

GIDDINGS & LEWIS Discounted Cash Flow Capital Investment Evaluation Procedure

CALCULATION SHEET FOR PAY BACK (Non-Discounted Cash Flow Basis)

Page No. 6–S&L

NET FUNDS REQUIRED FOR PROJECT (See Line 2-5 or Page 2-L) **69,562**

AFTER TAX CASH FLOW RECOVERY OF INVESTED FUNDS

		COLUMN 1	COLUMN 2	COLUMN 3	COLUMN 4	COLUMN 5	COLUMN 6	COLUMN 7	COLUMN 8	COLUMN 9	
		Depreciation Schedules Involved in Project	Total Depreciation Tax Credit from Request Form Pages 3-5 or 3-L (lines 10, 11, & 12)	Specific Year % Depreciation from CHART 6	Specific Year Depreciation Investment Tax Credit Col. 2 X Col. 3	After Tax Income From Operating Asset Request Form Pages 2-5 (line 10a) or 1-L (specific year)	Interest On Unrecovered Invested Funds *3.2% * (After Tax) X Prev. Balance Col. 8	Net Cash In-Flow Each Specific Year To Recover Invested Funds Col. 4 & Col. 5 Minus Col. 6	Year End Balance of Unrecovered Invested Funds Prev. Balance from Col. 8 Minus Col. 7	% Recovery of Invested Funds	
FIRST YEAR	10 Yr. / 3 Yr. / Yr.	40,975 / 1,650	.1000 / .3333	4,098 / 550	11,200	⟨2,226⟩	13,622	55,940	19.6%	FIRST YEAR
SECOND YEAR	10 Yr. / 3 Yr. / Yr.	40,975 / 1,650	.1800 / .4444	7,376 / 733	11,200	⟨1,790⟩	17,519	38,421	44.8%	SECOND YEAR
THIRD YEAR	10 Yr. / 3 Yr. / Yr.	40,975 / 1,650	.1440 / .1482	5,900 / 245	11,200	⟨1,229⟩	16,116	22,305	67.9%	THIRD YEAR
FOURTH YEAR	10 Yr. / 3 Yr. / Yr.	40,975 / 1,650	.1152 / .0741	4,720 / 122	11,200	⟨ 714⟩	15,328	6,977	89.9%	FOURTH YEAR
FIFTH YEAR	10 Yr. / Yr. / Yr.	40,975	.0922	3,778	11,200	⟨223⟩	14,755	⟨7,778⟩	111.2%	FIFTH YEAR
SIXTH YEAR	Yr. / Yr. / Yr.									SIXTH YEAR
SEVENTH YEAR	Yr. / Yr. / Yr.									SEVENTH YEAR
EIGHTH YEAR	Yr. / Yr. / Yr.									EIGHTH YEAR
NINTH YEAR	Yr. / Yr. / Yr.									NINTH YEAR
TENTH YEAR	Yr. / Yr. / Yr.									TENTH YEAR

＊ 7% X (1.0 - Tax Rate) 45% = 3.2%

INTERPOLATION FOR PAY BACK

NOTE:
"Pay Back" or number of years to recover investment is one measure of risk of investment. Not a good measure of profitability.

YEARS TO PAY BACK **4.5 (After Tax)**

"Yrs. to Pay Back" is read from graph at point where curve crosses the 100% line.

% RECOVERY OF INVESTMENT (Col. 9)

YEARS OF OPERATION

Figure 10-A-5. Example form and evaluation (p6.5).

Capital Project Evaluation Under Risk and Uncertainty Conditions

Chapter
11

introduction to risk and uncertainty

All of the economy study methods and illustrations in the chapters of Part 1 were for conditions of "assumed certainty"; i.e., all elements (parameters) considered were estimated or specified by a single figure. Generally, such elements as life, salvage value, and periodic incomes and costs are random variables rather than known constants. Hence, in many economy studies it is necessary or desirable to extend the results of assumed certainty analyses by directly considering the risk and uncertainty involved due to variability in the outcome of elements. Part 2 treats the subject of capital project evaluation under risk and uncertainty conditions.

Difference Between Risk and Uncertainty

The classical distinction between risk and uncertainty is that an element or analysis involves *risk* if the probabilities of the alternative, possible outcomes are known, while it is characterized by *uncertainty* if the frequency distribu-

251

tion of the possible outcomes is not known. The distinction between conditions of assumed certainty, risk, and uncertainty for a given element such as project life is portrayed graphically in Fig. 11-1.

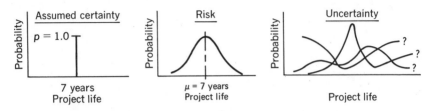

Figure 11-1. Illustrations of assumed certainty, risk, and uncertainty as applied to life of a project.

Another less restrictive distinction between risk and uncertainty is that *risk* is the dispersion of the probability distribution of the element being estimated or calculated outcome(s) being considered, while *uncertainty* is the degree of lack of confidence that the estimated probability distribution is correct. The word *risk* can be used to apply to the outcome of any element or measure of merit. Colloquially, the word is often used merely to denote variability of outcome, and oftentimes the only variability which is of concern is variability in an unfavorable direction.

There are several combinations of risk and assumed certainty which can specify a given element estimate over time. For example, Fig. 11-2 represents an assumed certain outcome amount (e.g., cash flow) at an assumed certain point in time, while Fig. 11-3 shows a risk amount at an assumed certain point in time. Fig. 11-4 represents an assumed certain amount at risk (dis-

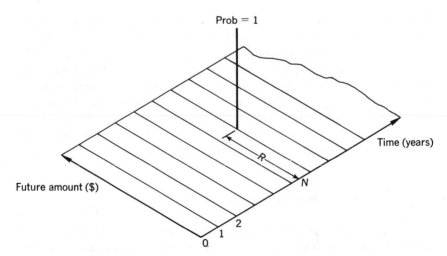

Figure 11-2. Assumed certain outcome at assumed certain point in time.

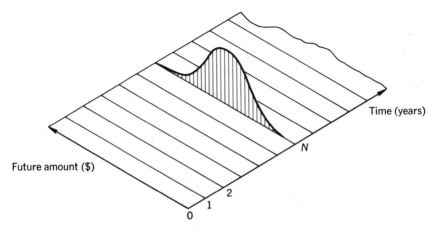

Figure 11-3. Risk amount at assumed certain point in time.

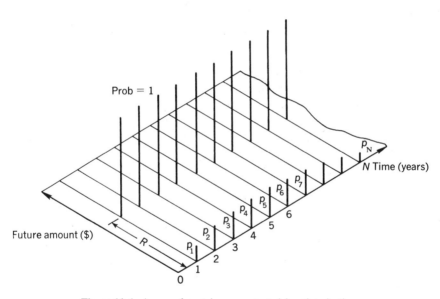

Figure 11-4. Assumed certain amount at risk points in time.

crete) points in time, while Fig. 11-5 represents random amounts at each of risk (discrete) points in time.

Causes of Risk and Uncertainty

Risk and uncertainty in project investment decisions are attributable to many possible sources. Below is a brief description of some main causes.

1. *Insufficient numbers of similar investments.* In general, a firm will have only

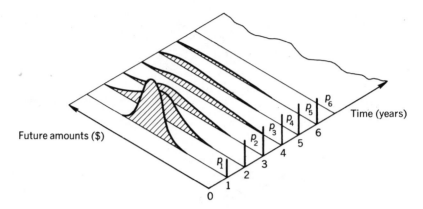

Figure 11-5. Risk amounts at risk points in time.

a few investments of a particular type. This means that there will be insufficient opportunity for the results of a particular investment type to "average out," i.e., for the effect of unfavorable outcomes to be virtually cancelled by favorable outcomes. This type of risk is dominant when the magnitude of the individual investment commitment is large compared to the financial resources of the firm.

2. *Bias in the data and its assessment.* It is common that individuals making or reviewing economic analyses have biases of optimism or pessimism or are unconsciously influenced by factors which should not be a part of an objective study. A pattern of consistent undue optimism or pessimism on the part of an analyst should be recognized through analysis review procedures.

3. *Changing external economic environment, invalidating past experience.* Whenever estimates are made of future conditions, the usual bases are past results for similar quantities, whenever available. While the past information is often valuable, there is risk in using it directly without adjustment for expected future conditions.

4. *Misinterpretation of data.* Misinterpretation may occur if the underlying factors behind elements to be estimated are so complex that the relationship of one or more factors to the desired elements is misunderstood.

5. *Errors of analysis.* Errors can occur either in analysis of the technical operating characteristics of a project or in the analysis of the financial implications of a project.

6. *Managerial talent availability and emphasis.* The performance of an industrial investment project or set of projects usually depends in substantial part on the availability and application of managerial talent once the project has been undertaken. In general, management talent is a very limited resource within a firm; hence, it follows that the results of some projects are going to suffer compared to the results of other projects. Thus, there is

risk due to lack of availability or neglect in needed managerial talent applied to investment projects.

7. *Salvageability of investment.* Of prime consideration in judging risk is the relative recoverability of investment commitments if a project, for performance considerations or otherwise, is to be liquidated. For example, an investment in special-purpose equipment which has no value to other firms entails more risk than an investment in general-purpose equipment which would have a high percentage salvage value if sold because of poor operating results. A descriptive synonym is "bail-outability."

8. *Obsolescence.* Rapid technological change and progress are characteristic of our economy. Not only do products become superseded, thus rendering productive facilities for those products less needed or useless, but also changes in process technology can render existing facilities obsolete.

Weakness in Probabilistic Treatment of Project Analyses Involving Risk

While the use of probabilities is freely made in analyses of projects involving risk, it should be pointed out that these probabilities are not generally objectively verifiable, and hence are generally *subjective* (sometimes called *personal*) probabilities. A further weakening fact is that the evidence supporting any given probability in an analysis may differ markedly in both quality and quantity from that for any other probability.

When probabilities are used, the risk and uncertainty concerning outcomes in question are not eliminated, but rather the uncertainty then becomes uncertainty connected with the probabilities on which the analysis is based. Nevertheless, it is often worthwhile to express degree of confidence in estimates through the use of probability distributions rather than through subjective verbal expressions.

Ways to Change or Influence Degree of Uncertainty

It is usually possible for the firm to take actions which will decrease the degree of uncertainty to which it is subject as a result of investment project selection. Several notable ways are

1. by increasing information obtained before decision, such as through additional market research or investigation of technical performance characteristics;

2. by increasing size of operations so as to have enough different investment projects to increase expectation that results will "average out"; and

3. by diversifying products, particularly by choosing product lines for which sales are affected differently by changes in business activity (i.e., when sales of some products decrease, then sales of other products can be expected to increase).

Return, Risk, and Choice

It is generally accepted that the riskier a project, the higher the apparent return it must promise to warrant acceptance. It would be desirable to determine differential risk allowances which would reduce all projects to a common basis. This cannot be done precisely, however, for the statement of differential risk allowances is very much a matter of subjective judgment.

Before a firm can make investment decisions to include allowances for risk, the firm's policy toward risk should be determined. The amount of risk a firm is prepared to undertake to secure a given actual or apparent monetary return is a general question of values. There is no rational or logical criterion by which the choice can be made. Rather, this is largely a function of the preferences of the decision-makers of the firm and the amount of risk to which the firm is already exposed.

In general, the relationship between expected return and risk (degree of variability of the return) can be represented as in Fig. 11-6. A refinement of the concept of Fig. 11-6 can be made if risk is subcategorized into the quantitative components of variability of returns and amount of investment. This is shown in Fig. 11-7.

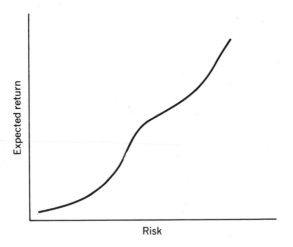

Figure 11-6. Relationship between return and risk.

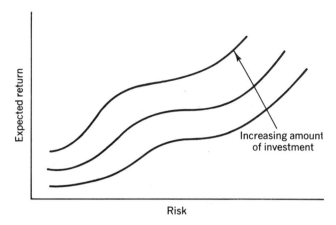

Figure 11-7. Relationship between return and risk, considering amount of investment.

Decision Guides on When and How Much to Consider Risk and Uncertainty

The question of the extent to which risk and uncertainty should be directly considered in economic analyses is of great concern and cannot be answered categorically. The concern stems from the fact that the risk and uncertainty of the future pervades most capital projects for which analyses are made. The impossibility of categorical answers stems from the fact that there is an infinite variety of sources of risk and relative degrees of risk for various projects and firms.

It is sometimes felt that the risk and uncertainty inherent in most investment decisions make it not worthwhile to engage in any complex or "sophisticated" methods of analysis. While this may be true in particular situations, the position is strongly suggested that it is, in general, very worthwhile to supplement judgment quantitatively and explicitly in the analysis of risk and uncertainty for investment projects. Analysis is needed to insure that the implementation of judgment is not accompanied by errors in quantification and omissions in factors considered. Indeed, with the increasing complexity and economic size of individual projects compared to the worth of the firm as a whole, quantitative consideration of risk and uncertainty in capital project analyses becomes increasingly important. This section provides some qualitative decision guides regarding this question.

A conceptual answer to the question of when and how much risk and uncertainty should be considered can be reduced to simple economics—that is, put more study effort into the analysis as long as the savings from further study is greater than the cost of further study (i.e., as long as marginal savings is greater than marginal cost). Since the marginal savings (and possibly marginal cost also) for a given amount of added study is a variable, it is necessary to modify the rationale. A reasonable modification is suggested then to be the consideration of expected values. Thus the rationale can be restated as: put more study effort into the analysis as long as the expected savings from further study is greater than the expected cost of that further study.

The great problem in applying this rationale in practice is that it is quite difficult to estimate the expected savings from further study. In economic analyses of mutually exclusive projects (i.e., when at most one project can be chosen), savings from further study occur if the further study correctly causes a reversal or change in decision as to the project accepted. In economic analyses of nonmutually exclusive projects (i.e., when the choice of one project does not affect the desirability of choice of any other project), savings from further study occur if the further study correctly causes the decision-maker to drop one or more projects previously accepted and/or correctly to add one or more projects not previously accepted. By "correctly" is meant "with favorable consequences." Other savings can be created by the added study. For example, the added study may provide information which will prove useful in future operating decisions and/or investment analyses.

The savings from further study can be conceptually determined as the discounted present value of the new project(s) accepted after the further study minus the present value of the project(s) accepted before the further study. However, the practical problem of determination of the expected savings from further study, as based on the amount of savings and the likelihood or probability of those savings, is generally quite difficult. It should be noted that the expected savings from added study may well not be a continuous function of the amount of the added study, but rather it is likely to change in discrete steps.

The expected cost of added study is more readily determinable than the expected savings from that study; nevertheless, it is not always apparent. Two common viewpoints on this cost are that it is equal to the direct cost of the resources devoted to the added study or that it is essentially zero on the grounds that the resources are available and paid for regardless of whether or not they are used on that added study. The most defensible cost of added study is based on the opportunity cost principle; that is, the cost of the added study should be determined by the value to the company of those study resources if put to best productive use on work other than that added study. While this opportunity cost is often hard to evaluate, it seems reasonable that in a well-managed company the cost will be at least as great as the direct cost of those resources.

Figure 11-8 shows a flow diagram which depicts a general recommended

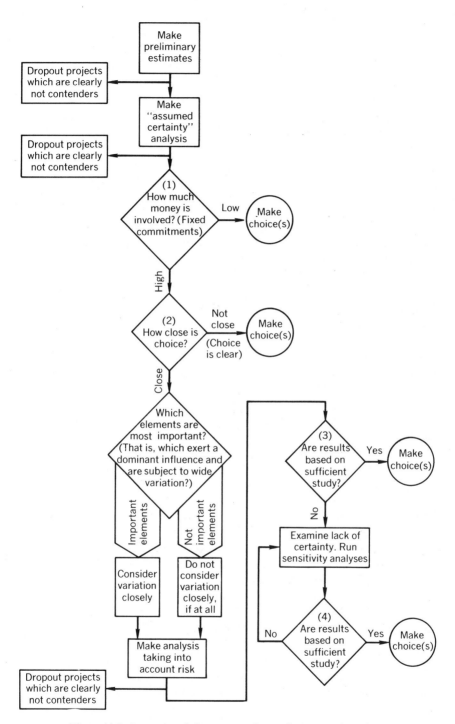

Figure 11-8. Recommended sequence of steps for economic analyses.

259

sequence of steps in making economic analyses and shows qualitative test points regarding the extent of the analysis. This sequence would be applicable to analyses of either groups of mutually exclusive or nonmutually exclusive projects. Note that the recommended sequence shown in the figure shows four different points at which the decision could be made concerning which project(s) to accept. Also, there are four stages at which provision is made for dropping from further consideration projects which analysis indicates are clearly not contenders worthy of further study.

The meaning of the test points included is worthy of discussion. The test points are depicted as diamond shapes and are numbered in parentheses. Test point 1 considers the magnitude of the fixed monetary commitments involved in the decision for purposes of deciding whether further study is justified. The relevant amount of money to consider is the total present value of the nonsalvageable investment costs as well as other fixed costs which the company would incur if it should accept that project. If the magnitude of the fixed commitments for each of the projects being considered is low compared to the cost of further study, then it may be decided that further study is not justified and that the choice(s) should be made. The break-even point concerning the size of fixed commitments to use as this criterion is rather subjective. Determined intuitively, it appears that this point would be related to the company's financial health, the size of the projects usually considered, and the availability of resources for further analysis.

Test point 2 in Fig. 11-8 considers how close is the choice between projects. In this case, "close" can be defined as the nearness of the measure of merit for the most preferred alternative to the next most preferred alternative. If the assumed certainty analysis results up to that point show that the decision is not at all close [i.e., the choice(s) is (are) apparent], then further study is hardly justified and the choice(s) should be made.

Test point 3 is concerned with the decision of whether the results of an initial analysis considering variation of elements (which would be essentially a risk analysis such as described in the following chapters) is based on sufficient study considering the economic importance of the decision and the closeness of the analysis results for the projects considered. If the decision is important enough in terms of worth of the fixed commitments for the projects considered and the analysis results are somewhat close, then further study should be performed before the choice(s) is (are) made. The further study would take the form of closer estimations of elements and sensitivity analyses.

Test point 4 in Fig. 11-8 is repetitious of test point 3. It shows that closer estimations and sensitivity analyses would be continued until it is decided that the results of the analyses are based on sufficient study and the choice(s) can be made.

The sequence suggested in Fig. 11-8 is subject to shortcuts in cases where warranted. For example, if a given analysis involves projects that are of extreme importance to the future of the company, it may be decided to perform directly a risk analysis which considers variation of multiple elements without bothering to perform an initial "assumed certainty" study.

The sequence of steps shown in Fig. 11-8 provides a conceptual basis for determining the extent to which economic analyses should be performed. The decisions in the sequence are rather intangible; nevertheless, the sequence of steps represents a formalized structure for thinking which the analyst or decision-makers can follow in determining the extent to which analyses should be carried out in particular situations. It should be recognized that all of the above steps of analyses involving a particular set of alternatives are not necessarily performed at a single level in the organization. In fact, the more money which is involved, the higher is the level in the organization to which the analysis is referred, in general, before a decision is made.

In summary, the justifiable extent of an economic analysis depends on the economic importance of the study. When the risks or potentials are substantial, systematic procedures are needed to reduce the uncertainties inherent and to give them appropriate weight in arriving at decisions.

General Model for Risk and Uncertainty Problems

In order to provide a framework for the subsequent discussion, it is useful to employ a general model of decision problems in which there are various possible outcomes (called *states of nature*) in combination with several alternative actions. As depicted in Table 11-1, m mutually exclusive

Table 11-1

GENERAL MODEL FOR RISK AND UNCERTAINTY PROBLEMS

Alternative	S_1 $P(S_1)$	$S_2 \ldots$ $P(S_2) \ldots$	$S_j \ldots$ $P(S_j) \ldots$	S_k $P(S_k)$
		State of nature (Probability of state)		
A_1	R_{11}	$R_{12} \ldots$	$R_{1j} \ldots$	R_{1k}
A_2	R_{21}	$R_{22} \ldots$	$R_{2j} \ldots$	R_{2k}
.	.	.	.	.
.	.	.	.	.
.	.	.	.	.
A_i	R_{i1}	$R_{i2} \ldots$	$R_{ij} \ldots$	R_{ik}
.	.	.	.	.
.	.	.	.	.
.	.	.	.	.
A_m	R_{m1}	$R_{m2} \ldots$	$R_{mj} \ldots$	R_{mk}

investment alternatives, $\{A_i\}$, and k mutually exclusive and collectively exhaustive states of nature, $\{S_j\}$, have been identified. The combination of action A_i and state of nature S_j yields a net result R_{ij}. The outcome, R_{ij}, is normally expressed in equivalent returns or costs, but it can be in any measure. (In fact, it may well be that the outcome is multidimensional; however, it is generally assumed that, in such cases, a one-dimensional utility measure can be obtained. For a discussion of this subject, see Chapter 20.) This tabular model is often descriptively called a *payoff table*.

When the decision problem is considered a decision under risk, then for $j = 1, \ldots, k$ estimates are provided of $P(S_j)$, the probability of state of nature S_j occurring. In the absence of such probabilities, the decision is considered to be a decision under uncertainty.

The general model is very useful in the case of a single decision. However, when sequential decisions are made, with each subsequent decision being influenced by a partial realization of the future state, then an alternative model is generally used. In Chapter 15 a decision tree model is used to represent decision problems under risk which involve sequential decisions.

Estimating in Terms of Probability Distributions

It is reasonable to estimate many element outcomes in terms of subjective, usually continuous, probability distributions. This can be most useful, either for purposes of calculating measures of merit which directly take these distributions into account or for purposes of merely judging the degree and effect of probable outcome variation. When it is desired to estimate the subjective probability distribution of an element and that element is not thought to fit one of the computationally convenient distributions, one good way is to estimate in terms of a cumulative probability distribution function and then convert the results to other forms if needed. For example, suppose you desire to estimate the life of a project (such as the length of time before your car will have a major breakdown). After considering the experience records for similar cars and making your subjective adjustments for future conditions, you may decide that, say, there is practically nil probability that the life will be equal to or less than 2 years; 0.10 probability that the life will be equal to or less than 3 years; and you keep making similar estimates until the life is reached at which you feel there is 100% chance that the life will not be exceeded. A complete set of estimates for this example is given in Table 11-2, and then graphed, assuming a continuous distribution, in Fig. 11-9. Figure 11-10 shows the same estimates converted into the more commonly portrayed probability density form. The reader may recall that the probability density function (height of the curve) for a continuous distribution

Table 11-2

Example Estimates Expressed in Cumulative Probability From

Life (yr)	Probability that life will be equal to or less than life given
2	0.0
3	0.1
4	0.3
5	0.7
6	0.9
7	1.0

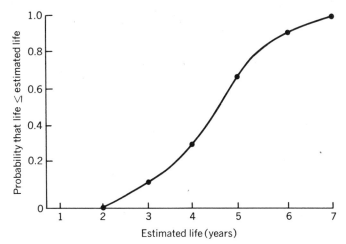

Figure 11-9. Cumulative probability distribution representation of data in Table 11-2.

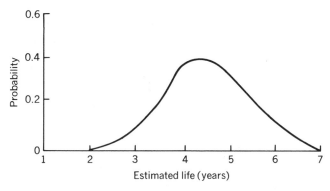

Figure 11-10. Alternative form of probability distribution (probability density) for data given in Table 11-2.

equals the slope of the cumulative probability distribution function over the entire range of the element estimated.

Another way to estimate in terms of a cumulative probability distribution which is probably even easier to do than that depicted above is to estimate median, quartile, and extreme values. Below are typical suggested questions and example answers for estimating, say, the labor cost for a new product.

For Median (50% Cumulative Probability):
At what value is the labor cost as likely to be above as below that value? (*Ex. Ans.:* $18)

For Upper Quartile (75% Cumulative Probability):
Given that the labor cost is above the median, $18, at what value is the labor cost as likely to be above as below that value? (*Ex. Ans.:* $28)

For Lower Quartile (25% Cumulative Probability):
Given that the labor cost is below the median, $18, at what value is the labor cost as likely to be above as below that value? (*Ex. Ans.:* $12)

For Upper Extreme (99% Cumulative Probability):
What value would the labor cost exceed only 1% of the time? (*Ex. Ans.:* $45)

For Lower Extreme (1% Cumulative Probability):
What value would the labor cost be lower than only 1% of the time? (*Ex. Ans.:* $8)

After having obtained the above answers one can either plot directly on a cumulative probability distribution or first check the answers for consistency and make adjustments by asking such questions such as:

1. Is the labor cost more likely to be within the two quartiles (i.e., $12 to $28) or outside the two quartiles (i.e., < $12 or > $28)?

2. Is the labor cost more likely to be less than the lower quartile estimate, $12, or greater than the upper quartile estimate, $28?

If the answers to the above questions aren't "... equally likely ...," then adjustments in one or more of the original estimates should be made until one is satisfied that the estimates represent the best judgments which can be made within the time and talent resources available. Let us suppose that after such adjustments the final estimates are as follows:

Median (M)	$19
Upper quartile (UQ)	30
Lower quartile (LQ)	12
Upper extreme (UE)	48
Lower extreme (LE)	8

Figure 11-11 shows the above results on a cumulative probability graph.

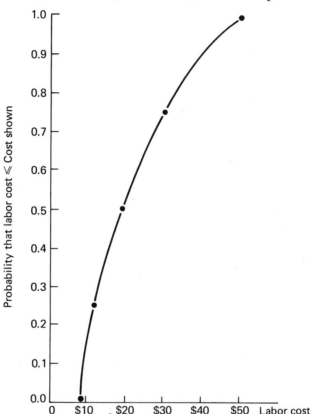

Figure 11-11. Cumulative probability graph.

The following two sections give simplified approximation procedures for estimating parameters of elements thought to be distributed according to the Beta distribution and to the normal distribution.

Beta II Distribution

The Beta II distribution is of interest because it can describe a wide range of left-skew and right-skew conditions of differing variances.*

The following Beta estimation procedure is based on a system developed for the PERT network planning and scheduling technique. It involves first

---

*Whereas the Beta I (normally called just Beta) distribution applies to variables ranging between 0 and 1, the Beta II distribution applies to variables ranging over any set of outcomes.

making an "optimistic" estimate, a "pessimistic" estimate, and a "most likely" estimate for the element. These estimates are to correspond to the lower (or upper) bound, upper (or lower) bound, and mode, respectively, of the assumed Beta II distribution describing the element. Figure 11-12 shows an assumed Beta distribution for a typical element together with the meaning of the above types of estimates. In this case, the distribution happens to be left-skewed.

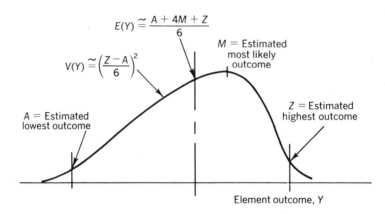

Figure 11-12. Demonstration of estimates with Beta distribution.

Once the three estimates of element outcome have been made, the approximate mean and variance of the Beta distribution for the element may be calculated as

$$E[Y] \approx \frac{A + 4M + Z}{6} \qquad\qquad 11\text{-}1$$

and

$$V[Y] \approx \left(\frac{Z - A}{6}\right)^2 \qquad\qquad 11\text{-}2$$

where $E[Y]$ = Estimated expected outcome
$V[Y]$ = Estimated variance of outcome
A = Estimated lowest outcome
M = Estimated most likely outcome
Z = Estimated highest outcome

It is worthy of note that the difference between the approximate expected values as calculated by Eq. (11-1) and the exact formula is relatively small for a wide range of Beta II distribution conditions. On the other hand, the difference between the approximate variance as calculated by Eq. (11-2) and the exact formula can be quite high, and the difference usually is in the direction of underestimation of the exact value.

If several elements, as estimated by the above procedure, are assumed to be independent and are added together, the distribution of the total outcome so obtained is, according to the central limit theorem, approximately normal. The mean of this total outcome distribution can be calculated by adding the means of the individual elements. Further, the variance of this total outcome distribution can be calculated by adding the variances of the distributions of the individual elements.

Normal Distribution

Quite often the best subjective estimate of the shape of the distribution of an element that can be made in practice is that the distribution is normal. It can be observed from tables of area under the normal distribution that the middle 50% of a normal distribution i.e. between the upper quartile and the lower quartile is within ± 0.675 standard deviations of the mean of that distribution as shown in Fig. 11-13. Thus, for a normally distributed element, if one is willing to estimate the smallest range $r \ (= UQ - LQ)$ within which that variable is expected to occur with 50% probability, then the standard deviation σ for that variable can be calculated by the relation $0.675\sigma = r/2$. In practice, it is generally sufficiently close to approximate the 0.675 with $\frac{2}{3}$.

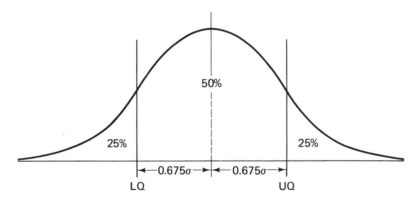

Figure 11-13. Estimating relationships for normal distribution.

This same idea for estimating the variance for normally distributed variables could be applied using any other number of standard deviations and the associated probabilities. The values suggested above, however, are probably most useful because of the relative ease of visualizing the minimum range which would include 50% probability of occurrence.

As an example, suppose that the investment for a project is estimated to be normally distributed, and it is thought that there is a 50% chance it will be between $9,000 and $12,000. The standard deviation for this distribution is calculated as $\frac{2}{3}\sigma = (\$12,000 - \$9,000)/2$; or $\sigma = \$2,250$. The mean for the distribution is, of course, $(\$12,000 + \$9,000)/2 = \$10,500$.

Responses to Risk and Uncertainty

Although it is generally agreed that risk and uncertainties exist in the conduct of economic analyses, there does not exist complete agreement on how such information is to be incorporated in the analysis. Some prefer to rely heavily on the recommendations obtained from analytical models; others choose to rely solely on intuition and judgment. The latter are most often associated with the claim that one's ability to make good decisions in the face of risk and uncertainty is what separates the "men from the boys."

There is great appeal in being able to specify quantitatively, completely, and accurately an "optimum" course of action in the face of risk and uncertainty. However, what is optimum to one individual might be very unsatisfactory to another. Hence, two approaches have emerged in performing economic analyses that explicitly incorporate risk and uncertainty conditions in the analysis. Each are described below.

One approach is to develop a *descriptive* model which *describes* the economic performance of an individual investment alternative. As an illustration, one might descriptively model the present worths of each of several alternatives. No recommendation would be forthcoming *from the model.* Rather, the decision-maker would be furnished descriptive information concerning each alternative; the final choice among the alternatives would require a separate action.

The second approach is to develop a *prescriptive* or *normative* model which includes an objective function to be maximized or minimized. The output from the model *prescribes* the course of action to be taken. In previous analyses under assumed certainty the objective was implicitly stated as the maximization of, say, present worth.

Chapters 12 and 13 are concerned with descriptive modeling of cash flow profiles in the face of risk and uncertainty. Chapters 14 and 15 present prescriptive modeling approaches that can be used to evaluate economic investment alternatives under risk and uncertainty conditions. It will be found that the analysis in Chapters 12 and 13 can be useful not only when the formal analysis is to terminate with descriptive modeling but also in providing the required inputs for the prescriptive models.

PROBLEMS

11-1. What distinction between risk and uncertainty do you think is most useful? Why?

11-2. Which of the eight causes of risk and uncertainty listed in this chapter may be said to be generally within the control (power to affect) of the economic analyst or the people from whom he obtains estimates?

11-3. Which of the three listed ways for a firm to change or influence degree of uncertainty is generally within the control of the economic analyst?

11-4. Under what circumstances might it be reasonable to start the analysis at the point immediately following decision point 2 in the sequence of steps shown in Fig. 11-8?

11-5. In Fig. 11-8, are there any points at which the step "Drop-out Projects Which Are Clearly Not Contenders" might reasonably be added or deleted to make it a more reasonable representation of ideal general practice? Explain your reasoning.

11-6. What are the pros and cons of descriptive modeling versus prescriptive modeling? Which do you prefer? Why?

11-7. Classify each of the following models as descriptive or prescriptive and justify your classifications:
   a. Linear programming model
   b. Replacement model
   c. Present worth model
   d. Dynamic programming model
   e. Inventory (EOQ) model
   f. Queueing model
   g. Simulation model
   h. Quality control model
   i. Reliability model
   j. Warehouse location model
   k. Rate of return model
   l. Forecasting model
   m. MAPI model
   n. Giddings & Lewis DCF Investment Evaluation Plan

11-8. If you were faced with the following decision problem under risk, which action would you choose? Why?

	S_1 (0.1)	S_2 (0.7)	S_3 (0.2)
A_1	$-\$40$	$\$30$	$\$20$
A_2	$-\$20$	$\$20$	$\$40$
A_3	$\$0$	$\$20$	$\$10$

11-9. If you were faced with the following decision problem under risk, which would you choose? Why?

	S_1 (0.4)	S_2 (0.6)
A_1	$110	−$20
A_2	−$40	$80
A_3	$0	$50

11-10. If the decision problems in Probs. 11-8 and 11-9 had been decisions under uncertainty, would your preferences change? Why or why not?

11-11. Estimate the expected total remaining life of a given car, either one you happen to own or some other car with which you are familiar, in terms of the following:
  a. Single best estimate
  b. Subjective continuous probability distribution (cumulative and probability density function)
  c. Beta II distribution (calculate the approximate mean and variance)
  d. Normal distribution (calculate the approximate mean and variance)

11-12. Work Probs. 11-11 except change the variable to be estimated to the number of basketball (or football) games to be won next year by the team of your choice. Of course, since the variable is discrete, the Beta II and normal distributions are only approximations.

11-13. Repair costs have been recorded as follows:

$225	$400	$ 75	$125
100	50	100	75
50	25	25	275
75	150	175	25
50	175	150	100

On the basis of the data above,
  a. Find the median value of the cost to repair.
  b. Estimate the probability that a given repair will cost less than $200.
  c. Show the data in graph form with "Cost to Repair in $" as the horizontal axis and "Estimated Probability That Repair Cost Will Not Exceed $____" as the vertical axis.

11-14. A heat exchanger is being installed as part of a plant modernization program. It costs $10,000, including installation, and is expected to reduce the overall plant fuel cost by $2,500 per year. Estimates of the useful life of the heat exchanger range from an optimistic 12 years to a pessimistic 4 years.

The most likely value is 5 years. Using the Beta II approximation formula, determine the expected before-tax rate of return.

11-15. Estimated maintenance expenses are very uncertain, but it is thought that there is a 50% chance they will be less than $14,000 and more than $10,000. Assuming the estimate can best be described by a normal distribution, what is:
a. The estimated mean and standard deviation?
b. The probability the expense will be more than $12,000?
c. The probability the expense will be more than $15,000? (*Hint:* Use Appendix F and the relation

$$S = \frac{\text{Upper limit cost} - \text{Expected (mean) cost}}{\text{Standard deviation}})$$

11-16. Using the Beta II distribution approximation formula and the fact that for independent elements (variables) being added the expected total = the sum of the expected elements and the variance of the total = the sum of the variances of the independent elements, find the expected total mean cost and variance of the cost for the following:

Cost element	Optimistic cost	Most likely cost	Pessimistic cost
1. Direct labor	$79	$95	$95
2. Direct material	60	66	67
3. Indirect expenses	93	93	96

Chapter

12

sensitivity analysis

There are a number of procedures for *describing* analytically the effects of risk and uncertainty on capital projects. Such procedures are generally categorized as *sensitivity* or *risk analyses*. In this chapter sensitivity analysis procedures are described. Risk analysis is considered in Chapter 13.

Sensitivity analyses are performed when conditions of uncertainty exist for one or more parameters. The objectives of a sensitivity analysis are to provide the decision-maker with information concerning (1) the behavior of the measure of economic effectiveness due to errors in estimating various values of the parameters and (2) the potential for reversals in the preferences for economic investment alternatives. The term sensitivity analysis is derived from the desire to measure the sensitivity of a decision to changes in the values of one or more parameters.

One-At-A-Time Procedure

One-at-a-time sensitivity analysis procedures consider the sensitivity of the measure of economic effectiveness due to changes in a single parameter.

Example:

An investment alternative is being considered by a firm. The following estimates have been provided:

Parameter	Estimate
Investment:	$10,000
Project life:	5 yr
Salvage value:	$ 2,000
Annual receipts:	$ 5,000
Annual disbursements:	$ 2,200
M.A.R.R. $= 8\%$	

A sensitivity analysis is to be performed for those parameters whose estimated values are most uncertain. In this case, project life, M.A.R.R., and annual disbursements are to be considered one at a time.

Solution:

The example problem illustrates the importance of knowing the context in which the investment occurs. Namely, if the investment is one which will be repeated a sufficient number of times that either an indefinite planning horizon or a least-common-multiple-of-lives planning horizon is appropriate, then it is easier to perform an A.W. analysis than, say, a P.W. analysis. However, if the investment will not be repeated, then a present worth analysis may be easier to perform. Both approaches will be used to illustrate the differences in the results. Annual worth approach:

$$\text{A.W.} = -\$10,000(A/P,i\%,N) + \$5,000 - D + \$2,000(A/F,i\%,N)$$

where D denotes the annual disbursement. The results of a one-at-a-time sensitivity analysis are depicted graphically in Fig. 12-1. The abscissa expresses the changes in i, N, and D as a percentage of the estimated values. Present worth approach:

$$\text{P.W.} = -\$10,000 + \$5,000(P/A,i\%,N) - D(P/A,i\%,N)$$
$$+ \$2,000(P/F,i\%,N)$$

The results of a one-at-a-time sensitivity analysis are depicted in Fig. 12-2. It appears, from the $\pm 20\%$ error regions, that both the A.W. and the P.W. are equally sensitive to changes in the project life and annual receipts. Both A.W. and P.W. are relatively insensitive to changes in the M.A.R.R. Furthermore, the project will be profitable, (A.W. > 0 and P.W. > 0), so long as either the project life is at least 80% of the estimated value, the M.A.R.R. is no more than twice the estimated value, or the annual disbursements do not increase by more than approximately 28%. The primary difference in the A.W. and P.W. analyses is the effect of project life. With A.W. the effect of changes in project life decreases at a faster rate, i.e., levels off sooner, than with P.W. In

273

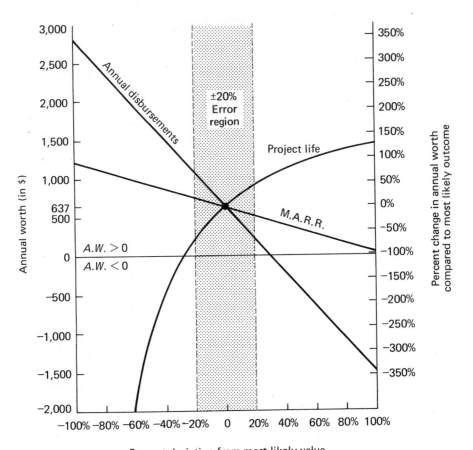

Figure 12-1. One-at-a-time sensitivity analysis of A.W.

the $\pm 20\%$ error region, however, the sensitivity of project life is relatively the same for both measures of economic effectiveness.

Example:

Four alternative incinerators are to be compared on the basis of the following estimates:

	Incinerator			
	A	*B*	*C*	*D*
First cost:	$3,000	$3,800	$4,500	$5,000
Life:	10 yr	10 yr	10 yr	10 yr
Salvage value:	0	0	0	0
Annual operating disbursements:	$1,800	$1,770	$1,470	$1,320
M.A.R.R. = 10%				

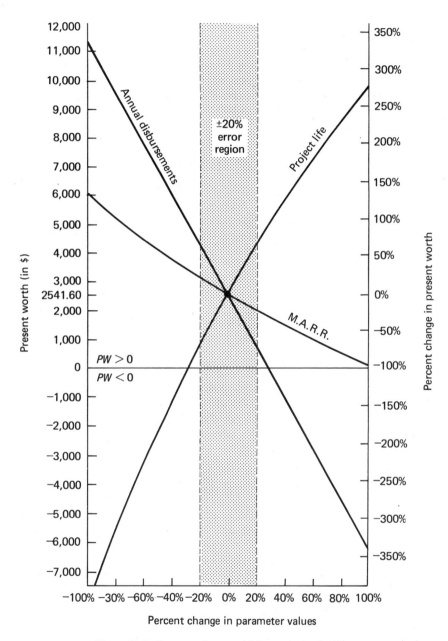

Figure 12-2. One-at-a-time sensitivity analysis of P.W.

275

It is desired to determine the sensitivity of the preferred alternative to either estimation errors or changes in the annual operating disbursements.

Solution:

The equivalent uniform annual cost is given in Fig. 12-3 for various percent changes in the annual operating disbursements. The choice will be between alternatives A and D because one or the other will have the minimum annual cost over the entire range. Setting the A.C.(A) = A.C.(D) and solving for the percent change in annual disbursements gives

$$\$3,000(A/P,10\%,10) + \$1,800(1 + x) = \$5,000(A/P,10\%,10)$$
$$+ \$1,320(1 + x)$$
$$\$2,000(A/P,10\%,10) = \$480(1 + x)$$
$$\$325.50 = \$480(1 + x)$$
$$x = -0.322 \quad \text{or} \quad -32.2\%$$

Thus, so long as the annual disbursements are at least 67.8% of the estimated value, then alternative D will be preferred. On the basis of the analysis, it might be concluded that the decision is relatively insensitive to changes in the annual disbursements.

Sensitivity to Decision Reversal

A related sensitivity test which is often quite valuable is to determine the relative (or absolute) change in one or more elements (parameters) which will just reverse the decision. Applied to the investment alternative example on pg. 273, this means the relative change which will decrease the net A.W. by $637 so that it reaches $0. Table 12-1 shows this and emphasizes that decision reversal is most sensitive to relative changes in annual savings and least sensitive to relative changes in the salvage value.

Table 12-1

EXAMPLE OF SENSITIVITY TO DECISION REVERSAL

	Most likely estimate	*To reverse decision (decrease A.W. to $0)*		
		Estimate outcome	*Change amount*	*Change amount as % of most likely*
Investment:	$10,000	$12,540	+$2,540	+ 25%
Life:	5 yr	3.7 yr	− 1.3	− 26%
Salvage value:	$ 2,000	− $1,740	−$3,740	−187%
Annual savings:	5,000	4,363	− 637	− 13%
Annual disbursements:	2,200	2,837	+ 637	+ 29%
Minimum attractive rate of return:	8%	16.2%	+ 8.2%	+103%

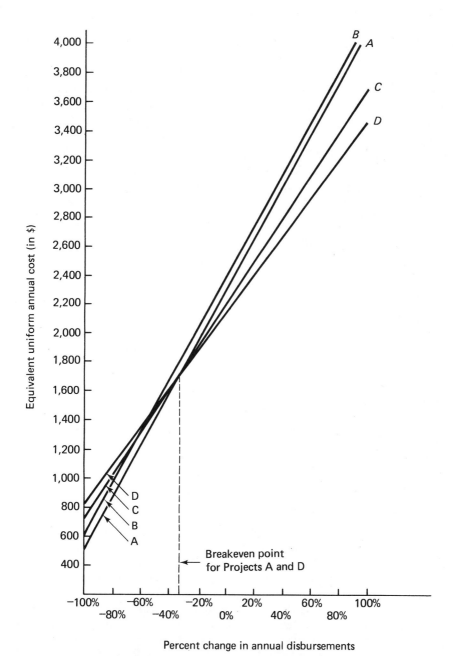

Figure 12-3. Sensitivity analysis of changes in operating disbursements
—incinerator example.

Multiparameter Procedures

The preceding discussion concentrated on the sensitivity of the measure of effectiveness to changes in a single parameter. Such an approach allows the most sensitive parameter to be identified. However, it overlooks the possibility of interaction among parameters. Additionally, since estimation errors will generally occur in more than one parameter, it is important to examine the sensitivity of the measure of effectiveness to multiple parameters.

Two approaches will be described in the consideration of multiparameter sensitivity analysis. First, the approach used in the one-at-a-time analysis will be extended to multiple parameters; second, an optimistic–pessimistic approach will be described.

Sensitivity Surface Approach

In the one-at-a-time analysis depicted in Figs. 12-1 and 12-2 sensitivity curves were obtained. If combinations of more than one parameter are analyzed, a sensitivity surface is required.

Example:

Consider the data which were used to develop Figs. 12-1 and 12-2. Suppose the most critical parameters are believed to be the initial investment and the annual receipts. Perform a multiparameter sensitivity analysis involving the two parameters.

Solution:

Let x denote the percent change in the initial investment and let y denote the percent change in the annual receipts. The annual worth can be given as

$$A.W. = -\$10,000(1 + x)(A/P,8\%,5) + \$5,000(1 + y) - \$2,200$$
$$+ \$2,000(A/F,8\%,5)$$
$$A.W. = \$636.32 - \$2,504.60x + \$5,000y$$

The investment will be profitable so long as A.W. ≥ 0 or

$$y \geq -0.127264 + 0.50092x$$

Plotting the inequality relationship yields the two regions depicted in Fig. 12-4. The favorable region (A.W. > 0) is dominant. If errors in estimating the values of the investment and annual receipts were statistically independent and uniformly distributed over the interval $\pm10\%$, then the probability of A.W. < 0 would be given by the ratio of the shaded area below the break-even line which is contained within the $\pm10\%$ error region to the total area in the error region. However, it is not generally the case that estimation errors are either statistically independent or uniformly distributed. Furthermore, the incorporation of probabilistic considerations in sensitivity analyses lies in the domain of risk analysis, to be considered subsequently. If it is anticipated

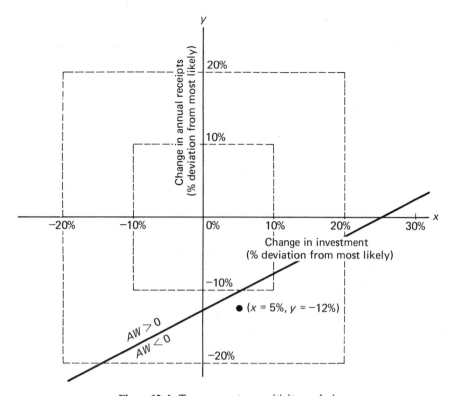

Figure 12-4. Two-parameter sensitivity analysis.

that $\pm 20\%$ estimation errors will be made, then there is greater concern for the profitability of the investment. For example, the combination of a 5% increase in the initial investment and a 12% reduction in annual receipts would result in a negative annual worth.

Example:

Suppose that in the previous example the life of the investment is also a critical parameter. Perform a multiparameter sensitivity analysis for the three parameters.

Solution:

It is difficult to develop a three-dimensional representation of the sensitivity surface. But it is possible to gain an insight into the sensitivity of annual worth to errors in estimating the three parameters by plotting a family of break-even lines for each possible value of project life. Letting A.W.(N) denote the annual worth as a function of N, the following results are obtained:

$$\text{A.W.}(N) = -\$10,000(1 + x)(A/P,8\%,N) + \$5,000(1 + y) - \$2,200$$
$$+ \$2,000(A/F,8\%,N) \geq 0$$
$$\text{A.W.}(2) = -\$1,846.62 - \$5,607.70x + \$5,000y \geq 0$$
$$y \geq 0.369324 + 1.12154x$$

A.W.(3) $= -\$464.24 - \$3,880.30x + \$5,000y \geq 0$

$y \geq 0.092848 + 0.77606x$

A.W.(4) $= \$224.64 - \$3,019.20x + \$5,000y \geq 0$

$y \geq -0.044928 + 0.60384x$

A.W.(5) $= \$636.32 - \$2,504.60x + \$5,000y \geq 0$

$y \geq -0.127264 + 0.50092x$

A.W.(6) $= \$909.44 - \$2,163.20x + \$5,000y \geq 0$

$y \geq -0.181888 + 0.43264x$

A.W.(7) $= \$1,121.15 - \$1,920.70x + \$5,000y \geq 0$

$y \geq -0.22423 + 0.38414x$

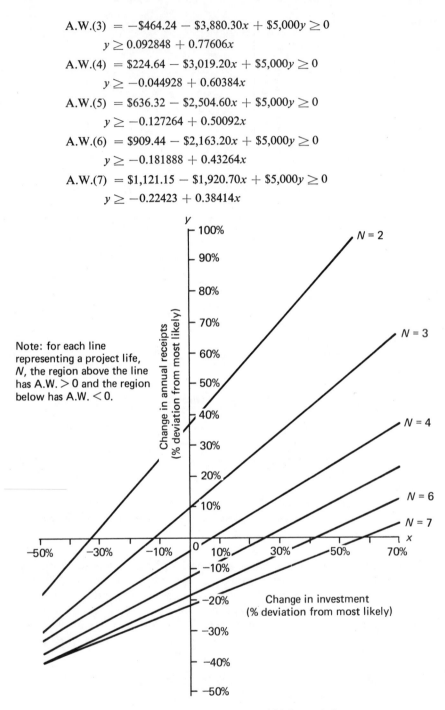

Figure 12-5. Three-parameter sensitivity analysis.

The family of break-even lines are given in Fig. 12-5. For $N = 4, 5, 6$ (a $\pm$ 20% range), the profitability of the investment continues to appear promising. However, for $N = 4$, there is very little opportunity for error in estimating the investment required and the annual receipts. In particular, if $N = 4$, then with a 10% increase in the investment there must be at least a 1.55% increase in annual receipts for the annual worth to be positive.

Optimistic–Pessimistic Approach

The optimistic–pessimistic approach, as its name implies, involves changing estimates of one or more elements in a favorable outcome (optimistic) direction and in an unfavorable outcome (pessimistic) direction to determine the effect of these various changes on the economy study result.

In using this method, it is desirable for the estimator to adopt a guideline philosophy of "how optimistic" and "how pessimistic" in making the estimates. One convenient way to do this is to adopt a probabilistic statement such as: "An optimistic estimate will mean a value of the element which we would expect to be bettered or exceeded in outcome no more than, say, 5% of the time, while a pessimistic estimate is a value of the element which we would expect to be more favorable than the final outcome no more than, say, 5% of the time." Figure 12-6 illustrates this.

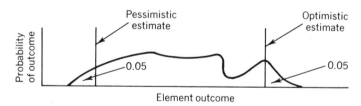

Figure 12-6. Illustration of estimates for optimistic-pessimistic approach.

Example:

For the single project example given above, suppose the optimistic, pessimistic, and most likely estimates are as follows:

	Estimation condition		
	Optimistic	*Most likely*	*Pessimistic*
Investment:	$10,000	$10,000	$10,000
Life:	7 yr	5 yr	4 yr
Salvage value:	$2,000	$2,000	$2,000
Annual receipts:	$6,000	$5,000	$4,500
Annual disbursements:	$2,200	$2,200	$2,400
Interest rate:	8%	8%	8%

Solution:

Using the annual worth method and the "repeatability" assumptions:

A.W.(optimistic) $= \$-10,000(A/P,8\%,7) + \$2,000(A/F,8\%,7) + \$3,800$

$\qquad\qquad\quad = \$2,103$

A.W.(most likely) $= \$-10,000(A/P,8\%,5) + \$2,000(A/F,8\%,5) + \$2,800$

$\qquad\qquad\quad = \$637$

A.W.(pessimistic) $= \$-10,000(A/P,8\%,4) + \$2,000(A/F,8\%,4) + \$2,100$

$\qquad\qquad\quad = -\$475$

The above example calculations are based on the assumption that the elements are going to all equal the pessimistic estimates, all equal the most likely estimates, or all equal the optimistic estimates. Of course, one can investigate the effect on calculated results when various elements equal to optimistic, most likely, or pessimistic estimates in various combinations. When this is done, it is usually helpful to summarize the results in tabular form.

Example:

For the above example, note that estimates for the three conditions differed only for the project life, annual receipts, and annual disbursements. Table 12-2 shows the calculated results for all combinations of estimating conditions— optimistic (O), most likely (M), and pessimistic (P)—for all elements that vary significantly. Displays such as Table 12-2 can be made more easily informative by the use of histogram bars or other symbols. For example, all outcomes greater than $1,500 are marked for emphasis in Table 12-2.

Table 12-2

Calculated Results for All Combinations of Estimating Conditions

	Net annual worth								
	Annual disb.—O			Annual disb.—M			Annual disb.—P		
Life	O	M	P	O	M	P	O	M	P
Annual O	$2,103*	$1,637*	$1,235	$2,103*	$1,637*	$1,235	$1,903*	$1,437	$1,035
receipts M	1,103	637	235	1,103	637	235	903	437	35
P	603	137	− 275	603	137	− 275	403	− 63	− 475

Key: *O* is optimistic outcome.

    M is most likely outcome.

    P is pessimistic outcome.

*Indicates Net A.W. > 1,500

PROBLEMS

12-1. A certain potential investment project is critical to a firm. The following are "best" or "most likely" estimates:

Investment:	$100,000
Life:	10 yr
Salvage value:	$20,000
Net annual cash flow:	$30,000
Minimum required rate of return:	10%

It is desired to show the sensitivity of a measure of merit (net annual worth) to variation, over a range of ±50% of the expected values, in the following elements: (a) life, (b) net annual cash flow, and (c) interest rate. Graph the results. To which element is the decision most sensitive?

12-2. Suppose that for a certain potential investment project the optimistic–pessimistic estimates are as follows:

	Optimistic	Most likely	Pessimistic
Investment:	$90,000	$100,000	$120,000
Life:	12 yr	10 yr	6 yr
Salvage value:	$30,000	$20,000	0
Net annual cash flow:	$35,000	$30,000	$20,000
Minimum required rate of return:	10%	10%	10%

a. What is the net annual worth for each of the three estimation conditions?
b. It is thought that the most critical elements are life and net annual cash flow. Develop a table showing the net annual worth for all combinations of estimates for those two elements assuming all other elements to be as expected.

12-3. Two pumps, A and B, are being considered for a given drainage need. Both pumps operate at a rated output of 8 kW (10.7 hp), but differ in initial cost and electrical efficiency. Electricity costs 2¢ per kWh and the minimum before-tax rate of return is 15%. Below are relevant data.

	Pump A	Pump B
Cost installed:	$3,500	$4,500
Expected life to termination at zero salvage value:	10 yr	15 yr
Maintenance cost per 1,000 hr of operation:	$50	$30
Efficiency:	60%	80%

a. The critical variable hardest to estimate is the number of hours of operation per year. Determine the break-even point for this variable.

b. If the operating time is greater than the break-even point in part a, which pump is better?

c. Plot the total annual costs of each pump as a function of hours of operation.

12-4. A new all-season hotel will require land costing $300,000 and a structure costing $500,000. In addition, fixtures will cost $150,000, and working capital of 30 days' gross income at 100% capacity will be required. While the land is nondepreciable, the investment in fixtures should be recovered in 8 years, and the investment in the structure should be recovered in 25 years.

When the hotel is operating at 100% capacity, the gross income will be $1,400 per day. Fixed operating expenses, exclusive of depreciation and interest, will amount to $120,000 per year. Operating expenses, which vary linearly in proportion to the level of operation, are $80,000 per year at 100% capacity.

a. At what percentage of capacity must the hotel operate to earn a before-tax minimum attractive rate of return of 20%?

b. Plot the revenue and total cost (including cost of capital) as a function of percentage of capacity. (*Note:* The point at which revenue and the total of all costs, including capital, are equal is commonly called the *unhealthy point.*)

12-5. It is desired to determine the most economic thickness of insulation for a large cold-storage room. Insulation is expected to cost $150 per 1,000 sq ft of wall area per in. of thickness installed and to require annual property taxes and insurance of 5% of first cost. It is expected to have 0 net salvage value after a 20-year life. The following are estimates of the heat loss per 1,000 sq ft of wall area for several thicknesses:

Insulation, in.	Heat loss, Btu per hr
3	4,400
4	3,400
5	2,800
6	2,400
7	2,000
8	1,800

The cost of heat removal is estimated at $0.01 per 1,000 Btu per hr. The minimum required yield on investment is 20%. Assuming continuous operation throughout the year, analyze the sensitivity of the optimal thickness to errors in estimating the cost of heat removal.

12-6. An industrial machine costing $1,000 will produce net savings of $400 per year. The machine has a 5-year economic life but must be returned to the factory for major repairs after 3 years of operation. These repairs cost $500.

The company's cost of capital is approximately 10%. What rate of return will be earned on purchase of this machine? Analyze the sensitivity of the internal rate of return by considering the repair cost to be the critical parameter.

12-7. The following alternatives are available to fill a given need which is expected to exist indefinitely. Each is expected to have 0 salvage value at the end of each life cycle.

	Plan A	Plan B	Plan C
First cost:	$2,000	$6,000	$12,000
Life cycle:	6 yr	3 yr	4 yr
Annual disbursements:	$3,500	$1,000	$400

  a. Analyze the sensitivity of the preferred plan due to errors in estimating the annual disbursements. Use a M.A.R.R. of 10%.
  b. Analyze the sensitivity of the preferred plan due to errors in estimating the M.A.R.R.

12-8. An improved facility costing $50,000 has been proposed. Construction time will be 2 years with expenditures of $20,000 the first year and $30,000 the second year. Savings beginning the first year after construction completion are as follows:

Year	Savings
1	$10,000
2	14,000
3	18,000
4	22,000
5	26,000

The facility will not be required after 5 years and will have a salvage value of $5,000. Analyze the sensitivity of annual worth due to errors in estimating both the savings in the first year and the magnitude of the gradient amount.

12-9. It is desired to determine the optimal height for a proposed building which is expected to last 40 years and then be demolished at zero salvage. The following are pertinent data:

	Number of floors			
	2	3	4	5
Building first cost:	$200,000	$250,000	$320,000	$400,000
Annual revenue:	40,000	60,000	85,000	100,000
Annual cash disbursements:	15,000	25,000	25,000	45,000

In addition to the building first cost, the land requires an investment of $50,000 and is expected to retain that value throughout the life period. Analyze the sensitivity of the decision due to errors in estimating the M.A.R.R.

12-10. There are five alternative machines to do a given job. Each is expected to have a salvage value of 100% of the investment amount at the end of its life of 4 years. The firm's minimum attractive rate of return is 12%. Analyze the sensitivity of the best choice due to the salvage value ranging from 0% to 100% of the initial investment.

	Machine				
	A	B	C	D	E
Investment:	$1,000	$1,400	$2,100	$2,700	$3,400
Net cash flow per yr:	110	180	280	340	445

12-11. Best estimates of the parameters for an investment are given below. It is expected that the investment will be repeated indefinitely.

Initial investment: $15,000
Net annual receipt: $ 2,500
Project life: 10 yr
Salvage value: 0
M.A.R.R. = 15%

a. Perform a one-at-a-time sensitivity analysis to determine the most critical parameter.
b. Perform a multiparameter sensitivity analysis using the sensitivity surface approach. Base the analysis on the initial investment and the net annual receipt.

12-12. An office building is considering converting from a coal burning furnace to one which burns either fuel oil or natural gas. The cost of converting to fuel oil is estimated to be $80,000 initially; annual operating costs are estimated to be $4,000 less than that experienced using the coal furnace. Approximately 140,000 Btu's are produced per gallon of fuel oil; fuel oil is anticipated to cost $0.13 per gallon.

The cost of converting to natural gas is estimated to be $60,000 initially; additionally, annual operating and maintenance costs are estimated to be $6,000 less than that for the coal-burning furnace. Approximately 1,000 Btu's are produced per cubic foot of natural gas; it is estimated natural gas will cost $0.0025 per cu ft.

A planning horizon of 20 years is to be used. Zero salvage values and a 10% M.A.R.R. are appropriate. Perform a sensitivity analysis for the annual Btu requirement for the heating system.

risk analysis

As was noted previously, *sensitivity analyses* are performed under *conditions of uncertainty* for an investment in order to *describe* the effects on the measure of effectiveness due to either estimation errors or changes in the values of one or more parameters. When *conditions of risk* are present, the process is referred to as *risk analysis.*

The term risk analysis has different interpretations among various government agencies and units, as well as nongovernment organizations. However, there is a growing acceptance that risk analysis involves the development of the probability distribution for the measure of effectiveness. Furthermore, the *risk* associated with an investment alternative is generally either given as the probability of an unfavorable value for the measure of effectiveness or measured by the variance of the measure of effectiveness.

Analytical Methods

Typical parameters for which conditions of risk can reasonably be expected to exist include the initial investment, yearly operating and maintenance expenses, salvage values, the life of an investment, the planning horizon, and the minimum attractive rate of return. The parameters can be statistically independent, correlated with time and/or correlated with each other. Analytical methods of performing risk analyses are described in this section.

Random Cash Flows

In order to determine analytically the probability distribution for the measure of effectiveness, a number of simplifying assumptions are normally made. The simplest situation is one involving a known number of random and statistically independent cash flows. As an example, suppose the random variable A_j denotes the net cash flow occurring at the end of period $j, j = 0, 1, \ldots, N$. Hence, the present worth is given by

$$\text{P.W.} = \sum_{j=0}^{N} (1 + i)^{-j} A_j \qquad 13\text{-}1$$

Since the expected value of a sum of random variables equals the sum of the expected values of the random variables, then the expected present worth is given by*

$$E[\text{P.W.}] = \sum_{j=0}^{N} (1 + i)^{-j} E[A_j] \qquad 13\text{-}2$$

where $E[\cdot]$ denotes the expected value. Furthermore, since the A_j's are statistically independent, then the variance of present worth is given by†

$$V[\text{P.W.}] = \sum_{j=0}^{N} (1 + i)^{-2j} V[A_j.] \qquad 13\text{-}3$$

where $V[\cdot]$ denotes the variance, and $\sigma[\cdot] = \sqrt{V[\cdot]}$ will denote the standard deviation.

The Central Limit Theorem, from probability theory, establishes that the sum of independently distributed random variables tends to be normally distributed as the number of terms in the summation increases.‡ Hence, as N increases, P.W. tends to be normally distributed with a mean value of $E[\text{P.W.}]$ and a variance of $V[\text{P.W.}]$.

---

*Recall that the expected value of a constant times a random variable equals the constant times the expected value of the random variable.

†Recall that the variance of a constant times a random variable equals the constant squared times the variance of the random variable.

‡An additional condition is that the random variables have finite moments. The condition is usually met in risk analysis.

288

Example:
   Consider the following data: M.A.R.R. $= 10\%$

j	$E[A_j]$	$V[A_j]$
0	$-\$10,000$	1×10^6
1–10	$\$ 1,800$	4×10^4

Determine the probability of a negative present worth.

Solution:

$$E[\text{P.W.}] = -\$10,000 + \sum_{j=1}^{10} (1.10)^{-j} \,\$1,800$$

$$= -\$10,000 + \$1,800(P/A,10\%,10)$$

$$= \$1,059.20$$

$$V[\text{P.W.}] = 1 \times 10^6 + (4 \times 10^4) \sum_{j=1}^{10} (1.10)^{-2j}$$

which reduces to*

$$V[\text{P.W.}] = 1 \times 10^6 + (4 \times 10^4)(P/A,10\%,20)/2.10$$

$$= 116.217 \times 10^4$$

The probability of P.W. ≤ 0 is obtained as follows:

$$Pr(\text{P.W.} \le 0) = Pr\left(S \le \frac{0 - E[\text{P.W.}]}{\sqrt{V[\text{P.W}]}}\right) \qquad \textit{13-4}$$

$$= Pr\left(S \le -\frac{1,059.20}{1,078.04}\right)$$

$$= Pr(S \le -0.982)$$

$$= 0.163$$

where S is the standard normal deviate for which a table of probabilities is given in Appendix F.

A slightly more complex situation involves a set of correlated cash flows. In particular, if the A_j's are not statistically independent, then the variance calculation is modified as follows:

$$V[\text{P.W.}] = \sum_{j=0}^{N} V[A_j](1 + i)^{-2j} + 2 \sum_{j=0}^{N-1} \sum_{k=j+1}^{N} \text{Cov}[A_j, A_k](1 + i)^{-(j+k)} \quad \textit{13-5}$$

where $\text{Cov}[A_j, A_k]$† is the covariance between A_j and A_k. Alternately, the

---

*The relation $\sum_{j=1}^{N} (1 + i)^{-2j} = (P/A,i\%,2N)/(2 + i)$ is used.

†Recall $\text{Cov}[X, Y] = E[XY] - E[X]E[Y]$.

variance can be given as

$$V[\text{P.W.}] = \sum_{j=0}^{N} V[A_j](1 + i)^{-2j} + 2 \sum_{j=0}^{N-1} \sum_{k=j+1}^{N} \rho_{jk}\sigma[A_j]\sigma[A_k](1 + i)^{-(j+k)}$$

13-6

where ρ_{jk} is the correlation coefficient between A_j and A_k.
If all A_j and A_k are perfectly correlated such that $\rho_{jk} = +1$, then

$$V[\text{P.W.}] = \left\{ \sum_{j=0}^{N} \sigma[A_j](1 + i)^{-j} \right\}^{2}$$

13-7

When dealing with correlated random variables there is greater uncertainty that a normal approximation is reasonable as the distribution for P.W. However, such an assumption is often made when a large number of random variables are involved and not all are correlated. In the absence of suitable conditions for the use of a normal approximation, Monte Carlo simulation is recommended.

In performing risk analyses involving correlated cash flows Hillier [203] argues that it is probably unrealistic to expect that accurate estimates of covariances can be obtained. Consequently, it is suggested that the net cash flow in any year be separated into those components of cash flow one can reasonably expect to be independent from year to year and those that are correlated over time. Specifically, Hillier assumes that the net cash flow in year j can be represented by

$$A_j = X_j + Y_{j1} + Y_{j2} + \cdots + Y_{jm}$$

13-8

where X_j denotes the component of cash flow that is statistically independent for all values of j and Y_{jk} denotes the component of cash flow which is *perfectly* correlated with $Y_{0k}, Y_{1k}, \ldots, Y_{Nk}$. Notice that $Y_{j1}, Y_{j2}, \ldots,$ and Y_{jm} are statistically independent. Thus, it is assumed that Y_{jk} is perfectly correlated over j and perfectly uncorrelated over k.

The resulting expected value of present worth and variance of present worth can be given as

$$E[\text{P.W.}] = \sum_{j=0}^{N} E[X_j](1 + i)^{-j} + \sum_{j=0}^{N} \sum_{k=1}^{m} E[Y_{jk}](1 + i)^{-j}$$

13-9

and

$$V[\text{P.W.}] = \sum_{j=0}^{N} V[X_j](1 + i)^{-2j} + \sum_{k=1}^{m} \left\{ \sum_{j=0}^{N} \sigma[Y_{jk}](1 + i)^{-j} \right\}^{2}$$

13-10

Example:
A firm is considering purchasing a numerically controlled milling machine. A firm quote indicates the machine can be purchased and installed for $150,000. A planning horizon of 10 years is used in the analysis. The salvage value is anticipated to be normally distributed with a mean of $25,000 and a standard deviation of $2,500. Labor costs are expected to be perfectly correlated; maintenance costs are also expected to be perfectly correlated; and

other annual operating costs are anticipated to be statistically independent. The expected values and standard deviations are estimated as follows:

$$E[\text{labor } j] = -\$10,000 - (j - 1)\$1,000$$
$$\sigma[\text{labor } j] = 0.10\ E[\text{labor } j]$$
$$E[\text{maintenance } j] = -\$1,000 - (j - 1)\$500$$
$$\sigma[\text{maintenance } j] = 0.20\ E[\text{maintenance } j]$$
$$E[\text{other } j] = -\$3,000$$
$$\sigma[\text{other } j] = \$500$$

Using a M.A.R.R. of 20% it is desired to determine $E[\text{P.W.}]$ and $\sigma[\text{P.W.}]$.

Solution:

$$\begin{aligned}
E[\text{P.W.}] = {} & -\$150,000 + \$25,000(P/F,20\%,10) \\
& - [\$10,000 + \$1,000(A/G,20\%,10)](P/A,20\%,10) \\
& - [\$1,000 + \$500(A/G,20\%,10)](P/A,20\%,10) \\
& - \$3,000(P/A,20\%,10) \\
= {} & -\$227,507
\end{aligned}$$

$$V[\text{P.W.}] = (500)^2 \sum_{j=1}^{10} (1.20)^{-2j} + (2,500)^2(1.20)^{-20}$$

$$+ \left\{ \sum_{j=1}^{10} [1,000 + 100(j-1)](1.20)^{-j} \right\}^2 + \left\{ \sum_{j=1}^{10} [200 + 100(j-1)](1.20)^{-j} \right\}^2$$

$$\begin{aligned}
V[\text{P.W.}] = {} & \frac{250,000(P/A,20\%,20)}{2.20} + 6,250,000(P/F,20\%,20) \\
& + \{[1,000 + 100(A/G,20\%,10)](P/A,20\%,10)\}^2 \\
& + \{[200 + 100(A/G,20\%,10)](P/A,20\%,10)\}^2
\end{aligned}$$

$$V[\text{P.W.}] \doteq 35.25 \times 10^6$$

Therefore, $\sigma[\text{P.W.}] = \$5,937$.

Example:

The firm described in the previous example is considering as an alternative a semiautomated milling machine which will cost $80,000 initially and have a normally distributed salvage value in 10 years with a mean of $15,000 and a standard deviation of $1,000. As with the numerically controlled alternative, yearly labor costs are perfectly correlated and yearly maintenance costs are perfectly correlated; other annual operating costs are anticipated to be statistically independent. The following expected values and standard deviations have been estimated:

$$E[\text{labor } j] = -\$20,000 - (j - 1)\$2,000$$
$$\sigma[\text{labor } j] = 0.15E[\text{labor } j]$$
$$E[\text{maintenance } j] = -\$500 - (j - 1)\$400$$
$$\sigma[\text{maintenance } j] = 0.20E[\text{maintenance } j]$$
$$E[\text{other } j] = -\$6,000$$
$$\sigma[\text{other } j] = \$1,000$$

Using a M.A.R.R. of 20% it is desired to determine the probability that the numerically controlled milling machine is the preferred alternative. The present worth of each alternative is assumed to be normally distributed.

Solution:

$$E[P.W.] = -\$80,000 + \$15,000(P/F,20\%,10)$$
$$- [\$20,000 + \$2,000(A/G,20\%,10)](P/A,20\%,10)$$
$$- [\$500 + \$400(A/G,20\%,10)](P/A,20\%,10) - \$6,000(P/A,20\%,10)$$
$$= -\$219,552$$

$$V[P.W.] = \frac{(1,000)^2(P/A,20\%,20)}{2.20} + (1,000)^2(P/F,20\%,20)$$
$$+ \{[3,000 + 300(A/G,20\%,10)](P/A,20\%,10)\}^2$$
$$+ \{[100 + 80(A/G,20\%,10)](P/A,20\%,10)\}^2$$
$$V[P.W.] \doteq 274.51 \times 10^6$$

Therefore, $\sigma[P.W.] = \$16,568$.

Letting $P.W._1$ denote the present worth of the numerically controlled milling machine and $P.W._2$ denote the present worth of the semiautomatic machine, then it is desired to determine $Pr(P.W._1 > P.W._2)$ or $Pr(P.W._1 - P.W._2 > 0)$. Letting $Y = P.W._1 - P.W._2$, if $P.W._1$ and $P.W._2$ are normally distributed, then Y will be normally distributed with an expected value of $E[Y] = E[P.W._1] - E[P.W._2]$ and a variance of $V[Y] = V[P.W._1] + V[P.W._2]$. Therefore,

$$E[Y] = -\$227,507 + \$219,552 = -\$7,955$$
$$V[Y] = (35.25 \times 10^6) + (274.51 \times 10^6) = 309.76 \times 10^6$$

and

$$Pr(Y > 0) = Pr\left(S > \frac{0 - (-\$7,955)}{\sqrt{309.76 \times 10^6}}\right) = Pr(S > 0.452)$$

or, using appendix F,

Pr (numerically controlled milling machine is the most economical) $= 0.3257$.

Example:

In the previous example suppose the machine is to be used to manufacture parts for a 10-year production contract yielding a guaranteed annual income of $57,500. What is the probability that the firm will not make at least a 20% internal rate of return on the investment for each alternative?

Solution:

So long as there do not exist multiple roots in determining the internal rate of return, then

$$Pr(i^* < M.A.R.R.) = Pr(P.W. < 0 | M.A.R.R.)$$

Therefore, for the numerically controlled milling machine,

$$Pr(i^* < 20\%) = Pr[\$57,500(P/A,20\%,10) + \text{P.W.}_1 < 0]$$

$$= Pr(\text{P.W.}_1 < -\$241,040)$$

$$= Pr\left(S > -\frac{13,533}{\sqrt{35.25 \times 10^6}}\right) = 0.0113$$

For the semiautomatic milling machine,

$$Pr(i^* < 20\%) = Pr(\text{P.W.}_2 < -\$241,040)$$

$$= Pr\left(S < -\frac{\$21,488}{\sqrt{274.51 \times 10^6}}\right) = 0.0973$$

The numerically controlled milling machine has the lowest expected present worth. However, because of its smaller variance, it has a smaller probability of failing to earn at least a 20% internal rate of return. Thus, there is a 1.13% risk associated with the numerically controlled machine, as opposed to a 9.73% risk for the semiautomatic machine.

Random Project Life

Next, we consider the case in which the project life is a random variable, N, defined over the positive integers, i.e., $N = 1, 2, \ldots$. In this case, the present worth is given by

$$\text{P.W.} = A_0 + \sum_{j=1}^{N} (1 + i)^{-j} A_j \qquad \textit{13-11}$$

If the A_j's are statistically independent random variables, then

$$E[\text{P.W.} | N] = E[A_0] + \sum_{j=1}^{N} (1 + i)^{-j} E[A_j] \qquad \textit{13-12}$$

and

$$E[\text{P.W.}] = E[A_0] + \sum_{N=1}^{\infty} \left(\sum_{j=1}^{N} (1 + i)^{-j} E[A_j] \right) \cdot P(N) \qquad \textit{13-13}$$

where $P(N)$ is the probability mass function for N.

The variance of P.W. is obtained by first determining $E[\text{P.W.}^2]$, where

$$E[\text{P.W.}^2 | N] = E\left\{ A_0 + \sum_{j=1}^{N} (1 + i)^{-j} A_j \right\}^2 \qquad \textit{13-14}$$

$$= E\left\{ A_0^2 + \sum_{j=1}^{N} (1 + i)^{-2j} A_j^2 \right\} + E\left\{ 2 \sum_{j=0}^{N-1} \sum_{k=j+1}^{N} (1 + i)^{-j-k} A_j A_k \right\}$$

If the A_j's are statistically independent, then

$$E[\text{P.W.}^2 | N] = E[A_0^2] + \sum_{j=1}^{N} (1 + i)^{-2j} E[A_j^2]$$

$$+ 2 \sum_{j=0}^{N-1} \sum_{k=j+1}^{N} (1 + i)^{-j-k} E[A_j] E[A_k]$$

However, since $E[X^2] = V[X] - E^2[X]$, then

$$E[\text{P.W.}^2 | N] = (V[A_0] + E^2[A_0]) + \sum_{j=1}^{N} (V[A_j] + E^2[A_j])(P/F,i\%,2j)$$

$$+ 2 \sum_{j=0}^{N-1} \sum_{k=j+1}^{N} E[A_j]E[A_k](P/F,i\%,j+k) \qquad\qquad 13\text{-}15$$

Therefore,

$$E[\text{P.W.}^2] = (V[A_0] + E^2[A_0]) + \sum_{N=1}^{\infty} \left\{ \sum_{j=1}^{N} (V[A_j] + E^2[A_j])(P/F,i\%,2j) \right.$$

$$\left. + 2 \sum_{j=1}^{N-1} \sum_{k=j+1}^{N} E[A_j]E[A_k](P/F,i\%,j+k) \right\} P(N) \qquad 13\text{-}16$$

Given the values of $E[\text{P.W.}]$ and $E[\text{P.W.}^2]$, the variance of present worth is obtained from the relation

$$V[\text{P.W.}] = E[\text{P.W.}^2] - [E[\text{P.W.}]]^2 \qquad\qquad 13\text{-}17$$

Example:

Consider an investment having the following expected values and variances for the statistically independent cash flows:

j	$E[A_j]$	$V[A_j]$
0	−$10,000	1×10^6
1	2,000	2×10^4
2	3,000	3×10^4
3	4,000	4×10^4
4	5,000	5×10^4
5	6,000	6×10^4

The life of the investment is a random variable with the following probability distribution:

N	$P(N)$
3	0.25
4	0.50
5	0.25

Using a M.A.R.R. of 10%, determine the expected value of present worth and variance of present worth.

Solution:

To determine the expected present worth, the following relation is applied:

$$E[\text{P.W.}] = E[\text{P.W.} | N = 3](0.25) + E[\text{P.W.} | N = 4](0.50)$$

$$+ E[\text{P.W.} | N = 5](0.25)$$

where

$$E[\text{P.W.}|N=3] = -\$10,000 + [\$2,000 + \$1,000(A/G,10\%,3)]$$
$$(P/A,10\%,3) = -\$2,688.22$$

$$E[\text{P.W.}|N=4] = -\$10,000 + [\$2,000 + \$1,000(A/G,10\%,4)]$$
$$(P/A,10\%,4) = \$714.60$$

$$E[\text{P.W.}|N=5] = -\$10,000 + [\$2,000 + \$1,000(A/G,10\%,5)]$$
$$(P/A,10\%,5) = \$4,443.71$$

Therefore,

$$E[\text{P.W.}] = -\$2,688.22(0.25) + \$714.60(0.50) + \$4,443.71(0.25)$$
$$= \$796.17$$

To determine the variance of present worth, the value of $E[\text{P.W.}^2]$ is first determined using Eq. 13-16.

$$E[\text{P.W.}^2] = (V[A_0] + E^2[A_0]) + \sum_{N=3}^{5} \left\{ \sum_{j=1}^{N} (V[A_j] + E^2 A_j])(P/F,10\%,2j) \right.$$

$$\left. + 2\sum_{j=1}^{N-1} \sum_{k=j+1}^{N} E[A_j]E[A_k](P/F,10\%,j+k) \right\} P(N)$$

The complete solution for this problem is left to the interested student. The answer is $E[\text{P.W.}^2] = 224 \times 10^6$. Thus, using Eq. 13-17

$$V[\text{P.W.}] = (224 \times 10^6) - (796.17)^2 = 223.366 \times 10^6$$

There exists a Central Limit Theorem for the *random* sum of independent random variables which asserts that the distribution of P.W. can be approximated by the normal distribution under rather general conditions. Assuming P.W. is normally distributed yields

$$Pr(\text{P.W.} < 0) = Pr\left(S < \frac{0 - 796.17}{\sqrt{223.366 \times 10^6}} \right) = Pr(S < -0.053) = 0.4789$$

Example:
An individual is considering an investment of $10,000 in a project that will return $3,000 per year for the duration of the project. The life of the investment is not known with certainty. The following probability distribution is felt to be reasonable for the life of the investment:

N	$P(N)$
1	0.10
2	0.15
3	0.20
4	0.25
5	0.15
6	0.10
7	0.05

It is desired to determine the probability of a positive present worth, the expected present worth, and the variance of present worth. A M.A.R.R. of 15% is to be used.

Solution:

Since the cash flows are deterministic, the probability of a positive present worth is given by

$$Pr(\text{P.W.} > 0) = Pr[-\$10,000 + \$3,000(P/A,15\%,N) > 0]$$
$$= Pr[(P/A,15\%,N) > 3.33]$$

From the interest tables it is seen that the $(P/A,15\%,N)$ factor is greater than 3.33 for values of N greater than or equal to 5. Therefore,

$$Pr(\text{P.W.} > 0) = Pr(N \geq 5) = 0.15 + 0.10 + 0.05 = 0.30$$

The expected present worth is given by

$$E[\text{P.W.}] = -\$10,000 + \$3,000 \sum_{N=1}^{7} (P/A,15\%,N)P(N)$$
$$= -\$10,000 + \$3,000[0.870(0.10) + 1.626(0.15)$$
$$+ 2.283(0.20) + 2.855(0.25) + 3.352(0.15)$$
$$+ 3.784(0.10) + 4.160(0.05)]$$
$$= -\$10,000 + \$3,000(2.59045) = -\$2,228.65$$

The variance of present worth is obtained as follows:

$$E[\text{P.W.}^2] = \sum_{N=1}^{7} [-\$10,000 + \$3,000(P/A,15\%,N)]^2 P(N)$$
$$= (-\$7,390)^2(0.10) + (-\$5,122)^2(0.15) + (-\$3,151)^2(0.20)$$
$$+ (-\$1,435)^2(0.25) + (\$3,136)^2(0.15) + (\$1,352)^2(0.10)$$
$$+ (\$2,480)^2(0.05) = 13.86 \times 10^6$$

Thus,

$$V[\text{P.W.}] = (13.86 \times 10^6) - (2,228.65)^2$$
$$= 8.90 \times 10^6$$

Example:

In the previous example suppose that each annual receipt will be identical but that the size of the first annual receipt is a random variable, A, with the following probability distribution:

A	P(A)
$2,000	0.20
$3,000	0.50
$4,000	0.30

Determine the probability of a profitable investment, the expected present worth, and the variance of present worth.

Solution:

The probability of a positive present worth can be obtained as follows:

$$Pr(\text{P.W.} > 0) = Pr(\text{P.W.} > 0 \,|\, A = \$2,000)(0.20)$$
$$+ Pr(\text{P.W.} > 0 \,|\, A = \$3,000)(0.50)$$
$$+ Pr(\text{P.W.} > 0 \,|\, A = \$4,000)(0.30)$$

or

$$Pr(\text{P.W.} > 0) = Pr[(P/A,15\%,N) > 5.00 \,|\, A = \$2,000](0.20)$$
$$+ Pr[(P/A,15\%,N) > 3.33 \,|\, A = \$3,000](0.50)$$
$$+ Pr[(P/A,15\%,N) > 2.50 \,|\, A = \$4,000](0.30)$$

which reduces to

$$Pr(\text{P.W.} > 0) = Pr(N \geq 10)(0.20) + Pr(N \geq 5)(0.50) + Pr(N \geq 4)(0.30)$$
$$= 0(0.20) + 0.30(0.50) + 0.55(0.30)$$
$$= 0.315$$

The expected present worth can be obtained in a similar manner, namely,

$$E[\text{P.W.}] = \sum_A \sum_N E[\text{P.W.} \,|\, N,A] P(N)P(A) \qquad \textit{13-18}$$
$$= \sum_A E[\text{P.W.} \,|\, A] P(A)$$

From previous calculations it is seen that

$$E[\text{P.W.} \,|\, A = \$2,000] = -\$10,000 + \$2,000(2.59045) = -\$4,819.10$$
$$E[\text{P.W.} \,|\, A = \$3,000] = -\$10,000 + \$3,000(2.59045) = -\$2,228.65$$
$$E[\text{P.W.} \,|\, A = \$4,000] = -\$10,000 + \$4,000(2.59045) = \$361.80$$

Therefore,

$$E[\text{P.W.}] = -\$4,819.10(0.20) - \$2,228.65(0.50) + \$361.80(0.30)$$
$$= -\$1,969.61$$

The variance of present worth is obtained as follows:

$$E[\text{P.W.}^2] = \left\{ \sum_{N=1}^{7} [-\$10,000 + \$2,000(P/A,15\%,N)]^2 P(N) \right\}(0.20)$$
$$+ \left\{ \sum_{N=1}^{7} [-\$10,000 + \$3,000(P/A,15\%,N)]^2 P(N) \right\}(0.50)$$
$$+ \left\{ \sum_{N=1}^{7} [-\$10,000 + \$4,000(P/A,15\%,N)]^2 P(N) \right\}(0.30)$$

The interested student can solve the above to find that $E[\text{P.W.}^2] = 16.23 \times 10^6$, and that $V[\text{P.W.}] = (16.23 \times 10^6) - (1,969.61)^2 = 12.35 \times 10^6$.

Monte Carlo Simulation

The Monte Carlo simulation technique is an especially useful means of analyzing situations involving risk to obtain approximate answers when a physical experiment or the use of analytical approaches is either too burdensome or not feasible. It has enjoyed widespread acceptance in practice because of the analytical power it makes possible without the necessity for complex mathematics. It is especially adaptable to computation by digital computers. Indeed, computer languages have been developed especially to facilitate Monte Carlo simulation.

The technique is sometimes descriptively called the *method of statistical trials*. It involves, first, the random selection of an outcome for each variable (element) of interest, the combining of these outcomes with any fixed amounts, and calculation if necessary to obtain one trial outcome in terms of the desired answer (measure of merit). This, done repeatedly, will result in enough trial outcomes to obtain a sufficiently close approximation of the mean, variance, distribution shape, or other characteristic of the desired answer. Figure 13-1 schematically shows this process applied to investment project analysis.

The key requisite of the Monte Carlo technique is that the outcomes of all variables of interest be *randomly* selected, i.e., that the probability of selection of all possible outcomes be in exact accord with their respective probability distributions. This is accomplished through the use of tables of random numbers and relating these numbers to the distributions of the variables. *Random numbers* are numbers which have been generated in such a way that there is an equal probability of any number appearing each time, regardless of what sequence is experienced at any prior time. Appendix C contains one page of these numbers. The simple example below will demonstrate the Monte Carlo technique.

Example:
> As an illustration of Monte Carlo simulation applied to one variable or element, suppose the annual net cash flow for a project is estimated to have the distribution shown in Table 13-1.
>
> This random simulation can be accomplished through tabular methods by assigning random numbers to each outcome in proportion to the probability of each outcome. Because two-digit probabilities are given in this case, sets of only two random digits are needed, and are shown in Table 13-2.
>
> Now one can generate net cash flow outcomes by picking random numbers* and determining the net cash flow which corresponds to each according to the above list. Table 13-3 lists ten two-digit random numbers taken arbi-

---

Note: The random numbers should be taken from the table in a way to assure randomness or nonrepetitiveness by randomly selecting a point to begin in the table and randomly selecting the direction of movement within the table (such as up, down, to right, etc.).

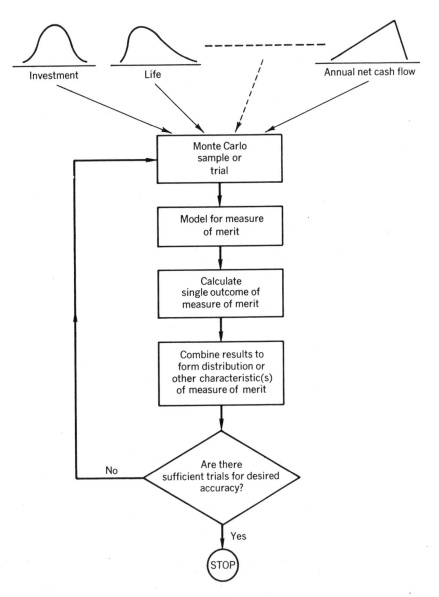

Figure 13-1. Schematic of Monte Carlo technique applied to investment project analysis.

trarily from a table of random numbers such as Appendix C, together with the corresponding net cash flows, taken from Table 13-2.

It may be of interest to note that the mean net cash flow based on the above simulated outcomes is $175,000/10 = $17,500. This compares with a

Table 13-1

EXAMPLE FREQUENCY DISTRIBUTION FOR
ANNUAL NET CASH FLOW

Net cash flow	P(Net cash flow)
$10,000	0.10
15,000	0.50
20,000	0.25
25,000	0.15

Table 13-2

ASSIGNMENT OF RANDOM NUMBERS FOR
EXAMPLE IN TABLE 13-1

Net cash flow	Random numbers
$10,000	00–09
15,000	10–59
20,000	60–84
25,000	85–99

Table 13-3

GENERATION OF OUTCOMES FOR EXAMPLE IN TABLE 13-1

Random number	Net cash flow outcome
47	$15,000
91	25,000
02	10,000
88	25,000
81	20,000
74	20,000
24	15,000
05	10,000
51	15,000
74	20,000

mean of $17,250 for the known distribution shown in Table 13-1. Results for ten simulated outcomes would not always turn out this close. However, in general, the larger the number of Monte Carlo trials, the closer the approximation to the desired answer(s).

For Monte Carlo simulations in which a computer is not used, it is sometimes helpful to use a graph of the distribution function (cumulative frequency function) instead of a table matching random numbers to the various outcomes. Figure 13-2 contains a graph of the distribution function for the example in Table 13-1. Once a graph such as in Fig. 13-2 has been construct-

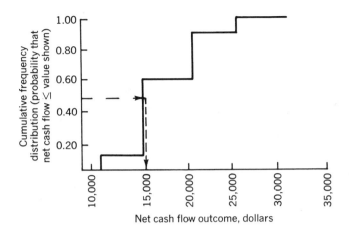

Figure 13-2. Sample cumulative frequency distribution for net cash flow.

ed, outcomes are generated as follows: A random number table such as Appendix C is used to obtain random values which correspond to the ordinate scale (vertical axis) with the decimal removed. For each random number, a horizontal line is drawn until it meets the curve. Then a vertical line is dropped to the abscissa (horizontal axis) and the outcome thus determined. The dotted line in Fig. 13-2 illustrates the generation of a sample cash flow outcome.

The above example is for a discrete outcome distribution, but it should be noted that the same principle applies for continuous distributions. For continuous distributions, the tabular method is usually impractical, but the graphical method is readily applicable as is shown in the next section.

Generation of Random Normal Values

It is quite common for random phenomena to possess a normal distribution and for element outcomes to be estimated as normally distributed. The Monte Carlo technique can be conveniently used for simulation of random outcomes in such cases.

The basic quantity needed to generate randomly distributed normal outcomes is called a *random normal deviate,* or random normal number. A random normal deviate is merely a random number of standard deviations from the mean of a standard normal distribution. Random normal deviates can be obtained directly from a graph of the cumulative standard normal distribution. Such a graph is shown in Fig. 13-3.

For a normal distribution, the probability of an occurrence near the mean is greater than the probability of an occurrence further from the mean.

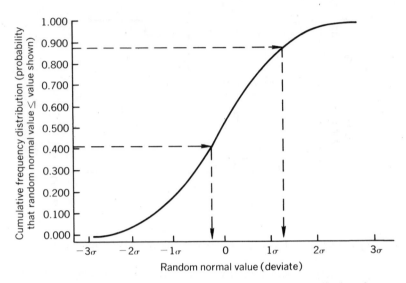

Figure 13-3. Cumulative standard normal frequency distribution for generation of random normal deviates.

This is reflected in Fig. 13-3, for the relative frequency of occurrence at each outcome value is proportional to the slope of the cumulative frequency curve.

To obtain random normal deviates, a table of random numbers is used to select numbers between 0.000 and 0.999 on the ordinate scale of the cumulative frequency distribution. (*Note:* More or less than three decimal places can be used as desired for accuracy.) For each random number a horizontal and vertical line can be drawn to find the corresponding random normal deviate. This is shown for two example random numbers in Fig. 13-3, and the results are summarized below.

Random number	*Random normal deviate*
405	−0.24
877	1.16

Tables of random normal deviates can be generated by a procedure such as the above. Such a table is presented in Appendix D. Tables of random normal deviates save much effort, for they enable us to generate a Monte Carlo sample from a normal distribution merely by using the relation, Outcome value = Mean + (R.N.D. × Standard deviation), where R.N.D. denotes the random normal deviate. As an example, suppose a project has a mean life of 8 years and a standard deviation of 2 years. Generated lives using the above random normal deviates, for example, can then be calculated as

$$8 - 0.24(2) = 7.52 \text{ yr}$$

and

$$8 + 1.16(2) = 10.32 \text{ yr}$$

Generation of Uniformly Distributed Values*

Whenever the cumulative distribution function of a random variable can be expressed mathematically, random outcomes of that variable can be generated from random numbers by direct mathematical substitution. An example is the following development of a mathematical model for the generation of uniformly distributed values.

A uniform continuous distribution with a minimum value a and a maximum value b has a density function and cumulative frequency distribution as shown in Fig. 13-4. For this distribution, the mean equals $(a + b)/2$, the variance equals $(b - a)^2/12$, and the range equals $(b - a)$.

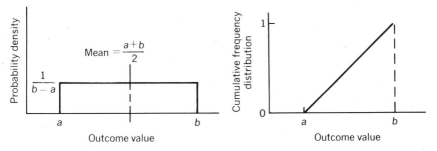

Figure 13-4. Density and distribution function for uniform continuous distribution.

To illustrate the generation of outcomes according to this distribution, let R.N. denote a random number, and R.N.$_m$ denote the highest–valued random number. By similar triangles, it can be seen that

$$\left.\begin{array}{l} \text{Outcome value} = a + \dfrac{\text{R.N.}}{\text{R.N.}_m}(b - a) \\[2mm] \qquad\qquad\quad = a + (\text{R.N. expressed as a decimal})(b - a) \end{array}\right\} \quad 13\text{-}19$$

An equivalent statement is

$$\text{Outcome value} = \frac{a + b}{2} - \frac{(b - a)}{2} + \frac{\text{R.N.}}{\text{R.N.}_m}(b - a) \qquad 13\text{-}20$$

*Methods of generating random variates from a variety of different probability distributions are given by Shannon [134] and White, Schmidt, and Bennett [148], among others.

If an element or variable is uniformly distributed with a mean of 8 and a range of 6, random outcomes can be generated using the relation

$$8 - \frac{6}{2} + \frac{R.N.}{R.N._m}(6) = 5 + (R.N. \text{ expressed as a decimal})(6)$$

Example:

Example of the use of Monte Carlo simulation for nonindependent elements: One of the valuable features of the Monte Carlo technique is that it provides an analysis tool for cases in which elements are not independent and thus are difficult or impossible to manipulate so as to obtain the desired answers analytically. For example, suppose that the life of a project is described by some distribution with a mean which is a function of the annual cash flow of the project. Further, suppose the annual cash flow itself is described by some distribution and that it is desired to determine the distribution of the P.W. (present worth) of those cash flows over the life of the project. The following illustrates the use of the Monte Carlo technique for this type of situation.

The annual net cash flow of a project is estimated to be normally distributed with a mean of $10,000 and standard deviation of $2,000. The life of the project is estimated to be uniformly distributed with a mean of 0.0005 of the annual net cash flow (rounded to the nearest integer year) and a range (difference between maximum and minimum life) of 6 years. Table 13-4 demonstrates the use of the Monte Carlo technique for ten trials to obtain an estimate of the mean of the P.W. of the cash flows, at an interest rate of 10%.

The estimated mean P.W. from the limited number of trials in Table 13-4 is $374,800/10 = $37,480. Repeated trials would doubtless result in a more accurate answer. It is worthy of note that the exact answer for this situation is not the same as $10,000 (P/A,10%,5) = $37,910, where $10,000 is the mean cash flow and 5 years is the mean life.

Example:

Example of Monte Carlo technique applied to economic analysis for a single project: To illustrate the use of the Monte Carlo technique to calculate the measure of merit for a single project for which the element outcomes are estimated as variables, consider a case in which the estimates are as follows:

Investment:	Normally distributed with mean of $100,000 and standard deviation of $5,000
Life:	Uniformly distributed with minimum of 4 yr and maximum of 16 yr (rounded to nearest integer)
Salvage value:	$10,000 (single outcome)
Annual net cash flow:	$14,000 with probability 0.4, $16,000 with probability 0.4, and $20,000 with probability 0.2.

It is assumed that all elements which are subject to variation vary independently of one another, and it is desired to obtain a good estimate of the distribution characteristics for the A.W. using an interest rate of 10%. For purposes of the illustration, only five repetitions of the Monte Carlo simula-

Table 13-4

MONTE CARLO EXAMPLE WITH NONINDEPENDENT ELEMENTS

Random normal deviate (R.N.D.)	Annual net cash flow (A.N.C.F.) [$10,000 + R.N.D.($2,000)]	Three random numbers (R.N.)	Project life N $\left[0.0005(A.N.C.F.) - 3 + \dfrac{R.N.}{999}(6)\right]$	Project life N to nearest integer	$(P/A,10\%,N)$	P.W. of cash flows [A.N.C.F. × $(P/A,10\%,N)$]
0.944	$ 8,112	443	3.65	4	3.170	$25,700
−1.140	7,720	511	3.64	4	3.170	24,500
1.353	12,706	549	6.54	7	4.868	62,000
0.466	10,912	169	3.48	3	2.487	27,100
0.732	11,464	656	6.65	7	4.868	56,000
−1.853	6,394	955	5.84	6	4.355	27,800
−0.411	9,188	783	6.29	6	4.355	40,100
0.488	10,976	197	5.92	6	4.355	48,000
−0.351	9,298	842	6.75	7	4.868	45,400
−1.336	7,328	372	2.89	3	2.487	18,200
						$\Sigma = $374,800

Table 13-5

MONTE CARLO EXAMPLE FOR A SINGLE PROJECT

Random normal deviate (R.N.D.)	Investment, P [$100,000 + R.N.D.($5,000)]	Three random numbers (R.N.)	Project life, N $\left[4 + \dfrac{R.N.}{1,000}(16-4)\right]$	Project life, N nearest integer	One random number	Annual receipts, A $\begin{bmatrix}\$14,000 \text{ for } 0\text{-}3\\ 16,000 \text{ for } 4\text{-}7\\ 20,000 \text{ for } 8\text{-}9\end{bmatrix}$	A.W. $\begin{bmatrix}-\{(P-F)(A/P,10\%,N)\\ + F(10\%)\} + A\end{bmatrix}$
0.30	$101,500	693	4 + 8.32	12	2	$14,000	−$ 400
−0.92	95,400	192	4 + 2.30	6	5	16,000	− 4,700
0.13	100,650	924	4 + 1.10	5	1	14,000	− 9,000
−0.16	99,200	490	4 + 5.87	10	4	16,000	+ 500
0.54	102,700	314	4 + 3.77	8	1	14,000	− 4,400
						$\Sigma =$	−$18,000

tion will be made. However, perhaps several thousand repetitions would be needed to obtain sufficiently accurate A.W. distribution information. Table 13-5 shows the calculations.

The estimate of the A.W. based on the very limited sample as calculated in Table 13-5 is $-$18,000/5 = -$3,600$.

An estimate of the standard deviation of the A.W. can be obtained from the relation

$$\sigma[\text{A.W.}] = \sqrt{\frac{\sum\limits_{i=1}^{k} (\text{A.W.}_{\cdot i} - E[\text{A.W.}])^2}{k-1}} \left.\vphantom{\sqrt{\frac{\sum\limits_{i=1}^{k}}{k}}}\right\} \quad 13\text{-}21$$

$$= \sqrt{\frac{58,100,000}{4}} = \$3,850$$

This estimate should also come closer to the true standard deviation with increasing numbers of Monte Carlo trials.

Example of Monte Carlo technique applied to economic comparison of two independent projects: Suppose two competing projects, A and B, have the following estimated distributions of A.W. and it is desired to estimate the distribution of the difference in A.W. between the projects using Monte Carlo simulation and assuming that the outcomes are independent of each other.

Project A		*Project B*
A.W.	*P(A.W.)*	
$-$ 5,000	0.10	A.W. is normally distributed
$10,000	0.30	with mean of $25,000 and
20,000	0.50	standard deviation of $10,000
30,000	0.10	

Sample calculations to obtain the desired answers are shown in Table 13-6. The mean difference in A.W. based on the limited simulation in Table 13-6

Table 13-6

MONTE CARLO COMPARISON OF TWO INDEPENDENT PROJECTS

One random number	*A.W. for project A* [$-$5,000 for 0, $10,000 for 1–3, 20,000 for 4–8, 30,000 for 9]	*Random normal deviate (R.N.D.)*	*A.W. for project B* [= $25,000 + R.N.D.($10,000)]	*Difference in A.W. for two projects*
4	$20,000	0.636	$31,360	$11,360
1	10,000	-0.179	22,210	11,210
4	20,000	-2.546	$-$ 460	$-$ 20,460
6	20,000	0.457	29,570	9,570
			$\Sigma =$	$11,680

is $11,680/5 = $2,816. To re-emphasize, a much larger number of Monte Carlo trials than illustrated is needed before meaningful estimates of the distribution of the difference in the A.W. for the two projects can be made.

Example of Monte Carlo technique applied to economic comparison of two projects with correlated elements: Two competing projects have the following outcome distribution characteristics:

	Project	
	A	B
Investment (normally distributed)		
Mean:	$50,000	$60,000
Standard deviation:	$20,000	$5,000
Life (uniformly distributed and		
rounded to the nearest year)		
Minimum:	3 yr	2 yr
Maximum:	7 yr	12 yr

It is thought that the investment outcomes are completely correlated for the two projects; i.e., when the investment for one project occurs high, the investment for the second project occurs correspondingly high, etc. On the other hand, the lives for the two projects are thought to be independently distributed. Table 13-7 demonstrates the use of the Monte Carlo technique for generating the distribution of the difference in the capital recovery costs

Table 13-7

Monte Carlo Comparison of Projects with Correlated Elements

Random normal deviate (R.N.D.)	Investment (P) for A [$50,000 + R.N.D. ($20,000)]	Investment (P) for B [$60,000 + R.N.D. ($5,000)]	Two random numbers	Life for A $\left[3 + \dfrac{R.N.}{99}(4)\right]$ (rounded)
0.178	$53,560	$60,890	95	8
−0.507	49,860	57,460	04	4
0.362	57,240	61,810	08	4

Two random numbers	Life for B $\left[2 + \dfrac{R.N.}{99}(10)\right]$ (rounded)	Capital recovery cost for A [P (A/P,10%,N)]	Capital recovery cost for B [P (A/P,10%,N)]	Difference in capital recovery cost [project B − project A]
16	4	$10,000	$19,150	$ 9,150
98	12	15,550	8,400	− 7,150
00	2	18,030	35,000	16,970

for the two projects. For purposes of the illustration, zero salvage value and 10% interest are assumed and only three trials are shown. Note that the investment amounts for the two projects are generated using the same random normal deviates, thus reflecting complete correlation. On the other hand, the lives for the two projects are generated using independent random digits, reflecting the independence of life outcomes.

Use of Computers

For typical practical problems, hundreds or even thousands of Monte Carlo trials are required in order to reduce sampling variation to a sufficiently low level so that the desired answers possess the level of accuracy thought necessary. This is often too laborious a task by hand methods, but it can be done very efficiently with digital computers. Appendix 13-A contains a short exposition on simulation languages and information on programs available for economic analyses.

Method for Determining Approximate Number of Monte Carlo Trials Required

An easy method for determining the approximate number of Monte Carlo trials required to obtain sufficiently accurate answers is to keep a running tally (plot) on the average answer(s) of interest for increasing numbers of trials and to judge the number of trials at which those answer(s) have become stable enough to be within the accuracy required.

It is to be expected that the average outcome(s) will dampen or stabilize with increasing numbers of trials. This phenomenon is illustrated in Fig. 13-5 by the wavy line. Figure 13-5 also shows how a given typical permissible

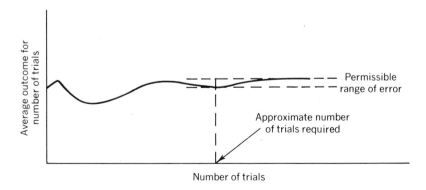

Figure 13-5. Number of trials.

range of error can result in an indicated approximate number of trials required.

Limitations

The Monte Carlo technique possesses real limitations which should be recognized. As for any analysis technique, the results can be no more accurate than the model and estimates used. The technique also inherently possesses the same problems of statistical variation and the need for experimental design that is encountered in direct physical experimentation. Finally, it should be emphasized that a sufficiently large number of Monte Carlo trials must be performed to reduce sampling variation (range of error) to a level which is tolerable in view of the accuracy needed and economically justified.

PROBLEMS

13-1. An individual is considering an investment of $10,000 in a venture. It is expected that annual receipts of $2,000 will occur over a 10-year period. However, the annual receipts are not guaranteed to occur at the expected level. The standard deviation for annual receipts is estimated to be $200 each year. A M.A.R.R. of 10% is to be used to determine the expected value and standard deviation of present worth assuming (a) annual receipts are statistically independent and (b) annual receipts are perfectly correlated.

13-2. A firm is considering purchasing a new 20-hp electric motor. Motor A sells for $800 and has an efficiency rating of 90%; motor B sells for $600 and has a rating of 84%. The cost of electricity is $0.038/kWh. An 8-yr study period is used; equal salvage values are assumed for the two motors. A M.A.R.R. of 20% is to be used. The annual usage of the motor is uncertain; the following probabilities have been estimated:

Annual usage	Probability
1,000 hr	0.20
2,000 hr	0.40
3,000 hr	0.30
4,000 hr	0.10

Assuming that annual usage is statistically independent, determine the probability that motor A is preferred to motor B. (Note: 1 hp = 3/4 kW.)

13-3. A manufacturing plant in Wisconsin has been contracting snow removal at a cost of $300/day. A snow removal machine can be purchased for $25,000; it is estimated to have a useful life of 10 years and a zero salvage value at that time. Annual costs for operating and maintaining the equipment are estimated to be $10,000. A M.A.R.R. of 10% is used by the plant. The number of days per year the snow removal equipment is required is a random variable with the following probability distribution:

No. days/yr x	Probability $P(x)$
20	0.10
40	0.20
60	0.30
80	0.30
100	0.10

Snow removal requirements in one year are independent of the requirements in any other year.
  a. Determine the mean and variance for P.W., A.W., and F.W. of the savings resulting from the purchase of the machine.
  b. Assuming normally distributed P.W., what is the probability of a positive equivalent savings by purchasing the machine?

13-4. An aluminum extrusion plant manufactures a particular product at a variable cost of $$X$/unit. The fixed cost associated with manufacturing the product equals $20,000/yr. The selling price for the product is $0.40/unit. The variable cost has the following estimated probability distribution:

x	$P(x)$
0.07	0.05
0.08	0.10
0.09	0.20
0.10	0.30
0.11	0.20
0.12	0.10
0.13	0.05

Develop the probability distribution for the break-even value of annual sales volume.

13-5. A deposit of $1,000 is to be made in a savings account. The interest rate paid each year is a random variable with the following probability distribution:

$i\%$	$P(i)$
5%	0.25
6%	0.50
7%	0.25

Develop the probability distribution for the amount in the fund after 4 years. Assume the interest rate is not autocorrelated, i.e., is independent over time.

13-6. An initial investment of $9,000 results in annual receipts of $2,500 until the project is terminated. The probability distribution for the life of the project is estimated to be as follows:

n	$P(n)$
4	0.10
5	0.25
6	0.45
7	0.15
8	0.05

Use a M.A.R.R. of 15% to determine the probability the investment is profitable.

13-7. In Prob. 13-6 suppose the M.A.R.R. is a random variable with the following probability distribution:

i	$P(i)$
10%	0.30
15%	0.40
20%	0.30

What is the probability the investment is profitable?

13-8. In Prob. 13-6 suppose the annual receipt is identical each year of the project, but let the first such receipt be distributed as follows:

R	$P(R)$
$2,000	0.25
2,500	0.50
3,000	0.25

What is the probability of the investment being profitable?

13-9. Combine the information provided in Probs. 13-6, 13-7, and 13-8 to determine the probability the investment is profitable. Assume all element (variable) outcomes are statistically independent of each other.

13-10. An investment of $8,000 is to be made; over a 3-year period annual receipts are estimated to occur with the following probabilities:

R	P(R)
$2,500	0.30
3,000	0.40
3,500	0.30

The annual receipts are statistically independent. Use a M.A.R.R. of 8% to develop the probability distribution for the external rate of return.

13-11. An investment of $15,000 is contemplated for a machine. The machine will be used for N years and will be disposed of at a salvage value of F. Maintenance and operating costs for the machine are estimated to increase by $500/yr, with the first year's cost being $1,500. Using the probability distributions given below, determine the expected value and variance for equivalent uniform annual cost given a M.A.R.R. of 12%.

		F		
N	$1,000	$2,000	$3,000	$4,000
6	0.00	0.05	0.10	0.15
8	0.05	0.10	0.15	0.05
10	0.15	0.15	0.05	0.00

13-12. The salvage value of a prospective asset is a random variable dependent upon the life of the asset according to the following table:

	Probability of salvage value				
Life	$5,000	$10,000	$15,000	$20,000	$25,000
2	——	——	0.20	0.50	0.30
4	——	0.20	0.50	0.20	0.10
6	0.30	0.30	0.30	0.10	——
8	0.30	0.50	0.20	——	——

It is thought that each of the asset lives is equally likely to occur. If the investment in the asset is $50,000 and the interest rate is 15%, show how one can obtain a distribution of the capital recovery cost for the asset by setting up a table and generating five trial outcomes.

13-13. The estimated element outcomes for a key project are as follows:

    Investment: Normally distributed with a mean of $1,000,000 and a variance of 16,000,000

    Life: 5 yr with probability 0.2

                              7 yr with probability 0.7

                              9 yr with probability 0.1

    Net annual cash flow: Uniformly distributed between $120,000 and $340,000 per yr

    Salvage value: 0

All element outcomes are independent of each other. Demonstrate how to obtain a distribution of the A.W. by generating five outcomes. From this obtain estimates of the mean and variance of the A.W. Assume a minimum attractive rate of return of 10%.

13-14. A certain project is expected to require an investment of $100,000 and to have a life which can be best described by a uniform distribution with a minimum of 5 years and a maximum of 15 years. The salvage value is expected to be $40,000 if the life is less than 8 years, $20,000 if the life is 8 to 12 years, and $15,000 if the life is 13 or more years. Show how to build a distribution of the capital recovery cost for this project by generating five outcomes using the Monte Carlo technique. Use an interest rate of 10% and round the project lives to the nearest whole year. From your results estimate the expected value and variance of the distribution of capital recovery cost.

13-15. Project X is expected to require an investment of $40,000 and to have a life which is normally distributed with a mean of 5 years and a standard deviation of 1 year (rounded to the nearest integer). The salvage value is expected to vary according to the relationship $8,000 − $1,000 × (life in yr).

Project Y is expected to require an investment of $50,000 and to have a life which is uniformly distributed between 5 and 15 years (rounded to the nearest integer). The salvage value is expected to be nil regardless of life. Show how to build a distribution of the difference in capital recovery costs for the two projects (X minus Y) by generating three outcomes using the Monte Carlo technique. Interest is 15%.

13-16. Records for a certain inventory item type indicate that the number of days lead time required for replenishment can be expected to have the following probability distribution:

Lead time (days)	Probability
1	0.25
2	0.50
3	0.25

Demand during any day of lead time is a normally distributed random variable independent of the number of days lead time and with a mean of 4 units and a standard deviation of 1 unit of the item. Inventory holding costs average $100 per unit per yr and the opportunity cost of a stock-out (failing to have a unit when demanded) is estimated at $70 per unit. Show how to use the Monte Carlo technique to determine the most economical size of safety stock for the item, where safety stock is defined as the difference between the number of units in inventory when the item is reordered and the expected demand during the lead time period. Illustrate by simulating five reorder periods with safety stocks of 0 units and then 4 units.

13-17. Two investment alternatives, A and B, are under consideration; one must be selected. Alternative A requires an initial investment of $15,000 in equipment; annual operating and maintenance costs are anticipated to be normally distributed, with a mean of $6,000 and a standard deviation of $600; the terminal salvage value at the end of the 10-year study period is anticipated to be normally distributed with a mean of $2,000 and a standard deviation of $500. Alternative B requires end-of-year annual expenditures over the study period, with the annual expenditure being normally distributed with a mean of $9,000 and a standard deviation of $900. Use a M.A.R.R. of 10%. What is the probability that alternative A is the preferred alternative?

13-18. Use the Monte Carlo simulation technique to obtain five pairs of present worth values for the alternatives described in Prob. 13-17. What percentage of the present worth combinations favors alternative A?

appendix 13-A

computer simulation languages and information on available programs for capital investment analyses

There are many simulation languages and programs to facilitate the use of digital computers in making economic analyses. Two of the most common simulation languages used in the early 1970's were GPSS III and SIM-SCRIPT. GPSS III was developed by IBM for its 7040/44, 7090/94, and 360 series of computers. SIMSCRIPT was developed by the Rand Corporation for the IBM 709/7090 series of computers. Such special languages reduce programming effort by providing routines to perform certain operations unique to simulation which would otherwise have to be programmed in detail. GPSS is used primarily for queuing and scheduling simulations, but does not require the user to have previous knowledge of computer programming unless certain special features are desired. SIMSCRIPT, on the other hand, does require some knowledge of computer programming, but it allows for greater flexibility than GPSS. If one desires the ultimate in program flexibility, a general-purpose language, such as Fortran IV, can be used for simulation.

Fleischer and Lubin* have published a very extensive catalogue of some 54 computer programs useful for engineering economy applications, indexed according to availability, user sophistication required, requisite hardware/ software, and primary use. Berger† has provided extensive information on 11 programs available for decision and risk analysis applications.

By the time of publication of this book, doubtless some of the programs will have become obsolete and many new programs will have become available. However, the addresses given should provide a good starting point for searches for desired programs. One good source of information on newly-released programs on many topics is *SKINNY*, an abbreviated issue of the *ICP Quarterly* published by International Computer Programs, Inc., 9000 Keystone Crossing, Carmel, Indiana.

---

*Fleischer, G. A. and Lubin, J. H., "Useful Computer Programs for Engineering Economy Applications," *Proceedings of the 1972 AIIE Conference and Convention*, 1972, pp. 63–71.

†Berger, Roger W., "Implementing Decision Analysis on Digital Computers," *Engineering Economist*, Vol. 17, No. 4 (July–Aug. 1972), p. 242.

Chapter

14

decision criteria and methods for risk and uncertainty

This chapter will be devoted first to numerous criteria for aiding in making decisions for what are classically called *risk problems*, i.e., problems in which probabilities of various possible outcomes can be estimated. These are:

1. dominance;
2. aspiration level;
3. most probable future;
4. expected value;
5. expectation-variance;
6. certain monetary equivalence;
7. expected utility.

The final section illustrates the use of several decision rules and principles which can be used for so-called uncertainty problems, i.e., when the probabilities of various possible outcomes cannot be estimated.

General Model for Risk Problems

Table 11-1 showed a general formulation for decision problems in which there are various possible outcomes (called *states of nature*) for which probabilities can be estimated.

A typical problem involving five alternatives and four states of nature together with associated probabilities is shown in Table 14-1. The numbers in the body of the table can be thought of as returns or payoffs in $M of net P.W., such that a negative number is a cost.

Table 14-1

EXAMPLE PROBLEM WITH PROBABILITIES KNOWN
—PAYOFFS IN $M OF NET P.W.

Alternatives	State of nature (probability of state)			
	S_1 (0.5)	S_2 (0.1)	S_3 (0.1)	S_4 (0.3)
I	3	−1	1	1
II	4	0	−4	6
III	5	−2	0	2
IV	2	−2	0	0
V	5	−4	−1	0

Decision Criteria

The following sections will describe and illustrate several criteria for decision making using the above example problems. Most of the criteria apply to classical risk problems in which probabilities of various outcomes can be estimated. However, the first two criteria or principles can be applied to decision problems even when the probabilities are not known.

Dominance Criterion or Elimination Check

The first step in making a decision when the results for all alternatives and states of nature can be quantified is to eliminate from consideration any alternatives which are clearly not to be preferred regardless of the state of nature which occurs. If the result for any alternative, X, is better than the result for some other alternative, Y, for all possible states of nature, then alternative X is said to *dominate* alternative Y, and thus Y can be dropped from further consideration.

Example:

Given the problem depicted in Table 14-1, check for dominance and take appropriate action.

Solution:

By systematic visual inspection, one can determine that alternative I dominates IV and that alternative III dominates V. (*Note:* Actually, III and V are equally good for state of nature S_1, but V is never better than III.) Thus, alternatives IV and V can both be eliminated from further consideration on the grounds that no rational decision-maker would choose either alternative.

The example problem in Table 14-1 can now be reduced to the problem shown in Table 14-2.

Table 14-2

EXAMPLE PROBLEM IN TABLE 14-1 AFTER
DOMINATED ALTERNATIVES HAVE BEEN
ELIMINATED—PAYOFFS IN $M OF NET P.W.

	State of nature (probability of state)			
Alternatives	S_1 (0.5)	S_2 (0.1)	S_3 (0.1)	S_4 (0.3)
I	3	−1	1	1
II	4	0	−4	6
III	5	−2	0	2

Aspiration Level Criterion

The aspiration level criterion involves selecting some level of aspiration and then choosing so as to maximize (or minimize) the probability of achieving this level. An aspiration level is simply some level of achievement (like profit) the decision-maker desires to attain or some level of negative results (like cost) to be avoided.

Example:

Given the decision problem in Table 14-2, determine which would be the best alternative if the decision-maker has each of the following aspiration levels: (a) possible result of at least 5; (b) possible negative result (loss) no worse than −1.

Solution:

a. Alternatives II and III have possible results of 5 or greater. The probabilities of these results are 0.3 and 0.5, respectively. Hence, alternative III .would be the choice.

b. Only alternative I has a possible result which is no more negative than -1. Thus, alternative I would be the choice.

It is commonly thought that some form of the aspiration level criterion is the most widely used of all principles in management decision making. The following are cases in which use of aspiration levels makes intuitive sense.

1. When it is costly or too time-consuming to determine what are all the reasonable alternatives and their prospective results, one may choose to search for alternatives only until an alternative is found that gives a reasonable probability of achieving the aspiration level.

2. Occasionally a given alternative is available for only a limited time and action must be taken before information on all the reasonable alternatives and their prospective results can be developed. For example, equipment at a particular price may be available only if an agreement to purchase is made within a matter of hours or days.

3. Sometimes it is difficult or impossible to evaluate the results for each alternative, but it may be possible to determine which alternatives do versus do not meet the aspiration level of the decision-maker. In this case, a reasonable criterion is to choose the alternative that maximizes the probability of achieving the aspiration level.

Most Probable Future Criterion

The most probable future criterion suggests that as the decision-maker considers the various possible outcomes in a decision, he overlooks all except the most probable one and acts as though it were certain.

Many decisions are based on this principle, since, in fact, only the most probable future is seriously considered (thus making the problem virtually one of "assumed certainty").

Example:

Given the decision problem in Table 14-2, determine which would be the best alternative using the most probable future criterion.

Solution:

The most probable future is state of nature S_1 (probability $= 0.5$). The results for S_1 range from 3 for alternative I to 5 for alternative III. Of these, alternative III has the best result and thus would be the choice.

Expected Value Criterion

Using the expectation principle and thereby choosing so as to optimize the expected payoff or cost (expressed in equivalent terms) simplifies a decision situation by weighting all dollar payoffs or costs by their probabilities. The criterion is often known as the *expected monetary value*, or *E.M.V.* As long as the dollar consequences of possible outcomes for each alternative are not very large in the eyes of the decision-maker, the expectation principle can be expected to be consistent with a decision-maker's behavior.

The general formula for finding the expected outcome (value) of a variable x for any alternative, A_i, having k discrete outcomes is:

$$E[x] = \sum_{j=1}^{k} x_j \cdot P(x_j) \qquad 14\text{-}1$$

where $E[x] =$ Expected value of x
$x_j = j$th outcome of x
$P(x_j) =$ Probability x_j occurring

If the notation for the general model in Table 14-1 is used, this can be expressed as:

$$E[A_i] = \sum_{j=1}^{k} R_{ij} \times P(S_j) \qquad 14\text{-}2$$

Example:
 Given the same decision problem in Table 14-3, show which alternative is best by the expected value criterion.

Solution:

Alternative, A_i	$E[A_i]$
I	$3(0.5) - 1(0.1) + 1(0.1) + 1(0.3) = 1.8$
II	$4(0.5) + 0(0.1) - 4(0.1) + 6(0.3) = 3.4$
III	$5(0.5) - 2(0.1) + 0(0.1) + 2(0.3) = 2.9$

Thus, alternative II, having the highest expected result, is best.

Expectation–Variance Criterion

The *expectation-variance criterion* or procedure, sometimes called the *certainty equivalence method*, involves reducing the economic desirability of a project into a single measure which includes consideration of the expected outcome as well as variation of that outcome. One simple example is

$$Q = E[x] - A \cdot \sigma[x] \qquad 14\text{-}3$$

where $Q =$ Expectation-variance measure
$E[x] =$ Mean or expected monetary outcome

$\sigma[x]$ = Standard deviation of monetary outcome
A = Coefficient of risk aversion*

The variance of a variable, x, for any alternative having k discrete outcomes is:

$$V[x] = \sum_{j=1}^{k} (x_j - E[x])^2 P(x_j) \qquad 14\text{-}4$$

where $V(x)$ = variance of x and all other symbols were defined with Eq. 14-1. A more convenient form for calculating $V(x)$, which corresponds to Eq. 13-17, is:

$$V[x] = \sum_{j=1}^{k} x_j^2 P(x_j) - (E[x])^2 \qquad 14\text{-}5$$

Example:

Given the decision problem in Table 14-2, determine which alternative is best using the criterion in Eq. 14-3, with $A = 0.7$. Also, determine the value of the coefficient of risk aversion, A, at which the two alternatives having the highest expected outcomes are equally desirable.

Solution:

Using Eq. 14-4 gives:

Alternative, A_i	$V[A_i]$
I	$(3)^2(0.5) + (-1)^2(0.1) + (1)^2(0.1) + (1)^2(0.3) - (1.2)^2 = 3.56$
II	$(4)^2(0.5) + (0)^2(0.1) + (-4)^2(0.1) + (6)^2(0.3) - (3.3)^2 = 9.51$
III	$(5)^2(0.5) + (-2)^2(0.1) + (0)^2(0.1) + (2)^2(0.3) - (3.0)^2 = 5.10$

Using Eq. 14-3 and calculated results for $E[x]$ from the above example of the expected value criterion gives:

Alternative	$Q = E[x] - 0.7\sqrt{V[x]}$
I	$1.2 - 0.7\sqrt{3.56} = -0.12$
II	$3.3 - 0.7\sqrt{9.51} = 1.14$
III	$3.0 - 0.7\sqrt{5.10} = 1.42$

*Donald Farrar (*The Investment Decision Under Uncertainty,* Englewood Cliffs, N.J.: Prentice-Hall, Inc., 1962) and others have shown that as long as there is a diminishing marginal utility of money, the correspondence between a firm's coefficient of risk aversion and its utility function of monetary outcome is

$$A = -\frac{U''(E[x])}{2}$$

That is, the coefficient of risk aversion is equal to the negative of one-half of the second derivative of the utility function evaluated at the expected monetary outcome.

Thus, alternative III is highest and thus the best by this particular expectation-variance criterion.

Alternatives II and III, having the highest expected outcomes, would be equally desirable by this expectation-variance criterion for a coefficient, A, calculated as follows:

$$3.3 - A\sqrt{9.51} = 3.0 - A\sqrt{5.10}$$

$$A = \frac{3.3 - 3.0}{\sqrt{9.51} - \sqrt{5.10}} = 0.36$$

There are innumerable other expection-variance criteria which can be applied depending on the risk preferences and sophistication of the decision-maker and his analyst. For example, Cramer and Smith, in a classic article,* recognize that the desirability of an investment project is a function of not only the expected value and variance but also of the investment amount in the individual project. Hence, they developed an evaluation model of the form

$$Q = E[x] - A\sigma[x]^a I^b \qquad 14\text{-}7$$

where Q = Certainty equivalence or expectation-variance measure
$E[x]$ = Expected monetary outcome
A = Coefficient of risk aversion
$\sigma[x]$ = Standard deviation of monetary outcome
I = Project investment amount
a and b = Constants

Cramer and Smith further show detailed examples of how one can empirically obtain all the constants for the use of the model. The following is a simple application.

Example:
Suppose the outcomes and investments required for two competing projects are estimated as follows:

Alternative	Outcomes in net P.W. $E[A.W.]$	$\sigma[A.W.]$	Investment required
A	$10,000	$25,000	$22,500
B	$ 8,000	$ 4,000	$40,000

It is desired to show which alternative would be preferred if each of the following criteria are used:
a. Expected value.

---

*R. H. Cramer and B. E. Smith, "Decision Models for the Selection of Research Projects," *Engineering Economist*, Vol. 9, No. 2, Winter 1964.

b. Expectation-variance, using Eq. 14-3 with a high coefficient of risk aversion, A, for both projects.

c. Expectation-variance, using Eq. 14-7 with $A = 0.40$ for project A and 0.75 for project B and constants $a = b = 0.50$.

Solution:

a. Project A is best; $E(\text{A.W.})_A > E(\text{A.W.})_B$.

b. Project B would be best, intuitively. (*Note:* This is true if the coefficient of risk aversion, A, for both projects were anything higher than 0.095.

$$A = \frac{\$10,000 - \$8,000}{\$25,000 - \$4,000} = 0.095$$

c. Project A:

$$Q = \$10,000 - 0.4(\$25,000)^{0.5}(\$22,500)^{0.5} = \$520$$

Project B:

$$Q = \$8,000 - 0.75(\$4,000)^{0.5}(\$40,000)^{0.5} = \$5,000$$

Thus, on the basis of the above calculated results, project B is best.

Certain Monetary Equivalence Criterion

An offshoot of the expectation-variance criterion is to subjectively determine the *certain monetary equivalence* of any set of results for any alternative. The *certain monetary equivalent*, or *C.M.E.*, is merely the monetary amount for certain at which the decision-maker would be indifferent between that amount and various possible monetary outcomes. This concept is very useful in practice and can be applied to situations involving gains (payoffs) or losses (costs). While it can be most meaningfully applied to risk situations in which various payoffs or costs and their respective probabilities are known, it can also be used in situations involving uncertainty regarding payoffs/costs, or probabilities, or both. Below are several examples.

Example:

Suppose a decision-maker is faced with either a possible loss of $100,000 with probability 0.01 or no loss with probability 0.99. He desires to decide what is the maximum amount he would be willing to pay in order to avoid the risk of loss.

Solution:

The desired quantity is a certain monetary equivalent. It is quite subjective, depending on the decision-maker's risk preferences, particularly considering the consequences of the possible monetary outcomes in relation to the total assets at the disposal of the decision-maker. As a guide, one might calculate the expected monetary value, E.M.V. as follows:

$$\text{E.M.V.} = -\$100,000(0.01) + \$0(0.99) = -\$1,000$$

If the possible $100,000 loss poses little threat in the eyes of the decision-maker so that he is so-called *risk-neutral* in this situation, he could reasonably designate the E.M.V. as his C.M.E. However, most decision-makers are at least somewhat *risk-averse* and thus will be willing to pay a certain amount of more than $1,000—say, $5,000—in order to avoid the chance of loss of $100,000. This illustrates why most people are willing to purchase liability insurance even though the known cost of the policy is higher than the expected losses to be covered by the policy. On the other hand, occasionally there are decision-makers who are *risk-seeking* in nature and would pay only something less than $1,000 for certain in order to avoid the risk of loss. A possible, but not necessarily rational, extreme is a decision-maker who enjoys the risk of loss of $100,000 so much (for example, he may like to boast about it to his friends) that he is unwilling to pay any amount to avoid the risk.

Example:

Suppose a decision-maker is again confronted with the example problem in Table 14-2 and desires to designate his C.M.E. for each alternative so as to choose the best.

Solution:

Again, the specification of C.M.E.'s is very subjective, reflecting the decision-maker's relative weighting of the consequences of the various possible gains and losses. As a starting point, one might consider the E.M.V.'s for alternatives I, II, and III which were previously calculated to be 1.2, 3.3, and 3.0, respectively. After considering this and the range of possible outcomes involved, a particular decision-maker might choose C.M.E.'s of, say, 1.0, 2.0, and 2.5, respectively. In this case, alternative III, with the highest C.M.E., would be preferred.

The C.M.E. criterion can also be used for situations in which probabilities are neither known nor estimable. In such cases, any C.M.E.'s determined are even more subjective than otherwise; nevertheless, they can express one's "gut feelings" about the uncertainties and risk preferences involved.

Example:

Suppose a decision-maker has a prospective project which is projected to bring the following possible equivalent returns (for which the respective probabilities are thought to be too nebulous to estimate):

Return in $M: −50, or 150, or 250

It is desired to demonstrate the determination of his C.M.E. for the project; i.e., what single lump amount would he accept as being just as valuable to him as the variable return.

Solution:

This requires very subjective judgment based on the decision-maker's intuitive feelings about the desirability (or nondesirability) of the possible gains or losses and their respective likelihoods. If he very much abhors the possible loss of $50M, he might be willing to pay something like $10M or $25M (C.M.E. = −$10M or −$25M) or more to avoid the risk. On the other hand, if he is strongly attracted to the possible gain of $150M or $250M, and if he thinks the probabilities of them are quite high, he might specify a C.M.E. approaching the $250M gain.

Expected Utility Criterion

The *expected utility criterion* or method has particular usefulness for analyzing projects in which the potential gain or loss is of significant size compared to the total funds available to the firm. More specifically, if the marginal utility or desirability of each dollar potentially to be gained or lost is not a constant, then the utility of dollars rather than just amount of dollars is relevant, and then it may be worthwhile to use the expected utility method rather than the probabilistic monetary method.

The expected utility method consists of determining the *cardinal utility*— e.g., relative degree of usefulness or desirability to the decision-maker—of each of the possible outcomes of a project or group of projects on some numerical scale and then calculating the expected value of the utility to use as the measure of merit.

The application of this method is based on the premise that it is possible to measure the attitudes of an individual or decision-maker toward risk. If the decision-maker is consistent with himself, then a relation between monetary gain or loss and the utility or relative desirability of that gain or loss can be obtained through the decision-maker's answers to a series of questions and resultant computations as explained below.

Steps in Deriving Utility-of-Money Function

1. Select two possible monetary outcomes within the range of interest. For example, say you pick $0 and $10,000.

2. Assign arbitrary utility indices to these monetary outcomes, the only restriction being that the index for the higher monetary outcome be higher than the index for the lower monetary outcome. For example, say you assign an index of 1 to a $0 outcome and 20 to a $10,000 outcome.

3. The utility value of other monetary outcomes can be found by having the decision-maker answer questions based on the following relation: Given any three monetary amounts, $X < $Y < Z, and known utility values for any two of these amounts, the utility of the third amount can be found by the equation:

$$U[\$Y] = P \times U[\$X] + (1 - P) \times U[\$Z] \qquad (14\text{-}8)$$

where $P = $ Probability

$$U[X] = \text{Utility of } \$X, \text{ etc.}$$

a. *To obtain utility values for monetary amounts within any two amounts,* $X and $Z, for which utility values have been assigned or calculated, ask questions such as, "What monetary amount for certain, $ Y, would you desire just as highly as a $P\%$ chance of $X and a $(1 - P\%)$ chance of $Z?" (*Note:* It is generally thought that it is easiest for decision-makers to think in terms of $P = 0.5$, though P can be any value between 0 and 1.)

For example, say you let $P = 50\%$ and suppose the decision-maker decides he would desire $3,000 for certain just as much as a 50% chance of $0 outcome and a 50% chance of $10,000 outcome. The utility of $3,000 can then be calculated as

$$U[\$3,000] = 0.5 \times U[\$0] + 0.5 \times U[\$10,000]$$
$$= 0.5 \times 1 + 0.5 \cdot 20$$
$$= 10.5$$

b. To obtain utility values for monetary outcomes less than or greater than those for which utility values have been assigned or calculated, ask questions such as, "What relative chances of monetary outcomes of $X vs. $Z would be just as desirable as a certain monetary outcome of $ Y?" (*Note:* $X or $Z is the amount for which the utility value is to be determined.)

For example, suppose it is desired to find the utility of $20,000 given the utility values which have been obtained above for $0, $3,000, and $10,000. Suppose the question posed is, "What relative chances of monetary outcomes of $3,000 vs. $20,000 would be just as desirable as a certain outcome of $10,000?" Suppose further that the considered answer by the decision-maker is 40% chance of $3,000 and 60% chance of $20,000. The utility value of $20,000 can then be calculated as

$$0.4 \times U[\$3,000] + 0.6 \times U[\$20,000] = U[\$10,000]$$
$$0.4 \times 10.5 + 0.6 \times U[\$20,000] = 20$$
$$U[\$20,000] = 26.3$$

4. Questions and computations in step 3 above can be continued as long as utility values are needed. These can, in turn, be graphed to show utility values for the entire range of monetary outcomes of interest. A graph based on the above values is shown in Fig. 14-1.

In carrying out the utility derivation procedure, inconsistencies in the decision-maker's replies may be discovered (e.g., two or more utility values calculated for the same monetary outcome or an extremely jagged utility-of-money function). If this happens, it becomes necessary to re-question to obtain judgments which are internally consistent.

The use of expected utility value as a decision criterion has a real advantage over the expected monetary value such as expected annual worth or

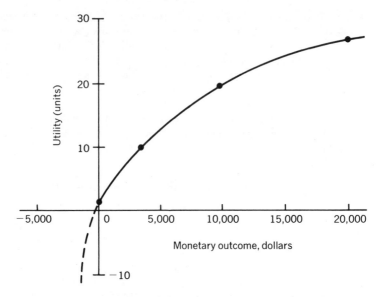

Figure 14-1. Utility-of-money function.

expected present worth. Procedures based on expected monetary values virtually overlook the severe consequences of widely varying possible outcomes and merely take a weighted average of all outcomes. The expected utility procedure overcomes this objection by incorporating these variance influences directly into the computations. A large loss may be assigned a large negative utility by the individual, or he may assign a very great positive utility to a large increment in wealth, thus automatically bringing variance influences into the calculated results. This is demonstrated in the example below.

Example:

As an example of calculation of expected utility, suppose the decision-maker having the utility-of-money function in Fig. 14-2 is faced with a project which is expected to have monetary outcomes according to the following probabilities:

Monetary outcome (in net P.W.)	Probability
$20M	0.05
10M	0.15
0M	0.30
− 2M	0.50

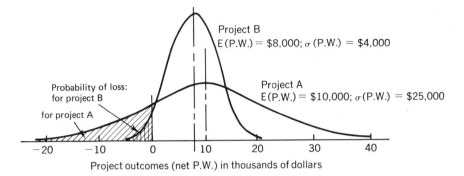

Figure 14-2. Outcome data for alternative projects assuming normal distributions.

It is desired to compare calculated results using expected utility and expected monetary value or outcome.

Solution:

The necessary calculations are shown in Table 14-3. Thus the expected utility method indicates an unfavorable project (expected utility is less than 1.0 when the utility of a monetary outcome of $0 is 1.0). In contrast, the expected monetary outcome (EMV) indicates a favorable project (expected new P.W. is greater than $0).

Table 14-3

CALCULATION OF EXPECTED MONETARY OUTCOME (E.M.V.) AND EXPECTED UTILITY

Monetary outcome (in net P.W.)	Probability of monetary outcome	Monetary outcome × Probability	Utility of outcome	Utility × Probability
$20M	0.05	$1.0M	26.3	1.31
10M	0.15	1.5M	20.0	3.00
0M	0.30	0M	1.0	0.30
− 2M	0.50	− 1.0M	−10.0	−5.00
	Expected Net P.W.: $\sum = \$1.5M$		Expected utility: $\sum = -0.39$	

Again, it should be emphasized that the expected utility method is useful for analyzing projects in which the potential gain or loss is of significant size compared to the monetary resources of the individual or firm for which the analysis is made. If a graph of the utility-of-money function can be closely approximated by a straight line over the range between the maximum and minimum monetary returns under consideration, then the expected monetary value can be used in place of the expected utility without significant error.

The Use of Utility Measurements

The method of assigning utilities to outcomes can be quite useful for gaining understanding of the rationale behind decisions made in situations involving risk. Indeed, if a decision-maker specifies a utility-of-money function and if the economic analyst can predict monetary outcomes of individual projects which are accepted or believed by the decision-maker, then the analyst can specify the project acceptance or rejection choices which would presumably turn out to be the same as those of the decision-maker (neglecting nonmonetary factors). Thus, the problem of the analyst in dealing with decisions under risk would be "solved." That is, the analyst could provide the manager with recommendations which are consistent with the manager's own thinking, thus relieving the manager for other problems.

Several limitations to use of the expected utility method should be recognized. First, it is often time-consuming and it is difficult to obtain a consistent utility-of-money function for an individual or organization. Second, responses for determining utility-of-money functions may well change over time; indeed, they may change even from day to day because of changes in the mood or temporary outlook of the person being questioned. Finally, a utility function for a particular set of alternative projects is not necessarily valid for another set of alternatives. Many intangible considerations fringe the choice of any specific weighting. A decision-maker might indicate a utility function which clearly shows a conservative approach in his attitudes toward corporate actions, but he might have an entirely different set of attitudes for gambling with his own personal finances, such as on the stock market.

Under some conditions, it is expedient to employ methods that retain the concepts of utility functions without having to enumerate the full range of utilities and continuing through formal expected utility calculations. These informal uses can serve well to solidify subjective evaluations of risk situations.

Expectation and Variance Criteria Applied to Investment Projects with One or More Discrete Probabilistic Variables or Elements

The following examples show how expectation and variance criteria may be calculated for a project in which one or more of the variables (elements) are thought to vary according to independent discrete probabilities. The same type of analysis could be used for comparison of two or more alternatives.

Example:

A single project is estimated to have a variable life and other element outcomes as follows:

Investment:	$10,000
Life:	3 yr, with probability = 0.3 5 yr, with probability = 0.4 7 yr, with probability = 0.3
Salvage value:	$2,000
Annual receipts:	$5,000
Annual disbursements:	$2,200

Find the expected annual worth and the standard deviation of the annual worth if interest on invested capital is 8%.

Solution:

For life = 3 yr, net A.W.:

$$\$5,000 - \$2,200 - [(\$10,000 - \$2,000)(A/P,8\%,3) + \$2,000(8\%)]$$
$$= -\$460$$

For life = 5 yr, net A.W.:

$$\$5,000 - \$2,200 - [(\$10,000 - \$2,000)(A/P,8\%,5) + \$2,000(8\%)] = \$630$$

For life = 7 yr, net A.W.:

$$\$5,000 - \$2,200 - [(\$10,000 - \$2,000)(A/P,8\%,7) + \$2,000(8\%)]$$
$$= \$1,110$$

$$E[\text{A.W.}] = \sum_{yr} \text{A.W.} \times P(\text{A.W.})$$
$$= -\$460(0.3) + \$630(0.4) + \$1,110(0.3) = \$446$$
$$V[\text{A.W.}] = \sum_{yr} (\text{A.W.})^2 \times P(\text{A.W.}) - (E[\text{A.W.}])^2$$
$$= (-\$460)^2 \times 0.3 + (\$630)^2 \times 0.4$$
$$+ (\$1,110)^2 \times 0.3 - (\$446)^2$$
$$= 401,000$$
$$\sigma(\text{A.W.}) = \sqrt{401,000} = \$631$$

Note that the expected net A.W. at an expected life of 5 years, which is $446, is less than the net A.W. at the assumed certain life of 5 years, which is $630. Variation of project life can have a very marked effect on the results of an economic evaluation. In general, the greater the life variation, the higher the expected capital recovery cost based on that variation compared to the capital recovery cost at the assumed certain life equal to the expected life.

Example:

Assume the same conditions as the example above except that annual receipts is also a random variable and is $7,000 with a probability of 0.33 or $4,000 with a probability of 0.67. Further, assume that the variation of project life occurs independently of variation of annual receipts. Show the net A.W. for all possible occurrences and compute the expected net A.W.

	Net Annual Worth Project life		
Annual receipts	*3 yr (P = 0.3)*	*5 yr (P = 0.4)*	*7 yr (P = 0.3)*
$7,000 (P = 0.33)	$1,540	$2,630	$3,110
$4,000 (P = 0.67)	− 1,460	− 370	110

Solution:

$$E[\text{A.W.}] = \sum_R \sum_N (\text{A.W.} \,|\, N, R) P(N) P(R)$$

where R denotes annual receipts and N denotes project life. Hence,

$$E[\text{A.W.}] = \$1,540(0.3)(0.33) + \$2,630(0.4)(0.33)$$
$$+ \$3,110(0.3)(0.33) - \$1,460(0.3)(0.67)$$
$$- \$370(0.4)(0.67) + \$110(0.3)(0.67)$$
$$= \$437$$

Comparing Alternatives with Continuous Distributions of Measure of Merit

In view of the risk and uncertainty regarding numerous variables or elements as typically found in economic analyses, it is commonly reasonable that the measure of merit or desirability for one or more projects can be expressed as one or more continuous distributions. As an illustration, if the net annual worths for projects A and B in the example using the expectation-variance criterion (above) were distributed normally, the situation could be depicted as in Fig. 14-2. It can be seen in Fig. 14-2 that the probability of a loss (negative net A.W.) for project A is much higher than for project B; hence, project B might be chosen. If the respective distributions are extremely skewed rather than normally distributed, the indicated decision may differ. For example, suppose that project A is skewed to the right and project B is skewed to the left as shown in Fig. 14-3. On the basis of these conditions, project B might no longer be considered the more desirable.

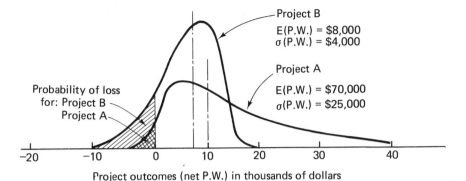

Figure 14-3. Same alternative projects as in Fig. 14-2, except with skewed distributions.

If a probabilistic monetary model involves simple mathematical functions for the individual elements considered, then it sometimes can be mathematically manipulated so as to obtain directly the desired parameters or characteristics of the measure of merit. Use of the Taylor series expansion is often convenient for obtaining analytical approximations of such distributions.* Chapter 13 described how Monte Carlo simulation can be used to obtain approximations for models of virtually unlimited complexity.

Miscellaneous Decision Rules for Complete Uncertainty

In this section we will describe some arbitrary decision rules or principles for choosing from among alternatives in situations in which there is complete uncertainty about certain probabilities. These decision rules apply to situations in which there are a number of alternatives (*courses of action*) and a number of possible outcomes (*states of nature*), and in which the *result* (effect) of each alternative on each possible outcome is known but the probability of occurrence of each possible outcome is not known.

The most difficult aspect of using these decision rules is deciding which one to use for making a decision. In effect, these decision rules reflect various degrees of optimism or pessimism and should be chosen according to which reflect certain management views involving intuition and appropriateness for a particular situation. The greatest defense for the use of any of these rules is that their use will promote explicitness and consistency in decision-making under complete uncertainty.

*See especially articles by Hillier (1963, 1964, and 1965) and by Canada and Wadsworth (1968) referenced in the Bibliography at the end of this book.

A representation of a typical problem is given by the matrix in Table 14-4.

Table 14-4

EXAMPLE PROBLEM INVOLVING COMPLETE UNCERTAINTY
PAYOFFS—NET P.W. ($M)

	State of nature			
Alternative	S_1	S_2	S_3	S_4
I	3	−1	1	1
II	4	0	−4	6
III	5	−2	0	2

Note that this problem is the same as the risk problem in Table 14-2 except that probabilities are not known. The following sections will explain and illustrate each of several decision rules for this type of problem.

Maximin or Minimax Rule

The *maximin rule* suggests that the decision-maker determine the minimum profit (payoff) associated with each alternative and then select the alternative which maximizes the minimum profit. Similarly, in the case of costs, the *minimax rule* suggests that the decision-maker determine the maximum cost associated with each alternative and then select the alternative which minimizes the maximum cost. These decision rules are conservative and pessimistic, for they direct attention to the worst outcome and then make the worst outcome as desirable as possible.

Example:
Given the payoffs for each of three alternatives and for each of four possible states of nature (chance occurrences) in Table 14-4, determine which alternative would maximize the minimum possible payoff.

Solution:
The minimum possible payoff for alternative I is −1, for alternative II is −4, for alternative III is −2. Hence, alternative I would be chosen as maximizing these minimum payoffs.

Maximax or Minimin Rule

The maximax or minimin rules are direct opposites of their counterparts discussed above, and thus reflect extreme optimism. The *maximax rule* suggests that the decision-maker determine the maximum profit associated with each alternative and then select the alternative which maximizes the maximum profit. Similarly, in the case of costs, the *minimin rule* indicates that the decision-maker should determine the minimum cost associated with each alternative and then select the alternative which minimizes the minimum cost.

Example:

Given the same payoff matrix as in Table 14-4, determine which alternative would maximize the maximum payoff.

Solution:

The maximum possible payoff for alternative I is 3. Similarly, for II the maximum payoff is 6, and for III it is 5. The highest of these is 6, which occurs with alternative II; so alternative II is the maximax choice.

Laplace Principle or Rule

The Laplace rule simply assumes that all possible outcomes are equally likely and that one can choose on the basis of expected outcomes as calculated using equal probabilities for all outcomes. There is a common tendency toward this assumption in situations where there is no evidence to the contrary, but the assumption (and, therefore, the rule) is of highly questionable merit.

Example:

Given the same payoff matrix as in Table 14-4, determine which alternative is best using the Laplace rule.

Solution:

$$E \text{ [alt. I]:} \quad 3 \times \tfrac{1}{4} - 1 \times \tfrac{1}{4} + 1 \times \tfrac{1}{4} + 1 \times \tfrac{1}{4} = 1.00$$

$$E \text{ [alt. II]:} \quad 4 \times \tfrac{1}{4} + 0 \times \tfrac{1}{4} - 4 \times \tfrac{1}{4} + 6 \times \tfrac{1}{4} = 1.50$$

$$E \text{ [alt. III]:} \quad 5 \times \tfrac{1}{4} - 2 \times \tfrac{1}{4} + 0 \times \tfrac{1}{4} + 2 \times \tfrac{1}{4} = 1.25$$

Thus, alternative II, giving the highest expected payoff, is best.

Hurwicz Principle or Rule

The Hurwicz rule is intended to reflect any degree of moderation between extreme optimism and extreme pessimism which the decision-maker may wish to choose. The rule may be stated explicitly as

Select an index of optimism, a, such that $0 \le a \le 1$. For each alternative, compute the weighted outcome: $a \times$ (Value of profit or cost if most favorable outcome occurs) $+ (1 - a) \times$ (Value of profit or cost if least favorable outcome occurs). Choose the alternative which optimizes the weighted outcome.

A practical difficulty of the Hurwicz rule is that it is difficult for the decision-maker to determine a proper value for a, the weighting factor. The

Hurwicz rule also lacks several of the desirable properties of a good decision rule, and it can even lead to results which are obviously counter to one's intuition.

Example:

Given the same payoff matrix as in Table 14-4, calculate which alternative would be best, using the Hurwicz rule, for an index of optimism of 0.75. Also graph the calculated payoff for each alternative over the entire range of the index of optimism.

Solution:

$$\text{Alt. I:} \qquad 0.75(3) + 0.25(-1) = 2.0$$

$$\text{Alt. II:} \qquad 0.75(6) + 0.25(-4) = 3.5$$

$$\text{Alt. III:} \qquad 0.75(5) + 0.25(-2) = 3.25$$

Thus, alternative II, giving the highest payoff, is best. The graph is shown in Fig. 14-4.

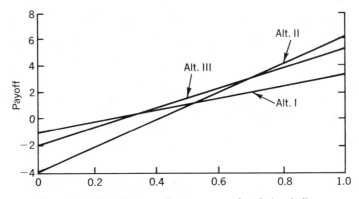

Figure 14-4. Graphed payoffs over range of optimism indices.

Minimax Regret Rule

The minimax regret rule, proposed by L.J. Savage, is similar to the minimax and maximin rules but is intended to counter some of the ultraconservative results given by those rules. This rule suggests that the decision-maker examine the maximum possible *regret* (loss because of not having chosen the best alternative for each possible outcome) associated with each alternative and then select the alternative which minimizes the maximum regret.

Example:

Given the same payoff matrix as in Table 14-4, show which alternative would be chosen on the basis of minimizing the maximum regret. Develop a regret matrix to obtain a solution.

Solution:

The result is shown in Table 14-5.

Table 14-5

REGRET MATRIX FOR PROBLEM OF TABLE 14-4

Alternative	State of nature				Maximum of states
	S_1	S_2	S_3	S_4	
I	$2(= 5 - 3)$	1	0	5	5
II	$1(= 5 - 4)$	0	5	0	5
III	$0(= 5 - 5)$	2	1	4	4 (Min. of all max.)

Thus, it can be seen that the worst (highest) regret for alternative I is 5, for alternative II is 5, and for alternative III is 4. The minimum of these maximum regrets is 4 for alternative III, and thus alternative III is the choice.

PROBLEMS

14-1. Given the following matrix of net P.W.'s (in $M) for four alternatives and various possible business conditions for which probabilities can be estimated:

Alternative	Business condition (and probability)		
	Excellent (0.3)	Fair (0.5)	Poor (0.2)
I	30	25	-15
II	15	15	15
III	35	30	-5
IV	45	10	-5

Show what can be determined, or which alternative is preferred, using each of the following criteria:

a. Does any alternative dominate all alternatives? Is any alternative dominated by any other alternative? Which alternative(s) is (are) left for consideration after checking for dominance?

b. If the aspiration level is to minimize the chance of a loss and maximize the chance to make at least 28

c. Most probable future

d. Expected value

    e. Expectation-variance, using the function in Eq. 14-3 where $\sigma[x]$ is approximated as (maximum outcome − minimum outcome)/5 and where $A = 1.0$

    f. Certain monetary equivalence, using your own subjective assessment assuming you are the top decision-maker for a firm with $100 million assets

14-2. Suppose you were faced with the same matrix of net P.W.'s as in Prob. 14-1 but you do not have probability estimates for the various business conditions. Show which alternative should be chosen using each of the following decision rules or principles:

    a. Maximin rule

    b. Maximax rule

    c. Laplace principle

    d. Hurwicz principle, with 0.5 optimism

    e. Minimax regret rule

14-3. Given the following matrix of equivalent annual costs (in $thousands) for four alternatives and various possible conditions as follows:

	State of nature (and probability)		
Alternative	*Kind* (0.3)	*Erratic* (0.6)	*Perverse* (0.1)
Alpha	20	28	40
Bravo	25	25	25
Charlie	11	27	45

Show what can be determined, or which alternative is preferred, using each of the following criteria:

    a. Is any alternative dominated?

    b. If the aspiration level is to have a possible cost no greater than 26

    c. The most probable future

    d. Expected value

    e. Certain monetary equivalence, using your own subjective assessment assuming you are a manager who is risk-neutral and thus you base your decisions on long-run averages

14-4. Suppose you are faced with the same matrix of equivalent annual costs as in Prob. 14-3 except that you feel the probability estimates are invalid and cannot be used. Show which alternative should be chosen using each of the following decision rules or principles:

    a. Minimax rule

    b. Minimin rule

    c. Laplace principle

    d. Hurwicz principle, with 0.8 index of optimism

    e. Minimax regret rule

14-5. Given the matrix of costs below, for various mutually exclusive alternatives, show which is best using the following decision rules or principles:
   a. Minimax rule
   b. Minimin rule
   c. Laplace principle
   d. Hurwicz principle with $\frac{2}{3}$ optimism
   e. Minimax regret rule

	State of nature			
Alternative	A	B	C	D
I	18	18	10	14
II	14	14	14	14
III	5	26	10	14
IV	14	22	10	10
V	10	12	12	10

14-6. Suppose the flip of a fair coin will determine whether you gain $\$X$ or lose $\$X$. What certain amount would you personally be willing to pay out (or accept) instead of the random outcome if $\$X$ is:
   a. $0.10
   b. $1.00
   c. $10
   d. $100
   e. $1,000
   f. $10,000

14-7. Suppose a business opportunity has a 0.25 chance of making a P.W. of $\$X$ and a 0.75 chance of making $0. For what certain amount would you be just willing to sell the opportunity if the money is for you personally and $\$X$ is:
   a. $1,000
   b. $10,000
   c. $100,000
   d. $1,000,000

14-8. Answer Prob. 14-7 if the money belongs to a large corporation for which you are the decision-maker. Are you more risk-averse if making such decisions for a corporation or for yourself personally?

14-9. Entrepreneur Y has a utility index of 108 for $11,000 and 75 for $0. He is indifferent between a 0.5 chance at $11,000 plus a 0.5 chance at a $20,000 loss and a certainty of $0. What is his utility index for a loss of $20,000?

14-10. Entrepreneur Z has a utility index of 10 for $18,750, 6 for $11,200, and zero for $0. What probability combination of $0 and $18,750 would make him indifferent to $11,200 for certain?

14-11. Two economists, Alfred M. Dismal and J. Maynard Science, are arguing about the relative merits of their respective decision rules. Dismal says he always takes the act with the greatest expected monetary value; Science says he always takes the act with the greatest expected utility, and his utility function for money is $U = 10 + 0.2M$, where M is the monetary payoff. For decisions involving monetary payoffs, who will make the better choices?

14-12. You have a date for the economic analysis ball; the admission is $20, which you do not have. On the day of the dance your psychology instructor offers you either $16 for certain or a 50–50 chance at nothing or $24. Which choice would you make, assuming you had no other source of funds or credit. Why? If the utility of $16 is 20, and the utility of $0 is zero, what does this imply about the utility of $20?

14-13. Develop a utility function for yourself for the monetary outcomes of −$100,000, −$10,000, +$10,000, +$40,000, and +$200,000. Start with the following monetary outcomes and arbitrarily assigned units:

Monetary outcome	Utility units
$ 1,000	10
15,000	30

Write out the questions which you ask yourself and show your calculations. Finally, plot the results with monetary outcome on the x-axis.

14-14. Suppose that the utility-of-money function of a decision-maker is described as Utility = ln (Monetary outcome in thousands of dollars) between the monetary outcome limits of $100 and $1,000,000. The monetary outcomes and associated probabilities for two competing projects are as follows:

Project	Monetary outcome (gain)	Probability
A	$ 1,000	0.33
	10,000	0.33
	19,000	0.33
B	$ 3,000	0.3
	10,000	0.4
	12,000	0.1
	13,000	0.2

Show which project is preferable by (a) the expected monetary method and by (b) the expected utility method. (*Note:* ln means logarithm to the base e.)

14-15. A certain project requires an investment of $10,000 and is expected to have net annual receipts minus disbursements of $2,800. The salvage value as a function of life, together with associated probabilities, is

Life	Salvage value	Probability
3	$4,000	0.25
5	2,000	0.50
7	0	0.25

Find the expected net A.W. and the standard deviation of net A.W. if interest on invested capital is 8%.

14-16. Work Prob. 14-15 with the change that the net annual receipts minus disbursements is a random variable which is independent of the life and is estimated to be $1,800 with probability 0.2, $2,800 with probability 0.6, and $3,800 with probability 0.2.

14-17. Project Stochastic is estimated to require an investment of $25,000, have a life of 5 years and 0 salvage value, and have an annual net cash flow of $5,000 with 30% probability, $10,000 with 50% probability, and $12,000 with 20% probability. If the minimum required rate of return is 15%, calculate the expected value and variance of the net A.W. for Project Stochastic.

14-18. Project Variate is estimated to require an investment of $25,000 and have an annual net cash flow of $16,000 and a 0 salvage value. The life for Project Variate is estimated to be 1 year with 10% probability, 5 years with 50% probability, and 10 years with 40% probability. If the minimum required rate of return is 15%, calculate the expected value and variance of the net A.W.

14-19. Plot a frequency histogram for the projects in Probs. 14-17 and 14-18, distinguishing between the two by shaded coding. Which project would probably be thought more desirable if the decision-maker were (a) conservative, thus not prone to take risks, and (b) a maximizer of expectations, regardless of risk.

14-20. Suppose that the expectation-variance decision function for a given project is equal to the net A.W. minus a constant times the standard deviation of the net A.W.
   a. For the projects in Probs. 14-17 and 14-18, determine which appears to be the more desirable if the constant coefficient is 0.6.
   b. At what value of the constant coefficient are the two projects equally desirable?

14-21. The mean and standard deviation of the rate of return for project X are estimated to be 15% and 5% respectively. Similarly, the mean and standard deviation of the rate of return for a competing project Y are estimated to be 25% and 18% respectively.
   a. If the expectation-variance function for the decision-maker is the expected rate of return minus 0.1 times the variance of the rate of return (in integer amounts), show which project would be more desirable.

b. For the function in part a, at what value of the coefficient applied to the variance would the projects be considered equally desirable?

14-22. Suppose that in Prob. 14-15 the interest on capital is 4% with probability 0.5 and 12% with probability 0.5, and suppose that interest varies independently of the life of the project.
a. Calculate the expected net A.W.
b. Plot histograms of outcomes for Prob. 14-15 and for this problem to compare variability.

14-23. A specific project requires an investment of $100,000 and is expected to have a salvage value of $20,000. It is thought equally likely that the life will turn out to be either 6, 10, or 12 years. The net annual cash inflow is twice as likely to be $30,000 as either $35,000 or $18,000. If the minimum required rate of return is 10%:
a. Develop a table showing the net A.W. for all combinations of the two variables.
b. Assuming that the variable outcomes are independent, calculate $E[A.W.]$ and $V[A.W.]$.

statistical decision techniques*

Numerous statistical techniques to aid in decision-making have been developed in the last two decades. Some of the more powerful of these techniques are included in the body of knowledge called *statistical decision theory*. Statistical decision theory is commonly characterized as the mathematical analysis of decision-making when, although the state of the world is uncertain, further information can yet be obtained by experimentation.

Statistical decision theory also often involves the use of subjective probabilities to express the decision-maker's degree of belief in the possible outcomes. A practice that is commonly associated with statistical decision theory is the use of Bayesian statistics, which is described briefly below.

*This chapter was written primarily by Nathan Wolf, International Business Machines Corp.

Bayesian Statistics

Bayesian statistics is characterized by the adjustment of "prior" probabilities for an unknown parameter or factor to more reliable "posterior" probabilities based on the results of sample evidence or evidence from further study. Bayes' theorem, usually employed in this adjustment, is developed with applications below.

Bayes' Theorem

Bayes' theorem is an extension of joint and conditional probability theory. The probability of two events occurring is given by probability theory as

$$P(A,B) = P(A \mid B)P(B) \qquad \text{15-1}$$

where $P(A,B)$ = Probability of the two events A and B occurring together

$P(A \mid B)$ = Probability of A occurring given that B has occurred

$P(B)$ = Probability of B occurring

It can be quickly reasoned that the probability of drawing the ace of spades from a standard deck of 52 cards is one in 52. As an example of the application of Eq. (15-1), this probability can also be computed as follows:

$$P(\text{Ace, Spade}) = P(\text{Ace} \mid \text{Spade})P(\text{Spade})$$
$$= (1 \text{ Ace}/13 \text{ Spades})(13 \text{ Spades}/52 \text{ cards})$$
$$= (1/13)(13/52) = 1/52$$

Note that the condition of getting the ace of spades is equivalent to drawing the spade ace. This leads to a second axiom:

$$P(A,B) = P(B,A)$$

Since $P(B,A) = P(B \mid A) \cdot P(A)$, then

$$P(A \mid B)P(B) = P(B \mid A)P(A) \qquad \text{15-2}$$

Bayes' theorem is derived from Eq. (15-2). Provided that $P(B)$ and $P(A) \neq 0$, then

$$\left. \begin{aligned} P(A \mid B) &= \frac{P(B \mid A)P(A)}{P(B)} \\[2mm] P(B \mid A) &= \frac{P(A \mid B)P(B)}{P(A)} \end{aligned} \right\} \qquad \text{15-3}$$

Thus, the probability of an ace, given a spade, can be computed in an indirect way using Eq. (15-3) as

$$P(\text{Ace} \mid \text{Spade}) = \frac{P(\text{Spade} \mid \text{Ace})P(\text{Ace})}{P(\text{Spade})}$$

$$= \frac{(1 \text{ Spade}/4 \text{ Aces})(4 \text{ Aces}/52 \text{ Cards})}{(13 \text{ Spades}/52 \text{ Cards})}$$

$$= \frac{(1/4)(1/13)}{(1/4)} = 1/13$$

In general, if there are n mutually exclusive, exhaustive possible outcomes $S_1, S_2, \ldots, S_n$, and the results of additional study, such as sampling or further investigation, is X, such that X is discrete and $P(X) \neq 0$, and prior probabilities $P(S_i)$ have been established, then Bayes' theorem for the discrete case can be written as

$$P(S_i \mid X) = \frac{P(X \mid S_i)P(S_i)}{P(X)} \qquad 15\text{-}4$$

The posterior probability $P(S_i \mid X)$ is the probability of outcome S_i given that additional study resulted in X. The probability of X and S_i occurring, $P(X \mid S_i)P(S_i)$, is the "joint" probability of X and S_i. The sum of all the joint probabilities is equal to the probability of X. Therefore, Eq. (15-4) can be written

$$P(S_i \mid X) = \frac{P(X \mid S_i)P(S_i)}{\sum_i P(X \mid S_i)P(S_i)} \qquad 15\text{-}5$$

A format for application is presented in Table 15-1.

Table 15-1

FORMAT FOR APPLYING BAYES' THEOREM IN DISCRETE OUTCOME CASES

(1) State	(2) Prior probability	(3) Probability of sample outcome, or confidence assessment, X	(4) = (2)(3) Joint probability	(5) = (4)/$\sum$ (4) Posterior probability, $P(S_i \mid X)$
S_1	$P(S_1)$	$P(X \mid S_1)$	$P(X \mid S_1)(P(S_1)$	$P(X \mid S_1)P(S_1)/P(X)$
S_2	$P(S_2)$	$P(X \mid S_2)$	$P(X \mid S_2)P(S_2)$	$P(X \mid S_2)P(S_2)/P(X)$
$\cdot$	$\cdot$	$\cdot$	$\cdot$	$\cdot$
$\cdot$	$\cdot$	$\cdot$	$\cdot$	$\cdot$
S_i	$P(S_i)$	$P(X \mid S_i)$	$P(X \mid S_i)P(S_i)$	$P(X \mid S_i)P(S_i)/P(X)$
$\cdot$	$\cdot$	$\cdot$	$\cdot$	$\cdot$
$\cdot$	$\cdot$	$\cdot$	$\cdot$	$\cdot$
S_n	$P(S_n)$	$P(X \mid S_n)$	$P(X \mid S_n)P(S_n)$	$P(X \mid S_n)P(S_n)/P(X)$
	$\sum_{i=1}^{n} P(S_i) = 1.0$		$\sum_{i=1}^{n} P(X \mid S_i)P(S_i) = P(X)$	$\sum_{i=1}^{n} P(S_i \mid X) = 1.0$

The columns in Table 15-1 are as follows:

Column

(1) S_i: the potential states of nature
(2) $P(S_i)$: the estimated prior probability of S_i (*Note:* This column sums to unity)
(3) $P(X|S_i)$: the conditional probability of getting sample or added study results X, given that S_i is the true state
(4) $P(X|S_i)P(S_i)$: the joint probability of getting X and S_i; the summation of this column is $P(X)$, which is the probability that the sample or added study results in outcome X
(5) $P(S_i|X)$: the posterior probability of S_i given that sample outcome resulted in X; numerically, the ith entry is equal to the ith entry of column (4) divided by the sum of column (4) [*Note:* Column (5) sums to unity]

As a side note of interest, when X has a continuous density function $f_1(X)$ and S has a continuous density function $f_2(S)$, such that all conditional density functions are continuous, then the continuous equivalent of Bayes' theorem states that

$$f_2(S|X) = \frac{f_1(X|S)f_2(S)}{\int_s f_1(X|S)f_2(S)\,dS} \qquad 15\text{-}6$$

Most examples in the remainder of this chapter will be devoted to discrete outcome cases.

Example:

Example involving sampling to revise probabilities for production process: Let us consider the following application: A production process requires that equipment be set up for a fixed run of 200 units. If the setup is good, defects occur with a probability of 0.05 and in a random fashion. A bad setup occurs randomly with a probability of 0.2 and then the random defect rate is 0.25. Letting S_1 represent a good setup, S_2 a bad setup, and X the event that a sample of one is found to be defective, it is desired to calculate the posterior probabilities that the setup is good or bad given that X has occurred. Table 15-2 shows the necessary calculations where $P(S_1)$ equals 0.8 and $P(S_2)$ equals 0.2.

Table 15-2

POSTERIOR PROBABILITY CALCULATION FOR PRODUCTION PROCESS

S_i	$P(S_i)$	$P(X\|S_i)$	$P(X\|S_i)P(S_i)$	$P(S_i\|X)$
S_1	0.80	0.05	0.04	$4/9 = 0.44$
S_2	0.20	0.25	0.05	$5/9 = 0.56$
	$\sum_i = 1.00$		$\sum_i = P(X) = 0.09$	$\sum_i = 1.00$

Thus, the prior probability that the setup is good, 0.8, is revised to a posterior probability of 0.44 based on the evidence that a sample unit is defective.

Example:

Example of use of Bayes' theorem for discrete outcome investment analysis: As a further example, consider an investment project with a return (expressed in net P.W.) of $6,000 if event S_1 occurs and $-$4,000$ if event S_2 occurs. The prior probability estimates are 0.4 for S_1 and 0.6 for S_2. Thus, the expected return, denoted $E[R]$, is

$$E[R] = 0.4(\$6,000) + 0.6(-\$4,000) = 0$$

The alternative of not investing also has an expected return of zero, for there would be no gain or loss. Additional study will result in either X_1, which indicates a net P.W. of $6,000, or X_2, which indicates a net present worth loss of $4,000. If S_1 will occur, then X_1 will be indicated with a probability of 0.8. Similarly, if S_2 will occur, X_2 will be indicated with a probability of 0.6. The problem is summarized as follows:

$$P(S_1) = 0.4 \qquad P(X_1|S_1) = 0.8$$
$$P(S_2) = 0.6 \qquad P(X_2|S_1) = 1.0 - P(X_1|S_1) = 0.2$$
$$E[S_1] = \$6,000 \qquad P(X_2|S_2) = 0.6$$
$$E[S_2] = -\$4,000 \qquad P(X_1|S_2) = 1.0 - P(X_2|S_2) = 0.4$$

The posterior probabilities resulting from the additional study can now be computed from the above information. New expected returns then can be computed and the decision to invest or not invest in the project can be determined as a function of the additional study outcome X.

Table 15-3

COMPUTATION OF POSTERIOR PROBABILITIES GIVEN X_1

S_i	$P(S_i)$	$P(X_1\|S_i)$	$P(X_1\|S_i)P(S_i)$	$P(S_i\|X_1)$
S_1	0.4	0.8	0.32	0.32/0.56 = 0.57
S_2	0.6	0.4	0.24	0.24/0.56 = 0.43
	$\sum_i = 1.0$		$\sum_i = P(X_1) = 0.56$	$\sum_i = 1.00$

Table 15-3 shows the computation of posterior probabilities if the added study results in X_1. When X_1 occurs, the probability of S_1 is revised from the "prior" 0.4 to the "posterior" 0.57. The expected return given X_1, denoted $E[R|X_1]$, can then be computed as

$$E[R|X_1] = 0.57(\$6,000) + 0.43(-\$4,000) = \$1714$$

Hence, if X_1 occurs, the project should be undertaken to obtain the positive expected net P.W. return.

The computation of posterior probabilities if the additional study results in X_2 is presented in Table 15-4. The occurrence of X_2 results in a posterior

Table 15-4

COMPUTATION OF POSTERIOR PROBABILITIES GIVEN X_2

S_i	$P(S_i)$	$P(X_2 \mid S_i)$	$P(X_2 \mid S_i)P(S_i)$	$P(S_i \mid X_2)$
S_1	0.4	0.2	0.08	0.18
S_2	0.6	0.6	0.36	0.82
	$\sum_i = 1.0$		$\sum_i = P(X_2) = 0.44$	$\sum_i = 1.00$

probability of S_1 of 0.18, and the expected return given X_2, denoted $E[R \mid X_2]$, is computed to be

$$E[R \mid X_2] = 0.18(\$6,000) + 0.82(-\$4,000) = -\$2,182$$

Since $E[R \mid X_2]$ is negative, the decision would be not to invest in the project if X_2 occurs, thus resulting in an expected return of zero.

Considering the decision rule, to invest if additional study results in X_1, and to reject the project if X_2 occurs, the overall expected return is now positive and is calculated to be

$$E[R] = \begin{cases} \$0 & \text{if } X = X_2 \\ \$1,714 & \text{if } X = X_1 \end{cases}$$

From Tables 15-3 and 15-4, $P(X_1) = 0.56$ and $P(X_2) = 0.44$. Thus, with sampling or additional study,

$$E[R] = E[R \mid X_1]P(X_1) + E[R \mid X_2]P(X_2)$$
$$= (\$1,714)0.56 + (\$0)0.44 = \$960$$

In general, the overall expected return, given additional study or sample information resulting in X_j, is

$$E[R \mid SI] = \sum_j \max \left(E[A_i] \mid X_j \right) P(X_j) \qquad 15\text{-}7$$

where $E[R \mid SI]$ is the expected return given sample information.

The change in the expected value from \$0 to \$960 is often called the *expected value of sample information* (EVSI). Expressed symbolically,

$$EVSI = E[R \mid SI] - E[R] \qquad 15\text{-}8$$

Expected Value of Perfect Information

The *expected value of perfect information* (EVPI) is the maximum possible EVSI and is the maximum expected loss due to imperfect information as to what will be the state of nature in a situation involving risk. Interpreted another way, the expected value of perfect information is the amount which could be gained, on the average, if the future regarding a particular decision situation became perfectly predictable and decisions changed to the optimal choice(s) based on the new known conditions. Another term synonymous with the expected value of perfect information is the *expected opportunity loss* (EOL).

Figure 15-1 shows the steps for computation of the EVPI for the usual situation of multiple alternatives and discrete outcomes. The discrete outcome investment project above will be used as an example of the application of EVPI. In this case, the alternatives are to invest or not to invest. If perfect information were available, the project would be accepted and have a net present value of $6,000 when S_1 is to occur or it would be rejected when S_2 is to occur. The expected present worth, given perfect information (certainty), denoted $E[R|PI]$, is thus $6,000 with an expected frequency of

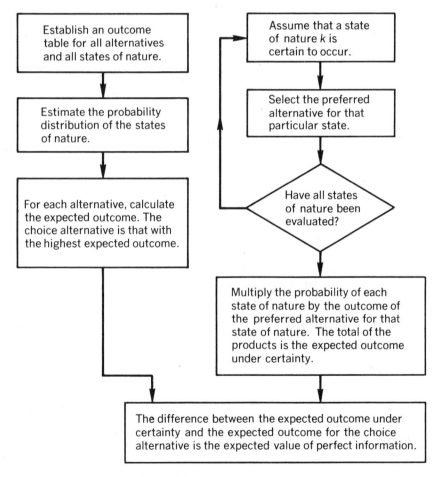

Figure 15-1. Computation of expected value of perfect information for multiple alternatives and discrete outcomes.

occurrence of 0.4, or it is \$0, occurring with a probability of 0.6. Overall,

$$E[R \,|\, PI] = 0.4(\$6,000) + 0.6(\$0) = \$2,400$$

This reasoning process corresponds to the right-hand side of Fig. 15-1.

Prior to sampling or added study, the expected return for the above investment project was computed to be \$0. This corresponds to the left-hand side of Fig. 15-1. Thus the EVPI is \$2,400 — \$0 or \$2,400. This is a measure of the maximum possible expected to be gained by sampling for further information. It should be noted from the previous section that the \$960 EVSI is expected to be gained (out of the \$2,400 EVPI) by sampling one unit.

In general, EVPI (EOL) can be expressed as

$$EVPI = EOL = E[R \,|\, PI] - E[R] \qquad\qquad 15\text{-}9$$

The general formula for computation of expected return under certainty is

$$E[R \,|\, PI] = \sum_i P(S_i) \cdot \max\,[\text{return }(A_1, \ldots, A_j, \ldots, A_m \,|\, S_i)] \quad 15\text{-}10$$

where
$$\begin{aligned}
E[R \,|\, PI] &= \text{Expected return given perfect} \\
&\quad\ \text{information} \\
P(S_i) &= \text{Probability of the } i\text{th outcome} \\
A_j &= \text{The } j\text{th alternative} \\
\text{return }(A_j \,|\, S_i) &= \text{Value of alternative } j \text{ given that } S_i \\
&\quad\ \text{outcome occurs} \\
\max\,[\text{return }(A_1, \ldots, A_j, \ldots, A_m \,|\, S_i)] &= \text{Decision rule that the value of the} \\
&\quad\ \text{returns, given that } S_i \text{ occurs, is the} \\
&\quad\ \text{maximum return over all } m \text{ alter-} \\
&\quad\ \text{natives}
\end{aligned}$$

Example:

> *Additional example of computation of* EOL *through use of opportunity loss concept:* The *expected opportunity loss* (EOL) concept will be further demonstrated with the multiple-alternative, discrete outcome example given in Table 15-5. In this example the returns (expressed in net P.W.) depend on whether

Table 15-5

OUTCOMES IN NET P.W. FOR THREE ALTERNATIVES GIVEN
DISCRETE BUSINESS CONDITIONS

	Business Condition		
	Good P(Good) = 0.25	*Average* P(Average) = 0.50	*Poor* P(Poor) = 0.25
Alternative I	\$300M	\$200M	−\$ 80M
Alternative II	400M	200M	− 200M
Alternative III	100M	240M	0M

business conditions are good, average, or poor. The probabilities of these three possible business conditions are given as 0.25, 0.50, and 0.25, respectively. The expected return for each alternative can be calculated as:

Alternative I: $300M(0.25) + $200M(0.50) − $80M(0.25) = $155M
Alternative II: $400M(0.25) + $200M(0.50) − $200M(0.25) = $150M
Alternative III: $100M(0.25) + $240M(0.50) + $0M(0.25) = $145M

Using the maximum expected return decision criterion, alternative I would be chosen. The *opportunity loss* (OL) for each business condition can be derived by the following rationale:

If good conditions prevail, alternative II would be preferred, and having chosen I incorrectly represents an OL of $400M − $300M or $100M. Similarly, if average business conditions occur, failure to select the optimal alternative III rather than alternative I represents an OL of $240M − $200M = $40M. If poor conditions resulted, alternative III would be the best choice at $0M. Choice of alternative I instead would cause an OL of $0M − (−$80M) = $80M.

Thus, for the above problem EOL is computed to be

$$EOL = ($100M)0.25 + ($40M)0.50 + ($80M)0.25 = $65M$$

In general, EOL can be computed as

$$EOL = \sum_i (OL \mid S_i)P(S_i) \tag{15-11}$$

This implies that the expected return for the above alternatives, given perfect information, would be $65M greater than the expected return with no added information. To confirm this implication, the expected return with perfect information should be equal to the expected return with no added information ($155M) plus the EOL ($65M), or $220M. The computation of $E[R \mid PI]$ is shown in Table 15-6 to be $220M.

Table 15-6

EXPECTED RETURN WITH PEFRECT INFORMATION

	Business condition (S_i)		
	Good	*Average*	*Poor*
Best alternative $\mid Si$	II	III	*III*
$P(S_i)$	0.25	0.50	0.25
Outcome for best alternative, $E(R \mid PI)_i$	$400M	$240M	$0M

$$E(R \mid PI) = \sum_i E(R \mid PI)_i P(S_i) = $100M(0.25) + $120M(0.50) + $0M(0.25) = $220M$$

Example:

As an example of evaluation of sample information schemes, suppose the Seyab Company is expanding its product line and a decision has to be made as to the size of additional facilities to add. The alternatives are to build a large plant (A_1), a modest plant (A_2), or to lease facilities as required (A_3). The possible outcomes in the strategy period are that demand will be high (S_1), good (S_2), fair (S_3), or low (S_4). Table 15-7 summarizes the net present value for each alternative for each of the four outcomes and also the best assessment by management of the (prior) probabilities of each possible demand outcome. From the data in Table 15-7, one can calculate the expected outcomes for each alternative as

$$E[A_1] = 0.2(\$18 \text{ million}) + 0.45(\$12 \text{ million}) + 0.25(\$6 \text{ million})$$
$$+ 0.1(-\$12 \text{ million}) = \$9.30 \text{ million}$$

$$E[A_2] = 0.2(\$12 \text{ million}) + 0.45(\$12 \text{ million}) + 0.25(\$9 \text{ million})$$
$$+ 0.1(-\$6 \text{ million}) = \$9.45 \text{ million}$$

$$E[A_3] = 0.2(\$13 \text{ million}) + 0.45(\$10 \text{ million}) + 0.25(\$6 \text{ million})$$
$$+ 0.1(-\$1 \text{ million}) = \$8.50 \text{ million}$$

Thus, based on the prior probabilities and expected outcomes, the indicated decision would be to build a modest plant (A_2) for an expected net P.W. of $9.45 million.

Table 15-7

SEYAB COMPANY RETURNS (IN NET P.W.)

	Demand and probability of demand			
	High, S_1	Good, S_2	Fair, S_3	Poor, S_4
	$P(S_1) = 0.2$	$P(S_2) = 0.45$	$P(S_3) = 0.25$	$P(S_4) = 0.1$
Alternative	*($ million)*	*($ million)*	*($ million)*	*($ million)*
Large plant (A_1)	$18	$12	$6	−$12
Modest plant (A_2)	12	12	9	− 6
Lease (A_3)	13	10	6	− 1

Suppose that a scheme for further consideration is that a market consultant be called in for further study. It is judged that the consultant will predict one of three possible ranges of demand outcome: good to high (X_1), fair to good (X_2), or poor to fair (X_3). The performance of the consultant based on management's subjective belief (or history) is given in Table 15-8. The interpretation of Table 15-8 is that if the demand is going to turn out to be high, the consultant will predict good–high with a probability of 0.6, i.e., $P(X_1 | S_1) = 0.6$; or he will predict fair–good with a probability of 0.3, i.e., $P(X_2 | S_1) = 0.3$; or he will predict poor–fair with a probability of 0.1, i.e., $P(X_3 | S_1) = 0.1$. Similarly, $P(X_1 | S_2) = 0.3, P(X_2 | S_2) = 0.5$, etc.

The expected value of the project, using the sample information (further study results) from the consultant can be computed by determining what the optimal expected return will be for each possible prediction (X_j) by the probability of each prediction occurring. Tables 15-9, 15-10, and 15-11 present the

Table 15-8

SEYAB COMPANY—INDICATIONS OF CONFIDENCE IN CONSULATANT'S STUDY

Given the demand will turn out to be _____ ...	... the probabilities the consultant will predict _____ are		
	Good–high X_1	Fair–good X_2	Poor–fair X_3
High (S_1)	0.6	0.3	0.1
Good (S_2)	0.3	0.5	0.2
Fair (S_3)	0.1	0.3	0.6
Poor (S_4)	0.1	0.1	0.8

Table 15-9

SEYAB COMPANY—COMPUTATION OF POSTERIOR PROBABILITIES GIVEN THAT THE CONSULTANT PREDICTS X_1

S_i	$P(S_i)$	$P(X_1 \mid S_i)$	$P(S_i)P(X_1 \mid S_i)$	$P(S_i \mid X_1)$
S_1	0.20	0.60	0.120	0.414
S_2	0.45	0.30	0.135	0.466
S_3	0.25	0.10	0.025	0.086
S_4	0.10	0.10	0.010	0.034
			$P(X_1) = 0.290$	

Table 15-10

SEYAB COMPANY—COMPUTATION OF POSTERIOR PROBABILITIES GIVEN THAT THE CONSULTANT PREDICTS X_2

S_i	$P(S_i)$	$P(X_2 \mid S_i)$	$P(S_i)P(X_2 \mid S_i)$	$P(S_i \mid X_2)$
S_1	0.20	0.30	0.060	0.162
S_2	0.45	0.50	0.225	0.608
S_3	0.25	0.30	0.075	0.203
S_4	0.10	0.10	0.010	0.027
			$P(X_2) = 0.370$	

computations of posterior probabilities given that X_1, X_2, or X_3 occur, respectively.

If X_1 is predicted, then the posterior probabilities of S_1, S_2, S_3, and S_4 are given in Table 15-9 as 0.414, 0.466, 0.086, and 0.034, respectively. The expected value of the alternatives can then be calculated as

$$E[A_1] = 0.414(\$18 \text{ million}) + 0.466(\$12 \text{ million}) + 0.086(\$6 \text{ million})$$
$$+ 0.034(-\$12 \text{ million}) = \$13.15 \text{ million}$$

Table 15-11

SEYAB COMPANY—COMPUTATION OF POSTERIOR PROBABILITIES GIVEN
THAT THE CONSULTANT PREDICTS X_3

S_i	$P(S_i)$	$P(X_3 \mid S_i)$	$P(S_i)P(X_3 \mid S_i)$	$P(S_i \mid X_3)$
S_1	0.20	0.10	0.020	0.059
S_2	0.45	0.20	0.090	0.265
S_3	0.25	0.60	0.150	0.441
S_4	0.10	0.80	0.080	0.235
			$P(X_3) = 0.340$	

$$E[A_2] = 0.414(\$12 \text{ million}) + 0.466(\$12 \text{ million}) + 0.086(\$9 \text{ million})$$
$$+ 0.031(-\$6 \text{ million}) = \$11.13 \text{ million}$$

$$E[A_3] = 0.414(\$13 \text{ million}) + 0.466(\$10 \text{ million}) + 0.086(\$6 \text{ million})$$
$$+ 0.034(-\$1 \text{ million}) = \$10.52 \text{ million}$$

Therefore, given X_1 is predicted, A_1 (large plant) would be the choice with an expected net P.W. of \$13.15 million.

Similarly if X_2 is predicted, then the posterior probabilities of S_1, S_2, S_3, and S_4 are calculated in Table 15-10 as 0.162, 0.608, 0.203, and 0.027, respectively. The expected return of each alternative can be similarly computed as \$11.11 million for A_1, \$10.91 million for A_2, and \$9.38 million for A_3. Thus, alternative A_1 is again preferred, but with an expected return of \$11.11 million.

Finally, if X_3 is predicted, the posterior probabilities of S_1, S_2, S_3, S_4 are calculated in Table 15-11 as 0.059, 0.265, 0.441, and 0.235, respectively. The expected returns in this instance are \$4.07 million for A_1, \$6.45 million for A_2, and \$5.83 million for A_3. Hence, A_2 is the optimal alternative with an expected return of \$6.45 million.

It should be noted from the summations in the fourth columns of Tables 15-9, 15-10, and 15-11 that the probabilities that X_1, X_2, and X_3 will be predicted are, respectively, 0.29, 0.37, and 0.34.

The expected return given sample information $E[R \mid SI]$, can now be computed using the general relationship

$$E[R \mid SI] = \sum_j \max \left(E[A_i \mid X_j] P(X_j) \right) \qquad 15\text{-}12$$

Thus, $E[R \mid SI] = (\$13.15 \text{ million})(0.29) + (\$11.11 \text{ million})(0.37) + (\$6.45 \text{ million})(0.34) = \$10.12$ million. To determine the EVSI, one need only compute

$$\text{EVSI} = E[R \mid SI] - E[R]$$
$$= \$10.12 \text{ million} - \$9.45 \text{ million} = \$0.67 \text{ million}$$

This result indicates that management, based on the expected monetary principle, should be willing to pay up to $0.67 million for the consultant's services in performing the added study if no other added study alternatives are available.

Suppose that the Seyab Company, rather than hiring a consultant, could follow the scheme of engaging its own staff in a fresh intensive study to predict outcomes. To evaluate the expected value of this new (sampling) information, management of the firm will again need to determine conditional probabilities that this type of added study will result in certain predictions given that the demand will turn out either high, good, fair, or poor. Table 15-12 shows the expected performance which reflects management's confidence in the added study. In this case, the staff will predict four possible outcomes corresponding to the actual expected demand—high, good, fair, or poor.

Table 15-12

SEYAB COMPANY—INDICATIONS OF CONFIDENCE IN STAFF STUDY

Given the demand will turn out to be _____ ...	... *the probabilities the staff will predict* _____ *are*			
	High X_1	*Good* X_2	*Fair* X_3	*Poor* X_4
High (S_1)	0.7	0.2	0.1	0.0
Good (S_2)	0.3	0.5	0.1	0.1
Fair (S_3)	0.1	0.3	0.4	0.2
Poor (S_4)	0.0	0.2	0.3	0.5

The posterior probabilities of demand turning out to be either S_1, S_2, S_3, or S_4 for each possible staff study prediction X_1, X_2, X_3, or X_4 can be calculated as shown in previous examples. Table 15-13 summarizes the results of these calculations. The expected returns for each alternative and each staff study prediction are summarized in Table 15-14.

Table 15-13

SEYAB COMPANY—SUMMARIZATION OF CALCULATED POSTERIOR PROBABILITIES FOR STAFF STUDY

S_i	*Posterior probability*			
	$P(S_i \mid X_1)$	$P(S_i \mid X_2)$	$P(S_i \mid X_3)$	$P(S_i \mid X_4)$
S_1	0.467	0.111	0.103	0.000
S_2	0.450	0.625	0.231	0.310
S_3	0.083	0.208	0.513	0.345
S_4	0.000	0.056	0.153	0.345

Table 15-14

SEYAB COMPANY—SUMMARIZATION OF EXPECTED RETURNS
FOR STAFF STUDY

	Prediction ($ million)			
Alternative	X_1	X_2	X_3	X_4
$E(A_1)$	$14.30	$10.07	$5.87	$1.65
$E(A_2)$	11.75	10.37	7.71	4.76
$E(A_3)$	11.07	8.89	6.51	4.83

Table 15-15

SEYAB COMPANY—CALCULATION OF EXPECTED RETURN
FOR STAFF STUDY

Staff prediction (X_j)	Expected return of best alternative ($ million)	$P(X_j)$	Expected return $\times P(X_j)$ ($ million)
X_1	$14.30	0.300	$4.29
X_2	10.37	0.360	3.73
X_3	7.71	0.195	1.50
X_4	4.83	0.145	0.71
			$\sum_j = 10.23 million

Table 15-15 indicates the expected return of the best alternative and also probabilities of staff prediction for X_1, X_2, X_3, and X_4, respectively. The expected returns come directly from Table 15-14, but the probabilities are the result of the posterior probability calculations not shown but for which the results were summarized in Table 15-13. The right-hand column of Table 15-15 shows the computation of the expected return given the sample (added study) information to be $10.23 million. From this the expected value of sample information can be calculated as $10.23 million $-$$9.45 million $=$ $0.78 million.

The difference between EVSI and the cost of additional study is called the *expected net value of sample information*, denoted ENVSI. Symbolically,

$$\text{ENVSI} = \text{EVSI} - \text{Cost of sample information} \qquad (15\text{-}13)$$

which is a more valuable decision criterion than EVSI alone. Suppose that for this example problem it is thought that the consultant would cost $0.50 million for the added study and that if the firm's staff conducted the study it would cost $0.65 million. In this event, the two alternatives for the added study can be compared through the following calculation:

Consultant:

ENVSI = $0.67 million $-$ $0.50 million $=$ $0.17 million

Staff:

$$ENVSI = \$0.78 \text{ million} - \$0.65 \text{ million} = \$0.13 \text{ million}$$

Thus, the expected net value of the sample information (added study) is slightly greater for the consultant alternative, and thus the consultant should be chosen on the basis of expectations.

Inventory example application: Consider a rather typical retailer's inventory problem with variable demand in which the objective is to minimize the sums of carrying costs and stock-out costs. Table 15-16 shows the costs totaled for each of four possible levels of demand S_i and four amounts of starting inventory A_k, as well as the prior probabilities of each level of demand. It is assumed that the product is highly seasonal and that the demand in a given time period is independent of demand in previous periods. The problem is to determine the optimal starting inventory.

Table 15-16

COSTS OF INVENTORY FOR LEVELS OF DEMAND
AND STARTING INVENTORY ALTERNATIVES

		Demand level			
Starting inventory	$P(S_i)$:	S_1 0.3	S_2 0.2	S_3 0.25	S_4 0.25
A_1		$ 0	$2	$6	$9
A_2		6	0	4	5
A_3		9	2	0	4
A_4		11	5	1	0

The expected costs of each alternative can be calculated to be

$$E[A_1] = 0.3(\$0) + 0.2(\$2) + 0.25(\$6) + 0.25(\$9) = \$4.15$$
$$E[A_2] = 0.3(\$6) + 0.2(\$0) + 0.25(\$4) + 0.25(\$5) = \$4.05$$
$$E[A_3] = 0.3(\$9) + 0.2(\$2) + 0.25(\$0) + 0.25(\$4) = \$4.10$$
$$E[A_4] = 0.3(\$11) + 0.2(\$5) + 0.25(\$1) + 0.25(\$0) = \$4.55$$

The objective, to minimize expected costs, is thus satisfied by inventory level A_2.

Suppose it is observed that the industry's output (production) level for a given period is a modest basis for prediction of the retailer's level of demand for the next period. The nature of this leading correlation is reflected in Table 15-17.

Table 15-17 can be interpreted as follows: If the industry output level for a given period is, say, X_3, then the probability the retailer's demand level for the next period will be S_1 is 0.2; the probability the retailer's demand will be S_2 is 0.3, etc. Another way of stating, which is more in line with previous examples, is that, given the retailer's demand level will turn out to be, say, S_3,

Table 15-17

PROBABILITIES OF INDUSTRY OUTPUT LEVEL
FOR EACH LEVEL OF RETAILER'S DEMAND IN FOLLOWING PERIOD

Given the retailer's demand level for the next period will turn out to be _____ ...	... the probabilities the industry output level is _____ are			
	X_1	X_2	X_3	X_4
S_1	0.5	0.2	0.2	0.1
S_2	0.2	0.4	0.3	0.1
S_3	0.1	0.3	0.4	0.2
S_4	0.0	0.2	0.3	0.5

the probability the industry produced, say, X_4 in the previous period is 0.2.

Using the results of Table 15-17, posterior probabilities can be calculated using the format suggested in Table 15-1 for each of the four outcome levels. The results are summarized in Table 15-18.

Table 15-18

INVENTORY EXAMPLE—SUMMARIZATION OF CALCULATED POSTERIOR
PROBABILITIES OF RETAILER'S DEMAND FOR EACH INDUSTRY OUTPUT LEVEL

S_i	$P(S_i \mid X_1)$	$P(S_i \mid X_2)$	$P(S_i \mid X_3)$	$P(S_i \mid X_4)$
S_1	0.698	0.226	0.203	0.133
S_2	0.186	0.302	0.203	0.089
S_3	0.116	0.283	0.340	0.222
S_4	0.000	0.189	0.254	0.556

Skipping the illustration of several computational steps, Table 15-19 summarizes the expected inventory costs for each alternative given the industry output level and also indicates the best alternative and probability for each output level.

The expected cost given the sample information (industry output level) is calculated to be

$$\text{Expected cost} \mid \text{SI} = \$1.07(0.215) + \$3.39(0.265) + \$3.25(0.295)$$
$$+ \$2.13(0.225) = \$2.57$$

The savings due to the additional study is

$$\text{EVSI} = \min E[A_i] - E[\text{cost} \mid \text{SI}]$$
$$= \$4.05 - \$2.57 = \$1.48$$

An interpretation of the above result is that if there is, say, a financial newsletter reporting service which publishes this industry's output level, their information would be expected to be worth up to $1.48 per demand period to

Table 15-19

EXPECTED COSTS FOR EACH RETAILER'S INVENTORY LEVEL
ALTERNATIVE, GIVEN INDUSTRY OUTPUT LEVEL IS X_J

	Industry output level			
Alternative	X_1	X_2	X_3	X_4
$E(A_1)$	$1.07	$4.00	$4.73	$6.51
$E(A_2)$	$4.65	$3.43	$3.85	$4.47
$E(A_3)$	$6.65	$3.39	$3.25	$3.60
$E(A_4)$	$8.72	$4.28	$2.13	$2.13
Best alternative:	A_1	A_2	A_3	A_4
$P(X_j)$:	0.215	0.265	0.295	0.225

the retailer. The numbers for this hypothetical problem are arbitrary and may appear to be insignificant. However, it is noteworthy that the EVSI of $1.48 represents 36% of the expected inventory costs before the additional study.

Classical and Bayesian Statistical Decision Approaches Compared

Implicit in all statistical decision techniques is that there are risks whenever information is less than perfect. Both classical and Bayesian techniques involve decision rules to minimize risk. Classical inference techniques are more widely used than Bayesian techniques, but Bayesian techniques are widely acknowledged as the more powerful. They will be compared briefly below.

Classical inference techniques categorize error as either Type I, the error due to the rejection of a hypothesis incorrectly, or Type II, the error of accepting a hypothesis when it is not correct. For example, consider a quality control situation where the hypothesis is that a production lot is acceptable from a defect standpoint. In this case, a Type I error occurs when a good lot is rejected, while a Type II error occurs when a bad lot is accepted. Typically, the classical technique objective is to minimize the Type II error subject to a restriction on the probability of committing a Type I error.

The Bayesian technique, on the other hand, is concerned with minimizing the expected opportunity loss (EOL) defined in Eq. 15-12. Another, more detailed definition is

$$\text{EOL} = \sum_i [P(e_i | S_i)\text{OL}(e_i | S_i)P(S_i)] \qquad 15\text{-}14$$

where $P(e_i | S_i) = $ Probability of erring given that state S_i is present

$\text{OL}(e_i | S_i) = $ Opportunity loss of not knowing that S_i is present

$P(S_i) = $ Prior probability of S_i occurring

Hence, the Bayesian technique is concerned not only with the probabilities of committing errors of accepting or rejecting the hypothesis incorrectly, but also with the opportunity losses due to error. Additionally, the prior probability of each hypothesis (state S_i) is factored into the decision rule.

As an example comparing the classical and Bayesian approaches, consider the following problem which neglects the time value of money. A firm, entering into a new product line, is trying to decide whether to buy fully automatic or semiautomatic equipment. The costs of equipment are $830,000 and $250,000, respectively. The variable unit costs of production are $60 for the fully automatic process; and $80 per unit for the first 29,000 units and $85 per unit in excess of the first 29,000 units for the semiautomatic equipment. The selling price is $100, and the estimated market ranges from 20,000 to 40,000 units. A sample technique is devised, and from this it is estimated that the probabilities of the total market demand being in the range of 20,000–25,000 units is 0.20, between 25,000–30,000 is 0.40, 30,000–35,000 is 0.30, and from 35,000–40,000 is 0.10. The expected demand determined by using the midpoints of each of these ranges is 29,000 units. At this quantity the profits using fully automatic equipment (A_1) can be calculated to be $330,000. The profit using semiautomatic equipment (A_2) also happens to be $330,000. Since this is a problem of uncertainty, the application of statistical decision techniques can be used as input for the decision as to which equipment to purchase.

The classical technique requires the establishment of a null hypothesis H_0 and an alternate hypothesis H_1. For this example, suppose H_0 is taken to be that the market demand is at least 29,000 units. The alternative hypothesis H_1 would be that the demand is less than 29,000 units. The classical analyst has the problem of establishing a specific point for H_1 that is tested by sampling through setting an acceptable Type I error level.

When the decision rule is to accept the alternative hypothesis H_1 if the sample indicates 29,000 units or less, the probability of committing a Type I error, denoted α, approaches 0.50 as the true demand approaches 29,000. Similarly, the probability of accepting the null hypothesis incorrectly, denoted β, is also a maximum of 0.50 when the true demand is 29,000 units. The analyst can change his cut-off point for the acceptance of H_1 to a lower value—for example, 27,000 units. If this policy is adopted, the probability of α is reduced but β is increased. Figure 15-2 illustrates this point and indicates how α and β values change for varying levels of market demand.

To apply the Bayesian technique to this problem, one must consider the opportunity losses as well as the probabilities. If the demand is greater than 29,000 units and the semiautomatic equipment was chosen, then OL would be $(S - 29,000) \cdot \$25$, where S is true market demand and $25 is the $85 − $60 difference in unit costs. If the demand is less than 29,000 units and fully automatic equipment is chosen, the OL would be $(29,000 - S) \cdot \$20$. Figure

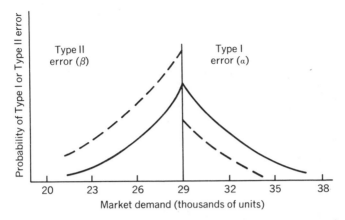

Figure 15-2. Probability of committing Type I and Type II errors for decision rule accept H_1 at or below 29,000 (solid line) and for decision rule accept H_1 at or below 27,000 (dashed line).

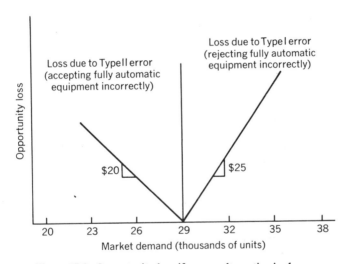

Figure 15-3. Opportunity loss if wrong alternative is chosen.

15-3 illustrates this loss function. The Bayesian technique would require further sampling, computation of the posterior probabilities, and calculation of the EOL for each alternative. The decision would be to choose that alternative which would minimize the EOL. The following section gives convenient means of calculating the EOL when the possible outcomes are normally distributed. After that section, yet another example will be used to illustrate the calculation of EOL for a general two-alternative decision problem.

EOL with Continuous Distribution of Outcomes

If a project has a distribution of outcomes (expressed, say, in net P.W.) which ranges from positive to negative, then opportunity loss occurs whenever the outcome of the project is negative (or below some break-even cut-off point S_b). If the distribution of outcomes, denoted $f(S)$, is continuous, then the expected opportunity loss (expected value of perfect information) is the product of the amount the outcome is on the unfavorable side of the break-even point times $f(S)$ summed over all possible outcomes on that side of the break-even point. Thus,

$$\text{EOL} = \int_{-\infty}^{S_b} |S_b - S| \cdot f(S) \, dS \qquad \text{15-15}$$

As an example, suppose project Z has an expected net P.W., $E(S)$, of \$20 million, that the outcomes are continuous, that the standard deviation $\sigma(S)$ is \$15 million, and that the project is acceptable if the return in net P.W. is greater than or equal to the break-even value ($S_b = \$0$). Figure 15-4

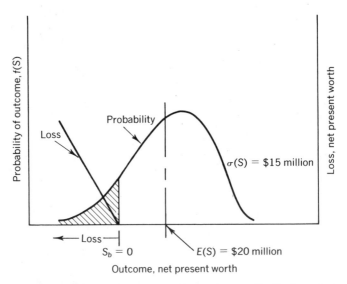

Figure 15-4. Example project Z, with continuous distribution of outcome.

represents this belief in the outcome of the project. Figure 15-5 represents the curve of the product of the distribution of S and the magnitude of the loss $S_b - S$. The area under the curve in Fig. 15-5 represents EOL.

When the outcome is normally distributed, convenient utilization of a

362

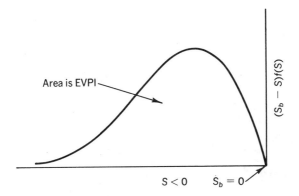

Figure 15-5. Product of the probability of outcome S by the magnitude of loss, $S_b - S$.

"unit normal loss integral"* table (see Appendix E) can be made by the formula

$$EOL = \sigma[S] \cdot UNLI \text{ at } D \qquad 15\text{-}16$$

where UNLI denotes the *unit normal loss integral*, and D equals $[E[S] - S_b]/\sigma[S]$. For the project Z example, given the outcome is normally distributed, UNLI at $D = (\$20 \text{ million} - 0)/\$15 \text{ million} = 1.33$ and can be found to be 0.0427 in Appendix E, and the expected opportunity loss can now be calculated as

$$EOL = \$15 \text{ million} \cdot UNLI \text{ at } D = 1.33$$

$$= \$15 \text{ million}(0.0427) = \$0.6405 \text{ million}$$

Thus, the expected gain is $0.6405 million if the outcomes were known with certainty so that the investment in project Z could be averted when the net P.W. outcome is going to be negative.

The concept of UNLI can also be applied when the difference between the outcomes for the two projects can be expressed as a continuous normal distribution. For example, suppose two projects are each distributed normally as in Fig. 15-6.

The expected difference between the two projects is $7M - $6M = $1M. If the outcomes for the two projects are statistically independent, then

---

*The "unit normal loss integral" is derived on p. 453 of Robert Schlaifer, *Probability and Statistics for Business Decisions* (New York: McGraw-Hill Book Company, 1958), and is equal to

$$f(S_b)\left[\frac{E[S] - S_b}{\sigma[S]}\right] \int_{-\infty}^{S_b} f(S)\, dS$$

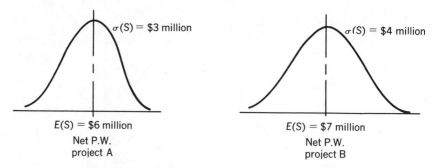

Figure 15-6. Outcome distributions for example projects.

the standard deviation of the distribution of the difference between the two projects is

$$\sigma_d[S] = \sqrt{(\$3M)^2 + (\$4M)^2} = \$5M$$

and that distribution is normal. Thus, the distribution of the difference between the two projects is as shown in Fig. 15-7.

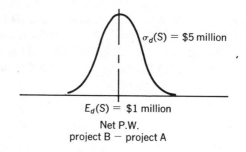

Figure 15-7. Distribution of difference between example projects.

The expected opportunity loss for the difference between the two projects can be calculated as

$$\$5M \times \text{UNLI at } D = \frac{\$1M - 0}{\$5M} = \$5M \times 0.3069 = \$1.535M$$

This is a measure of the expected amount which can be gained by the perfect prediction of when project A will turn out better than project B (even though project B has a higher expected outcome) and then choosing project A at those times.

Example:

An example two-alternative problem in which outcome is normally distributed: As a further example of the use of expected opportunity loss concepts and computational tools, suppose a firm is confronted with a decision as to which type of advertising contract to take with a trade journal. The second alternative A_2 is to pay a fixed rate of \$3,000. The first alternative A_1 is to pay \$30 per unit for the first 100 units sold and \$5 per unit thereafter. The usual range of units sold is from 60 to 150 units because of the journal advertising. Additional information from the publisher gives the firm confidence that the number of units of this type and price sold through advertisement in this journal is normally distributed with a mean of 105 units and standard deviation of 15 units.

The loss functions can be generated from the above information. The break-even quantity S_b is 100 units at which the advertisement cost is \$3,000 for either contract. The opportunity loss function for A_2 occurs if the number of units sold is less than 100 and is

$$\text{OL}(A_2 \,|\, S \leq 100) = \$30(S_b - S)$$

Similarly, the loss function for A_1 occurs if the number of orders received is greater than 100 and is

$$\text{OL}(A_1 \,|\, S \geq 100) = \$5(S - S_b)$$

Both the opportunity losses and the outcome function are depicted in Fig. 15-8.

The characteristics of this type of problem in general are:
1. S is a random variable which is normally distributed.
2. There are two alternatives available. One alternative is preferred over one range of S; the other alternative is preferred over a second range of S.

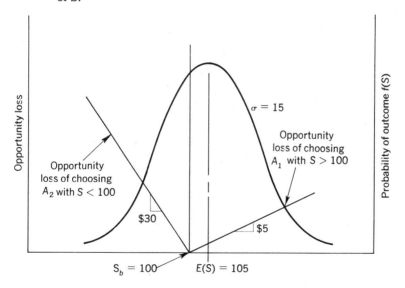

Figure 15-8. Example two-alternative decision problem involving two steps in determination of UNLI.

3. There is a value of S, denoted S_b, at which the two alternatives are equally desirable.
4. A loss function equal to the opportunity loss due to the selection of the wrong alternative is definitive and is one or more linear functions of $|S - S_b|$.

The EOL for each alternative in the example depicted in Fig. 15-8 can now be computed. The UNLI for choosing the fixed contract A_2 is 0.2555 from the table in Appendix E when $D = (105 - 100)/15 = 0.33$. The UNLI for A_1 has to be calculated by adding two segments. Since the loss for choosing A_1 occurs when S is above 100 and since the mean is 105, then the section between 100 and 105 is one segment and from 105 to infinity or the right half of the normal curve is the other segment. From Appendix E, the UNLI at $D = 0.0$ is 0.3989. The UNLI at $D = (105 - 100)/15 = 0.33$ beyond the mean is the complement of the UNLI for one-half the curve less the UNLI for the portion beyond $D = 0.33$. From Appendix E, this is $0.3989 - 0.2555$, or 0.1434. Thus, the total UNLI for A_1 is $0.3989 + 0.1434$ or 0.5423.

The loss value of one standard deviation from the break-even value S_b is equal to $30 per unit times 15 units or $450 for A_2, and is $5 per unit times 15 units or $75 for A_1. The EOL for each alternative can now be computed as

$$\text{EOL}[A_2] = \sigma[A_2] \cdot \text{UNLI}(A_2)$$
$$= \$450(0.2555) = \$115$$

and

$$\text{EOL}[A_1] = \sigma[A_1] \cdot \text{UNLI}(A_1)$$
$$= \$75(0.5423) = \$41$$

where (A_1) and (A_2) denote "for those alternatives," respectively. Since $\text{EOL}[A_1]$ is less than $\text{EOL}[A_2]$, alternative A_1, the variable rate contract, should be chosen.

Note that the probability of getting orders in excess of 100 is more likely than getting orders of less than 100—i.e., $P(S_i \geq 100) = 0.63$, per Appendix F. Thus, the probability that A_1 is the wrong alternative is 0.63 even though the indicated decision is to choose A_1. This decision considers not only probability of error but also the magnitude of loss due to error. Herein lies the main difference between the classical inference and the Bayesian techniques.

PROBLEMS

15-1. The Quick Key Lock Company produces two types of locks and two models of each type. Below are summarized the probabilities of demand for each type and model:

Model	Type	
	Cartridge (C)	Bolt (B)
Standard (S)	0.5	0.1
Pick-proof (P)	0.2	0.2

a. What is $P(S)$? $P(P)$? $P(C)$? $P(B)$?
b. What is the conditional probability of a lock being type B given that the lock is model P?
c. What is $P(B|S)$?
d. What is the joint probability of the bolt type being the pick-proof model?
e. If one knew that a lock drawn randomly was of the bolt type, what is the probability that that particular lock is the standard model?

15-2. The Parcel Delivery Service has analyzed costs and longevity of their trucks. The length of service varies from $2\frac{1}{2}$ to $4\frac{1}{2}$ years with rare exception. The average cost per mile ranges from $0.105 to $0.165. The following matrix summarizes experience with 1,000 vehicles in which the ages and costs are shown discretely for simplicity.

	Cost per mile	
Length of service	$0.12	$0.15
3 yr	120	280
4	270	330

a. What is the prior probability of the cost of $0.12 per mile? Of $0.15 per mile? Of 3 yr of service? Of 4 yr?
b. What are the following conditional probabilities: $P(\$0.12|3\text{ yr})$? $P(\$0.15|3\text{ yr})$? $P(\$0.12|4\text{ yr})$? $P(\$0.15|4\text{ yr})$?
c. A truck at retirement is found to be in the $0.12 per mile category. What is the posterior probability that it is 4 yr old?

15-3. The Carolina Clay Company manufactures brick. A grading process occurs after each firing. A sample is drawn and a quality test is made. Grades A, B, and C have a 0.95, 0.75 and 0.50 proportion passing the quality test, respectively. Historically, the distribution of grade A, B, and C lots has been 32%, 44%, and 24%, respectively.

	Pass	Fail	Total
Grade A			
Grade B			
Grade C			
Total			

a. One brick is randomly drawn from each of 1,000 random lots. Fill in the matrix with the expected results.
b. What is the probability of pass? Fail?
c. A lot of unknown grade was sampled once. The brick passed the test. What are the posterior probabilities that the brick was drawn from a grade A lot? Grade B lot? Grade C lot?

15-4. The returns (in P.W.) for three investment alternatives are summarized below:

	Business condition		
Alternative	Good ($P = 0.30$)	Fair ($P = 0.60$)	Poor ($P = 0.10$)
A_1	$120,000	$60,000	-$100,000
A_2	90,000	70,000	- 40,000
A_3	- 30,000	50,000	90,000

a. Based on the decision rule to maximize expected return, which alternative is best?
b. Which alternative(s) would be chosen if it were known with certainty that business conditions would be good, fair, or poor, respectively?
c. What would be the expected return if perfect information were available?
d. What is the expected value of perfect information?
e. Construct an opportunity loss matrix.
f. On the basis of the decision rule to minimize EOL, which alternative should be chosen?

15-5. In Prob. 15-4, additional information conditional upon sample outcomes X_1 and X_2 is obtainable. The prior and posterior probabilities are presented below:

	Business conditions		
Probability	Good	Fair	Poor
Prior probability	0.30	0.60	0.10
Posterior probability if X_1 occurs	0.40	0.50	0.10
Posterior probability if X_2 occurs	0.15	0.65	0.20

The probabilities of X_1 or X_2 occurring are equally likely:

$$[P(X_1) = P(X_2) = 0.5]$$

a. Compute the $E[R]$ for each alternative if X_1 occurs; if X_2 occurs.
b. What is the $E[R]$ if sample information is obtained?
c. What is the value of the sample information?
d. What is the expected net gain if the sample information costs $5,000?

15-6. The net A.W. for project A is estimated to be normally distributed with a mean of $20,000 and a standard deviation of $12,000. What is the expected opportunity loss?

15-7. The net A.W. for project B is estimated to be normally distributed with a mean of $18,000 and a standard deviation of $6,000. What is the expected opportunity loss?

15-8. Given the two projects in Probs. 15-6 and 15-7, which is the better investment? Assuming that the outcomes for the two projects are independent, what is the expected opportunity loss for the difference between the two projects?

Chapter

16

*decision tree analysis**

Decision trees, also commonly called *decision flow networks* and *decision diagrams*, are powerful means for depicting and facilitating the analysis of important problems, especially those that involve sequential decisions and variable outcomes over time. Decision trees have great usefulness in practice because they make it possible to look at a large complicated problem in terms of a series of smaller simple problems and they enable objective analysis and decision making which includes explicit consideration of the risk and effect of the future.

The name *decision tree* is descriptive of the appearance of a graphical portrayal, for it shows branches for each possible alternative for a given decision and branches for each possible outcome (event) which can result from each alternative. Such networks reduce abstract thinking to a logical

*This chapter is based partially on J. R. Canada, "Decision Flow Networks," *Industrial Engineering* (May–June, 1974), by permission of the publisher.

visual pattern of cause and effect. When costs and returns are associated with each branch and probabilities are estimated for each possible outcome, then analysis of the flow network can clarify choices and risks.

Deterministic Example

The most basic form of decision tree occurs when each alternative can be assumed to result in a single outcome—that is, when certainty is assumed. The replacement problem in Fig. 16-1 illustrates this. The problem as shown reflects that the decision on whether to replace the old machine with the new machine is not just a one-time decision, but rather one which recurs periodically. That is, if the decision is made to keep the old machine at decision point 1, then later, at decision point 2, a choice again has to be made. Similarly, if the old machine is chosen at decision point 2, then a choice again has to be made at decision point 3. For each alternative, the cash inflow is shown above the arrow and the cash investment opportunity cost is shown below the arrow.

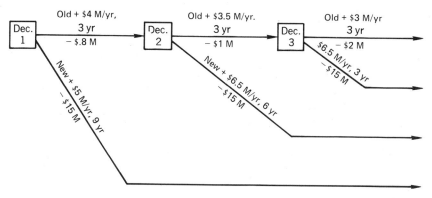

Figure 16-1. Deterministic replacement example.

For this problem, one is concerned initially with which alternative to choose at decision point 1. But an intelligent choice at decision point 1 should take into account the later alternatives and decisions which stem from it. Hence, the correct procedure in analyzing this type of problem is to start at the most distant decision point, determine the best alternative and quantitative result of that alternative, and then "roll back" to each successive decision point, repeating the procedure until finally the choice at the initial or present decision point is determined. By this procedure, one can make a present decision which directly takes into account the alternatives and expected decisions of the future.

For simplicity in this example, timing of the monetary outcomes will first be neglected, which means that a dollar has the same value regardless of the year in which it occurs. Table 16-1 shows the necessary computations and decisions. Note that the monetary outcome of the best alternative at decision point 3 ($7.0M for the "Old") becomes part of the outcome for the "Old" alternative at decision point 2. Similarly, the best alternative at decision point 2 ($24.0M for the "New") becomes part of the outcome for the "Old" alternative at decision point 1.

Table 16-1

MONETARY OUTCOMES AND DECISIONS AT EACH
POINT—DETERMINISTIC REPLACEMENT EXAMPLE OF FIG. 16-1

Decision point	Alternative	Monetary outcome		Choice
3	Old	$3M(3) − $2M	= $ 7.0M	Old
	New	$6.5M(3) − $15M	= $ 4.5M	
2	Old	$7M + $3.5M(3) − $1M	= $16.5M	
	New	$6.5M(6) − $15M	= $24.0M	New
1	Old	$24M + $4M(3) − $0.8M	= $35.2M	Old
	New	$5M(9) − $15M	= $30.0M	

By following the computations in Table 16-1, one can see that the answer is to keep the "Old" now and plan to replace it with the "New" at the end of 3 years. But this does not mean that the old machine should necessarily be kept for a full 3 years and then a new machine bought without question at the end of 3 years. Conditions may change at any time, thus necessitating a fresh analysis—probably a decision tree analysis—based on estimates which are reasonable in light of conditions at that later time.

Deterministic Example Considering Timing

For decision tree analyses, which involve working from the most distant decision point to the nearest decision point, the easiest way to take into account the timing of money is to use the present worth approach and thus discount all monetary outcomes to the decision points in question. To demonstrate, Table 16-2 shows computations for the same replacement problem of Fig. 16-1 using a discount rate of 25% per year.

Note from Table 16-2 that when taking into account the effect of timing by calculating present worths at each decision point, the indicated choice is not only to keep the "Old" at decision point 1, but also to keep the "Old"

Table 16-2

DECISIONS AT EACH POINT WITH INTEREST = 25% PER YR FOR
DETERMINISTIC REPLACEMENT EXAMPLE OF FIG. 16-1

Decision point	Alternative	P.W. of monetary outcome		Choice
3	Old	$3M($P/A$,3) − $2M$		
		$3M(1.95) − $2M	= $3.85M	Old
	New	$6.5M($P/A$,3) − $15M		
		$6.5M(1.95) − $15M	= −$2.33M	
2	Old	$3.85($P/F$,3) + $3.5M($P/A$,3) − $1M		
		$3.85(0.512) + $3.5M(1.95) − $1M	= $7.79M	Old
	New	$6.5M($P/A$,6) − $15M		
		$6.5M(2.95) − $15M	= $4.18M	
1	Old	$7.89M($P/F$,3) + $4M($P/A$,3) − $0.8M		
		$7.89M(0.512) + $4M(1.95) − $0.8M	= 10.98M	Old
	New	$5.0M($P/A$,9) − $15M		
		$5.0M(3.46) − $15M	= $2.30M	

at decision points 2 and 3 as well. This result is not surprising since the high interest rate tends to favor the alternatives with lower initial investments, and it also tends to place less weight on long-term returns.

Consideration of Random Outcomes

The deterministic replacement example of Fig. 16-1 discussed above did not include one of the most powerful elements in the use of decision trees: the formal consideration of variable outcomes to which probabilities of occurrence can be assigned. Suppose that for each alternative there are two possible monetary outcomes, depending on whether the demand is "high" or "low." In such a case, the decision tree problem of Fig. 16-1 would appear as in Fig. 16-2. Note that for each alternative in Fig. 16-2 there is shown a circle from which are drawn arrows to represent each possible chance event or state of nature which can result, such as demand being either "high" or "low."

In order to solve this problem—that is, to determine the best alternative for each decision point, etc.—it is necessary first to determine the outcome (usually expressed in monetary units) and the probability of occurrence for each possible chance event. Then the criterion (measure of merit) for choice (usually expected P.W. of monetary outcomes) can be decided and the solution computed by the same procedure as before; that is, criterion outcomes and decisions are determined for the most distant decision points first, and

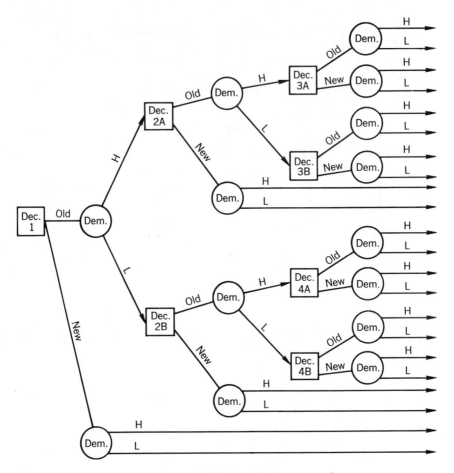

Figure 16-2. Probabilistic replacement example.

then the procedure is successively repeated, moving back in time until the decision for decision point 1 is determined.

Typical Problem and Solution

The following is a brief description of a classical problem for which decision trees are very useful for analysis and solution.*

An oil wildcatter must decide whether to drill or not to drill at a given site before his option expires. He is uncertain whether the hole will turn out to be dry, wet, or a gusher. The net payoffs (in present worths) for each

*H. Raiffa, *Decision Analysis: Introductory Lectures on Choices Under Uncertainty* (Reading, Mass.: Addison-Wesley, 1968).

state are $70,000, $50,000, and $200,000, respectively. The initially estimated probabilities that each state will occur are 0.5, 0.3, and 0.2, respectively. Figure 16-3 is a decision flow network depicting this simple situation. Table 16-3 shows calculations to determine that the best choice for the wildcatter is to drill based on an expected monetary value of $30,000 versus $0 if he does not drill. Nevertheless, this may not be a clear-cut decision because of the risk of a $70,000 loss and because the wildcatter might reduce the risk by obtaining further information.

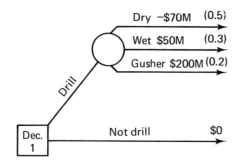

Figure 16-3. Oil wildcatter problem diagram, before consideration of seismic soundings.

Table 16-3

EXPECTED MONETARY CALCULATIONS FOR
THE OIL WILDCATTER PROBLEM BEFORE
CONSIDERATION OF SEISMIC SOUNDINGS

Drill: −$70,000(0.5) + $50,000(0.3)	
+ $200,000(0.2)	= $30,000
Not drill:	= $0

Suppose it is possible for the wildcatter to take seismic soundings at the cost of $1,000. The soundings will disclose whether the terrain below has no structure (outcome NS), or open structure (outcome OS), or closed structure (outcome CS).

Instead of using Bayesian methods for revision of probabilities at this point, let us assume that the probabilities of the various possible well outcomes given the various seismic sounding outcomes are as shown in Fig. 16-4, which is a flow diagram for the entire problem.* The solution of the problem using the EMV criterion is shown in Table 16-4. It should be noted

---

*Problem 16-12 at end of this chapter is a statement of the sampling or added-study probabilities which, when combined with the prior probabilities in Fig. 16-3, result in the posterior probabilities in Fig. 16-4.

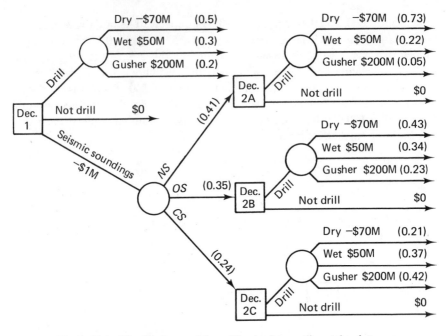

Figure 16-4. Oil wildcatter problem with seismic soundings taken into consideration.

Table 16-4

EXPECTED MONETARY CALCULATIONS FOR THE OIL WILDCATTER
PROBLEM WITH CONSIDERATION OF SEISMIC SOUNDINGS

Decision point	Alternative	Expected monetary value	Choice
2A	Drill	$-\$70M(0.73) + \$50M(0.22)$ $+ \$200M(0.05) \quad = -\$30M$	
	Not drill	$\$0$	Not drill
2B	Drill	$-\$70M(0.43) + \$50M(0.34)$ $+ \$200M(0.23) \quad = \quad \$33M$	Drill
	Not drill	$\$0$	
2C	Drill	$-\$70M(0.21) + \$50M(0.37)$ $+ \$200M(0.42) \quad = \quad \$98M$	Drill
	Not drill	$\$0$	
1	Drill	$\$30M$	
	Not drill	$\$0$	
	Seismic soundings	$\$0(0.41) + \$33M(0.35)$ $+ \$98M(0.24) - \$1M$ $= \quad \$33M$	Seismic soundings

that the alternative "seismic soundings" is now best with an expected monetary outcome of $33,000.

Decision Tree Steps

Now that decision trees (diagrams) have been introduced and the mechanics of using the diagrams to arrive at an initial decision have been illustrated, the steps involved can be summarized as:

1. Identify the points of decision and alternatives available at each point.
2. Identify the points of uncertainty and the type or range of possible outcomes at each point. (Layout of decision flow network.)
3. Estimate the values needed to make the analysis, especially the probabilities of different outcomes and the costs/returns for various outcomes and alternative actions.
4. Analyze the alternatives, starting with the most distant decision point(s) and working back, to choose the best initial decision.

The above example used the expected monetary value (E.M.V.) as the decision criterion. However, if outcomes can be expressed in terms of utility units, then the decision-maker can use the expected utility as a decision criterion. Alternatively, the decision-maker may be willing to express his certain monetary equivalent (C.M.E.) for each chance outcome node and use that as his decision criterion as explained in a later section.

Because a decision diagram can quickly become discouragingly, if not unmanageably, large, it is generally best to start out by structuring a problem simply by considering only major alternatives and outcomes in order to get an initial understanding or "feel" for the problem. Then one can develop more information on alternatives and outcomes which seem sufficiently important to affect the final decision until one is satisfied that the study is sufficiently complete in view of the nature and importance of the problem and the time and study resources available.

General Principles of Diagramming

The proper diagramming of a decision problem is, in itself, generally very useful to the understanding of the problem, and it is essential to correct subsequent analysis.

The placement of decision points and chance outcome nodes from the initial decision point to the base of any later decision point should give a correct representation of the information that will and will not be available when the decision-maker actually has to make the choice represented by the decision point in question. The decision tree diagram should show the following:

1. all initial or immediate alternatives among which the decision-maker wishes to choose;

2. all uncertain outcomes and future alternatives that the decision-maker wishes to consider because they may directly affect the consequences of initial alternatives;

3. all uncertain outcomes that the decision-maker wishes to consider because they may provide information that can affect his future choices among alternatives and hence indirectly affect the consequences of initial alternatives.

It should also be noted that the alternatives at any decision point and the outcomes at any outcome node must be:

1. mutually exclusive, i.e., no more than one can possibly be chosen; and

2. collectively exhaustive, i.e., some one must be chosen or something must occur if the decision point or outcome node is reached.

Use of Bayesian Method to Evaluate the Worth of Further Investigative Study

One alternative that frequently exists in an investment decision problem is further research or investigation before deciding on the investment. This means making an intensive objective study, hopefully by a fresh group of people. It may involve such aspects as undertaking additional research and development study, making a new analysis of market demand, or possibly studying anew future operating costs for particular alternatives.

The concepts of Bayesian statistics provide a means for utilizing subsequent information to modify estimates of probabilities and also a means for estimating the value of further economic investigation study.

To illustrate, consider the one-stage decision situation shown in Fig. 16-5, in which each alternative has two possible chance outcomes: "high" or "low" demand. It is estimated that each outcome is equally likely to occur, and the monetary result expressed as P.W. is shown above the arrow for each outcome. Again, the amount of investment for each alternative is shown below the respective lines. Based on these amounts, the calculation of the expected monetary outcome (net P.W.) is shown in Table 16-5, which indicates that the "Old" should be chosen.

To demonstrate the use of Bayesian statistics, suppose that one is considering the advisability of undertaking a fresh intensive investigation before

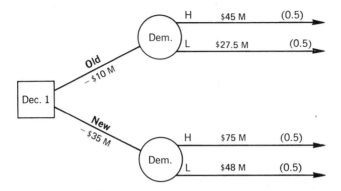

Figure 16-5. One-stage replacement problem.

Table 16-5

EXPECTED MONETARY VALUES FOR PROBLEM IN FIG. 16-5

Old: $45M(0.5) + $27.5M(0.5) − $10M = $26.25M
New: $75M(0.5) + $43M(0.5) − $35M = $24.0M

deciding upon the "Old" versus the "New." Suppose also that this further study would cost $0.1M. In order to use the Bayesian approach, it is necessary for management to assess the conditional probabilities that the intensive investigation will yield certain results. These probabilities reflect explicit measures of management's confidence in the ability of the investigation to predict the outcome. Sample assessments are shown in Table 16-6. As an explanation, $P(h|H)$ means the probability that the predicted demand is "high," given that the actual demand will turn out to be "high."

Chapter 15 contains a formal statement of Bayes' theorem as well as a tabular format for ease of calculations in the discrete outcome case. Tables

Table 16-6

MANAGEMENT'S ASSESSMENT OF CONFIDENCE
IN INVESTIGATION RESULTS

$P(h\|H) = 0.70$
$P(h\|D) = 0.20$
$P(d\|H) = 0.30$
$P(d\|D) = 0.80$

Key:	*Investigation-predicted demand*	*Actual demand*
	h = High	H = High
	d = Low	D = Low

16-7 and 16-8 use this format for revision of probabilities based on the data in Table 16-6 and the prior probabilities of 0.5 that the demand will be high and 0.5 that the demand will be low.

Table 16-7

COMPUTATION OF POSTERIOR PROBABILITIES GIVEN
THAT INVESTIGATION-PREDICTED DEMAND IS HIGH (*h*)

(1)	(2)	(3)	(4) = (2)(3)	(5) = (4)/Σ (4)
State (actual demand)	Prior probability P (state)	Confidence assessment P (h|state)	Joint probability	Posterior probability P (state|h)
H	0.5	0.70	0.35	0.78
D	0.5	0.20	0.10	0.22
			$\Sigma = 0.45$	

Table 16-8

COMPUTATION OF POSTERIOR PROBABILITIES GIVEN THAT
INVESTIGATION-PREDICTED DEMAND IS LOW (*d*)

(1)	(2)	(3)	(4) = (2)(3)	(5) = (4)/Σ (4)
State (actual) demand	Prior probability P (state)	Confidence assessment P (d|state)	Joint probability	Posterior probability P (state|d)
H	0.5	0.30	0.15	0.27
D	0.5	0.80	0.40	0.73
			$\Sigma = 0.55$	

The probabilities calculated in Tables 16-7 and 16-8 can now be used to assess the alternative of further investigation. Figure 16-6 shows a decision tree diagram for this alternative as well as the two original alternatives. Note the demand probabilities entered on the branches according to whether the investigation indicates "high" or "low" demand.

The expected outcome for the alternative of further investigation can now be calculated. This is done by the standard decision tree principle of determining the decision at the most distant points and working back. This is shown in Table 16-9. It is worthy of note that the 0.45 and 0.55 probabilities that investigation-predicted demand will be "high" and "low," respectively, are obtained from the total in column (4) of the Bayesian revision calculations shown in Tables 16-7 and 16-8.

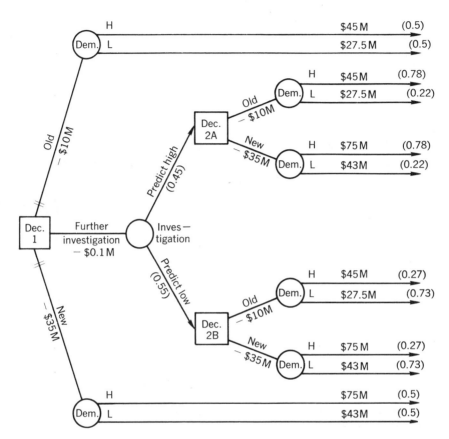

Figure 16-6. Replacement problem with alternative of further investigation.

Table 16-9

EXPECTED MONETARY OUTCOME FOR REPLACEMENT PROBLEM OF FIG. 16-6

Decision point	Alternative	Expected monetary outcome		Choice
2a	Old	$45M(0.78) + $27.5M(0.22) − $10M	= $31.15M	
	New	$75M(0.78) + $43M(0.22) − $35M	= $32.96M	New
2b	Old	$45M(0.27) + $27.5M(0.73) − $10M	= $22.23M	Old
	New	$75M(0.27) + $43M(0.73) − $35M	= $16.64M	
1	Further investigation	$32.96M(0.45) + $22.23M(0.55) − $0.1M	= $26.96M	Further investigation
	Keep old	(from Table 16-5):	26.25M	
	New	(from Table 16-5):	24.00M	

Thus, from Table 16-9, it can be seen that the alternative of further investigation, with an expected return of $26.96M, is the best present course of action by a slight margin. While the figures used here do not reflect much advantage to the further investigation, the advantage potentially can be great.

Expected Value of Perfect Information

Calculations of the expected value of perfect information (EVPI), which was introduced in Chapter 15, for the example replacement problem of Fig. 16-5 are shown in Table 16-10.

Table 16-10

EXPECTED VALUE OF PERFECT INFORMATION FOR ONE-STAGE
REPLACEMENT PROBLEM OF FIG. 16-5

If demand is	...then the preferred alternative is	And the monetary outcome is	The prior probability estimate is	Thus, the expected value is
High	New	$ 40M	0.5	$20.00M
Low	Old	17.5M	0.5	8.75M

Expected outcome with perfect foreknowledge: $\sum$ = $28.75M

EVPI = EOL = $28.75M − $26.25M = $2.5M

From Table 16-10, It can be seen that the expected outcome with perfect foreknowledge, $28.75M, is greater than the expected value of the preferred alternative before the further investigation, $26.25M, by $2.5M, which is a measure of the maximum expected value of further investigation. For the example problem in Fig. 16-5 and Table 16-9, the further investigation resulted in an increase in the expected net value of only $0.71M of this $2.5M; i.e., $26.96M − $26.25M = $0.71M.

There is a practical limit to the amount of expenditure for further investigation which can be justified by the potential expected gains from that investigation. In general, the principle of diminishing marginal returns applies in this type of situation.

Useful Notation Conventions

It is often thought useful to show results of calculations and choices between alternatives directly on the decision diagrams. For example, the replacement problem in Fig. 16-6 (and the calculated results and choices in Table 16-9) might be shown as in Fig. 16-7. The numbers in small boxes next

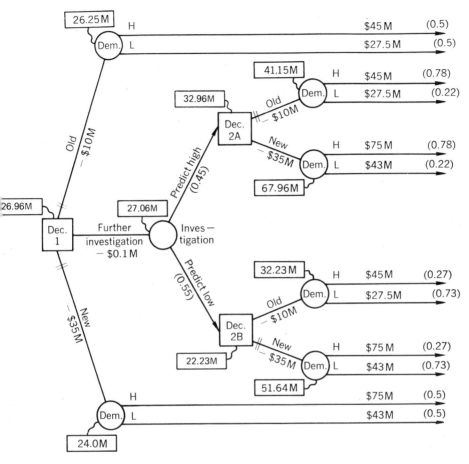

Figure 16-7. Replacement problem with alternative of further investigation (showing useful notation conventions).

to each outcome node represent the expected value (or other indicator of desirability) of outcomes beyond that point. The "double slash" marks for all alternatives except one emanating from each decision point indicate alternatives that would not be chosen. The number in the small box next to each decision point indicates the value of the best alternative at each point.

Alternate Method of Analysis

Some analysts and decision-makers prefer to show the criterion values (like expected monetary value) at the end of each possible path through the tree. (*Note:* If the monies along the path are at significantly different points in time, the criterion values should be expressed in terms of equivalent worths, such as P.W. or A.W.) Then, the "roll back" technique can be used to determine the optimal choice at each decision point and obtain the same initial decision as when using the previous method. For example, the problem in Fig. 16-6 and Fig. 16-7 could be shown as in Fig. 16-8, which also includes the "notation conventions" explained in the last section. The criterion values at the end of each branch are placed in oval boxes to distinguish them from the other outcome and investment values emanating from each chance node and decision point. As an example, the criterion value for the third path from the top, $34.9M, in Fig. 16-8 is obtained by adding −$0.1M,

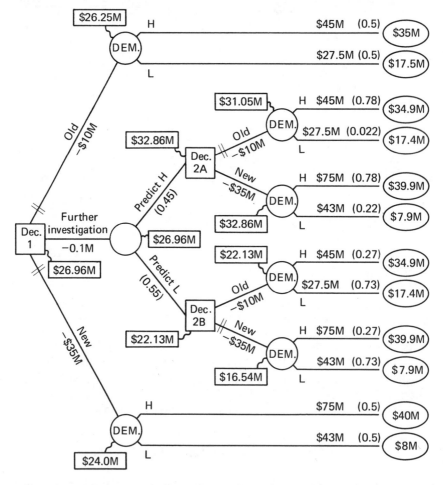

Figure 16-8. Replacement problem with alternative of further investigation (showing outcomes at end of each branch and subsequent analysis).

Table 16-11

EXPECTED MONETARY OUTCOMES FOR REPLACEMENT
PROBLEM OF FIGURE 16-8

Decision point	Alternative	Expected monetary outcome	Choice
2A	Old	$34.9M(0.78) = 17.4M(0.22) = 31.05M	
	New	$39.9M(0.78) + 7.9M(0.22) = 32.86M	New
2B	Old	$34.9M(0.27) + 17.4M(0.73) = 22.13M	Old
	New	$39.9M(0.27) + 7.9M(0.73) = 16.54M	
1	Further investigation	$32.86M(0.45) + 22.13M(0.55) = 26.96M	Further investigation
	Old	35M(0.5) + 17.5M(0.5) = 26.25M	
	New	40M(0.5) + 8M(0.5) = 24.0M	

—$10M, and $45M for that path as shown in Fig. 16-7. Calculations of expected monetary outcomes for Fig. 16-8 are shown in Table 16-11.

Certain Monetary Equivalents

Any problem involving variable outcomes, such as the replacement problem in Fig. 16-8, could just as well be analyzed using the so-called certain monetary equivalent (C.M.E. or C.E.) criterion rather than the expected monetary value (E.M.V.) criterion. A decision-maker's certain monetary equivalent for a set of uncertain cash flow outcomes should depend on the complete context in which the flow occurs, i.e., on everything which would precede or follow the set of uncertain outcomes. For example, the decision-maker should be particularly cognizant of his overall financial position when deciding on a C.M.E. One way this could be taken into account is to specify the decision-maker's asset position before the initial decision is to be made. For example, perhaps *net liquid assets* (such as net assets that can be converted into cash within a month or within a year) might be taken as the most appropriate measure of asset position.

Suppose, for the replacement problem in Fig. 16-8, it is desired to evaluate the alternatives using the certain monetary equivalent criterion while formally considering that the decision-maker's initial asset position is, say, $10M. Figure 16-9 depicts this as well as a hypothetical solution to the problem. Note that the initial asset position is shown in a dotted oval to the left of the initial decision point. Because the initial asset position amount is common to all paths through the decision tree, the $10M is added to the criterion values in oval blocks at the end of all paths.

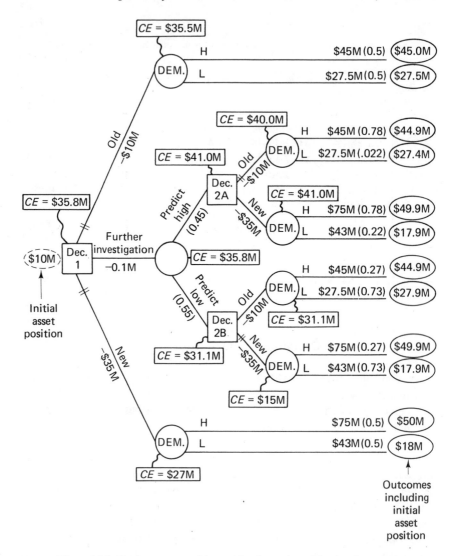

Figure 16-9. Replacement problem with alternative of further investigation (showing outcomes at the end of each branch and subsequent analysis using C.M.E. (or C.E.) criterion).

To complete the solution, the decision-maker must specify his C.M.E.
for all chance outcome nodes. Suppose, for the top node, the decision-maker
decides that a certain $35.5M is just as desirable as 0.5 chance at $45M and
0.5 chance at $27.5M. This is shown in the small block above the node. Other
subjectively determined C.M.E.'s are shown at all nodes. The "roll back"
analysis procedure is again applied, with double slash marks used to show

which alternatives would not be preferred. In this case, the preferred initial alternative is again "Further Investigation," but in general one should not expect to get the same answer by the C.M.E. criterion as by the E.M.V. criterion. Further, the C.M.E. for any situation can be expected to differ among decision makers and from time to time.

Stochastic Decision Trees

It is generally true that the number of possible outcomes that could result from the choice of an alternative is greater than the few outcomes typically assumed in decision tree problems so that the number of branches is kept to manageable size. Hence, information (and sometimes, objectivity) is sacrificed by the assumed reduction of branches. It is common that the possible outcomes emanating from an alternative could be described most adequately as a continuous distribution. These networks are called *stochastic decision trees* or *stochastic decision flow networks*.

As an example of a problem for which some kind of stochastic decision tree analysis is probably applicable, consider the classic oil wildcatter problem in Fig. 16-3. Only three possible outcomes were considered in case the well were drilled. However, the problem would have been more adequately modeled if, say, ten or more possible monetary outcomes were considered if the well were drilled, taking into account the variable costs of drilling and the variable barrels of oil which might be found. Indeed, the problem probably can be represented best by continuous probability distributions such as shown in Fig. 16-10. Monte Carlo simulation, can be used to analyze such decision situations efficiently to arrive at probability distributions of the decision criterion for all initial alternatives. Chapter 13 explained Monte Carlo simulation in general. An excellent article by Hespos and Strassman* provides further discussion of the application of Monte Carlo simulation to decision tree problems.

It is common that outcomes are thought to have a continuous distribution but the decision-maker or analyst feels that it is not feasible or reasonable to specify the distribution, i.e., the decision problem fits the classical definition of uncertainty. A useful way to diagram an uncertain outcome for a decision tree problem is shown in Fig. 16-11. Note that this outcome "fan" can show maximum and minimum values if these can be estimated.

As a further example, suppose the above wildcatter problem involved continuous outcomes for which probabilities cannot be estimated but for which the minimum and maximum extremes for each outcome can be esti-

---

*Hespos, R.F. and P.A. Strassman, "Stochastic Decision Trees for the Analysis of Investment Decision," *Management Science* (August, 1965).

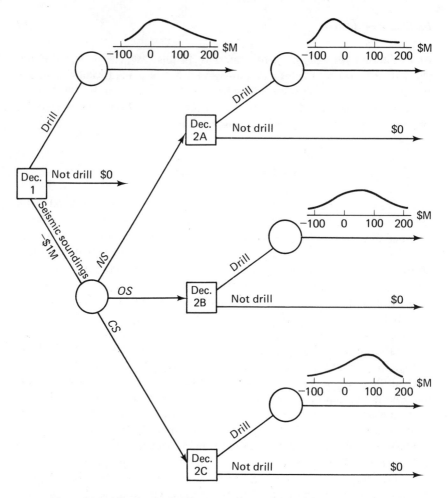

Figure 16-10. Stochastic decision flow network for oil wildcatter problem, showing conceptual probability distributions.

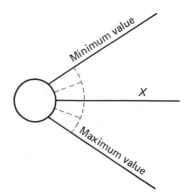

Figure 16-11. Representation of a continuous outcome for which probabilities are not known.

mated. In this case, a diagram representing the problem (with assumed maximums and minimums) could be as shown in Fig. 16-12. Note that even the outcome of the seismic soundings is represented to have a continuous, but unknown, probability distribution. While information in this form does not lend itself to mathematical calculation of decision criteria such as E.M.V., the mere diagramming of the problem can be very helpful in reaching a decision. Indeed, a decision-maker can be asked to determine his C.M.E. at any outcome node even though probabilities of the various outcomes are not known. Any such C.M.E. would be a gross guesstimate (certainly it

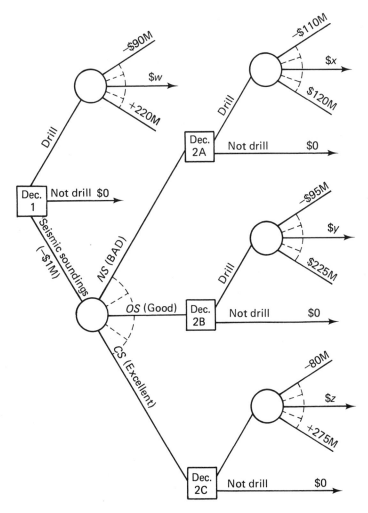

Figure 16-12. Oil wildcatter problem assuming continuous outcomes for which probabilities are not known, but extremes can be estimated.

would be more subjective than if probabilities were known), but at least it represents the decision-maker's intuitive judgment under the circumstances and can be used for comparing alternatives.

Examples of Decision Tree Applications

The decision tree technique can be useful in a very wide range of decision situations. To give some idea of the breadth of potential application, several examples follow.

Small versus Large Asset

Figure 16-13 shows a situation in which a firm is initially faced with the decision between a small machine and a large machine for a use in which demand for the machine is uncertain but subject to probabilistic estimates. Further, if the firm should invest in a small machine now, it has the future choice of whether to invest in another small machine according to the anticipated demand at the time of that future decision.

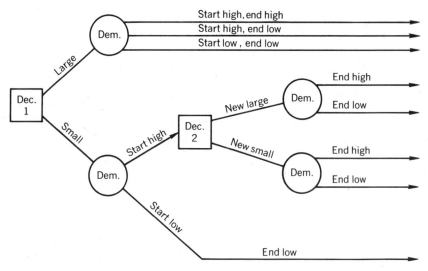

Figure 16-13. Small versus large machine example.

Facilities Modernization

Figure 16-14 shows a situation in which a firm is faced with the decision of whether to invest in major automation of the plant's facilities. The new equipment is supposed to result in reduced labor cost, but its technical performance is critical and subject to variation. Also, the monetary outcome is

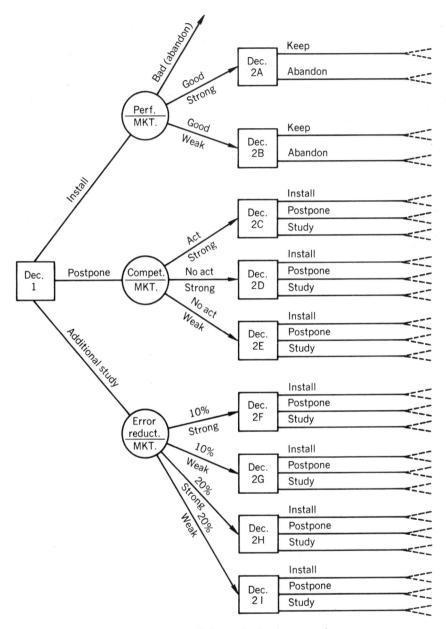

Figure 16-14. Facilities modernization example.

influenced strongly by the total market demand for the product and by whether or not competitors also automate. The diagram shows two decision stages, but, of course, further stages can be enumerated if that is thought desirable.

Buy versus Lease Building

Figure 16-15 depicts a simple buy versus lease decision for building space in which three stages are considered and the amount of use of the space is the critical outcome subject to variation. Note that if initial use is high, there is no further decision, regardless of whether the decision is to buy or lease in the first stage. However, if use is low, then there are subsequent decisions concerning whether to keep, abandon, or perhaps replace with a smaller building.

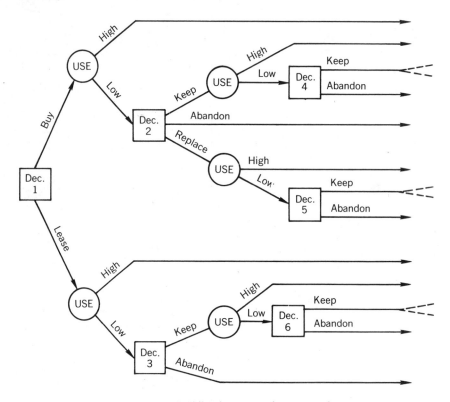

Figure 16-15. Building buy versus lease example.

Advantages and Disadvantages of Decision Tree Analysis

The systematic approach of decision tree analysis has its merits and demerits. Indeed, what is a pro to some analysts and decision-makers may well be a con to others. The following is a synthesis of often claimed advantages:

392

1. *Makes uncertainty explicit.* The uncertainty which the analyst feels about estimates or projects is recognized and incorporated in the analysis.

2. *Promotes more reasoned estimating procedures.* By requiring that estimates be given as probability distributions rather than as single values, and by requiring that these estimates be broken into elements, forces more attention on the estimating.

3. *Encourages consideration of whole problem.* The systematic approach forces the analyst or decision-maker to come to quantitative grips with the interactions between various facets of his problem.

4. *Helps communication.* It facilitates the provision of inputs in an unambiguous quantitative manner from experts and analysts as needed and it provides these results to the decision-maker in a clear manner.

5. *Helps determine need for data and study.* The systematic examination of the value of information in a decision context helps suggest the gathering and compilation of data from new sources.

6. *Stimulates generation of new alternatives.* Detailed decision analysis helps the decision-maker and his staff to think hard about new, viable alternative actions.

7. *Helps "sell" decision.* A hard, thorough analysis can be used to emphasize that a decision has not been made frivolously and to rally support for the decision.

8. *Provides framework contingency planning.* Decision analysis not only results in an initial decision but it can be used as a basis for continuous reevaluation of a decision problem that has a distant time horizon.

The following is a synthesis of often claimed disadvantages:

1. *Tends to exclude consideration of intangibles.* Because a well-done decision analysis is thorough, there is a tendency to place too great a reliance on the quantitative results.

2. *The clear basic questions are often most difficult.* Often the decision-maker would rather take refuge in the fuzziness and complexity of real-life situations than reveal preferences in a number of broken-down or starkly simple decision situations.

3. *Requires expert articulation of the thought process.* A decision-maker may be a great synthesizer of interconnected considerations through subconscious thinking, but he may be unable to give a verbal description of his thought process, thus making it appear that he is much more restricted in the complexity of his analysis than is actually true.

4. *Decision analysts tend to lack compassion.* Persons who elect to get into formalized, systematic analysis are so prone to attach numbers to everything that they tend to exclude many human and artistic qualities and therefore they inhibit creativity.

SUMMARY

The decision tree approach may appear to be complex, but it needs to be no more complex than the decision situation involved. Any investment problem can be examined at many levels of detail. A major difficulty in setting up a decision tree analysis is to strike the appropriate level. In general, the appropriate level is one which allows decision-makers to consider major future alternatives commensurate with the consequences of those alternatives without becoming so concerned with detail and refinement that the key factors are obscured.

Use of decision tree methodology as a basis for investment analysis, evaluation, and decision is a means for making explicit the process which should be at least intuitively present in good investment decision-making. Use of this methodology will help force a consideration of alternatives, define problems for further investigation, and clarify for the decision-maker the nature of the risks he faces and the estimates he must make.

PROBLEMS

16-1. Because of shifting rock formations, a community will be in danger of the collapse of an upstream dam for a year starting now. A permanent replacement dam has been started, but it will take a year to complete. If there is a dam collapse, it will destroy the town, but no deaths would be expected because there is an efficient warning system.

One alternative is to make temporary repairs on the existing dam and to construct temporary levees. Such repairs would greatly decrease the probability of the collapse of he dam. If the collapse should occur, the levees might or might not hold the water back from the town.

The decision-maker in this problem has decided to call in experts to give opinions. Because the collapse of the old dam depends in part on the underlying geological features of the area, the experts can better assess the likelihood of dam collapse if they conduct some geological tests which are expensive.

Diagram the decision-maker's problem in the form of a tree.

16-2. The president of the High Point Carolina Company, Bob Foscue, must decide quickly whether or not to lease a large manufacturing area that has become available adjacent to the firm's present facilities. He is convinced that if he does not lease the extra space now, it will not be feasible for him to move or otherwise expand his plant capacity for at least 2 years. If he does not lease the space and runs out of production capacity during the period, may be forced next year to make a difficult decision that could be critical to the future of his small business. This decision will be between (a) failure to fill all customer orders by rationing limited supplies among existing accounts and (b) using outside contract furniture builders to produce for demand in excess of the firm's capacity. The consequences of choice (a) would be a significant slowing of the firm's aggressive growth momentum. However, choice (b) has an excellent chance of working out well except for two potentially fatal dangers: the contract suppliers might develop dangerous competition with the firm's designs or they might fail to meet quality and shipping quantity requirements.

Foscue believes that if he does not lease the additional space, the question of whether or not he will run out of production capacity and be forced to choose between (a) and (b) depends on two key factors: (1) retailer demand for his furniture during the coming year's buying season and (2) his own decision on whether or not to continue an existing merchandising arrangement with a large direct-mail catalog firm. The direct merchandising arrangement provides an outlet for considerable sales volume, but at modest prices. Foscue is very sure that the merchandising firm will not offer materially improved prices or terms. His own final decision about renewal of the contract will depend on his overall evaluation of supply and demand factors at the time. His current decision about the lease, by limiting the amount of furniture he can supply without going to outside contractors, may have some impact on his subsequent decision on the renewal of the contract. However, Foscue does not consider it feasible or worthwhile to lay out all of the important developments occurring prior to the time of renegotiation. He is fairly confident, however, that if he does not renew the contract, then total demand will be low enough so that he can meet it fully without either expanding beyond his present manufacturing space or relying upon contract producers.

Draw a decision tree that would be appropriate for a first model of Foscue's problem.

16-3. A purchasing manager is faced with deciding whether or not to stock a large supply of metal. The uncertain variable is the future price of the metal. The following are present worths of consequences and prior probabilities for the various perceived outcomes:

Future price	P(Future price)	P.W. if stock	P.W. if don't stock
High	0.3	$100,000	$0
Medium	0.5	− 10,000	$0
Low	0.2	−100,000	$0

For $6,000 it is possible to hire a consulting firm that would be able to make a fairly accurate forecast in terms of whether the price will go up or down as follows:

If the future is going to be:	Then the probabilities the consultant will predict the price will go up or down are as follows:	
	Up	Down
High	0.9	0.1
Medium	0.4	0.6
Low	0.8	0.2

a. Diagram the problem in the form of a decision tree.
b. Determine what would be the best alternative using the E.M.V. criterion.
c. Determine the maximum expected value of the consulting firm's services if the firm could perfectly predict the future.
d. Determine the best alternative if you were the decision-maker using your own unique C.M.E. values.

16-4. The Norva Company has already spent $80,000 developing a new electronic gage and is now considering whether or not to market it. Tooling for production would cost $50,000. If the gage is produced and marketed, the company estimates that there is only one chance in four that the gage would be successful. If successful, the net cash inflows would be $100,000 per year for 8 years. If not successful, the net cash outflows would be $30,000 per year for 2 years, after which time the venture would be terminated. The minimum attractive rate of return on money is 20% per year.

a. Draw a decision tree and determine the best alternative using the E.M.V. criterion based on present worths.
b. If there is a market research group that can provide perfect information about the success of this product, what would be the most the company should be willing to pay for the group's service?
c. Suppose the market research group can make a market survey that with probability 0.8 will predict a success if the gage will actually turn out to be a success and with probability 0.9 will predict failure if the gage will turn out to be unsuccessful. Should the survey be undertaken first? What is the expected value of the survey to the company?

16-5. Suppose, given the alternatives in the small versus large machine example in Fig. 16-13, the demands are assumed to be random variables with present worths of outcomes as follows:

At Decision Point 1:
    If "Large," normal distribution with:
        Expected outcome $= $500M
        Standard deviation $= $200M
    If "Small," discrete distribution with:
        P(Start high) $= 0.70$
        P(Start low) $= 0.30$, with outcome
                "End Low" having uniform distribution between $150M and $450M

At Decision Point 2:
    If "New Large," normal distribution with:
        Expected outcome $= $650M
        Standard deviation $= $250M
    If "New Small," normal distribution with:
        Expected outcome $= $550M
        Standard deviation $= $150M

Demonstrate the use of Monte Carlo simulation for developing data to approximate the distribution of the difference between the present worths of the "Large" and "Small" alternatives at decision point 1. Set up a table to show your random numbers and random normal deviates and the subsequent calculations and demonstrate by generating five full outcomes for the desired distribution.

16-6. Given the following two-stage decision situation shown below in Fig. P16-6, determine which is the best initial decision. Use the expected P.W. method and a minimum R.R. of 12%. To give the problem a physical context, the following letter symbols have been employed for each alternative:

  BSW—Build small warehouse
  RLW—Rent large warehouse
  BA—Build addition
  NC—No change

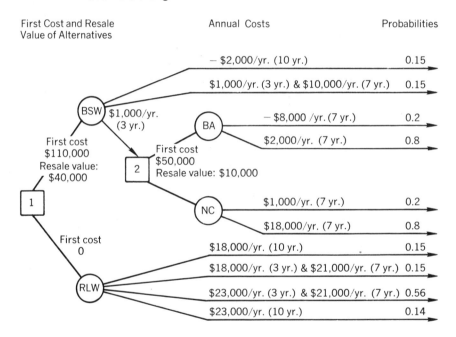

Figure P16-6. Two-stage decision situation for Problem 16-6.

16-7. A firm must decide between purchasing an automatic machine which costs $50,000 and will last 10 years and have 0 salvage value or purchasing a manual machine which costs $20,000 and will last 5 years and have 0 salvage value. If the manual machine is purchased initially, after 5 years a decision will have to be between a manual machine having the same characteristics affecting cost as the first manual machine and a semiautomatic machine costing $40,000 which would have a $20,000 salvage value after 5 years of life. The annual operating costs for each of the machines is as follows: automatic, $10,000; manual, $14,000; semiautomatic, $11,000.

a. Graphically construct a decision tree to represent this situation.

    b. Determine which decision would be made at each point using the **P.W.** method and an interest of 10%.

    c. At what interest rate would the decision between the manual and semi-automatic machine be reversed?

16-8. Suppose one is faced with the same alternatives and dollar outcome consequences as in the replacement problem depicted in Fig. 16-6. However, the initial estimates of probability of demand are: high, 0.6; low, 0.4. Furthermore, management's assessment of confidence in further investigation results, using the notation in Table 16-6 are

$$P(h|H) = 0.80$$
$$P(h|D) = 0.40$$
$$P(d|H) = 0.20$$
$$P(d|D) = 0.60$$

Calculate the choice at each decision point to determine the best initial decision. How close is the initial decision with these revised probabilities to the initial decision for the original problem depicted in Fig. 16-6?

16-9. Figure P16-9 is a decision tree portrayal of a building lease vs. buy problem

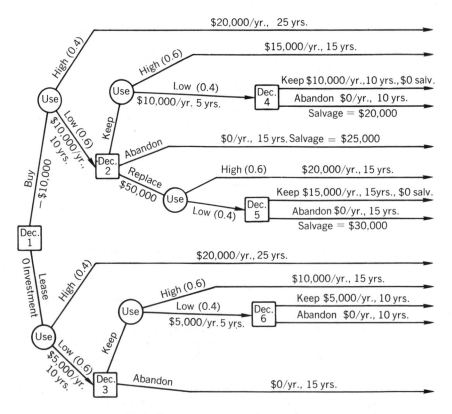

Figure P16-9. Decision tree for Prob. 16-9.

with input data supplied. Investment requirements are shown as negative numbers; probabilities associated with each outcome are shown in parentheses. The annual cash savings and duration of those savings are shown together at each relevant outcome. Salvage values in the cases of abandonments are assumed to occur at the end of the 25-year study period. Determine the best decision using the expected net P.W. method with a minimum required R.R. of 0%.

16-10. Figure P16-10 is a simplified portrayal of the relevant factors for deciding whether to start an applied research project. Determine the answer assuming that the decision points are each 1 year apart and the minimum required R.R. is 20%. Use the expected net P.W. method.

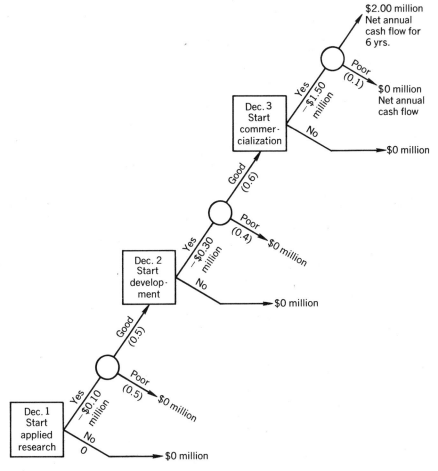

Figure P16-10. Simplified tree showing only relevant information, for Prob. 16-10.

16-11. Set up a decision tree to reflect the personal automobile alternatives which you expect over the next several years. Carry the tree far enough in time to show several decision points at which a decision must be made between keeping an old car and buying a new car (from a possible choice of several). Show your roughly estimated assumed certain investment costs and salvage values and annual operating costs for each alternative and determine the best initial decision using the P.W. method and a 10% minimum personal opportunity cost of money.

16-12. Suppose, for the oil wildcatter problem for which prior probabilities are shown in Fig. 16-3, the probabilities of the possible outcomes for the added study (seismic soundings) are as follows:

Given that the well state will turn out to be:	*Then the probability that the seismic soundings will indicate____structure is:*		
	No	*Open*	*Closed*
Dry	0.6	0.3	0.1
Wet	0.3	0.4	0.3
Soaking	0.1	0.4	0.5

Given the structure indicated by the seismic sounding, use Bayes' theorem to calculate the posterior probabilities regarding what the well state will turn out to be. Check your results against the probabilities shown in Fig. 16-4.

Selected Topics for Economic Evaluation of Investment Decisions

replacement models

The investment problem involving the replacement of assets was explored in Chapter 7. In this chapter we present a number of mathematical models for use in determining the optimum replacement policy for an asset over the planning horizon.

Two types of replacement problems are considered. First, we consider the replacement of assets that deteriorate gradually over time. Second, we consider assets that fail suddenly.

Replacement of Assets Not Subject to Sudden Failure

The following sections consider replacement analysis models for assets that do not suddenly fail in service, but rather are subject to deterioration or at least to decreases in relative desirability over time. The following models are based on common, noncomplex assumptions and serve to indicate the variety of models of the type that can be utilized.

Model I*

As a beginning, assume a zero interest rate, no salvage value at any time, and a minimum equivalent uniform annual cost per period is desired. To facilitate the development the following notation is introduced. Let

A.C.(N) = Equivalent uniform annual cost based on an N period replacement interval

P = Initial investment in the asset

C_j = Sum of operating and maintenance costs in period j, where $C_{j-1} \leq C_j$ for $j = 2, 3, \ldots$

Thus,

$$\text{A.C.}(N) = \frac{P}{N} + \frac{1}{N} \sum_{j=1}^{N} C_j \qquad\qquad 17\text{-}1$$

Denoting N^* as the value of N which minimizes A.C.(N), it must be true that

$$\text{A.C.}(N^* + 1) \geq \text{A.C.}(N^*) \qquad\qquad 17\text{-}2$$

and

$$\text{A.C.}(N^* - 1) \geq \text{A.C.}(N^*) \qquad\qquad 17\text{-}3$$

Substituting Eq. 7-1 into Eq. 7-2 gives

$$\frac{P}{N^* + 1} + \frac{1}{N^* + 1} \sum_{j=1}^{N^*+1} C_j \geq \frac{P}{N^*} + \frac{1}{N^*} \sum_{j=1}^{N^*} C_j$$

which may be written as

$$\frac{P}{N^* + 1} + \frac{1}{N^* + 1} \left[\sum_{j=1}^{N^*} C_j + C_{N^*+1} \right] - \frac{P}{N^*} - \frac{1}{N^*} \sum_{j=1}^{N^*} C_j \geq 0$$

or

$$\frac{P}{N^* + 1} - \frac{P}{N^*} + \left[\frac{1}{N^* + 1} - \frac{1}{N^*} \right] \sum_{j=1}^{N^*} C_j + \frac{C_{N^*+1}}{N^* + 1} \geq 0$$

Multiplying both sides of the inequality by $N^*(N^* + 1)$ gives

$$-P - \sum_{j=1}^{N^*} C_j + N^* C_{N^*+1} \geq 0$$

or

$$C_{N^*+1} \geq \frac{1}{N^*} \left[P + \sum_{j=1}^{N^*} C_j \right] = \text{A.C.}(N^*) \qquad\qquad 17\text{-}4$$

*Based on a development by W.T. Morris in *Engineering Economic Analysis* (Reston, Va.: Reston Publishing Company, 1976).

Substituting Eq. 17-1 into Eq. 17-3 gives

$$\frac{P}{N^* - 1} + \frac{1}{N^* - 1} \sum_{j=1}^{N^*-1} C_j \geq \frac{P}{N^*} + \frac{1}{N^*} \sum_{j=1}^{N^*} C_j$$

Collecting common terms yields

$$P\left[\frac{1}{N^* - 1} - \frac{1}{N^*}\right] + \sum_{j=1}^{N^*} C_j\left[\frac{1}{N^* - 1} - \frac{1}{N^*}\right] - \frac{C_{N^*}}{N^* - 1} \geq 0$$

which reduces to

$$\frac{P}{N^*(N^* - 1)} + \frac{\sum_{j=1}^{N^*} C_j}{N^*(N^* - 1)} - \frac{N^* C_{N^*}}{N^*(N^* - 1)} \geq 0$$

Multiplying both sides of the inequality by $N^*(N^* - 1)$ gives

$$P + \sum_{j=1}^{N^*} C_j \geq N^* C_{N^*}$$

or

$$\text{A.C.}(N^*) \geq C_{N^*} \qquad\qquad 17\text{-}5$$

Combining Eqs. 17-4 and 17-5 indicates the optimum service life is that value, N^*, such that

$$C_{N^*} \leq \text{A.C.}(N^*) \leq C_{N^*+1} \qquad\qquad 17\text{-}6$$

The replacement policy indicated here is the decision rule that *replacement should not take place as long as the equivalent uniform annual cost is greater than the cost of extending the life of the asset by an additional year. As soon as the equivalent uniform annual cost becomes less than the added cost of keeping the asset another year, replace the asset.*

It should be noted that it has been implicitly assumed, with this model, that the replacement machines will have identical cash flow profiles. Further, it is assumed that such replacements will take place indefinitely.

Example:

To illustrate the use of Model I, suppose a machine tool can be purchased for $6,000 and that its operating and maintenance costs are anticipated to increase at a rate of $500 per year, with the first year's cost being $2,000. A zero salvage value and discount rate are assumed.

Solution:

The equivalent uniform annual cost (A.C.) calculations are summarized in Table 17-1. As shown, the optimum replacement interval is 5 years. The operating and maintenance cost of $4,500 for the sixth year would be greater than the A.C. of $4,200 for 5 years of service. Hence, the equipment should be replaced at the end of the fifth year. Rather than employ a tabular solution,

Table 17-1

EXAMPLE FOR MODEL I

N	P/N	$\sum_{j=1}^{N} C_j$	$\frac{1}{N}\sum_{j=1}^{N} C_j$	$A.C.(N)$
1	6,000	2,000	2,000	8,000
2	3,000	4,500	2,250	5,250
3	2,000	7,500	2,500	4,500
4	1,500	11,000	2,750	4,250
5	1,200	15,000	3,000	4,200
6	1,000	19,500	3 250	4,250

an analytical approach can also be used since $C_j = 1,500 + 500j$ for $j = 1,$ $\cdots, N$. Thus,

$$\sum_{j=1}^{N} C_j = 1,500N + 500N(N + 1)/2$$

Hence,

$$\text{A.C.}(N) = \frac{6,000}{N} + 1,500 + 250(N + 1)$$

The condition for an optimum solution is

$$1,500 + 500N^* \le \frac{6,000}{N^*} + 1,500 + 250(N^* + 1) \le 1,500 + 500(N^* + 1)$$

or

$$500N^{*2} \le 6,000 + 250N^*(N^* + 1) \le 500N^*(N^* + 1)$$

Breaking the inequalities into two parts gives

(i) $500N^{*2} - 250N^*(N^* + 1) \le 6,000$

$\qquad 250N^{*2} - 250N^* \le 6,000$

$\qquad\quad N^*(N^* - 1) \le 24$

(ii) $250N^*(N^* + 1) \ge 6,000$

$\qquad\quad N^*(N^* + 1) \ge 24$

or

$$N^*(N^* - 1) \le 24 \le N^*(N^* + 1)$$

and $N^* = 5$.

Model II*

As an enrichment of Model I it is now assumed that the salvage value and interest rate are not zero. Thus, the present worth of an indefinite sequence of identical machines, with salvage values of S_j at time j would be given as

---

*Based on a development by W.T. Morris, in *Engineering Economic Analysis, op. cit.*

$$P.W.(N) = \left[P + \frac{C_1}{(1+i)} + \cdots + \frac{C_N}{(1+i)^N} - \frac{S_N}{(1+i)^N} \right]$$

$$+ \frac{1}{(1+i)^N} \left[P + \frac{C_1}{(1+i)} + \cdots + \frac{C_N}{(1+i)^N} - \frac{S_N}{(1+i)^N} \right] + \cdots$$

$$+ \frac{1}{(1+i)^{kN}} \left[P + \frac{C_1}{(1+i)} + \cdots + \frac{C_N}{(1+i)^N} - \frac{S_N}{(1+i)^N} \right] + \cdots$$

17-7

$$P.W.(N) = \left[P + \sum_{j=1}^{N} \frac{C_j}{(1+i)^j} - \frac{S_N}{(1+i)^N} \right] \sum_{k=0}^{\infty} \left[\frac{1}{(1+i)^N} \right]^k$$

17-8

$$P.W.(N) = \left\{ P + \sum_{j=1}^{N} \left[\frac{C_j}{(1+i)^j} \right] - \frac{S_N}{(1+i)^N} \right\} \left\{ \frac{1}{\left[1 - \frac{1}{(1+i)^N} \right]} \right\}$$

17-9

$$P.W.(N) = \frac{P + \sum_{j=1}^{N} \frac{C_j}{(1+i)^j} - \frac{S_N}{(1+i)^N}}{\frac{(1+i)^N - 1}{(1+i)^N}}$$

17-10

Morris shows that the conditions for a minimum may be conveniently expressed as

$$A.C.(N^*) \le C_{N^*+1} + S_{N^*}(1+i) - S_{N^*+1}$$

17-11

$$A.C.(N^* - 1) \ge C_{N^*} + S_{N^*-1}(1+i) - S_{N^*}$$

17-12

where $A.C.(N) = P.W.(N) \cdot i$. Again the decision rule is *do not replace as long as the equivalent uniform annual cost is greater than the cost of extending the life of the asset by an additional year. As soon as the equivalent uniform annual cost becomes less than the added cost of keeping the asset another year, replace the asset.*

Example:

Model II can be illustrated by recalling the compressor replacement problem considered in Chapter 7. Recall that the compressor cost $5,000 initially. Operating and maintenance costs for year j were given by $C_j = \$1,400(1.10)^{j-1}$; salvage values after N years service were given by

$$S_N = \begin{cases} \$500 + \$50(9 - N)(10 - N) & N = 1, \ldots, 9 \\ \$500 & N > 9 \end{cases}$$

and a M.A.R.R. equal to 10% was given.

Solution:

From Table 17-2 it is seen that the optimality conditions for Model II are satisfied for $N = 5$. Also, it appears that replacing the asset too soon is preferable to replacing it too late!

Table 17-2

EXAMPLE FOR MODEL II

N	C_N	S_N	A.C.(N)		$C_{N+1} + S_N(1+i) - S_{N+1}$
1	1,400	4,100	2,800	>	2,750
2	1,540	3,300	2,776	>	2,724
3	1,694	2,600	2,761	>	2,723
4	1,863	2,000	2,753	>	2,750
5	2,050	1,500	2,751	<	2,805
6	2,255	1,100	2,759	<	2,890
7	2,480	800	2,773	<	3,008
8	2,728	600	2,793	<	3,161
9	3,001	500	2,819	<	3,351

Model III*

The previous analysis assumed that an asset was always replaced by an identical asset. However, technological improvements are very likely to occur. Hence, improved candidates for replacement will exist. In order to illustrate one method of incorporating technological improvement explicitly in the replacement model, suppose an asset is owned currently and at most one replacement can occur during the planning horizon of N years. The following notation will be used:

S_n = Salvage value of presently owned asset if replaced n years from the present, $n = 0, 1, \ldots, N$

P_n = Purchase price (including installation) for the replacement if purchased n years from the present

C_{0j} = Operating and maintenance cost for year j for the presently owned asset

C_{1k}^n = Operating and maintenance cost for the kth year of service for the replacement asset, given replacement occurs n years from the present

F_n = Salvage value of the replacement asset at the end of the planning horizon, if replacement occurs n years from the present

The present worth cost for the replacement problem can be given by

$$P.W.(n) = [P_n + \sum_{k=1}^{N-n} C_{1k}^n (1+i)^{-k} - S_n](1+i)^{-n}$$

$$17\text{-}13$$

$$+ \sum_{j=1}^{n} C_{0j}(1+i)^{-j} - F_n(1+i)^{-N}$$

Hence, the objective is to find the value of n which minimizes P.W.(N). As anticipated, the optimality condition remains the same; namely, *replace as*

*Based on a development by W.T. Morris in *Engineering Economic Analysis*, op cit.

soon as the marginal cost of keeping the old asset one additional year is greater than the marginal savings of postponing replacement one additional year.

Example:

As an illustration of how to use Model III consider a situation for which the following data are appropriate:

$$N = 10 \text{ years}$$
$$S_n = \$5,000(0.75)^n$$
$$P_n = \$15,000(1.10)^n$$
$$C_{0j} = \$8,500 + \$750j$$
$$C_{1k} = (\$3,500 + 800k)(0.90)^n$$
$$F_n = P_n(0.80)^{N-n}$$
$$i = 10\%$$

Solution:

$$\text{P.W.}(n) = [15,000(1.10)^n + \sum_{k=1}^{10-n} (3,500 + 800k)(0.90)^n(1.10)^{-k}$$

$$-5,000(0.75)^n](1.10)^{-n} + \sum_{j=1}^{n} (8,500 + 750j)(1.10)^{-j}$$

$$-15,000(1.10)^n(0.80)^{10-n}(1.10)^{-10}$$

As shown in Table 17-3, the minimum value of P.W.(n) occurs for $n = 1$; however, round-off error could account for the $1 difference in P.W.(1) and P.W.(2). Hence, it is anticipated that the current asset should be replaced in either one or two years.

Table 17-3

VALUES OF P.W.(n) FOR THE
MODEL III EXAMPLE

n	$P.W.(n)$
0	54,753
1	52,111
2	52,112
3	53,612
4	56,161
.	.
.	.
.	.
10	73,911

Model IV

At this point it is possible to develop a generalized replacement model for a planning horizon of N years. Letting M equal the maximum number of replacements allowed to occur during the planning horizon and letting n_k

denote the number of years service for replacement k, then the present worth function to be minimized can be written

$$P.W.(n_0, n_1, \ldots, n_k, \ldots, n_M)$$

$$= \sum_{j=1}^{n_0} C_{0j}(1 + i)^{-j} - S_{n_0}(1 + i)^{-n_0}$$

$$+ \left[P_1 + \sum_{j=1}^{n_1} C_{1j}(1 + i)^{-j} - S_{n_1}(1 + i)^{-n_1} \right](1 + i)^{-n_0}$$

$$+ \left[P_2 + \sum_{j=1}^{n_2} C_{2j}(1 + i)^{-j} - S_{n_2}(1 + i)^{-n_2} \right](1 + i)^{-n_0-n_1} + \cdots$$

$$+ \left[P_M + \sum_{j=1}^{n_M} C_{Mj}(1 + i)^{-j} - S_{n_M}(1 + i)^{-n_M} \right](1 + i)^{-n_0-n_1-\cdots-n_{M-1}}$$

17-14

where n_0 is the number of years before the currently owned asset is replaced. As before, P_k, S_{n_k}, and C_{kj} denote the initial investment, salvage value, and yearly operating and maintenance costs for replacement k.

A dynamic programming solution procedure can be used to minimize the present worth expression given by Eq. 17-14. The stage variable denotes the number of replacements that have been made and is related to the index k. The state variable, N_k, corresponds to the number of years remaining in the planning horizon at the kth stage. The following recursive equation can be defined, for $k = 0, 1, \ldots, M$,

$$f_k(N_k) = \min_{n_k} [r_k(n_k, N_k) + f_{k+1}(N_{k+1})(1 + i)^{-n_k}] \qquad \textit{17-15}$$

where the state variable transformation is given by

$$N_{k+1} = N_k - n_k$$

and the individual stage return function, $r_k(n_k, N_k)$, represents the "present" worth of the cash flows associated with the kth replacement, i.e.,

$$r_k(n_k, N_k) = \begin{cases} P_k + \sum_{j=1}^{n_k} C_{kj}(1 + i)^{-j} - S_{n_k}(1 + i)^{-n_k} & k = 1, \ldots, M \\ \sum_{j=1}^{n_0} C_{0j}(1 + i)^{-j} - S_{n_0}(1 + i)^{-n_0} \end{cases} \qquad \textit{17-16}$$

Example:

As an illustration of Model IV, consider the data for the previous example. Suppose a maximum of two replacements is allowed during the 10-year planning horizon. Naturally, for the second stage $n_2^* = N_2$. Additionally, $f_3(N_3) \equiv 0$ and

$$f_2(N_2) = 15,000(1.10)^{10-N_2} + \sum_{j=1}^{N_2} (3,500 + 800j)(0.90)^{10-N_2}(1.10)^{-j}$$

$$- 15,000(1.10)^{10-N_2}(0.80)^{N_2}(1.10)^{-N_2}$$

or

$$f_2(N_2) = 15{,}000(F/P{,}10\%{,}10 - N_2)[1 - (0.80)^{N_2}(P/F{,}10\%{,}N_2)]$$
$$+ [4{,}300 + 800(A/G{,}10\%{,}N_2)](0.90)^{10-N_2}(P/A{,}10\%{,}N_2)$$

(*Note:* $f_2(N_2 = 0) \equiv 0$.)

Stage 1 calculations involve the stage return function

$$f_1(n_1, N_1) = 15{,}000(1.10)^{10-N_1} + \sum_{j=1}^{n_1} (3{,}500 + 800j)(0.90)^{10-N_1}(1.10)^{-j}$$
$$- 15{,}000(1.10)^{10-N_1}(0.80)^{n_1}(1.10)^{-n_1}$$

or

$$r_1(n_1, N_1) = 15{,}000(P/F{,}10\%{,}10 - n_1)[1 - (0.80)^{n_1}(P/F{,}10\%{,}n_1)]$$
$$+ [4{,}300 + 800(A/G{,}10\%{,}N_1)](0.90)^{10-N_1}(P/A{,}10\%{,}n_1)$$

Additionally, the recursive relation is given by

$$f_1(N_1) = \min_{n_1}[r_1(n_1, N_1) + f_2(N_1 - n_1)(P/F{,}10\%{,}n_1)]$$

Values of $f_1(N_1)$ and n_1^* are given in Table 17-4. The stage 0 calculations are somewhat simplified since it is known that $N_0 = 10$ years. Hence,

$$r_0(n_0, 10) = \sum_{j=1}^{n_0} (8{,}500 + 750j)(1.10)^{-j} - 5{,}000(0.75)^{n_0}(1.10)^{-n_0}$$

or

$$r_0(n_0, 10) = [9{,}250 + 750(A/G{,}10\%{,}n_0)](P/A{,}10\%{,}n_0) - 5{,}000(0.75)^{n_0}$$
$$(P/F{,}10\%{,}n_0)$$

and the recursive relation is given by

$$f_0(N_0 = 10) = \min_{n_0}[r_0(n_0, 10) + f_1(10 - n_0)(P/F{,}10\%{,}n_0)]$$

As shown in Table 17-4, $n_0^* = 1$; hence, $N_1 = 10 - 1 = 9$ and, from Table 17-4, $n_1^* = 4$. Thus, $n_2^* = N_2 = 9 - 4 = 5$. In summary, the currently owned asset should be retained for one more year; the new asset should be used for 4 years and then replaced by an asset which should be used for the duration of the planning horizon.

Replacement of Assets Subject to Sudden Failure

Some assets, such as light bulbs, electronic parts, and missiles, do not exhibit significant deterioration in capabilities over time, but they are usually subject to increasing opportunities for failure as usage or age increases. The usual objective in this type of problem is to determine the amount and timing of replacement (or maintenance) of such assets. Three types of problems are as follows:

Table 17-4

STAGE 1 AND STAGE 0 CALCULATIONS FOR THE MODEL IV EXAMPLE

Stage 1 Calculations

N_1	0	1	2	3	4	5	6	7	8	9	10	$f_1(N_1)$	n_1^*
							n_1						
0	0	—	—	—	—	—	—	—	—	—	—	0	0
1	6,014	6,014	—	—	—	—	—	—	—	—	—	6,014	0, 1
2	9,651	11,481	9,651	—	—	—	—	—	—	—	—	9,651	0, 2
3	13,975	14,815	14,643	13,975	—	—	—	—	—	—	—	13,975	0, 3
4	19,065	18,746	17,627	18,514	19,065	—	—	—	—	—	—	17,627	2
5	25,029	23,373	21,200	21,226	23,191	25,029	—	—	—	—	—	21,200	2
6	31,938	28,795	25,406	24,474	25,657	28,780	31,938	—	—	—	—	24,474	3
7	39,930	35,076	30,335	28,299	28,610	31,621	35,333	39,940	—	—	—	28,299	3
8	49,111	42,341	36,045	32,779	32,086	34,574	37,386	43,016	49,111	—	—	32,086	4
9	59,631	50,688	42,649	37,970	36,160	38,050	39,827	44,883	51,917	59,631	—	36,160	4
10	71,663	60,252	50,236	43,974	40,879	42,124	42,700	47,102	53,613	62,182	71,663	40,879	4

Stage 0 Calculations

N_0	0	1	2	3	4	5	6	7	8	9	10	$f_1(N_0)$	n_0^*
							n_0						
10	40,879	37,872	40,875	44,434	48,239	52,639	56,982	61,424	65,621	70,218	73,911	37,872	1

1. Should a group of such assets be replaced in entirety, or should they be individually replaced upon failure?

2. If group replacement is the best policy, what is the optimum group-replacement interval?

3. How much and how often should preventive maintenance be performed?

To solve the first type of problem the cost of group replacement can be compared with that of individual replacement upon failure. Whenever group replacement can lead to reduced costs (through labor savings, materials discounts, etc.), the optimum group-replacement interval can be computed using calculus or arithmetic approximation methods. The same methods may be used to solve preventive-maintenance problems. Group-replacement and preventive-maintenance interval problems can also be solved by dynamic programming.

An Illustrative Model

Let us assume that failures occur only at the end of a period. Thus, replacements of failures which occur at the end of, say, the third period will be age zero at the beginning of the fourth period. During the first $(N - 1)$ time intervals, all failures are replaced as indicated in the foregoing. At the end of the Nth time interval, all units are replaced regardless of their ages. The problem is to find the value of N that minimizes total cost per period. If it is assumed that the entire replacement interval in question is of short duration such that the time value of money can be neglected, then the total cost from time of group installation until the end of N periods can be given by

$$K(N) = QC_1 + C_2 \sum_{x=1}^{N-1} f(x) \qquad \qquad 17\text{-}17$$

where $K(N) =$ Expected total cost for N periods
$\qquad C_1 =$ Unit cost of replacement in a group
$\qquad C_2 =$ Unit cost of individual replacement after failure
$\qquad f(x) =$ Expected number of failures in the xth period
$\qquad Q =$ Number of units in the group

The objective is to find the value of N which minimizes $K(N)/N$. If an individual unit fails during the jth period with probability $P(j)$, then $f(x)$ is obtained as follows:

$$f(1) = QP(1)$$
$$f(2) = QP(2) + f(1)P(1)$$
$$f(3) = QP(3) + f(1)P(2) + f(2)P(1)$$
$$\cdot$$
$$\cdot$$
$$\cdot$$
$$f(x) = QP(x) + f(1)P(x-1) + f(2)P(x-2) + \cdots + f(x-1)P(1)$$

or

$$f(x) = QP(x) + \sum_{k=1}^{x-1} f(k)P(x - k) \qquad\qquad 17\text{-}18$$

Equation 17-18 is based on the assumption that failures occur independently. If the failure of a unit affects the probability of another unit's failing, then $f(x)$ cannot be computed using Eq. 17-18.

Costs are minimized for a policy of group replacing after $\hat{N}$ periods if

$$\frac{K(\hat{N})}{\hat{N}} \leq \frac{K(\hat{N}+1)}{\hat{N}+1} \quad \text{and if} \quad \frac{K(\hat{N})}{\hat{N}} \leq \frac{K(\hat{N}-1)}{\hat{N}-1} \qquad 17\text{-}19$$

Considering the first condition, from Eq. 17-17 it is seen that

$$\frac{QC_1}{\hat{N}} + \frac{C_2 \sum\limits_{x=1}^{\hat{N}-1} f(x)}{\hat{N}} \leq \frac{QC_1}{\hat{N}+1} + \frac{C_2 \sum\limits_{x=1}^{\hat{N}} f(x)}{\hat{N}+1}$$

reduces to

$$QC_1(\hat{N}+1) + C_2(\hat{N}+1)\sum_{x=1}^{\hat{N}-1} f(x) \leq QC_1\hat{N} + C_2\hat{N}\sum_{x=1}^{\hat{N}-1} f(x) + C_2\hat{N}f(\hat{N})$$

Cancelling like terms on both sides of the inequality gives

$$QC_1 + C_2 \sum_{x=1}^{\hat{N}-1} f(x) \leq C_2\hat{N}f(\hat{N})$$

or

$$\frac{K(\hat{N})}{\hat{N}} \leq C_2 f(\hat{N}) \qquad\qquad 17\text{-}20$$

Similarly, the second condition gives

$$\frac{K(\hat{N}-1)}{(\hat{N}-1)} \geq C_2 f(\hat{N}-1) \qquad\qquad 17\text{-}21$$

Hence, the following interpretation is obtained: *Group replacement should be performed at the end of period $\hat{N}$ if the average cost per period to date is less than the cost of individual replacements during the period. So long as the average cost per period is greater than the cost of replacing individual units during the period, do not group replace.*

If $\hat{N}$ is the optimum group-replacement interval, then $K(\hat{N})/\hat{N}$ should be compared with the expected cost of the policy of replacing only individual units. Namely, group replacement should occur if and only if

$$\frac{K(\hat{N})}{\hat{N}} < \frac{C_2 Q}{E[N]}$$

where $E[N]$ is the expected service life of an individual unit, i.e.,

$$E[N] = \sum_{N=1}^{\infty} NP(N)$$

Example:

As an illustration of the calculations of the optimal group-replacement interval for a situation that fits the model represented by Eq. 17-17, suppose that for a group of 10,000 electronic parts subject to sudden failure the unit cost of group replacement is \$0.50 and the unit cost of individual replacement is \$2.00. Further, the failure probabilities are as shown in Table 17-5. Table 17-6 shows the calculations for $f(x)$. As shown in Table 17-7, the lowest cost is

Table 17-5

FAILURE PROBABILITIES

j	$P(j)$
1	0.05
2	0.10
3	0.20
4	0.30
5	0.20
6	0.10
7	0.05

Table 17-6

COMPUTATION OF $f(x)$ VALUES

x	$f(x)$	
1	500	= 500.00
2	1,000 + 25	= 1,025.00
3	2,000 + 50 + 51.25	= 2,101.25
4	3,000 + 100 + 102.50 + 105.06	= 3,307.56
5	2,000 + 150 + 205.00 + 210.12 + 165.38	= 2,730.50
6	1,000 + 100 + 307.50 + 420.25 + 330.76 + 136.52	= 2,295.03

Table 17-7

DETERMINATION OF THE
OPTIMUM GROUP-REPLACEMENT INTERVAL

N	$\sum_{x=1}^{N-1} f(x)$	$K(N)$	$K(N)/N$
1	0	\$5,000.00	\$5,000.00
2	500.00	6,000.00	3,000.00
3	1,525.00	8,050.00	2,683.33
4	3,626.25	12,252.50	3,063.13
5	6,933.81	18,867.62	3,773.52
6	9,664.31	24,328.62	4,054.77

obtained if group replacement is performed every three periods. The expected cost per period with individual replacements alone is found to be

$$\frac{C_2 Q}{E[N]} = \frac{\$2(10,000)}{4} = \$5,000 > \$2,683.33$$

where, from Table 17-5, $E[N] = 1(0.05) + \cdots + 7(0.05) = 4$. Therefore, the group-replacement policy is an optimum policy.

In a number of cases the values of $P(j)$ are not available. Rather, failure data are collected such that $f(x)$ values are obtained directly. This situation is commonly encountered when a group-replacement policy is already in use.

Example:

As an illustration of the determination of the optimum group-replacement interval when $f(x)$ values are given directly, consider a situation involving 50 cutting tools on a number of numerically controlled milling machines. Data collected on the number of replacements of cutting tools per day are given in Table 17-8. A unit cost of $10.00 occurs when group replacement is performed; a unit cost of $50.00 applies to individual replacement. The calculations shown in Table 17-9 indicate the optimum replacement interval is 3 days. (Notice that there are two local minima at $N = 3$ and $N = 8$.)

Table 17-8

FAILURE DATA FOR THE EXAMPLE

x	$f(x)$	x	$f(x)$
1	2	6	7
2	4	7	6
3	7	8	9
4	7	9	7
5	8	10	8

Table 17-9

COMPUTATION OF THE OPTIMUM
REPLACEMENT INTERVAL

N	$\sum_{x=1}^{N-1} f(x)$	$K(N)$	$K(N)/N$
1	0	$500	$500
2	2	600	300
3	6	800	267
4	13	1,150	288
5	20	1,500	300
6	28	1,900	317
7	35	2,250	321
8	41	2,550	319
9	50	3,000	333
10	57	3,350	335

Unfortunately, when the $f(x)$ values are given directly, there is no convenient way to determine the expected service life of an individual unit. Hence, one cannot determine the expected cost of a policy of only individual replacements. In the previous example it is clear that the failures did not occur independently. To show this, recall

$$f(1) = QP(1)$$

or

$$2 = 10P(1)$$
$$P(1) = 0.20$$

Similarly,

$$f(2) = QP(2) + f(1)P(1)$$

or

$$4 = 10P(2) + 2(0.20)$$
$$P(2) = 0.36$$

Finally,

$$f(3) = QP(3) + f(1)P(2) + f(2)P(1)$$

or

$$7 = 10P(3) + 2(0.36) + 4(0.20)$$
$$P(3) = 0.548$$

But

$$P(1) + P(2) + P(3) = 0.20 + 0.36 + 0.548 > 1.0$$

Therefore, Eq. 17-18 is not valid for this case.

PROBLEMS

17-1. Consider a replacement situation involving an indefinite sequence of replacements. Does the replacement interval increase or decrease as the minimum attractive rate of return increases? Why?

17-2. The initial installed cost of a compressor is $6,000. Operation and repair costs are $1,000 for the first year and increase by $300 each year thereafter. The expected salvage value is $3,600 after 1 year and decreases by $400 each year thereafter until the compressor reaches a maximum life of 8 years. If the minimum required rate of return is 15% before taxes, determine, by a before-tax annual cost analysis, the most economical year in which to replace the compressor. Assume an indefinite planning horizon.

17-3. A new machine is expected to cost $25,000. Its salvage value is expected to be $15,000 at the end of the first year and to decrease by $1,500 each year thereafter for as long as the machine is kept. The operation and maintenance costs are expected to be $8,000 the first year and to increase by $4,000 each year thereafter. If interest on invested capital is 20% before taxes and a machine of this type is expected to be needed indefinitely, determine the most economical replacement interval by a before-tax annual cost analysis.

17-4. A machine originally costs \$10,000. Operating and maintenance costs for year j are equal to \$1,000 + \$100(j − 1). A 50% tax rate, 10% investment tax credit, straight line depreciation, zero salvage value at all times, 10% minimum attractive rate of return after taxes, and indefinite planning horizon are to be assumed. The machine must be used for at least 5 years and cannot be used more than 10 years. Determine the optimum replacement interval under the assumption of identical replacements.

17-5. Solve Prob. 17-4 for the case of operating and maintenance costs for year j equal to \$1,000(1.10)$^{j-1}$. Use a before-tax analysis and a minimum attractive rate of return of 20%.

17-6. Find the optimal replacement policy for machines having an initial cost of \$20,000, no salvage value, and annual operating costs of \$1,500 + (N − 1) (\$400), where N is the age of the machine in years. Interest is 10% per yr and an indefinite planning horizon is assumed. (*Hint: $N^* \geq 10$ yr.*)

17-7. Work Prob. 17-6 except assume that the salvage value varies according to the function \$8,000 − \$300N.

17-8. A machine tool can be purchased for \$9,000. Operating and maintenance costs for year j are equal to \$3,000 + \$750(j − 1). Using a zero salvage value, zero discount rate, and an 8-year planning horizon, determine the optimum replacement policy. What is the optimum replacement policy assuming a minimum attractive rate of return of 20%?

17-9. A compressor costs \$10,000(1.10)N if purchased at the end of year N. Operating and maintenance costs during the jth year of service for a compressor purchased at the end of year N equals \$3,000(1.10)$^{N+j-1}$. The salvage value for a compressor purchased at the end of year N and used for k years is given by 10,000(1.10)^N(0.80)^k. A minimum attractive rate of return of 10% is used. Consider a planning horizon of 8 years. If at most one replacement can be made during the planning horizon, what is the optimum replacement strategy?

17-10. Suppose there are 1,000 identical independent electronic components, the failure rate of which as a function of days of use, t, is $f(t) = 50 + 60t$. The unit cost of replacement of the entire group is \$0.30, while the unit cost of individual replacement after failure is \$2.00. Find the most economical replacement interval.

17-11. The probability that a certain critical machine component will last t hours is given by

	t			
	20	40	60	80
$P(t)$	0.90	0.70	0.45	0.15

If the component fails during production, the machine is stopped and a cost of $400 is incurred for downtime and repairs. Preventive replacement of the component costs approximately $50. Find the replacement policy which will minimize total expected costs.

17-12. Past experience has indicated that the probability of an electronic part's failing during the jth period of service is given by the relation

$$P(j) = \alpha^{j-1}(1 - \alpha) \qquad j = 1, 2, \ldots$$

where $\alpha = 0.80$. Show that group replacement is not preferred over a policy of individual replacements alone.

Chapter

18

mathematical programming for capital budgeting

A number of mathematical programming algorithms have been used to assist management in developing capital budgets. Some of the commonly used mathematical programming approaches are outlined in this chapter. The emphasis of the chapter is on the formulation of capital budgeting problems rather than on the details of the algorithms. Consequently, in a number of instances, heuristic approaches are used to obtain solutions to the example problems.

Indivisible, Independent Investment Opportunities

In order to illustrate the use of mathematical programming in capital investment decision analyses, we will consider a situation in which m new independent, indivisible* investment *opportunities* are available. Investment

*An investment opportunity is indivisible if it cannot be broken up into parts; either it is undertaken as a whole or it is not undertaken at all.

opportunity i has a present worth of p_i, an initial investment of c_i, and annual operating and maintenance costs of a_i. There exists a capital budget limitation of $\$C$ for new investments; similarly, a limitation of $\$A$ exists on total annual operating and maintenance costs for new investments. It is desired to select the set of investment opportunities which maximizes present worth subject to the budgetary limitations.

Letting x_i be defined to be 0 if opportunity i is not selected for investment and letting x_i be defined to be 1 if opportunity i is selected for investment, the following mathematical programming formulation of the investment decision problem is obtained.

$$\text{Maximize} \quad p_1x_1 + p_2x_2 + \cdots + p_mx_m$$
$$\text{subject to} \quad c_1x_1 + c_2x_2 + \cdots + c_mx_m \leq C$$
$$a_1x_1 + a_2x_2 + \cdots + a_mx_m \leq A$$
$$x_i = (0, 1) \quad i = 1, \ldots, m$$

The optimum set of investment opportunities can be determined by solving the binary linear programming problem formulated above. Branch and bound, implicit enumeration, and dynamic programming are examples of solution procedures that can be used to solve the budget allocation problem. A number of heuristic approaches also exist for determining "good," if not optimum, solutions to the problem.

With m investment opportunities there exist 2^m combinations of the m binary decision variables. As depicted in Fig. 18.1, for $m = 5$ there exist 32 combinations to be considered. Even though a number of the combinations might be infeasible because of the constraints which exist, for large firms faced with numerous investment opportunities the number of feasible combinations can still be very large. Hence, it is desirable to use mathematical programming algorithms to achieve a systematic and objective selection process; total enumeration of all possible combinations is obviously not a feasible solution procedure.

Indivisible, Dependent Investment Opportunities

The previous discussion considered budgetary constraints in a situation involving independent investment opportunities. In a number of instances investment opportunities are *dependent*. As an illustration, two or more investment opportunities might be *mutually exclusive*. Similarly, the selection of one particular opportunity might be *contingent* upon the selection of one or more other opportunities.

If opportunities j and k are mutually exclusive, then the following constraint can be added to the mathematical programming formulation: $x_j + x_k \leq 1$. Similarly, if the selection of opportunity e is contingent upon the

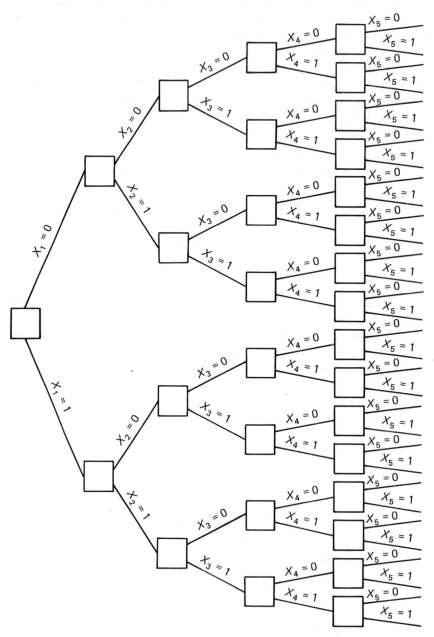

Figure 18-1. Tree representation of combinations of a binary linear programming problem with five investment opportunities.

selection of either opportunity f or g, then the following constraint applies: $x_e \leq x_f + x_g$ or $x_e - x_f - x_g \leq 0$. (As before, the x's are zero-one decision variables.)

Example:

A firm is considering two different computing systems (1 and 2) and three different software packages (1, 2, and 3). Software packages 1 and 2 can be used only on computing system 1; software package 3 can be used on either computing system. Alternatively, the firm can develop its own software. In this instance the following investment opportunities are defined:

1. Purchase computing system 1.
2. Purchase computing system 2.
3. Purchase software package 1.
4. Purchase software package 2.
5. Purchase software package 3.
6. Prepare own software package.

The following constraints apply for this situation:

$$x_1 + x_2 \leq 1$$
$$x_3 + x_4 + x_5 + x_6 \leq 1$$
$$-x_1 + x_3 + x_4 \leq 0$$
$$-x_1 - x_2 + x_5 + x_6 \leq 0$$

The first two constraints indicate that the two computing systems and four software options are mutually exclusive investment opportunities, respectively. The remaining three constraints express the contingency relationships between software packages and computing systems.

One approach that can be used when dependencies exist is to solve the problem first assuming all investment opportunities are independent. If the solution satisfies the dependency constraints, then an optimum solution has been obtained. On the other hand, if one or more of the dependency constraints are violated, then a branch and bound approach can be used.

Example:

Consider a situation in which 6 investment opportunities are available. Opportunities 1 and 3 are mutually exclusive and opportunity 2 is contingent upon opportunity 5 being selected. The following mathematical programming formulation is obtained (all monetary amounts are expressed in $1,000's).

Maximize $20x_1 + 15x_2 + 18x_3 + 24x_4 + 8x_5 + 4x_6$

subject to $60x_1 + 50x_2 + 40x_3 + 80x_4 + 30x_5 + 20x_6 \leq 180$

$5x_1 + 8x_2 + 10x_3 + 4x_4 + 12x_5 + 9x_6 \leq 30$

$x_1 + x_3 \leq 1$

$x_2 - x_5 \leq 0$

$x_i = (0, 1) \quad i = 1, \ldots, 6$

The resulting solution to the binary integer programming problem is $x_1 = x_4 = x_5 = 1$ and $x_2 = x_3 = x_6 = 0$ for a maximized objective of 52.

Independent Collections of Mutually Exclusive Opportunities

To be considered next is a capital budgeting problem involving indivisible investment opportunities consisting of independent collections of mutually exclusive investment opportunities. To motivate the discussion, let us consider a firm that has m sources of investment opportunities, with source i providing n_i mutually exclusive investment opportunities for consideration. A single budgetary constraint limits the total amount invested. Extending the notation introduced to date, we see that the budget allocation problem is formulated as follows:

$$\text{Maximize } \sum_{i=1}^{m} \sum_{j=1}^{n_i} p_{ij} x_{ij}$$

$$\text{subject to } \sum_{i=1}^{m} \sum_{j=1}^{n_i} c_{ij} x_{ij} \leq C$$

$$\sum_{j=1}^{n_i} x_{ij} \leq 1 \qquad i = 1, \ldots, m$$

$$x_{ij} = (0, 1) \text{ for all } i, j$$

where m = Number of sources of investment opportunities

n_i = Number of mutually exclusive investment opportunities available from source i

p_{ij} = Present worth of investment opportunity j from source i

c_{ij} = Initial investment required for investment opportunity j from source i

$x_{ij} = \begin{cases} 1, & \text{if investment opportunity } j \text{ from source } i \text{ is selected} \\ 0, & \text{otherwise} \end{cases}$

C = Budget limit

The first constraint expresses the budget limitation; the remaining generalized upper-bound constraints express the mutually exclusive conditions on all opportunities from the same source.

The budget allocation problem is a generalized upper-bound variation of the classic knapsack problem, studied extensively in the mathematical programming literature. Exact solution procedures exist for such a formulation and are computationally feasible for several hundred x_{ij}.

From a historical perspective, to solve this particular capital budgeting problem, Lorie and Savage [212] suggested the following heuristic approach:

1. Let α be a non-negative multiplier; let $f_{ij}(\alpha) = p_{ij} - \alpha c_{ij}$; and let j^* be the index j having the maximum $f_{ij}(\alpha)$ value for each i; if $\max_j f_{ij}(\alpha) \leq 0$, then j^* is undefined.

2. Find the smallest value of α such that

$$\sum_{i=1}^{m} c_{ij^*} \leq C$$

where $c_{ij^*} = 0$ when j^* is undefined. The investment opportunities having investments c_{ij^*} are to be funded.

In the case in which all opportunities are independent, the *Lorie–Savage problem* is formulated as

$$\text{maximize} \quad \sum_{i=1}^{m} p_i x_i$$

$$\text{subject to} \quad \sum_{i=1}^{m} c_i x_i \leq C$$

$$x_i = (0, 1)$$

Applying the Lorie–Savage procedure given above for independent collections of mutually exclusive opportunities is equivalent to ranking the opportunities in decreasing order of p_i/c_i and funding opportunities in order until further funding would exceed the budget limit. If the last opportunity funded is opportunity k, then the quantity $p_i - \alpha c_i \geq 0$ for funded opportunities; for those opportunities not funded, $p_i - \alpha c_i < 0$, where

$$\alpha \epsilon \left[\frac{p_{k+1}}{c_{k+1}}, \frac{p_k}{c_k} \right]$$

Example:
    A firm has available \$275,000 for allocation among three plants. Plant A has available three mutually exclusive investment opportunities; plant B has available a single investment opportunity; and plant C has available two mutually exclusive investment opportunities. The net present worths for the investment opportunities are given in Table 18.1, along with the required initial investments. Determine the budget allocation using the Lorie–Savage procedure.

Table 18-1

DATA FOR THE LORIE–SAVAGE EXAMPLE

i	j	Net present worth	Initial investment
1	1	\$60,000	\$110,000
	2	66,000	150,000
	3	68,000	215,000
2	1	9,000	50,000
3	1	37,000	120,000
	2	38,000	165,000

1. Let $\alpha = 0$ $C = 275$

i	j	p_{ij}	c_{ij}	$f_{ij}(\alpha)$	$\max\limits_{j} f_{ij}(\alpha)$	j^*	c_{ij^*}
1	1	60	110	60	—	—	—
	2	66	150	66	—	—	—
	3	68	215	68	68	3	215
2	1	9	50	9	9	1	50
3	1	37	120	37	—	—	—
	2	38	165	38	38	2	165
				279			430 > 275

2. Let $\alpha = 0.10$

i	j	p_{ij}	c_{ij}	$f_{ij}(\alpha)$	$\max\limits_{j} f_{ij}(\alpha)$	j^*	c_{ij^*}
1	1	60	110	49.0	—	—	—
	2	66	150	51.0	51	2	150
	3	68	215	46.5	—	—	—
2	1	9	50	4.0	4	1	50
3	1	37	120	25.0	25	1	120
	2	38	165	21.5	—	—	—
							320 > 275

3. Let $\alpha = 0.15$

i	j	p_{ij}	c_{ij}	$f_{ij}(\alpha)$	$\max\limits_{j} f_{ij}(\alpha)$	j^*	c_{ij^*}
1	1	60	110	43.50	—	—	—
	2	66	150	43.50	43.50	1,2	110
	3	68	215	35.75	—	—	—
2	1	9	50	1.50	1.50	1	50
3	1	37	120	19.00	19.00	1	120
	2	38	165	13.25	—	—	—
							280 > 275

4. Let $\alpha = 0.20$

i	j	p_{ij}	c_{ij}	$f_{ij}(\alpha)$	$\max\limits_{j} f_{ij}(\alpha)$	j^*	c_{ij^*}
1	1	60	110	38	38	1	110
	2	66	150	36	—	—	—
	3	68	215	25	—	—	—
2	1	9	50	−1	−1	Undefined	—
3	1	37	120	13	13	1	120
	2	38	165	5	—	—	—
							230 < 275

The recommended budget allocation is to undertake opportunity 1 ($j = 1$) at plant A ($i = 1$) and opportunity 1 ($j = 1$) at plant C ($i = 3$) for a present worth of 97. It should be noted that the Lorie–Savage procedure did not yield an optimum solution; in this instance, investments in opportunity 2 at plant A and opportunity 1 at plant C will yield a present worth of 103 and satisfy the budget constraint. (As an exercise at the end of the chapter, the reader is asked to solve this example using the branch and bound method).

Lorie and Savage proposed an extension of their procedure to obtain budget allocations for *multiperiod* problems. They noted that if undertaking an investment opportunity requires investments in multiple periods, then the impact on subsequent budgets should be considered.

For simplicity, suppose investments are required only for the first 2 years of each investment opportunity. Let c_{1i} and c_{2i} denote the investment required for opportunity i in years 1 and 2, respectively; let C_1 and C_2 be the respective budget limits for years 1 and 2; and let p_i denote the present worth for opportunity i. The problem can be formulated mathematically as

$$\text{maximize} \quad \sum_{i=1}^{m} p_i x_i$$

$$\text{subject to} \quad \sum_{i=1}^{m} c_{1i} x_i \leq C_1$$

$$\sum_{i=1}^{m} c_{2i} x_i \leq C_2$$

$$x_i = (0, 1) \text{ for all } i$$

The Lorie–Savage procedure for solving the budgeting problem can be summarized as follows:

1. Let α_1 and α_2 be non-negative multipliers; let $f_i(\alpha_1, \alpha_2) = p_i - \alpha_1 c_{1i} - \alpha_2 c_{2i}$; and let i^* denote those opportunities for which $f_{i^*}(\alpha_1, \alpha_2) > 0$.
2. Find the smallest values of α_1 and α_2 such that $\sum_{i^*} c_{1i^*} \leq C_1$ and $\sum_{i^*} c_{2i^*} \leq C_2$. The investment opportunities having index i^* are to be funded.

Example:
   Lorie and Savage solve an example problem for which the data given in Table 18-2 are appropriate. With budget limitations of $C_1 = 50$ and $C_2 = 20$ they find that opportunities 1, 3, 4, 6, and 9 should be selected; their recommendation is based on values of $\alpha_1 = 0.33$ and $\alpha_2 = 1.00$.

For the example problem, a solution involving the allocation of funds for opportunities 1, 3, 4, 6, and 9 must satisfy the following Lorie–Savage inequalities:

$$14 - 12\alpha_1 - 3\alpha_2 \geq 0$$
$$17 - 54\alpha_1 - 7\alpha_2 \leq 0$$

$$17 - 6\alpha_1 - 6\alpha_2 \geq 0$$
$$15 - 6\alpha_1 - 2\alpha_2 \geq 0$$
$$40 - 30\alpha_1 - 35\alpha_2 \leq 0$$
$$12 - 6\alpha_1 - 6\alpha_2 \geq 0$$
$$14 - 48\alpha_1 - 4\alpha_2 \leq 0$$
$$10 - 36\alpha_1 - 3\alpha_2 \leq 0$$
$$12 - 18\alpha_1 - 3\alpha_2 \geq 0$$

Table 18-2

DATA FOR THE MULTIPERIOD BUDGETING PROBLEM

Investment opportunity (i)	Year 1 investment (c_{1i})	Year 2 investment (c_{2i})	Present worth (p_i)
1	12	3	14
2	54	7	17
3	6	6	17
4	6	2	15
5	30	35	40
6	6	6	12
7	48	4	14
8	36	3	10
9	18	3	12

Plotting the inequalities yields the feasible combinations of α_1 and α_2 given in Fig. 18.2. As can be seen, the combination $\alpha_1 = 0.33$ and $\alpha_2 = 1.0$ is a feasible point. Furthermore, when used with the Lorie–Savage procedure, the combination yields a feasible budget allocation with $\sum_{i^*} c_{1i^*} = 48$ and $\sum_{i^*} c_{2i^*} = 20$. From Fig. 18.2 it does not appear that any reversals of inequalities would yield an improved solution.

Divisible Investment Opportunities

In some cases, investment opportunities are divisible. Namely, it is possible to undertake some portion of the investment instead of being forced to "do all" or "nothing." A number of such investments can be formulated as linear programming problems using continuous decision variables; others can be formulated as integer linear programming problems.

Example:

A major industrial firm has $60 million available for the coming year to be allocated among three processing plants. Because of personnel levels and ongoing projects at the plants, it is necessary that at least $6 million be allo-

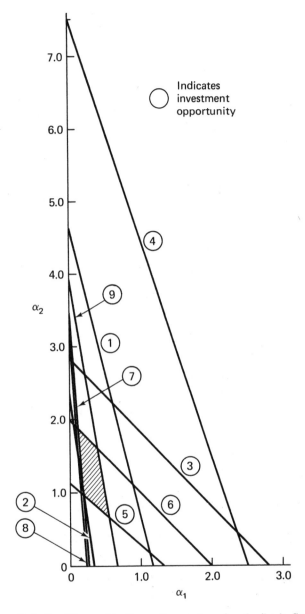

Figure 18-2. Feasible combinations of α_1 and α_2 for the Lorie–Savage example.

cated to plant 1, $16 million be allocated to plant 2, and $10 million be allocated to plant 3. Because of the production facilities available at plant 3, no more than $34 million can be utilized without major new capital expansion; such expansion cannot be undertaken at this time. A number of investment opportunities exist at the various plants. Each plant has submitted budget requests in which the opportunities are grouped into categories by anticipated rate of return. For simplicity, the rate of return is expressed as a percentage of investment. Upper limits have been placed on the investment in each category. The data for the budgeting problem are given in Table 18-3.

Table 18-3

DATA FOR THE LINEAR PROGRAMMING EXAMPLE PROBLEM

Plant	Budget category	Rate of return	Maximum investment
1	1	16%	$12 million
	2	12%	10 million
	3	14%	18 million
2	4	20%	12 million
	5	12%	6 million
3	6	10%	14 million
	7	16%	20 million
	8	18%	8 million

A linear programming formulation of the problem is given as follows:

$$\text{Maximize} \quad 0.16x_1 + 0.12x_2 + 0.14x_3 + 0.20x_4$$
$$+ 0.12x_5 + 0.10x_6 + 0.16x_7 + 0.18x_8$$

$$\text{subject to} \quad x_1 + x_2 + x_3 + x_4 + x_5 + x_6 + x_7 + x_8 \leq 60$$
$$x_1 + x_2 + x_3 \geq 6$$
$$x_4 + x_5 \geq 16$$
$$x_6 + x_7 + x_8 \geq 10$$
$$x_6 + x_7 + x_8 \leq 34$$

$$0 \leq x_1 \leq 12, \quad 0 \leq x_2 \leq 10, \quad 0 \leq x_3 \leq 18$$
$$0 \leq x_4 \leq 12, \quad 0 \leq x_5 \leq 6, \quad 0 \leq x_6 \leq 14$$
$$0 \leq x_7 \leq 20, \quad 0 \leq x_8 \leq 8$$

where x_j represents the amount (in millions) to be invested in budget category j.

An optimum solution to the linear programming problem can be obtained by using the simplex method. The optimum solution will be found to be $x_1 = 12$, $x_2 = 0$, $x_3 = 4$, $x_4 = 12$, $x_5 = 4$, $x_6 = 0$, $x_7 = 20$, and $x_8 = 8$. Hence, $16 million will be allocated to plant 1, $16 million will be allocated to plant 2, and $28 million will be allocated to plant 3.

If it is assumed that an individual investment opportunity is divisible such that fractional opportunities or projects can be pursued, then a number of the binary linear programming formulations considered previously can be solved by replacing the binary requirement with the restriction $0 \leq x_i \leq 1$.

Weingartner [146] proves that the number of fractional-valued x_i's will be no greater than the number of inequality constraints. Hence, if the first

Lorie–Savage example problem is solved as a linear programming problem, at most one fractional x_i will occur.

In the past decade significant breakthroughs have occurred in the development of mathematical programming code, for large-scale optimization problems. Hence, reliance on heuristic procedures, such as the Lorie-Savage procedure or Senju-Toyoda [230] procedure, is probably not necessary for problems you will encounter in practice. We presented the Lorie-Savage procedure because of its historic value, rather than as the recommended procedure for the future.

The M.A.R.R. Controversy

The controversy over the establishment of the minimum attractive rate of return has been alluded to in earlier chapters. However, because of the intensity of the issue as it relates to the mathematical formulation of capital budgeting problems, it deserves additional consideration. The essential issue is "what should be the value of the M.A.R.R. in present worth calculations for capital budget determinations when a constraint exists on capital available for investment?"

The issue was first dealt with explicitly by Baumol and Quandt [155]; they concluded that a meaningful discount rate cannot be determined simultaneously with capital budgeting. Lusztig and Schwab [213] later contended otherwise. Bernhard [160] studied the issue and came to the following conclusion:

As concluded by Baumol and Quandt, in programming models of the Lorie–Savage type, internal procurement of economically meaningful values of the discount rate, k, is not possible. We have seen here . . . that the more recently proposed procedure of Mao, and of Lusztig and Schwab, does not, in general, give meaningful results and hence does not counter the earlier finding of Baumol and Quandt.

In developing the mathematical programming formulations, assumption was made that the M.A.R.R. is based on the opportunity cost of capital. Unfortunately, the opportunity cost will be dependent upon the collection of investments accepted (and rejected!). Bernhard [160] recommends that the manager's utility function for reinvestment funds made available over time be used to determine the budget allocation. Independently, Atkins and Ashton [154] considered the Lorie–Savage formulation allowing fractional investments and concluded, "Our analysis, while questioning the logic of the Baumol and Quandt paper, does not question the correctness of their conclusion that a capital budgeting model which ignores the owners' consumption preference over time is of no practical importance."

Although the M.A.R.R. controversy is an important issue, from a pragmatic point of view the objective in using mathematical programming formulations is to obtain budget allocations which are better than would otherwise be obtained. Final decisions will generally be different from the output from the mathematical model because of the nonquantifiables, multiple criteria, and changing conditions. Consequently, in an operating setting, it is felt that the M.A.R.R. used by the firm in evaluating mutually exclusive investment alternatives will yield results which "satisfice," if not optimize!

Capital Rationing

The capital rationing problem, considered in Chapter 10, can be formulated as a special type of linear programming problem, the transportation problem. Recall that a number of sources of investment funds may be available, along with a number of investment opportunities. Each dollar borrowed from source j costs c_j; each dollar invested in investment opportunity i returns r_i. The dollar amount available from source j is denoted b_j; the maximum amount that can be invested in opportunity i is denoted a_i. The net return resulting from borrowing a dollar from source j and investing it in opportunity i is denoted $c_{ij} = r_i - c_j$. The amount borrowed from source j and invested in opportunity i is denoted x_{ij}.

In order to insure that money will not be invested unless it is profitable to do so, a dummy source of funds is defined with

$$b_{n+1} = \sum_{i=1}^{m} a_i \quad \text{and} \quad c_{i,n+1} = 0$$

similarly, in order to insure that money is not borrowed unless it is profitable to do so, a dummy investment opportunity is defined with

$$a_{m+1} = \sum_{j=1}^{n} b_j \quad \text{and} \quad c_{m+1,j} = 0$$

The capital rationing problem is formulated as follows:

$$\text{Maximize} \quad \sum_{i=1}^{m+1} \sum_{j=1}^{n+1} c_{ij} x_{ij}$$

$$\text{subject to} \quad \sum_{i=1}^{m+1} x_{ij} = b_j \quad j = 1, \ldots, n+1$$

$$\sum_{j=1}^{n+1} x_{ij} = a_i \quad i = 1, \ldots, m+1$$

$$x_{ij} \geq 0 \quad \text{for all } i, j$$

The capital rationing problem is formulated using the well-known transportation problem formulation. It is interesting to note that the optimum solution to the capital rationing problem is that given in Chapter 10: *Invest the cheapest money in the opportunity with the greatest return; continue until the marginal cost of securing a dollar is equal to or greater than the marginal return obtained.*

Example:

Consider a situation in which three sources of funds are available and five investment opportunities exist. Suppose $c_1 = 0.10$, $c_2 = 0.12$, $c_3 = 0.15$, $r_1 = 0.30$, $r_2 = 0.20$, $r_3 = 0.14$, $r_4 = 0.11$, and $r_5 = 0.08$; similarly, $b_1 = 100$, $b_2 = 50$, $b_3 = 20$, $a_1 = 15$, $a_2 = 25$, $a_3 = 40$, $a_4 = 65$, and $a_5 = 70$. Since

$$\sum_{i=1}^{5} a_i = 215 \quad \text{and} \quad \sum_{j=1}^{3} b_j = 170$$

a "dummy" source is defined with $b_4 = 215$ and $c_4 = 0$; also a "dummy" investment opportunity is defined with $a_6 = 170$ and $r_6 = 0$.

As given in Fig. 18-3, the optimum solution is to borrow 100 from source

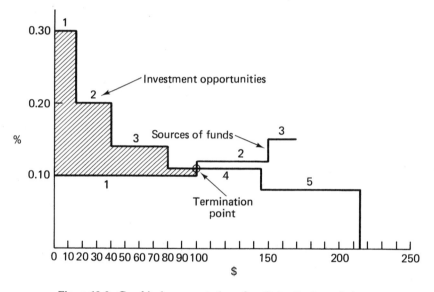

Figure 18-3. Graphical representation of capital rationing solution.

1; 15 is invested in opportunity 1, 25 is invested in opportunity 2, 40 is invested in opportunity 3, and 20 is invested in opportunity 4. The solution is obtained by allocating as much as possible to the cells having the greatest c_{ij} values.

Solving this capital rationing problem as a transportation problem gives the solution illustrated in Fig. 18-4. Opportunities 1, 2, and 3 are completely funded from source 1; 20 is borrowed from source 1 and is invested in opportunity 4.

Portfolio Selection

A class of investment problems that has received considerable attention among researchers is that referred to by Markowitz [103] as the portfolio selection problem. The portfolio problem involves the selection of an optimal set of investments (the portfolio) based on the expected yields, the risks associated with the investments, and the utility of the investor.

Markowitz used the variance of the return obtained as a surrogate for risk. He assumed the objective of the investor to be the maximization of

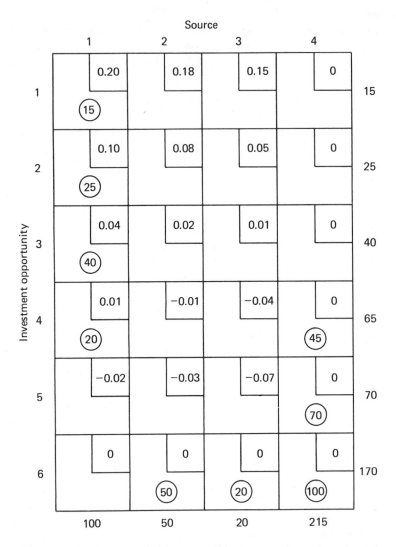

Figure 18-4. Transportation tableau solution for the capital rationing problem.

expected utility, where expected utility can be expressed as a function of the expected value and variance of return.

If y_i is defined as the percentage of the available funds invested in investment opportunity i and if R_i is a random variable denoting the return obtained from opportunity i, then the expected value and variance of return are given as

$$E[R] = \sum_{i=1}^{m} y_i E[R_i]$$

$$V[R] = \sum_{i=1}^{m} \sum_{j=1}^{m} y_i y_j \, \text{Cov}\,[R_i, R_j]$$

where Cov $[R_i, R_j]$ is the covariance of R_i and R_j and Cov $[R_i, R_i]$ $= V[R_i]$.

Multiple values of the y_i can yield the same variance; similarly, the same expected return can be obtained for multiple combinations of the y_i (portfolios). The risk-averse investor will want to select one of the portfolios that yields either minimum variance ($\mho$) for a given expected return ($\mathcal{E}$) or maximum $\mathcal{E}$ for a given $\mho$. Such portfolios are referred to as *mean-variance* ($\mathcal{E}$-$\mho$) *efficient portfolios.*

As depicted in Fig. 18.5 (by the bold line segment), a number of $\mathcal{E}$-$\mho$ efficient portfolios can exist. If the utility function can be represented in such a way that the expected utility is given as $E[U] = f(\mathcal{E}, \mho)$, then some $\mathcal{E}$-$\mho$ efficient portfolio will maximize $E[U]$. In Figure 18.6 isoutility curves are shown with $E[U_1] > E[U_2] > E[U_3]$. The optimum portfolio is portfolio Y, as shown.

If it is assumed that the investor's utility function is at least twice differentiable, the utility function may be expanded by Taylor's series about its mean to yield

$$U(R) = U(\mu) + U'(\mu)[R - \mu] + \frac{U''(\mu)}{2}[R - \mu]^2 + \cdots$$

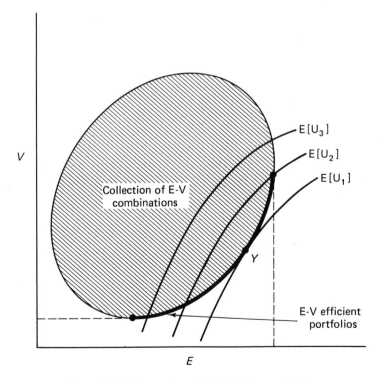

Figure 18-5. Mean-variance ($\mathcal{E}$-$\mho$) efficient portfolios.

where $\mu = E[R]$ and $U'(\mu)$ is the first derivative of U evaluated at μ. The expected utility is given by

$$E[U(R)] = \mu + \frac{U''(\mu)}{2}\sigma^2 + \cdots$$

where $\sigma^2 = V[R]$. Letting $\theta = -U''(\mu)/2$, which was defined in Chapter 14 as the coefficient of risk aversion, then dropping all terms beyond those given above yields

$$E[U(R)] \doteq \mu - \theta\sigma^2$$

If the investor is risk-averse, $\theta > 0$.

The above result indicates the expected utility can be approximated by a linear function of $\mathcal{E}$ and $\mathcal{V}$. Hence, the portfolio problem can be formulated as a quadratic programming problem:

$$\text{Maximize} \quad \sum_{i=1}^{m} E[R_i]y_i - \theta \sum_{i=1}^{m} \sum_{j=1}^{m} \text{Cov}\,[R_i, R_j]y_i y_j$$

$$\text{subject to} \quad \sum_{i=1}^{m} y_i \leq 1$$

$$y_i \geq 0$$

A number of different objective functions have been proposed in the literature, including the maximization of $\mu - \theta\sigma$. As noted in Chapter 14, empirical results by Cramer and Smith [175] tend to support the use of the standard deviation instead of the variance in approximating the utility function.

Among the several criteria which may be used in selecting the portfolio are the following:*

1. expected value criterion
    maximize $E[R]$

2. portfolio criterion
    minimize $V[R]$
    subject to $E[R] \geq \alpha$

3. aspiration level criterion
    maximize $P[R \geq \beta]$

4. fractile criterion
    maximize z
    subject to $P[R \geq z] \geq \gamma$

5. chance constrained criterion
    maximize $E[R]$
    subject to $P[R \geq \delta] \geq \epsilon$

---

*The constraints $\sum_{i=1}^{m} y_i \leq 1$ and $y_i \geq 0$ are required for each formulation.

where $E[\cdot]$, $V[\cdot]$ and $P[\cdot]$ denote the expected value, variance, and probability operations, respectively, and α, β, γ, δ, and ϵ are appropriately defined constants. For discussions of one or more of the criteria and their relationships, see Baumol [156], Farrar [78], Geoffrion [188], Hanssman [192], Markowitz [103], Peterson and Laughhunn [222], Pyle and Turnovsky [224], and Sengupta and Portillo-Campbell [229], among others.

Example:

Consider a simplified portfolio situation involving only two investment opportunities with the following formulation:

$$\text{maximize} \quad z = 10y_1 + 12y_2 - 4y_1^2 - 6y_1y_2 - 5y_2^2$$

$$\text{subject to} \quad y_1 + y_2 \leq 1$$

$$y_i \geq 0 \quad i = 1, 2$$

Taking the partial derivatives of z with respect to y_1 and y_2, setting the results equal to zero, and solving give

$$\left. \begin{aligned} \frac{\partial z}{\partial y_1} &= 10 - 8y_1 - 6y_2 = 0 \\ \frac{\partial z}{\partial y_2} &= 12 - 6y_1 - 10y_2 = 0 \end{aligned} \right\} \quad y_1 = \frac{7}{11} \quad \text{and} \quad y_2 = \frac{9}{11}$$

Since

$$y_1 + y_2 = \frac{16}{11} > 1$$

the constraint will be active and $y_1 + y_2 = 1$. Thus, $y_2 = 1 - y_1$ and the objective function becomes

$$z = 10y_1 + 12(1 - y_1) - 4y_1^2 - 6y_1(1 - y_1) - 5(1 - y_1)^2$$

or

$$z = 7 + 2y_1 - 3y_1^2$$

Differentiating z with respect to y_1, setting the result equal to zero, and solving give $y_1 = \frac{1}{3}$; hence, $y_2 = \frac{2}{3}$.

Goal Programming

The concept of goal programming was developed by Charnes and Cooper [69]; Ijiri [92] reinforced and refined the concept. A number of applications and extensions of the technique are described by Ignizio [91] and Lee [99].

The goal programming approach involves the specification of several desired levels of attainment (goals) and the establishment of priorities for the goals. Generally, the priorities are expressed as either ordinal or cardinal priorities. In the case of ordinal priorities, the most important goal is satisfied first, followed by the satisfaction of as many other goals as possible, in rank order. When a cardinal scale is used, it is typically assumed that "goal attainment" is additive and an aggregate, linear objective function is developed.

Goal programming was developed initially in conjunction with linear programming formulations. More recently the concept has been applied in conjunction with both integer programming and nonlinear programming.

In terms of capital investment decision-making, it is generally the case that managers have multiple goals. Although the number of reported applications of the use of goal programming in capital budgeting is small, the approach seems promising. For this reason, the goal programming approach will be illustrated with the following example.

Example:

Consider a production manager who must schedule the production of two products on three machines. The unit profits, machining times, and production capacities of the equipment are summarized below:

	Machines			
Product	1	2	3	
1	0.2 hr	0.4 hr	0.3 hr	Time/unit
2	0.4 hr	0.1 hr	0.3 hr	Time/unit
Capacity	40 hr	40 hr	40 hr	Time/week

Product	*Maximum demand*	*Profit*
1	80/wk	$5/unit
2	80/wk	$20/unit

The linear programming formulation of the production scheduling problem is given as follows:

$$\text{Maximize } 5x + 20y$$
$$\text{subject to } 0.2x + 0.4y \le 40$$
$$0.4x + 0.1y \le 40$$
$$0.3x + 0.3y \le 40$$
$$x \qquad \le 80$$
$$y \le 80$$
$$x \ge 0 \quad y \ge 0$$

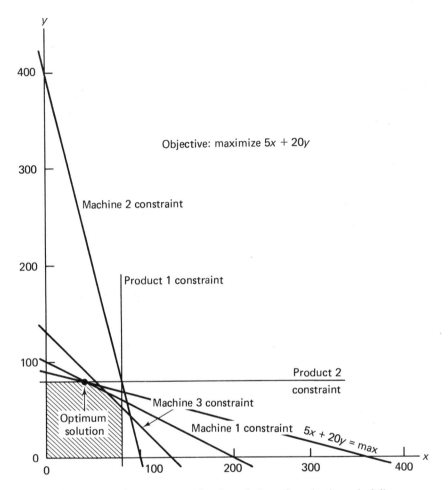

Figure 18-6. Linear programming formulation of production scheduling problem.

As depicted in Fig. 18-6, the optimum solution is $x = 40$ and $y = 80$. The unused machining capacities for the machines are 0, 16, and 4 hours per week, respectively. Hence, machine 2 will be only 60% utilized.

The manager is concerned not only with the utilization of the machines but also with the profits realized for the firm. He also recognizes that the market forecasts of 80 units per week for the products could be in error.

The manager would prefer to have the three machines equally loaded, but he does not want to sacrifice profits unduly. The maximum profit condition ($x = 40$, $y = 80$) would result in an $1,800 profit. He feels that a satisfactory minimum profit level would be $1,500.

The following alternative formulation is being considered:

$$\text{Minimize } (d_1^-, d_2^- + d_3^- + d_4^-)$$

$$\text{subject to} \quad 5x + 20y + d_1^- - d_1^+ = \$1,500$$

$$0.2x + 0.4y + d_2^- \quad = \quad 40$$

$$0.4x + 0.1y + d_3^- \quad = \quad 40$$

$$0.3x + 0.3y + d_4^- \quad = \quad 40$$

$$x \quad \leq \quad 80$$

$$y \quad \leq \quad 80$$

$$x, y, d_j^-, d_j^+ \leq 0$$

The slack variable, d_j^-, and surplus variable, d_j^+, measure the deviation from the right-hand side of the constraints. (Since the upper limit of 40 hours production capacity cannot be exceeded, the surplus variables are omitted for $j = 2, 3, 4$.) The objective function is expressed using an ordinal scaling of the profit goal (make at least a \$1,500 profit) and the machine balance goal (minimize the sum of unused capacities).* To solve the problem, the set of optimum solutions is determined using the following objective: Minimize d_1^-. The resulting set of solutions is depicted in Fig. 18-7, for $d_1^- = 0$.

Next, the following linear programming problem is solved:

$$\text{Minimize } d_2^- + d_3^- + d_4^-$$

$$\text{subject to } 0.2x + 0.4y + d_2^- = \quad 40$$

$$0.4x + 0.1y + d_3^- = \quad 40$$

$$0.3x + 0.3y + d_4^- = \quad 40$$

$$5x + 20y - d_1^+ = 1,500$$

$$x \quad \leq \quad 80$$

$$y \quad \leq \quad 80$$

$$x, y, d_j^-, d_1^+ \geq 0$$

The optimum solution is $x = 700/9$, $y = 500/9$, $d_2^- = 20/9$, $d_3^- = 10/3$, $d_4^- = 0$, and $d_1^+ = 0$. Hence, the profit obtained is \$1,500, with machine utilizations of 94.44%, 91.67%, and 100.00%.

An alternative expression of the machine balance goal is to minimize the maximum difference in the d_j^- values, i.e.,

$$\text{Minimize maximum } (|d_2^- - d_3^-|, |d_2^- - d_4^-|, |d_3^- - d_4^-|)$$

$$\text{subject to } 0.2x + 0.4y + d_2^- = \quad 40$$

$$0.4x + 0.1y + d_3^- = \quad 40$$

*An alternate expression of the machine balance goal will be considered subsequently.

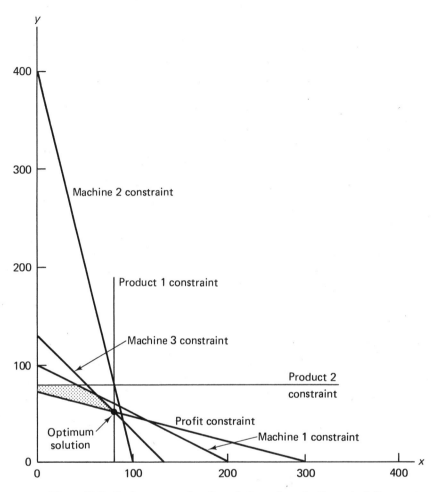

Figure 18-7. Goal programming formulation of production scheduling problem.

$$0.3x + 0.3y + d_4^- = 40$$
$$5x + 20y - d_1^+ = 1{,}500$$
$$x \leq 80$$
$$y \leq 80$$
$$x, y, d_j^-, d_1^+ \geq 0$$

Letting z denote the maximum absolute deviation among the slack variables, the formulation becomes:

Minimize z

subject to $z \geq |d_2^- - d_3^-|$

$$z \geq |d_2^- - d_4^-|$$

$$z \geq |d_3^- - d_4^-|$$

$$0.2x + 0.4y + d_2^- = \quad 40$$

$$0.4x + 0.1y + d_3^- = \quad 40$$

$$0.3x + 0.3y + d_4^- = \quad 40$$

$$5x + 20y - d_1^+ = 1{,}500$$

$$x \qquad\qquad\quad \leq \quad 80$$

$$y \quad \leq \quad 80$$

$$x, y, d_j^-, d_1^+ \geq 0$$

The first three constraints insure that the minimum value of z will equal the maximum absolute deviation among the slack variables. A constraint of the form

$$|u - v| \leq w$$

can be written as two linear constraints

$$u - v \leq w$$

$$u - v \geq -w$$

Therefore, the optimization problem can be written:

Minimize z

subject to $d_2^- - d_3^- - z \leq 0$

$$-d_2^- + d_3^- - z \leq 0$$

$$d_2^- - d_4^- - z \leq 0$$

$$-d_2^- + d_4^- - z \leq 0$$

$$d_3^- - d_4^- - z \leq 0$$

$$-d_3^- + d_4^- - z \leq 0$$

$$0.2x + 0.4y + d_2^- = \quad 40$$

$$0.4x + 0.1y + d_3^- = \quad 40$$

$$0.3x + 0.3y + d_4^- = \quad 40$$

$$5x + 20y - d_1^+ = 1{,}500$$

$$x \qquad\qquad\quad \leq \quad 80$$

$$y \quad \leq \quad 80$$

A linear programming solution to the above problem yields the following values for the decision variables: $x = 700/9$, $y = 500/9$, $d_1^+ = 0$, $d_2^- = 20/9$, $d_3^- = 10/3$, $d_4^- = 0$, and $z = 10/3$. Hence, a profit of \$1,500 is obtained, along with machine utilizations of 94.44%, 91.67%, and 100.00%. For this example the same solution is obtained for the goal programming problem using a minimax objective and an objective of minimizing the sum of the deviations.

Goal programming problems are special cases of multicriterion optimization problems. In the past decade considerable research has been performed on the general class of multicriterion optimization problems. Although multicriterion optimization offers considerable potential for improved decision-making in capital budgeting, further development is required before it will receive widespread application. Based on the research performed to date, it appears that interactive approaches involving the decision-maker will be used. For a discussion of interactive approaches in multicriterion optimization, see Geoffrion, Dyer, and Feinberg [190]. Chapter 19 contains several commonly-recognized techniques for consideration of multiple objectives and criteria.

PROBLEMS

18-1. Use an exact solution procedure to solve the following capital budgeting formulation:

$$\text{Maximize } 18x_1 + 20x_2 + 15x_3 + 22x_4$$

$$\begin{aligned}
\text{subject to} \quad 4x_1 + 6x_2 + 5x_3 + 6x_4 &\leq 15 \\
5x_1 + 3x_2 + 6x_3 + 4x_4 &\leq 12 \\
10x_1 + 5x_2 + 4x_3 + 12x_4 &\leq 30 \\
x_j = (0, 1) \quad j &= 1, \ldots, 4
\end{aligned}$$

18-2. In Prob. 18-1 suppose investment opportunities 1 and 3 are mutually exclusive. Suppose investment opportunity 2 is contingent on the selection of opportunity 4. Solve the problem using total enumeration.

18-3. Consider the following capital budgeting formulation:

$$\text{Maximize } 6x_1 + 12x_2 + 8x_3 + 15x_4 + 10x_5 + 9x_6 + 5x_7 + 14x_8$$

$$\text{subject to } 12x_1 + 30x_2 + 12x_3 + 25x_4 + 16x_5 + 20x_6 + 4x_7 + 20x_8 \leq 75$$

$$x_j = (0, 1) \quad j = 1, 2, \ldots, 8$$

Determine the budget allocation using
a. The Lorie–Savage procedure.
b. An exact solution procedure.

18-4. A firm is confronted with ten investment opportunities. The investment opportunities will require commitments of investment funds for up to 3 years. The present worths and investment requirements (for each of the first 3 years) are given below. Opportunity 2 is contingent on the selection of opportunity 7; opportunity 3 is contingent on the selection of both opportunities 1 and 4; and opportunity 6 is contingent on the selection of either mutually exclusive opportunity 8, 9, or 10. Determine the budget allocation which maximizes present worth using an exact solution procedure.

Investment opportunity (i)	Present worth (p_i)	Investments		
		Year 1 (c_{1i})	Year 2 (c_{2i})	Year 3 (c_{3i})
1	20	24	16	6
2	16	12	10	2
3	11	8	6	6
4	4	6	4	7
5	4	1	6	9
6	18	18	18	20
7	7	13	8	0
8	19	14	8	12
9	24	16	20	24
10	4	4	6	8
Budget limit		50	30	30

18-5. A firm has available $300,000 to be allocated among four production plants. Plant 1 has proposed three mutually exclusive projects; plant 2 has available two mutually exclusive projects; plant 3 has proposed three mutually exclusive investment opportunities; and plant 4 has available two mutually exclusive projects. The relevant data are given below. Use the Lorie–Savage procedure to obtain an allocation and compare the result with that obtained using an exact solution procedure.

Investment source i	Mutually exclusive investment opportunity (by source)	Initial investment required	Present worth
1	1	$100,000	$25,000
	2	125,000	20,000
	3	175,000	22,000
2	1	80,000	20,000
	2	100,000	15,000
3	1	50,000	10,000
	2	75,000	15,000
	3	90,000	12,000
4	1	40,000	10,000
	2	60,000	12,000
Budget limitation		$300,000	

18-6. A firm has available six sources of investment funds and ten independent investment opportunities. The interest costs of the investment capital and the rates of return for the investment opportunities are given below. Assuming divisible investment opportunities, determine the optimum borrowing and investment program.

Source of funds	Interest cost	Maximum investment funds available
1	8%	$ 50,000
2	9%	80,000
3	10%	150,000
4	12%	250,000
5	15%	500,000
6	18%	$1,000,000

Investment opportunity	Rate of return	Maximum amount of investment
1	5%	$ 30,000
2	8%	80,000
3	20%	50,000
4	15%	80,000
5	12%	100,000
6	10%	200,000
7	25%	50,000
8	10%	75,000
9	12%	40,000
10	7%	60,000

18-7. In Prob. 18-6, if the investment opportunities are not divisible, how would you solve the problem? Develop a mathematical formulation of the capital rationing problem for indivisible investment opportunities when borrowed funds are to be used. What are the potential pitfalls of using a criterion involving rates of return instead of present worths?

18-8. An individual has identified two investment opportunities. Every $100 invested in opportunity 1 yields a present worth of $20; in opportunity 2 a present worth of $24 is anticipated for every $100 invested. A maximum of $10,000 is available for investment. The individual wishes to hedge against risk by diversifying his investment; it is required that the amount invested in opportunity 1 be from 40% to 60% of the total. Formulate the investment problem as a linear programming problem and determine the optimum investment program.

18-9. In Prob. 18-8, suppose a goal programming approach is to be taken. The individual has a primary objective of investing the $10,000 in such a way that a present worth of at least $2,230 is obtained. A secondary goal is to minimize the difference in the amount invested in each opportunity. Determine the investment program that would result.

18-10. Consider a portfolio selection problem involving three investment opportunities with the following data:

i Investment opportunity	$E[R_i]$	$V[R_i]$	i	j	$Cov[R_i, R_j]$
1	0.06	0.0004	1	2	0.0005
2	0.12	0.0036	1	3	0.0002
3	0.30	0.0625	2	3	0.0015

The coefficient of risk aversion, θ, equals 20. Determine the portfolio mix that maximizes expected utility.

18-11. In Prob. 18-8, determine the effect on the optimum solution resulting from the presence of a third investment which has a present worth of $22 per $100 investment. It will be required that from $30,000 to $40,000 be invested in each opportunity rather than from 40 % to 60 % be invested in opportunity 1.

18-12. Determine the effect on the solution to Prob. 18-9 due to the additional investment opportunity described in Prob. 18-11. The primary and secondary objectives remain unchanged.

18-13. Use the branch and bound method to solve the Lorie–Savage example problem given on page 425.

18-14. Use an exact solution procedure to solve the Lorie–Savage example problem given on pages 427–28.

consideration of multiple objectives and criteria

Although it is very useful to use cost or profit as a measure of desirability, many decisions between alternatives cannot be measured only in these terms. Most firms have other objectives, such as customer service, good will, community reputation, job satisfaction, safety, employment stability, etc. These factors, which cannot be expressed directly in cost or profit terms, often are called *intangibles* or *irreducibles*.

Even though a decision-maker may have readily definable objectives, he might still have a significant problem defining the criteria (sometimes also called *attributes* or *decision factors*) by which the attainment of objectives can be measured. For example, the attainment of a "safety" objective in an automobile purchase decision might be measured by such criteria as weight, maximum possible speed, and interior padding.

The ultimate aim of the analyst, or decision-maker, with respect to multiple objectives and criteria, should be to use rational methods of evaluating them so that a single measure of value may be associated with each alternative in a decision problem. Techniques to achieve this ultimate aim now fall far short of full development and widespread use in practice. This means that in most instances multiple objectives/criteria must be evaluated by some process of judgment exercised by the decision-maker. Indeed, if his personal objectives differ from those of the firm, there may be little to prevent their inclusion in the decisions he makes.

Numerous methods have been developed over the past decade to facilitate analysis. To give the readers an introduction to the diversity and application of available methods, we will concentrate on the following, which are given in approximate order of increasing complexity and power:

1. alternatives–objectives score card;
2. indifference curves;
3. ordinal scaling;
4. weighting factors;
5. weighted evaluation of alternatives;
6. multi-criteria utility models.

Alternatives–Objectives Score Card

One of the most palatable and useful ways to handle multiple-objective/criteria problems in which it is particularly difficult to determine ordinal rankings or weightings of those multiple factors is to display a matrix of alternatives versus objectives together with numbers and/or other symbols to represent how well each alternative meets each objective. Table 19-1 is a simple example. The numbers are illustrative only.

Using such a display, the decision-maker should be aided in his selection according to his subjective weightings of objectives and the corresponding measures. If he is particularly concerned about costs and fuel economy, then the Honda would probably be the choice. On the other hand, . . . you make the choice!

Indifference Curves

A simple way to express relative weightings of two or three factors or decision criteria is to construct indifference curves. Even though the method of expression (displaying) is simple, the determination of the relative weightings over a wide range may not be. Figure 19-1 shows a typical example for three factors.

Table 19-1

Sᴀᴍᴘʟᴇ Aʟᴛᴇʀɴᴀᴛɪᴠᴇs–Oʙᴊᴇᴄᴛɪᴠᴇs Sᴄᴏʀᴇ Cᴀʀᴅ

Alternative

Criteria (factors)	Toyota Celica	Buick Wagon	Olds Cutlass	Honda Civic
First cost	$4,500	($6,500)	$5,500	[$3,000]
Avg. mi./gal.	20	(13)	17	[30]
Total equiv. ann. cost	$2,000	($3,000)	$2,700	[$1,500]
Servicibility (miles to dealer)	10	[5]	[5]	(30)
Comfort (rank)	3	2	[1]	(4)
Size flexibility (equiv. no passengers)	4	[9]	5	(3)

Key: ▢ Best alternative for factor.

⬭ Worst alternative for factor.

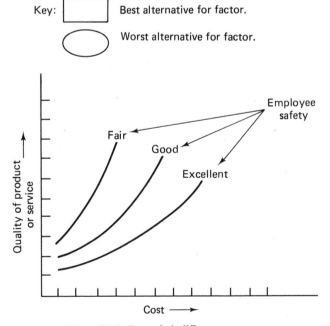

Figure 19-1. Example indifference curves.

Ordinal Scaling*

An ordinal scaling is simply a ranking of factors in order of preference. This scaling may be done by merely presenting the decision-maker with a list of factors and asking him to rank them in order of preference. There is, however, a simple device that makes this task easier and provides a check on the internal consistency of the value judgments obtained. This is called the *method of paired comparisons* and is illustrated by example below.

Suppose there are five factors (objectives) considered to be important, and they are designated as follows:

A—Profit (Cost Minimization)
B—Stable Employment
C—Product Quality
D—Appearance
E—Employee Safety

The method of paired comparisons suggests that the factors be submitted to the decision-maker two at a time for a preference judgment. In general, if there are n factors, $n(n-1)(1/2)$ pairs must be judged. Assume that the results of this process are indicated by the following list of preference statements (the symbol $>$ should be read "is preferred to"):

1.	$A > B$	6.	$B > D$
2.	$A > C$	7.	$B < E$
3.	$A > D$	8.	$C > D$
4.	$A > E$	9.	$C < E$
5.	$B < C$	10.	$D < E$

The first step in deducing the ordinal scale from the results is to rearrange the list so that all the "is preferred to" signs point in the same direction.

1.	$A > B$	6.	$B > D$
2.	$A > C$	7.	$E > B$
3.	$A > D$	8.	$C > D$
4.	$A > E$	9.	$E > C$
5.	$C > B$	10.	$E > D$

The factor ranking first on the ordinal scale must be preferred to four other factors in this problem, and thus it should appear four times on the left-hand side of our list. The factor A appears four times on the left, and thus ranks at the top of the ordinal scale. Similarly, the factor that ranks second must be preferred to three other factors and should appear three times on the left-hand side of the list. In general, if there are n factors, the

*Adapted from W.T. Morris, *Engineering Economic Analysis* (Reston, Va: Reston Publishing Company. 1976).

factor whose rank is r on the resulting ordinal scale will appear $n - r$ times on the left-hand side of a list such as constructed above. In this problem the resulting ordinal scale is:

Rank	Factor	$n - r$
1	A	4
2	E	3
3	C	2
4	B	1
5	D	0

Thus, the final ranking is:

$$A > E > C > B > D$$

Suppose the above scheme of deducing the ordinal scale from the results of paired comparisons does not work out just the way the example suggests. For example, suppose the decision-maker, in comparison 8 on the above list, had judged $D > C$ rather than $C > D$. In this case, the second list would show C, B, and D all appearing one time on the left-hand side; thus the rule for deducing the ordinal scale would then fail. This indicates that there is an apparent inconsistency in the judgments made by the decision-maker with respect to the relative rankings of those three alternatives. One should then check comparison statements involving all combinations on these three alternatives, which are as follows:

$$C > B \quad \text{(comparison 5)}$$
$$B > D \quad \text{(comparison 6)}$$
$$D > C \quad \text{(comparison 8)}$$

The first two comparisons together say that $C > B > D$, which means that C should be $> D$. But this contradicts comparison 8, and thus indicates the need for the decision-maker to rethink his ordering of these alternatives so that he will have logical consistency in his judgments.

Weighting Factors*

Consider k factors $A, B, C, \ldots J, K$, or $F_1, F_2, \ldots, F_k$, such as objectives of a firm or nonmonetary factors, which should be considered in an analysis. The following method of weighting factors requires two assumptions:

*This section is adapted from William T. Morris, *The Analysis of Management Decisions* (Homewood, Ill.: Richard D. Irwin, Inc., 1964), pp. 417–424, with permission of the publisher.

1. It must be possible for the decision-maker to consider and judge the relative weight of any combination of factors. That is, it must be possible to consider not only the weight of F_1, but also the weight of both F_1 and F_2.

2. Weights are assumed to be additive. That is, given the weight of F_1 and the weight of F_2, the weight of both F_1 and F_2 is the sum of their individual weights.

The decision-maker should proceed in weighting the factors as follows:

1. Rank the factors according to decreasing preference or importance by any method such as ordinal scaling illustrated above. Once this is done, it might be desirable to assign or reassign subscripts to indicate the rankings. Thus, F_1 is ranked first, F_2 is ranked second, etc.

2. Let the weight of F_1 equal 100 [i.e., $W(F_1) = 100$] and weight the other factors so as to reflect judgment of their weight relative to the weight of F_1. Thus, the weights of $F_2 \cdots F_k$ will range from a possible high value of 100 to a possible low value of 0. All further steps (3 through 6) serve to refine these initial weighting judgments and to insure they are internally consistent.

3. Compare F_1 with the combination of $F_2 + F_3$ (the plus sign here means "and"). If F_1 is considered to have less weight than $F_2 + F_3$, then the weights assigned in step 2 above must satisfy the relation $W(F_1) < W(F_2) + W(F_3)$. If the assigned weights do not satisfy this relation, then $W(F_1)$ should be adjusted until the relation above corresponds to the judgment on relative weights. If, on the other hand, F_1 is considered to have greater weight than $F_2 + F_3$, then the inequality sign of the above relation would be reversed, and, if necessary, the weight of F_1 may be adjusted.

4. Compare F_1 with the combination $F_2 + F_3 + F_4$, and repeat the process of adjusting the value of $W(F_1)$ if necessary.

5. The process of comparison and adjustment is continued according to the following pattern (for a given problem, it is to be expected that many of these comparisons will not be needed, thus shortening the process):

$$\text{Compare } F_1 \text{ with } F_2 + F_3 + F_4 + F_5$$

$$\vdots$$

$$\text{Compare } F_1 \text{ with } F_2 + F_3 + F_4 + F_5 + \cdots + F_k$$
$$\text{Compare } F_2 \text{ with } F_3 + F_4$$
$$\text{Compare } F_2 \text{ with } F_3 + F_4 + F_5$$

$$\vdots$$

$$\text{Compare } F_2 \text{ with } F_3 + F_4 + F_5 + \cdots + F_k$$

$$\vdots$$

$$\text{Compare } F_{k-2} \text{ with } F_{k-1} \quad + F_k$$

6. Once the weights $[W(F_1) + W(F_2) + \cdots + W(F_k)]$ have been adjusted and checked for consistency to the satisfaction of the decision-maker, it is common to "normalize" them to sum to 100 points by multiplying each individual weight by $\dfrac{100}{\sum\limits_{i=1}^{k} W(F_i)}$.

Example:

Suppose management desires to establish weights for the four most important factors or objectives identified in the above section on ordinal scaling. The following are identifications and initial weighting assignments.

Factor	Ordinal scaling identification	Reassigned identification	Initial weighting assignment
Profit	A	F_1	$W(F_1) = 100$
Safety	E	F_2	$W(F_2) = 65$
Quality	C	F_3	$W(F_3) = 40$
Employment	B	F_4	$W(F_4) = 30$

The first consistency check is to compare F_1 with $F_2 + F_3$. Suppose the decision-maker feels that F_1 is less important than the combination of F_2 and F_3. This judgment checks with the initial assignment of weights. That is,

$$W(F_1) = 100 < W(F_2) + W(F_3) = 65 + 40 = 105$$

The next comparison is between F_1 and $F_2 + F_3 + F_4$. It is reasonable that F_1 should be considered less important than the combination of F_2 and F_3 and F_4. This, too, checks with the initial assignment of weights. That is,

$$W(F_1) = 100 < W(F_2) + W(F_3) + W(F_4) = 65 + 40 + 30 = 135$$

The next comparison is between F_2 and $F_3 + F_4$. Suppose the decision-maker feels F_2 is more important than the combination of F_3 and F_4. A check of this compared to the assigned weights shows

$$W(F_2) = 65 < W(F_3) + W(F_4) = 40 + 30 = 70$$

Thus there is an inconsistency to be resolved. This might be done by increasing $W(F_2)$ by more than 5 points (i.e., $70 - 65$), by decreasing $W(F_3)$ and/or $W(F_4)$ by more than 5 points, or by some combination of these adjustments for consistency. Suppose it is judged that $W(F_2)$ should be increased by 5 points and that $W(F_4)$ should be decreased by 10 points. With these changes,

$$W(F_2) = 70 > W(F_3) + W(F_4) = 40 + 20 = 60$$

which agrees with the original judgment that F_2 is more important than the combination of F_3 and F_4. If adjustments in point assignments are sufficient, it may be necessary to redo prior consistency checks.

Table 19-2 shows the normalization of the factor weights which have been checked for consistency.

Table 19-2

CALCULATION OF NORMALIZED FACTOR WEIGHTS

Factor	Weight $[= W(F_i)]$	Normalized factor weight $\left[= \dfrac{W(F_i)}{\sum\limits_{i=1}^{4} W(F_i)} \times 100\right]$
F_1	100	44
F_2	70	30
F_3	40	17
F_4	20	9
$\sum\limits_{i=1}^{4} W(F_i) = 230$		$\sum = 100$

Weighted Evaluation of Alternatives

Once weights have been assigned to factors, the next step is to assign numerical values regarding the degree to which each alternative satisfies each factor. This is generally a difficult judgment task using an arbitrary scale of, say, between 0 and 10 or between 0 and 100 to reflect relative evaluations for each alternative and each factor.

Example:

Suppose we are comparing two alternatives on the basis of how well they satisfy the four factors with the weights developed in the example above. The factors, together with the subjective evaluation of how well each alternative meets each on the basis of a scale of 0 to 10 is shown in Table 19-3.

Table 19-3

EXAMPLE EVALUATION RATING OF HOW WELL EACH
ALTERNATIVE SATISFIES EACH FACTOR

Factor	Alternative A	Alternative B
Profit	10	9
Employee safety	6	7
Product quality	5	10
Stable employment	7	7

Once the evaluations have been made, the results can be calculated as in Table 19-4 to arrive at weighted evaluations of factors for each alternative. Thus, the summed weighted evaluation is 76.8 for alternative A and 83.9 for alternative B, indicating that alternative B is the better, even though it showed a lower profit in Table 19-3.

Table 19-4

CALCULATION OF WEIGHTED EVALUATIONS OF ALTERNATIVES

	Normalized factor weight (From Table 17-1)	Alternative A		Alternative B	
Factor		Evaluation rating	Weighted evaluation*	Evaluation rating	Weighted evaluation*
Profit	44	10	44.0	9	39.6
Employee safety	30	6	18.0	7	21.0
Product quality	17	5	8.5	10	17.0
Stable employment	9	7	6.3	7	6.3
			$\Sigma = 76.8$		$\Sigma = 83.9$

*Weighted evaluation = Normalized factor weight $\times \dfrac{\text{Evaluation rating}}{10}$

Multi-Criteria Utility Models

Significant developments in the theory and practice of using multi-criteria (e.g., multiple objectives, attributes, or factors) utility models have been summarized in a definitive work by Keeney and Raiffa.* The following is a condensed version that incorporates the essential elements for use but does not include extensive explanation of the theory.

In general, the utility, $U(x) = U(x_1, x_2, \ldots, x_n)$, of any combination of outcomes $(x_1, x_2, \ldots, x_n)$ for n criteria $(X_1, X_2, \ldots, X_n)$ can be expressed as either (a) an additive or (b) a multiplicative function of the individual criteria utility functions $U_1(x_1), U_2(x_2), \ldots, U_n(x_n)$ provided that each pair of criteria is:

1. preferentially independent of its complement (i.e., the preference order of consequences for any pair of criteria does not depend on the levels at which all other criteria are held); and

2. utility independent of its complement (i.e., the conditional preference order for lotteries involving only changes in the levels for any pair of criteria does not depend on the levels at which all other criteria are held).

Additive Utility Model

Another way of stating the above applicability provisions as they apply to the additive utility function is that the criteria should be *additively independent* (i.e., that preferences in lotteries involving two or more criteria

*R. L. Keeney, and H. Raiffa, *Decisions with Multiple Objectives: Preferences and Value Tradeoffs* (New York: John Wiley & Sons, Inc., 1976).

depend only on their marginal probability distributions and not on their joint probability distribution). This will be true if the $\sum_{i=1}^{n} k_i = 1$ in the model as given below in Eq. 19-1.

The utility $U(x)$ of any combination of outcomes for n criteria $(X_1, X_2, \ldots, X_n)$ can be expressed as

$$U(x) = \sum_{i=1}^{n} U(x_i, \bar{x}_i^0) = \sum_{i=1}^{n} k_i \cdot U_i(x_i) \qquad 19\text{-}1$$

where $U(x_i, \bar{x}_i^0) =$ The utility of the outcome for the ith criterion, x_i, and the worst possible outcome for the complement of the ith criterion, $\bar{x}_i^0$ (*Note:* By complement of the ith criterion, $\bar{x}_i$, is meant all criteria other than the ith criterion)

$\qquad\qquad k_i =$ The weighting for the ith criterion

$\qquad U_i(x_i) =$ The utility of the outcome x_i for the ith criterion

Further conditions and explanations for the additive utility model are as follows:

1. U is normalized by $U(x_1^0, x_2^0, \ldots, x_n^0) = 0$ and $U(x_1^*, x_2^*, \ldots, x_n^*) = 1$. (Note: x_i^0 means worst outcome of x_i and x_i^* means best outcome of x_i.)

2. U_i is a conditional utility function of X_i normalized by $U_i(x_i^0) = 0$ and $U_i(x_i^*) = 1$, for $i = 1, 2, \ldots, n$ criteria.

3. $k_i = U(x_i^*, \bar{x}_i^0)$, for $i = 1, 2, \ldots, n$ criteria.

As mentioned above, the additive model applies when $\sum_{i=1}^{n} k_i = 1.0$. Otherwise, the multiplicative model (explained below) applies.

Multiplicative Utility Model

The utility $U(x)$ of any combination of outcomes of n criteria can be obtained from the solution to the following equation:

$$K \cdot U(x) + 1 = \prod_{i=1}^{n} [K \cdot k_i \cdot U_i(x_i) + 1] \qquad 19\text{-}2$$

Solving for $U(x)$ gives

$$U(x) = \frac{\prod_{i=1}^{n} [K \cdot k_i \cdot U_i(x_i) + 1] - 1}{K} \qquad 19\text{-}3$$

where

1. U is normalized by $U(x_1^0, x_2^0, \ldots, x_n^0) = 0$ and $U(x_1^*, x_2^*, \ldots, x_n^*) = 1$.

2. $U_i(x_i)$ is a conditional utility function on X_i normalized by $U_i(x_i^0) = 0$ and $U_i(x_i^*) = 1$, for $i = 1, 2, \ldots, n$.

3. $k_i = U(x_i^*, \bar{x}_i^0)$.

4. K is a scaling constant that is a solution to

$$1 + K = \prod_{i=1}^{n} (1 + K \cdot k_i) \qquad 19\text{-}4$$

and must be found iteratively. When utility independence applies, as assumed by the model, $-1 < K < 0$.

Determination of Utility Functions for Individual Criteria

To use either of the above models, a utility function must be specified for each criterion, X_i, where $U_i(x_i^0) = 0$ and $U_i(x_i^*) = 1.0$. In words, the worst outcome for each criterion should be assigned a utility of 0, and the best outcome for each criterion should be assigned a utility of 1.0. The shape of each utility function depends on the decision-maker's subjective judgment on the relative desirability of various outcomes. As noted on p. 327, this can be done by obtaining answers to a series of questions such as the following:

For criterion X_i, what certain outcome, x_i, would be equally as desirable as a $P\%$ chance of the highest outcome and a $(1 - P)\%$ chance of the lowest outcome? This can be expressed in utility terms, using the extreme values x_i^* and x_i^0, as $U(x_i = ?) = P \cdot U(x_i^*) + (1 - P) \cdot U(x_i^0)$.

To obtain plotting points for the utility function, one can vary P as desired. Alternatively, one could specify the certain outcome, x_i over a range of values and ask questions such as: At what P is the certain outcome x_i equally desirable as $P \cdot U(x_i^*) + (1 - P) \cdot U(x_i^0)$.

Example:
Suppose it is desired to define an approximate utility function for, say, the number of pollutants caused by a process. The best conceivable number might be specified as 3 and the worst conceivable number might be specified as 15. These would be given utility values of 1 and 0, respectively. One question might be: "What number of pollutants for certain would be as desirable as a 50% chance of 3 and a 50% chance of 15?" If the answer is, say, 12, then the new utility value could be calculated as:

$$U(x = 12) = 0.5 \cdot U(x = 3) + 0.5 \cdot U(x = 15)$$
$$U(x = 12) = 0.5 \cdot 1 + 0.5 \cdot 0$$
$$U(x = 12) = 0.5$$

Figure 19-2 shows the results up to this point with a possible curve dotted in. Other points can be calculated and plotted until one is satisfied with the "accuracy" of his utility representation. Alternatively, one can use his intuitive judgment to "draw in" an approximation. It is typical that the scale for the criterion be arranged so that the worst outcome is on the left and the best

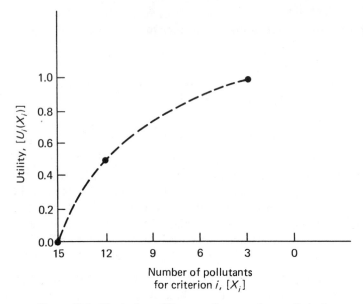

Figure. 19-2. Illustrative utility curve for example re pollutants.

outcome is on the right, but this can be reversed if desired. In any case, the criterion values and utility values should be shown on linear scales for ease of graphical comparison.

Determination of Weighting or Scaling Factors

Once utility functions for all criteria have been determined, the next step is to determine the weighting for each criterion, k_i. From the explanations for both the additive and multiplicative utility models, $k_i = U(x_i^*, \bar{x}_i^0)$ where $0 \leq k_i \leq 1$. In words, k_i is the utility if the outcome for criterion i is at its best value, x_i^*, and the outcome for all criteria except i are at their respective worst values, $\bar{x}_i^0$.

Two types of questions often helpful in assessing the k_i's are given below:

Question A:

For what probability P are you indifferent between:

1. the lottery giving a P chance at $x^*(= x_1^*, x_2^*, \ldots, x_n^*)$ and a $1 - P$ chance at $x^0(= x_1^0, x_2^0, \ldots, x_n^0)$; and
2. the consequence $(x_1^0, \ldots, x_{i-1}^0, x_i^*, x_{i+1}^0, \ldots, x_n^0)$.

The above is shown diagramatically and in words in Fig. 19-3. The result of such an assessment is that $P = k_i$.

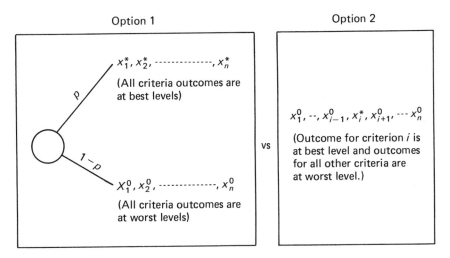

Figure 19-3. Illustration of Question A for finding weighting or scaling factor, k_i for the ith criterion.

Question B:

Select a level of X_i (e.g., x_i') and a level of X_j (e.g., x_j') so that, for any fixed levels of all other attributes, you are indifferent between:

1. an outcome yielding x_i' and x_j^0 together; and
2. an outcome yielding x_j' and x_i^0 together.

Thus, you can use the relation

$$k_i \cdot U_i(x_i') = k_j \cdot U_j(x_j')$$

to solve for either k_i or k_j, depending on which is unknown.

Suggested good practice in assessing the k_i's would be first to rank them, then to use Question A to evaluate the largest k_i, and then to use Question B successively to evaluate the magnitude of the other k_i's relative to the largest k_i, or relative to any other k_i which has already been determined.

The rank ordering of the k_i's can be done by intuitive judgment or by asking the decision-maker, for instance, whether he prefers $(x_1^*, \bar{x}_1^0)$ or $(x_2^*, \bar{x}_2^0)$. If the former is preferred, then $k_i > k_2$, and if the latter is preferred, then $k_2 > k_1$. This can be done for as many combinations of weighting factors as deemed needed to check for consistency.

Example:

The criteria for a decision problem, together with rankings for order of importance and the range for worst to best outcomes, might be as follows:

Criterion	Ranking	Range
X_1 Profit index	1	0–10
X_2 No. of pollutants	3	15–3
X_3 Quality level	2	90–99
X_4 Downtime	4	18–8

The utility functions for each of the criteria are given in Fig. 19-4. It is desired to illustrate how one might determine the scaling factors, k_i.

We will first use Question A (above) to obtain the scaling factor for the highest-ranked criterion, X_1. The question might be phrased as follows:

> What probability of all criteria outcomes at their best levels versus all criteria outcomes at their worst levels would be as desirable as profit at its best level and all other criteria at their worst levels?

Let us suppose that the answer to the above question is, say, 0.4. Thus, the scaling factor for the profit criterion, k_1, = 0.4.

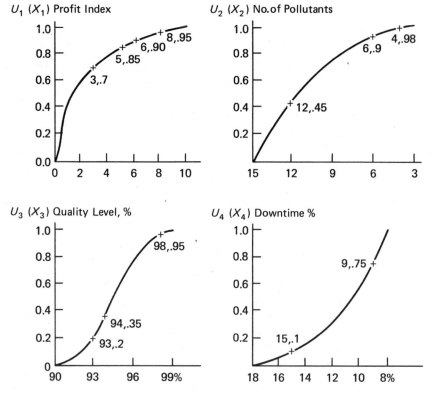

Figure 19-4. Illustrative utility curves for example with four criteria (certain plotting points are shown).

Next, let us illustrate how one can obtain the scaling factor for the quality level criterion, k_3, by using Question B (above). The question might be phrased as follows:

What profit index, given quality level at its worst (i.e., 90) would be as desirable as what quality level, given profit at its worst (i.e., 0)?

Let us suppose that the answer is:

$$\text{Profit index, } x_1' = 5$$

$$\text{Quality level, } x_3' = 98$$

We can now use the relation below (and the graphs in Fig. 19-4 to find utility values) and solve for k_3.

$$k_1 \cdot U_1(x_1') = k_3 \cdot U_3(x_3')$$

$$k_1 \cdot U_1(5) = k_3 \cdot U_3(98)$$

$$k_1 \cdot 0.85 = k_3 \cdot 0.95$$

$$k_3 = 0.894 \cdot k_1$$

$$= 0.894(0.4) = 0.357$$

Scaling factors for the other criteria can be obtained by successive use of Question B to find indifference equivalents and then converting this into the desired factors. Table 19-5 summarizes the results obtained above as well as for k_2 and k_4. The following calculations are based on the indifference equivalents stated in Table 19-5.

Table 19-5

SUMMARY OF SCALING FACTOR DETERMINATION FOR EXAMPLE PROBLEM

Criterion	Rank	Range	Indifference equivalent	Relative scaling factor	Scaling factor k_i
X_1 Profit	1	0–10		k_1	0.4
X_2 No. of pollutants	3	15–3	3 of $X_1 \sim$ 6 of X_2	$k_2 = 0.778k_1$	0.311
X_3 Quality	2	90–99	5 of $X_1 \sim$ 98 of X_3	$k_3 = 0.894k_1$	0.357
X_4 Downtime	4	18–8	94 of $X_3 \sim$ 9 of X_4	$k_4 = 0.467k_3$	0.167
				$\sum = 1.235$	

To find k_2—(3 of $X_1 \sim$ 6 of X_2):

$$k_1 \cdot U_1(x_1) = k_2 \cdot U_2(X_2)$$

$$k_1 \cdot U_1(3) = k_2 \cdot U_2(6)$$

$$k_1 \cdot 0.7 = k_2 \cdot 0.9$$

$$k_2 = 0.778k_1$$

$$= 0.778(0.4) = 0.311$$

To find k_4—(94 of $X_3 \sim$ 9 of X_4):

$$k_3 \cdot U_3(X_3) = k_4 \cdot U_4(X_4)$$
$$k_3 \cdot U_3(94) = k_4 \cdot U_4(9)$$
$$k_3 \cdot 0.35 = k_4 \cdot 0.75$$
$$k_4 = 0.467 \cdot k_3$$
$$= 0.467(0.357) = 0.167$$

One can note from the right-hand column of Table 19-5 that the sum of the scaling factors, $\sum k_i = 1.235$. Since this sum $\neq 1.0$, the multiplicative, rather than the additive, utility model is applicable. We will now illustrate the use of that model for the evaluation of alternatives.

Example:

Suppose that the organization for which the above criteria, utility functions, and scaling factors are applicable desires to determine which of two major investment or operating alternatives is preferable based on composite utility. The following is information on the outcomes expected for each criterion:

	Outcome, x_i, for alternative:	
Criterion	I	II
X_1 Profit index	8	6
X_2 No. of pollutants	12	4
X_3 Quality level, %	94	93
X_4 Downtime, %	9	15

One can quickly convert the above outcomes to utility values using the curves in Fig. 19-4. The approximate utilities of the outcomes given are:

	Utility, $U_i(x_i)$, for alternative:	
Criterion:	I	II
X_1	0.95	0.90
X_2	0.45	0.98
X_3	0.35	0.20
X_4	0.75	0.10

In order to apply the multiplicative utility function, one needs first to find iteratively (by trial and error) the $-1 < K < 0$ at which

$$K = \prod_{i=1}^{n} (1 + K \cdot k_i) - 1$$

applied to this example by using the scaling factors, k_i, in Table 19-5:

$$K = (1 + 0.4K)(1 + 0.311K)(1 + 0..357K)(1 + 0.167K) - 1$$

Trying $K = -0.1$:

$$-0.1 \stackrel{?}{=} (1 - 0.04)(1 - 0.0311)(1 - 0.0357)(1 - 0.0167) - 1$$

$$-0.1 \neq -0.12$$

Thus, the next trial K should be more negative than -0.1.
Trying $K = -0.4$:

$$-0.4 \stackrel{?}{=} (1 - 0.16)(1 - 0.1244)(1 - 0.1428)(1 - 0.0668) - 1$$

$$-0.4 \neq -0.412$$

Thus, the next trial K should be more negative than -0.4.
Trying $K = -0.6$:

$$-0.6 \stackrel{?}{=} (1 - 0.24)(1 - 0.1866)(1 - 0.2142)(1 - 0.1002)$$

$$-0.6 \neq -0.562$$

Thus, the next trial K should be less negative than -0.6. Further trial and error would result in finding K approximately equal to -0.47. We can now apply the multiplicative model of Eq. 19-3:

$$U(x) = \prod_{i-1}^{n} \frac{[K \cdot k_i U_i(x_i) + 1] - 1}{K}$$

For Alternative I:

$$U(x) = \frac{(-0.47 \cdot 0.4 \cdot 0.95 + 1)(-0.47 \cdot 0.311 \cdot 0.45 + 1)}{(-0.47 \cdot 0.357 \cdot 0.35 + 1)(-0.47 \cdot 0.167 \cdot 0.75 + 1) - 1}{-0.47}$$

$$= 0.682$$

For Alternative II:

$$U(x) = \frac{(-0.47 \cdot 0.4 \cdot 0.90 + 1)(-0.47 \cdot 0.311 \cdot 0.98 + 1)}{(-0.47 \cdot 0.357 \cdot 0.2 + 1)(-0.47 \cdot 0.167 \cdot 0.10 + 1) - 1}{-0.47}$$

$$= 0.676$$

Thus, alternative I has a slightly greater utility than alternative II.

SUMMARY

This chapter has outlined some approaches to resolving the multiple objective, criterion, attribute, and/or factor problem by having the decision-maker compare his alternatives on the basis of one factor at a time. Most such simple comparisons, judgments, or ratings generally are relatively easy to make. Then the decision-maker or his analyst can combine these into an overall evaluation for each alternative. This should make the decision-maker more confident and ultimately make his job easier. The following is a guiding principle:

> Use analysis to accept as inputs simple judgment decisions well within a decision-maker's experience and to logically extend the consequences of these inputs to situations not within his experience and easy intuition.

The determination of what model(s) to use depends on the nature of the decision problem and the preferences of the decision-maker(s). While this determination is a very inexact science, it can be shown that the use of widely differing models (and subjective probability distributions, if applicable) will often have less effect on the probable quality of the solution than does the unintended deletion of possible outcomes, alternatives, or important criteria.

PROBLEMS

19-1. A young man, considering his first job, decides that starting salary and promotion possibilities are of primary importance to him. Faced with an array of job offers, he tries to make an orderly description of his preferences. He decides that promotion possibilities in a company are roughly indicated by the mean time (in years) that it has taken people to become vice-presidents. For several jobs he obtains data on starting salary and mean time to vice-president and, using the method of paired comparisons, and ranks them. The results are shown below (equal ranks denote indifference):

Job	Starting salary	Mean time to vice-president (years)	Rank
A	$15,000	9	3
B	15,500	8	2
C	16,000	12	3
D	16,500	8	1
E	16,500	11	2
F	17,000	10	1
G	17,500	13	2
H	18,000	12	1
I	18,000	15	3

a. Sketch a rough approximation to the indifference map of this man in the region for which data are available.
b. Predict his preference between the two jobs below:

Job	Starting salary	Mean time to vice-president (*years*)
X	$15,500	9
Y	17,000	11

19-2. Draw an indifference curve to reflect your personal preferences or trade-offs between two main factors in selecting a car. The factors should be expressible on some more-or-less continuous scale.

19-3. List the three or four most important factors you would consider in selecting a car. Using the method of paired comparisons, rank those factors on an ordinal scale.

19-4. Select a class or type of decision problem in your organization or personal life involving multiple objectives or factors. Name three to five most important objectives for that class of problem, as you see them, and do the following:
   a. Using the method of paired comparisons, rank them by ordinal scaling.
   b. Weight them and check for consistency and then normalize the weight to sum to 100.
   c. Identify two to four alternatives for the decision problem and evaluate how well each alternative meets each objective on a scale of 0 to 10. Then multiply the evaluation ratings by the objective factor weights and sum these for each factor to compute a weighted evaluation for each alternative.

19-5. Select a class or type of significant decision problem in your organization or personal life. Name the three or more significant objectives or factors to be considered for that class of problem. Assume that the weighting of these factors is nebulous so you think it desirable to develop only a matrix of alternatives versus objectives, with entries to show how well each alternative meets each objective in whatever measures are appropriate, such as in $, time, rank, etc. Then use colors or other symbol codings to highlight the ease of intrepretation of these measures by the persons making the final selection among the alternatives.

19-6. a. Weight the relative importance of the three or four most important factors you would consider in selecting a job. Assume these are the only factors you will quantitatively consider. Show how you make comparisons for internal consistency and normalize the factor weights to sum to 100.
   b. Using the factor weights developed above, obtain a weighted evaluation of two alternative jobs in which you might be interested by evaluating how well each job satisfies each factor using a scale of from 0 to 10.

19-7. a. Weight the relative importance of the three to six most important factors you would consider in selecting a personal car. Assume these are the only factors you will quantitatively consider. Show how you make comparisons for internal consistency and normalize the factor weights to sum to 1,000.

b. Using the factor weights developed above, obtain a weighted evaluation of three alternative makes of cars you might consider for purchase by evaluating how well each make of car satisfies each factor. Use a scale of from 0 to 20.

19-8. Weight the relative importance of your significant personal goals or objectives. These should include work-related goals as well as those not related to your work. Show how you make comparisons for internal consistency and normalize the factor weights to sum to 1,000.

19-9. Suppose a new decision-maker desires to arrive at his own scaling factors for the same criteria for which utilities are given in Fig. 19-4. By asking himself question type A for criterion 1, he judges that $p = 0.7$. Thus, the scaling factor $k_1 = 0.7$. Further, his indifference equivalents are as follows:

$$4 \text{ of } X_1 \sim 5 \text{ of } X_2$$
$$9 \text{ of } X_2 \sim 97 \text{ of } X_3$$
$$2 \text{ of } X_1 \sim 8 \text{ of } X_4$$

Determine all k_i scaling factors.

19-10. Using the scaling factors obtained in Prob. 19-9 and the utility functions in Fig. 20-4, determine the utility for alternatives which are expected to have the following outcomes:

| | Alternatives | |
Criterion	A	B
x_1 Profit	5	8
x_2 No. of pollutants	6	15
x_3 Quality, %	92	97
x_4 Downtime, %	8	12

19-11. Work Prob. 19-10, except use the following scaling factors: $k_1 = 0.2$, $k_2 = 0.4$, $k_3 = 0.3$, and $k_4 = 0.1$.

19-12. Work Prob. 19-10, except use the following scaling factors: $k_1 = 0.3$, $k_2 = 0.7$, $k_3 = 0.4$, and $k_4 = 0.6$.

Appendices

tables of discrete compounding interest factors (for various common values of i from 1/4% to 50%)

DISCRETE COMPOUNDING; $i = 1/4\%$

	SINGLE PAYMENT		UNIFORM SERIES				
	Compound Amount Factor	Present Worth Factor	Compound Amount Factor	Present Worth Factor	Sinking Fund Factor	Capital Recovery Factor	
N	To find F Given P F/P	To find P Given F P/F	To find F Given A F/A	To find P Given A P/A	To find A Given F A/F	To find A Given P A/P	N
1	1.0025	0.9975	1.0000	0.9975	1.0000	1.0025	1
2	1.0050	0.9950	2.0025	1.9925	0.4994	0.5019	2
3	1.0075	0.9925	3.0075	2.9851	0.3325	0.3350	3
4	1.0100	0.9901	4.0150	3.9751	0.2491	0.2516	4
5	1.0126	0.9876	5.0250	4.9627	0.1990	0.2015	5
6	1.0151	0.9851	6.0376	5.9478	0.1656	0.1681	6
7	1.0176	0.9827	7.0527	6.9305	0.1418	0.1443	7
8	1.0202	0.9802	8.0703	7.9107	0.1239	0.1264	8
9	1.0227	0.9778	9.0905	8.8885	0.1100	0.1125	9
10	1.0253	0.9753	10.1132	9.8638	0.0989	0.1014	10
11	1.0278	0.9729	11.1385	10.8367	0.0898	0.0923	11
12	1.0304	0.9705	12.1663	11.8072	0.0822	0.0847	12
13	1.0330	0.9681	13.1967	12.7753	0.0758	0.0783	13
14	1.0356	0.9656	14.2297	13.7409	0.0703	0.0728	14
15	1.0382	0.9632	15.2653	14.7041	0.0655	0.0680	15
16	1.0408	0.9608	16.3035	15.6650	0.0613	0.0638	16
17	1.0434	0.9584	17.3442	16.6234	0.0577	0.0602	17
18	1.0460	0.9561	18.3876	17.5795	0.0544	0.0569	18
19	1.0486	0.9537	19.4335	18.5331	0.0515	0.0540	19
20	1.0512	0.9513	20.4821	19.4844	0.0488	0.0513	20
21	1.0538	0.9489	21.5333	20.4333	0.0464	0.0489	21
22	1.0565	0.9466	22.5872	21.3799	0.0443	0.0468	22
23	1.0591	0.9442	23.6436	22.3241	0.0423	0.0448	23
24	1.0618	0.9418	24.7027	23.2659	0.0405	0.0430	24
25	1.0644	0.9395	25.7645	24.2054	0.0388	0.0413	25
26	1.0671	0.9371	26.8289	25.1425	0.0373	0.0398	26
27	1.0697	0.9348	27.8959	26.0773	0.0358	0.0383	27
28	1.0724	0.9325	28.9657	27.0098	0.0345	0.0370	28
29	1.0751	0.9302	30.0381	27.9399	0.0333	0.0358	29
30	1.0778	0.9278	31.1132	28.8678	0.0321	0.0346	30
35	1.0913	0.9163	36.5291	33.4723	0.0274	0.0299	35
40	1.1050	0.9050	42.0130	38.0197	0.0238	0.0263	40
45	1.1189	0.8937	47.5659	42.5107	0.0210	0.0235	45
50	1.1330	0.8826	53.1884	46.9460	0.0188	0.0213	50
55	1.1472	0.8717	58.8817	51.3262	0.0170	0.0195	55
60	1.1616	0.8609	64.6464	55.6521	0.0155	0.0180	60
65	1.1762	0.8502	70.4836	59.9244	0.0142	0.0167	65
70	1.1910	0.8396	76.3941	64.1436	0.0131	0.0156	70
75	1.2059	0.8292	82.3788	68.3105	0.0121	0.0146	75
80	1.2211	0.8189	88.4388	72.4257	0.0113	0.0138	80
85	1.2364	0.8088	94.5748	76.490	0.0106	0.0131	85
90	1.2520	0.7987	100.788	80.504	0.0099	0.0124	90
95	1.2677	0.7888	107.079	84.467	0.0093	0.0118	95
100	1.2836	0.7790	113.45	88.382	0.0088	0.0113	100
∞				400.0		0.0025	∞

DISCRETE COMPOUNDING; $i = 1/2\%$

	SINGLE PAYMENT		UNIFORM SERIES				
	Compound Amount Factor	Present Worth Factor	Compound Amount Factor	Present Worth Factor	Sinking Fund Factor	Capital Recovery Factor	
	To find F Given P	To find P Given F	To find F Given A	To find P Given A	To find A Given F	To find A Given P	
N	F/P	P/F	F/A	P/A	A/F	A/P	N
1	1.0050	0.9950	1.0000	0.9950	1.0000	1.0050	1
2	1.0100	0.9901	2.0050	1.9851	0.4988	0.5038	2
3	1.0151	0.9851	3.0150	2.9702	0.3317	0.3367	3
4	1.0202	0.9802	4.0301	3.9505	0.2481	0.2531	4
5	1.0253	0.9754	5.0502	4.9259	0.1980	0.2030	5
6	1.0304	0.9705	6.0755	5.8964	0.1646	0.1696	6
7	1.0355	0.9657	7.1059	6.8621	0.1407	0.1457	7
8	1.0407	0.9609	8.1414	7.8229	0.1228	0.1278	8
9	1.0459	0.9561	9.1821	8.7790	0.1089	0.1139	9
10	1.0511	0.9513	10.2280	9.7304	0.0978	0.1028	10
11	1.0564	0.9466	11.2791	10.6770	0.0887	0.0937	11
12	1.0617	0.9419	12.3355	11.6189	0.0811	0.0861	12
13	1.0670	0.9372	13.3972	12.5561	0.0746	0.0796	13
14	1.0723	0.9326	14.4642	13.4887	0.0691	0.0741	14
15	1.0777	0.9279	15.5365	14.4166	0.0644	0.0694	15
16	1.0831	0.9233	16.6142	15.3399	0.0602	0.0652	16
17	1.0885	0.9187	17.6973	16.2586	0.0565	0.0615	17
18	1.0939	0.9141	18.7857	17.1727	0.0532	0.0582	18
19	1.0994	0.9096	19.8797	18.0823	0.0503	0.0553	19
20	1.1049	0.9051	20.9791	18.9874	0.0477	0.0527	20
21	1.1104	0.9006	22.0839	19.8879	0.0453	0.0503	21
22	1.1160	0.8961	23.1944	20.7840	·0.0431	0.0481	22
23	1.1216	0.8916	24.3103	21.6756	0.0411	0.0461	23
24	1.1272	0.8872	25.4319	22.5628	0.0393	0.0443	24
25	1.1328	0.8828	26.5590	23.4456	0.0377	0.0427	25
26	1.1385	0.8784	27.6918	24.3240	0.0361	0.0411	26
27	1.1442	0.8740	28.8303	25.1980	0.0347	0.0397	27
28	1.1499	0.8697	29.9744	26.0676	0.0334	0.0384	28
29	1.1556	0.8653	31.1243	26.9330	0.0321	0.0371	29
30	1.1614	0.8610	32.2799	27.7940	0.0310	0.0360	30
35	1.1907	0.8398	38.1453	32.0353	0.0262	0.0312	35
40	1.2208	0.8191	44.1587	36.1721	0.0226	0.0276	40
45	1.2516	0.7990	50.3240	40.2071	0.0199	0.0249	45
50	1.2832	0.7793	56.6450	44.1427	0.0177	0.0227	50
55	1.3156	0.7601	63.1256	47.9813	0.0158	0.0208	55
60	1.3488	0.7414	69.7698	51.7254	0.0143	0.0193	60
65	1.3829	0.7231	76.5818	55.3773	0.0131	0.0181	65
70	1.4178	0.7053	83.5658	58.9393	0.0120	0.0170	70
75	1.4536	0.6879	90.7262	62.4135	0.0110	0.0160	75
80	1.4903	0.6710	98.0674	65.8022	0.0102	0.0152	80
85	1.5280	0.6545	105.594	69.107	0.0095	0.0145	85
90	1.5666	0.6383	113.311	72.331	0.0088	0.0138	90
95	1.6061	0.6226	121.22	75.475	0.0082	0.0132	95
100	1.6467	0.6073	129.33	78.542	0.0077	0.0127	100
∞				200.0		0.0050	∞

DISCRETE COMPOUNDING; $i = 3/4\%$

	SINGLE PAYMENT		UNIFORM SERIES				
	Compound Amount Factor	Present Worth Factor	Compound Amount Factor	Present Worth Factor	Sinking Fund Factor	Capital Recovery Factor	
N	To find F Given P F/P	To find P Given F P/F	To find F Given A F/A	To find P Given A P/A	To find A Given F A/F	To find A Given P A/P	N
1	1.0075	0.9926	1.0000	0.9926	1.0000	1.0075	1
2	1.0151	0.9852	2.0075	1.9777	0.4981	0.5056	2
3	1.0227	0.9778	3.0226	2.9556	0.3308	0.3383	3
4	1.0303	0.9706	4.0452	3.9261	0.2472	0.2547	4
5	1.0381	0.9633	5.0756	4.8894	0.1970	0.2045	5
6	1.0459	0.9562	6.1136	5.8456	0.1636	0.1711	6
7	1.0537	0.9490	7.1595	6.7946	0.1397	0.1472	7
8	1.0616	0.9420	8.2132	7.7366	0.1218	0.1293	8
9	1.0696	0.9350	9.2748	8.6716	0.1078	0.1153	9
10	1.0776	0.9280	10.3443	9.5996	0.0967	0.1042	10
11	1.0857	0.9211	11.4219	10.5207	0.0876	0.0951	11
12	1.0938	0.9142	12.5076	11.4349	0.0800	0.0875	12
13	1.1020	0.9074	13.6014	12.3423	0.0735	0.0810	13
14	1.1103	0.9007	14.7034	13.2430	0.0680	0.0755	14
15	1.1186	0.8940	15.8136	14.1370	0.0632	0.0707	15
16	1.1270	0.8873	16.9322	15.0243	0.0591	0.0666	16
17	1.1354	0.8807	18.0592	15.9050	0.0554	0.0629	17
18	1.1440	0.8742	19.1947	16.7791	0.0521	0.0596	18
19	1.1525	0.8676	20.3386	17.6468	0.0492	0.0567	19
20	1.1612	0.8612	21.4912	18.5080	0.0465	0.0540	20
21	1.1699	0.8548	22.6523	19.3628	0.0441	0.0516	21
22	1.1787	0.8484	23.8222	20.2112	0.0420	0.0495	22
23	1.1875	0.8421	25.0009	21.0533	0.0400	0.0475	23
24	1.1964	0.8358	26.1884	21.8891	0.0382	0.0457	24
25	1.2054	0.8296	27.3848	22.7187	0.0365	0.0440	25
26	1.2144	0.8234	28.5902	23.5421	0.0350	0.0425	26
27	1.2235	0.8173	29.8046	24.3594	0.0336	0.0411	27
28	1.2327	0.8112	31.0282	25.1707	0.0322	0.0397	28
29	1.2420	0.8052	32.2609	25.9758	0.0310	0.0385	29
30	1.2513	0.7992	33.5028	26.7750	0.0298	0.0373	30
35	1.2989	0.7699	39.8537	30.6826	0.0251	0.0326	35
40	1.3483	0.7416	46.4464	34.4469	0.0215	0.0290	40
45	1.3997	0.7145	53.2900	38.0731	0.0188	0.0263	45
50	1.4530	0.6883	60.3941	41.5664	0.0166	0.0241	50
55	1.5083	0.6630	67.7686	44.9315	0.0148	0.0223	55
60	1.5657	0.6387	75.4239	48.1733	0.0133	0.0208	60
65	1.6253	0.6153	83.3706	51.2962	0.0120	0.0195	65
70	1.6871	0.5927	91.6198	54.3045	0.0109	0.0184	70
75	1.7514	0.5710	100.183	57.2026	0.0100	0.0175	75
80	1.8180	0.5500	109.072	59.9943	0.0092	0.0167	80
85	1.8872	0.5299	118.300	62.6837	0.0085	0.0160	85
90	1.9591	0.5104	127.879	65.275	0.0078	0.0153	90
95	2.0337	0.4917	137.822	67.770	0.0073	0.0148	95
100	2.1111	0.4737	148.14	70.175	0.0068	0.0143	100
∞				133.333		0.0075	∞

DISCRETE COMPOUNDING; $i = 1\%$

	SINGLE PAYMENT		UNIFORM SERIES				
	Compound Amount Factor	Present Worth Factor	Compound Amount Factor	Present Worth Factor	Sinking Fund Factor	Capital Recovery Factor	
N	To find F Given P F/P	To find P Given F P/F	To find F Given A F/A	To find P Given A P/A	To find A Given F A/F	To find A Given P A/P	N
1	1.0100	0.9901	1.0000	0.9901	1.0000	1.0100	1
2	1.0201	0.9803	2.0100	1.9704	0.4975	0.5075	2
3	1.0303	0.9706	3.0301	2.9410	0.3300	0.3400	3
4	1.0406	0.9610	4.0604	3.9020	0.2463	0.2563	4
5	1.0510	0.9515	5.1010	4.8534	0.1960	0.2060	5
6	1.0615	0.9420	6.1520	5.7955	0.1625	0.1725	6
7	1.0721	0.9327	7.2135	6.7282	0.1386	0.1486	7
8	1.0829	0.9235	8.2857	7.6517	0.1207	0.1307	8
9	1.0937	0.9143	9.3685	8.5660	0.1067	0.1167	9
10	1.1046	0.9053	10.4622	9.4713	0.0956	0.1056	10
11	1.1157	0.8963	11.5668	10.3676	0.0865	0.0965	11
12	1.1268	0.8874	12.6825	11.2551	0.0788	0.0888	12
13	1.1381	0.8787	13.8093	12.1337	0.0724	0.0824	13
14	1.1495	0.8700	14.9474	13.0037	0.0669	0.0769	14
15	1.1610	0.8613	16.0969	13.8650	0.0621	0.0721	15
16	1.1726	0.8528	17.2578	14.7178	0.0579	0.0679	16
17	1.1843	0.8444	18.4304	15.5622	0.0543	0.0643	17
18	1.1961	0.8360	19.6147	16.3982	0.0510	0.0610	18
19	1.2081	0.8277	20.8109	17.2260	0.0481	0.0581	19
20	1.2202	0.8195	22.0190	18.0455	0.0454	0.0554	20
21	1.2324	0.8114	23.2391	18.8570	0.0430	0.0530	21
22	1.2447	0.8034	24.4715	19.6603	0.0409	0.0509	22
23	1.2572	0.7954	25.7162	20.4558	0.0389	0.0489	23
24	1.2697	0.7876	26.9734	21.2434	0.0371	0.0471	24
25	1.2824	0.7798	28.2431	22.0231	0.0354	0.0454	25
26	1.2953	0.7720	29.5256	22.7952	0.0339	0.0439	26
27	1.3082	0.7644	30.8208	23.5596	0.0324	0.0424	27
28	1.3213	0.7568	32.1290	24.3164	0.0311	0.0411	28
29	1.3345	0.7493	33.4503	25.0657	0.0299	0.0399	29
30	1.3478	0.7419	34.7848	25.8077	0.0287	0.0387	30
35	1.4166	0.7059	41.6602	29.4085	0.0240	0.0340	35
40	1.4889	0.6717	48.8863	32.8346	0.0205	0.0305	40
45	1.5648	0.6391	56.4809	36.0945	0.0177	0.0277	45
50	1.6446	0.6080	64.4630	39.1961	0.0155	0.0255	50
55	1.7285	0.5785	72.8523	42.1471	0.0137	0.0237	55
60	1.8167	0.5505	81.6695	44.9550	0.0122	0.0222	60
65	1.9094	0.5237	90.9364	47.6265	0.0110	0.0210	65
70	2.0068	0.4983	100.676	50.1684	0.0099	0.0199	70
75	2.1091	0.4741	110.912	52.5870	0.0090	0.0190	75
80	2.2167	0.4511	121.671	54.8881	0.0082	0.0182	80
85	2.3298	0.4292	132.979	57.0776	0.0075	0.0175	85
90	2.4486	0.4084	144.86	59.161	0.0069	0.0169	90
95	2.5735	0.3886	157.35	61.143	0.0064	0.0164	95
100	2.7048	0.3697	170.48	63.029	0.0059	0.0159	100
∞				100.000		0.0100	∞

DISCRETE COMPOUNDING; $i = 1\text{-}1/2\%$

	SINGLE PAYMENT		UNIFORM SERIES				
	Compound Amount Factor	Present Worth Factor	Compound Amount Factor	Present Worth Factor	Sinking Fund Factor	Capital Recovery Factor	
	To find F Given P	To find P Given F	To find F Given A	To find P Given A	To find A Given F	To find A Given P	
N	F/P	P/F	F/A	P/A	A/F	A/P	N
1	1.0150	0.9852	1.0000	0.9852	1.0000	1.0150	1
2	1.0302	0.9707	2.0150	1.9559	0.4963	0.5113	2
3	1.0457	0.9563	3.0452	2.9122	0.3284	0.3434	3
4	1.0614	0.9422	4.0909	3.8544	0.2444	0.2594	4
5	1.0773	0.9283	5.1523	4.7826	0.1941	0.2091	5
6	1.0934	0.9145	6.2295	5.6972	0.1605	0.1755	6
7	1.1098	0.9010	7.3230	6.5982	0.1366	0.1516	7
8	1.1265	0.8877	8.4328	7.4859	0.1186	0.1336	8
9	1.1434	0.8746	9.5593	8.3605	0.1046	0.1196	9
10	1.1605	0.8617	10.7027	9.2222	0.0934	0.1084	10
11	1.1779	0.8489	11.8632	10.0711	0.0843	0.0993	11
12	1.1956	0.8364	13.0412	10.9075	0.0767	0.0917	12
13	1.2136	0.8240	14.2368	11.7315	0.0702	0.0852	13
14	1.2318	0.8118	15.4504	12.5434	0.0647	0.0797	14
15	1.2502	0.7999	16.6821	13.3432	0.0599	0.0749	15
16	1.2690	0.7880	17.9323	14.1312	0.0558	0.0708	16
17	1.2880	0.7764	19.2013	14.9076	0.0521	0.0671	17
18	1.3073	0.7649	20.4893	15.6725	0.0488	0.0638	18
19	1.3270	0.7536	21.7967	16.4261	0.0459	0.0609	19
20	1.3469	0.7425	23.1236	17.1686	0.0432	0.0582	20
21	1.3671	0.7315	24.4705	17.9001	0.0409	0.0559	21
22	1.3876	0.7207	25.8375	18.6208	0.0387	0.0537	22
23	1.4084	0.7100	27.2251	19.3308	0.0367	0.0517	23
24	1.4295	0.6995	28.6335	20.0304	0.0349	0.0499	24
25	1.4509	0.6892	30.0630	20.7196	0.0333	0.0483	25
26	1.4727	0.6790	31.5139	21.3986	0.0317	0.0467	26
27	1.4948	0.6690	32.9866	22.0676	0.0303	0.0453	27
28	1.5172	0.6591	34.4814	22.7267	0.0290	0.0440	28
29	1.5400	0.6494	35.9986	23.3761	0.0278	0.0428	29
30	1.5631	0.6398	37.5386	24.0158	0.0266	0.0416	30
35	1.6839	0.5939	45.5920	27.0756	0.0219	0.0369	35
40	1.8140	0.5513	54.2678	29.9158	0.0184	0.0334	40
45	1.9542	0.5117	63.6141	32.5523	0.0157	0.0307	45
50	2.1052	0.4750	73.6827	34.9997	0.0136	0.0286	50
55	2.2679	0.4409	84.5294	37.2714	0.0118	0.0268	55
60	2.4432	0.4093	96.2145	39.3802	0.0104	0.0254	60
65	2.6320	0.3799	108.803	41.3378	0.0092	0.0242	65
70	2.8355	0.3527	122.364	43.1548	0.0082	0.0232	70
75	3.0546	0.3274	136.97	44.8416	0.0073	0.0223	75
80	3.2907	0.3039	152.71	46.4073	0.0065	0.0215	80
85	3.5450	0.2821	169.66	47.8607	0.0059	0.0209	85
90	3.8189	0.2619	187.93	49.2098	0.0053	0.0203	90
95	4.1141	0.2431	207.61	50.4622	0.0048	0.0198	95
100	4.4320	0.2256	228.80	51.6247	0.0044	0.0194	100
∞				66.667		0.0150	∞

DISCRETE COMPOUNDING; $i = 2\%$

	SINGLE PAYMENT		UNIFORM SERIES				
	Compound Amount Factor	Present Worth Factor	Compound Amount Factor	Present Worth Factor	Sinking Fund Factor	Capital Recovery Factor	
N	To find F Given P F/P	To find P Given F P/F	To find F Given A F/A	To find P Given A P/A	To find A Given F A/F	To find A, Given P A/P	N
1	1.0200	0.9804	1.0000	0.9804	1.0000	1.0200	1
2	1.0404	0.9612	2.0200	1.9416	0.4950	0.5150	2
3	1.0612	0.9423	3.0604	2.8839	0.3268	0.3468	3
4	1.0824	0.9238	4.1216	3.8077	0.2426	0.2626	4
5	1.1041	0.9057	5.2040	4.7135	0.1922	0.2122	5
6	1.1262	0.8880	6.3081	5.6014	0.1585	0.1785	6
7	1.1487	0.8706	7.4343	6.4720	0.1345	0.1545	7
8	1.1717	0.8535	8.5830	7.3255	0.1165	0.1365	8
9	1.1951	0.8368	9.7546	8.1622	0.1025	0.1225	9
10	1.2190	0.8203	10.9497	8.9826	0.0913	0.1113	10
11	1.2434	0.8043	12.1687	9.7868	0.0822	0.1022	11
12	1.2682	0.7885	13.4121	10.5753	0.0746	0.0946	12
13	1.2936	0.7730	14.6803	11.3484	0.0681	0.0881	13
14	1.3195	0.7579	15.9739	12.1062	0.0626	0.0826	14
15	1.3459	0.7430	17.2934	12.8493	0.0578	0.0778	15
16	1.3728	0.7284	18.6393	13.5777	0.0537	0.0737	16
17	1.4002	0.7142	20.0121	14.2919	0.0500	0.0700	17
18	1.4282	0.7002	21.4123	14.9920	0.0467	0.0667	18
19	1.4568	0.6864	22.8405	15.6785	0.0438	0.0638	19
20	1.4859	0.6730	24.2974	16.3514	0.0412	0.0612	20
21	1.5157	0.6598	25.7833	17.0112	0.0388	0.0588	21
22	1.5460	0.6468	27.2990	17.6580	0.0366	0.0566	22
23	1.5769	0.6342	28.8449	18.2922	0.0347	0.0547	23
24	1.6084	0.6217	30.4218	18.9139	0.0329	0.0529	24
25	1.6406	0.6095	32.0303	19.5234	0.0312	0.0512	25
26	1.6734	0.5976	33.6709	20.1210	0.0297	0.0497	26
27	1.7069	0.5859	35.3443	20.7069	0.0283	0.0483	27
28	1.7410	0.5744	37.0512	21.2813	0.0270	0.0470	28
29	1.7758	0.5631	38.7922	21.8444	0.0258	0.0458	29
30	1.8114	0.5521	40.5681	22.3964	0.0246	0.0446	30
35	1.9999	0.5000	49.9944	24.9986	0.0200	0.0400	35
40	2.2080	0.4529	60.4019	27.3555	0.0166	0.0366	40
45	2.4379	0.4102	71.8927	29.4902	0.0139	0.0339	45
50	2.6916	0.3715	84.5793	31.4236	0.0118	0.0318	50
55	2.9717	0.3365	98.5864	33.1748	0.0101	0.0301	55
60	3.2810	0.3048	114.051	34.7609	0.0088	0.0288	60
65	3.6225	0.2761	131.126	36.1975	0.0076	0.0276	65
70	3.9996	0.2500	149.978	37.4986	0.0067	0.0267	70
75	4.4158	0.2265	170.792	38.6771	0.0059	0.0259	75
80	4.8754	0.2051	193.772	39.7445	0.0052	0.0252	80
85	5.3829	0.1858	219.144	40.7113	0.0046	0.0246	85
90	5.9431	0.1683	247.16	41.5869	0.0040	0.0240	90
95	6.5617	0.1524	278.08	42.3800	0.0036	0.0236	95
100	7.2446	0.1380	312.23	43.0983	0.0032	0.0232	100
∞				50.0000		0.0200	∞

DISCRETE COMPOUNDING; $i = 3\%$

	SINGLE PAYMENT		UNIFORM SERIES				
	Compound Amount Factor	Present Worth Factor	Compound Amount Factor	Present Worth Factor	Sinking Fund Factor	Capital Recovery Factor	
N	To find F Given P F/P	To find P Given F P/F	To find F Given A F/A	To find P Given A P/A	To find A Given F A/F	To find A Given P A/P	N
1	1.0300	0.9709	1.0000	0.9709	1.0000	1.0300	1
2	1.0609	0.9426	2.0300	1.9135	0.4926	0.5226	2
3	1.0927	0.9151	3.0909	2.8286	0.3235	0.3535	3
4	1.1255	0.8885	4.1836	3.7171	0.2390	0.2690	4
5	1.1593	0.8626	5.3091	4.5797	0.1884	0.2184	5
6	1.1941	0.8375	6.4684	5.4172	0.1546	0.1846	6
7	1.2299	0.8131	7.6625	6.2303	0.1305	0.1605	7
8	1.2668	0.7894	8.8923	7.0197	0.1125	0.1425	8
9	1.3048	0.7664	10.1591	7.7861	0.0984	0.1284	9
10	1.3439	0.7441	11.4639	8.5302	0.0872	0.1172	10
11	1.3842	0.7224	12.8078	9.2526	0.0781	0.1081	11
12	1.4258	0.7014	14.1920	9.9540	0.0705	0.1005	12
13	1.4685	0.6810	15.6178	10.6349	0.0640	0.0940	13
14	1.5126	0.6611	17.0863	11.2961	0.0585	0.0885	14
15	1.5580	0.6419	18.5989	11.9379	0.0538	0.0838	15
16	1.6047	0.6232	20.1569	12.5611	0.0496	0.0796	16
17	1.6528	0.6050	21.7616	13.1661	0.0460	0.0760	17
18	1.7024	0.5874	23.4144	13.7535	0.0427	0.0727	18
19	1.7535	0.5703	25.1168	14.3238	0.0398	0.0698	19
20	1.8061	0.5537	26.8703	14.8775	0.0372	0.0672	20
21	1.8603	0.5375	28.6765	15.4150	0.0349	0.0649	21
22	1.9161	0.5219	30.5367	15.9369	0.0327	0.0627	22
23	1.9736	0.5067	32.4528	16.4436	0.0308	0.0608	23
24	2.0328	0.4919	34.4264	16.9355	0.0290	0.0590	24
25	2.0938	0.4776	36.4592	17.4131	0.0274	0.0574	25
26	2.1566	0.4637	38.5530	17.8768	0.0259	0.0559	26
27	2.2213	0.4502	40.7096	18.3270	0.0246	0.0546	27
28	2.2879	0.4371	42.9309	18.7641	0.0233	0.0533	28
29	2.3566	0.4243	45.2188	19.1884	0.0221	0.0521	29
30	2.4273	0.4120	47.5754	19.6004	0.0210	0.0510	30
35	2.8139	0.3554	60.4620	21.4872	0.0165	0.0465	35
40	3.2620	0.3066	75.4012	23.1148	0.0133	0.0433	40
45	3.7816	0.2644	92.7197	24.5187	0.0108	0.0408	45
50	4.3839	0.2281	112.797	25.7298	0.0089	0.0389	50
55	5.0821	0.1968	136.071	26.7744	0.0073	0.0373	55
60	5.8916	0.1697	163.053	27.6756	0.0061	0.0361	60
65	6.8300	0.1464	194.332	28.4529	0.0051	0.0351	65
70	7.9178	0.1263	230.594	29.1234	0.0043	0.0343	70
75	9.1789	0.1089	272.630	29.7018	0.0037	0.0337	75
80	10.6409	0.0940	321.362	30.2008	0.0031	0.0331	80
85	12.3357	0.0811	377.856	30.6311	0.0026	0.0326	85
90	14.3004	0.0699	443.35	31.0024	0.0023	0.0323	90
95	16.5781	0.0603	519.27	31.3227	0.0019	0.0319	95
100	19.2186	0.0520	607.29	31.5989	0.0016	0.0316	100
∞				33.3333		0.0300	∞

DISCRETE COMPOUNDING; $i = 4\%$

	SINGLE PAYMENT		UNIFORM SERIES				
	Compound Amount Factor	Present Worth Factor	Compound Amount Factor	Present Worth Factor	Sinking Fund Factor	Capital Recovery Factor	
N	To find F Given P F/P	To find P Given F P/F	To find F Given A F/A	To find P Given A P/A	To find A Given F A/F	To find A Given P A/P	N
1	1.0400	0.9615	1.0000	0.9615	1.0000	1.0400	1
2	1.0816	0.9246	2.0400	1.8861	0.4902	0.5302	2
3	1.1249	0.8890	3.1216	2.7751	0.3203	0.3603	3
4	1.1699	0.8548	4.2465	3.6299	0.2355	0.2755	4
5	1.2167	0.8219	5.4163	4.4518	0.1846	0.2246	5
6	1.2653	0.7903	6.6330	5.2421	0.1508	0.1908	6
7	1.3159	0.7599	7.8983	6.0021	0.1266	0.1666	7
8	1.3686	0.7307	9.2142	6.7327	0.1085	0.1485	8
9	1.4233	0.7026	10.5828	7.4353	0.0945	0.1345	9
10	1.4802	0.6756	12.0061	8.1109	0.0833	0.1233	10
11	1.5395	0.6496	13.4863	8.7605	0.0741	0.1141	11
12	1.6010	0.6246	15.0258	9.3851	0.0666	0.1066	12
13	1.6651	0.6006	16.6268	9.9856	0.0601	0.1001	13
14	1.7317	0.5775	18.2919	10.5631	0.0547	0.0947	14
15	1.8009	0.5553	20.0236	11.1184	0.0499	0.0899	15
16	1.8730	0.5339	21.8245	11.6523	0.0458	0.0858	16
17	1.9479	0.5134	23.6975	12.1657	0.0422	0.0822	17
18	2.0258	0.4936	25.6454	12.6593	0.0390	0.0790	18
19	2.1068	0.4746	27.6712	13.1339	0.0361	0.0761	19
20	2.1911	0.4564	29.7781	13.5903	0.0336	0.0736	20
21	2.2788	0.4388	31.9692	14.0292	0.0313	0.0713	21
22	2.3699	0.4220	34.2480	14.4511	0.0292	0.0692	22
23	2.4647	0.4057	36.6179	14.8568	0.0273	0.0673	23
24	2.5633	0.3901	39.0826	15.2470	0.0256	0.0656	24
25	2.6658	0.3751	41.6459	15.6221	0.0240	0.0640	25
26	2.7725	0.3607	44.3117	15.9828	0.0226	0.0626	26
27	2.8834	0.3468	47.0842	16.3296	0.0212	0.0612	27
28	2.9987	0.3335	49.9676	16.6631	0.0200	0.0600	28
29	3.1187	0.3207	52.9663	16.9837	0.0189	0.0589	29
30	3.2434	0.3083	56.0849	17.2920	0.0178	0.0578	30
35	3.9461	0.2534	73.6522	18.6646	0.0136	0.0536	35
40	4.8010	0.2083	95.0255	19.7928	0.0105	0.0505	40
45	5.8412	0.1712	121.029	20.7200	0.0083	0.0483	45
50	7.1067	0.1407	152.667	21.4822	0.0066	0.0466	50
55	8.6464	0.1157	191.159	22.1086	0.0052	0.0452	55
60	10.5196	0.0951	237.991	22.6235	0.0042	0.0442	60
65	12.7987	0.0781	294.968	23.0467	0.0034	0.0434	65
70	15.5716	0.0642	364.290	23.3945	0.0027	0.0427	70
75	18.9452	0.0528	448.631	23.6804	0.0022	0.0422	75
80	23.0498	0.0434	551.245	23.9154	0.0018	0.0418	80
85	28.0436	0.0357	676.090	24.1085	0.0015	0.0415	85
90	34.1193	0.0293	827.98	24.2673	0.0012	0.0412	90
95	41.5113	0.0241	1012.78	24.3978	0.0010	0.0410	95
100	50.5049	0.0198	1237.62	24.5050	0.0008	0.0408	100
∞				25.0000		0.0400	∞

DISCRETE COMPOUNDING; $i = 5\%$

	SINGLE PAYMENT		UNIFORM SERIES				
	Compound Amount Factor	Present Worth Factor	Compound Amount Factor	Present Worth Factor	Sinking Fund Factor	Capital Recovery Factor	
N	To find F Given P F/P	To find P Given F P/F	To find F Given A F/A	To find P Given A P/A	To find A Given F A/F	To find A Given P A/P	N
1	1.0500	0.9524	1.0000	0.9524	1.0000	0.5378	1
2	1.1025	0.9070	2.0500	1.8594	0.4878	0.5378	2
3	1.1576	0.8638	3.1525	2.7232	0.3172	0.3672	3
4	1.2155	0.8227	4.3101	3.5460	0.2320	0.2820	4
5	1.2763	0.7835	5.5256	4.3295	0.1810	0.2310	5
6	1.3401	0.7462	6.8019	5.0757	0.1470	0.1970	6
7	1.4071	0.7107	8.1420	5.7864	0.1228	0.1728	7
8	1.4775	0.6768	9.5491	6.4632	0.1047	0.1547	8
9	1.5513	0.6446	11.0266	7.1078	0.0907	0.1407	9
10	1.6289	0.6139	12.5779	7.7217	0.0795	0.1295	10
11	1.7103	0.5847	14.2068	8.3064	0.0704	0.1204	11
12	1.7959	0.5568	15.9171	8.8633	0.0628	0.1128	12
13	1.8856	0.5303	17.7130	9.3936	0.0565	0.1065	13
14	1.9799	0.5051	19.5986	9.8986	0.0510	0.1010	14
15	2.0789	0.4810	21.5786	10.3797	0.0463	0.0963	15
16	2.1829	0.4581	23.6575	10.8378	0.0423	0.0923	16
17	2.2920	0.4363	25.8404	11.2741	0.0387	0.0887	17
18	2.4066	0.4155	28.1324	11.6896	0.0355	0.0855	18
19	2.5269	0.3957	30.5390	12.0853	0.0327	0.0827	19
20	2.6533	0.3769	33.0659	12.4622	0.0302	0.0802	20
21	2.7860	0.3589	35.7192	12.8212	0.0280	0.0780	21
22	2.9253	0.3418	38.5052	13.1630	0.0260	0.0760	22
23	3.0715	0.3256	41.4305	13.4886	0.0241	0.0741	23
24	3.2251	0.3101	44.5020	13.7986	0.0225	0.0725	24
25	3.3864	0.2953	47.7271	14.0939	0.0210	0.0710	25
26	3.5557	0.2812	51.1134	14.3752	0.0196	0.0696	26
27	3.7335	0.2678	54.6691	14.6430	0.0183	0.0683	27
28	3.9201	0.2551	58.4026	14.8981	0.0171	0.0671	28
29	4.1161	0.2429	62.3227	15.1411	0.0160	0.0660	29
30	4.3219	0.2314	66.4388	15.3725	0.0151	0.0651	30
35	5.5160	0.1813	90.3203	16.3742	0.0111	0.0611	35
40	7.0400	0.1420	120.800	17.1591	0.0083	0.0583	40
45	8.9850	0.1113	159.700	17.7741	0.0063	0.0563	45
50	11.4674	0.0872	209.348	18.2559	0.0048	0.0548	50
55	14.6356	0.0683	272.713	18.6335	0.0037	0.0537	55
60	18.6792	0.0535	353.584	18.9293	0.0028	0.0528	60
65	23.8399	0.0419	456.798	19.1611	0.0022	0.0522	65
70	30.4264	0.0329	588.528	19.3427	0.0017	0.0517	70
75	38.8327	0.0258	756.653	19.4850	0.0013	0.0513	75
80	49.5614	0.0202	971.228	19.5965	0.0010	0.0510	80
85	63.2543	0.0158	1245.09	19.6838	0.0008	0.0508	85
90	80.7303	0.0124	1594.61	19.7523	0.0006	0.0506	90
95	103.035	0.0097	2040.69	19.8059	0.0005	0.0505	95
100	131.501	0.0076	2610.02	19.8479	0.0004	0.0504	100
∞				20.0000		0.0500	∞

DISCRETE COMPOUNDING; $i = 6\%$

	SINGLE PAYMENT		UNIFORM SERIES				
	Compound Amount Factor	Present Worth Factor	Compund Amount Factor	Present Worth Factor	Sinking Fund Factor	Capital Recovery Factor	
N	To find F Given P F/P	To find P Given F P/F	To find F Given A F/A	To find P Given A P/A	To find A Given F A/F	To find A Given P A/P	N
1	1.0600	0.9434	1.0000	0.9434	1.0000	1.0600	1
2	1.1236	0.8900	2.0600	1.8334	0.4854	0.5454	2
3	1.1910	0.8396	3.1836	2.6730	0.3141	0.3741	3
4	1.2625	0.7921	4.3746	3.4651	0.2286	0.2886	4
5	1.3382	0.7473	5.6371	4.2124	0.1774	0.2374	5
6	1.4185	0.7050	6.9753	4.9173	0.1434	0.2034	6
7	1.5036	0.6651	8.3938	5.5824	0.1191	0.1791	7
8	1.5938	0.6274	9.8975	6.2098	0.1010	0.1610	8
9	1.6895	0.5919	11.4913	6.8017	0.0870	0.1470	9
10	1.7908	0.5584	13.1808	7.3601	0.0759	0.1359	10
11	1.8983	0.5268	14.9716	7.8869	0.0668	0.1268	11
12	2.0122	0.4970	16.8699	8.3838	0.0593	0.1193	12
13	2.1329	0.4688	18.8821	8.8527	0.0530	0.1130	13
14	2.2609	0.4423	21.0151	9.2950	0.0476	0.1076	14
15	2.3966	0.4173	23.2760	9.7122	0.0430	0.1030	15
16	2.5404	0.3936	25.6725	10.1059	0.0390	0.0990	16
17	2.6928	0.3714	28.2129	10.4773	0.0354	0.0954	17
18	2.8543	0.3503	30.9056	10.8276	0.0324	0.0924	18
19	3.0256	0.3305	33.7600	11.1581	0.0296	0.0896	19
20	3.2071	0.3118	36.7856	11.4699	0.0272	0.0872	20
21	3.3996	0.2942	39.9927	11.7641	0.0250	0.0850	21
22	3.6035	0.2775	43.3923	12.0416	0.0230	0.0830	22
23	3.8197	0.2618	46.9958	12.3034	0.0213	0.0813	23
24	4.0489	0.2470	50.8155	12.5504	0.0197	0.0797	24
25	4.2919	0.2330	54.8645	12.7834	0.0182	0.0782	25
26	4.5494	0.2198	59.1563	13.0032	0.0169	0.0769	26
27	4.8223	0.2074	63.7057	13.2105	0.0157	0.0757	27
28	5.1117	0.1956	68.5281	13.4062	0.0146	0.0746	28
29	5.4184	0.1846	73.6397	13.5907	0.0136	0.0736	29
30	5.7435	0.1741	79.0581	13.7648	0.0126	0.0726	30
35	7.6861	0.1301	111.435	14.4982	0.0090	0.0690	35
40	10.2857	0.0972	154.762	15.0463	0.0065	0.0665	40
45	13.7646	0.0727	212.743	15.4558	0.0047	0.0647	45
50	18.4201	0.0543	290.336	15.7619	0.0034	0.0634	50
55	24.6503	0.0406	394.172	15.9905	0.0025	0.0625	55
60	32.9876	0.0303	533.128	16.1614	0.0019	0.0619	60
65	44.1449	0.0227	719.082	16.2891	0.0014	0.0614	65
70	59.0758	0.0169	967.931	16.3845	0.0010	0.0610	70
75	79.0568	0.0126	1300.95	16.4558	0.0008	0.0608	75
80	105.796	0.0095	1746.60	16.5091	0.0006	0.0606	80
85	141.579	0.0071	2342.98	16.5489	0.0004	0.0604	85
90	189.464	0.0053	3141.07	16.5787	0.0003	0.0603	90
95	253.546	0.0039	4209.10	16.6009	0.0002	0.0602	95
100	339.301	0.0029	5638.36	16.6175	0.0002	0.0602	100
∞				18.182		0.0600	∞

DISCRETE COMPOUNDING; $i = 8\%$

	SINGLE PAYMENT		UNIFORM SERIES				
	Compound Amount Factor	Present Worth Factor	Compound Amount Factor	Present Worth Factor	Sinking Fund Factor	Capital Recovery Factor	
N	To find F Given P F/P	To find P Given F P/F	To find F Given A F/A	To find P Given A P/A	To find A Given F A/F	To find A Given P A/P	N
1	1.0800	0.9259	1.0000	0.9259	1.0000	1.0800	1
2	1.1664	0.8573	2.0800	1.7833	0.4808	0.5608	2
3	1.2597	0.7938	3.2464	2.5771	0.3080	0.3880	3
4	1.3605	0.7350	4.5061	3.3121	0.2219	0.3019	4
5	1.4693	0.6806	5.8666	3.9927	0.1705	0.2505	5
6	1.5869	0.6302	7.3359	4.6229	0.1363	0.2163	6
7	1.7138	0.5835	8.9228	5.2064	0.1121	0.1921	7
8	1.8509	0.5403	10.6366	5.7466	0.0940	0.1740	8
9	1.9990	0.5002	12.4876	6.2469	0.0801	0.1601	9
10	2.1589	0.4632	14.4866	6.7101	0.0690	0.1490	10
11	2.3316	0.4289	16.6455	7.1390	0.0601	0.1401	11
12	2.5182	0.3971	18.9771	7.5361	0.0527	0.1327	12
13	2.7196	0.3677	21.4953	7.9038	0.0465	0.1265	13
14	2.9372	0.3405	24.2149	8.2442	0.0413	0.1213	14
15	3.1722	0.3152	27.1521	8.5595	0.0368	0.1168	15
16	3.4259	0.2919	30.3243	8.8514	0.0330	0.1130	16
17	3.7000	0.2703	33.7502	9.1216	0.0296	0.1096	17
18	3.9960	0.2502	37.4502	9.3719	0.0267	0.1067	18
19	4.3157	0.2317	41.4463	9.6036	0.0241	0.1041	19
20	4.6610	0.2145	45.7620	9.8181	0.0219	0.1019	20
21	5.0338	0.1987	50.4229	10.0168	0.0198	0.0998	21
22	5.4365	0.1839	55.4567	10.2007	0.0180	0.0980	22
23	5.8715	0.1703	60.8933	10.3711	0.0164	0.0964	23
24	6.3412	0.1577	66.7647	10.5288	0.0150	0.0950	24
25	6.8485	0.1460	73.1059	10.6748	0.0137	0.0937	25
26	7.3964	0.1352	79.9544	10.8100	0.0125	0.0925	26
27	7.9881	0.1252	87.3507	10.9352	0.0114	0.0914	27
28	8.6271	0.1159	95.3388	11.0511	0.0105	0.0905	28
29	9.3173	0.1073	103.966	11.1584	0.0096	0.0896	29
30	10.0627	0.0994	113.283	11.2578	0.0088	0.0888	30
35	14.7853	0.0676	172.317	11.6546	0.0058	0.0858	35
40	21.7245	0.0460	259.056	11.9246	0.0039	0.0839	40
45	31.9204	0.0313	386.506	12.1084	0.0026	0.0826	45
50	46.9016	0.0213	573.770	12.2335	0.0017	0.0817	50
55	68.9138	0.0145	848.923	12.3186	0.0012	0.0812	55
60	101.257	0.0099	1253.21	12.3766	0.0008	0.0808	60
65	148.780	0.0067	1847.25	12.4160	0.0005	0.0805	65
70	218.606	0.0046	2720.08	12.4428	0.0004	0.0804	70
75	321.204	0.0031	4002.55	12.4611	0.0002	0.0802	75
80	471.955	0.0021	5886.93	12.4735	0.0002	0.0802	80
85	693.456	0.0014	8655.71	12.4820	0.0001	0.0801	85
90	1018.92	0.0010	12723.9	12.4877	a	0.0801	90
95	1497.12	0.0007	18071.5	12.4917	a	0.0801	95
100	2199.76	0.0005	27484.5	12.4943	a	0.0800	100
∞				12.5000		0.0800	∞

a Less than 0.0001.

DISCRETE COMPOUNDING; $i = 10\%$

	SINGLE PAYMENT		UNIFORM SERIES				
	Compound Amount Factor	Present Worth Factor	Compound Amount Factor	Present Worth Factor	Sinking Fund Factor	Capital Recovery Factor	
N	To find F Given P F/P	To find P Given F P/F	To find F Given A F/A	To find P Given A P/A	To find A Given F A/F	To find A Given P A/P	N
1	1.1000	0.9091	1.0000	0.9091	1.0000	1.1000	1
2	1.2100	0.8264	2.1000	1.7355	0.4762	0.5762	2
3	1.3310	0.7513	3.3100	2.4869	0.3021	0.4021	3
4	1.4641	0.6830	4.6410	3.1699	0.2155	0.3155	4
5	1.6105	0.6209	6.1051	3.7908	0.1638	0.2638	5
6	1.7716	0.5645	7.7156	4.3553	0.1296	0.2296	6
7	1.9487	0.5132	9.4872	4.8684	0.1054	0.2054	7
8	2.1436	0.4665	11.4359	5.3349	0.0874	0.1874	8
9	2.3579	0.4241	13.5795	5.7590	0.0736	0.1736	9
10	2.5937	0.3855	15.9374	6.1446	0.0627	0.1627	10
11	2.8531	0.3505	18.5312	6.4951	0.0540	0.1540	11
12	3.1384	0.3186	21.3843	6.8137	0.0468	0.1468	12
13	3.4523	0.2897	24.5227	7.1034	0.0408	0.1408	13
14	3.7975	0.2633	27.9750	7.3667	0.0357	0.1357	14
15	4.1772	0.2394	31.7725	7.6061	0.0315	0.1315	15
16	4.5950	0.2176	35.9497	7.8237	0.0278	0.1278	16
17	5.0545	0.1978	40.5447	8.0216	0.0247	0.1247	17
18	5.5599	0.1799	45.5992	8.2014	0.0219	0.1219	18
19	6.1159	0.1635	51.1591	8.3649	0.0195	0.1195	19
20	6.7275	0.1486	57.2750	8.5136	0.0175	0.1175	20
21	7.4002	0.1351	64.0025	8.6487	0.0156	0.1156	21
22	8.1403	0.1228	71.4027	8.7715	0.0140	0.1140	22
23	8.9543	0.1117	79.5430	8.8832	0.0126	0.1126	23
24	9.8497	0.1015	88.4973	8.9847	0.0113	0.1113	24
25	10.8347	0.0923	98.3470	9.0770	0.0102	0.1102	25
26	11.9182	0.0839	109.182	9.1609	0.0092	0.1092	26
27	13.1100	0.0763	121.100	9.2372	0.0083	0.1083	27
28	14.4210	0.0693	134.210	9.3066	0.0075	0.1075	28
29	15.8631	0.0630	148.631	9.3696	0.0067	0.1067	29
30	17.4494	0.0573	164.494	9.4269	0.0061	0.1061	30
35	28.1024	0.0356	271.024	9.6442	0.0037	0.1037	35
40	45.2592	0.0221	442.592	9.7791	0.0023	0.1023	40
45	72.8904	0.0137	718.905	9.8628	0.0014	0.1014	45
50	117.391	0.0085	1163.91	9.9148	0.0009	0.1009	50
55	189.059	0.0053	1880.59	9.9471	0.0005	0.1005	55
60	304.481	0.0033	3034.81	9.9672	0.0003	0.1003	60
65	490.370	0.0020	4893.71	9.9796	0.0002	0.1002	65
70	789.746	0.0013	7887.47	9.9873	0.0001	0.1001	70
75	1271.89	0.0008	12708.9	9.9921	a	0.1001	75
80	2048.40	0.0005	20474.0	9.9951	a	0.1000	80
85	3298.97	0.0003	32979.7	9.9970	a	0.1000	85
90	5313.02	0.0002	53120.2	9.9981	a	0.1000	90
95	8556.67	0.0001	85556.7	9.9988	a	0.1000	95
100	13780.6	a	137796	9.9993	a	0.1000	100
∞				10.0000		0.1000	∞

a Less than 0.0001.

DISCRETE COMPOUNDING; $i = 12\%$

	SINGLE PAYMENT		UNIFORM SERIES				
	Compound Amount Factor	Present Worth Factor	Compound Amount Factor	Present Worth Factor	Sinking Fund Factor	Capital Recovery Factor	
N	To find F Given P F/P	To find P Given F P/F	To find F Given A F/A	To find P Given A P/A	To find A Given F A/F	To find A Given P A/P	N
1	1.1200	0.8929	1.0000	0.8929	1.0000	1.1200	1
2	1.2544	0.7972	2.1200	1.6901	0.4717	0.5917	2
3	1.4049	0.7118	3.3744	2.4018	0.2963	0.4163	3
4	1.5735	0.6355	4.7793	3.0373	0.2092	0.3292	4
5	1.7623	0.5674	6.3528	3.6048	0.1574	0.2774	5
6	1.9738	0.5066	8.1152	4.1114	0.1232	0.2432	6
7	2.2107	0.4523	10.0890	4.5638	0.0991	0.2191	7
8	2.4760	0.4039	12.2997	4.9676	0.0813	0.2013	8
9	2.7731	0.3606	14.7757	5.3282	0.0677	0.1877	9
10	3.1058	0.3220	17.5487	5.6502	0.0570	0.1770	10
11	3.4785	0.2875	20.6546	5.9377	0.0484	0.1684	11
12	3.8960	0.2567	24.1331	6.1944	0.0414	0.1614	12
13	4.3635	0.2292	28.0291	6.4235	0.0357	0.1557	13
14	4.8871	0.2046	32.3926	6.6282	0.0309	0.1509	14
15	5.4736	0.1827	37.2797	6.8109	0.0268	0.1468	15
16	6.1304	0.1631	42.7533	6.9740	0.0234	0.1434	16
17	.6.8660	0.1456	48.8837	7.1196	0.0205	0.1405	17
18	7.6900	0.1300	55.7497	7.2497	0.0179	0.1379	18
19	8.6128	0.1161	63.4397	7.3658	0.0158	0.1358	19
20	9.6463	0.1037	72.0524	7.4694	0.0139	0.1339	20
21	10.8038	0.0926	81.6987	7.5620	0.0122	0.1322	21
22	12.1003	0.0826	92.5026	7.6446	0.0108	0.1308	22
23	13.5523	0.0738	104.603	7.7184	0.0096	0.1296	23
24	15.1786	0.0659	118.155	7.7843	0.0085	0.1285	24
25	17.0001	0.0588	133.334	7.8431	0.0075	0.1275	25
26	19.0401	0.0525	150.334	7.8957	0.0067	0.1267	26
27	21.3249	0.0469	169.374	7.9426	0.0059	01.259	27
28	23.8839	0.0419	190.699	7.9844	0.0052	0.1252	28
29	26.7499	0.0374	214.583	8.0218	0.0047	0.1247	29
30	29.9599	0.0334	241.333	8.0552	0.0041	0.1241	30
35	52.7996	0.0189	431.663	8.1755	0.0023	0.1223	35
40	93.0509	0.0107	767.091	8.2438	0.0013	0.1213	40
45	163.988	0.0061	1358.23	8.2825	0.0007	0.1207	45
50	289.002	0.0035	2400.02	8.3045	0.0004	0.1204	50
55	509.320	0.0020	4236.00	8.3170	0.0002	0.1202	55
60	897.596	0.0011	7471.63	8.3240	0.0001	0.1201	60
65	1581.87	0.0006	13173.9	8.3281	a	0.1201	65
70	2787.80	0.0004	23223.3	8.3303	a	0.1200	70
75	4913.05	0.0002	40933.8	8.3316	a	0.1200	75
80	8658.47	0.0001	72145.6	8.3324	a	0.1200	80
∞				8.333		0.1200	∞

a Less than 0.0001.

DISCRETE COMPOUNDING; $i = 15\%$

	SINGLE PAYMENT		UNIFORM SERIES				
	Compound Amount Factor	Present Worth Factor	Compound Amount Factor	Present Worth Factor	Sinking Fund Factor	Capital Recovery Factor	
N	To find F Given P F/P	To find P Given F P/F	To find F Given A F/A	To find P Given A P/A	To find A Given F A/F	To find A Given P A/P	N
1	1.1500	0.8696	1.0000	0.8696	1.0000	1.1500	1
2	1.3225	0.7561	2.1500	1.6257	0.4651	0.6151	2
3	1.5209	0.6575	3.4725	2.2832	0.2880	0.4380	3
4	1.7490	0.5718	4.9934	2.8550	0.2003	0.3503	4
5	2.0114	0.4972	6.7424	3.3522	0.1483	0.2983	5
6	2.3131	0.4323	8.7537	3.7845	0.1142	0.2642	6
7	2.6600	0.3759	11.0668	4.1604	0.0904	0.2404	7
8	3.0590	0.3269	13.7268	4.4873	0.0729	0.2229	8
9	3.5179	0.2843	16.7858	4.7716	0.0596	0.2096	9
10	4.0456	0.2472	20.3037	5.0188	0.0493	0.1993	10
11	4.6524	0.2149	24.3493	5.2337	0.0411	0.1911	11
12	5.3502	0.1869	29.0017	5.4206	0.0345	0.1845	12
13	6.1528	0.1625	34.3519	5.5831	0.0291	0.1791	13
14	7.0757	0.1413	40.5047	5.7245	0.0247	0.1747	14
15	8.1371	0.1229	47.5804	5.8474	0.0210	0.1710	15
16	9.3576	0.1069	55.7175	5.9542	0.0179	0.1679	16
17	10.7613	0.0929	65.0751	6.0472	0.0154	0.1654	17
18	12.3755	0.0808	75.8363	6.1280	0.0132	0.1632	18
19	14.2318	0.0703	88.2118	6.1982	0.0113	0.1613	19
20	16.3665	0.0611	102.444	6.2593	0.0098	0.1598	20
21	18.8215	0.0531	118.810	6.3125	0.0084	0.1584	21
22	21.6447	0.0462	137.632	6.3587	0.0073	0.1573	22
23	24.8915	0.0402	159.276	6.3988	0.0063	0.1563	23
24	28.6252	0.0349	184.168	6.4338	0.0054	0.1554	24
25	32.9189	0.0304	212.793	6.4641	0.0047	0.1547	25
26	37.8568	0.0264	245.712	6.4906	0.0041	0.1541	26
27	43.5353	0.0230	283.569	6.5135	0.0035	0.1535	27
28	50.0656	0.0200	327.104	6.5335	0.0031	0.1531	28
29	57.5754	0.0174	377.170	6.5509	0.0027	0.1527	29
30	66.2118	0.0151	434.745	6.5660	0.0023	0.1523	30
35	133.176	0.0075	881.170	6.6166	0.0011	0.1511	35
40	267.863	0.0037	1779.09	6.6418	0.0006	0.1506	40
45	538.769	0.0019	3585.13	6.6543	0.0003	0.1503	45
50	1083.66	0.0009	7217.71	6.6605	0.0001	0.1501	50
55	2179.62	0.0005	14524.1	6.6636	a	0.1501	55
60	4384.00	0.0002	29220.0	6.6651	a	0.1500	60
65	8817.78	0.0001	58778.5	6.6659	a	0.1500	65
70	17735.7	a	118231	6.6663	a	0.1500	70
75	35672.8	a	237812	6.6665	a	0.1500	75
80	71750.8	a	478332	6.6666	a	0.1500	80
∞				6.667		0.1500	∞

a Less than 0.0001.

DISCRETE COMPOUNDING; $i = 20\%$

	SINGLE PAYMENT		UNIFORM SERIES				
	Compound Amount Factor	Present Worth Factor	Compound Amount Factor	Present Worth Factor	Sinking Fund Factor	Capital Recovery Factor	
N	To find F Given P F/P	To find P Given F P/F	To find F Given A F/A	To find P Given A P/A	To find A Given F A/F	To find A Given P A/P	N
1	1.2000	0.8333	1.0000	0.8333	1.0000	1.2000	1
2	1.4400	0.6944	2.2000	1.5278	0.4545	0.6545	2
3	1.7280	0.5787	3.6400	2.1065	0.2747	0.4747	3
4	2.0736	0.4823	5.3680	2.5887	0.1863	0.3863	4
5	2.4883	0.4019	7.4416	2.9906	0.1344	0.3344	5
6	2.9860	0.3349	9.9299	3.3255	0.1007	0.3007	6
7	3.5832	0.2791	12.9159	3.6046	0.0774	0.2774	7
8	4.2998	0.2326	16.4991	3.8372	0.0606	0.2606	8
9	5.1598	0.1938	20.7989	4.0310	0.0481	0.2481	9
10	6.1917	0.1615	25.9587	4.1925	0.0385	0.2385	10
11	7.4301	0.1346	32.1504	4.3271	0.0311	0.2311	11
12	8.9161	0.1122	39.5805	4.4392	0.0253	0.2253	12
13	10.6993	0.0935	48.4966	4.5327	0.0206	0.2206	13
14	12.8392	0.0779	59.1959	4.6106	0.0169	0.2169	14
15	15.4070	0.0649	72.0351	4.6755	0.0139	0.2139	15
16	18.4884	0.0541	87.4421	4.7296	0.0114	0.2114	16
17	22.1861	0.0451	105.931	4.7746	0.0094	0.2094	17
18	26.6233	0.0376	128.117	4.8122	0.0078	0.2078	18
19	31.9480	0.0313	154.740	4.8435	0.0065	0.2065	19
20	38.3376	0.0261	186.688	4.8696	0.0054	0.2054	20
21	46.0051	0.0217	225.026	4.8913	0.0044	0.2044	21
22	55.2061	0.0181	271.031	4.9094	0.0037	0.2037	22
23	66.2474	0.0151	326.237	4.9245	0.0031	0.2031	23
24	79.4968	0.0126	392.484	4.9371	0.0025	0.2025	24
25	95.3962	0.0105	471.981	4.9476	0.0021	0.2021	25
26	114.475	0.0087	567.377	4.9563	0.0018	0.2018	26
27	137.371	0.0073	681.853	4.9636	0.0015	0.2015	27
28	164.845	0.0061	819.223	4.9697	0.0012	0.2012	28
29	197.814	0.0051	984.068	4.9747	0.0010	0.2010	29
30	237.376	0.0042	1181.88	4.9789	0.0008	0.2008	30
35	590.668	0.0017	2948.34	4.9915	0.0003	0.2003	35
40	1469.77	0.0007	7343.85	4.9966	0.0001	0.2001	40
45	3657.26	0.0003	18281.3	4.9986	a	0.2001	45
50	9100.43	0.0001	45497.2	4.9995	a	0.2000	50
55	22644.8	a	113219	4.9998	a	0.2000	55
60	56347.5	a	281732	4.9999	a	0.2000	60
∞				5.0000		0.2000	∞

a Less than 0.0001.

	SINGLE PAYMENT		UNIFORM SERIES				
	Compound Amount Factor	Present Worth Factor	Compound Amount Factor	Present Worth Factor	Sinking Fund Factor	Capital Recovery Factor	
N	To find F Given P F/P	To find P Given F P/F	To find F Given A F/A	To find P Given A P/A	To find A Given F A/F	To find A Given P A/P	N
1	1.2500	0.8000	1.0000	0.8000	1.0000	1.2500	1
2	1.5625	0.6400	2.2500	1.4400	0.4444	0.6944	2
3	1.9531	0.5120	3.8125	1.9520	0.2623	0.5123	3
4	2.4414	0.4096	5.7656	2.3616	0.1734	0.4234	4
5	3.0518	0.3277	8.2070	2.6893	0.1218	0.3718	5
6	3.8147	0.2621	11.2588	2.9514	0.0888	0.3388	6
7	4.7684	0.2097	15.0735	3.1611	0.0663	0.3163	7
8	5.9605	0.1678	19.8419	3.3289	0.0504	0.3004	8
9	7.4506	0.1342	25.8023	3.4631	0.0388	0.2888	9
10	9.3132	0.1074	33.2529	3.5705	0.0301	0.2801	10
11	11.6415	0.0859	42.5661	3.6564	0.0235	0.2735	11
12	14.5519	0.0687	54.2077	3.7251	0.0184	0.2684	12
13	18.1899	0.0550	68.7596	3.7801	0.0145	0.2645	13
14	22.7374	0.0440	86.9495	3.8241	0.0115	0.2615	14
15	28.4217	0.0352	109.687	3.8593	0.0091	0.2591	15
16	35.5271	0.0281	138.109	3.8874	0.0072	0.2572	16
17	44.4089	0.0225	173.636	3.9099	0.0058	0.2558	17
18	55.5112	0.0180	218.045	3.9279	0.0046	0.2546	18
19	69.3889	0.0144	273.556	3.9424	0.0037	0.2537	19
20	86.7362	0.0115	342.945	3.9539	0.0029	0.2529	20
21	108.420	0.0092	429.681	3.9631	0.0023	0.2523	21
22	135.525	0.0074	538.101	3.9705	0.0019	0.2519	22
23	169.407	0.0059	673.626	3.9764	0.0015	0.2515	23
24	211.758	0.0047	843.033	3.9811	0.0012	0.2512	24
25	264.698	0.0038	1054.79	3.9849	0.0009	0.2509	25
26	330.872	0.0030	1319.49	3.9879	0.0008	0.2508	26
27	413.590	0.0024	1650.36	3.9903	0.0006	0.2506	27
28	516.988	0.0019	2063.95	3.9923	0.0005	0.2505	28
29	646.235	0.0015	2580.94	3.9938	0.0004	0.2504	29
30	807.794	0.0012	3227.17	3.9950	0.0003	0.2503	30
35	2465.19	0.0004	9856.76	3.9984	0.0001	0.2501	35
40	7523.16	0.0001	30088.7	3.9995	a	0.2500	40
45	22958.9	a	91831.5	3.9998	a	0.2500	45
50	70064.9	a	280256	3.9999	a	0.2500	50
∞				4.0000		0.2500	∞

a Less than 0.0001.

DISCRETE COMPOUNDING; $i = 30\%$

	SINGLE PAYMENT		UNIFORM SERIES				
	Compound Amount Factor	Present Worth Factor	Compound Amount Factor	Present Worth Factor	Sinking Fund Factor	Capital Recovery Factor	
N	To find F Given P F/P	To find P Given F P/F	To find F Given A F/A	To find P Given A P/A	To find A Given F A/F	To find A Given P A/P	N
1	1.3000	0.7692	1.000	0.769	1.0000	1.3000	1
2	1.6900	0.5917	2.300	1.361	0.4348	0.7348	2
3	2.1970	0.4552	3.990	1.816	0.2506	0.5506	3
4	2.8561	0.3501	6.187	2.166	0.1616	0.4616	4
5	3.7129	0.2693	9.043	2.436	0.1106	0.4106	5
6	4.8268	0.2072	12.756	2.643	0.0784	0.3784	6
7	6.2749	0.1594	17.583	2.802	0.0569	0.3569	7
8	8.1573	0.1226	23.858	2.925	0.0419	0.3419	8
9	10.604	0.0943	32.015	3.019	0.0312	0.3312	9
10	13.786	0.0725	42.619	3.092	0.0235	0.3235	10
11	17.922	0.0558	56.405	3.147	0.0177	0.3177	11
12	23.298	0.0429	74.327	3.190	0.0135	0.3135	12
13	30.287	0.0330	97.625	3.223	0.0102	0.3102	13
14	39.374	0.0254	127.91	3.249	0.0078	0.3078	14
15	51.186	0.0195	167.29	3.268	0.0060	0.3060	15
16	66.542	0.0150	218.47	3.283	0.0046	0.3046	16
17	86.504	0.0116	285.01	3.295	0.0035	0.3035	17
18	112.46	0.0089	371.52	3.304	0.0027	0.3027	18
19	146.19	0.0068	483.97	3.311	0.0021	0.3021	19
20	190.05	0.0053	630.16	3.316	0.0016	0.3016	20
21	247.06	0.0040	820.21	3.320	0.0012	0.3012	21
22	321.18	0.0031	1067.3	3.323	0.0009	0.3009	22
23	417.54	0.0024	1388.5	3.325	0.0007	0.3007	23
24	542.80	0.0018	1806.0	3.327	0.0005	0.3005	24
25	705.64	0.0014	2348.8	3.329	0.0004	0.3004	25
26	917.33	0.0011	3054.4	3.330	0.0003	0.3003	26
27	1192.5	0.0008	3971.8	3.331	0.0003	0.3003	27
28	1550.3	0.0006	5164.3	3.331	0.0002	0.3002	28
29	2015.4	0.0005	6714.6	3.332	0.0002	0.3002	29
30	2620.0	0.0004	8730.0	3.332	0.0001	0.3001	30
31	3406.0	0.0003	11350.	3.332	a	0.3001	31
32	4427.8	0.0002	14756.	3.333	a	0.3001	32
33	5756.1	0.0002	19184.	3.333	a	0.3001	33
34	7483.0	0.0001	24940.	3.333	a	0.3000	34
35	9727.8	0.0001	32423.	3.333	a	0.3000	35
∞				3.333		0.3000	∞

a Less than 0.0001

DISCRETE COMPOUNDING; $i = 40\%$

	SINGLE PAYMENT		UNIFORM SERIES				
	Compound Amount Factor	Present Worth Factor	Compound Amount Factor	Present Worth Factor	Sinking Fund Factor	Capital Recovery Factor	
N	To find F Given P F/P	To find P Given F P/F	To find F Given A F/A	To find P Given A P/A	To find A Given F A/F	To find A Given P A/P	N
1	1.4000	0.7143	1.000	0.714	1.000	1.4000	1
2	1.9600	0.5102	2.400	1.224	0.4167	0.8167	2
3	2.7440	0.3644	4.360	1.589	0.2294	0.6294	3
4	3.8416	0.2603	7.104	1.849	0.1408	0.5408	4
5	5.3782	0.1859	10.946	2.035	0.0934	0.4914	5
6	7.5295	0.1328	16.324	2.168	0.0613	0.4613	6
7	10.541	0.0949	23.853	2.263	0.0419	0.4419	7
8	14.758	0.0678	34.395	2.331	0.0291	0.4291	8
9	20.661	0.0484	49.153	2.379	0.0203	0.4203	9
10	28.925	0.0346	69.814	2.414	0.0143	0.4143	10
11	40.496	0.0247	98.739	2.438	0.0101	0.4101	11
12	56.694	0.0176	139.23	2.456	0.0072	0.4072	12
13	79.371	0.0126	195.93	2.469	0.0051	0.4051	13
14	111.12	0.0090	275.30	2.478	0.0036	0.4036	14
15	155.57	0.0064	386.42	2.484	0.0026	0.4026	15
16	217.80	0.0046	541.99	2.489	0.0018	0.4019	16
17	304.91	0.0033	759.78	2.492	0.0013	0.4013	17
18	426.88	0.0023	1064.7	2.494	0.0009	0.4009	18
19	597.63	0.0017	1491.6	2.496	0.0007	0.4007	19
20	836.68	0.0012	2089.2	2.497	0.0005	0.4005	20
21	1171.4	0.0009	2925.9	2.498	0.0003	0.4003	21
22	1639.9	0.0006	4097.2	2.498	0.0002	0.4002	22
23	2295.9	0.0004	5737.1	2.499	0.0002	0.4002	23
24	3214.2	0.0003	8033.0	2.499	0.0001	0.4001	24
25	4499.9	0.0002	11247.	2.499	a	0.4001	25
26	6299.8	0.0002	15747.	2.500	a	0.4001	26
27	8819.8	0.0001	22047.	2.500	a	0.4000	27
28	12348.	0.0001	30867.	2.500	a	0.4000	28
29	17287.	0.0001	43214.	2.500	a	0.4000	29
30	24201.	a	60501.	2.500	a	0.4000	30
∞				2.500		0.4000	∞

a Less than 0.0001

DISCRETE COMPOUNDING; $i = 50\%$

	SINGLE PAYMENT		UNIFORM SERIES				
	Compound Amount Factor	Present Worth Factor	Compound Amount Factor	Present Worth Factor	Sinking Fund Factor	Capital Recovery Factor	
N	To find F Given P F/P	To find P Given F P/F	To find F Given A F/A	To find P Given A P/A	To find A Given F A/F	To find A Given P A/P	N
1	1.5000	0.6667	1.000	0.667	1.0000	1.5000	1
2	2.2500	0.4444	2.500	1.111	0.4000	0.9000	2
3	3.3750	0.2963	4.750	1.407	0.2101	0.7105	3
4	5.0625	0.1975	8.125	1.605	0.1231	0.6231	4
5	7.5938	0.1317	13.188	1.737	0.0758	0.5758	5
6	11.391	0.0878	20.781	1.824	0.0481	0.5481	6
7	17.086	0.0585	32.172	1.883	0.0311	0.5311	7
8	25.629	0.0390	49.258	1.922	0.0203	0.5203	8
9	38.443	0.0260	74.887	1.948	0.0134	0.5134	9
10	57.665	0.0173	113.33	1.965	0.0088	0.5088	10
11	86.498	0.0116	171.00	1.977	0.0059	0.5059	11
12	129.75	0.0077	257.49	1.985	0.0039	0.5039	12
13	194.62	0.0051	387.24	1.990	0.0026	0.5026	13
14	291.93	0.0034	581.86	1.993	0.0017	0.5017	14
15	437.89	0.0023	873.79	1.995	0.0011	0.5011	15
16	656.84	0.0015	1311.7	1,997	0.0008	0.5008	16
17	985.26	0.0010	1968.5	1.998	0.0005	0.5005	17
18	1477.9	0.0007	2953.8	1.999	0.0003	0.5003	18
19	2216.8	0.0005	4431.7	1.999	0.0002	0.5002	19
20	3325.3	0.0003	6648.5	1.999	0.0002	0.5002	20
21	4987.9	0.0002	9973.8	2.000	0.0001	0.5001	21
22	7481.8	0.0001	14962.	2.000	a	0.5001	22
23	11223.	0.0001	22443.	2.000	a	0.5000	23
24	16834.	0.0001	33666.	2.000	a	0.5000	24
25	25251.	a	50500.	2.000	a	0.5000	25
∞				2.000		0.5000	∞

a Less than 0.0001

Table A-20

GRADIENT TO PRESENT WORTH CONVERSION FACTOR FOR DISCRETE COMPOUNDING. (TO FIND P, GIVEN G)

$$(P/G, i\%, N) = \frac{1}{i}\left[\frac{(1+i)^N - 1}{i(1+i)^N} - \frac{N}{(1+i)^N}\right]$$

n	1%	2%	4%	6%	8%	10%	12%	15%	20%	25%	n
1	0.00	0.00	0.00	0.00	0.00	0.00	0.00	0.00	0.00	0.00	1
2	0.98	0.96	0.92	0.89	0.86	0.83	0.80	0.76	0.69	0.64	2
3	2.92	2.85	2.70	2.57	2.45	2.33	2.22	2.07	1.85	1.66	3
4	5.80	5.62	5.27	4.95	4.65	4.38	4.13	3.79	3.30	2.89	4
5	9.61	9.24	8.55	7.93	7.37	6.86	6.40	5.78	4.91	4.20	5
6	14.32	13.68	12.50	11.46	10.52	9.68	8.93	7.94	6.58	5.51	6
7	19.92	18.90	17.07	15.45	14.02	12.76	11.64	10.19	8.26	6.77	7
8	26.38	24.88	22.18	19.84	17.81	16.03	14.47	12.48	9.88	7.95	8
9	33.69	31.57	27.80	24.58	21.81	19.42	17.36	14.75	11.43	9.02	9
10	41.84	38.95	33.88	29.60	25.98	22.89	20.25	16.98	12.89	9.99	10
11	50.80	47.00	40.38	34.87	30.27	26.40	23.13	19.13	14.23	10.85	11
12	60.57	55.67	47.25	40.34	34.63	29.90	25.95	21.18	15.47	11.60	12
15	94.48	85.20	69.74	57.55	47.89	40.15	33.92	26.69	18.51	13.33	15
20	165.46	144.60	111.56	87.23	69.09	55.41	44.97	33.58	21.74	14.89	20
25	252.89	214.26	156.10	115.97	87.80	67.70	53.10	38.03	23.43	15.56	25
30	355.00	291.72	201.06	142.36	103.46	77.08	58.78	40.75	24.26	15.83	30
35	470.15	374.88	244.88	165.74	116.09	83.99	62.61	42.36	24.66	15.94	35
40	596.85	461.99	286.53	185.96	126.04	88.95	65.12	43.28	24.85	15.98	40
45	733.70	551.56	325.40	203.11	133.73	92.45	66.73	43.81	24.93	15.99	45
50	879.41	642.36	361.16	217.46	139.59	94.89	67.76	44.10	24.97	16.00	50
60	1192.80	823.70	423.00	239.04	147.30	97.70	68.81	44.34	24.99	—	60
70	1528.64	999.83	472.48	253.33	151.53	98.99	69.21	44.42	—	—	70
80	1879.87	1166.79	511.12	262.55	153.80	99.56	69.36	44.47	—	—	80
90	2240.55	1322.17	540.77	268.39	154.99	99.81	—	—	—	—	90
100	2605.76	1464.75	563.12	272.05	155.61	99.92	—	—	—	—	100

GRADIENT TO UNIFORM SERIES CONVERSION FACTOR FOR DISCRETE COMPOUNDING. (TO FIND A, GIVEN G)

$$(A/G, i\%, N) = \left[\frac{1}{i} - \frac{N}{(1+i)^N - 1}\right]$$

n	1%	2%	4%	6%	8%	10%	12%	15%	20%	25%	n
1	0.0001	0.0000	0.0000	0.0000	0.0000	0.0000	0.0000	0.0000	0.0000	0.0000	1
2	0.4974	0.4950	0.4902	0.4854	0.4808	0.4762	0.4717	0.4651	0.4545	0.4444	2
3	0.9932	0.9868	0.9739	0.9612	0.9487	0.9366	0.9246	0.9071	0.8791	0.8525	3
4	1.4874	1.4752	1.4510	1.4272	1.4040	1.3812	1.3589	1.3263	1.2742	1.2249	4
5	1.9799	1.9604	1.9216	1.8836	1.8465	1.8101	1.7746	1.7228	1.6405	1.5631	5
6	2.4708	2.4422	2.3857	2.3304	2.2763	2.2236	2.1720	2.0972	1.9788	1.8683	6
7	2.9600	2.9208	2.8433	2.7676	2.6937	2.6216	2.5515	2.4498	2.2902	2.1424	7
8	3.4476	3.3961	3.2944	3.1952	3.0985	3.0045	2.9131	2.7813	2.5756	2.3872	8
9	3.9335	3.8680	3.7391	3.6133	3.4910	3.3724	3.2574	3.0922	2.8364	2.6048	9
10	4.4177	4.3367	4.1773	4.0220	3.8713	3.7255	3.5847	3.3832	3.0739	2.7971	10
11	4.9003	4.8021	4.6090	4.4213	4.2395	4.0641	3.8953	3.6549	3.2893	2.9663	11
12	5.3813	5.2642	5.0343	4.8113	4.5957	4.3884	4.1897	3.9082	3.4841	3.1145	12
15	6.8141	6.6309	6.2721	5.9260	5.5945	5.2789	4.9803	4.5650	3.9588	3.4530	15
20	9.1692	8.8433	8.2091	7.6051	7.0369	6.5081	6.0202	5.3651	4.4643	3.7667	20
25	11.4829	10.9744	9.9925	9.0722	8.2254	7.4580	6.7708	5.8834	4.7352	3.9052	25
30	13.7555	13.0251	11.6274	10.3422	9.1897	8.1762	7.2974	6.2066	4.8731	3.9628	30
35	15.9869	14.9961	13.1198	11.4319	9.9611	8.7086	7.6577	6.4019	4.9406	3.9858	35
40	18.1774	16.8885	14.4765	12.3590	10.5699	9.0962	7.8988	6.5168	4.9728	3.9947	40
45	20.3271	18.7033	15.7047	13.1413	11.0447	9.3740	8.0572	6.5830	4.9877	3.9980	45
50	22.4362	20.4420	16.8122	13.7964	11.4107	9.5704	8.1597	6.6205	4.9945	3.9993	50
60	26.5331	23.6961	18.6972	14.7909	11.9015	9.8023	8.2664	6.6530	4.9989	—	60
70	30.4701	26.6632	20.1961	15.4613	12.1783	9.9113	8.3082	6.6627	—	—	70
80	34.2490	29.3572	21.3718	15.9033	12.3301	9.9609	8.3241	6.6656	—	—	80
90	37.8723	31.7929	22.2826	16.1891	12.4116	9.9831	—	—	—	—	90
100	41.3424	33.9863	22.9800	16.3711	12.4545	9.9927	—	—	—	—	100

tables of continuous compounding interest factors (for various common values of r from 2% to 25%)

CONTINUOUS COMPOUNDING; $r = 2\%$

	Discrete Flows				Continuous Flows		
	SINGLE PAYMENT		UNIFORM SERIES		UNIFORM SERIES		
	Compound Amount Factor	Present Worth Factor	Compound Amount Factor	Present Worth Factor	Compound Amount Factor	Present Worth Factor	
N	To find F Given P F/P	To find P Given F P/F	To find F Given A F/A	To find P Given A P/A	To find F Given $\overline{A}$ $F/\overline{A}$	To find P Given $\overline{A}$ $P/\overline{A}$	N
1	1.0202	0.9802	1.0000	0.9802	1.0101	0.9901	1
2	1.0408	0.9608	2.0202	1.9410	2.0405	1.9605	2
3	1.0618	0.9418	3.0610	2.8828	3.0918	2.9118	3
4	1.0833	0.9231	4.1228	3.8059	4.1644	3.8442	4
5	1.1052	0.9048	5.2061	4.7107	5.2585	4.7581	5
6	1.1275	0.8869	6.3113	5.5976	6.3748	5.6540	6
7	1.1503	0.8694	7.4388	6.4670	7.5137	6.5321	7
8	1.1735	0.8521	8.5891	7.3191	8.6755	7.3928	8
9	1.1972	0.8353	9.7626	8.1544	9.8609	8.2365	9
10	1.2214	0.8187	10.9598	8.9731	11.0701	9.0635	10
11	1.2461	0.8025	12.1812	9.7756	12.3038	9.8741	11
12	1.2712	0.7866	13.4273	10.5623	13.5625	10.6686	12
13	1.2969	0.7711	14.6985	11.3333	14.8465	11.4474	13
14	1.3231	0.7558	15.9955	12.0891	16.1565	12.2108	14
15	1.3499	0.7408	17.3186	12.8299	17.4929	12.9591	15
16	1.3771	0.7261	18.6685	13.5561	18.8564	13.6925	16
17	1.4049	0.7118	20.0456	14.2678	20.2474	14.4115	17
18	1.4333	0.6977	21.4505	14.9655	21.6665	15.1162	18
19	1.4623	0.6839	22.8839	15.6494	23.1142	15.8069	19
20	1.4918	0.6703	24.3461	16.3197	24.5912	16.4840	20
21	1.5220	0.6570	25.8380	16.9768	26.0981	17.1477	21
22	1.5527	0.6440	27.3599	17.6208	27.6354	17.7982	22
23	1.5841	0.6313	28.9126	18.2521	29.2037	18.4358	23
24	1.6161	0.6188	30.4967	18.8709	30.8037	19.0608	24
25	1.6487	0.6065	32.1128	19.4774	32.4361	19.6735	25
26	1.6820	0.5945	33.7615	20.0719	34.1014	20.2740	26
27	1.7160	0.5827	35.4435	20.6547	35.8003	20.8626	27
28	1.7507	0.5712	37.1595	21.2259	37.5336	21.4395	28
29	1.7860	0.5599	38.9102	21.7858	39.3019	22.0051	29
30	1.8221	0.5488	40.6962	22.3346	41.1059	22.5594	30
35	2.0138	0.4966	50.1824	24.9199	50.6876	25.1707	35
40	2.2255	0.4493	60.6663	27.2591	61.2770	27.5336	40
45	2.4596	0.4066	72.2528	29.3758	72.9802	29.6715	45
50	2.7183	0.3679	85.0578	31.2910	85.9141	31.6060	50
55	3.0042	0.3329	99.2096	33.0240	100.208	33.3564	55
60	3.3201	0.3012	114.850	34.5921	116.006	34.9403	60
65	3.6693	0.2725	132.135	36.0109	133.465	36.3734	65
70	4.0552	0.2466	151.238	37.2947	152.760	37.6702	70
75	4.4817	0.2231	172.349	38.4564	174.084	38.8435	75
80	4.9530	0.2019	195.682	39.5075	197.652	39.9052	80
85	5.4739	0.1827	221.468	40.4585	223.697	40.8658	85
90	6.0496	0.1653	249.966	41.3191	252.482	41.7351	90
95	6.6859	0.1496	281.461	42.0978	284.295	42.5216	95
100	7.3891	0.1353	316.269	42.8023	319.453	43.2332	100

CONTINUOUS COMPOUNDING; $r = 5\%$

	Discrete Flows				Continuous Flows		
	SINGLE PAYMENT		UNIFORM SERIES		UNIFORM SERIES		
	Compound Amount Factor	Present Worth Factor	Compound Amount Factor	Present Worth Factor	Compound Amount Factor	Present Worth Factor	
N	To find F Given P F/P	To find P Given F P/F	To find F Given A F/A	To find P Given A P/A	To find F Given $\overline{A}$ $F/\overline{A}$	To find P Given $\overline{A}$ $P/\overline{A}$	N
1	1.0513	0.9512	1.0000	0.9512	1.0254	0.9754	1
2	1.1052	0.9048	2.0513	1.8561	2.1034	1.9033	2
3	1.1618	0.8607	3.1564	2.7168	3.2367	2.7858	3
4	1.2214	0.8187	4.3183	3.5355	4.4281	3.6254	4
5	1.2840	0.7788	5.5397	4.3143	5.6805	4.4240	5
6	1.3499	0.7408	6.8237	5.0551	6.9972	5.1836	6
7	1.4191	0.7047	8.1736	5.7598	8.3814	5.9062	7
8	1.4918	0.6703	9.5926	6.4301	9.8365	6.5936	8
9	1.5683	0.6376	11.0845	7.0678	11.3662	7.2474	9
10	1.6487	0.6065	12.6528	7.6743	12.9744	7.8694	10
11	1.7333	0.5759	14.3015	8.2512	14.6651	8.4610	11
12	1.8221	0.5488	16.0347	8.8001	16.4424	9.0238	12
13	1.9155	0.5220	17.8569	9.3221	18.3108	9.5591	13
14	2.0138	0.4966	19.7724	9.8187	20.2751	10.0683	14
15	2.1170	0.4724	21.7862	10.2911	22.3400	10.5527	15
16	2.2255	0.4493	23.9032	10.7404	24.5108	11.0134	16
17	2.3396	0.4274	26.1287	11.1678	26.7929	11.4517	17
18	2.4596	0.4066	28.4683	11.5744	29.1921	11.8686	18
19	2.5857	0.3867	30.9279	11.9611	31.7142	12.2652	19
20	2.7183	0.3679	33.5137	12.3290	34.3656	12.6424	20
21	2.8577	0.3499	36.2319	12.6789	37.1530	13.0012	21
22	3.0042	0.3329	39.0896	13.0118	40.0833	13.3426	22
23	3.1582	0.3166	42.0938	13.3284	43.1639	13.6673	23
24	3.3201	0.3012	45.2519	13.6296	46.4023	13.9761	24
25	3.4903	0.2865	48.5721	13.9161	49.8069	14.2699	25
26	3.6693	0.2725	52.0624	14.1887	53.3859	14.5494	26
27	3.8574	0.2592	55.7317	14.4479	57.1485	14.8152	27
28	4.0552	0.2466	59.5891	14.6945	61.1040	15.0681	28
29	4.2631	0.2346	63.6443	14.9291	65.2623	15.3086	29
30	4.4817	0.2231	67.9074	15.1522	69.6338	15.5374	30
35	5.7546	0.1738	92.7346	16.1149	95.0921	16.5245	35
40	7.3891	0.1353	124.613	16.8646	127.781	17.2933	40
45	9.4877	0.1054	165.546	17.4484	169.755	17.8920	45
50	12.1825	0.0821	218.105	17.9032	223.650	18.3583	50
55	15.6426	0.0639	285.592	18.2573	292.853	18.7214	55
60	20.0855	0.0498	372.247	18.5331	381.711	19.0043	60
65	25.7903	0.0388	483.515	18.7479	495.807	19.2245	65
70	33.1155	0.0302	626.385	18.9152	642.309	19.3961	70
75	42.5211	0.0235	809.834	19.0455	830.422	19.5296	75
80	54.5981	0.0183	1045.39	19.1469	1071.963	19.6337	80
85	70.1054	0.0143	1347.84	19.2260	1382.308	19.7147	85
90	90.0171	0.0111	1736.20	19.2875	1780.342	19.7778	90
95	115.584	0.0087	2234.87	19.3354	2291.686	19.8270	95
100	148.413	0.0067	2875.17	19.3727	2948.263	19.8652	100

CONTINUOUS COMPOUNDING; $r = 10\%$

	Discrete Flows				Continuous Flows		
	SINGLE PAYMENT		UNIFORM SERIES		UNIFORM SERIES		
	Compound Amount Factor	Present Worth Factor	Compound Amount Factor	Present Worth Factor	Compound Amount Factor	Present Worth Factor	
	To find F Given P	To find P Given F	To find F Given A	To find P Given A	To find F Given $\overline{A}$	To find P Given $\overline{A}$	
N	F/P	P/F	F/A	P/A	$F/\overline{A}$	$P/\overline{A}$	N
1	1.1052	0.9048	1.0000	0.9048	1.0517	0.9516	1
2	1.2214	0.8187	2.1052	1.7236	2.2140	1.8127	2
3	1.3499	0.7408	3.3266	2.4644	3.4986	2.5918	3
4	1.4918	0.6703	4.6764	3.1347	4.9182	3.2968	4
5	1.6487	0.6065	6.1683	3.7412	6.4872	3.9347	5
6	1.8221	0.5488	7.8170	4.2900	8.2212	4.5119	6
7	2.0138	0.4966	9.6391	4.7866	10.1375	5.0341	7
8	2.2255	0.4493	11.6528	5.2360	12.2554	5.5067	8
9	2.4596	0.4066	13.8784	5.6425	14.5960	5.9343	9
10	2.7183	0.3679	16.3380	6.0104	17.1828	6.3212	10
11	3.0042	0.3329	19.0563	6.3433	20.0417	6.6713	11
12	3.3201	0.3012	22.0604	6.6445	23.2012	6.9881	12
13	3.6693	0.2725	25.3806	6.9170	26.6930	7.2747	13
14	4.0552	0.2466	29.0499	7.1636	30.5520	7.5340	14
15	4.4817	0.2231	33.1051	7.3867	34.8169	7.7687	15
16	4.9530	0.2019	37.5867	7.5886	39.5303	7.9810	16
17	5.4739	0.1827	42.5398	7.7713	44.7395	8.1732	17
18	6.0496	0.1653	48.0137	7.9366	50.4965	8.3470	18
19	6.6859	0.1496	54.0634	8.0862	56.8589	8.5043	19
20	7.3891	0.1353	60.7493	8.2215	63.8906	8.6466	20
21	8.1662	0.1225	68.1383	8.3440	71.6617	8.7754	21
22	9.0250	0.1108	76.3045	8.4548	80.2501	8.8920	22
23	9.9742	0.1003	85.3295	8.5550	89.7418	8.9974	23
24	11.0232	0.0907	95.3037	8.6458	100.232	9.0928	24
25	12.1825	0.0821	106.327	8.7278	111.825	9.1791	25
26	13.4637	0.0743	118.509	8.8021	124.637	9.2573	26
27	14.8797	0.0672	131.973	8.8693	138.797	9.3279	27
28	16.4446	0.0608	146.853	8.9301	154.446	9.3919	28
29	18.1741	0.0550	163.298	8.9852	171.741	9.4498	29
30	20.0855	0.0498	181.472	9.0349	190.855	9.5021	30
35	33.1155	0.0302	305.364	9.2212	321.154	9.6980	35
40	54.5981	0.0183	509.629	9.3342	535.982	9.8168	40
45	90.0171	0.0111	846.404	9.4027	890.171	9.8889	45
50	148.413	0.0067	1401.65	9.4443	1474.13	9.9326	50
55	244.692	0.0041	2317.10	9.4695	2436.92	9.9591	55
60	403.429	0.0025	3826.43	9.4848	4024.29	9.9752	60
65	665.142	0.0015	6314.88	9.4940	6641.42	9.9850	65
70	1096.63	0.0009	10417.6	9.4997	10956.3	9.9909	70
75	1808.04	0.0006	17182.0	9.5031	18070.7	9.9945	75
80	2980.96	0.0003	28334.4	9.5051	29799.6	9.9966	80
85	4914.77	0.0002	46721.7	9.5064	49137.7	9.9980	85
90	8103.08	0.0001	77037.3	9.5072	81020.8	9.9988	90
95	13359.7	a	127019	9.5076	133587	9.9993	95
100	22026.5	a	209425	9.5079	220255	9.9995	100

a Less than 0.0001.

CONTINUOUS COMPOUNDING; $r = 15\%$

	Discrete Flows				Continuous Flows		
	SINGLE PAYMENT		UNIFORM SERIES		UNIFORM SERIES		
	Compound Amount Factor	Present Worth Factor	Compound Amount Factor	Present Worth Factor	Compound Amount Factor	Present Worth Factor	
N	To find F Given P F/P	To find P Given F P/F	To find F Given A F/A	To find P Given A P/A	To find F Given $\overline{A}$ $F/\overline{A}$	To find P Given $\overline{A}$ $P/\overline{A}$	N
1	1.1618	0.8607	1.0000	0.8607	1.0789	0.9286	1
2	1.3499	0.7408	2.1618	1.6015	2.3324	1.7279	2
3	1.5683	0.6376	3.5117	2.2392	3.7887	2.4158	3
4	1.8221	0.5488	5.0800	2.7880	5.4808	3.0079	4
5	2.1170	0.4724	6.9021	3.2603	7.4467	3.5176	5
6	2.4596	0.4066	9.0191	3.6669	9.7307	3.9562	6
7	2.8577	0.3499	11.4787	4.0168	12.3843	4.3337	7
8	3.3201	0.3012	14.3364	4.3180	15.4674	4.6587	8
9	3.8574	0.2592	17.6565	4.5773	19.0495	4.9384	9
10	4.4817	0.2231	21.5139	4.8004	23.2113	5.1791	10
11	5.2070	0.1920	25.9956	4.9925	28.0465	5.3863	11
12	6.0496	0.1653	31.2026	5.1578	33.6643	5.5647	12
13	7.0287	0.1423	37.2522	5.3000	40.1913	5.7182	13
14	8.1662	0.1225	44.2809	5.4225	47.7745	5.8503	14
15	9.4877	0.1054	52.4471	5.5279	56.5849	5.9640	15
16	11.0232	0.0907	61.9348	5.6186	66.8212	6.0619	16
17	12.8071	0.0781	72.9580	5.6967	78.7140	6.1461	17
18	14.8797	0.0672	85.7651	5.7639	92.5315	6.2186	18
19	17.2878	0.0578	100.645	5.8217	108.585	6.2810	19
20	20.0855	0.0498	117.933	5.8715	127.237	6.3348	20
21	23.3361	0.0429	138.018	5.9144	148.907	6.3810	21
22	27.1126	0.0369	161.354	5.9513	174.084	6.4208	22
23	31.5004	0.0317	188.467	5.9830	203.336	6.4550	23
24	36.5982	0.0273	219.967	6.0103	237.322	6.4845	24
25	42.5211	0.0235	256.565	6.0338	276.807	6.5099	25
26	49.4024	0.0202	299.087	6.0541	322.683	6.5317	26
27	57.3975	0.0174	348.489	6.0715	375.983	6.5505	27
28	66.6863	0.0150	405.886	6.0865	437.909	6.5667	28
29	77.4785	0.0129	472.573	6.0994	509.856	6.5806	29
30	90.0171	0.0111	550.051	6.1105	593.448	6.5926	30
35	190.566	0.0052	1171.36	6.1467	1263.78	6.6317	35
40	403.429	0.0025	2486.67	6.1638	2682.86	6.6501	40
45	854.059	0.0012	5271.19	6.1719	5687.06	6.6589	45
50	1808.04	0.0006	11166.0	6.1757	12046.9	6.6630	50
55	3827.63	0.0003	23645.3	6.1775	25510.8	6.6649	55
60	8103.08	0.0001	50064.1	6.1784	54013.9	6.6658	60
65	17154.2	a	105993	6.1788	114355	6.6663	65
70	36315.5	a	224393	6.1790	242097	6.6665	70
75	76879.9	a	475047	6.1791	512526	6.6666	75
80	162755	a	1005680	6.1791	1085030	6.6666	80

^{a} Less than 0.0001.

CONTINUOUS COMPOUNDING; $r = 20\%$

	Discrete Flows				Continuous Flows	
	SINGLE PAYMENT		UNIFORM SERIES		UNIFORM SERIES	
	Compound Amount Factor	Present Worth Factor	Compound Amount Factor	Present Worth Factor	Compound Amount Factor	Present Worth Factor
N	To find F Given P F/P	To find P Given F P/F	To find F Given A F/A	To find P Given A P/A	To find F Given $\overline{A}$ $F/\overline{A}$	To find P Given $\overline{A}$ $P/\overline{A}$	N
1	1.2214	0.8187	1.0000	0.8187	1.1070	0.9063	1
2	1.4918	0.6703	2.2214	1.4891	2.4591	1.6484	2
3	1.8221	0.5488	3.7132	2.0379	4.1106	2.2559	3
4	2.2255	0.4493	5.5353	2.4872	6.1277	2.7534	4
5	2.7183	0.3679	7.7609	2.8551	8.5914	3.1606	5
6	3.3201	0.3012	10.4792	3.1563	11.6006	3.4940	6
7	4.0552	0.2466	13.7993	3.4029	15.2760	3.7670	7
8	4.9530	0.2019	17.8545	3.6048	19.7652	3.9905	8
9	6.0496	0.1653	22.8075	3.7701	25.2482	4.1735	9
10	7.3891	0.1353	28.8572	3.9054	31.9453	4.3233	10
11	9.0250	0.1108	36.2462	4.0162	40.1251	4.4460	11
12	11.0232	0.0907	45.2712	4.1069	50.1159	4.5464	12
13	13.4637	0.0743	56.2944	4.1812	62.3187	4.6286	13
14	16.4446	0.0608	69.7581	4.2420	77.2232	4.6959	14
15	20.0855	0.0498	86.2028	4.2918	95.4277	4.7511	15
16	24.5325	0.0408	106.288	4.3325	117.663	4.7962	16
17	29.9641	0.0334	130.821	4.3659	144.820	4.8331	17
18	36.5982	0.0273	160.785	4.3932	177.991	4.8634	18
19	44.7012	0.0224	197.383	4.4156	218.506	4.8881	19
20	54.5981	0.0183	242.084	4.4339	267.991	4.9084	20
21	66.6863	0.0150	296.682	4.4489	328.432	4.9250	21
22	81.4509	0.0123	363.369	4.4612	402.254	4.9386	22
23	99.4843	0.0101	444.820	4.4713	492.422	4.9497	23
24	121.510	0.0082	544.304	4.4795	602.552	4.9589	24
25	148.413	0.0067	665.814	4.4862	737.066	4.9663	25
26	181.272	0.0055	814.227	4.4917	901.361	4.9724	26
27	221.406	0.0045	995.500	4.4963	1102.03	4.9774	27
28	270.426	0.0037	1216.91	4.5000	1347.13	4.9815	28
29	330.299	0.0030	1487.33	4.5030	1646.50	4.9849	29
30	403.429	0.0025	1817.63	4.5055	2012.14	4.9876	30
35	1096.63	0.0009	4948.60	4.5125	5478.17	4.9954	35
40	2980.96	0.0003	13459.4	4.5151	14899.8	4.9983	40
45	8103.08	0.0001	36594.3	4.5161	40510.4	4.9994	45
50	22026.5	a	99481.4	4.5165	110127	4.9998	50
55	59874.1	a	270426	4.5166	299366	4.9999	55
60	162755	a	735103	4.5166	813769	5.0000	60

a Less than 0.0001.

CONTINUOUS COMPOUNDING; $r = 25\%$

	Discrete Flows				Continuous Flows		
	SINGLE PAYMENT		UNIFORM SERIES		UNIFORM SERIES		
	Compound Amount Factor	Present Worth Factor	Compound Amount Factor	Present Worth Factor	Compound Amount Factor	Present Worth Factor	
N	To find F Given P F/P	To find P Given F P/F	To find F Given A F/A	To find P Given A P/A	To find F Given $\overline{A}$ $F/\overline{A}$	To find P Given $\overline{A}$ $P/\overline{A}$	N
1	1.2840	0.7788	1.0000	0.7788	1.1361	0.8848	1
2	1.6487	0.6065	2.2840	1.3853	2.5949	1.5739	2
3	2.1170	0.4724	3.9327	1.8577	4.4680	2.1105	3
4	2.7183	0.3679	6.0497	2.2256	6.8731	2.5285	4
5	3.4903	0.2865	8.7680	2.5121	9.9614	2.8540	5
6	4.4817	0.2231	12.2584	2.7352	13.9268	3.1075	6
7	5.7546	0.1738	16.7401	2.9090	19.0184	3.3049	7
8	7.3891	0.1353	22.4947	3.0443	25.5562	3.4587	8
9	9.4877	0.1054	29.8837	3.1497	33.9509	3.5784	9
10	12.1825	0.0821	39.3715	3.2318	44.7300	3.6717	10
11	15.6426	0.0639	51.5539	3.2957	58.5705	3.7443	11
12	20.0855	0.0498	67.1966	3.3455	76.3421	3.8009	12
13	25.7903	0.0388	87.2821	3.3843	99.1614	3.8449	13
14	33.1155	0.0302	113.073	3.4145	128.462	3.8792	14
15	42.5211	0.0235	146.188	3.4380	166.084	3.9059	15
16	54.5982	0.0183	188.709	3.4563	214.393	3.9267	16
17	70.1054	0.0143	243.307	3.4706	276.422	3.9429	17
18	90.0171	0.0111	313.413	3.4817	356.068	3.9556	18
19	115.584	0.0087	403.430	3.4904	458.337	3.9654	19
20	148.413	0.0067	519.014	3.4971	589.653	3.9730	20
21	190.566	0.0052	667.427	3.5023	758.265	3.9790	21
22	244.692	0.0041	857.993	3.5064	974.768	3.9837	22
23	314.191	0.0032	1102.69	3.5096	1252.76	3.9873	23
24	403.429	0.0025	1416.88	3.5121	1609.72	3.9901	24
25	518.013	0.0019	1820.30	3.5140	2068.05	3.9923	25
26	665.142	0.0015	2338.31	3.5155	2656.57	3.9940	26
27	854.059	0.0012	3003.46	3.5167	3412.23	3.9953	27
28	1096.63	0.0009	3857.52	3.5176	4382.53	3.9964	28
29	1408.10	0.0007	4954.15	3.5183	5628.42	3.9972	29
30	1808.04	0.0006	6362.26	3.5189	7228.17	3.9978	30
35	6310.69	0.0002	22215.2	3.5203	25238.8	3.9994	35
40	22026.5	a	77547.5	3.5207	88101.9	3.9998	40
45	76879.9	a	270676	3.5208	307516	3.9999	45
50	268337	a	944762	3.5208	1073350	4.0000	50

a Less than 0.0001.

table of random numbers*

48867	33971	29678	13151	56644	49193	93469	43252	14006	47173
32267	69746	00113	51336	36551	56310	85793	53453	09744	64346
27345	03196	33877	35032	98054	48358	21788	98862	67491	42221
55753	05256	51557	90419	40716	64589	90398	37070	78318	02918
93124	50675	04507	44001	06365	77897	84566	99600	67985	49133
98658	86583	97433	10733	80495	62709	61357	66903	76730	79355
68216	94830	41248	50712	46878	87317	80545	31484	03195	14755
17901	30815	78360	78260	67866	42304	07293	61290	61301	04815
88124	21868	14942	25893	72695	56231	18918	72534	86737	77792
83464	36749	22336	50443	83576	19238	91730	39507	22717	94719
91310	99003	25704	55581	00729	22024	61319	66162	20933	67713
32739	38352	91256	77744	75080	01492	90984	63090	53087	41301
07751	66724	03290	56386	06070	67105	64219	48192	70478	84722
55228	64156	90480	97774	08055	04435	26999	42039	16589	06757
89013	51781	81116	24383	95569	97247	44437	36293	29967	16088
51828	81819	81038	89146	39192	89470	76331	56420	14527	34828
59783	85454	93327	06078	64924	07271	77563	92710	42183	12380
80267	47103	90556	16128	41490	07996	78454	47929	81586	67024
82919	44210	61607	93001	26314	26865	26714	43793	94937	28439
77019	77417	19466	14967	75521	49967	74065	09746	27881	01070
66225	61832	06242	40093	40800	76849	29929	18988	10888	40344
98534	12777	84601	56336	00034	85939	32438	09549	01855	40550
63175	70789	51345	43723	06995	11186	38615	56646	54320	39632
92362	73011	09115	78303	38901	58107	95366	17226	74626	78208
61831	44794	65079	97130	94289	73502	04857	68855	47045	06309
42502	01646	88493	48207	01283	16474	08864	68322	92454	19287
89733	86230	04903	55015	11811	98185	32014	84761	80926	14509
01336	66633	26015	66768	24846	00321	73118	15802	13549	41335
72623	56083	65799	88934	87274	19417	84897	90877	76472	52145
74004	68388	04090	35239	49379	04456	07642	68642	01026	43810
09388	54633	27684	47117	67583	42496	20703	68579	65883	10729
51771	92019	39791	60400	08585	60680	28841	09921	00520	73135
69796	30304	79836	20631	10743	00246	24979	35707	75283	39211
98417	33403	63448	90462	91645	24919	73609	26663	09380	30515
56150	18324	43011	02660	86574	86097	49399	21249	90380	94375
76199	75692	09063	72999	94672	69128	39046	15379	98450	09159
74978	98693	21433	34676	97603	48534	59205	66265	03561	83075
85769	92530	04407	53725	96963	19395	16193	51018	70333	12094
63819	65669	38960	74631	39650	39419	93707	61365	46302	26134
18892	43143	19619	43200	49613	50904	73502	19519	11667	53294
32855	17190	61587	80411	22827	38852	51952	47785	34952	93574
29435	96277	53583	92804	05027	19736	54918	66396	96547	00351
36211	67263	82064	41624	49826	17566	02476	79368	28831	02805
73514	00176	41638	01420	31850	41380	11643	06787	09011	88924
90895	93099	27850	29423	98693	71762	39928	35268	59359	20674
69719	90656	62186	50435	77015	29661	94698	56057	04388	33381
94982	81453	87162	28248	37921	21143	62673	81224	38972	92988
84136	04221	72790	04719	34914	95609	88695	60180	58790	12802
58515	80581	88442	65727	72121	40481	06001	13159	55324	93591
20681	59164	75797	08928	68381	12616	97487	84803	92457	88847

*Reproduced with permission from the Rand Corporation, *A Million Random Numbers*. (New York: The Free Press, 1955).

498

table of random normal deviates*

1.102	− .944	.401	.226	1.396	−1.030	−1.723	− .368	2.170	.393
.148	−1.140	.492	−1.210	− .998	.573	.893	− .855	−2.209	− .267
2.372	1.353	− .900	− .554	− .343	.470	−1.033	−1.026	2.172	.195
− .145	.466	.854	− .282	−1.504	.431	− .060	.952	− .343	.735
.104	.732	.604	− .016	− .266	1.372	− .925	−1.594	−2.004	1.925
1.419	−1.853	− .347	.155	−1.078	.623	− .024	.498	.466	.049
.069	− .411	− .661	− .037	.703	.532	− .177	.395	− .278·	.240
.797	.488	−1.070	− .721	−1.412	− .976	−1.953	− .206	1.848	.632
− .393	− .351	.222	.557	−1.094	1.403	.173	− .113	.806	.939
− .874	−1.336	.523	.848	.304	− .202	−1.279	.501	.396	.859
.125	−1.170	− .192	1.387	2.291	− .959	.090	1.031	.180	−1.389
−1.091	− .649	− .514	− .232	−1.198	.822	.240	.951	−1.736	.270
2.304	.481	− .987	−1.222	.549	−1.056	.277	− .919	.148	1.517
− .961	2.057	− .546	− .896	.165	− .343	.696	.628	− .929	− .965
− .783	.854	− .139	1.087	.515	− .876	− .448	.485	.589	− .804
.487	.557	.327	1.280	−1.731	− .339	.295	− .724	.720	.331
− .299	.979	− .924	− .649	.574	1.407	− .292	− .775	− .511	.026
1.831	− .937	−1.321	−1.734	1.677	−1.393	−1.187	− .079	− .181	− .844
.243	.466	−1.330	1.078	−1.102	1.123	− .421	− .674	2.951	− .743
−2.181	−1.854	−1.059	− .478	−1.119	.272	− .800	.841	− .061	2.261
.154	− .333	1.011	−1.565	1.261	.776	1.130	1.552	− .563	.558
−1.065	1.610	.463	.062	− .086	.021	1.633	1.788	.480	2.824
1.083	− .760	− .012	.183	.155	.676	−1.315	.067	.213	2.380
.615	− .594	− .028	− .506	− .054	3.173	.817	.210	1.699	1.950
.178	− .500	1.100	1.613	1.048	2.323	− .174	− .033	2.220	− .661
− .507	−1.273	.596	.690	−1.724	−1.689	.163	− .199	− .450	.244
.362	− .588	−1.386	.072	.778	− .591	.365	.465	2.472	1.049
.775	1.546	.217	−1.012	.778	.246	1.055	1.071	.447	− .585
.818	.561	−1.024	2.105	− .868	.060	− .385	1.089	.017	− .873
.014	.240	− .632	− .225	− .844	.448	1.651	1.423	.425	.252
−1.236	−1.045	−1.628	.687	.983	− .840	−1.835	−1.864	1.327	− .408
− .567	−1.161	.010	− .853	.111	1.145	1.015	.056	.141	1.471
.278	−1.783	.170	− .358	.705	− .054	1.098	.707	− .585	− .305
− .959	− .497	.688	− .268	−1.431	− .791	− .727	.958	.237	.092
1.249	.037	.497	.579	− .227	.860	.349	2.355	2.184	−1.744
− .915	− .164	−1.166	1.529	.008	.636	−1.080	− .688	2.444	−1.316
.132	2.809	−1.918	−1.083	− .642	− .179	.339	.637	.063	− .079
− .156	−1.664	1.140	.295	1.086	−2.546	− .002	− .672	.205	− .039
.538	−1.143	− .390	.165	− .160	.457	−1.307	.273	− .670	− .988
.027	− .057	.742	− .149	− .801	1.702	− .346	− .053	.892	−1.181
.023	.423	1.051	− .831	− .325	− .795	−1.129	− .287	.172	− .793
− .196	−1.457	1.060	.557	− .190	− .891	− .768	.282	−1.432	− .447
.133	.577	− .332	−1.932	.220	.189	−1.521	.896	− .781	− .899
.020	− .217	− .856	.605	.072	.520	1.222	− .181	− .266	−1.222
1.405	1.065	1.350	1.353	−2.289	−1.003	.375	1.621	−1.126	.937
.178	−1.237	− .520	− .603	−1.615	− .358	.605	− .407	−2.579	−1.811
−1.438	.104	−1.821	− .390	− .630	1.294	1.470	.991	− .355	−1.285
1.768	− .175	− .450	.915	− .221	− .019	1.864	.038	.058	1.212
.099	1.076	2.348	−1.550	.458	.147	−1.223	.994	−1.657	1.264
.951	.252	−1.261	− .963	.221	− .036	− .395	− .252	−1.379	1.885

*Reproduced with permission from the Rand Corporation, *A Million Random Numbers.* (New York: The Free Press, 1955).

unit normal loss integral (UNLI)*

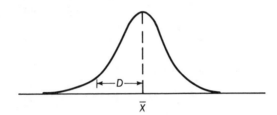

D	.00	.01	.02	.03	.04	.05	.06	.07	.08	.09
.0	.3989	.3940	.3890	.3841	.3793	.3744	.3697	.3649	.3602	.3556
.1	.3509	.3464	.3418	.3373	.3328	.3284	.3240	.3197	.3154	.3111
.2	.3069	.3027	.2986	.2944	'2904	.2863	.2824	.2784	.2745	.2706
.3	.2668	.2630	.2592	.2555	.2518	.2481	.2445	.2409	.2374	.2339
.4	.2304	.2270	.2236	.2203	.2169	.2137	.2104	.2072	.2040	.2009
.5	.1978	.1947	.1917	.1887	.1857	.1828	.1799	.1771	.1742	.1714
.6	.1687	.1659	.1633	.1606	.1580	.1554	.1528	.1503	.1478	.1453
.7	.1429	.1405	.1381	.1358	.1334	.1312	.1289	.1267	.1245	.1223
.8	.1202	.1181	.1160	.1140	.1120	.1100	.1080	.1061	.1042	.1023
.9	.1004	.09860	.09680	.09503	.09328	.09156	.08986	.08819	.08654	.08491
1.0	.08332	.08174	.08019	.07866	.07716	.07568	.07422	.07279	.07138	.06999
1.1	.06682	.06727	.06595	.06465	.06336	.06210	.06086	.05964	.05844	.05726
1.2	.05610	.05496	.05384	.05274	.05165	.05059	.04954	.04851	.04750	.04650
1.3	.04553	.04457	.04363	.04270	.04179	.04090	.04002	.03916	.03831	.03748
1.4	.03667	.03587	.03508	.03431	.03356	.03281	.03208	.03137	.03067	.02998
1.5	.02931	.02865	.02800	.02736	.02674	.02612	.02552	.02494	.02436	.02380
1.6	.02324	.02270	.02217	.02165	.02114	.02064	.02015	.01967	.01920	.01874
1.7	.01829	.01785	.01742	.01699	.01658	.01617	.01578	.01539	.01501	.01464
1.8	.01428	.01392	.01357	.01323	.01290	.01257	.01226	.01195	.01164	.01134
1.9	.01105	.01077	.01049	.01022	$.0^2 9957$	$.0^2 9698$	$.0^2 9445$	$.0^2 9198$	$.0^2 8957$	$.0^2 8721$
2.0	$.0^2 8491$	$.0^2 8266$	$.0^2 8046$	$.0^2 7832$	$.0^2 7623$	$.0^2 7418$	$.0^2 7219$	$.0^2 7024$	$.0^2 6835$	$.0^2 6649$
2.1	$.0^2 6468$	$.0^2 6292$	$.0^2 6120$	$.0^2 5952$	$.0^2 5788$	$.0^2 5628$	$.0^2 5472$	$.0^2 5320$	$.0^2 5172$	$.0^2 5028$
2.2	$.0^2 4887$	$.0^2 4750$	$.0^2 4616$	$.0^2 4486$	$.0^2 4358$	$.0^2 4235$	$.0^2 4114$	$.0^2 3996$	$.0^2 3882$	$.0^2 3770$
2.3	$.0^2 3662$	$.0^2 3556$	$.0^2 3453$	$.0^2 3352$	$.0^2 3255$	$.0^2 3159$	$.0^2 3067$	$.0^2 2977$	$.0^2 2889$	$.0^2 2804$
2.4	$.0^2 2720$	$.0^2 2640$	$.0^2 2561$	$.0^2 2484$	$.0^2 2410$	$.0^2 2337$	$.0^2 2267$	$.0^2 2199$	$.0^2 2132$	$.0^2 2067$
2.5	$.0^2 2005$	$.0^2 1943$	$.0^2 1883$	$.0^2 1826$	$.0^2 1769$	$.0^2 1715$	$.0^2 1662$	$.0^2 1610$	$.0^2 1560$	$.0^2 1511$
3.0	$.0^3 3822$	$.0^3 3689$	$.0^3 3560$	$.0^3 3436$	$.0^3 3316$	$.0^3 3199$	$.0^3 3087$	$.0^3 2978$	$.0^3 2873$	$.0^3 2711$
3.5	$.0^5 5848$	$.0^5 5620$	$.0^5 5400$	$.0^5 5188$	$.0^4 4984$	$.0^4 4788$	$.0^4 4599$	$.0^4 4417$	$.0^4 4242$	$.0^4 4073$
4.0	$.0^5 7145$	$.0^5 6835$	$.0^5 6538$	$.0^5 6253$	$.0^5 5980$	$.0^5 5718$	$.0^5 5468$	$.0^5 5227$	$.0^5 4997$	$.0^5 4777$

*Reprinted from R. Schlaifer, *Probability and Statistics for Business Decisions* (New York: McGraw-Hill Book Company, 1959) by permission of the publisher.

Key: Exponents after 0 means number of 0's before significant digits. For example, UNLI at D of 2.51 = $.0^2 1943$ = .001943

the standardized normal distribution function, F(S)*

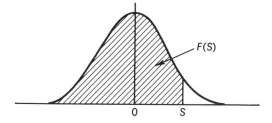

s	0.00	0.01	0.02	0.03	0.04	0.05	0.06	0.07	0.08	0.09
0.0	0.5000	0.5040	0.5080	0.5120	0.5160	0.5199	0.5239	0.5279	0.5319	0.5359
0.1	0.5398	0.5438	0.5478	0.5517	0.5557	0.5596	0.5636	0.5675	0.5714	0.5753
0.2	0.5793	0.5832	0.5871	0.5910	0.5948	0.5987	0.6026	0.6064	0.6103	0.6141
0.3	0.6179	0.6217	0.6255	0.6293	0.6331	0.6368	0.6406	0.6443	0.6480	0.6517
0.4	0.6554	0.6591	0.6628	0.6664	0.6700	0.6736	0.6772	0.6808	0.6844	0.6879
0.5	0.6915	0.6950	0.6985	0.7019	0.7054	0.7088	0.7123	0.7157	0.7190	0.7224
0.6	0.7257	0.7291	0.7324	0.7357	0.7389	0.7422	0.7454	0.7486	0.7517	0.7549
0.7	0.7580	0.7611	0.7642	0.7673	0.7703	0.7734	0.7764	0.7794	0.7823	0.7852
0.8	0.7881	0.7910	0.7939	0.7967	0.7995	0.8023	0.8051	0.8078	0.8106	0.8133
0.9	0.8159	0.8186	0.8212	0.8238	0.8264	0.8289	0.8315	0.8340	0.8365	0.8389
1.0	0.8413	0.8438	0.8461	0.8485	0.8508	0.8531	0.8554	0.8577	0.8599	0.8621
1.1	0.8643	0.8665	0.8686	0.8708	0.8729	0.8749	0.8770	0.8790	0.8810	0.8830
1.2	0.8849	0.8869	0.8888	0.8907	0.8925	0.8944	0.8962	0.8980	0.8997	0.90147
1.3	0.90320	0.90490	0.90658	0.90824	0.90988	0.91149	0.91309	0.91466	0.91621	0.91774
1.4	0.91924	0.92073	0.92220	0.92364	0.92507	0.92647	0.92785	0.92922	0.93056	0.93189
1.5	0.93319	0.93448	0.93574	0.93699	0.93822	0.93943	0.94062	0.94179	0.94295	0.94408
1.6	0.94520	0.94630	0.94738	0.94845	0.94950	0.95053	0.95154	0.95254	0.95352	0.95449
1.7	0.95543	0.95637	0.95728	0.95818	0.95907	0.95994	0.96080	0.96164	0.96246	0.96327
1.8	0.96407	0.96485	0.96562	0.96638	0.96712	0.96784	0.96856	0.96926	0.96995	0.97062
1.9	0.97128	0.97193	0.97257	0.97320	0.97381	0.97441	0.97500	0.97558	0.97615	0.97670
2.0	0.97725	0.97778	0.97831	0.97882	0.97932	0.97982	0.98030	0.98077	0.98124	0.98169
2.1	0.98214	0.98257	0.98300	0.98341	0.98382	0.98422	0.98461	0.98500	0.98537	0.98574
2.2	0.98610	0.98645	0.98679	0.98713	0.98745	0.98778	0.98809	0.98840	0.98870	0.98899
2.3	0.98928	0.98956	0.98983	0.9^20097	0.9^20358	0.9^20613	0.9^20863	0.9^21106	0.9^21344	0.9^21576
2.4	0.9^21802	0.9^22024	0.9^22240	0.9^22451	0.9^22656	0.9^22857	0.9^23053	0.9^23244	0.9^23431	0.9^23613
2.5	0.9^23790	0.9^23963	0.9^24132	0.9^24297	0.9^24457	0.9^24614	0.9^24766	0.9^24915	0.9^25060	0.9^25201
3.0	0.9^28650	0.9^28649	0.9^28736	0.9^28777	0.9^28817	0.9^28856	0.9^28893	0.9^28930	0.9^28965	0.9^28999
3.5	0.9^37674	0.9^37759	0.9^37842	0.9^37922	0.9^37999	0.9^38074	0.9^38146	0.9^38215	0.9^38282	0.9^38347
4.0	0.9^46833	0.9^46964	0.9^47090	0.9^47211	0.9^47327	0.9^47439	0.9^47546	0.9^47649	0.9^47748	0.9^47843

For example: $F(2.41) = 0.9^22024 = 0.992024$

*Reprinted from A. Hald, *Statistical Tables and Formulas* (New York: John Wiley & Sons, Inc., 1952), by permission of the publisher.

glossary of commonly used symbols and terminology

Mathematical Operations

$E[\cdot]$ Expected value of $[\cdot]$. Also, mean of $[\cdot]$.

$V[\cdot]$ Variance of $[\cdot]$.

$P(\cdot)$ or $Pr(\cdot)$ Probability of $(\cdot)$.

$\sigma[\cdot]$ Standard deviation of $[\cdot]$. Also, $\sqrt{V[\cdot]}$.

$U(\cdot)$ Utility of $(\cdot)$.

$\sum$ Summation.

∂ Partial derivative.

Economic Analysis Methods and Costs

A.W.	Annual worth (method, or equivalent).
A.C.	Annual cost (method, or equivalent).
C.R.	Capital recovery cost (equivalent annual cost of depreciation plus interest on investment).
E.R.R.	External rate of return.
E.R.R.R.	Explicit reinvestment rate of return.
F.W.	Future worth (method, or equivalent).
I.R.R.	Internal rate of return.
M.A.R.R.	Minimum attractive rate of return.
P.W.	Present worth (method, or equivalent).
R.R.	Rate of return.

bibliography

Part 1—Books

1. DeGarmo, E.P., J.R. Canada, and W.G. Sullivan, *Engineering Economy*, Sixth Edition. New York: Macmillan Publishing Co., Inc., 1979.

2. *Engineering Economy*, Second Edition. New York: American Telephone and Telegraph Company, Engineering Department, 1963.

3. Fleischer, G.A., *Capital Allocation Theory*. New York: Appleton-Century-Crofts, 1969.

4. Grant, E.L., W.G. Ireson, and R.S. Leavenworth, *Principles of Engineering Economy*, Sixth Edition. New York: The Ronald Press Company, 1976.

5. Jeynes, P.H., *Profitability and Economic Choice*. Ames, Iowa: The Iowa State University Press, 1968.

6. Newnan, D.G., *Engineering Economic Analysis*. San Jose, Calif.: Engineering Press, 1976.

7. Reisman, A., *Managerial and Engineering Economics*. Boston: Allyn and Bacon, Inc., 1971.

8. Riggs, J., *Engineering Economics*. New York: McGraw-Hill Book Company, 1977.

9. Smith, G.A., *Engineering Economy*, Second Edition. Ames, Iowa: The Iowa State University Press, 1973.

10. Tarquin, A.J., and L.T. Blank, *Engineering Economy: A Behavioral Approach*. New York: McGraw-Hill Book Company, 1976.

11. Taylor, G.A., *Managerial and Engineering Economy*, Second Edition. New York: Van Nostrand Reinhold Company, 1975.

12. Thuesen, H.G., W.J. Fabrycky, and G.J. Thuesen, *Engineering Economy*, Fifth Edition. Englewood Cliffs, N.J.: Prentice-Hall, Inc., 1977.

13. White, J.A., M.H. Agee, and K.E. Case, *Principles of Engineering Economic Analysis*. New York: John Wiley & Sons, Inc., 1977.

14. Woods, D.R., *Financial Decision Making in the Process Industry*. Englewood Cliffs, N.J.: Prentice-Hall, Inc., 1975.

references

Part 1—Articles

15. Adler, M., "The True Rate of Return and the Reinvestment Rate," *The Engineering Economist*, Vol. 15, No. 3, 1970, 185–187.

16. Athanasopoulos, P.J., "A Note on the Modified Internal Rate of Return and Investment Criterion," *The Engineering Economist*, Vol. 23, No. 2, 1978, 131–133.

17. Baldwin, R.H., "How to Assess Investment Proposals," *Harvard Business Review*, Vol. 37, No. 3, 1959, 98–99.

18. Beenhakker, H.L., "Discounting Indices Proposed for Capital Investment Evaluation: A Further Examination," *The Engineering Economist*, Vol. 18, No. 3, 1973, 149–168.

19. Bernhard, R.H., "Discount Methods for Expenditure Evaluation—A Clarification of Their Assumptions," *The Journal of Industrial Engineering*, Vol. 13, No. 1, 1962, 19–27.

20. ———, "On the Inconsistency of the Soper and Strum-Kaplan Conditions for Uniqueness of the Internal Rate of Return," *The Journal of Industrial Engineering*, Vol. 18, No. 8, 1967, 498–500.

21. ———, "A Comprehensive Comparison and Critique of Discounting Indices Proposed for Capital Investment Evaluation," *The Engineering Economist*, Vol. 16, No. 3, 1971, 157–186.

22. ———, "Comments on Horowitz, Ira, 'Engineering Economy: An Economist's Perspective,'" *AIIE Transactions*, Vol. 8, No. 4, 1976, 438–442.

23. Bullinger, C.E., "Comments on 'A Critical Evaluation of the Field of Engineering Economy,'" *The Journal of Industrial Engineering*, Vol. 15, No. 6, 1964, 316–318.

24. Canada, J.R., "Capital Budgeting: Its Nature, Present Practice and Needs for the Future," *The Journal of Industrial Engineering*, Vol. 15, No. 2, 1964, 82–86.

25. ———, "Rate of Return: A Comparison Between the Discounted Cash Flow Model and a Model Which Assumes an Explicit Reinvestment Rate for the Uniform Income Flow Case," *The Engineering Economist*, Vol. 9, No. 3, 1964, 1–15.

26. de Faro, C., "On the Internal Rate of Return Criterion," *The Engineering Economist*, Vol. 19, No. 3, 1974, 165–194.

504

27. Fleischer, G.A., "Two Major Issues Associated with the Rate of Return Method for Capital Allocation: The 'Ranking Error' and 'Preliminary Selection,' " *The Journal of Industrial Engineering*, Vol. 17, No. 4, 1966, 202–208.

28. ———, and T.L. Ward, "Classification of Compound Interest Models in Economic Analysis," *The Engineering Economist*, Vol. 23, No. 1, 1977, 13–30.

29. Grant, E.L., "Reinvestment of Cash Flow Controversy—A Review of: *Financial Analysis in Capital Budgeting* by Pearson Hunt," *The Engineering Economist*, Vol. 11, No. 3, 1966, 23–29.

30. Heebink, D.V., "Rate of Return, Reinvestment and the Evaluation of Capital Expenditures," *The Journal of Industrial Engineering*, Vol. 13, No. 1, 1962, 48–49.

31. Hirshleifer, J., "On the Theory of Optimal Investment Decision," *Journal of Political Economy*, Vol. 66, No. 5, 1958, 329–352.

32. Horowitz, I., "Engineering Economy: An Economist's Perspective," *AIIE Transactions*, Vol. 8, No. 4, 1976, 430–437.

33. Hsu, J.I.S., "A Survey of Equipment Replacement Practices," *Managerial Planning*, March-April, 1975.

34. Jeynes, P.H., "Minimum Acceptable Return," *The Engineering Economist*, Vol. 9, No. 4, 1964, 9–25.

35. ———, "Comment on Ralph O. Swalm's Letter," *The Engineering Economist*, Vol. 10, No. 3, 1965, 38–42.

36. ———, "The Significance of Reinvestment Rate," *The Engineering Economist*, Vol. 11, No. 1, 1965, 1–9.

37. Kirshenbaum, P.S., "A Resolution of the Multiple Rate-of-Return Paradox," *The Engineering Economist*, Vol. 10, No. 1, 1964, 11–16.

38. Klausner, R.F., "Communicating Investment Proposals to Corporate Decision-Makers," *The Engineering Economist*, Vol. 17, No. 1, 1971, 45–55.

39. Kulonda, D.J., "Replacement Analysis with Unequal Lives—The Study Period Method," *The Engineering Economist*, Vol. 23, No. 3, 1978, 171–179.

40. Lin, S.A., "The Modified Internal Rate of Return and Investment Criterion," *The Engineering Economist*, Vol. 21, No. 4, 1976, 237–247.

41. Lutz, R.P., "Tell the Boss—in His Terms," *Industrial Engineering*, Vol. 10, No. 7, 1978, 22–25.

42. Mao, J.C.T., "The Internal Rate of Return as a Ranking Criterion," *The Engineering Economist*, Vol. 11, No. 4, 1966, 1–13.

43. ———, "An Analysis of Criteria for Investment and Financing Decisions Under Certainty: A Comment," *Management Science*, Vol. 13, No. 3, 1966, 289–291.

44. Miller, M. H., and F. Modigliani, "Dividend Policy, Growth and the Valuation of Shares," *Journal of Business*, Vol. 34, No. 4, 1961, 411–433.

45. ———, "The Cost of Capital, Corporation Finance and the Theory of Investment," *American Economic Review*, Vol. 48, No. 3, 1958, 261–297.

46. Negrete, G.L., "The Modified Internal Rate of Return and Investment Criterion; A Reply," *The Engineering Economist*, Vol. 23, No. 2, 1978, 133–134.

47. Oakford, R.V., S.A. Bhimjee, and J.V. Jucker, "The Internal Rate of Return, The Pseudo Internal Rate of Return, and NPV and Their Use in Financial Decision Making," *The Engineering Economist*, Vol. 22, No. 3, 1977, 187–201.

48. Prest, A.R., and R. Turvey, "Cost-Benefit Analysis: A Survey," *Economic Journal*, Dec. 1965, 683–735.

49. Radnor, M., "A Critical Evaluation of the Field of Engineering Economy," *The Journal of Industrial Engineering*, Vol. 15, No. 3, 1964, 133–140.

50. Renshaw, E., "A Note on the Arithmetic of Capital Budgeting Decisions," *The Journal of Business*, Vol. 30, No. 3, 1957, 193–204.

51. Solomon, E., "The Arithmetic of Capital Budgeting Decisions," *The Journal of Business*, Vol. 29, No. 2, 1956, 124–129.

52. Swalm, R.O., "On Calculating the Rate of Return on an Investment," *The Journal of Industrial Engineering*, Vol. 9, No. 2, 1958, 99–103.

53. ———, "Comment on 'Minimum Acceptable Return' by Paul H. Jeynes," *The Engineering Economist*, Vol. 10, No. 3, 1965, 35–38.

54. ———, J.L.L. Leoutand, "Maximizing Future Wealth—A Consummation Devoutly to Be Wished," *Proceedings of the 1976 Spring Annual Conference of the American Institute of Industrial Engineers.*

55. Teichroew, D., A.A. Robicheck, and M. Montalbano, "Mathematical Analysis of Rates of Return Under Certainty," *Management Science*, Vol. 11, No. 3, 1965, 395–403.

56. ———, "An Analysis of Criteria for Investment and Financing Decisions Under Certainty," *Management Science*, Vol. 12, No. 3, 1965, 151–179.

57. Thuesen, G.J., "Selecting a Discount Rate: Let's Help the User," *Proceedings of 1975 Spring Annual Conference of American Institute of Industrial Engineers.*

58. Weaver, J.B., "False and Multiple Solutions by the Discounted Cash Flow Method for Determining Interest Rate of Return," *The Engineering Economist*, Vol. 3, No. 4, 1958, 1–31.

59. White, J.A., K.E. Case, and M.H. Agee, "Rate of Return: An Explicit Reinvestment Rate Approach," *Proceedings of the 1976 Spring Annual Conference of the American Institute of Industrial Engineers.*

Parts 2 and 3—Books

60. Abdelsamad, M.A., *Guide to Capital Expenditure Analysis*. New York: American Management Association, 1973.

61. Agee, M.H., R.E. Taylor, and P.E. Torgersen, *Quantitative Analysis for Management Decisions*. Englewood Cliffs, N.J.: Prentice-Hall, Inc., 1976.

62. Archer, S.H., and C.A. D'Ambrosio, *The Theory of Business Finance: A Book of Readings*. New York: Macmillan Publishing Co., Inc., 1967.

63. Barish, N.N., *Economic Analysis for Engineering and Managerial Decision Making*. New York: McGraw-Hill Book Company, 1962.

64. Bierman, H. Jr., and S. Smidt, *The Capital Budgeting Decision*, Fourth Edition. New York: Macmillan Publishing Co., Inc., 1974.

65. Bowman, E.H., and R.B. Fetter, *Analysis for Production and Operations Management*. Homewood, Ill.: Richard D. Irwin, Inc., 1967.

66. Brown, R.V., A.S. Kahr, and C. Peterson, *Decision Analysis for the Manager*. New York: Holt, Rinehart and Winston, 1974.

67. Carr, C.R., and C.W. Howe, *Quantitative Decision Procedures in Management and Economics*. New York: McGraw-Hill Book Company, 1964.

68. Carter, E.E., *Portfolio Aspects of Corporate Capital Budgeting*. Lexington, Mass.: D.C. Heath & Company, 1974.

69. Charnes, A., and W.W. Cooper, *Management Models and Industrial Applications of Linear Programming*. New York: John Wiley & Sons, Inc., 1961.

70. Cohen, J.B., and E.D. Zinbarg, *Investment Analysis and Portfolio Management*. Homewood, Ill.: Richard D. Irwin, Inc., 1967.

71. Cochrane, J.L., and M. Zeleny, *Multiple Criteria Decision Making*. Columbia, S.C.: University of South Carolina Press, 1973.

72. DeNeufville, R., and J.H. Stafford, *Systems Analysis for Engineers and Managers*. New York: McGraw-Hill Book Company, 1971.

73. Dewhurst, R.F.J., *Business Cost-Benefit Analysis*. New York: McGraw-Hill Book Company, 1972.

74. Dyckman, T.R., S. Smidt, and A.K. McAdams, *Management Decision Making Under Uncertainty*. New York: Macmillan Publishing Co., Inc., 1969.

75. Egerton, R.A.D., *Investment Decisions Under Uncertainty*. Liverpool, England: Liverpool University Press, 1960.

76. English, J.M., *Cost Effectiveness: Economic Evaluation of Engineered Systems*. New York: John Wiley & Sons, Inc., 1968.

77. Fama, E.F., and M.H. Miller, *The Theory of Finance*. New York: Holt, Rinehart and Winston, 1972.

78. Farrar, D.E., *The Investment Decision Under Uncertainty*. Reprint of Ph. D. Dissertation, Harvard University, 1961. Englewood Cliffs, N.J.: Prentice-Hall, Inc., 1962.

79. Fellner, W., *Probability and Profit*. Homewood, Ill.: Richard D. Irwin, Inc., 1965.

80. Fishburn, P.C., *Decision and Value Theory*. New York: John Wiley & Sons, Inc., 1964.

81. Fleischer, G.A., *Risk and Uncertainty: Non-Deterministic Decision Making in Engineering Economy*, Publication EE-75-1, Norcross, Ga: American Institute of Industrial Engineers, 1975.

82. ———, *Symbolic Scorecard Methodology*, Industrial and Systems Engineering Report 76–4, Los Angeles, University of Southern California, 1976.

83. Fredrikson, E.B., *Frontiers of Investment Analysis*. Scranton, Pa.: International Textbook Co., 1965.

84. Grayson, C.J., Jr., *Decisions Under Uncertainty*. Boston, Mass.: Harvard Business School Press, 1960.

85. Giffin, W.C., *Transform Techniques for Probability Modeling*. New York: Academic Press, Inc., 1975.

86. Hackney, J.W., *Control and Management of Capital Projects*. New York: John Wiley & Sons, Inc., 1965.

87. Hanssman, F., *Operations Research Techniques for Capital Investment*. New York: John Wiley & Sons, Inc., 1968.

88. Haynes, W.W., *Managerial Economics: Analysis and Cases*, Revised Edition. Austin, Texas: Business Publications, Inc., 1969.

89. Hester, D.D., and J. Tobin, *Risk Aversion and Portfolio Choice*. Cowles Monograph 19. New York: John Wiley & Sons, Inc., 1967.

90. House, W.C., *Sensitivity Analyses in Making Capital Investment Decisions*. Research Monograph No. 3. New York: National Association of Accountants, 1968.

91. Ignizio, J.P., *Goal Programming and Extensions*. Lexington, Mass.: D.C. Heath & Company, 1976.

92. Ijiri, Y., *Management Goals and Accounting for Control*. Chicago, Ill.: Rand McNally College Publishing Company, 1965.

93. Istvan, D.F., *Capital-Expenditure Decisions: How They Are Made in Large Corporations*. Indiana Business Report No. 33. Bloomington, Ind.: Indiana University Press, 1961.

94. Jelen, F.C., *Cost and Optimization Engineering*. New York: McGraw-Hill Book Company, 1970.

95. Kaufman, G., *Statistical Decisions and Related Techniques in Oil and Gas Exploration*. Ph.D. Dissertation, Harvard University, 1961.

96. Keeney, R.L., and H. Raiffa, Decisions with Multiple Objectives: Preferences and Value Tradeoffs. New York: John Wiley & Sons, Inc, 1976.

97. Kempster, J.H., *Financial Analysis to Guide Capital Expenditures*. New York: National Association of Accountants, 1967.

98. Lasser, J.K., *Your Income Tax*. New York: Simon and Schuster, Inc. (see latest edition).

99. Lee, S.M., *Goal Programming for Decision Analysis*. Philadelphia, Pa.: Auerbach Publishers, Inc., 1972.

100. Mao, J.C.T., *Corporate Financial Decisions*. Pavan Publishers, 1976.

101. ———, *Quantitative Analysis of Financial Decisions*. New York: Macmillan Publishing Co., Inc., 1969.

102. Marglin, S.A., *Public Investment Criteria: Benefit—Cost Analysis for Planned Economic Growth*. Cambridge, Mass.: The MIT Press, 1967.

103. Markowitz, H.M., *Portfolio Selection: Efficient Diversification of Investments*. New York: John Wiley & Sons, Inc., 1959.

104. Massé, P., *Optimal Investment Decisions: Rules for Action and Criteria for Choice*. Englewood Cliffs, N.J.: Prentice-Hall, Inc., 1962.

105. Meier, R.C., W.T. Newell, and L. Pazer, *Simulation in Business and Economics*. Englewood Cliffs, N.J.: Prentice-Hall, Inc., 1969.

106. Merrett, A.J., and A. Sykes, *The Finance and Analysis of Capital Projects*. New York: John Wiley & Sons, Inc., 1963.

107. Mock, E.J., *Financial Decision Making*. Scranton, Pa.: International Textbook Co., 1967.

108. Moore, P.G., *Risk in Business Decision*. New York: John Wiley & Sons, Inc. 1973.

109. Morris, W.T., *Engineering Economic Analysis*. Reston, Va.: Reston Publishing Company, 1976.

110. ———, *The Analysis of Management Decisions*. Homewood, Ill.: Richard D. Irwin, Inc., 1964.

111. Murdick, R.G., and D.D. Deming, *The Management of Capital Expenditures*. New York: McGraw-Hill Book Company, 1968.

112. Muth, E.J., *Transform Methods With Applications to Engineering and Operations Research*. Englewood Cliffs, N.J.: Prentice-Hall, Inc., 1977.

113. Oakford, R.V., *Capital Budgeting: A Quantitative Evaluation of Investment*. New York: The Ronald Press Company, 1970.

114. Optner, S.L., *Systems Analysis for Business and Industrial Problem Solving*. Englewood Cliffs, N.J.: Prentice-Hall, Inc., 1965.

115. Ostwald, P.F., *Cost Estimating for Engineering and Management*. Englewood Cliffs, N.J.: Prentice-Hall, Inc., 1974.

116. Park, C.M., *Quantitative Methods for Managerial Decisions*. New York: McGraw-Hill Book Company, 1973.

117. Park, W.R., *Cost Engineering Analysis*. New York: John Wiley & Sons, 1973.

118. Pessemier, E.A., *New-Product Decisions: An Analytical Approach*. New York: McGraw-Hill Book Company, 1966.

119. Peters, W.S., and G.W. Summers, *Statistical Analysis for Business Decisions*. Englewood Cliffs, N.J.: Prentice-Hall, Inc., 1968.

120. Peterson, D.E., *A Quantitative Framework for Financial Management*. Homewood, Ill.: Richard D. Irwin, Inc., 1969.

121. Pflomm, N.E., *Managing Capital Expenditures*. Studies in Business Policy No. 107. New York: National Industrial Conference Board, 1963.

122. Quirin, G.D., *The Capital Expenditure Decision*. Homewood, Ill.: Richard D. Irwin, Inc., 1967.

123. Raiffa, H., *Decision Analysis: Introductory Lectures on Choices Under Uncertainty*. Reading, Mass.: Addison-Wesley Publishing Co., Inc., 1968.

124. Rakowski, M., *Efficiency of Investment in a Socialist Economy*. New York: Pergamon Press, 1966.

125. Reisman, A., *Engineering Economics: A Unified Approach*. New York: Reinhold Publishing Corp., 1969.

126. Reutlinger, S., *Techniques for Project Appraisal Under Uncertainty*. Baltimore, Md.: The Johns Hopkins University Press, 1970.

127. Riggs, J.L., *Economic Decision Models for Managers and Engineers*. New York: McGraw-Hill Book Company, 1967.

128. Robichek, A.A., and S.C. Myers, *Optimal Financing Decisions*. Englewood Cliffs, N.J.: Prentice-Hall, Inc., 1965.

129. Schlaifer, R., *Analysis of Decisions Under Uncertainty, Vol. I*. New York: McGraw-Hill Book Company, 1969.

130. ———, *Probability and Statistics for Business Decisions*. New York: McGraw-Hill Book Company, 1959.

131. Schmidt, J.W., *Mathematical Foundations of Management Science and Systems Analysis*. New York: Academic Press, Inc., 1974.

132. Schweyer, H.E., *Analytical Models for Managerial and Engineering Economics*. New York: Reinhold Publishing Corp., 1964.

133. Seiler, K., III, *Introduction to Systems Cost-Effectiveness*. New York: Wiley-Interscience, 1969.

134. Shannon, R.E., *Systems Simulation: The Art and Science*. Englewood Cliffs, N.J.: Prentice-Hall, Inc., 1975.

135. Shuckett, D.H., and E.J. Mock, *Decision Strategies in Financial Management*. New York: American Management Association, 1973.

136. Simon, J.L., *Applied Managerial Economics*. Englewood Cliffs, N.J., Prentice-Hall, Inc., 1975.

137. Solomon, E., *The Management of Corporate Capital*. New York: The Free Press, 1959.

138. ———, *The Theory of Financial Management*. New York: Columbia University Press, 1963.

139. Spencer, M.H., *Managerial Economics*, Third Edition. Homewood, Ill.: Richard D. Irwin, Inc., 1968.

140. Terborgh, G., *Business Investment Management*. Washington: Machinery and Allied Products Institute, 1967.

141. U.S. Treasury Department, *Your Federal Income Tax: Edition for Individuals*. IRS Publication No. 17 (revised annually).

142. ———, *Tax Guide . . . for Small Businesses* (Individuals, Corporations, Partnerships). IRS Publication No. 334 (revised annually).

143. ———, *Depreciation, Investment Credit, Amortization, Depletion.* IRS Publication No. 5050, December, 1965.

144. Vernon, I.R., Editor, *Realistic Cost Estimating for Manufacturing.* Dearborn, Mich.: ASTME Manufacturing Data Series, 1968.

145. Walter, J.E., *The Investment Process.* Boston: Graduate School of Business, Harvard University, 1962.

146. Weingartner, H.M., *Mathematical Programming and the Analysis of Capital Budgeting Problems.* Chicago: Markham Publishing Co., 1967.

147. Weston, J.F., and E.F. Brigham, *Financial Management*, Fourth Edition. New York: Holt, Rinehart, and Winston, 1972.

148. White, J.A., J.W. Schmidt, and G.K. Bennett, *Analysis of Queueing Systems.* New York: Academic Press, Inc., 1975.

149. Wilson, F.W., and P.D. Harvey, *Manufacturing Planning and Estimating Handbook.* New York: ASTME, McGraw-Hill, Book Company, 1963.

150. Wilkes, F.M., *Capital Budgeting Techniques.* New York: John Wiley and Sons, 1977.

151. Winkler, R.L., *Introduction to Bayesian Inference and Decision.* New York: Holt, Rinehart, and Winston, 1972.

152. Woolsey, R.E.D., and H.S. Swanson, *Operations Research for Immediate Application: A Quick and Dirty Manual.* New York: Harper & Row, Publishers, Inc., 1975.

Parts 2 and 3 Articles

153. Angell, W., "Uncertainty, Likelihoods, and Investment Decisions," *Quarterly Journal of Economics*, Vol. 74, No. 1, 1960, 1–28.

154. Atkins, D.R., and D.J. Ashton, "Discount Rates in Capital Budgeting: A Reexamination of the Baumol and Quandt Paradox." *The Engineering Economist*, Vol. 21, No. 3, 1976, 159–172.

155. Baumol, W.J., "An Expected Gain-Confidence Limit Criterion for Portfolio Selection," *Management Science*, Vol. 10, No. 1, 1963, 174–182.

156. ———, and R.E. Quandt, "Investment and Discount Rates Under Capital Rationing—A Programming Approach," *The Economic Journal*, Vol. 75, No. 298, 1965, 317–329.

157. Beenhakker, H.L., and V. Narayanan, "Algorithms for Scheduling Projects with Limited Resources," *The Engineering Economist*, Vol. 21, No. 2, 1976, 119–140.

158. Bernhard, R.H., "On the Choice of a Cutoff Rate for the Internal Rate of Return," *Journal of Industrial Engineering*, Vol. 16, No. 3, 1965, 201–207.

159. ———, "Mathematical Programming Models for Capital Budgeting—A Survey, Generalization, and Critique," *Journal of Financial and Quantitative Analysis*, Vol. 4, No. 2, 1969, 111–158.

160. ———, "Some Problems in the Use of a Discount Rate for Constrained Capital Budgeting," *AIIE Transactions*, Vol. 3, No. 3, 1971, 180–184.

161. ———, "State Preference Synthesis of Utility and Interest with Critical Implications for Discounting Under Risk," *The Engineering Economist*, Vol. 22, No. 3, 1977, 203–217.

162. Bernoulli, D. (1700–1782), "Exposition of a New Theory on the Measurement of Risk," English translation by Louise Sommer, *Econometrica*, Vol. 22, 1954, 23–26.

163. Bower, R.S., and D.R. Lessard, "An Operational Approach to Risk Screening," *The Journal of Finance*, Vol. 28, No. 2, 1973, 321–327.

164. Buck, J.R., and T.W. Hill, "Additions to the Laplace Transform Methodology for Economic Analysis," *The Engineering Economist*, Vol. 20, No. 3, 1975, 197–208.

165. ———, "Alpha/Beta Difference Equations and Their Zeta Transforms in Economic Analysis," *AIIE Transactions*, Vol. 7, No. 3, 1975, 330–338.

166. ———, "Laplace Transforms for the Economic Analysis of Deterministic Problems in Engineering," *The Engineering Economist*, Vol. 16, No. 4, 1971, 247–264.

167. Canada, J.R., "Decision Flow Networks," *Industrial Engineering*, Vol. 6, No. 6, 1974, 30–37.

168. ———, and W.G. Sullivan, "To Understand the Decision Problem, Say It With Pictures," *Proceedings of Spring Annual Conference of the American Institute of Industrial Engineers,* 1977.

169. ———, and H.W. Wadsworth, "Methods for Quantifying Risk in Economic Analysis of Capital Project," *Journal of Industrial Engineering*, Vol. 19, No. 1, 1968, 32–37.

170. *Capital Investment Series*, Parts I and II (bound sets of reprints from *Harvard Business Review*, Boston, 1964, 1969.

171. Carter, E.E., "What Are the Risks in Risk Analysis?" *Harvard Business Review*, Vol. 50, No. 4, 1972, 1–20.

172. Chasteen, L.G., "Implicit Factors in the Evaluation of Lease Versus Buy Alternatives," *The Accounting Review*, October, 1973, 764–767.

173. Chen, A.H., and A.J. Boness, "Effects of Uncertain Inflation on the Investment and Financing Decisions of a Firm," *The Journal of Finance*, Vol. 30, No. 2, 1975, 469–483.

174. Cord, J., "A Method for Allocating Funds to Investment Projects When Returns Are Subject to Uncertainty," *Management Science*, Vol. 10, No. 2, 1964, 335–341.

175. Cramer, R.H., and B.E. Smith, "Decision Models for the Selection of Research Projects," *The Engineering Economist*, Vol. 9, No. 2, 1964, 1–20.

176. Dean, B.V., "Replacement Theory," *Progress in Operations Research*, Vol. 1, edited by R.L. Ackoff. New York: John Wiley & Sons, Inc., 1961.

177. Dreyfus, S.E., "A Generalized Equipment Replacement Study," *Journal of the Society for Industrial and Applied Mathematics*, Vol. 8, No. 3, 1960, 425–435.

178. Dyer, J.S., "Interactive Goal Programming," *Management Science*, Vol. 19, No. 1, 1972, 62–70.

179. Eisen, M., and M. Leibowitz, "Replacement of Randomly Deteriorating Equipment," *Management Science*, Vol. 9, No. 2, 1963, 268–276.

180. English, J.M., "A Discount Function for Comparing Economic Alternatives," *Journal of Industrial Engineering*, Vol. 16, No. 2, 1965, 115–118.

181. ———, "Economic Comparison of Projects Incorporating a Utility Criterion in the Rate of Return," *The Engineering Economist*, Vol. 10, No. 2, 1965, 1–14.

182. ———, "New Approaches to Economic Comparison for Engineering Projects," *Journal of Industrial Engineering*, Vol. 12, No. 6, 1961, 375–378.

183. Epstein, B., "Some Applications of the Mellin Transform in Statistics," *Annals of Mathematical Statistics*, Vol. 19, 1948, 370–379.

184. Fishburn, P.L., "Decision Under Uncertainty: An Introductory Exposition," *Journal of Industrial Engineering*, Vol. 17, No. 7, 1960, 341–353.

185. Fisher, J.L., "A Class of Stochastic Investment Problems," *Operations Research*, Vol. 9, No. 1, 1961, 53–65.

186. Fleischer, G.A., "A Technique for Determination of Project Priority When Considering Irreducibles," *The Engineering Economist*, Vol. 11, No. 2, 1966, 13–28.

187. ———, and J.H. Lubin, "Useful Computer Programs for Engineering Economy Application," *Proceedings, 23rd Annual Conference*, American Institute of Industrial Engineers, May, 1972, 63–82.

188. Geoffrion, A.M., "Stochastic Programming with Aspiration on Fractile Criteria," *Management Science*, Vol. 13, No. 9, 1967, 672–679.

189. ———, "Proper Efficiency and the Theory of Vector Maximization," *Journal of Mathematical Analysis and Applications*, Vol. 22, No. 3, 1968, 618–630.

190. ———, J.S. Dyer, and A. Feinberg, "An Interactive Approach for Multi-Criterion Optimization, With an Application to the Operation of an Academic Department," *Management Science*, Vol. 19, No. 4, 1972, 357–368.

191. Green, P.E., "Risk Attitudes and Chemical Investment Decisions," *Chemical Engineering Progress*, Vol. 59, No. 1, 1963, 35.

192. Hanssmann, F., "Probability of Survival as an Investment Criterion," *Management Science*, Vol. 15, No. 1, 1968, 33–48.

193. Harris, L., "A Decision-Theoretic Approach on Deciding When a Sophisticated Forecasting Technique Is Needed," *Management Science*, Vol. 13, No. 2, 1966, 66–69.

194. Harvey, R.K., and A.V. Cabot, "A Decision Theory Approach to Capital Budgeting Under Risk," *The Engineering Economist*, Vol. 20, No. 1, 1974, 37–50.

195. Hayes, R.H., "Incorporating Risk Aversion into Risk Analysis," *Engineering Economist*, Vol. 20, No. 2, 1975, 99–122.

196. Heebink, D.W., "Isoquants and Investment Decisions," *The Engineering Economist*, Part I, Vol. 7, No. 4, 1962; Part II, Vol. 8, No. 1, 1962.

197. Herschleifer, J., "The Bayesian Approach to Statistical Decision: an Exposition," *The Journal of Business*, Vol. 34, No. 4, 1961, 471–489.

198. Hertz, D.B., "Risk Analysis in Capital Investments," *Harvard Business Review*, Vol. 42, No. 1, 1964, 95–106.

199. ———, "Investment Policies That Pay Off," *Harvard Business Review*, Vol. 46, No. 1, 1968, 96–108.

200. Hetrick, J.C., "Mathematical Models in Capital Budgeting," *Harvard Business Review*, Vol. 39, No. 1, 1961, 49–64.

201. Hill T.W., and J.R. Buck, "Zeta Transforms, Present Value, and Economic Analysis," *AIIE Transactions*, Vol. 6, No. 2, 1974, 120–125.

202. Hillier, F.S., "A Basic Model for Capital Budgeting of Risky Interrelated Projects," *The Engineering Economist*, Vol. 17, No. 1, 1971, 1–30.

203. ———, "The Derivation of Probabilistic Information for the Evaluation of Risky Investments," *Management Science*, Vol. 9, No. 3, 1963, 443–457.

204. ———, "Supplement to 'The Derivation of Probabilistic Information for the Evaluation of Risky Investments,'" *Management Science*, Vol. 11, No. 3, 1965, 485–487.

205. ———, "The Evaluation of Risky Interrelated Investments," Technical Report No. 73, Department of Statistics, Stanford University, July 24, 1964.

206. Ignizio, J.P., "An Approach to the Capital Budgeting Problem With Multiple Objectives," *The Engineering Economist*, Vol. 21, No. 4, 1976, 259–272.

207. Jarrett, J.E., "An Abandonment Decision Model," *The Engineering Economist*, Vol. 19, No. 1, 1973, 35–46.

208. Keeney, R.L., "Decision Analysis With Multiple Objectives: The Mexico City Airport," *Bell Journal of Economics and Management Science*, Vol. 4, No. 1, 1973, 101–117.

209. Keown, A.J., and J.D. Martin, "A Chance Constrained Goal Programming Model for Working Capital Management," *The Engineering Economist*, Vol. 22, No. 3, 1977, 153–174.

210. Lintner, J., "The Cost of Capital and Optimal Financing of Corporate Growth," *Journal of Finance*, Vol. 18, No. 2, 1963, 292–310.

211. ———, "The Valuation of Risk Assets and the Selection of Risky Investments in Stock Portfolios and Capital Budgets," *Review of Economics and Statistics*, Vol. 47, No. 1, 1965, 13–37.

212. Lorie, J.H., and L.J. Savage, "Three Problems in Capital Rationing," *Journal of Business*, Vol. 28, No. 4, 1955, 229–239.

213. Lusztig, P., and B. Schwab, "A Nóte on the Application of Linear Programming to Capital Budgeting," *Journal of Financial and Quantitative Analysis*, Vol. 3, No. 4, 1968, 426–431.

214. Magee, J.F., "Decision Trees for Decision Making," *Harvard Business Review*, Vol. 42, No. 4, 1964, 126–138.

215. ———, "How to Use Decision Trees in Capital Investment," *Harvard Business Review*, Vol. 42, No. 5, 1964, 79–96.

216. Morris, W.T., "Value Clarification: An Engineering Approach," *AIIE Transactions*, Vol. 7, No. 4, 1974, 356–362.

217. Naik, M.D., and K.P. Nair, "Multistage Replacement Strategies," *Journal of the Operations Research Society of America*, Vol. 13, No. 2, 1965, 279–290.

218. Naslund, B., and A. Whinston, "A Model of Multi-Period Investment Under Uncertainty," *Management Science*, Vol. 8, No. 2, 1962, 184–200.

219. Norton, J.H., "The Role of Subjective Probability in Evaluating New Project Ventures," *Chemical Engineering Progress Symposium Series*, Vol. 59, No. 42, 1963.

220. Peterson, C.C., "A Capital Budgeting Heuristic Algorithm Using Exchange Operations," *AIIE Transactions*, Vol. 6, No. 2, 1974, 143–150.

221. ———, "Solution of Capital Budgeting Problems Having Chance Constraints; Heuristic and Exact Methods," *AIIE Transactions*, Vol. 7, No. 2, 1975, 153–158.

222. Peterson, D.E., and D.J. Laughhunn, "Capital Expenditure Programming and Some Alternative Approaches to Risk," *Management Science*, Vol. 17, No. 5, 1971, 320–336.

223. Petty, J.W., D.F. Scott, and M.M. Bird, "The Capital Expenditure Decision Making Process of Large Corporations," *The Engineering Economist*, Vol. 20, No. 3, 1975, 159–172.

224. Pyle, D.H., and S.J. Turnovsky, "Safety-First and Expected Utility Maximization in Mean-Standard Deviation Portfolio Analysis," *Review of Economics and Statistics*, Vol. 52, No. 1, 1970, 75–81.

225. Reisman, A., "Capital Budgeting for Interrelated Projects," *Journal of Industrial Engineering*, Vol. 16, No. 1, 1965, 59–63.

226. ———, and E.S. Buffa, "A General Model for Investment Policy," *Management Science*, Vol. 8, No. 3, 1962, 304–310.

227. Rosenthal, R.E., "The Variance of Present Worth of Cash Flows Under Uncertain Timing," *The Engineering Economist*, Vol. 23, No. 3, 1978, 163–170.

228. Sartoris, W.L., and M.L. Spruill, "Goal Programming and Working Capital Management," *Financial Management*, Vol. 3, No. 1, 1974, 67–74.

229. Sengupta, J.K., and J.H. Portillo-Campbell, "A Fractile Approach to Linear Programming Under Risk," *Management Science*, Vol. 16, No. 5, 1970, 298–308.

230. Senju, S., and Y. Toyoda, "An Approach to Linear Programming with 0–1 Variables," *Management Science*, Vol. 15, No. 4, 1968, 196–207.

231. Sharpe, W., "A Simplified Model for Portfolio Analysis," *Management Science*, Vol. 9, No. 2, 1963, 277–293.

232. Shore, B., "Replacement Decisions Under Capital Budgeting Constraints," *The Engineering Economist*, Vol. 20, No. 4, 1975, 243–256.

233. Smith, G.W., "Engineering Economy Abstracts" (collections of annotated bibliographies of selected articles in approximately 25 publications; first collection covered 1965–70 and updated collections have been published for each subsequent year through at least 1976) Dept. of Industrial Engineering, Iowa State University.

234. ———, "Decreasing Utility for Money and Optimal Corporate Debt Ratios," *The Engineering Economist*, Vol. 13, No. 2, 1968.

235. Springer, M.D., and W.E. Thompson, "The Distribution of Products of Independent Random Variables," *SIAM Journal of Applied Mathematics*, Vol. 14, No. 3, 1966, 511–526.

236. Stone, B.K., "A Linear Programming Formulation of the General Portfolio Selection Problem," *Journal of Financial and Quantitative Analysis*, Vol. 6, 1973, p.p. 1263–1276.

237. Swalm, R.O., "Capital Expenditure Analysis—A Bibliography," *The Engineering Economist*, Vol. 13, No. 2, 1968, 105–129.

238. ———, "Utility Theory—Insights Into Risk-Taking," *Harvard Business Review*, Vol. 44, No. 6, 1966, 123–135.

239. Terry, H., "Comparative Evaluation of Performance Using Multiple Criteria," *Management Science*, Vol. 9, No. 3, 1963, 431–442.

240. Tersine, R.J., and W. Rudko, "A Bivariate Stochastic Approach to Capital Investment Decisions," *The Engineering Economist*, Vol. 17, No. 3, 1972, 157–176.

241. Thompson, W.W., Jr., "Some Mathematical Models for Evaluating Investment Strategies," *Journal of Industrial Engineering*, Vol. 17, No. 2, 1966, 99–105.

242. Van Horne, J., "Capital Budgeting Decisions Involving Combinations of Risky Investments," *Management Science*, Vol. 13, No. 10, 1966, 84–92.

243. Van Horne, J.C., "Variation of Project Life as a Means for Adjusting for Risk," *The Engineering Economist*, Vol. 21, No. 3, 1976, 151–158.

244. Virts, J.R., and R.W. Garrett, "Weighing Risk in Capacity Expansion," *Harvard Business Review*, May-June, 1970, Vol. 48, No. 3, 1970, 132–141.

245. White, J.M., "Some Comments on Decision Theory Under Uncertainty and Minimax," *The Engineering Economist*, Vol. 8, No. 4, 1963, 1–9.

246. Yarmowich, E.P., "Estimating Plant Construction by Probabilistic Analysis," *Plant Engineering*, May, 1974, 137–148.

247. Young, D.B., and L. Contreras, "Expected Present Worths of Cash Flows Under Uncertian Timing," *The Engineering Economist*, Vol. 20, No. 4, 1975, 257–268.

answers to selected even-numbered problems

Chapter 1

4. (a) $3.20/ft², (b) No charge, (c) $4.00/ft². **6.** Use A from 5,001 through 15,000; use B otherwise. **8.** (a) Use New, (b) Use New, (c) Use Old.

Chapter 2

2. $10,725, **4.** 24 mos., **6.** $29.03, **8.** $4,166, **10.** $6,020, **12.** $6,212, **14.** (a) $2,762.80, (b) $18,605.90, **16.** (a) $16,041, (b) $75,000, **18.** $496,764, **20.** $13,495, **22.** $11,912.

Chapter 3

2. P.W.*(A)* = −$2,500 (best), P.W.*(B)* = −$4,002, **4.** $34,229, **6.** A.C.(3″) = $500.35, A.C.(4″) = $451.06, A.C.(5″) = $436.80, A.C.(6″) = $440.06, A.C.(7″) = $443.33, A.C.(8″) = $464.11, 5″ insulation is most economic, **8.** F.C.*(A)* = $48,955 (best), F.C.*(B)* = $54,319, **10.** P.C. (Owning) = $8,304,

517

P.C. (Contracting) = \$7,582 (best) **12.** F.W.(2) = −\$22,438,500, F.W.(3) = −\$18,040,750, F.W.(4) = \$7,686,090 (best), F.W.(5) = −\$22,638,400, **14.** P.W.*(A)* = \$245, P.W.*(B)* = \$288, A.W.*(A)* = \$78, A.W.*(B)* = \$91, F.W.*(A)* = \$359, F.W.*(B)* = \$424. **16.** P.W.*(A)* = − \$3,127, P.W.*(B)* = \$862, P.W.*(C)* = −\$2,487, P.W.*(D)* = −\$4,101, P.W.*(E)* = −\$290, P.W.*(F)* = −\$6,200.

Chapter 4

2. i ≐ 15.6%, **4.** i_{B-A} = 15%; build facility, **6.** Recommend Machine *E,* **8.** Recommend Machine *B,* **10.** Recommend Opportunities *B* and *C,* **12.** Recommend Incinerator *D,* **14.** (a) reject, (b) accept, (c) E.R.R. indicates accept; I.R.R. recommendation not clear, (d) reject.

Chapter 5

2. Leasing is recommended (*B/C* = 2.12), **4.** Repair machine (*B/C* = 1.60), **6.** Recommend II (△*B/C* = 1.165), **8.** Recommend *B* (△*B/C* = 1.058), **10.** Recommend *D* (△*B/C* = 1.098).

Chapter 6

2. (a) D_s = \$2,800; BV_s = \$18,000, (b) D_s = \$3,055; BV_s = \$11,636, (c) D_s = \$2,621; BV_s = \$10,486, **6.** D_4 = \$2,000; BV_4 = \$11,000, **8.** Total of \$8,300 in taxes, **10.** P.W.(15%) = \$43,079, **12.** *i* = 11.7%, **14.** (a) Tax = \$5,454, (b) Savings in taxes = \$12,000, (c) Savings in taxes = \$7,500, **16.** (a) Method I is best, (b) Method I is best, **20.** With I.T.C.: *i* = 12.8%, Without I.T.C.: *i* = 10.9%.

Chapter 7

2. Replace, △P.W. = \$1,981, **4.** Replace, △A.W. = \$1,185, **6.** Keep old drill, **8.** Recommend *A,* **10.** (a) I.R.R. = 2.8%, (b) I.R.R. = 0.7%.

Chapter 8

2. (a) *B/C* Ratio = 3.44, (b) P.W. = \$199,260, **4.** (a) *B/C* Ratio = 1.86, (b) △Investment = \$4,307,850, **6.** Private vehicles: \$0.22 fee, Commercial vehicles: \$1.10 fee, **8.** P.W. = \$2,539,860, **10.** Install 800-pair cable now, △P.W. = \$18,395, **12.** Choose Plan II, △P.W. = \$24,944, **14.** Choose A, △P.W. = \$2,655.

Chapter 9

4. \$16,450,000 **6.** (a) \$28,495, (b) \$10,000, \$9,615, and \$11,095, (c) \$28,414, **8.** Real rate = 2%, **10.** (a) \$33,463; \$30,278, (b) \$24,800; \$25,080, **12.** (a) \$321,644; \$354,600, (b) \$390,958; \$431,016 (Time 0; Real \$), \$562,555; \$620,195 (Time 4;

Actual $), **14.** $90,039, **16.** Approximately $45, **20,** (a) $Y = -5.83 + 1.41x$, (b) $757,000, (c) $p = 0.98$.

Chapter 10

8. (a) Lease, $\triangle$ P.W. = $805, Capital gain = $1,000, Capital loss = $200, (b) Operate without truck, **10.** Purchase is preferred to lease.

Chapter 11

14. 13.11% **16.** $E[x]$ = $251, $V[x]$ = 8.72.

Chapter 12

2. (a) A.W.(0) = $23,192, A.W.$(M)$ = $14,976, A.W.$(P)$ = −$7,552, (b) A.W.(0,0) = $21,256, A.W.(0,$M$) = $19,976, A.W.(0,$P$) = $14,632, A.W.$(M,0)$ = $16,256, A.W.$(M,M)$ = $14,976, A.W.$(M,P)$ = $9,632, A.W.$(P,0)$ = $6,256, A.W.$(P,M)$ = $4,976, A.W.$(P,P)$ = −$368, **4.** Breakeven value = 76.23% capacity **8.** A.W. = 0.7719 + 1.38x + y 0

Chapter 13

2. Using normal distribution, approximately 0.524

4.

V	P(V)
$60,606	0.05
62,500	0.10
64,500	0.10
64,516	0.20
66,667	0.30
68,966	0.20
71,429	0.10
74,074	0.05

6. 0.65, **8.** 0.65, **10.** 27 probability values required; Pr(E.R.R. > M.A.R.R.) = 0.360.

Chapter 14

2. (a) II, (b) III, (c) III, (d) IV, (e) III or IV, **4.** (a) Bravo, (b) Charlie, (d) Charlie, **10.** $P = 0.40$, **14.** B is best, **16.** $\sigma_{A.W.}$ = $677, **18.** V[A.W.] = 100,950,000, **20.** (a) Project in Problem 14-17 is best, (b) $A = 0.58$, **22.** E[A.W.] = $546.

Chapter 15

2. (a) $P($0.12) = 0.39, $P($0.15) = 0.61, P(3 yrs) = 0.40, P(4 yrs) = 0.60, (b) $P($0.12|3 yrs) = 0.30, $P($0.15|3 yrs) = 0.70, $P($0.12|4 yrs) = 0.45,

$P(\$0.15 | 4 \text{ yrs})$ 6 $= 0.55$, (c) $P(4 \text{ yrs} | \$0.12) = 0.69$, **4.** (a) A_2, (b) Good: A_1, Fair: A_2, Poor: A_3, (c) $E[R | PI] = \$87$, (d) E.V.P.I. $= \$22$, (f) A_2, **6.** \$236.

Chapter 16

4. Conduct survey; Expected value $= \$48,302$ **6.** RLW best choice, **8.** Further investigation recommended, **10.** Initiate applied research.

Chapter 17

2. 5 years, **4.** 10 years, **6.** 12 years, **8.** 5 years, **10.** Replace after 2 periods.

Chapter 18

2. $x_1 = x_3 = 0$, $x_2 = x_4 = 1$, objective function $= 42$, **4.** $x_2 = x_4 = x_7 = x_8 = 1$, all other $x_j = 0$, objective function $= 46$, **6.** $x_{32} = 50$, $x_{42} = 30$, $x_{4,3} = 50$, $x_{5,3} = 100$, $x_{7,1} = 50$, *all other* $x_{ij} = 0$, **8.** $x_1 = \$4,000$; $x_2 = \$6,000$, **10.** $y_2 = 100\%$ of investment, **12.** $x_1 = 4,000$; $x_2 = 5,500$; $x_3 = 500$; and $z = 5,000$, **14.** $x_1 = x_3 = x_4 = x_6 = x_9 = 1$; $z = 70$.

Chapter 19

10. $K = -0.95482$, $U(A) = 0.92005$, $U(B) = 0.85297$, **12.** $K = -0.93023$, $U(A) = 0.931$, $U(B) = 0.633$.

index